Contributions to Economics

The series *Contributions to Economics* provides an outlet for innovative research in all areas of economics. Books published in the series are primarily monographs and multiple author works that present new research results on a clearly defined topic, but contributed volumes and conference proceedings are also considered. All books are published in print and ebook and disseminated and promoted globally. The series and the volumes published in it are indexed by Scopus and ISI (selected volumes).

Biagio Bossone

Trailblazing Visions of Money in Economic Theory

Essence, Genesis, and Economic Ramifications

Springer

Biagio Bossone
Rome, Italy

ISSN 1431-1933 ISSN 2197-7178 (electronic)
Contributions to Economics
ISBN 978-3-031-82543-9 ISBN 978-3-031-82544-6 (eBook)
https://doi.org/10.1007/978-3-031-82544-6

This Springer imprint is published by the registered company Springer Nature Switzerland AG
The registered company address is: Gewerbestrasse 11, 6330 Cham, Switzerland

I dedicate this book to the cherished memory of my beloved parents, Luciano Bossone and Manuela Pellitteri; my grandparents Pietro e Anna Pellitteri, and uncle Beppe Pellitteri; to the loves of my life, my wife Ornella and my son Blasco; to my dearest cousin, Marcello Pellitteri, who is more a brother to me; and for all my other relatives, to my cousin Maria Luisa Leuzzi, a treasured sentiment for many years and now back again in my life.

Preface

The journey that led me to write this book is one rooted not in academic tradition, but in the dynamic interplay of research and practical experience that has characterized my life since I graduated from university. Over nearly four decades, I have moved through various public and private sector roles, each giving me a unique perspective on the complexities of economics, and more specifically the intricate workings of money.

The essays and analyses that readers will encounter in this book are the result of continuous dialogue between the two worlds I have inhabited: the theoretical realm of economic models and the tangible realities of economic and financial systems. This duality has been at the heart of my professional evolution, shaping my views and deepening my curiosity about the subject of money.

This book is for those who, like me, believe that the study of money is enriched when theory meets practice and when research informs action.

I invite readers to join me in this exploration, where the real and the theoretical converge, offering a deeper understanding of one of the most powerful forces shaping our economic world: money.

Rome, Italy — Biagio Bossone

Acknowledgements

Intellectual Acknowledgements

I wish to express my gratitude to the following esteemed economists who have greatly influenced my work and shaped my ideas throughout my professional lifetime. Each of them has played a significant role in my intellectual development and understanding of economics.

I would like to express my sincere gratitude to Tony Aspromourgos for deepening my understanding of the "economics of Keynes," distinct from what is commonly referred to as "Keynesian economics." His guidance has also significantly enhanced my appreciation of Keynes' policy conservatism, providing clarity that transcends the often-simplified interpretations of his views.

I am deeply indebted to Willem Buiter for being an example of exceptional analytical rigor and his ability to seamlessly merge theory and policy, which I have tried to emulate in my own work. His work has consistently inspired and guided my research efforts.

I also owe a tremendous debt to Paul Davidson, whose teachings have enlightened my understanding of the fundamental role of time, uncertainty, and non-ergodicity in the study of money. His insights have been invaluable in shaping my perspective.

Another influential figure in my intellectual journey is Augusto Graziani, who instilled in me a passion for economics that has remained with me since my early days as a university student. His enthusiasm and knowledge have been instrumental in shaping my research activity.

My deep appreciation goes to Frank Hahn, for his through-provoking attitude and the extraordinary ability to apply high theory to reality, never forgetting the ultimate purpose of Economics as a discipline to comprehend human societies.

I am grateful to Ian Kregel for introducing me to the profound insights of Keynes. Through his guidance, I have come to appreciate the significance of Keynes's economics in our understanding of the world.

I am also grateful to Axel Leijonhufvud, who, by stressing the role of money and finance in causing instability through coordination failures, helped me understand the "economics of Keynes."

During my early years at the Bank of Italy, Rainer Masera, the head of research, epitomized the qualities of a central bank economist. I thank him for leaving such a lasting impression on me.

Hyman Minsky's groundbreaking research on the intersection of finance and economics has been fundamental in to my understanding of capitalism and its inherent instability. I credit him for illuminating the crucial connection between these two disciplines.

I must acknowledge the influence of Tommaso Padoa-Schioppa, deputy director general of the Bank of Italy during my tenure, for his commitment to intellectual discipline and his role as an exemplary central banker, which have had a long-lasting impact on me to this day.

I also thank Thomas Palley, whose brilliant vision of economics—in the true tradition of Keynes—I always find inspirational.

My wholehearted gratitude goes to Gabriele Morello and Gustav Schacter—both my university professors and tutors, who played a key role in helping me achieve my dream of studying economics in the USA. Gustav Schacter's guidance and mentorship in the field of economic development have been invaluable throughout my career.

My gratitude goes also to Joe Stiglitz, chief economist of the World Bank during my tenure there as a financial policy advisor. His profound understanding of the impact of finance on the economic development of nations has greatly influenced my work and broadened my perspective.

My sincerest appreciation to Larry Summers—who I have always admired for his unique ability to combine theoretical capacity, policy-making skills, and the exercise of power—for having encouraged me to pursue the Portfolio Theory of Inflation.

I am grateful to Lance Taylor, for his focus on the interactions between economic structures (institutions, income distribution, technology, trade patterns) and macroeconomic dynamics, especially in developing economies. I heavily drew from his teachings in my early years of academic education in the US.

I want to express my gratitude to Charles Wyplosz for being a source of inspiration for my recent research on credibility and policy effectiveness, which originated from comments he kindly shared with me, years ago, in email exchanges.

I am also grateful to my former colleagues of the Group on Fiscal Money—Marco Cattaneo, Massimo Costa, and Stefano Sylos Labini—for the great intellectual spirit that has animated our courageous cooperative effort.

A special sentiment connects me to Guido Maria Brera, financier, writer, and filmmaker. The *Global investors* ofmyPortfolioTheory of Inflation closely resemble the *Devils* of his famous TV series.

I would like to finally extend my gratitude to my co-authors of the works reflected in this book: Fabio Bagarello, Massimo Costa, Michael Heines, and Abdou Sarr. However, I cannot conclude this list without acknowledging my indebtedness to

Corrado Augias (journalist, writer, TV host, screenwriter, and many other roles) for the profound impact his works have hadon my spirit over the years.

Professional Acknowledgements

I wish to remember the renowned figures of Carlo Azeglio Ciampi, former governor of the Bank of Italy, minister of the Italian government, and president of the Italian republic; Lamberto Dini, former director general of the Bank of Italy and minister of the Italian government; Giulio Tremonti, former minister of the Italian government, and Antonio Fazio, former governor of the Bank of Italy. They have played a crucial role as mentors and in supporting my professional career at important turns, and I wish to express my gratefulness and appreciation to them. For the consideration I received from them, I also wish to thank Giorgio La Malfa and Elio Lannutti, former senators of the Italian republic; Diego Cammarata, former mayor of Palermo; Gianfranco Micciché, former deputy minister of the Italian government; Alessandro Pagano, former member of the Italian parliament; the late Fabrizio Saccomanni, my former boss at the Bank of Italy; and my Bank of Italy's colleague the late Curzio Giannini. A special thought to the late Angelo Randazzo, Cavaliere del Lavoro della Repubblica Italiana.

Thanks to My Friends

Since this book represents a life milestone for me, I want to acknowledge some dear friends who have been important milestones along my life.

Raoul Ascari
I still think of you a lot, Fratello, though we have lost touch.

Sergio Barducci
Your willingness to listen whenever I felt like talking has always been a gift to me.

Marcello Chiodi ("Clodoveus") and Gugliemo Di Noto ("Gughi")
We met at the university on the very first morning of our first graduate course. I have loved you since then and always will.

Massimo Cirasino ("Max")
Your profound humanity, which you often conceal and many fail to appreciate, makes you a very special friend to me.

Alessandro Cusimano ("Cusi")
You are one of the treasures of my life, and you are in my thoughts far more than you can think (or perhaps you know…).

Vincenzo D'Alberti
The youngest of my friends, you are indeed very dear to me for your generosity, candor, loving care, and readiness to help.

Andrea Del Vecchio
Your unwavering support has been a source of strength for me, and I am genuinely thankful for it.

Enrico Gorgone
We have been great friends since we were kids, but the more time has passed since then, the more I realize how precious you are to me.

Maria Guarcello, Luigi Montesani, Bernard Mullane, Paola Sconzo, and Emanuele Vitrano
When I called out, you were there.

Giovanni La Barbera ("Pasquino")
We were so close, then things changed. I've never had bad feelings since we parted ways, only reckoned about our inability to be true to ourselves... I still treasure our old good times. Rest in peace, dear Pasquino.

Claudio Marchese
You were not given to live most of your life, while I have now lived most of mine. I miss you since that tragic day. Rest in peace, my beloved.

Gabriele Palpacelli ("Ga")
You, too, have gone too early. Your courage and determination have been an inspiration to me throughout the years, much as your attitude of "never surrender." Rest in peace, dearest Ga.

Alessandro Pagano
From the moment we met, it was natural closeness.

Luigi Passamonti
What began as a professional partnership has quickly blossomed into a special friendship.

Salvatore Paterna ("Salvino")
Your friendship and wisdom have enriched my life ever since we met as colleagues at work. I am deeply grateful for it.

Franco Patti ("Pallo")
We have been brothers, pal. We really shared our souls during the best years of our youth. I hope you are forever happy.

Giancarlo Pirrone
You ignited within me—then teenager—the passion for philosophy, science, and music and you taught me the importance of inner self-development. My profoundest gratitude.

Benni Priolisi
So different and yet so connected, until our lives took different turns. I deeply regret not being there during your final years. Rest in peace, my friend.

Franz Salerno ("FriFro")
I have always had great affection and high consideration for you, dearest Franz.

Francesco Vitale ("Zut")
You don't know how glad I still am that you once called me in DC and came back to my life after we had long missed each other.

Alberto Vourvoulias
Even though our friendship is relatively new, I truly appreciate that we "see" each other (as Avatars would say), and that means a lot to me.

I thank you all, dear friends. If there is anything good in me, this is also on you.

Thanks to My Wife

I cannot finish my list of thanks without expressing my infinite gratitude to my wife Ornella, for her steadfast support throughout the years.

Competing Interests The author has no competing interests to declare that are relevant to the content of this manuscript.

Contents

Part III On Money Effectiveness

About the Author

Biagio Bossone is a financial advisor to international organizations, including the African Development Bank, Bank for International Settlements, the International Monetary Fund, the International Organization of the Securities Commissions, and the World Bank. Biagio Bossone is an economic advisor to governments and financial institutions in Africa, Europe, and the Middle East. He has been, executive director of the World Bank Group, member of the Executive Board of the IMF, and has been a banker and central banker. Biagio Bossone has been the coordinator and a member of the public investment evaluation unit at Italy's Presidency of the Council of Ministers and general accountant and director general of the budget in the government of the Sicilian region. Biagio Bossone has been assistant director, Bank of Italy, and member of G10 and European central banking working groups and task forces. Biagio Bossone has served as an expert in the High-Level Commission on World Bank Reform chaired by Mexico's former president Ernesto Zedillo. He has taught international finance at the Universities of Palermo and Salento, Italy, and is author and coauthor of several studies on economics, banking, and finance.

Chapter 1
Introduction

I have never considered myself an academic, though I have occasionally participated in academic activities. Nevertheless, economic research has been a constant companion throughout my professional journey since graduating from college. Over nearly four decades, my research endeavors have seamlessly intertwined with my roles as a practical economist. I have been in the staff of public institutions, collaborated with national and international agencies, served as an economic policy advisor, and acted as a financial sector consultant. I have also been an administrator of public finances, a central banker, and a private sector banker. In each of these capacities, research has not only informed my views and decisions but has also enriched my understanding of the complexities of the economic landscape. At the same time, my applied experience has continuously enhanced my research work.

Throughout my activities, "money" has been the common thread connecting them all, and my most important area of economic interest. The integration of research with a real-world perspective has allowed me to explore this topic from various relevant angles. For example, when I was offered the opportunity to lead the division handling the operational and policy aspects of cross-border payments at the Bank of Italy, I felt a wave of uncertainty. I had no previous experience in this area, and initially, I even approached the operational side of the job with some disdain. However, I quickly realized—by doing the job—that no monetary economist can fully claim the title without practical experience in how money functions as a medium of exchange and settlement of obligations in the real world—especially as theory has prevalently emphasized the role of money as a store of value rather than means of payment and settlement instrument (Appendix 1).

Taking that job enabled me to exploit both theory and practice and to improve on them both: My direct involvement in payment operations deepened my understanding of how payment system rules and technologies affect the process of money creation, and my economic background empowered me to contribute to the policy aspects of payment systems.

B. Bossone, *Trailblazing Visions of Money in Economic Theory*, Contributions to Economics, https://doi.org/10.1007/978-3-031-82544-6_1

At a broader and deeper level, the interplay between theory and practice has placed me firmly on the camp of those for whom money "neutrality" (and "super-neutrality") is a fallacious notion: Money matters in both the short and the long runs, and it does so in a fundamental way. Hence my interest in it.

1.1 Money Is Non-neutral

I have always rejected the notion that money merely acts as a "veil" in the exchange process and is neutral in its impact on the economy and that essentially because of the foundational relationship that links money to historical time.

In the history of humankind, money has emerged as a rational response developed by societies to navigate the uncertainty and ignorance of the future that time inherently brings. As Prof. Frank Hahn once remarked, "A world in which all conceivable contingent future contracts are possible neither needs nor wants intrinsically worthless money." (Hahn, 1983, p. 1).

Money has taken many different forms over the past millennia—and continues to do so—yet all its forms serve the purpose of an instrument functioning as a medium that can be readily liquidated and exchanged against anything in the economy, with anyone, everywhere, at no cost, and at a sure nominal value. The purchasing power that money contains allows its holders to make exchanges and settle-related debts in the face of unknown and uninsurable future events. Without this basic understanding, money lacks any rationale for existence.

Yet, money is not only a response to uncertainty. It affects the motivations and decisions of those who hold it and is itself a source of uncertainty in a world with an unknown future, with consequences of great importance. The unpredictability of how, when, and why individuals decide to spend it creates an inherent uncertainty, making it difficult to foresee the impacts of economic and financial decisions at any given moment. Also, given that "ergodicity" is precluded by the uncertainty intrinsic to economic reality (Davidson, 1972), it cannot even be assumed that the spending decisions of multiple agents over time will guarantee that the economy achieves and maintains full-employment equilibrium or that it returns to it after disruptive shocks, once ridded of all rigidities and frictions.

Furthermore, as monetary flows keep accumulating in the economy and are used to finance asset acquisitions, the importance of stock variables—both real and financial—grows over time, their market valuations (as reflecting people's expectations on asset risks and returns) become crucial to resource allocation decisions by agents, and agents' liquidity preferences take precedence over the prices of loanable funds as drivers of their resource allocation decisions (Box 1). Agent decisions concern the stock of accumulated savings—wealth—at any point in time, rather than any new flow of saving exclusively; therefore, the equilibrium rates of interest on assets are not determined by the supply of and demand for (flows of) saving, but by the supply of and demand for (stocks of) assets into which holdings of wealth can be placed, and are influenced by agents' expectations and states of confidence (Tily, 2012).

Box 1. From Flows to Stocks in Monetary Economies In monetary economies where money is primarily generated through the credit channel (an aspect that will be explored in detail throughout this book), conditions must be in place that not only supports but also enhances the role of financial assets and credit in driving economic activity. This is essential for the ongoing growth and persistence of the significance of stock variables. These conditions include:

Continuous Credit Creation and Debt Growth

Credit creation must continue at a sustained or increasing rate, meaning that new loans must keep flowing into the economy, potentially exceeding the rate at which old loans are repaid. If new borrowing slows significantly or stops, the accumulated money flows would contract as debt repayments siphon off existing money. This ongoing credit creation keeps money circulating and prevents liquidity contraction. This can occur if there is high confidence among lenders and borrowers, supported by stable or growing income levels, which reduce default risk and enable debt expansion.

Asset Price Appreciation and Collateral Expansion

As monetary flows are directed toward asset acquisitions (like real estate, stocks, and bonds), rising asset prices increase the value of collateral, allowing more borrowing against these assets. This creates a feedback loop where rising asset values justify further lending, which in turn keeps monetary flows circulating in the economy. This appreciation sustains the importance of stock variables, as the financial value of assets (e.g., housing, equities) grows relative to the real economy's flow variables (like GDP or income), thereby amplifying the influence of financial stocks on economic activity.

Low Interest Rates

Low interest rates make credit cheaper, encouraging both borrowing and asset acquisitions. When rates are low, the burden of debt repayment is reduced, allowing a larger share of credit to be directed toward investment and consumption rather than just servicing debt. If central banks adopt accommodative policies to support economic activity, especially in low-growth or low-inflation environments, this can lead to asset price inflation, enhancing the significance of stock variables.

Economic Growth and Income Expansion

If incomes and output in the economy are growing, borrowers are more likely to have the means to repay loans without needing to reduce consumption or liquidate assets. Economic growth effectively "absorbs" the repayment burden, maintaining the money flows within the economy and allowing the stock of outstanding credit to rise without triggering widespread defaults. In this context, as income rises, both the capacity to borrow and the value of accumulated stocks increase, reinforcing the importance of stock variables over time.

Sector Imbalances and Financialization

The economy must have sectoral imbalances, where certain sectors (often financial or property sectors) accumulate a disproportionate amount of wealth or income. This concentration supports a shift toward financial asset accumulation, inflating the role of financial stock variables in the economy. On the other hand, financialization—whereby economic activity is increasingly driven by financial rather than productive activities—redirects credit into asset markets rather than productive investments. This shift in allocation boosts asset prices, making stock variables more influential over time.

Stable or Increasing Velocity of Money in Financial Markets

If the velocity of money in financial markets remains high, transactions involving financial assets occur frequently, effectively recycling monetary flows and ensuring that these flows remain significant in the economy. This can result in an economy where financial transactions (stocks and bonds trading, for example) grow faster than transactions involving goods and services, amplifying the importance of financial stock variables relative to real variables.

As (Keynes, 1936a) stressed, preferences for liquidity (due to high uncertainty) could keep interest rates higher than what is necessary for full employment. If interest rates are too high, investment falls, reducing aggregate demand. The resulting equilibrium is characterized by unemployment because firms are not producing at full capacity, and owing to the monetary character of the economy, there are not self-re-equilibrating mechanisms that can move the economy out of the high liquidity preference state and into full-employment equilibrium. Price (and wage) flexibility would not serve that purpose and might reduce aggregate demand further, as firms and households' purchasing power declines, thereby worsening the recession.[1] Moreover, if firms and households believe that the economy is in a prolonged downturn, they may reduce spending and investment, which would reinforce the downturn as a result.

On the other hand, overly optimistic expectations can lead agents to develop high preferences for illiquidity or to mistakenly believe that markets will always remain liquid. This can result in asset price inflation and increase the risk of financial and economic instability.

Beliefs can endure even when objective circumstances indicate otherwise. This is because individuals base their decisions on shared expectations that act as a social

[1] For the very same reasons, it can be argued that price (and wage) sluggishness during recessions act as stabilizers, mitigating the negative impact on aggregate demand by preserving firms' and households' purchasing power.

framework and shape how people interpret information and optimize their choices. Without external shocks—such as government interventions—there is no incentive for any individual to deviate from this equilibrium.

Shared expectations reinforce collective behavior, creating a self-fulfilling loop where individuals' actions align with their beliefs and those of others, perpetuating the status quo. This dynamic can trap an economy in a suboptimal state, as the inertia of collective belief systems resists changes that would otherwise be driven by objective improvements or opportunities, highlighting the critical role of coordinated interventions in breaking such equilibria.

In such circumstances, fiscal and monetary policies become necessary to change expectations and outcomes. In fact, the higher and more persistent the agents' preference for liquidity, the more intense and immediate the policy actions needed to avoid that path-dependence and hysteresis transform the recession into permanent stagnation and vice versa when preferences for illiquidity are high.

Various contributions and research programs have supported the existence of suboptimal (less than full employment) economic equilibria (Appendix 2). Yet, none of them has eventually resisted (and survived) the attraction that New Classical Macroeconomics has exercised on the mainstream, starting from the early 1980s and for several subsequent decades. NCM's abstraction from time—and the actual removal of time as a fundamental characteristic of reality—has stripped money of its essential relationship with uncertainty. This shift was driven by NCM's embrace of rational expectations, ergodicity, and the premise of continuously clearing markets as foundational theoretical assumptions. Consequently, money became a redundant and essentially neutral economic variable, losing its significance both as a response to uncertainty and as a source of uncertainty.

This extreme unrealism did not change perceptibly even after mainstream economic thinking evolved into New Keynesian Economics (NKE). NKE's models of the economy—today largely in use—typically generate long-run, full-employment, steady-state solutions for the key endogenous variables. In the long run, all variables settle on paths that grow consistently with each other in a sustainable equilibrium, while short-run dynamics are handled by embedding these long-run solutions in equilibrium-correction equations in which short-run frictions can explain temporary deviations from them and do not affect them (with exceptions discussed in Appendix 2).[2] NKE's underlying tenet is that the economy is never very far from its full-employment state-steady (optimal) equilibrium.

Returning to reality should lead one to realize that money matters not just in the short term, but also in the long run and in a fundamental way. The economy can drift significantly away from optimal equilibrium and remain there, without intervention.

Several important questions arise that any theory seriously engaging with the nature of reality should address. Specifically, these questions relate to how money affects real economic and financial processes and the consequences that follow. Some of them are: How is money created and injected into the economy? By whom is it

---

[2] For a comprehensive and critical review of New Keynesian economic modelling, see (Vines Wills, 2018).

created and introduced, through which channels, and under which conditions, and at which stage of the economic process? What criteria determine its allocation to various uses? When and on what is the money spent? How is the money distributed across the economy, who receives it and who doesn't, and what are the consequences for the level and type of spending of different distributions? What impact does this spending have on the quantities and prices of the goods and assets exchanged, and what about if the money is not spent or circulates more slowly? How does the money creation power influence the economics of a multi-sector economy? Does it generate hierarchical relationships within it? Are rents associated with the exploitation of these hierarchical relationships? What are their macroeconomic implications in terms of output, inflation, and resource distribution?

Moreover, critical policy questions arise when considering the effectiveness of monetary (and fiscal) policy: Is this effectiveness influenced by the beliefs that economic agents hold regarding the functioning of the economy—specifically, the structural models they consciously or unconsciously employ to formulate expectations and make predictions? If money effectiveness is indeed influenced, how does this effectiveness change when some agents possess sufficient market power to assert their beliefs about the economy? In other words, if the resource allocation decisions of these agents—rooted in their beliefs—are substantial enough to shape market dynamics, how do they impact the effectiveness of macroeconomic policies?

The different ways in which these questions are addressed in the real world not only affect the short-term performance of an economy; they also determine its potential for growth and its actual growth path by influencing the agents' intertemporal economic decision and specifically the quantity and quality of capital accumulation over time.

1.2 This Book

Based on these premises, and years after studying monetary theories and observing the effectiveness of monetary (and fiscal) policy in various national and international contexts, I have decided to write a book on money. My aim was to encapsulate the insights I have gained through my research and experience in this field and to provide answers to some of the questions raised above.

This book is the result of that decision. It is a collection of some of my earlier writings on money and related topics, largely revisited and revised to bring fresh insights and clarity. Each chapter serves as a "trailblazer" (hence the book's title) illuminating new ideas such as, inter alia, the equity nature of money, the intersection of commercial bank money and Quantum Physics, and the concept of Fiscal Money. Some chapters illustrate innovative methodologies, like the utility-based theory of money and the proposed new systems of money creation based on non-credit forms of money. Some others offer new perspectives on familiar topics (e.g., the use of liquidity preference as a micro-founded explanation of Secular Stagnation or the role of credibility in shaping the effectiveness of macroeconomic policies). Others yet apply old ideas to new problems (e.g., the application of Modigliani–Miller neutrality theorem to money and debt as public finance instruments in globally financially integrated economies). Lastly, some chapters highlight the collaborative projects I have undertaken with co-authors from diverse scientific backgrounds and show the unique insights that have emerged from blending our distinct perspectives.

The book is organized in fifteen chapters (excluding this introduction and the concluding section), each of which is presented by a preamble that explains the origin of the topic discussed and its relevance in the context of economic research. The chapters are articulated in three parts.

Part I of the book "On Money" focuses on the foundational aspects of money and consists of six chapters. Chapter 2—What is Money: Debt or Equity?—starts with one of my most recent works on the nature of money, is money debt or equity? The chapter illustrates the Accounting View of Money (AVM). The AVM shows that the fiat monies issued by the state (typically, cash, banknotes, and central bank money) are not debt and that only a share of commercial bank money can be regarded as debt (in fractional reserve regimes). The AVM argues, instead, that state monies as well as the non-debt share of commercial bank money is net wealth of their holders and net worth (equity) of their issuers. The AVM points to the correct way to account for the above forms of money in the financial statements of the issuing institutions, clarifies what the different accounting treatments imply for a correct understanding of the concept of money, and evaluates the related economic and economic policy implications.

Chapter 3—The Utility of Money—investigates the utility that money (and other financial assets) delivers to agents by serving as means of payment and settlement instrument in a world with time, uncertainty and changing market sentiment, a long-dated work effort of mine. Rather than assuming money in the utility function, it explains why and how money enters the utility function. The theory provides a unifying tool that allows money to be comparable to, and to be compared with, anything else—goods, services, and other assets—anytime and anywhere. It builds on three blocks: (i) a choice-theoretic model that determines the utility that the agents derive from holding assets with different liquidity; (ii) a variable (endogenously determined) cost structure of asset liquidation, which reflects the (in)efficiencies of the financial infrastructure and changes in market moods; and (iii) a model of expectations formation under uncertainty and changing market sentiment. While rich in structure, the approach offers a simple analytical framework to investigate resource allocation decisions and asset price dynamics under various sources of uncertainty and to explore the microeconomics of speculative bubbles and boom–bust sequences. The use of a possible market-specific prudential policy tool is discussed.

Having dealt with the nature of money, Chap. 4—Money in a Sequence Economy—considers how the money that we all prevalently use (i.e., demand deposits issued by commercial banks) is injected in an economy with time as an essential factor and illustrates the approach derived from monetary circuit theory to analyze the integrated functions of banking and finance in a monetary production economy—a topic that has attracted my interest ever since I was a college student. A micro-founded, circuit-sequenced model of a decentralized-decisions economy is used to this end, where production, exchange, and investment from households and firms are integrated through money creation and where funds allocation is operated, respectively, by banks and non-bank financial intermediaries. The model is used to investigate the special nature of (commercial) banks as money creators and the role of non-bank financial intermediaries in the saving-investment process, the relationship between saving and investment, and the channels through which finance may cause the circuit process to break down. The chapter discusses how the circuit approach can be used for an integrated analysis of economic and financial structural change. Importantly, the model used in the chapter is extended to show how circuit theory can explain the special role of banks as money creators also in contemporary "financialized" economies, where the financial dimension of capitalism far exceeds the sheer sphere of production.

Chapter 5—Money Creation by Banks—further elaborates on the role of banks as money creators and focuses on two aspects of bank money: its creation process and the extraction of seigniorage by banks being able to create money at a lower cost than its value. The recently flourishing literature on banks as money creators is reviewed, noting the still scant work traceable on bank seigniorage. The chapter analyzes how banks create money and the constraints on their money creation process deriving from the banks' payments activity and from the rules and technologies adopted by the payment system(s) where they operate. The chapter also analyzes how banks extract seigniorage from the economy and how seigniorage differs from the profits derived from pure financial intermediation, and it concludes with considerations on the nature of bank seigniorage.

Chapter 6—Money, Banks, and Seigniorage—delves deeper into the topic of bank seigniorage, highlighting its relative neglect in existing research. Remarkably, very few studies have sought to assess the effects of bank seigniorage on the economy. The chapter outlines the method I have employed to address this gap. A general aggregate production function is used to analyze the effects of seigniorage on the economy's aggregate output and to show how equilibrium prices and wages change when banks extract seigniorage from the economy, and a multi-sector model of the economy is used to study the impact of seigniorage on resource distribution across the economy. The chapter draws preliminary political-economy implications and discusses policy measures to eliminate, mitigate, or redistribute seigniorage across the economy.

As a final contribution to the first part of the book, Chapter 7—Money Quanta—focuses on the hybrid nature of bank money as it emerges from the Accounting View of Money (AVM) introduced in Chap. 2. With demand deposits being shown by the AVM to encompass both debt and equity components (in a mix that depends on factors that relate to the issuing banks and to the environment where they operate and interact), the idea is explored that they can be treated as objects of quantum physics—which typically feature a dual nature—and therefore be subject to quantum analysis. The chapter evaluates the merits of the idea and illustrates the work done using a quantum model to describe how the banks' power to create money is affected by the interactions taking place among the banks and between the banks and their environments. The chapter reports the main conclusions of numerical simulations run based on the afore-mentioned interactions and discusses how the information extracted through this process can be used for drawing financial stability considerations.

Part II of the book "On 'sound' money" explores how monetary instruments and their supporting systems can be (re)designed to reduce the financial instability risks associated with credit-based monies. Chapter 8—Preventing Banks from Creating Money—delves into the long-dated proposal to narrow the scope of banks as a measure to enhance financial stability. Accordingly, deposit-issuing banks would be prohibited from lending to the private sector and non-bank intermediaries would be restricted from funding investments with demand deposits. The chapter reviews the literature on the subject, contrasts the concept of narrow banking with contemporary banking theories, evaluates the potential consequences of narrow banking on finance and the real economy, and draws policy implications. The study also reports an early attempt to run an empirical exercise to estimate the economic costs of bank narrowness.

Two alternative system designs are then described in this part of the book, which feature characteristics of so-called "superstability." Chapter 9—Superstable Money (I): Separating Bank Money Creation from Lending—introduces the first "superstable" system design. It begins by highlighting that financial crises typically prompt demands for reforming financial systems that have either demonstrated vulnerability to shocks or have contributed to the crises themselves. The chapter contends that a fundamental issue with the current systems is that bank money is generated through the process of lending. It then illustrates the advantages of an alternative system where money creation occurs through specialized commercial institutions that issue money on a non-lending basis and free of charge (rather than lending at an interest) and supply payment services to customers. The chapter shows that the operation of these institutions, supported by an appropriate financial system policy framework, generates non-inflationary purchasing power without raising private-sector debt, allows broader access to purchasing power, fuels domestic output growth through higher domestic demand, reduces the economy's financial risks, and preserves the flow of money to the economy during crises.

Chapter 10—Superstable Money (II): Separating Money Creation from Banks—explores a different "superstable" system design. It starts by noting that fractional reserve banking inherently breeds instability, whereas full reserve systems (like narrow banking) eliminate this fragility but at the cost of suppressing banks' function as lenders. The chapter then highlights that a central bank digital currency (CBDC), as today widely discussed in the central banking literature, can offer a more secure type of domestic currency, but that the introduction of CBDC may pose significant challenges to traditional bank lending, and to banking intermediation more broadly. The chapter shows how such challenges can be avoided by implementing the "CBDC next-level model," whereby the central bank creates money by lending to banks and banks on-lend the proceeds to the economy (based on their own selection and allocation criteria). In this model—which the chapter fully describes—deposits are transferred from banks' balance sheets to that of the central bank, effectively removing the risk of bank runs while preserving their lending operations. This arrangement would ensure that no losses or defaults from individual banks or borrowers can undermine the central bank's capital or pose risks to depositors. Borrowers and banks remain obligated to fully repay their debts; failure to do so would result in their exit from the market or potential bankruptcy. The chapter describes how the transition would take place between conventional banking to the new CBDC-based system. The "CBDC next-level model" promises a level of financial stability that is far superior to that of current banking systems.

Finally, Part III of the book "On Money Effectiveness" focuses on the efficacy of monetary and fiscal policies as instruments to use "public" money for macroeconomic stabilization purposes. It comprises five chapters. Chapter 11—On Money Effectiveness: Beyond the Lucas Critique—presents my early attempt to address Lucas Critique, showing that a policy regime's effectiveness hinges on the reference model people believe reflects the economy: If the reference model itself changes, people's expectations and behaviors will also change, altering the impact of new policy rules compared to the old model. The chapter reaches the conclusion whereby in an economy agents do not only adjust their behavior in response to policy changes, thereby altering historical responses; they also modify their response to policy changes based on the model of the economy they believe correctly represents the economy. Consequently, monetary policy may or may not be effective depending on: i) the economic model adopted (albeit conventionally) by the agents and ii) the behaviors that agents consider rational (in accordance with the accepted convention) and consequently adopt. Importantly, in evaluating the effectiveness of monetary policy, understanding the prevailing conventions that lead agents to accept a model as "true" is more important than pinpointing the ontologically "true" model of the economy.

Chapter 12—Money and Secular Stagnation—analyzes the Secular Stagnation phenomenon as the consequence of strong liquidity preference in the economy caused by the upsurge and persistence of agents' pessimistic expectations. Using a micro-founded approach based on the utility theory of money illustrated in Chapter 3, Secular Stagnation is shown to emerge from money and other asset stock dynamics ultimately driven by liquidity preference (in Keynes's tradition), rather than by investment-saving relations. This approach is used to analytically evaluate alternative policies aimed at driving the economy out of Secular Stagnation and their effectiveness in doing so.

The conditions for policy effectiveness are the topic of Chap. 13—The Portfolio Theory of Inflation and Money (In)Effectiveness—which examines the influence of global investors on the value of money and other financial instruments that are issued in financially integrated economies and traded internationally. This analysis is grounded in the Portfolio Theory of Inflation (PTI), which studies the interplay between capital allocation decisions made by global investors and monetary and fiscal policies in today's interconnected economies. It explores how these decisions shape the policy space available for national authorities to implement active macroeconomic policies, thus impacting their effectiveness.

Chapter 14—Indifference Between State Money and Public Debt—further dwells on the value of money and other instruments issued by the public sector when they are traded in globalized markets and its reflections on macro-policy effectiveness. The famous capital structure irrelevance principle of (Modigliani & Miller, 1958) is used to show that when international capital allocation choices are determined by well-informed, deep-pocketed global investors, there are no net gains a government of a financially integrated economy can consistently extract from resorting to one type of deficit financing (say, debt) versus another (say, money) or by issuing debt in one form versus another. In particular, the approach is used to show that the cost of the capital needed by governments to finance their deficits is independent of whether: (i) financing originates from debt or money, (ii) debt is denominated in domestic or foreign currency, and (iii) money and debt are issued under floating or fixed exchange rates. The theorem's two corollaries show that governments seeking to monetize their deficits must remunerate money holdings with a real return that varies inversely with credibility and directly with the stock of money.

Chapter 15—The Fatal Flaws of Modern Money Theory—considers international financial integration as key to evaluate the effectiveness of the macroeconomic policy propounded by the supporters of Modern Money Theory (MMT)—a theory that has recently attracted the sympathy of a growing share of heterodox economists. The chapter shows that when the value of the domestic currency is determined by markets that are dominated by global investors, the monetization of fiscal deficits—which is central to MMT—cannot work as an effective and sustainable macroeconomic policy program aimed to achieve and maintain full-employment output in economies suffering from Keynesian unemployment or underemployment (unless very special and country-specific circumstances hold). Financially integrated economies that implemented MMT policies would either see their money stock grow unsustainably large, or they would have to adjust domestic interest rates to levels that would be inconsistent with the policy objective, leading to economic and financial instability instead.

Finally, Chapter 16—Fiscal Money—focuses on the concept of "Fiscal Money," a policy tool that was proposed in the aftermath of the European sovereign debt crisis of 2010 by a group of researchers, to stimulate domestic demand in highly indebted Eurozone countries without further increasing their public debt or violating Eurozone rules. The Fiscal Money proposal was a way to trigger economic recovery in countries that were trapped in stagnation and deflation and yet could not resort to conventional policies because of financial or institutional constraints. The chapter presents the work done to design Fiscal Money and illustrates a simulation of its application to the Italian economy, showing how it would operate in practice and evaluating its effectiveness.

The final chapter—Conclusion—wraps up the book by summarizing the main topics and viewpoints discussed throughout.

A remark before closing this Introduction. This book, notably the chapters of Part III, covers the work I have done in recent years, which enquires into the effectiveness of macro-policies. These chapters conclude that when national economies are highly financially integrated internationally ('globalized'), their credibility—as perceived by the markets—shapes the policy space available to their authorities and affects the effectiveness of their policy choices. When credibility is weak, the effectiveness of these policy choices is low or negligible, and vice versa.

This conclusion is not in contradiction with my earlier ones on the non-neutrality of money. The reason lies in the power that global market players hold to impose their views on the markets where they operate, through their investment decisions. To put it simply—though this may come across as an oversimplification—given the power of these players, if they believe that a country's policy choices are ineffective and not sustainable, those policies will ultimately prove to be so in practice.

It is not that global players necessarily know best or are more aware than others that certain policy choices are inherently ineffective; rather, they have the leverage to impose their own models and expectations on market outcomes, making those policy choices ineffective in the end.

The conclusion is that the more countries engage with these players, the more they become subject to their will and whims, regardless of the validity of the economic models used by them agents and the consistency of their expectations.

Appendix 1: Money in Economic Theory

Economic theory, particularly traditional monetary theory and the theory of finance, has predominantly treated money as a store of value while often giving less emphasis to its role as a means of payment and settlement instrument. This reflects the historical focus of economic models and the particular assumptions they make. Without pretending to be exhaustive, the following is a very cursory look at the literature.

Economic Theory and Money

In classical and neoclassical models, money is largely treated as a store of value and, to some extent, as a unit of account. These models emphasize money's role in holding wealth over time rather than as a medium of exchange (Brunner & Meltzer, 1971). Models like the Quantity Theory of Money and the Solow Growth Model deal with the effects of changes in the money supply on prices, output, and growth, without focusing much on the transactional role of money.

Even in New Keynesian models, money's role is simplified, and the analysis centers around how changes in the money supply or interest rates affect aggregate demand, inflation, and output (Woodford, 2003). These models prioritize understanding macroeconomic relationships involving money, leading to less attention to its everyday use in transactions.

Modeling Simplifications and Assumptions

To make macroeconomic modeling tractable, assumptions about money often emphasize its function as a store of value. This allows models to focus on intertemporal choices—how individuals and firms allocate resources over time—without delving into the complexities of the monetary system used for daily transactions (Lucas, 1980).

Monetary theory has typically abstracted away from the micro-level details of how money is used to facilitate transactions. For example, many models assume cash-in-advance constraints, treating money as a necessary condition to buy goods but not explicitly modeling the complexities involved in payment systems (Clower, 1967).

Money as a Medium of Exchange and Settlement Instrument

The role of money as a medium of exchange and settlement instrument is less formally represented in traditional economic models. Monetary exchange models such as those developed by Kiyotaki and Wright do address the transactional role of money, but these models are relatively niche and have not been the focus of mainstream monetary theory (Kiyotaki & Wright, 1989).

In financial theory, money is often treated as an asset in a portfolio, with its main role being to preserve value over time (Tobin, 1958). As such, the focus tends to be on how money fits into an optimal portfolio rather than on its use in settling transactions.

Practical Implications

The emphasis on money as a store of value has been helpful for understanding macroeconomic stability, inflation, and the conduct of monetary policy. However, it has limited applicability for understanding how payment systems evolve, how financial innovations affect the use of money, or how transaction frictions impact economic outcomes (Goodhart, 1989).

Ignoring the transactional role of money can overlook the impact of financial frictions and the importance of liquidity in everyday economic life. Understanding money's role as a means of settlement is crucial in contexts like financial crises, where payment systems freeze, and the ability to make transactions is fundamentally disrupted (Bernanke, 1983).

Modern Developments: Payment Systems

Recent developments in monetary economics have begun to emphasize the means of payment aspect, especially in the context of evolving payment technologies and digital currencies. Researchers are increasingly looking at how different payment mechanisms (e.g., cash, credit cards, cryptocurrencies) affect economic efficiency, liquidity constraints, and monetary policy (Rogoff, 2016).

New Monetarist models, such as those involving search and matching frameworks, have started to explicitly model money's transactional role, acknowledging that the medium of exchange function is essential for understanding real-world economic activity (Williamson & Wright, 2010).

With advancements in financial technology (FinTech) and digital payment systems, the role of money as a means of payment is gaining more theoretical and practical importance. This has spurred new interest in understanding the settlement dynamics and the institutional arrangements that underpin the payment system, aspects that traditional models have often neglected (Carstens, 2021).

Part I of this book considers the role of money as payment and settlement instrument and its theoretical implications, from different angles. Section B in the main text below.

Appendix 2: On the Non-neutrality of Money

In mainstream economics, money is neutral. If not in the short term, certainly in the long-term. The trajectory of an economy's output is typically determined by supply-side factors such as labor, capital, and technological progress, all of them fully employed or employed at capacity, if prices are sufficiently flexible. Consequently, money can only change prices proportionally, with no (long term) effects on real output. In such a context, thrift supports the growth of capital, through the investment of savings, and productivity is the manifestation of the supply-side factors working together effectively. These factors dictate the economy's potential output, and aggregate demand is seen primarily as a short-term influence that temporarily moves the economy away from or toward that potential.

Several non-mainstream economic theories incorporate **demand-side and monetary factors** into the determination of long-run output. These approaches argue that demand and monetary policies can (and do) have lasting effects on an economy's productive capacity, investment patterns, and overall growth trajectory. (Kaldor, 1966), a post-Keynesian economist, developed **demand-driven growth models** that emphasize the feedback loops between demand and supply-side factors. According to Kaldor-Verdoorn's Law, higher demand, particularly external demand for exports, drives output growth, which in turn improves productivity through economies of scale and learning-by-doing. Also, (Kaldor, 1972) idea of cumulative causation suggested that the initial increase in demand leads to greater production, which raises productivity, thereby reinforcing further increases in demand. This process is self-sustaining: Higher demand boosts output, which in turn fuels more demand, creating a virtuous cycle of growth. Kaldor's work challenges the neoclassical notion that supply-side factors alone determine long-term output and argues that persistent demand is crucial for sustaining economic growth (McCombie & Thirlwall, 1994).

In his work on **general equilibrium theory**, (Hahn, 1977) examined the idea that market processes might fail to reach full-employment equilibrium through the notion of "conjectural equilibria," even in economic models where time is not an essential feature. Hahn's conjectural equilibrium refers to the idea that markets, under certain conditions, may fail to achieve full employment or Pareto efficiency due to coordination failures and misaligned expectations among economic agents. The role of coordination failures in generating macroeconomic instability had already been emphasized by (Leijonhufvud, 1968), which noted that markets often fail to clear not because of price or wage rigidities, but due to misaligned expectations and the lack of coordination among economic agents. Leijonhufvud highlighted how decentralized decision-making and incomplete information can trap economies in suboptimal states, such as prolonged recessions or unemployment.

All this closely relates to the **disequilibrium macroeconomics** of the 1970s, a field that emerged as economists sought to explain persistent unemployment and market failures that neoclassical models could not account for. This line of theory focused on situations where wages and prices do not adjust instantly to clear markets, leading to persistent unemployment, excess supply, or demand, and failures in reaching full-employment equilibria (see, for instance, Bénassy, (Benassy, 1982).

One of the central theories that incorporates demand into long-run output determination comes from **post-Keynesian economics**, which emphasizes that the level of aggregate demand shapes the economy's long-term performance. Post-Keynesians argue that if demand is insufficient, the economy can operate below its potential for an extended period, resulting in a demand-constrained growth path (Lavoie, 2014).[3]

Another perspective that emphasizes the role of demand in long-run growth comes from **theories of endogenous Money**, particularly within post-Keynesian and monetary circuit theory frameworks (Fontana, 2003). According to this view, money is not neutral even in the long run and money creation by banks (through the extension of credit) plays a crucial role in stimulating investment, consumption, and economic growth (Lavoie, 1992). Over time, higher levels of investment lead to greater capital formation, technological advancements, and productivity improvements, which can boost long-term output (Graziani, 2003). In this way, demand driven by credit creation and monetary factors is a key determinant of long-run economic growth.

As an evolution of this view on growth, the **theory of the supermultiplier** builds on demand-driven growth models by emphasizing the role of autonomous demand components (such as exports, government spending, and investment) in driving long-term economic growth (Serrano, 1995), and (Serrano et al., 2022). Unlike traditional demand-driven growth models, this theory focuses on autonomous demand components (like government spending and exports) as the key drivers of long-term growth, rather than investment; it considers investment as endogenous to demand and emphasizes stable, cumulative demand effects that shape productive capacity over time, leading to more sustained and stable growth compared to traditional models, which focus on short-term cycles or supply-side factors.

Even within **New Keynesian economics**, which represents the current mainstream thinking, there is recognition that demand-side factors can influence long-term output through hysteresis (Blanchard & Summers, 1987). New Keynesian models traditionally focus on short-term price and wage rigidities, but some also incorporate the idea that persistent demand shocks can have long-lasting effects on an economy's productive capacity (Failed, 2009; Failed, 2009). For instance, a prolonged recession can result in long-term unemployment, which can reduce the economy's potential output. In this framework, the role of monetary policy becomes crucial not only for stabilizing short-term fluctuations but also for preventing long-term damage to the economy's

[3] An important concept here is "hysteresis," which refers to the idea that temporary downturns in demand can have permanent negative effects on an economy's potential output. For example, during a recession, firms reduce investment, and workers may become unemployed for extended periods (Blanchard & Summers, 1986). This not only reduces current output but also weakens the future productive capacity of the economy. Long-term unemployment leads to skill deterioration, which reduces labor market efficiency, while lower investment hampers capital accumulation and innovation (Stockhammer, 2011). Therefore, post-Keynesians assert that aggregate demand must be actively managed to ensure sustained growth and avoid long-term economic stagnation.

capacity. By preventing deep recessions, monetary policy can help maintain investment and labor market participation, thereby preserving the economy's productive potential.

In **structuralist models**, particularly in the context of developing economies, aggregate demand is considered a key driver of structural transformation and long-term growth (Taylor, 1991). These models emphasize the importance of demand in shifting resources from low-productivity sectors (such as agriculture) to high-productivity sectors (such as manufacturing and services). Government spending, external demand, and investment are seen as critical factors in promoting this structural change. By driving demand in higher productivity sectors, these models suggest that long-term economic growth can be accelerated, demonstrating that demand-side policies are essential for sustainable development.

Finally, the **secular stagnation hypothesis**, revived by (Summers, 2014), also emphasizes the role of demand in determining long-term output. Accordingly, advanced economies may face a persistent shortfall of aggregate demand, even with low interest rates, leading to chronically weak growth. This lack of demand results in low investment, subdued technological innovation, and a slowdown in labor force growth, which together contribute to long-term economic stagnation. In this framework, boosting aggregate demand through fiscal or monetary policy is crucial for sustaining long-run output growth. Without sufficient demand, economies may remain trapped in a low-growth equilibrium, where potential output remains below what it could be.

References

Ball, L. (2009). Hysteresis in unemployment: Old and new evidence. NBER Working Paper Series, March, 8–21.

Benassy, J. P. (1982). *The economics of market disequilibrium*. Academic Press.

Bernanke, B. S. (1983). Nonmonetary effects of the financial crisis in the propagation of the great depression. *American Economic Review, 73*(3), 257–276

Blanchard, O. J., & Summers, L. H. (1986). Hysteresis and the European unemployment problem. *NBER Macroeconomics Annual, 1*, 15–78.

Blanchard, O. J., & Summers, L. H. (1987). Hysteresis in unemployment. *European Economic Review, 31*(1–2), February–March, 288–295.

Brunner, K., & Meltzer, A. H. (1971). The uses of money: money in the theory of an exchange economy. *American Economic Review, 61*(5), 784–805.

Carstens, A. (2021), *Central bank digital currencies and the future of money*. BIS Speech, Bank for International Settlements, Basel.

Clower, R. W. (1967). A reconsideration of the microfoundations of monetary theory. *Western Economic Journal, 6*(1), 1–8.

Davidson, P. (1972). Money and the real world. *The Economic Journal, 82*(325), 101–115.

Humphrey, D. B. (2009). Retail payments: Integration and innovation payment scale economies, competition, and pricing. ECB Working Paper Series, No. 1136.

Fontana, G. (2003). Post Keynesian approaches to endogenous money: A time framework explanation. *Review of Political Economy, 15*(3), 291–314.

Goodhart, C. A. E. (1989). *Money, information, and uncertainty*. Palgrave Macmillan.

Graziani, A. (2003). *The monetary theory of production*. Cambridge University Press.
Hahn, F. H. (1977). Keynesian economics and general equilibrium theory: reflections on some current debates. In G. C. Harcourt (Eds.), *The microeconomic foundations of macroeconomics*. Other International Economic Association Publications Series. Palgrave Macmillan, London.
Hahn, F. H. (1983). *Money and inflation*. MIT Press.
Kaldor, N. (1966). *Causes of the slow rate of economic growth of the United Kingdom*. Cambridge University Press.
Kaldor, N. (1972). The irrelevance of equilibrium economics. *The Economic Journal, 82*(328), 1237–1255.
Keynes, J. M. (1936a). *The general theory of employment*. Macmillan, Cambridge University Press.
Kiyotaki, N., & R. Wright (1989). On money as a medium of exchange. *Journal of Political Economy, 97*(4), 927–954.
Lavoie, M. (1992). *Foundations of Post-Keynesian economic analysis*. Edward Elgar.
Lavoie, M. (2014). *Post-Keynesian economics: New foundations*. Edward Elgar Publishing.
Leijonhufvud, A. (1968). *On keynesian economics and the economics of Keynes*. Oxford University Press.
Lucas, R. E. (1980). Two illustrations of the quantity theory of money. *American Economic Review, 70*(5), 1005–1014.
McCombie, J., & Thirlwall, A. P. (1994). *Economic growth and the balance-of-payments constraint*. St. Martin's Press.
Modigliani, F., & Miller, M. (1958). The cost of capital, corporation finance and the theory of investment. *American Economic Review, 48*(3), 261–297.
Rogoff, K. (2016). *The curse of cash*. Princeton University Press.
Serrano, F. (1995). Long period effective demand and the sraffian supermultiplier. *Contributions to Political Economy, 14*, 67–69.
Serrano, F., Summa, R., & Freitas, F. (2022). Autonomous demand-led growth and the supermultiplier: The theory, the model and applications. In: *26th FMM Conference: post-Keynesian Economics and Global Challenges*.
Stockhammer, E. (2011). Wage-led growth: An introduction. *International Journal of Labour Research, 3*(2), 145–178.
Summers, L. H. (2014). U.S. Economic prospects: secular stagnation, hysteresis, and the zero lower bound. *Business Economics, 49*(2), 65–73.
Taylor, L. (1991). *Income distribution, inflation, and growth* (Vol 9). MIT Press.
Tily, G. (2012). *Keynes's monetary theory of interest*. BIS Paper No. 65c..
Tobin, J. (1958). Liquidity preference as Behavior towards risk. *Review of Economic Studies, 25*(2), 65–86.
Vines, D., & Wills, S., (Eds.) (2018). Rebuilding macroeconomic theory. *Oxford Review of Economic Policy, 34*(1 2), 1 12.
Williamson, S., & Wright, R. (2010). New monetarist economics: models. *Federal Reserve Bank of St. Louis Review, 92*(4), 265–302.
Woodford, M. (2003). *Interest and prices: Foundations of a theory of monetary policy*. Princeton University Press.

Part I
On Money

Part I focuses on the foundational aspects of money and consists of six chapters, each providing a perspective on the complex interplay between money, banking, and economic theory.

Chapter 2
What is Money: Debt or Equity?

Abstract This chapter explores the Accounting View of Money (AVM), a theoretical framework developed in collaboration with Prof. Massimo Costa, and investigates various forms of money, including traditional coins, modern banking deposits, and emerging digital currencies, through the lens of international accounting standards. The AVM fundamentally redefines the nature of fiat money. Traditionally seen as debt of the issuer, the AVM posits that state-issued currencies—such as cash, banknotes, and central bank reserves—should instead be viewed as net wealth for holders and net worth (equity) for issuers. The AVM also shows that, in fractional reserve regimes, only a share of commercial bank money (demand deposits) can be regarded as debt. The AVM points to the correct way to account for the above forms of money in the financial statements of the issuing institutions, clarifies what the different accounting treatments imply for a correct understanding of the concept of money, and evaluates the related economic and economic policy implications.

2.1 Preamble

This chapter illustrates the Accounting View of Money (AVM), which I have developed in collaboration with Prof. Massimo Costa, a leading expert in Accounting theory and practice. The AVM challenges the traditional view of money as a debt of the issuer and, instead, examines the equity nature of money, exploring the implications that follow from the new view. Our attempt to publish our article on the AVM faced fierce opposition from peer-reviewers of different perspectives, before finally being accepted (once hopes of this happening had almost gone…).

A common cause of such resistance was the momentum of "tradition" and the very persistent habit of established scholars to cling to old (and comfortable) ideas, while (pre)judging any new (and uncomfortable) thinking as incorrect. Another reason, related to the nature of the AVM, was that it is difficult to find good economists who have solid knowledge of Accounting, and good accountants who have solid knowledge of Economics: being deliberately at the intersection of Economics and Accounting, the AVM ended up facing a lot of unfounded criticism. Eventually, as

B. Bossone, *Trailblazing Visions of Money in Economic Theory*, Contributions to Economics, https://doi.org/10.1007/978-3-031-82544-6_2

Massimo and I advanced with the formulation of our theory, we pleasantly discovered that we were not alone. Other reputable researchers were heading in the same direction as ours; in fact, as mentioned below, some had even anticipated one of the fundamental tenets of our AVM (which we recognized only lately).

I wanted to start this book on money with the question of what money is. For that, I had to rely on my latest ideas on the topic, and I inevitably began with the AVM, which is one of my most recent works and precedes by far others that will appear later in the book. I want to reiterate that the AVM was the outcome of the (still ongoing) collaboration between Massimo and myself and the result of the combination of our two fields. Neither of us could have developed the AVM alone.

Right at the time of writing this chapter, Massimo and I are revisiting some aspects of the AVM that, in our view, promise to bear new interesting implications. We hope the AVM will contribute to pushing forward the frontier of the theory of money.

2.2 Introduction

The AVM reassesses the essence of money, examining it through the lens of internationally recognized accounting principles. It encompasses a wide spectrum of money, ranging from traditional coins, among the earliest forms of currency, and banknotes to contemporary manifestations such as bank deposits, electronic monies, and digital currencies. Coins retain their status as legal tender across numerous national jurisdictions, recognized as indebtedness of issuing states and consequently recorded as part of national public debt in accordance with prevailing accounting standards (European System of Accounts [ESA], 2010). Similarly, central bank-issued banknotes, alongside reserves, are accounted for as liabilities owed by central banks to holders thereof, a principle that extends to future digital currency iterations, and demand deposits issued by commercial banks, representing liabilities of the issuing institutions, are claims held by depositors against their respective banks.

However, the traditional legal characterization of money as "debt" is cast into doubt by a thorough application of extant accounting principles. While debt entails obligations for borrowers to transfer economic resources to lenders (International Accounting Standards Board [IASB], 2018), the obligations associated with public holdings of coins or financial institutions holding banknotes and reserves are less straightforward.[1] Moreover, non-debt monetary liabilities, often a source of income

[1] Here, I wish to set the record straight. When Massimo Costa and I developed the AVM, we missed to notice (and therefore refer to) the previous study by (Dyson and Hodgson 2016). This study had questioned the debt nature of state money and had concluded that it is a form of equity (as the AVM does), consistently with the International Financial Reporting Standards and the International Public Sector Accounting Standards. Thus, while, as discussed in this chapter, the AVM goes beyond this recognition, extends it to other forms of money, and considers its implications to a broader and deeper extent than the work by Dyson and Hodgson, the latter must be acknowledged as the first contribution to this new way of thinking about money—at least, to our knowledge so far. In any case, (Covick and Davis 1990) are the first authors (at least, to the best of our knowledge) to have argued

for issuers, known as "seigniorage," pose questions regarding their appropriate accounting treatment and the adequacy of current practices.

Distinct accounting methodologies are advocated by the AVM for state-issued and private-issued monies, shedding light on their economic implications. The AVM reconciles the divergence between formal reporting rules and the economic essence of money, aiming to redefine accurate representations of money in accounting terms. It addresses inconsistencies arising from outdated representations that fail to align with evolving economic contexts.

Throughout this chapter, analogies are drawn to the "selling" and "leasing" of money. Money is "sold" when it is exchanged for other forms of value (e.g., goods, services, real or financial assets, or other currencies) and its ownership changes hands, and it is "leased" when it is exchanged against a promise to be returned at some future date.[2]

Methodologically, while accounting practices may vary across jurisdictions and institutions, and in particular across central banks (Archer & Moser-Boehm, 2013), the AVM draws primarily upon the Conceptual Framework for Financial Reporting, the backbone of International Financial Reporting Standards (IFRS) for private-sector entities,[3] and the Conceptual Framework for General Purpose Financial Reporting by Public-Sector Entities for public bodies.[4] The IFRS and IPSAS, embodying globally recognized accounting principles, fosters consistency in financial reporting across diverse entities.

The chapter is organized as follows: Sect. 2.3 reviews the existing literature on accounting practices pertaining to currency in the financial statements of currency issuers, alongside discussions on seigniorage. Section 2.4 delineates the AVM, elucidating the treatment of various forms of currency and identifying sources of seigniorage. It also outlines how different types of currency should be treated based on relevant international accounting principles. With specific reference to commercial banks, the section delineates their hybrid nature of their deposit liabilities (as partly debt and partly equity) and the associated complexities in accounting for them as financial instruments. Section 2.5 explores the implications of the AVM for theory and policy, both at a corporate and societal level. Section 2.6 offers concluding

---

against considering banknotes as state liabilities, proposing instead that they should be accounted for as a source of revenues (seignior age), with implications for the public debt.

[2] Selling or leasing involves a "revenue" for the entity that sells or leases a resource over which it has control, exactly as money is a resource controlled (and produced) by the issuing entity. Quoting IPSAS no. 47, revenue "comprises gross inflows of economic benefits or service potential received and receivable by the entity, which represents an increase in net assets/equity, other than increases relating to contribution from owners". The International Public Sector Accounting Standards (IPSAS) are the accounting standards for public bodies and are derived from the IFRS used for the private sector. The case of repurchase agreements, for instance, points to how a lending operation can be structured, both legally and economically, as a temporary sale of money with an obligation from the seller to repurchase the money at a future date. Yet, strict legal terminology is not necessarily relevant in Accounting and the general principle of "Prevalence of substance over form" holds, whereby if an exchange bears the substance of a sale, it is indeed a sale.

[3] See International Financial Reporting Standards Foundation (IFRSF 2018).

[4] See International Public Sector Accounting Standard Board (IPSASB 2020).

remarks. The chapter is supplemented with three appendixes: The first discusses how primary seigniorage on money issuance should be accounted for correctly; the second addresses the question of whether money should be considered as a liability of the financial sector; the third and final one offers further clarifications on commercial bank money (partially) sharing the nature of equity.

Before proceeding, a note on terminology may be useful to clarify the correct use of some key accounting terms, especially to the benefit of economist readers. The balance sheet or statement of financial position of (financial and non-financial) companies consists of two sections: the right and left sections. The right section is a composite one as it includes equity and liabilities. In the accounting jargon, this section is called the "Credit," highlighting the fact that from the accounting standpoint, both equity and liabilities credit the account of the company. At a deeper level, however, what connects these two elements is that they are both "claims" that third parties hold on the company. Thus, the right section is conventionally termed the "Claims" side of the balance sheet. As to the left side, which in jargon is called "Debit," noting that from the economic and functional viewpoints the opposite of "claims" is "resources," it is correctly called the "Resources" side of the balance sheet, which is to be preferred to the "Assets" side denomination that is more commonly used by the economists. Throughout the following, the accounting terminology will be used referring to "Claims" and "Resources." As a result, when references will be made in this chapter (and in the whole book, for that matter) to money and public debt, these will be considered as government claims or claims issued by the public sector (not as public liabilities, as is usually done).

2.3 Review of the Literature

Until recently, the realm of accounting literature concerning money liabilities remained notably limited, as evidenced by the financial accounting practices survey conducted by Beatty & Liao (2014). This lack of scholarly interest can be traced back to historical origins: Traditionally, money liabilities were perceived as straightforward debt obligations and were accordingly accounted for in the financial statements of issuing institutions without much further inquiry; inertia has largely perpetuated this perspective. This perspective is echoed, for example, in Mehrling (2012) hierarchy of money, and is even more explicitly articulated in the theory of state money, originally proposed by Knapp (1905) and revisited in recent years (see Wray, 1998), which posits all forms of money as debt and asserts that the acceptance of state money for tax payments renders it a liability of the government. However, this outlook is challenged by the AVM and other contemporary contributions, as discussed in Sect. 2.4. Recent research has begun to invigorate this subject, potentially paving the way for intriguing new developments.

In the context of central bank money accounting, an influential contribution comes from the work of Archer and Moser-Boehm (cit.), which replaces the narrow concept of equity capital with the broader notion of "positive comprehensive net worth." This expanded definition encompasses not only conventional shareholder equity but also the inventory of outstanding banknotes and the present value of future seigniorage income. Regarding banknotes specifically, the authors contend that they "...act more like equity capital than debt obligations. As they bear no interest and are perpetual in character, they provide a stable funding base for income generation. To the extent that net income can be retained when needed, a large share of banknote liabilities provides a base for rebuilding equity if it has been depleted by a negative shock" (pp. 33–34). However, Archer and Moser-Boehm refrain from delving deeper into this line of inquiry and do not extend the sources of income beyond banknotes, a point which the AVM addresses.

As noted, Dyson & Hodgson (2016) took a significant step farther, concluding that all state monies (including central bank reserves) are a form of equity, and Reis (2019) posits that banknotes should not be considered a liability of the central bank but rather as durable goods produced and sold by the central bank; this author further argues that central bank money could indeed be viewed as part of the public debt, but this would then require including the associated seigniorage as a source of funds. This perspective aligns with the AVM.

In line with the AVM, Zellweger-Gutnecht (2019) questions whether central bank money can be classified as a form of (quasi) equity, arguing that it no longer obligates the central bank to exchange it for an asset other than central bank money. However, unlike the AVM, Zellweger-Gutnecht associates the nature of money with the time profile of its creation, suggesting that money created permanently through outright transactions should be considered equity, while money created through temporary operations remains closer to classical debt. This divergence from the AVM's stance is discussed later in this chapter, which maintains that the time profile of money creation does not determine its nature as equity.

Importantly, the perspectives articulated by Kumhof et al. (2020) substantially converge with those of the AVM regarding state money, as the authors themselves acknowledge reference to earlier work cited. They concur that central bank money cannot be characterized as a liability of the central bank, as in fiat money systems, the central bank is under no legal obligation to repay money holders with anything other than central bank money. However, they refrain from categorizing it as equity, instead considering it a hybrid financial instrument termed "social equity." The AVM asserts that its view of money as equity does not lead to misunderstandings regarding associated rights and obligations.

The AVM intersects with the discourse on the ontology of money, as hosted by the Cambridge Journal of Economics in a special issue dedicated to the topic. In this regard, it transcends the conventional dichotomy between commodity-based and credit-based money, proposing neither a commodity nor a credit theory of money but rather an "equity theory" of money (with specific qualifications for commercial bank money). As discussed below, the AVM underscores that recipients of money claims acquire generalized purchasing power over national wealth, while entities with the authority to issue money claims generate a form of income equal in nominal value, which must be duly recorded. While Heinsohn & Steiger (2013) also conceive of money as a non-physical title to property, they diverge in their assertion that money is never net worth to its issuer, whereas money as equity constitutes the essence of the AVM.

Furthermore, the connection between the AVM and Bezmer's (2016) work warrants acknowledgment, particularly his emphasis on the necessity of incorporating an " "accounting view" of the economy when reimagining money and banking. While Bezmer employs this view to advocate for the credit theory of money, the AVM employs accounting principles to establish a new, alternative perspective on contemporary forms of money.

The AVM's characterization of money as equity also extends to a portion of commercial bank money, as discussed further in this chapter. However, there exists scant literature on the accounting treatment of commercial bank money (demand deposits) beyond categorizing them as commercial bank liabilities, and the topic is overlooked by the international accounting standards (IFRS), national accounting standards (GAAP), and existing national banking regulations. Nevertheless, for the purposes of the AVM, the literature on hybrid financial instruments is highly pertinent. According to PAAinE (2008), Schmidt, (2013), and PWC(2017), PWC (2017), the distinction between liabilities and equity as fundamental sources of bank funding is no longer as clear-cut as in the past, raising questions about the conventional definition of equity capital. For a company, equity capital serves as a funding source like debt liabilities, with the distinction that, unlike the latter, equity capital need not be repaid to the company's owners unless and until the company undergoes liquidation.

The application of the AVM to commercial bank money—demand deposits—builds upon Costa (2009), which traces the historical evolution of deposits from debt to equity, and Bossone (2000), my early exploration of how payment settlement rules influence this transformation—an issue which I then re-explored more recently in Bossone (2020a) and will be discussed in Chap. 4 of this book.

The AVM considers deposits as a hybrid instrument, partly debt and partly equity, based on stochastic considerations. The pronouncement by IPSASB (2020) on liabilities and probabilities lends significant support to the AVM, at least for Central Bank or State money. Chapter 5 of this book will deem the "duality" of deposits inherent in their hybrid nature as a reason to treat them as objects of quantum physics and show that subjecting them to quantum analytical methods can extract valuable economic information.

The tax accounting literature (Flynn, 1999) is also relevant to the AVM, as its distinction between capital gains and revenues facilitates the application of accounting definitions of hybrid financial instruments to commercial bank money liabilities within the AVM framework.

The concept of money as equity presupposes that seigniorage income accrues to money issuers. Regarding state seigniorage, extensive literature exists (see Baltensperger & Jordan, 1997; Haslag, 1998; Burdekin, 2009), the review by Bjerg et al., (2017), and the comprehensive work by Reich (2017). The AVM introduces novel components into the definition and measurement of seigniorage, distinguishing between primary and secondary seigniorage in a manner conceptually similar to the distinction drawn by Bjerg et al. (cit.) between monetary and opportunity cost seigniorage, albeit with different definitions and measurements based on correct accounting principles. As discussed below, this has significant financial and fiscal implications warranting further exploration. Concerning the seigniorage extracted by commercial banks, references to the relevant literature are reported in Chap. 5 of this book.

2.4 The Accounting View of Money

The AVM examines the various forms of fiat money currently in widespread use globally as legal tender or settlement instruments and the money issued by commercial banks as demand deposits and reevaluates their essence based on the accurate application of relevant international financial accounting principles. It addresses state money and commercial bank money separately.

2.4.1 *State Money*

Historically, sovereigns ensured that the coins they minted contained specific amounts of precious metals. Under conditions where debasement was avoided, full-bodied golden or silver coins were not considered to generate debt obligations for the issuing sovereigns according to accounting standards. However, the introduction of banknotes later allowed holders to claim conversion into silver or gold, thus creating genuine debt obligations for the issuers. Subsequently, central banks faced similar obligations as holders of their reserve liabilities, predominantly commercial banks. Both banknotes and central bank reserves thus constituted true debt obligations legally binding on their issuers.

Today, the convertibility of all three forms of money has nearly disappeared. Coins have largely been supplanted by paper money and, increasingly, electronic money, convertible only into cash and bank deposits. Banknote convertibility was halted globally before World War II and never reinstated, effectively abolishing it in practice. The abandonment of the gold-exchange standard further eradicated " "debt" banknotes internationally. Presently, reserve deposits held by commercial banks, or other authorized financial intermediaries, and national treasuries at central banks are disconnected from conversion obligations into commodities or third-party liabilities, except in cases where fixed exchange rate arrangements, dollarization of the economy, or currency board regimes apply. A liability that the issuer may settle using either itself or another of the issuer's own liability is not truly a liability; and yet, if it is accepted in the economy for settling payments and other debts, it is a generic asset, while it is a credit on the issuer.[5] This is exactly what central bank

[5] Mehrling (cit.) claims that, "From the point of view of the system as a whole, every liability is someone else's asset," (p 6). Yet, this is not necessarily always the case. In (Buiter 2003) words, "Base money (…) does not have to be redeemed by the government – ever. It is the final means of

money is: not a true liability of the issuing central bank, and yet an asset that the economy uses as settlement instrument. As an asset, it is a claim on the real resources that the economy produces but does not involve any obligation for its issuer to deliver those resources.

Consequently, although all the aforementioned forms of money are classified as debt in public finance statistics and central bank financial statements, they do not constitute debt in the sense of implying creditor rights.[6]

The AVM dismisses the idea that all money is debt and that debt obligations arise when money issuers commit to accepting their own money from borrowers for debt settlement. Debt denotes a current obligation of an agent to transfer, not accept, an economic resource due to past events. Fiat money represents a claim on real resources; thus, when returned to the state for tax payments, it signifies a transfer of real resources from the economy to the state. The state accepts money like any other agent in the economy. But the state's commitment to extinguishing tax obligations as it receives claims on real resources at settlement is not debt. When the state absolves itself of its obligations to redeem the money received into anything but its liabilities, no debt-credit relationships remain outstanding between the state and the taxpayers. Other compelling arguments, consistent with the AVM, against the notion that state money is debt are provided by Kumhof et al. (2020).

Financial Reporting

The IPSASB has stated that when there is a substantial engagement to give something to the holder, a true debt exists; when the outflow of resources is probable, a provision is made; when the outflow of resources is possible, a contingent liability arises; and when the outflow of resources is remote, no liability exists. This pronouncement supports the AVM's conclusion that irredeemable money is not a liability of the issuing entity.

However, if irredeemable fiat money is not a liability, what else is state money then? And how should it be accounted for correctly in financial reports?

When the state issues irredeemable fiat money and spends it on goods and services or lends it in exchange for credit claims, the proceeds generate a form of income, specifically " "revenue income," corresponding to the resources that fiat money enables the state to acquire. Issuing state money thus generates seigniorage income for the state, particularly when it is used to finance government expenditures directly. Under current accounting practices, this income is incorrectly unreported in the

settlement of government obligations vis-à-vis the private sector. It does not represent a claim on the issuer other than the same amount of itself." As shown by (Costa 2009), with fiat money being irredeemable, no holder may ask the issuing entity to exchange it into anything else, and thus the money ceases to be a liability and becomes a source of undistributed income, that is net worth or equity (see further below). See also Reis (2019) and Kumhof (cit.).

[6] In the EU, for instance, according to Eurostat, also the coins issued by central governments in the euro area are, by convention, treated as liabilities of the national central banks, which as a counterpart hold a notional claim on general government. See item 5.2.2. of the Classification of Financial Transactions, Regulation (EU) No 549/2013 of the European Parliament and of the Council of 21 May 2013.

income statement of the issuing entity. For instance, in the case of central bank money, it is incorrectly reported under the central bank's liabilities.

In fact, when money is issued by a public-sector entity, the income should accrue to the entity's owners—the citizens, as ideal "shareholders" of the "res publica,"[7] and when money is issued by a privately owned central bank, the income from seigniorage that is undistributed to the state treasury accrues to the central bank's shareholders. If the income is not distributed to the owners, it should be recorded as retained earnings, becoming equity, consistent with BIS's Archer and Moser-Boehm. Issuing money is akin to producing and selling goods, as money bears value as any goods does.[8] When money is sold or loaned, it falls under IFRS 15 and 16, respectively. The proceeds from selling money should be accounted for as revenue, reflecting the fair value of the goods, services, or assets received in exchange for money. The margin between this revenue and the cost of issuing money constitutes "primary" seigniorage.

On the other hand, when money is leased, the money issuer is treated as a lessor in a finance lease. In this case, the leased money is accounted for as credit, while the interest accrued should be recorded as revenue, not a liability. The lessee accounts for the leased money as an asset, recorded as cash, while the associated debt is accounted for as a liability. The margin between the interest revenue and the costs of issuing the loan is termed "secondary" seigniorage and should be recorded as revenue in the financial statements of the issuing institution. Notice that when fiat money is loaned, the income to the issuing entity combines both primary and secondary seigniorage, originating from the use of fiat money to purchase real resources. From an accounting perspective, the permanent or temporary time profile of the transaction is irrelevant. Income is generated through a money creation transaction and can be undone through a transaction of opposite sign, which destroys previously created money. Furthermore, mutual offsetting of entries is not permissible in accounting because it affects the clarity of financial reports. When money is issued and leased, capital increases, and any increases in capital are equity, while the reverse holds when money is returned as loan repayments. Yet, the sequence of offsetting transactions does not alter the nature of money as equity. Additionally, to the extent that a net positive stock of money issued as loans exists, this represents income for the issuer, i.e., primary seigniorage, to be recorded as equity.

Presently, only a fraction of secondary seigniorage, specifically that on banknotes, is recorded in central bank financial statements, while primary seigniorage on banknotes and reserves and secondary seigniorage on reserves are concealed. The former is recorded on the claims side of the balance sheet, among the liabilities, while the latter is mingled with other revenues and expenses on the income statement and not properly identified.

The current practice exhibits an evident inconsistency between the correct accounting rule adopted for the lessee and the incorrect one adopted for the lessor. Accumulated incomes, in the form of primary and secondary seigniorage, constitute

[7] Kumhof et al. (cit.) share the same view.

[8] Chapter 2 will show that money (and other financial assets) bears utility much like any goods, will identify the origin of its utility, and will illustrate its analytical foundations.

equity for the issuing institution. Assimilating money to equity necessitates moving beyond the distinction between equity and liabilities. Recognizing that state money is not debt by the issuing state, a proper application of the IFRS should acknowledge its nature as equity. According to the International Accounting Standard (IAS) 32, an equity instrument is defined as "any contract that exhibits a residual interest in the assets of an entity after subtracting all its liabilities." Under these definitions, state money is neither "credit" for its holders nor "debt" for its issuer (Appendix 1). It instead represents net wealth for the holders and net worth (equity) for the issuer.

Money accounted as issuer's equity implies ownership rights. However, these rights do not confer any possession entitlement to money holders over the entity issuing the money. Unlike shares, the equity associated with money holdings does not grant money holders residual claims on the net assets of the issuing entity, akin to consumers purchasing goods from firms not acquiring ownership rights over the selling firms. Money holders possess rights identical to those obtained by consumers purchasing goods from firms, as selling goods that deliver utility to consumers conceptually parallels selling an instrument, like money, which enables settlement of financial obligations.

The rights vested in money holdings consist of claims on nominal shares of national wealth, exercisable at any time by money holders (Appendix 2), granting generalized purchasing power on national wealth. Issuers of these claims receive a form of gross income equivalent to the real resources they can acquire with the issued claims.

Under the AVM, based on double-entry rules, money is recorded as equity on the Claims side of the balance sheet and cash on the Resources side. When money is "sold" or "leased," the value received in exchange replaces cash on the Resources side, while the Claims side remains unchanged. Providing distinct evidence of the source of income separate from general revenues and distinguishing between primary and secondary seigniorage ensures clarity for stakeholders of financial statements.

This distinction aids in avoiding confusion between the two sources of income, facilitating appropriate recognition of revenues and assets related to money issuance: Only the state can appropriate directly and spend the income from primary seigniorage through coins' issuance; all other issuing-money agents can only accumulate primary seigniorage into equity. On the other hand, secondary seigniorage is duly reported in the Income Statement but gets confused among several types of intermediation revenues.

2.4.2 Commercial Bank Money

It is nowadays generally accepted, included by mainstream economists, that commercial banks (henceforth, "banks") create money by lending demand deposits (henceforth, "deposits") to borrowers or by selling deposits to their clients, or other traders, against securities. While the next chapter will review the literature on bank money creation and analyze relevant aspects of the bank money creation process that are ignored by existing theories, this section discusses the nature of bank money through the lens of the AVM and the implications that derive from the AVM understanding of money.

Financial Reporting

At its essence, bank money is deemed to represent a debt liability for deposit-issuing banks. Banks are contractually obligated to convert deposits into cash upon clients' demand or to transfer value and mobilize funds to execute transfers or payments ordered by their clients. The transfers or payments from and to clients of different banks originate interbank payments that require the movement of funds consisting of specific settlement instruments across banks.[9] These settlement instrument typically consist of central bank reserves or liabilities issued by other entities (typically other banks), depending on the settlement rules or practices adopted by the payment systems used.[10] The contractual obligation of a bank toward its clients to convert their deposits into cash or to mobilize funds, on demand, form the basis of the debt relationship between the bank and its depositors, with the bank assuming the responsibility to honor their deposit claims promptly. An important implication of this obligation is that, unless the bank serves as the settlement agent, it must deliver a costly resource—the settlement instrument—to its creditors by the due date. How banks can optimize their use of this costly resource is discussed next.

Bank deposits, thus, represent "claims" on banks that banks have issued to customers in exchange for the funds that customers have deposited with them (which consist of cash, central bank reserves, or the instruments used for settlement). These claims represent rights for the depositing customers (depositors) and obligations of the deposit banks to relinquish cash or to transfer equivalent funds back to the depositors or to third parties, upon their demand. Depositors may exercise the rights

---

[9] No movements of funds take place when the transfers or payments are made to/from clients of the same bank. In this case, the bank simply debits the account of the paying client (payer) and credits the account of the receiving client (payee), and both accounts are held on its own books. In these cases, settlement does not involve any interbank transactions and does not require the use of any settlement instrument. These payments are called "on us.".

[10] The pivotal role of central bank money (reserves) in payment systems must be balanced against the business decision of any commercial bank to use the payment services of another commercial bank rather than those of the central bank. These decisions lead to varying degrees of tiering within interbank payment systems, characterized by multiple layers of settlement. In this context, when the central bank serves as the settlement institution, some banks act as direct participants (top-tier banks) that settle transactions using central bank money. Conversely, lower-tier banks often rely on top-tier banks to facilitate their interbank payments. This tiered structure is standard practice in international banking, where correspondent banks are used to handle cross-border transactions. Similarly, in domestic banking, smaller institutions typically depend on larger banks for payment services. Consequently, a transaction between two banks can be settled in different ways: exclusively in commercial bank money (if both are lower-tier banks utilizing the same top-tier bank), entirely in central bank money (if both are top-tier banks), or through a combination of both (for example, when two lower-tier banks do not share the same top-tier bank). See (CPSS 2003). Settling in the liabilities issued by commercial banks was the norm in the clearinghouse arrangements adopted in the US and UK in the past centuries (Norman et al., 2011),

associated to the claims at any time, either by requesting that the banks redeem the claims in legal tender at par or by disposing of their transfers to third parties.[11]

In fractional reserve systems,[12] banks maintain reserves as a fraction of their total outstanding deposits. These reserves act as a buffer to facilitate the settlement of interbank obligations, with only a fraction of the reserves being utilized for this purpose ex post. The volume of reserves required by banks is influenced by factors such as the extent of cash usage in the economy and the economies of scale enabled by payment system rules and clients' asynchronous deposit mobilization. As economies of scale increase, banks can create more deposits with reduced reserve coverage, optimizing their use of reserves and lowering the cost of raising and maintaining reserve balances.

Payment system rules play a pivotal role in shaping reserve utilization and settlement mechanisms, as discussed in Chap. 5. These rules dictate whether settlements occur through netting or gross settlement processes and influence the technological advancements adopted by banks. Modern technologies have integrated elements of netting into gross settlement processes, accelerating reserve circulation and allowing banks to economize on reserves for settled payments. In a hypothetical scenario of a fully consolidated banking system in a cashless economy, where all accounts are held with a single bank, reserves would be unnecessary for transaction settlement.

In real-world economies, multiple banks engage in payment activities that generate interbank settlement obligations. However, within the fractional reserve regime, and benefiting from economies of scale facilitated by payment system rules and depositors' asynchronous deposit mobilization, banks require reduced volumes of reserves to back their debts. As economies of scale increase, banks can expand their liabilities while decreasing reserve margins for coverage. Consequently, a more consolidated banking system, all else being equal, enables individual banks to maintain lower coverage of their liabilities at a reduced cost compared to a less concentrated system.

In a broader context, unless extreme economic or market contingencies prompt depositors to convert their claims into cash or transfer them across banks, deposits represent only partial debt liabilities of the issuing bank, necessitating cash and reserve coverage. For instance, in a scenario where debts are settled with reserves and banks issue deposit claims by lending them to clients, the outstanding stock of deposits created by banks is only partially backed with reserves. In such cases, the "unbacked" portion of deposits, comprising interest-earning loaned deposits net of costly reserves, serves as a free resource for banks.

In fractional reserve regimes, the uncovered segment of banks' deposit liabilities constitutes a previously non-existent free resource, which is a form of income. To the extent that this income remains accumulated and undistributed, it amounts to

---

[11] Notice that when customers acquire bank deposit claims, they relinquish funds to the issuing banks and the banks become the new owners of the funds received. On this and the legal underpinnings of the change in ownership, see (Bossone 2020a).

[12] That is, where banks are not required to back up with central bank reserves the totality of all their (demand) deposit claims issued.

equity and should be reflected as such in accounting practices. Consequently, demand deposits comprise both "debt-deposits" and "equity-deposits," a proposition further elaborated in Appendix 3 for additional clarity.

Debt-deposits represent the portion of deposits that are backed by reserves and constitute a contractual obligation of the issuing bank. In contrast, equity-deposits comprise the unbacked portion of deposits, which banks can create at will to purchase revenue-earning assets. This unbacked portion resembles equity in banks' balance sheets and should be accounted for as such, reflecting the accumulated and undistributed income generated by deposits.

Deposits exhibit a *stochastic* double nature, where each deposit unit can be either a debt-deposit or an equity-deposit upon issuance. In this context, "stochastic" denotes the probabilistic nature wherein a bank, upon creating a unit of deposit, anticipates that only a portion of that unit will likely translate into debt, while the remaining portion will probably not be subject to conversion into cash or cause reserve outflows. Banks back up deposit units with reserves based on the expected value of associated debt events, considering factors such as market conditions and behavioral dynamics. During periods of market stress and uncertainty, the share of debt-deposits tends to increase, requiring more reserve provisions, reflecting heightened demand for liquidity and risk aversion among depositors, and vice versa during period of high confidence. Policy and structural measures that enhance such confidence, such as central bank liquidity provision or deposit insurance mechanisms, boost the proportion of equity-deposits.

This argument holds true for both the entire banking system and banks taken individually, albeit to varying degrees depending on factors such as bank size, payment settlement system characteristics, cash usage, and risk profile. Bank size, defined by the volume and value of payment transactions intermediated relative to the total transactions in the system, influences the time distribution of debt-deposits and equity-deposits. Generally, smaller banks exhibit a higher share of debt-deposits, while larger banks have a greater proportion of equity contained within their deposit liabilities.

The "hybrid" (dual) nature of bank money has suggested the idea, discussed in Chap. 7 that the latter could be treated as an object of quantum physics, and has led to investigating whether and how the application of quantum analytical methods to money with dualistic features can be used to extract valuable economic information, notably as regards the study of how the money creation process is affected by the interactions among issuing banks of different size and between the issuing banks and their operating environments.

In conclusion, while the conventional perspective regards bank money (demand deposits) as a liability (debt) of the issuing commercial banks, the AVM contends that, within a fractional reserve regime, commercial bank money constitutes only partially a debt obligation, with the remaining portion representing equity in the form of accumulated and undistributed income for the same commercial bank. This equity, akin to the accumulated and undistributed income generated by deposits, should not be conflated with the bank's capital and its associated rights and obligations.[13]

Thus, at the time of issuance, a deposit can be classified as either a debt-deposit (if there is a certain probability of requests for cash conversion or interbank settlement) or an equity-deposit (with the complementary probability). Faced with this stochastic duality of its money, a bank typically provisions the issued deposit unit with reserves equivalent only to the expected value of the associated debt event (possibly supplemented by an unexpected variation margin), rather than the full value of the deposit unit issued.

The stochastic double nature of bank money is consistent with the definition of liability provided by the Conceptual Framework under IASB (2018), whereby, "*a liability is a present obligation of the entity to transfer an economic resource as a result of past events*" (section 4.26, Conceptual Framework) and "*Financial reports represent economic phenomena in words and number. To be useful, financial information must not only represent relevant phenomena, but it must also represent the substance of the phenomena that it purports to represent. In many circumstances, the substance of an economic phenomenon and its legal form are the same. If they are not the same, providing information only about the legal form would not faithfully represent the economic phenomenon*" (section 2.12, Conceptual Framework).

According to these definitions, demand deposits represent a "hybrid" instrument, embodying elements of both debt and revenue. The debt component pertains to the portion of deposits that are likely to be converted into banknotes on demand or reserved for payment settlement purposes, reflecting the substantive obligation inherent in the deposit contract. Conversely, the revenue component relates to the share of deposits expected never to be converted into banknotes or reserves.

This revenue-generating segment accumulates over time, ultimately transforming into equity. It is noteworthy that equity-deposits are not necessarily dormant; they primarily consist of deposit flows within the same bank's accounts and flows that offset each other before settlement, none of which necessitate reserves.

Given the absence of explicit accounting standards governing hybrid financial instruments, IAS 32 is applicable (by analogy stated in IAS 8), mandating the separation of the debt and equity components. Consequently, once the debt portion is identified, the residual portion constitutes equity. In the context of deposits, the proportion of deposits unlikely to translate into debt liabilities represents retained earnings or equity capital.

The application of IAS 32 serves as a classic example, requiring the financial statements of the issuing bank to include only the portion of deposits giving rise to a substantial obligation to transfer economic resources as debts, while the remaining portion should be reported in the income statement as revenue. Additionally, since

[13] The dual nature of deposits and their variable debt-vs-equity composition determine an intrinsic instability that prevents deposits from being a true source of capital – which must be available when needed. While the equity nature of bank deposits in a fractional reserve regime is undisputed, as the AVM shows, its intrinsic instability makes it an inferior instrument vis-à-vis capital, for the purposes that the latter must serve.

the profits attributable to this revenue remain undistributed, they contribute to the bank's equity.

Supporting the validity of this approach is the perspective offered by IAS 37 (on risk provisioning, charges, and contingent liabilities), which categorizes as debt all commitments falling under the Conceptual Framework's definition of "liability," specifically those resulting in outflows of economic resources with a probability exceeding 0.5. Liabilities falling below this threshold are considered contingent liabilities and must only be disclosed in the financial statements' notes. Furthermore, the innovation by IPSASB (2020), discussed below, aligns closely with the AVM.[14]

The implication is clear: The mere existence of formal claims does not suffice for a liability to be classified as debt; the essential criterion is the probable outflows of economic resources. Moreover, this probability is significant only if it facilitates a faithful representation of the transactions involved, aiming to provide useful information to investors, lenders, and other creditors. In the case of commercial bank money, the part of deposits that do not constitute debt liabilities must be recognized as revenue. However, since this revenue is not explicitly reported in the income statement, it should be reflected as retained earnings or equity.

A New Classification for Bank Money?

Although, theoretically, the distinction between liabilities and equity appears to preclude any intermediate category, the AVM posits the potential for introducing a novel accounting subclassification within the equity realm. Traditionally, equity encompasses capital, capital reserves, and retained earnings, with a recent addition being "reserves deriving from other comprehensive income" (formerly known as "capital maintenance adjustments").

The rationale behind the AVM underscores the necessity for a fresh category termed "cash reserves," reflecting the equity component of money issuance. Consequently, a new breed of hybrid instruments would emerge, distinct from conventional hybrids like securities and shares, but rather bridging securities and revenues. Upon capitalization, these revenues would amalgamate within the proposed cash reserves subcategory.

Notably, the proposed accounting treatment of money bears striking parallels with the treatment of insurance liabilities outlined in international standards. As per IFRS 17 (pertaining to insurance contracts), when premium payments are collected or upon issuance of a new policy contract, the insurer's cash or credit position is adjusted equivalently on the Resources side of its balance sheet. On the Claims side, only a portion of the insurer's obligations becomes debt, reflecting the present value of its anticipated future commitments to customers, adjusted for risks and other factors. The remaining portion, which is not earmarked for fulfilling future obligations to customers, is temporarily classified as a liability. Subsequently, since it represents

[14] While IPSASB primarily applies to the public sector, its innovative treatment of liabilities holds relevance for private sector entities as well, emphasizing the importance of them adhering to general principles, particularly regarding liabilities.

"deferred income," it is recognized as revenue and spread across future financial statements, based on an amortization schedule that considers the insurer's provision of future services. The revenue spreads over several years, because it corresponds to a series of forthcoming offsetting obligations and may not be fully "earned" by the insurer at once; as these future obligations materialize, the revenue is reflected in the insurer's financial records; if not distributed, it is allocated to equity.

In the context of bank money, since there are no residual obligations for the issuing bank to fulfill beyond the liquidity it provides to depositors on a fractional basis (i.e., central bank reserves), the non-debt portion of the deposits held with it can be entirely classified as revenue in the financial statements. Unlike the insurer's scenario, this revenue is instantly "earned" by the issuing bank and can thus be attributed to equity.

2.5 Implications

Implications for Central Banks

The previous arguments bear several crucial financial and fiscal implications. Firstly, they suggest that there is systematic concealment of seigniorage income, which is not appropriately reflected in the central banks' income statement where it logically should be; it is rather recorded under debt liabilities on the balance sheet, resulting in inaccurate accounting practices.

Secondly, they point to the importance of differentiating between primary and secondary seigniorage. Primary seigniorage originates from the creation of money ex nihilo and through fiat decisions, which can be utilized to finance various exchanges of value. In contrast, secondary seigniorage is derived from the interest income generated on issued and loaned money. Notably, the state does not benefit from secondary seigniorage from coins, as they are not loaned. Central banks, however, earn primary seigniorage from banknotes and reserve issuances, yet they often account for only the former, neglecting the latter. Additionally, central banks receive secondary seigniorage from reserve lending. Notably, primary seigniorage on coins and secondary seigniorage on banknotes, even though they now represent negligible amounts, are generally granted to the states.

Thirdly, central banks possess the power to generate their own capital as needed. This power ensures that central banks, by retaining the ability to issue money, never face the necessity of seeking recapitalization from the government. Central bank independence, thus, remains secure from undercapitalization issues and the "optimality" of central bank capital should thus be defined only in relation to the monetary policy objectives that the central bank is mandated to pursue. That is why central bank capital matters: A structural tendency toward negative capital, for instance, which would require continuous "self-creation" of capital by the central bank, would be inconsistent—and therefore suboptimal—vis-à-vis a low inflation objective, while a structural tendency to a too high level of capital would be inconsistent—and therefore, again, suboptimal—vis-a vis a full-employment objective (Archer & Moser-Boehm, 2013).[15]

Fourthly, the delineation of responsibilities clarifies the entity responsible for providing the ultimate crisis backstop. Discussions on the backstop function often involve a circular argument: When the risk of government default arises, the central bank can act as the last-resort remedy through debt monetization (IMF, 2022a); conversely, when the central bank faces financial losses, the government is expected to provide additional capital to restore equity. However, the true backstop can only be the entity with the power to issue currency.

A short digression on this point. Buiter (2008) correctly argues that the taxpayer, through the state treasury, is the ultimate and only guarantor of central bank solvency. Accordingly, the backstop function can ultimately work only if real resources are available that can be extracted from the economy (through either explicit taxation or the implicit (inflation) tax via money creation) for the purpose of financing the backstop. It should be noted, however, that even prior to getting to the (extreme) point where real resources are physically exhausted, a confidence crisis in an economy might be such that wealth holders would want to dump both government debt and cash in exchange for foreign securities, thereby neutralizing the ultimate backstop role of the central bank. Under such circumstances, the backstop function (its financing) could only be provided by an entity supplying foreign resources. The key conclusion, here, is that while financial capital is not a constraint on central banks (in the sense that central banks can always "produce" their own capital by issuing the domestic currency), they should never want to find themselves in situations where their capital position is inconsistent with their policy objectives and the need to protect their (internal and external) credibility.

Finally, the underappreciation of seigniorage under current accounting practices warrants attention. Identifying all sources of seigniorage, estimating their impact, and ensuring transparency in fiscal budgets and central bank balance sheets through accurate financial accounting principles are imperative. Moreover, the argument could be made that the government is entitled to receive the correctly estimated seigniorage extracted by the central bank, after covering the central bank's operational and capital costs. This transfer would not weaken the central bank's financial position, allowing it to focus on pursuing monetary policy objectives without concern for its equity level. However, the use of seigniorage income by the government should be subject to the

[15] The capacity to create one's own capital exemplifies what economists term a "free lunch." The social benefit of this free lunch depends on whether the newly created purchasing power is utilized to mobilize untapped resources and stimulate new output. However, if no unused capacity exists, this power may only lead to increased prices without yielding net social benefits. Even in this extreme case, however, the money issuer would still retain a claim on real resources that it would not have, absent its money creation power. This would result in a redistribution of the economy's resources to its own benefit: Following money issuances, the whole "pie" of real resources would be smaller for each eater (due to the price effect), but a share of the pie would then go to the one eater who has not contributed to its preparation: a free lunch for the money issuer, and a loss for those who actually contributed the pie. Obviously, if the money creation power were abused and engender hyperinflation, not even the money issuer would be able to appropriate a positive share of the pie and the whole pie might shrink for all.

country's political process, considering distributional and macroeconomic aspects, while acknowledging that seigniorage ultimately belongs to the citizens' wealth.

2.5.1 Implications for Commercial Banks

Several implications arise from the duality of bank money, which represent novel contributions of the AVM alongside those pertaining to state money. Firstly, a considerable portion of deposits, classified by banks in their financial statements as " "debt toward clients," generates revenues akin to the seigniorage rents obtained by the state or central bank through the issuance of legal tender (coins and banknotes) and central bank reserves. This has ramifications for calculating banks' capital, contingent upon the probability factor outlined earlier, which varies for each bank based on its size, role in the payment system, and risk profile.

Before entering into this, it should be clarified that seigniorage here refers to bank profits exceeding the "norm." Seigniorage, that is, is any revenue accruing to banks as money creators in excess of the competitive remuneration of the inputs they use to produce money.[16] A "normal" profit rate would therefore remunerate banks for the value they add to the economy by creating and allocating money—in a competitive economy—as a public good that the public demands (and is willing to hold) for the services it delivers. This is not only important to establish conceptual clarity, it would also matter for any empirical attempt to estimate bank seigniorage—especially should this become a topic for tax considerations.

The counterargument to this perspective is that the creation of demand deposits cannot serve as a source of income since, in the event of insolvency, all deposits would be withdrawn (to the extent they are covered with assets or guaranteed). Nevertheless, international accounting standards like the IFRS operate under the assumption of a going concern, not liquidation. Under liquidation, money becomes a liability to holders, similar to how equity shares of a firm become liabilities toward shareholders for any remaining value of the firm. However, this change in status does not affect the representation of transactions in accounting terms, as substance must always take precedence over form under normal conditions. In the case of bank money, according to the AVM, only secondary seigniorage is appropriated and potentially distributable to shareholders, while primary seigniorage is a distinct component of equity, not to be settled to holders (which would classify it as a liability) or distributed to shareholders, but rather retained within the bank.

Secondly, like demand deposits, banks, too, are "hybrid" entities. As issuers of debt-deposits (through lending activities), they act as pure intermediaries. Conversely, as issuers of equity-deposits, they function as money creators. Due to

[16] For the determination of "normal" profits in an economy, one could 'neoclassically' expect that, in the absence of frictions and as competition increases in the banking sector, bank profits (net of risk reward) tend to gravitate around zero-excess profits. Or one could take a 'Sraffian' perspective and consider that a uniform (net of risk) rate of profit attains across all sectors as an inherent technical feature of the economy.

the economies of scale in reserve utilization discussed earlier, smaller banks tend to lean toward the former category, while larger banks gravitate toward the latter. This distinction will be subject to quantum analysis in Chap. 7. Notably, while income earned on debt-deposits stems from intermediation, income on equity-deposits constitutes seigniorage, one of the topics of Chaps. 5and6.

Third, the equity derived from seigniorage should be accurately estimated and accounted for, with stakeholders, including authorities, being able to identify it. Appropriate accounting standards and value estimates of seigniorage would offer reliable indicators of banks' strength and true market power. This underscores the importance of one of the fundamental qualitative characteristics of financial information: faithful representation. The fact that issuing money enhances the equity of the issuer must be faithfully recognized and represented.

2.6 Conclusion

Based on the accurate application of international accounting principles, the Accounting View of Money (AVM) illustrated in this chapter contends that fiat currencies issued by the state, typically encompassing cash, banknotes, and central bank reserves, do not constitute debt. Furthermore, within a fractional reserve system, only a portion of commercial bank money can be classified as debt. By addressing these distinct categories of money separately, the AVM delineates the appropriate accounting treatment for various forms of money in the financial statements of issuing institutions. This clarification elucidates the implications of different accounting methodologies for a comprehensive understanding of money, and the consequent policies, both at a corporate and at a social level. In more practical terms, it serves to reconcile the apparent incongruity between the formal reporting rules governing money liabilities in current financial statements of issuing institutions and the economic essence of these money liabilities as portrayed in the statements.

The AVM brings fresh insights into diverse issues such as the essence of central bank capital, the character of bank money as a hybrid instrument blending debt and equity components, and the identity of banks as hybrid entities embodying aspects of both pure financial intermediaries and money creators.

Having discussed the nature of money, let us now dive into why money is useful and how its usefulness can be evaluated—the topics of the next chapter.

Appendix 1: Primary Seigniorage in Accounting

Once fiat money is generated, it represents value capable of acquiring various forms of worth, including goods, services, financial assets, and tangible assets. For example, the central bank can use fiat money in repurchase agreements, officially termed as transactions where money is sold against assets (typically, though not exclusively, government bonds) with a pledge from the counterparty to repurchase the bonds for money at a later date. (In practice, even when the central bank extends loans to borrowers, it effectively "sells" money and acquires debt obligations from the borrowers in return.)

The crucial point lies in the fact that the value created by the central bank "out of nothing" is traded by the central bank for tangible resources or commitments to obtain tangible resources. The value of the money created through fiat and utilized to procure (claims on) tangible resources serves as a revenue stream for the issuing central bank in accounting terms, and any such income left undistributed represents equity in accounting principles.

When commodities are sold, the entries in a double-entry scheme are as follows:

By Receivables To Revenues
By Cost of sale To Commodities

where Receivables and Commodities are assets in the balance sheet and Revenues and Cost of sale are items of the income statement. Their difference accrues to equity as income (i.e., changes of equity).

When money is produced and allocated, it should be identically represented as:

By Securities To Money Revenues
By Cost of money production To Money

Here, the assets exchanged are Securities and Money (rather than Receivables and Commodities, as under commodities) and the Cost of sales and Revenues are the same: respectively, the decrease of equity needed for producing the good (either money or commodities) and the increase of equity obtained from its sale. All undistributed net revenues—that is, the primary seigniorage—accrue to equity (i.e., changes of equity).

Appendix 2: Money: A Liability of the Financial Sector?

The economy's total net worth is in the balance sheets of real-sector agents. Money is their asset. Every financial asset is some counterparty's liability, and the only counterparty for real-sector agents as a consolidated sector is the financial sector (including the central bank). Isn't thus money a liability of the financial sector?

No, It Is Not

Representing the economy in two consolidated entities, the real sector and the financial sector, respectively, yields the two following balance sheets:

Real Sector

Resources	Claims
Physical goods (among which money, as a product used for exchange purposes) Money	Liabilities = Debts toward the financial sector Equity = Difference between resources and liabilities (part of which is kept by the financial sector as shares)

Financial Sector

Resources	Claims
Resources = credits toward the real sector + money + shares in the real sector equity	Liabilities = None Equity = Difference between resources and liabilities

Money is an "output" produced by the financial sector. Once "sold," it accrues to financial sector equity and becomes a good in the full possession of the real sector. Money produced and not yet sold would temporarily transit from the Resources side of the financial sector's balance sheet, as it would be the case of coins produced by the treasury and not yet sold to the real sector; however, this is not reflected in the above representation. Moreover, the real sector holds nothing to claim on the financial sector in exchange for money.

In what a sense is money a credit for the real sector and a debt for the financial sector? It is only an output that the real sector uses within itself and not for claiming anything from the financial sector.

After consolidating the balance sheets across all sectors of the economy, money ends up on the Resources side of the consolidated balance sheet, while net revenues from money issuances end up on the Claims side of the balance sheet (thereby becoming net worth or equity).

The financial sector owes no debt to the real sector.

Appendix 3: Bank Money as Equity: Further Clarifications

This is how the AVM addresses common critical views on its tenets. These views are:

1. Bank money does not grant to its holders any residual claims on the issuing banks; therefore, it cannot be equity.
2. Selling goods and selling money are different things.
3. While this argument might apply to state-issued currency, it doesn't necessarily apply to bank money.
4. This brings up the notion of probability: How does this notion relate to the liability nature of deposits?
5. What prompts a contingent liability to turn into revenue?

6. How do deposits serve as both a revenue stream for the issuing bank and as assets for their holders?
7. Lastly, if a deposit serves as credit for the depositor, it should logically be considered a debt for the issuing bank.

Let's discuss them in turn.

Bank money does not grant to its holders any residual claims on the issuing banks; therefore, it cannot be equity.

The AVM adopts the distinction between "equity" and "capital," the latter being one component of the former. The other component is "retained earnings." The issuance of commercial bank money generates revenues for the issuing banks, exactly like the sale of goods does for a firm. Those who purchase deposits (depositors in exchange for funds and borrowers in exchange for credit claims) do not get residual claims on the issuing banks any more than buyers or leasers of goods do on the selling or leasing firms.

Selling goods and selling money are different things.

Money grants access to economic benefits much as any other consumer good does. Goods deliver utility from consumption; money delivers utility from its ability to settle transactions. For money sellers, money is a source of revenue, much as goods are for producing firms. For firms, revenue equals the money received in exchange for selling goods; for banks, revenue is the cash, reserves, or credit claims received in exchange for selling deposit claims.

While this argument might apply to state-issued currency, it doesn't necessarily apply to bank money.

Banks are liable to convert deposits into cash on demand and to cover them with central bank reserves for settlement purposes. Yet, due to scale economies in payment systems and depositors' asynchronous mobilization of deposits, banks operating in fractional reserve regimes need to back only a fraction of their deposit liabilities with cash or central bank reserves. The fraction of uncovered deposits is a source of revenue which, once accumulated and undistributed, becomes equity. The circumstances that partial coverage raises risk and that the share of uncovered deposits is uncertain ex ante do not change the fact that they are a source of revenue.

This brings up the notion of probability: how does this notion relate to the liability nature of deposits?

The international accounting standards indicate that the concept of probability becomes relevant to determine how a liability is to be reflected in the financial statements. When liabilities show low probability of generating financial obligations, they may be recorded as "contingent liabilities" in the Notes to the financial statements (not in the financial statements themselves) and may even go unrecorded if the probability is very low.

What prompts a contingent liability to turn into revenue?

Revenues, like all components of equity, are a residual between assets and liabilities. The purpose of equity is to ensure that the fundamental identity Asset - Liabilities = Equity holds at all times. If a liability is written off, the resulting gap determines residually an addition to net worth (hence, it constitutes revenue). This conclusion is inescapable.

How do deposits serve as both a revenue stream for the issuing bank and as assets for their holders?

As discussed in the text, deposits are a hybrid instrument. Ex ante, they can be either a liability or equity. And fractional coverage ensures that, under most contingencies (including extreme economic and financial situations, as the global financial crisis has shown), a share of deposits will become equity, and the banking system won't find itself under an obligation to convert all outstanding deposits into cash or central bank reserves. Indeed, the institutional arrangements supporting the banking system (e.g., central banks acting as lenders of last resort, other liquidity provision mechanisms, deposit insurance guarantee schemes, etc.) ensure that a fraction of outstanding deposits will—under most circumstances—feature the nature of equity.

Lastly, if a deposit serves as credit for the depositor, it should logically be considered a debt for the issuing bank.

Demand deposits are never reported as credit or financial assets in the financial statements of their holders; they are reported instead as cash and equivalents on hand. The correct question, therefore, is: if they are not credit, why should they be debt? In fact, they are not; they entail for the issuing banks an obligation that is similar to debt. A demand deposit is a contract where the depositor swaps cash or funds with its bank against claims to access those cash and funds on demand. The bank commits to ensuring that such conversion is guaranteed at all times it is requested. As above, however, the share of claims that remain unconverted are a source of revenue for the bank and are thus part of its equity.

References

Archer, D., & Moser-Boehm, P. (2013). Central Bank Finances," BIS Papers, No 71, Bank for International Settlements.

Baltensperger, E., & Jordan, T. J. (1997). Seigniorage, banking, and the optimal quantity of money. *Journal of Banking and Finance 21*(6), 781–796.

Beatty, A., & Liao, S. (2014). Financial accounting in the banking industry: A review of the empirical literature. *Journal of Accounting and Economics, 58*(2014), 339–383.

Bezemer, D. J. (2016). Towards an "accounting view" on money, banking and the macroeconomy: History, empirics, theory. *Cambridge Journal of Economics, 40*(5), 1275–1295

Bjerg, O., McCann, D., Macfarlane, L., Nielsen, R.H., & Ryan-Collins, J. (2017). Seigniorage in the 21st Century: A study of the profits from money creation in the United Kingdom and Denmark," CBS Working Paper.

Bossone, B. (2000), What makes banks special? A study on banking, finance, and economic development, Policy Research Working Paper, WPS2408, The World Bank.

Bossone, B. (2020a). Money and customer funds in the world of digital finance: Who really owns what? *Journal of Payments Strategy and Systems, 15*(1), 37–53.

Buiter, W. H. (2003). 'Helicopeter money: irredeemable fiat money and the liquidity trap,' Working Paper 10163, National Bureau of Economic Research.

Buiter, W. H. (2008). Can central banks go broke? CEPR Policy Insight, no 24.

Burdekin, R. C. K. (2009),"Seigniorage." In K. A. Reinert, R. S. Rajan, A. J. Glass, & L. S. Davis (Eds.), *The Princeton encyclopedia of the world economy*. Princeton University Press.
Costa, M. (2009), *Sulla natura contabile delle "passività monetarie" nei bilanci bancari*, Quaderni Monografici Rirea, n. 85.
Covick, O., & Davis, K. (1990). Accounting for Seigniorage. Accounting and Finance, pp 57–72.
CPSS. (2003). The role of central bank money in payment systems, report by the Committee on Payment and Settlement Systems, Bank for International Settlements, Basel.
Dyson, B., & Hodgson, G. (2016). Accounting for sovereign money: Why state-issued money is not 'Debt'," Positive Money.
ESA. (2010). *European system of accounts*. Eurostat, European Commission.
Flynn, M. (1999). Distinguishing between income and capital receipts – a search for principle JIATax 14. *Journal of Australian Taxation, 2*(3), 155.
Haslag, J. H. (1998). Seigniorage revenue and monetary policy economic review. Third Quarter, Federal Reserve Bank of Dallas.
Heinsohn, G., & Steiger, O. (2013). Ownership Economics: On the foundations of interest, money, markets, business cycles and economic development. In F. Decker (Ed.), Routledge.
IASB. (2018). *Conceptual framework for financial reporting*. International Accounting Standards Board, IFRS Foundation.
IFRS (2018). Conceptual Framework 2018, International Financial Reporting Standards.
IMF. (2022a). Monetary finance: Do not touch, or handle with care? IMF Departmental Papers, DP/2022/001, prepared by I. Agur, D. Capelle, G. Dell'Ariccia, and D. Sandri, International Monetary Fund.
IPSASB. (2020). *Non-authoritative amendments to IPSAS 41, financial instruments*. International Public Sector Accounting Standard.
Knapp, G. F. (1905). The state theory of money, abridged and translated by H. M. Lucas and J. Bonar. Macmillan & Company Ltd. (1924).
Kumhof, M., Allen, J. G., Bateman, W., Lastra, R. M., Gleeson, S., & Omarova, S. T. (2020). Central bank money: Liability, asset, or equity of the nation? Cornell Legal Studies Research Paper, pp. 20–46.
Mehrling, P. (2012). The inherent hierarchy of money. Prepared for Duncan Foley Festschrift Volume, and Conference April 20–21.
Norman, B., Shaw, R., & Speight G. (2011). The history of interbank settlement arrangements: exploring central banks' role in the payment system Working Paper No. 412, Bank of England.
PAAinE. (2008). Distinguishing between Liabilities and Equity. In: Pro-active accounting in Europe, discussion paper, European financial reporting advisory group.
PWC. (2017). *Distinguishing liabilities from equity*. Price Waterhouse Cooper.
Reich, J. (2017). *Seigniorage: on the revenue from the creation of money*. Springer International Publishing.
Reis, R. (2019). 'Can the Central Bank Alleviate Fiscal Burdens?.' In D. G. Mayes, P. L. Siklos, & J. E. Sturm (Eds.), *The Oxford Handbook of the Economics of Central Banking*, Oxford University Press.
Schmidt, M. (2013). Equity and liabilities—a discussion of IAS 32 and a critique of the classification. *Accounting in Europe, 10*(2), 201–222.
Zellweger-Gutknecht, C. (2019). Developing the right regulatory regime for cryptocurrencies and other value data. In Fox, D., Green S. (eds.), Private and Public Law Implications of Cryptocurrencies, Oxford University Press.

Chapter 3
The Utility of Money

Abstract This chapter explores the utility of money as a fundamental economic asset serving as a means of payment and a source of liquidity for individuals and societies. It positions money within a broader context of financial assets, examining how its utility derives from its immediate convertibility into goods and services. The theory allows money to be compared with goods, services, and assets and builds on three foundational components: (i) a choice-theoretic model assessing utility from assets with various liquidity levels; (ii) a variable cost structure for asset liquidation that reflects financial inefficiencies and market mood changes; and (iii) a model for expectations formation amid uncertainty. The theory integrates elements of neoclassical economics, emphasizing a choice-theoretic model that evaluates utility based on liquidity levels and the costs associated with asset liquidation. By dissecting how market sentiment and uncertainty influence resource allocation and asset prices, the chapter formulates a framework that captures the dynamics between consumption, money, and non-money assets.

3.1 Preamble

As the asset that serves as means of payment and settlement instrument in the exchange process, money provides liquidity services to the individuals and societies that utilize it, and such services are a source of utility to them. Yes, that provided by money is a form of indirect utility, since it ultimately rests on the exchangeability of money with anything that has direct intrinsic usefulness. But it is utility nonetheless, much like the utility provided by a vehicle transporting things from one place to another.

In investigating the role of money in the economy, economic theory has never explored the utility of money thoroughly enough. With few exceptions, economic models have integrated money in the utility function of representative agents as an "as if" assumption, without inquiring into the nature of such utility and using it as a convenient formal expedient to derive optimal resource allocation choices.

B. Bossone, *Trailblazing Visions of Money in Economic Theory*, Contributions to Economics, https://doi.org/10.1007/978-3-031-82544-6_3

The utility of money was one of my first interests in studying monetary economics. If money can buy anything—I thought—its utility must originate from its power to be immediately convertible into things that provide utility and must be comparable with their utility and that of consumption commodities. By extension—I further argued—this must hold for all other assets as well since these, too, can be converted into things that provide utility, though less instantly and possibly with greater (and riskier) store-of-value capacity than money. Therefore, I came to view money and non-money assets as competing "vehicles," each characterized by its own "speed" and "power" to access "useful" resources, and each thereby providing utility to their holders.

I then considered that neoclassical theory was the natural tool to frame this utility-based conception of money, assets, and consumption commodities within an intertemporal general equilibrium setting. On that ground, I established a formal model through which utility comparisons could be run under specific assumptions concerning the preferences of the individuals taking part in their exchange and the conditions underpinning the process of exchange. I started developing the utility theory of money in the nineties (Bossone, 1996, 1997) and arrived at a more complete configuration of it years after (Bossone, 2014). This chapter illustrates this theory and its uses.

3.2 Introduction

This chapter examines the role of money (alongside other financial assets) in providing utility to its holders in an economy with time, uncertainty, and changing market sentiment because of its specific role as the asset that serves as means of payment and settlement instrument in the exchange process. It explores the characteristics of the utility delivery mechanism of money (and other assets) that the theory incorporates and its repercussions on resource allocation and the dynamics of asset prices.

The utility theory of money builds on three blocks: first, a choice-theoretic model to gauge the utility that the economic agents derive from holding assets with varying liquidity levels and store-of-value capacity. Second, a flexible cost structure model for asset liquidation, influenced by i) optimal asset trading under uncertainty, ii) the efficiency of the financial infrastructure, and iii) changing market sentiments. Third, a model for agents forming expectations amid uncertainty and changing market sentiment.

A distinctive feature of this theory is that institutions like money and monetary exchange emerge from it, rather than being assumed by it. The theory enables the assessment of how rational agents, seeking to maximize intertemporal utility, adjust resource allocation between consumption, money, and non-money assets in response to various shocks, while also analyzing the nature of bubble-bust sequences. The proposal is discussed of employing the market-specific policy tools that emerge from the model to prevent financial bubbles.

The approach used for the utility theory of money minimizes assumptions while drawing on both general and realistic behavioral and structural functions. Despite its complexity, it offers a straightforward analytical framework for exploring pertinent economic issues, relying solely on the imposition of first-order conditions.

Aligned with the research by Frydman and Goldberg (2011) but adopting a distinct methodological approach, this study incorporates imperfect knowledge and non-economic determinants of market sentiments within a rational choice-theoretic framework, illustrating how these factors can lead the economy into disequilibria or suboptimal equilibria.

Broadly speaking, the utility theory of money presented in this chapter offers a unifying approach that uses utility as a benchmark to compare such different things as (consumer and capital) goods with (real and financial) assets within and across dates in time. The theory also tells which of the goods and assets available in an economy can emerge featuring the characteristics that are required for anything to be used and accepted as money.

The chapter is organized as follows: Sect. 3.3 reviews the various strands of the literature that relate to the foundations of the theory discussed in this chapter, characterized by a utility-based conception of money and assets and the combination of rational expectations and market sentiment. Section 3.4 illustrates the model underpinning the theory, describing the economy, defining and formalizing money and non-money asset utility, and introducing expectations formation under uncertainty and changing market sentiment; the section then derives optimal resource allocation rules and asset equilibrium prices. Section 3.5 analyzes the implications of the model, investigating the effects of uncertainty and changing market sentiment on resource allocations and asset prices including speculative bubble-and-bust consequences and policy responses thereto. Section 3.6 concludes the chapter, and Appendix describes simple indicators that can be used to construct an efficient market sentiment variable.

3.3 Review of the Literature

The model illustrated in this chapter relates to various strands of the literature. The first is the literature on the utility of money. As noted in the Preamble, this literature is quite limited and most of the contributions assume money as an argument of the household's utility function without analyzing how this utility originates. Early contributions to this literature were Samuelson (1948), Patinkin (1965), Sidrauski (1967), and Friedman (1969),[1] who simply argued that including real money balances in the utility function represented a "reduced form" equation in a world of transactions costs or uncertainty. This argument was criticized on the grounds that it amounted

[1] References to these contributions are reported by Feenstra (1986), which also refers to subsequent works that used the money-in-the-utility-function assumption in dynamic (growth) models to examine stability under perfect foresight, finding the uniqueness of equilibria to be sensitive to utility-function parameters such as the cross-derivative between money and the consumption good.

to "implicit theorizing," which did not allow for consistent modeling (Kareken & Wallace, 1980). More generally, many economists consider including money in a utility function as an incorrect practice since money provides liquidity services, which affects agents only through their budget constraints (Croushore, 1993). Despite this criticism, Poterba and Rosemberg (1986), innovatively, studied household asset demands by allowing money and other assets to contribute to household utility and estimated the parameters of an aggregate utility function that included both consumption and liquidity services, with the latter depending on the level of various asset stocks. Ganchev (2010) has inquired into the concept of utility of money, defined as the ability to generate additional income, and has proposed a model where the utility of money is maximized by equalizing dynamic marginal utility of money and marginal cost, showing that individuals' utility-of-money maximization objectives may be aggregated at macro level and can be used for monetary policy optimization.

My earliest attempts at identifying the analytical foundations of money-in-the-utility function had worked out a definition of money utility that would reflect the power of money to access real resources or claims thereon (Bossone, 1996, 1997). I later corrected and refined the original analytical structure of the utility function of money and other assets, integrating it into a more comprehensive choice-theoretic framework that would contemplate uncertainty and market sentiment (Bossone, 2014), as discussed next.

The second relevant strand of literature to which my work relates is, in fact, on the economic and financial analysis of uncertainty and market sentiment. This literature has so far proceeded following two separate threads. The first and longer dated thread has devoted large attention to the effects of uncertainty on resource allocation and investment decisions, as well as to the analysis of how risk and uncertainty affect asset prices. While the related literature is much too extended for a comprehensive review here, important contributions and references to earlier works can be found in Kacperczyk and Damien (2011). More recently, Douglas de Medeiros (2022) studied how economic uncertainty interacts with the informational structure of sentiment and finds that, ex ante, uncertainty precedes sentiment, while sentiment helps predict the informational structure of fundamental uncertainty, ex-post. Birru and Young (2023) found a significant amplifying role for market uncertainty in the relation between sentiment and aggregate investment, and their evidence suggests that the importance of sentiment for corporate decisions varies over time and depends crucially on the underlying level of market uncertainty.

The second thread of the literature on uncertainty and market sentiment, which has received a major important boost from the development of behavioral economics, has focused on the effects of changing market sentiment on asset prices. For a survey of the first studies of the topic, see Scherbina (2013). More recent references are reported in Berardi (2022), which also proposes a way to model sentiments in asset prices, showing that the source of noise generating uncertainty, whether fundamental or informational, has important consequences for the effect of sentiments—specifically, while more informational noise always amplifies the impact of psychological shocks on prices, more fundamental noise can reduce such impact, depending on the elasticity of sentiments to uncertainty. My earlier work had indeed introduced a model of expectations and market sentiment that features those same properties (see below) and, in addition, incorporates a mechanism whereby new incoming information corrects the distortions originating from market sentiment, that is, the gaps between the agent's *perceived* state of the world relative to the state of the world that would be reasonable to expect to prevail based on the agent's knowledge and information available.

The model used in this chapter, also, is fundamentally about liquidity and asset prices, an issue that has been analyzed by several scholars, most notably, Kiyotaki and Moore (2005), who developed a model of a monetary economy to examine the interaction between liquidity, asset prices, and aggregate economic activity, and Amihud et al. (2005), who focused on how liquidity affects the required returns of capital assets. Lagos (2010) developed an asset-pricing where financial assets are valued for their liquidity (that is, the extent to which they are useful in facilitating exchange) as well as for being claims to streams of consumption goods, and studies the implications of this liquidity channel for average asset returns, the equity-premium puzzle, and the risk-free rate puzzle and, more recently, Foucault et al. (2023) studied how liquidity affects the returns required by investors (and hence asset prices), it examines how prices in illiquid markets may diverge from underlying long-run values, especially in the context of market freezes and financial crises, and it then highlights that noise trading can play an important role in pushing securities prices away from fundamental values.

The utility theory of money, discussed in this chapter, contributes to the literature by using choice theory to combine the two strands of research referred to above, showing how changes in the state of uncertainty and market sentiment affect the agents' liquidity preference, and how changes in the agents' liquidity preference, in turn, affects resource allocations and asset prices.

3.4 The Model

3.4.1 The Economy

The economy consists of a representative infinitely-lived, intertemporal utility-maximizing household, a representative firm, the government, the central bank, and four asset types: money M, which is used as a store of value and as the instrument for executing payment transactions, a short-term treasury bill T, a long-term government bond B, and non-liquid asset that can be thought of as a claim on the economy's productive capital stock K. Each asset trades at price $P^{Q(=M,T,B,K)}$, where $P^M = 1$ under normal conditions.

For the purpose of analyzing secular stagnation in the context of a purely demand-driven economy, a simplifying assumption on the supply side of the economy is adopted whereby the representative firm sells all the output demanded by the household at the going price, and output adjusts immediately to changes in demand.[2] Similarly, it is assumed that the firms accumulate as much capital as households are willing to hold in the form of capital shares, while labor employment depends on the level of capital used. Therefore, household expectations—as influenced by the prevailing market sentiment—determine capital accumulation, output, and employment thereby providing the closure of the model.

The Household

The household supplies the hours of work that are demanded by firms, at competitive nominal compensation rate, y, and receives from the government a non-pecuniary public good, G, in the form of a material and immaterial services (e.g., law & order, education, financial stability, etc.) The household orders its preferences across consumption C, M, T, B, and K, according to a strictly quasi-concave, time-separable, and well-behaved utility function $u(\cdot)$, with $u'''(\cdot) > 0$ (that is, decreasing absolute and relative risk aversion). All assets deliver utility to their holders, as discussed below. In this chapter, utility from money and other assets is not just assumed (as it is done in the money-in-the-utility-function literature[3]); it is derived and formalized (Sect. 3.2.2, below), and is used to make assets and consumption all mutually comparable in a general state-dependent equilibrium context driven by optimal microeconomic choices from rational agents. In the utility-based model used here, and as discussed below, asset liquidation costs are variable, and agent expectations are rational but distortable by changes in the state of market sentiment that are ultimately driven by changes in economic observables.

In each period, the household earns asset nominal returns $r^{Q=(M,T,B,K)} = (1+\rho^Q)(1+\pi^Q)$, where ρ is the nominal interest rate or the dividend paid on the assets and π^Q is rate of change of asset price P^Q. The real rate of return on asset Q is $R^{Q=(M,T,B,K)} = (1+\rho^Q)(1+\pi^Q)(1-\pi^C)$, where π^C is the rate of consumer price inflation. As discussed below, R^Q reflects the liquidity and riskiness characterizing each asset as determined by the market.

In calculating its intertemporal budget constraint, the household evaluates its future income perspectives by considering its job value, that is, the present discounted value of the future difference between a worker's productivity and the worker's current pay (Hall, 2013),

$$JV_t = E_t\left[\sum_{\tau=t+1}^{\infty}\prod_{i=t}^{\tau}\beta_i(p_\tau x_\tau - y_t)|\omega_\tau\right], \tag{3.1}$$

[2] The model could be enriched by incorporating in it a standard New-Keynesian price adjustment model. Yet, since this would add nothing substantial to the analysis for the purpose at hand, I use the simpler assumption of quantity adjustments. The role of relative price adjustment and its ineffectiveness under distorted rational expectations are discussed in Sect. 3.5.3.

[3] See Blanchard and Fischer (1989), Chap. 5.

where x and y are, respectively, the household's output and remuneration, and expectations reflect changing market moods ω at time t (to be discussed later): The job value declines with pessimistic prospects about future levels of remuneration and risk of unemployment (and vice versa with optimistic prospects). It is assumed that the household reads through the job value as estimated by the firm:

$$E_t[y_\tau|\omega_t] = E_t\left[y_\tau^{\{[JV_\tau(\omega_t)/\overline{\Pi}]\}}\right], \tag{3.2}$$

where $\overline{\Pi}$ is the normal rate of profit, $\frac{JV_t}{\overline{\Pi}} = 1$ holds under normal economic conditions, and $\frac{JV_t}{\overline{\Pi}} > 1(< 1)$ under optimistic (pessimistic) expectations, as reflect4ed by indicator $\omega > 1(< 1)$, , to be explained later: The household expects a higher or lower future income level (or an interruption of income) depending on how the prevailing market sentiment affects its own expectations (and those of the enterprises) and reflects on the job value estimates. Equation (3.2) can be considered as an expression for household permanent income built on expectations and market sentiment and provides an important channel to which uncertainty (and, specifically, idiosyncratic uninsurable risks) can be introduced in the model. Equations (3.1)–(3.2) introduce two very important features of the model:

- First, household future income does not just stochastically fluctuate around its full-employment level: households do factor into their plans the possibility of protracted periods of underemployment or unemployment income. This feature is consistent with the findings by Guvenen (2017) on income risk.
- Second, although (as discussed below) price responses to demand shocks are not considered in this chapter, Eqs. (3.1)–(3.2) suggest that, especially in deflationary environments, price adjustments might not provide simple equilibrating mechanisms since expected price (and wage) dynamics enter the job value estimates and reflect on the demand responses (see Sect. 3.4d).

The Firm

The firm employs physical capital K and labor L to produce composite output Y, consisting of consumption and investment goods, through a standard neoclassical production function,

$$Y = C + k = Y(K, L).$$

The supply of C is an increasing function of consumption good price:

$$C_t = C\left(P_t^C\right), \text{with} \quad C' > 0$$

and the demand, which is derived from first principles below, can be written in a general form as a function of relative prices:

$$C_t = C\left(P_t^C, P_t^T, P_t^B, P_t^K\right), \text{with } C'_C < 0, C'_T > 0, C'_B > 0, C'_K > 0.$$

Each period the firm adds investment k to its existing capital stock,

$$K = K_{-1} + k.$$

The firm finances investment k by selling shares of K to the households. In each period, capital K earns real return $r^K = (1 + y^K)(1 + \pi^K)(1 - \pi^C)$, where y^K is capital's unit output rate, and π^K is rate of change of capital price P^K. The firms decide the stock of K to hold based on the stream of future expected real rates of return on K as reflected in its current price,

$$K_t = K\left(P_t^K\right) \text{ with } K' > 0.$$

On their side, households buy new shares and decide how much stock of K to hold in their portfolio based on the stream of future expected real rates of return on K as reflected in its current price,

$$K_t = K\left(P_t^K\right) \text{ with } K' < 0,$$

The demand function for K is derived from first principles below. Capital K embodies a technology that employs household labor at competitive nominal compensation rate y. Based on capital K, the firm hires household labor L

$$L_t = L(K_t) \text{ with } K' > 0.$$

The Government

The government produces a non-pecuniary public good G and finances production by issuing earlier defined bills and bonds, respectively T and B, to match household portfolio preferences of different maturity and liquidity services),

$$G_\tau + r_{\tau-1}^T P_\tau^T T_\tau + r_{\tau-1}^B P_\tau^T B_\tau = P_\tau^T T_\tau + P_\tau^B B_\tau + Tax_\tau, \tag{3.3}$$

under an intertemporal constraint whereby all state expenditures must eventually be paid through tax revenues

$$\sum_{t=0}^{\infty} \beta^i \prod_{i=t}^{\tau-1} [(G_\tau + P_{\tau-1}^T T_{\tau-1} r_{\tau-1}^T + P_{\tau-1}^B B_{\tau-1} r_{\tau-1}^B) - Tax_\tau] = 0. \tag{3.4}$$

The government sells as many T and B as households wish to buy and on the respective prices. The functional form of the household demand for bills and bonds is derived from first principles below, but they can be written here respectively in the general form:

$$T_t = T\left(P_t^T, P_t^C, P_\tau^B, P_t^K\right), \quad \text{with} \quad T_T' < 0, T_C' > 0, T_B' > 0, T_K' > 0.$$

$$B_t = T\left(P_t^B, P_t^C, P_\tau^T, P_t^K\right) \quad \text{with} \quad B_B' < 0, B_C' > 0, B_T' > 0, B_K' > 0.$$

The Central Bank

The supply of M is governed by central bank's policy rule:

$$M_\tau = M\left(r^* - r_\tau^T\right), \quad \text{with} \quad M' > 0 \text{ if } r^* - r_\tau^T < 0, \tag{3.5}$$

whereby the central bank governs the supply of M so as to minimize deviations over time between the nominal interest rate on (short-term and risk-less) treasury bills T and the neutral rate of interest r^*, which holds when real-sector supply and demand are in intertemporal equilibrium and consumer price inflation is constant ($\pi^C = 0$). The central bank thus fully accommodates the demand for M.

3.4.2 *The Utility-Based Choice Framework*

The model of household choices builds upon three blocks: (i) the utility derived by the households from their holding assets, (ii) the cost of liquidating assets, and (iii) rational expectations distorted by (changes in) market sentiment. Each block is discussed in turn.

Block 1: Assets Provide Utility to Their Holders

Asset Utility. Financial assets, from money to tradeable claims on physical (productive) capital, goods, and commodities, are here thought of as "vehicles" to immediate and/or future consumption, each characterized by its own peculiar "*speed*" (i.e., the time and cost for it to be exchanged for consumption flows) and "*power*" (i.e., its capacity to store and increase value, and to protect value against adverse events). Greater speed typically comes at the cost of some power loss, and vice versa. The speed is the greatest for that asset (i.e., money) that in the exchange process is accepted by all agents, at anytime, anywhere (within the relevant jurisdiction(s)), and at par against all goods, services, and assets traded in the economy—that is, the asset that acts in the economy as means of payment and instrument for settling all (present and future) financial obligations, whether in force of a legal requirement or by societal choice. Because of such property, as formalized below, money delivers to its holders a utility margin (or liquidity premium) that all other (less speedy) assets must compensate by paying some extra returns. These extra returns enhance their power as stores of value and, in equilibrium, offset their lower speed.

At every instant in time, an asset holder is faced with the likelihood of having to liquidate the asset for her to be able to absorb a consumption shock: changes in likelihood affect differently the utility derived from assets featuring different speeds and power loads. The advantage of a framework where money and assets are "competing vehicles" for accessing consumption flows is that it removes the need for assuming money, exogenously, as "the" asset that can buy commodities (such as under cash-in-advance, or Clower, constraint)s, and instead, it makes money emerge (spontaneously or by design) out of many assets as the one that exchanges against consumption flows at the shortest time interval and at the lowest (information and transaction) cost. Notice that money is convertible into consumption or into other assets that are themselves claim on (or convertible into) consumption, implying that the utility of money derives also from its power to support transactions (e.g., financial transactions) that are not directly related to consumption.

The utility of asset Q at date t is obtained by summing over two terms: i) the utility derived from converting the asset into consumption at the next date $t + 1$ with probability ϑ_{t+1} and ii) the utility from holding the asset available to access consumption at some later date with residual probability $(1 - \vartheta_{t+1})$. Taking ω_τ to represent market sentiment (to be defined below) at time τ, and calling s_t a shock to consumption at some future date t, for $t > \tau$, the subjective probability of event ϑ_t whereby the asset holder must finance consumption shock s_t is defined as:

$$\vartheta_t \equiv Pr_\tau[(s_{t=\tau+\varepsilon}), \varepsilon \to 0] = \vartheta(\tau_\tau),\ \vartheta' < 0,\ \vartheta_t = \begin{cases} \lim\limits_{\omega \to 1} \vartheta(\omega_\tau) \\ \lim\limits_{\omega \to 0} \vartheta(\omega_\tau) \end{cases},\ \omega \in (0, \infty). \tag{3.6}$$

Relation (3.6) means that the higher the state of pessimism, the more asset holders expect consumption shocks to occur in the nearest future, whereas strong optimism leads holders to expect smooth consumption in the near as well as foreseeable future. Indicator Ω is explained below (see Block 3). In the following, $\beta = 1/(1 + \delta)$ is the household's time discount factor, where δ is the household's rate of time preference. For ease of exposition, gross returns $R^{Q=M,T,B,K}$ are assumed constant and the price of consumption is set at $P^C = 1.$. (Later, these assumptions will be removed.) Substituting iteratively for $u(Q)$ at each forward date yields

$$\begin{aligned}
u(Q_t) &= \beta R^Q \Big\{ E_t\Big[u\Big(P^Q_{t+1} Q_t\Big)\vartheta_{t+1}\Big] + u(Q_t)(1 - \vartheta_{t+1})\Big\} \\
&= \beta R^Q E_t\Big[u\Big(P^Q_{t+1} Q_t\Big)\vartheta_{t+1}\Big] \\
&+ \beta^2 R^{Q2}(1 - \vartheta_{t+1})\Big\{E_t\Big[u\Big(P^Q_{t+2} Q_t\Big)\vartheta_{t+2}\Big] + u(Q_t)(1 - \vartheta_{t+2})\Big\} \\
&= \beta R^Q E_t\Big[u\Big(P^Q_{t+1} Q_t\Big)\vartheta_{t+1}\Big] + \beta^2 R^{Q2}(1 - \vartheta_{t+1}) E_t\Big[u\Big(P^Q_{t+2} Q_t\Big)\vartheta_{t+2}\Big] \\
&+ \beta^3 R^{Q3}(1 - \vartheta_{t+1})(1 - \vartheta_{t+2})\Big\{E_t\Big[u\Big(P^Q_{t+3} Q_t\Big)\vartheta_{t+3}\Big] + u(Q_t)(1 - \vartheta_{t+3})\Big\} \\
&= \beta R^Q E_t\Big[u\Big(P^Q_{t+1} Q_t\Big)\vartheta_{t+1}\Big] + \beta^2 R^{Q2}(1 - \vartheta_{t+1}) E_t\Big[u\Big(P^Q_{t+2} Q_t\Big)\vartheta_{t+2}\Big] + \\
&\ldots \beta^i R^{Qi}(1 - \vartheta_{t+1}) \ldots (1 - \vartheta_{t+i-1})\Big\{E_t\Big[u\Big(P^Q_{t+i} Q_t\Big)\vartheta_{t+i}\Big] + u(Q_t)(1 - \vartheta_{t+i})\Big\}
\end{aligned}$$

$$= \beta R^Q E_t \left\{ \begin{array}{c} \left[u\left(P^Q_{t+1}Q_t\right)\vartheta_{t+1}\right] + \beta R^Q(1-\vartheta_{t+1})E_t\left[u\left(P^Q_{t+2}Q_t\right)\vartheta_{t+2}\right] + \\ \ldots \beta^i R^{Qi}(1-\vartheta_{t+1})\ldots(1-\vartheta_{t+i})\left\{E_t\left[u\left(P^Q_{t+i+1}Q_t\right)\vartheta_{t+i+1}\right]\right. \\ \left. +u(Q_t)(1-\vartheta_{t+i})\right\} \end{array} \right\},$$

And so on for each subsequent substitution of $u(Q)$. Assuming the household consumes all its wealth throughout its time horizon, thereby implying that the holding of any asset Q vanishes in the limit since $\lim_{i \to \infty} u(Q_t)(1-\vartheta_{t+i}) = 0$; relaxing the constancy of R^Q and $P^C = 1$; considering $\vartheta_t = \vartheta_t(\omega_\tau)$; and summing over the household's infinite time horizon, the utility function of asset Q at date t can be written in the following general form as

$$u(Q_t) = u(Q_t|\omega_t) = E_t\left\{\beta R^Q_{t+1}\left\{u\left(\frac{P^Q_{t+1}Q_t}{P^C_{t+1}}\right)\vartheta_{t+1}(\omega_t) + \sum_{\tau=t+1}^{T=\infty}\beta^\tau \prod_{\tau=t+1}^{T=\infty} u\left(\frac{P^Q_\tau Q_t}{P^C_\tau}\right)R^Q_\tau[1-\vartheta_\tau(\Omega_t)]\vartheta_T(\omega_t)\right\}\right\} \tag{3.7}$$

It should be noted that since current and future expectations at any given point in time are conditional on the information available at that time, markets are necessarily incomplete since uncertainty is not eliminable and future probability distributions are subject to shifts that cannot be predicted. This fundamental feature strengthens the support that this model offers to Keynes's liquidity preference theory (LPT) as the foundation to the (intra- and intertemporal) resource allocation mechanism that underpins the utility-of-money theory discussed here. At the same time, the utility-of-money theory offers a way to ground the LPT on microeconomic foundations (see at the end of this section). The LPT combined with money utility theory will prove instrumental to provide an explanatory hypothesis of the Secular Stagnation phenomenon, examined in Chap. 12.

Anticipating Block 3 below, notice that in the hypothetical event of the highest possible level of pessimism ($\omega_t = 0$), the second term on the right-hand side of Eq. (3.7) would equal zero since $\vartheta_{t+1} = 1$ (that is, Q_t must be liquidated at $t + 1$ with probability 1), and the utility of Q_t would derive from the conversion of the liquidation value of Q_t into consumption at date $t + 1$. In the alternative hypothetical event of high optimism ($\omega_t = 1$), the household would not expect to be facing any consumption shock in the immediate or distant future and would then hold Q until maturity, when it would either consume its capitalized value or reinvest it into a new asset. In either case, the utility of Q_t would derive from converting its future (capitalized) value into consumption at some point in the indefinite future (date T).

Block 2: Variable Cost of Asset Liquidation

Transaction Costs. Every asset Q features an optimal "speed," defined as the shorter time interval possible $\Delta\tau^*_Q$ for the asset to be sold at price $(1-q)P^Q$, where

$q^* \in (0, 1)$ is minimum possible liquidation unit cost for asset Q.[4] Asset optimal speeds are structural parameters determined by the economy's level of institutional and technological development: All else equal, a more efficient and safe financial infrastructure allows asset liquidation to be effected more rapidly and at lower costs. Asset optional speeds vary depending on the assets' different degree of liquidity: Some assets can be liquidated immediately and at very low or no cost; they can thus serve as monies in the exchange system. Liquidating other assets, especially riskier ones, takes longer and involves costs such as for information acquisition; search; analysis, evaluation, and verification; advisory, legal, and administrative requirements and services; and bargaining and negotiations. Having to liquidate an asset at a higher than its optimal speed (owing, for instance, to immediate and unexpected consumption needs) results in higher liquidation costs or forces the household to accept larger discounts on the asset sale price. Denoting $\Delta\ell$ as the time interval available to the asset holder for liquidating asset Q, and with a given level of financial infrastructure development, unit liquidation cost q is determined endogenously based on the following conditions:

i. If $0 < \Delta\ell_Q^* < \Delta\ell$, then $q = q^* > 0$, that is, the seller has enough time to liquidate Q at minimum unit cost q^*.
ii. If $\Delta\ell_Q^* > \Delta\ell \geq 0$, then $q > q^*$, that is, the seller has not enough time and sells Q at a unit cost higher than q^*.
iii. As $\lim_{\Delta\ell^* > \Delta\ell, \Delta\ell \to 0} q = 1$, the unit cost of liquidation increases since the time available for the seller to sell Q shortens up.
iv. If $\Delta\ell_Q^* = 0$ then $q^* = 0$, that is, Q is a perfectly liquid asset (i.e., cash),

where $\Delta\ell_Q^* = \Delta\ell\left(\psi^Q, \omega\right)$, with $\Delta\ell_\psi' < 0$, $\Delta\ell_\omega' < 0$, is the minimum time interval required for the owner of asset Q to sell it optimally (i.e., at no loss on its market value). This time interval decreases with structural variable ψ^Q, which reflects the level of financial system's safety and efficiency (S&E) – including such features as technology, market development, legal basis, governance, risk management, etc.— and their effects on the trading of asset Q, and increases with ω, to be defined below, which captures optimistic market sentiment for trading Q. Thus, all else equal, greater (lower) S&F of the financial infrastructure supporting the market where Q is traded, combined with a "seller" ("buyer") market, would shorten (lengthen) $\Delta\ell_Q^*$ and lower (raise) liquidation unit cost q^Q. Thus, for a given level of financial system efficiency, ψ^Q, liquidation unit cost q^Q can be written as a function $q^Q = q^Q(\omega) = q\left(\frac{\Delta\ell_Q^*}{\Delta\ell(\omega)}\right)$, with $q' > 0$.

Notice that "trust" is a key variable determining the optimal timing for asset trading (that is, the greater the trust, the lower the minimum time interval required for the owner of asset Q to sell it optimally).[5] In complex systems characterized by

[4] The link between asset liquidation and optimal timing was explored by Lippman and McCall (1986).

[5] "Trust" is here defined as the confidence that parties involved in a transaction or interaction will act reliably, ethically, and in good faith. It involves the expectation that each side will fulfill

numerous agents who may not know and trust one another, a financial infrastructure with high S&E serves as a "trusted third party" and reduces transactions costs in asset trading. Market mood interacts with agent expectations and trust in that they speed up transactions (under optimism) and slow them down (under pessimism).[6]

Denote ξ^Q the expected utility lost to Q's liquidation as a fraction of the expected utility from the consumption financed through the proceeds from the sale of Q at date τ,

$$\xi_\tau^Q = \left\{ \frac{E_t\left[u\left(\frac{q(\Omega)_\tau P_\tau^Q Q_t}{P_\tau^C}\right)\right]}{E_t\left[u\left(\frac{P_\tau^Q Q_t}{P_\tau^C}\right)\right]} \right\} = \xi^Q(\omega)_\tau, \text{ with } \xi' > 0. \tag{3.8}$$

Then, Eq. (3.7) can then be rewritten as:

$$u(Q_t) = u(Q_t|\omega_t) = E_t\left\{\beta R_{t+1}^Q \left\{u\left(\frac{P_{t+1}^Q Q_t}{P_{t+1}^C}\right)\vartheta_{t+1}(\omega_t)\right.\right.$$
$$\left.\left.+ \sum_{\tau=t+1}^{T=\infty} \beta^\tau \prod_{\tau=t+1}^{T} u\left(\frac{P_\tau^Q Q_t}{P_\tau^C}\right) R_\tau^Q[1-\vartheta_\tau(\omega_t)][1-\xi_\tau^Q(\Omega_t)]\vartheta_T(\omega_t)\right\}\right\}. \tag{3.7b}$$

Asset Price Volatility. The asset holder faces the risk that, at any time when the asset needs to be liquidated, she might have to sell it at a loss due to market price volatility. Asset price volatility affects risk-averse agent choices. The utility of each asset, therefore, responds inversely to changes in the expected volatility of the asset price, and Jensen's inequality holds such that,

$$E_t\left[u\left(\frac{P_\tau^Q Q_t}{P_\tau^C}\right)\right] < u\left[E_t\left(\frac{P_\tau^Q Q_t}{P_\tau^C}\right)\right].$$

Call σ_τ^Q the ratio of the expected utility loss caused by price volatility to the expected utility from the consumption financed by Q's liquidation at date τ,

$$\sigma_\tau^Q = \left\{ \frac{\left\{u\left[E_t\left(\frac{P_\tau^Q Q_t}{P_\tau^C}\right)\right] - E_t\left[u\left(\frac{P_\tau^Q Q_t}{P_\tau^C}\right)\right]|\omega_t\right\}}{E_t\left[u\left(\frac{P_\tau^Q Q_t}{P_\tau^C}\right)\right]} \right\} = \sigma^Q(\omega_t)_\tau, \text{ with } \sigma' > 0. \tag{3.9}$$

---

their promises or obligations, without exploitation or deceit, facilitating smooth and cooperative exchanges.

[6] When market sentiment is positive (e.g., during economic growth or a bull market), trust in the exchange process increases. Buyers and sellers are more confident in future returns, leading to quicker transactions. For example, during a housing boom, people may rush to buy properties, believing prices will keep rising. In contrast, when market sentiment is negative (e.g., during a recession or bear market), trust erodes, and agents become more cautious. This slows down transactions, as buyers fear future losses and sellers worry about falling prices. For instance, during a financial crisis, investors may hesitate to trade stocks, fearing further market declines.

Ratio σ_τ^Q varies directly with the dispersion of the distribution functions of P^Q and P^C, if they are negatively correlated, and with market pessimism. From Eq. (3.8), Eq. (3.7b) can be further expanded as

$$u(Q_t) = u(Q_t|\omega_t) = E_t\left\{\beta R_{t+1}^Q \left\{u\left(\frac{P_{t+1}^Q Q_t}{P_{t+1}^C}\right)\vartheta_{t+1}(\omega_t)\right.\right.$$
$$\left.\left.+\sum_{\tau=t+1}^{T=\infty}\beta^\tau \prod_{\tau=t+1}^{T=\infty} u\left(\frac{P_\tau^Q Q_t}{P_\tau^C}\right)R_\tau^Q[1-\vartheta_\tau(\omega_t)][1-\xi_\tau^Q(\omega_t)][1-\sigma_\tau^Q(\Omega_t)]\vartheta_{t+1}(\omega_t)\right\}\right\} \tag{3.7c}$$

where $u'_Q > 0$, $u'_{P^Q} > 0$, $u'_{P^C} < 0$, $u'_\beta < 0$, $u'_\theta > 0$, $u'_\xi < 0$, $u'_\sigma < 0$.

Equation (3.7c) determines the utility of assets across the whole spectrum of liquidity, with variable liquidation costs and price volatility, under rational expectations and changing market sentiment as influenced by economic observables. In the case of a fully liquid asset (i.e., money), with $\Delta_Q^* = \xi^M = \rho^M = 0$, Eq. (3.7c) reduces to:

$$u(M_t) = u(M_t|\omega_t) = E_t\left\{\beta\left(1-\pi_{t+1}^c\right)\left\{u\left(\frac{M_t}{P_{t+1}^C}\right)\vartheta_{t+1}(\omega_t)\right.\right.$$
$$\left.\left.+\sum_{\tau=t+1}^{T=\infty}\beta^\tau \prod_{\tau=t+1}^{T=\infty} u\left(\frac{M_t}{P_\tau^C}\right)\left(1-\pi_\tau^c\right)[1-\vartheta_\tau(\omega_t)][1-\sigma_\tau^M(\omega_t)]\vartheta_{t+1}(\omega_t)\right\}\right\}, \tag{3.7d}$$

that is, as a perfectly liquid asset, money trades against any goods or assets at a sure nominal price, $P^M = 1$, at zero transaction cost, and bears a zero nominal interest rate.[7] Note that the lower the probability of the household having to mobilize liquidity any time soon, the lower the utility derived from holding M, and vice versa.

Block 3: Rational Expectations and Market Sentiment

Expectations Formation. Let $X_\tau = [Y_\tau, \boldsymbol{P}_\tau]$, with $\tau = t+1, \infty$, where Y refers to future income levels and vector $\boldsymbol{P}$ denotes the vector of future prices of goods and assets. The expected values of the X variables coincide with those determined by the model of the economy. At each date, the representative household uses current

[7] In economies characterized by sophisticated financial market infrastructures and a government boasting a strong fiscal reputation, short-term (risk-free) treasury bill T tends to be highly traded in liquid monetary markets, featuring low liquidation costs and interest rates. As such, it is often viewed as a viable alternative to money. Conversely, longer-term government bonds, corporate bonds, and equities exhibit lower liquidity levels, incur higher liquidation costs, are subject to increased risks and price fluctuations, and consequently demand higher return premiums to entice investor participation. Holding all other factors constant, a surge in pessimistic expectations diminishes the appeal of more liquid assets (and conversely enhances it for optimistic expectations), thus influencing their demand and the equilibrium rates of return. This approach broadens the scope of the framework initially proposed by Giovannini (1989).

information set $i_t \in I$ to form and update expectations of the future values of X, as a solution of the economy's model. The agent operates transformation $\boldsymbol{T} : \boldsymbol{iT} \in (\mathrm{I} \times \mathrm{R}) \rightarrow i \in (0, 1)$, which converts every information set i into a real number Ω drawn from the interval (0,1), reflecting the state of knowledge and information of the agents: As ω moves up (down) along the interval, it reflects a higher (lower) level of knowledge and information about the economy, and hence more (less) precise expectations about of the future values of X, which the agent extracts from the information set available and processes through her accumulated knowledge of the economy. At each date t, the evolution of the agent's expectations of the future values of X is governed by the following distribution function:

$$F_t(X_T|\Omega_t) = \sum_{n=1}^{N|\iota}(w_{nT}|\Omega_t)F_{tn}(X_T),\ T > t, \tag{3.10}$$

where w_T:$0 \leq w_{nT} \leq 1$; $\sum_n w_{nT} = 1$, and where the weights w's and the order N of the set of selected distribution functions are conditional on state of knowledge and information Ω_t. Equation (3.9) associates a specific structure of weights to N different probability distribution functions of X. A "high" value of state variable Ω, reflecting strong knowledge and good information, implies a small set (i.e., a small N) of narrowly dispersed distribution functions of X, each with a large w_T attached, leading to more precise predictions of future X's: in the limit case of $\Omega_t = 1$ (that is, perfect knowledge and full information), then $N = 1$ and $w_T = 1$, such that $F_t(X_T|1) = F_t(X_T)$. On the other hand, a low value of ω, reflecting poor knowledge and limited information, implies a broad set (i.e., a large N) of dispersed distribution functions, each with a small w_T attached: No single distribution dominates the others in the agent's expectations, and each has a very low probability of being the "true" one. In "fan chart" diagram terms, the band would be very large and all predicted values within it would have the same shadings since none would have a higher likelihood than the others. In the extreme case of a value of ω very proximate to 0, then $w_{nT} \cong 0, \forall n$, and the distribution $F_t(X_T)$ would be indeterminate (the width of the fan-chart band would be infinite).

Market Sentiment. Agent expectations are affected by (changes in) market mood, that is, the sentiment about the state of the world, which prevails in the environment where the agents operate and interacts with their information and knowledge on the state of the economy.[8] Market sentiment ranges between (a maximum level of) "optimism" and a (minimum level of) "pessimism:" optimism (pessimism) is the state of mind inducing an agent to expect superior (inferior) outcomes of future events than would be reasonable for the agent to anticipate on the exclusive basis of the knowledge and the information available to her. Formally, expectations are said to be "optimistic" when

[8] For a recent empirical analysis of how market moods translate into narratives and affect the macroeconomic performance, see Flynn and Sastry (2024).

$$E_t(X_T|\Omega_t') \succ E_t(X_T|\Omega_t).$$

or

$W_t[E_t(X_T|\Omega_t')] > W_t[E_t(X_T|\Omega_t)]\text{for } T > t \text{ and } \Omega_t' > \Omega_t,$

where W the welfare associated with the expected value of X and the reverse sign holds in both expressions for "pessimistic" expectations, and where the *perceived* state of the world Ω' is the result of information "distortive" process $\boldsymbol{D} : iD \in (I \times R) \rightarrow \Omega' > \Omega \text{for} \Omega < 1, or\Omega' \langle \Omega \text{for} \Omega \rangle 0$, with $\Omega', \Omega \in (0, 1)$, so that $\omega = \frac{\Omega'}{\Omega} \in (0, \infty)$ is the market sentiment indicator introduced earlier.

Process $\boldsymbol{D}$ distorts the expected value of the variables that are relevant to the agent to an extent that depends on the intensity of the prevailing emotions, much as individuals experience in real-life situations when they see the very same contingency under a different light depending on the underlying state of their mind, often under the influence of the prevailing social context. This process can be understood as the product of (changing) individual "animal spirits" as these may be socially influenced by the individuals' mutual observation of others' moods and behaviors, as well as by individual psychological attitudes.

Optimism (pessimism), therefore, introduces a distortion in the way agents process and interpret the information available to them. As knowledge progresses, better information becomes available, and new feedback is received from the observed reality, agents adjust their perceptions possibly causing their "distorted" (optimistic or pessimistic) expectations to converge (though not necessarily linearly) toward their correct ("undistorted") equivalent. However, it is also possible that, at least for some length of time, "distorted" expectations are confirmed ex-post by real events or prove to be self-fulfilling, determining new equilibria; it is even possible that new information causes expectations to shoot in the opposite direction leading to other distortions.

The special feature of this model is that it incorporates uncertainty and market sentiment as separate and interacting dimensions of the economy, which affect expectations' formation. Their interaction is captured in Chart 3.1.

The (extreme) combinations reported in the chart should clarify the relationship between the two state variables Ω and Ω' and their different economic interpretations. An agent can have very pessimistic and yet very accurate expectations about the future, if she has enough knowledge and information to back them up, or she can have very optimistic and yet very uncertain expectations due to not having enough knowledge and information.

Market Sentiment and the Economic Environment. Market moods respond to the evolving economic environment. While changes in market sentiment necessarily reflect subjective, psychological processes of individual human beings and the mechanisms governing their social interactions, this chapter assumes that they are nonetheless influenced by the observation of reality as filtered through knowledge (Frydman & Goldberg, 2011). Among the factors that drive changes in market sentiment critical are: (a) the perceptions of general economic (in)stability; (b) the performance of relevant markets; and (c) relevant news, innovations, and forecasts.

Table 3.1 Combinations of state variables concerning uncertainty and market sentiment (under extreme assumptions)

Values of Ω' (market mood)	Values of Ω (information/knowledge)	
	Very low	Very high
Very low	$\Omega' \cong \Omega \cong 0$ Strong pessimism High uncertainty $\Rightarrow$ Indefinite expectations of extremely bad outcomes	$0 \cong \Omega' < \Omega \cong 1$ Strong pessimism Quasi certainty $\Rightarrow$ Definite (accurate) expectations of extremely bad outcomes
Very high	$1 \cong \Omega' > \Omega \cong 0$ Strong optimism High uncertainty $\Rightarrow$ Indefinite expectations of extremely good outcomes	$\Omega' \cong \Omega \cong 1$ Strong optimism Quasi certainty $\Rightarrow$ Definite (accurate) expectations of extremely good outcomes

Through simple indicators, Appendix shows how these three classes of factors influence market sentiment. The relevance of the indicators does not lie in their specific form, but in that they reflect the notion whereby agent emotions are not unexplained "sunspots" and derive, instead, from the ongoing interactions of human states of mind with information, knowledge, and rationality and their influence on agent responses to real circumstances. Integrating or replacing the algorithms formulated in Appendix with others would not alter this basic understanding.

3.4.3 *Optimal Resource Allocations and Equilibrium Prices*

The household maximizes her intertemporal utility:

$$U = \mathrm{Max}_{C,M,T,B,K}\beta^{\tau} E_t \left\{ \left[\sum_{t=\tau}^{\infty} u(C_\tau, M_\tau, T_\tau, B_\tau, K_\tau,) \right] |\omega_t \right\} \tag{3.11}$$

subject to budget constraint

$$\begin{aligned} P^C_\tau C_\tau + P^T_\tau T_\tau + P^B_\tau B_\tau + P^K_\tau K_\tau + M_\tau &= y_\tau - Tax_\tau + M_{\tau-1} \\ + r^T_{\tau-1} P^T_\tau T_\tau + r^B_{\tau-1} P^T_\tau B_\tau + r^K_{\tau-1} P^K_\tau K_\tau, \end{aligned} \tag{3.12}$$

where

$$C_\tau, M_\tau, T_\tau, B_\tau, K_\tau \geq 0, \tag{3.13}$$

and subject to transversality condition

$$\sum_{t=0}^{\infty} \beta^{\tau}(P_{\tau}^{C}C_{\tau} + P_{\tau}^{T}T_{\tau} + P_{\tau}^{B}B_{\tau} + P_{\tau}^{K}K_{\tau} + M_{\tau} - y_{\tau}) = 0. \qquad (3.14)$$

Plans (3.11)–(3.14) are the household's program to allocate resources optimally between current consumption, money and non-money assets with a view to maximizing—both within each date and over time—the streams of utility derived from each, subject to the given resource constraint. The Bellman's equation to solve the plan is:

$$\begin{aligned} &V(y_t, C_t, M_t, T_t, B_t, K_t|\omega_t) \\ &= \mathrm{Max}_{(C,M,T,B,K)}[u(C_t, M_t, T_t, B_t, K_t|\omega_t) \\ &\quad + \beta V(y_{t+1}, C_{t+1}, M_{t+1}, T_{t+1}, B_{t+1}, K_{t+1})\boldsymbol{R}'|\omega_t] \end{aligned}$$

The Euler equation is:

$$u'(C_t, M_t, T_t, B_t, K_t|\omega_t) = \beta E_t\big[u'(C_{t+1}, M_{t+1}, T_{t+1}, B_{t+1}, K_{t+1})\boldsymbol{R}'|\omega_t\big],$$

which determines the optimal intertemporal path for consumption and asset holdings, conditional on state variable ω_t. The optimal intra-date allocation across consumption and assets, conditional on ω_t, is derived as a solution to Eq. (3.11), subject to constraints (3.12)–(3.14) in the text, which yields the following first-order conditions:

$$U'(C_t) = \left\{u'(C_t)\beta^i E_t\left[\left(\frac{1}{P_t^C}\right)\prod_{i=0}^{t} R_i\right]|\omega_t\right\} - \lambda_t = 0,$$

where R is the real gross rate of household wealth growth,

$$U'(M_t) = \left\{u'(M_t)\beta^i E_t\left[\left(\frac{1}{P_t^C}\right)\prod_{i=0}^{t} R_i^M\right]|\omega_t\right\} - \lambda_t = 0,$$

$$U'(T_t) = \left\{u'(T_t)\beta^i E_t\left[\left(\frac{1}{P_t^C}\right)\prod_{i=0}^{t} R_i^T\right]|\omega_t\right\} - \lambda_t = 0,$$

$$U'(B_t) = \left\{u'(B_t)\beta^i E_t\left[\left(\frac{1}{P_t^C}\right)\prod_{i=0}^{t} R_i^B\right]|\omega_t\right\} - \lambda_t = 0,$$

$$U'(K_t) = \left\{u'(K_t)\beta^i E_t\left[\left[\left(\frac{1}{P_t^C}\right)\prod_{i=0}^{t} R_i^K\right]\right]|\omega_t\right\} - \lambda_t = 0,$$

$$\begin{aligned} &\lambda_t E_t\{P_{\tau}^{C}C_{\tau} + P_{\tau}^{T}T_{\tau} + P_{\tau}^{B}B_{\tau} + P_{\tau}^{K}K_{\tau} + M_{\tau} + Tax_{\tau} - M_{\tau-1} \\ &-r_{\tau-1}^{T}P_{\tau}^{T}T_{\tau} - r_{\tau-1}^{B}P_{\tau}^{T}B_{\tau} - r_{\tau-1}^{K}P_{\tau}^{K}K_{\tau} = y_{\tau}]|\omega_t\}\lambda_t \geq 0. \end{aligned}$$

These conditions, including the general and well-behaved functional forms assumed in the model, imply that at planning date *t*, and for expected real gross returns $(R_\tau^M, R_\tau^T, R_\tau^B, R_\tau^K)$ for all τ's, the household selects allocation $(C_\tau^*, M_\tau^*, T_\tau^*, B_\tau^*, K_\tau^*)$ and the economy determines the equilibrium price set $(P_\tau^{C*}, 1, P_\tau^{T*}, P_\tau^{B*}, P_\tau^{K*})$ which exists, is unique, and clears the markets for goods and (money and non-money) assets.

For future expected real rates of return on assets $(R_\tau^M, R_\tau^T, R_\tau^B, R_\tau^K)$, for all τ's, for the value of ω that does not distort expectations, and for the given resource constraints, the solution determines the path to optimal intertemporal consumption and a sequence of allocations $(C_\tau^*, M_\tau^*, T_\tau^*, B_\tau^*, K_\tau^*)$ that satisfy the optimal intra-date rule of weighted marginal utility (w. m. u.) equality at each future date $\tau = t+1, \ldots, \infty$, and clear the markets for the economy's goods and assets at prices $(P_\tau^{C*}, 1, P_\tau^{T*}, P_\tau^{B*}, P_\tau^{K*})$:

$$\begin{aligned}\left[u'(C_\tau^*)\left(\frac{1}{P_\tau^{C*}}\right)|\omega_t\right] &= \left[u'(M_\tau^*)|\omega_t\right] = \left[u'(T_\tau^*)\left(\frac{1}{P_\tau^{T*}}\right)|\omega_t\right] \\ &= \left[u'(B_\tau^*)\left(\frac{1}{P_\tau^{B*}}\right)|\omega_t\right] = \left[u'(K_\tau^*)\left(\frac{1}{P_\tau^{K*}}\right)|\omega_t\right] = \lambda_\tau,\end{aligned} \tag{3.15}$$

which requires equating the marginal utilities of *M* and all other assets holdings, each weighted with its own price, and

$$\lambda_\tau/\lambda_{\tau+1} = \beta E_t R_{\tau+1}^M = \beta E_t R_{t+1}^{B_D} = \beta E_t R_{\tau+1}^T = \beta E_t R_{\tau+1}^K. \tag{3.16}$$

The optimal intra-date and intertemporal allocation rules optimal rules (3.15) and (3.16), respectively lie at the core of the analysis of this chapter. Rule (3.15) requires the household to equate at each date the w. m. u. of consumption and monetary and financial assets. Rule (3.16) requires that all real rates of return on money and assets, in present (discounted) value and net of default risk, are equalized at each date and intertemporally.

The consistency of rule (3.15) with plan (3.11)–(3.14) can be seen by considering any alternative allocation path incorporating allocations such as, for example, $(C_\tau^0, M_\tau^0, T_\tau^0, B_\tau^0, K_\tau^0) \neq (C_\tau^*, M_\tau^*, T_\tau^*, B_\tau^*, K_\tau^*)$. If, at equilibrium prices $(P_\tau^{C*}, 1, P_\tau^{T*}, P_\tau^{B*}, P_\tau^{K*})$ across all $\tau = t, \infty$, it was the case that $(C_\tau^0, M_\tau^0, T_\tau^0, B_\tau^0, K_\tau^0) \succ (C_\tau^*, M_\tau^*, T_\tau^*, B_\tau^*, K_\tau^*)$, then allocation $(C_\tau^0, M_\tau^0, T_\tau^0, B_\tau^0, K_\tau^0)$ would violate constraints (3.13)–(3.15) and would therefore be unfeasible. If, on the other hand, $(C_\tau^0, M_\tau^0, T_\tau^0, B_\tau^0, K_\tau^0) \prec (C_\tau^*, M_\tau^*, T_\tau^*, B_\tau^*, K_\tau^*)$, then the allocation could be improved upon without violating constraints (3.12)–(3.14) and so on, until optimal allocation $(C_\tau^*, M_\tau^*, T_\tau^*, B_\tau^*, K_\tau^*)$ is reached and no further improvement is possible.

The consistency of rule (3.16) with plans (3.11)–(3.14) can be similarly established considering any alternative allocations $(C_\tau, M_\tau, T_\tau, B_\tau, K_t)$ and $(C_{\tau+1}, M_{\tau+1}, T_{\tau+1}, B_{\tau+1}, K_{\tau+1})$, across all $\tau = t, \infty$, such that the ratio $\lambda_\tau/\lambda_{\tau+1} \neq \beta E_t R_{\tau+1}^M = \beta E_t R_{t+1}^{B_D} = \beta E_t R_{\tau+1}^T = \beta E_t R_{\tau+1}^K$, then, for given real rates, reallocations would be possible (at no additional costs) that would improve household welfare.

Otherwise, if households do prefer those allocations, then real rates must adjust until equilibrium is reached.

Optimal rules (3.15)–(3.16) require that: *In equilibrium, at each date the household derives the same level of utility from each marginal unit of consumption and asset holdings, and all real rates of return on money and assets, in present (discounted) value, and net of default risk, are equalized at each date and intertemporally.*

Optimal rules (3.15)–(3.16) hold under expected real interest rates and asset returns conditional on the knowledge of, and information on, the economy and its prospects at the times expectations are formed. Full-employment general equilibrium would require that agent expectations are rational and undistorted by market sentiment ($\omega = 1$). Distorted expectations (by pessimistic or optimistic beliefs) ($\omega \neq 1$) lead the economy to suboptimal equilibria with less than full resource employment or higher than optimal inflation.

Importantly, from a theoretical standpoint, rules (3.15)–(3.16) provide the microfoundations to Keynes's Liquidity Preference Theory (LPT), whereby equilibrium asset prices (interest rates) are not determined by the relationship between saving and investment flows (as in loanable fund theories), but by agents deciding how to allocate their stocks of wealth (Tily, 2012). In other words, LPT is about agents deciding the degree of liquidity at which their accumulated savings are held.[9] These are decisions concerning the stock of wealth at any point in time, rather than just the new flows of saving generated out of income. Therefore, where money and other financial assets are recognized as instruments that deliver utility to their holders, equilibrium asset prices (rates of interest) are determined by the supply of and demand for assets into which holdings of wealth can be placed, not by the supply of and demand for (flows of) saving. As such, they influenced by agent expectations and states of confidence.

3.5 Implications

Three types of uncertainty are analyzed in this section, concerning respectively nominal income, financial asset prices, and real-sector prices. In this model, the uncertainty surrounding income and prices originates from the higher likelihood of future shocks affecting the stream of real returns on labor and/or wealth, which are expected to increase their variability. Faced with higher uncertainty, the risk-averse

[9] I wish to take this opportunity to point out that several critiques of LPT stem from the erroneous conflation of "liquidity" with "money." This conflation leads to confusion between the demand for money and the demand for liquidity. The demand for money refers specifically to the market for the asset that an economy accepts as means of exchange and payment instrument. In contrast, liquidity is a characteristic that all existing assets—both real and financial—possess to different degrees (and bearing in mind that such degrees can change over time based on circumstances). Therefore, the demand for liquidity encompasses all asset markets and reflects agents' preferences for each asset relative to others regarding its liquidity. Notice that the demand for money aligns with a partial equilibrium approach, while the demand for liquidity corresponds to a general equilibrium approach. Thus understood, the demand for liquidity extends to all types of agents (households, firms, and financial intermediaries) and determines their spending and financing decisions.

agent solving plans (3.11)–(3.14) reduce intertemporal consumption and devote at each date more resources to asset accumulation. The following analysis focuses on intra-date portfolio decisions to allocate resources across assets of different liquidity and their impact on asset prices.

3.5.1 Income Uncertainty

Under greater uncertainty (at $\omega < 1$, so that greater uncertainty is not offset by optimistic expectations), an anticipated increase in the variability of nominal income raises the risk-averse agent's need to stand ready to absorb its potential impact on consumption by mobilizing the purchasing power stored in her asset portfolio. In terms of Eq. (3.7c), this means that a decrease in ω_t below 1 leads to an increase in the probability of the agent having to accelerate asset liquidation. It follows that the utility of each asset is affected differently by the prospects of accelerated sale via the effect on liquidation cost. As the time-distance between the planning date and the expected date of asset liquidation draws shorter than the time interval needed for optimal asset sale, that is, $T - t = \Delta \mathscr{t}_{Q}^{*}$, from Eqs. (3.7c) and (3.7d) it follows that the asset price discount factor ξ_{τ}^{Q} increases and reduces the utility of Q, while leaving the utility of M unaffected. The increase in ξ_{τ}^{Q} (and the consequent decrease in Q's utility) grows with the size of the asset's optimal interval $\Delta \mathscr{t}_{Q}^{*}$ (which is zero in the case of M). The agent, therefore, has an incentive to adjust her optimal portfolio mix by moving away from less liquid assets and into relatively more liquid assets, specifically those with smaller $\Delta \mathscr{t}_{Q}^{*}$'s and for which $T - t = \Delta \mathscr{t}_{Q}^{*}$. As a result, the agent shifts her portfolio from A to M, until a new equilibrium allocation $(C_{\tau}^{**}, M_{\tau}^{**}, T_{\tau}^{**}, B_{\tau}^{**}, K_{\tau}^{**})$ obtains, consistent with optimal rules (3.15)–(3.16). Obviously, for the economy as a whole, if the supplies of M and A are both rigid, or sluggish, equilibrium requires price P_{T}^{A} to adjust downward, implying a higher return on A. That is, the agents prefer to stay liquid, and the economy converges toward a suboptimal (Pareto-inefficient, typically Keynesian under-investment) equilibrium. Notice that if the effects of uncertainty are large, restoring full employment equilibrium would require incentivizing the agents to reduce their liquid holdings and to spend them on consumption and investment activities. The return on M should thus be lowered to the point where its holders find it convenient to exchange it for more consumption goods and for less liquid assets. In those cases where the nominal interest rate on M was brought down to zero, only unconventional monetary policies (and fiscal measures) can be used to generate desired economic stimuli.

3.5.2 Asset Price Uncertainty

In the above model, greater asset price uncertainty is defined by more dispersed asset price distributions conditional on lower values of Ω_t. These work their effects on portfolio allocations and asset returns by increasing the expected values of the σ_T^Q's—as in can be seen from Eq. (3.7c) and optimal rules (3.15)–(3.16). Larger σ_T^Q's reduces the utility of less liquid assets, while they leave the utility of liquid assets unchanged, and therefore induce holders to shrink the portfolio shares of less liquid assets relative to more liquid assets: Greater uncertainty causes higher liquidity preference. This, in turn, raises (lowers) the equilibrium returns on less (more) liquid assets. The results are unambiguous.

3.5.3 Real-Sector Price Uncertainty

If the distribution of expectations regarding the future dynamics of the general level of prices for goods and services becomes more uncertain, due to, say, possible supply shocks or changes in monetary policy,from Eqs. (3.9) and (3.7c), at any date t, this leads to an increase in the ratio of expected utility loss, σ_τ^Q, for $T > t$. Assume that inflation variability and relative price variability are associated with mean inflation, in line with empirical findings,[10] and assume that money grows at the expected inflation rate π^C. Inspecting the w. m. u. expressions for money M and any other asset Q to be equalized under rule (3.15), yields the following equations.

For M:

$$
\begin{aligned}
u(M_t) = u(M_t|\omega_t) = E_t\Bigg\{\beta\left(1-\pi_{t+1}^c\right)\Bigg\{u\left(\frac{M_t}{P_{t+1}^C}\right)\vartheta_{t+1}(\omega_t) \\
+\sum_{\tau=t+1}^{T=\infty}\beta^\tau\prod_{\tau=t+1}^{T=\infty}u\left(\frac{M_t}{P_\tau^C}\right)\left(1-\pi_\tau^c\right)[1-\vartheta_\tau(\omega_t)]\left[1-\sigma_\tau^M(\omega_t)\right]\vartheta_{t+1}(\omega_t)\Bigg\}\Bigg\}
\end{aligned}
\tag{3.17}
$$

Equation (3.17) shows that the m. u. of M is lowered by expectations of future higher inflation π^C and the expected loss to utility ratio, σ^M, due to larger price variability.

---

[10] Positive correlations between mean inflation, inflation variability, and relative price variability have been consistently observed in many inflationary episodes worldwide. For empirical research and references on these relationships, see Fernández Valdovinos and Gerling (2011), and Caporale et al. (2010). More recently, Baglan et al. (2016) found that the inflation-relative price variability is linear in high-inflation regimes but nonlinear and U-shaped in more stable environments. Regarding the relationship between inflation and inflation variability, see Barnett et al. (2020). On the theory of the effects of inflation on relative prices and their impact on welfare, see Ball and Romer (2003). On the theory of the relationship between inflation and inflation uncertainty, see Ball (1992).

For Q:

$$u(Q_t) = u(K_t|\omega_t) = E_t\left\{\beta R^Q_{t+1}\left\{u\left(\frac{P^Q_{t+1}Q_t}{P^C_{t+1}}\right)\vartheta_{t+1}(\omega_t)\right.\right.$$
$$\left.\left. + \sum_{\tau=t+1}^{T=\infty}\beta^\tau \prod_{\tau=t+1}^{T=\infty} u\left(\frac{P^Q_\tau Q_t}{P^C_\tau}\right) R^Q_\tau[1-\vartheta_\tau(\omega_t)]\left[1-\xi^Q_\tau(\omega_t)\right]\left[1-\sigma^Q_\tau(\omega_t)\right]\vartheta_{t+1}(\omega_t)\right\}\right\} \tag{3.18}$$

Equation (3.18) indicates that asset K is affected by the same two variables ξ and σ as M, but its m. u. depends crucially on the correlation between the price of Q and the price of consumption. In the event of perfect negative correlation, as σ increases the cost of Q's liquidation rises, thus lowering factor $\left(1-\xi^Q_\tau\right)$ and, hence, the value of its m. u. The opposite holds under perfect positive correlation, to the point that, in cases of extreme price uncertainty (e.g., hyperinflation) an asset with such a property would become a perfect hedge against consumer price variability, its cost of liquidation would go down to zero, and eventually it might even replace money as a store of value and medium of exchange. Given rules (3.15)–(3.16), under real-sector price uncertainty, at any future time t the agents would prefer a new optimal resource allocation $C^{**}_t < C^*_t$ $M^{**}_t < M^*_t$ and $Q^*_t \gtreqless Q^*_t$, where the equilibrium demand for Q depends on the correlation between its price and the price of consumption: Assets with higher (lower) positive correlation would be in higher (lower) demand. Correspondingly, the poor performance of money as a store of value would require a higher equilibrium rate of interest, whereas the required return on Q would be lower (higher) the higher (lower) the correlation between its price and the price of consumption.

Where the reduction in intertemporal consumption matters is especially for the demand for physical (productive) capital K, whose m. u. would be affected by a lower stream of real returns (due to lower expected future sales). Inflation discourages the accumulation of real (productive) capital.

3.5.4 Financial Sector Implications

An important implication of the variable (endogenous) cost structure of liquidation introduced in Sect. 3.3.2b is that, by making all assets relatively more liquid, economies with more developed financial systems tend to reduce the impact of higher levels of income uncertainty on equilibrium portfolio allocations and asset returns, for two reasons. First, by lowering $\Delta^*_{\not Q}$'s, a more developed financial system reduces the required (equilibrium) return on less liquid assets, which can be traded more efficiently, and thereby facilitates portfolio diversification away from money and quasi-money assets and into less liquid assets. Second, for higher values of ω_t, a lower $\Delta^*_{\not Q}$, reduces the probability of $T - t = \Delta^*_{\not Q}$, thus making the economy more resilient to shocks. Conversely, in less developed economies, where agents have lower stocks of wealth available to absorb income shocks, and where financial markets are less liquid and less efficient, portfolios tend to be more liquid, and the accumulation of risky capital is thereby discouraged.

3.5.5 Speculative Bubbles and Booms and Busts

The methodology discussed in this chapter allows performing an instructive dissection of the dynamics involved in the microeconomics of "bubble" phenomena, leading also to policy indications on how to intervene on them. Take the example of a new production technology K being launched in the market, which promises to yield large increases of output productivity r^K. The offer stock price of K and the shares of stock K held in the portfolios are both initially very low, rendering the w. m. u. of the asset abnormally high relative to that of consumption and the other assets available. In terms of rules (3.15)–(3.16), conditional on the information available at time t, the situation looks like:

$$\left[u'(C_\tau^*)\left(\frac{1}{P_\tau^{C*}}\right)|\omega_t\right] = \left[u'(M_\tau^*)|\omega_t\right]\left[u'(T_\tau^*)\left(\frac{1}{P_\tau^{T*}}\right)|\omega_t\right]$$
$$= \left[u'(B_\tau^*)\left(\frac{1}{P_\tau^{B*}}\right)|\omega_t\right] \ll \left[u'(K_\tau^*)\left(\frac{1}{P_\tau^{K*}}\right)|\omega_t\right],$$

featuring a very high w. m. u. of asset K, and a consequent large market incentive waiting to be arbitraged out by the agents. Under complete knowledge and full certainty ($\omega' \cong \omega \cong 1$), and assuming a fully flexible supply of K, both price P^K and quantity K settle instantly at their rational expectations equilibrium levels, so that,

$$\left[u'(C_\tau^*)\left(\frac{1}{P_\tau^{C*}}\right)|\omega_t = 1\right] = \left[u'(M_\tau^*)|\omega_t = 1\right] = \left[u'(T_\tau^*)\left(\frac{1}{P_\tau^{T*}}\right)|\omega_t = 1\right]$$
$$= \left[u'(B_\tau^*)\left(\frac{1}{P_\tau^{B*}}\right)|\omega_t = 1\right] = \left[u'(K_\tau^{**})\left(\frac{1}{P_\tau^{K**}}\right)|\omega_t = 1\right],$$

with $K_\tau^{**} > K_\tau^*$ and P_τ^{K**} being feasible only if $C_\tau^{**} < C_\tau^*$, and/or $T_\tau^{**} < T_\tau^*$, and/or $B_\tau^{**} < B_\tau^*$ since within the given budget constraints agents could obtain higher shares of K only by reallocating resources away from current consumption and liquid holdings. However, in a highly globalized economy under a monetary regime with "excess elasticity" (Borio & Disyatat, 2011), the higher demand for K would be accommodated through endogenous money creation from the banking systems, and the dynamics of asset price P^K would be left unanchored. This would be particularly critical if expectations were sensible to changes in market sentiment. Under optimistic expectations, and a sluggish supply of K (due to, say, short-term production rigidities), the dynamics would be much richer and might give origin to financial boom-and-bust phenomena. By inspecting the m. u. expression for K using Eq. (3.7c), here rewritten as:

$$u(K_t) = E_t\left\{\beta R^{K}_{t+1}\left\{u\left(\frac{P^{K}_{t+1}K_t}{P^{C}_{t+1}}\right)\vartheta_{t+1} + \sum_{\tau=t+1}^{T=\infty}\beta^{\tau}\prod_{\tau=t+1}^{T=\infty}u\left(\frac{P^{K}_{\tau}K_t}{P^{C}_{\tau}}\right)R^{K}_{\tau}[1-\vartheta_{\tau}]\left[1-\xi^{K}_{\tau}\right]\left[1-\sigma^{K}_{\tau}\right]\vartheta_{t+1}\right\}|\omega' > 1\right\}. \tag{3.7e}$$

One notices that, if a consistent flow of positive news about K leads the agents to expect an increasing trend of P^K, then, an upbeat market for K shortens Δt^*_Q and feeds into lower expected values of ξ^Q_τ. Also, the positive news reduces the expected values of σ^K_τ. Throughout this progression, to the extent that agents do not anticipate being forced to liquidate their holdings of K ahead of time to hedge against possible future consumption shocks, they solve Eq. (3.7e) using $1 - \vartheta_{\tau+i-1}$ for all i's and pushing $\vartheta_T = 1$ forward in time, thus delaying the time of asset liquidation. Meanwhile, as the supply physical capital of K adjusts only slowly to the high demand for it, K's rate of return increases as both Y^K and P^K rise fast. All this contributes to keeping the relative w. m. u. of K (and, hence, the demand for it) rising. But as the supply of K responds slowly to increasing demand, optimal rules (3.15)–(3.16) require that P^K overshoots its rational-expectations equilibrium consistent with optimum K, that is, the level of K that clears the market for K at the equilibrium real rate of return. Price overshooting feeds into high values of Ω and causes P^K to stay above equilibrium (or to rise further up) even as the supply of K starts adjusting to match demand.

Optimistic expectations may induce a large increase in the perceived w. m. u. of asset K, giving rise to market incentive, $\mathcal{M}$, defined as:

$$\mathcal{M}\left(K_t, P^K_t\right) = \left\{\left[u'\left(K^*_\tau\right)\left(\frac{1}{PK*_\tau}\right)|\omega'_t > 1\right] - \left[u'\left(K^*_\tau\right)\left(\frac{1}{PK*_\tau}\right)|\omega_t = 1\right]\right\} > 0,$$

which can cause a temporary equilibrium (or a sequence of temporary equilibria) characterized by higher values of K and P^K than their rational-expectations, full-information equivalents, thereby feeding bubble $\mathcal{B}$, defined as:

$$\mathcal{B}\left(K_t, P^K_t\right) = \left\{\left(K^*_\tau, P^{K*}_\tau\right)|\omega'_t > 1 \gg \left(K^*_\tau, P^{K*}_\tau\right)|\omega_t = 1\right\},$$

characterized by over-extended portfolios in asset K and inflation of asset price P^K. This result explains the seeming paradox of a rising asset stock driving a rising asset price, well-illustrated by Phelps (2009) as applying to the housing sector. The magnitudes of $\mathcal{M}$ and $\mathcal{B}$, together, provide a "measure" of the market's "irrational exuberance."

Size and duration of the bubble vary with the agents' space to fund new purchases of K, including through portfolio reallocations and, even more relevantly, by accessing external financing. The relationship between asset price bubbles and external financing and their policy implications are analyzed by Borio and Lowe (2004). In fact, the elasticity with which the financial system accommodates the demand for financing asset purchases from agents anticipating asset price growth becomes itself a critical factor that feeds into further asset price growth. The latter, in turn, magnifies optimistic expectations and stimulates higher demands for asset purchase financing. In the model above, external financing for growing investment in asset K would show up as an increasing supply of M, which would be reallocated from transaction balances to higher shares of K within the agents' portfolios. Sustained increases in portfolio absorption of K and reassessments of market sentiment Ω eventually lead P^K to revert its growth trend and to begin a corrective descent, thus pricking bubble $\mathcal{B}$ and arbitraging market incentive $\mathcal{M}$ out.

Throughout the adjustment process, both P^K and K may oscillate around their new equilibrium values given by

$$\left[u'(C_\tau^{***})\left(\frac{1}{P_\tau^{C*}}\right)|\omega_t = 1\right] = \left[u'(M_\tau^{***})|\omega_t = 1\right] = \left[u'(T_\tau^{*})\left(\frac{1}{P_\tau^{T*}}\right)|\omega_t = 1\right]$$
$$= \left[u'(B_\tau^{*})\left(\frac{1}{P_\tau^{B*}}\right)|\omega_t = 1\right] = \left[u'(K_\tau^{***})\left(\frac{1}{P_\tau^{K*}}\right)|\omega_t = 1\right],$$

where

$$\mathcal{M}\left(K_t^{***}, P_t^{K***}\right) = \mathcal{B}\left(K_t^{***}, P_t^{K***}\right) = 0.$$

Oscillations around equilibrium follow from the dynamics of P^K and K conditional, in turn, on the prevailing market sentiment. To the extent, for example, that pessimism sets in, price P^K might undershoot its equilibrium level, while agents might squeeze their portfolio shares of K much below their equilibrium values. A boom–bust sequence would ensue along the convergence process.

3.5.6 *Preventing Bubbles*

The model points to the possible introduction of a macro-prudential policy tool, which could be used when the price dynamics in specific asset markets are subject to significant speculative activity and "excessive" volatility. Bubble growth in the market for any asset Q could be pre-empted by increasing Q's unit liquidation cost q^Q through an ad hoc fee that would "throw sand in the wheel" of Q's trading, forcing the economy to settle at an equilibrium with a lower level of Q than in the absence of the fee.

Compared with the alternative of using monetary policy to prick bubbles (Roubini, 2006), the ad hoc fee tool above would have the advantage of being market- (or asset-) specific, thus reducing the larger impact on the rest of the economy that would likely follow from coarser (non-selective) instruments like interest rates or credit restraints (Posen, 2009). The ad hoc fee tool would also have the advantage that its level could be calibrated as necessary to discourage, or to halt, excess trading of any specific asset— a flexibility feature that is not available to the monetary authorities under traditional interest rate policy (Bernanke, 2004).[11]

3.6 Conclusion

This chapter has presented an in-depth exploration of my proposed utility theory of money. The theory offers a unifying approach that uses utility as a benchmark to compare such different things as (consumer and capital) goods with (real and financial) assets within and across dates in time. The theory builds on three blocks. First, money and non-money assets provide their holders with utility associated to their "speed" and "power" to access consumption across time. Second, less liquid assets trade at a variable, endogenously determined transaction cost, reflecting financial system's (in)efficiencies and trading under uncertainty and changing market sentiment. Third, a general model of expectations formation incorporates agents' information and prevailing market mood. These blocks together allow for studying how rational agents exposed to uncertainty and changing market moods allocate resources between consumption and assets, and across assets, to maximize lifetime utility under uncertainty and changing market sentiment.

Using parsimonious assumptions, and very general behavioral and structural functions, the theory provides a consistent and simple framework to analyze—from first principles—the microeconomics of income and price uncertainty, speculative bubbles, and boom-and-bust sequences.

By allowing to integrate Keynes' liquidity preference theory within a microfounded framework with rational choices and market sentiment, the theory can be used to explain the occurrence of Keynesian macroeconomic underemployment equilibria (Chap. 12).

Having explored the utility of money, the next chapter will delve into the effects of injecting money into the economy, examining its circulation and the various frictions that may impede this process.

Appendix: Market Sentiment

A simple way to build variable Ω', which reflects the agents' *perceived* state of the world, introduced in block 3 of the model, is to use backward and forward indicators that capture, respectively, past and future economic dynamics. Simple examples of such indicators include the following:

---

[11] For references to the literature on the pros and cons of the role of monetary policy vis-à-vis asset bubbles, see Hördahl and Packer (2007) and the discussion therein, and see also the more recent Bonchi (2021).

(a) *General economic stability:* This is evaluated in terms of social loss function $L = L(\overline{x})$, where $\overline{x}$ is the set of arguments representing the key macroeconomic policy objectives pursued by the policymakers, and each argument is expressed as a deviation between actual and target values. Agents know that policymakers pursue socially optimal target $T^* = \min L(\overline{x})$. They, thus, observe the actual values of T and compare them to T^*, and grant equal weight to negative and positive deviations of equal value. Looking backward, say τ periods from current date t_0, the agents evaluate economic stability using the quadratic function:

$$S = -\sum_{t=t_0-\tau}^{t_{0-1}} \left(\frac{1}{t}\right)\left(T_t - T^*\right)^2 = S(\Lambda, t), \text{ where } \left(T_t - T^*\right) \equiv \Lambda_t \text{with } S'_{\Lambda}\langle 0,\ S'_{t}\rangle 0, \tag{3.19}$$

where recent deviations Λ weigh more heavily than distant ones. Note that S increases with lower Λ and with higher scalar factor t, which determines the duration of (in)stability: All else equal, a value of S calculated over a longer time interval is more informative than if calculated over a shorter interval. In words: protracted stability (instability) feeds optimism (pessimism).

(b) *Past economic performances:* These are measured as observed changes in the past realizations of some relevant variables (e.g., GDP growth, inflation, unemployment, etc.) over a given period:

$$PEP_t = \sum_{t=t_0-\tau}^{t_{0-1}} \left(\frac{1}{t}\right)(X_t - X_{t-1}), \tag{3.20}$$

where observations distant in time weigh less than those closer to the present and persistent same-directional changes increase the value of the indicator.

(c) *Expected future performances:* These are measured as future discounted expected values of relevant variable market performances over a foreseeable period:

$$FEP_t = \sum_{t=t_0-\tau}^{t_{0-1}} \left(\frac{1}{t}\right)E_{t_0}(X_t - X_{t-1}). \tag{3.21}$$

From Eqs. (3.23)–(3.25), define

$$\Omega' = \Omega'(S, PEP, FEP) \text{ with } \Omega'_S, \Omega'_{PEP}, \Omega'_{FEP} > 0, \tag{3.22}$$

that is, increasing perceptions of economic stability, improving past market performances, and improving expected future market performance, generate greater optimism and vice versa.

As noted in the text, the relevance of the above indicators does not lie in their specific form, but in that they reflect the notion that agent emotions are not unexplained "sunspots" and derive, instead, from the ongoing interactions of human states of mind with information, knowledge, and rationality and their influence on agent responses to real circumstances. Integrating or replacing these indicators with others, including more sophisticated ones and covering other aspects of the economy, would not alter this basic understanding.

References

Amihud, Y., Mendelson, H., & Pedersen, L. H. (2005). Liquidity and asset prices. *Foundations and Trends in Finance, 1*(4), 269–364.

Baglan, D., Yazgan, M., Yilmazkuday, H. (2016). Relative price variability and inflation: New evidence. *Journal of Macroeconomics, 48*, 263–282.

Ball, L. (1992). Why does high inflation raise inflation uncertainty. *Journal of Monetary Economics, 29*(3), 371–388.

Ball, L., & Romer, D. (2003). Inflation and the Informativeness of Prices. *Journal of Money, Credit and Banking, 35*(2), 177–196, April, Blackwell Publishing.

Barnett, W. A., J. Fredj, & Ftiti, Z. (2020). Causal relationships between inflation and inflation uncertainty. *Studies in Nonlinear Dynamics & Econometrics, 24*(5), 20190094. https://doi.org/10.1515/snde-2019-0094.

Berardi, M. (2022). Uncertainty and sentiments in asset prices. *Journal of Economic Behavior & Organization, 202*, 498–516, Elsevier.

Bernanke, B. (2004). The logic of monetary policy. Remarks Before the National Economists Club.

Birru, J., & Young, T. (2023). The real effects of sentiment and uncertainty. Fisher College of Business Working Paper No. 2023-03-011and Charles A. Dice Working Paper No. 2023-11.

Bonchi, J. (2021). Asset price bubbles and monetary policy: Revisiting the nexus at the zero lower bound. Working Paper 11/2021.

Borio, C., & Lowe, P. (2004). Securing sustainable price stability: should credit come back from the wilderness?. BIS Working Papers No 157.

Borio, C., & Disyatat, P. (2011). Global imbalances and the financial crisis: Link or no link? BIS Working Papers No 346, Basel: Bank for International Settlements.

Bossone, B. (1996). Time and trust in the demand for money and assets. *International Review of Economics and Business, October/November*, 793–816.

Bossone, B. (1997). On trust, uncertainty and liquidity. *Quaderni di Economia e Finanza, Anno VI, 2*, 109–152.

Bossone, B. (2014). Liquidity and capital under uncertainty and changing market sentiment: A simple analysis. *Review of Financial Economics, 23*(2), 98–105.

Blanchard, O. J., & Fischer, S. (1989). *Lectures on macroeconomics*. MIT Press.

Caporale, G. M., Onorante, L., & Paesani, P. (2010). Inflation and inflation uncertainty in the euro area. Working Paper Series No. 1229, Luiss, School of European Political Economy.

Croushore, D. (1993). Money in the utility function: Functional equivalence to a shopping-time model. *Journal of Macroeconomics, 15*(1), 175–182.

Douglas de Medeiros, F. (2022). Expectations, Economic Uncertainty, and Sentiment. *Revista de Administração Contemporânea, 26*(5).

Feenstra, R. C. (1986). Functional equivalence between liquidity costs and the utility of money. *Journal of Monetary Economics, 17*, 271–291.

Flynn, J., & Sastry, K. (2024). *The macroeconomics of narratives*. NBER Working Paper 32602.

Foucault, T., Pagano, M., Röell, A. (2023). Liquidity and asset prices," Chapter 10 of Foucault. In T. M. Pagano & A. Röell (Eds.), *Market Liquidity: Theory, Evidence, and Policy*, 2nd edn. Oxford Academic, pp. 307–349

Friedman, M. (1969). *Optimum quantity of money*. Aldine Publishing Company.

Frydman, R., & Goldberg M. D. (2011). *Beyond mechanical markets: asset price swings, risk, and the role of the state*. Princeton University Press.

Ganchev, G. T. (2010). On the utility of money. *Economic Studies Journal, Issue, 1*, 32–60.

Giovannini, A. (1989). Uncertainty and liquidity. *Journal of Monetary Economics, 23*(2), 239–258.

Guvenen, F. (2017). Understanding income risk: New insights from big data—large data sets reveal new insights into the risks individuals face from fluctuating incomes, Federal reserve Bank of Minneapolis

Hall, R. E. (2013). The routes into and out of the zero lower bound. Prepared for the Federal Reserve Bank of Kansas City's Jackson Hole Symposium, Global Dimensions of Unconventional Monetary Policy, August 23, 2013.

Hördahl. P., & Packer, F. (2007). Understanding asset prices: an averview. BIS Papers, No. 34, 30 March.

Kareken, J. H., & Wallace, N. (Eds.) (1980). Models of monetary economies. Federal Reserve Bank, Minneapolis.

Kacperczyk, M. T., Damien, P., Walker, S. G. (2011). A new class of bayesian semiparametric models with applications to option pricing. In NYU Stern School of Business Working Paper, McCombs Research Paper Series No. IROM-08-05, April 13.

Kiyotaki, N., & Moore, J. (2005). Lawrence R. Klein Lecture: Liquidity and Asset Prices. *International Economic Review, 46*(2), 317–349.

Lagos, R. (2010). Asset prices and liquidity in an exchange economy. *Journal of Monetary Economics, 57*(8), 913–930.

Lippman, S. A., & McCall, J. J. (1986). An operational measure of liquidity. *American Economic Review, 76*(1), 43–55.

Patinkin, D. (1965). Money, interest, and prices: An integration of monetary and value theory. 2nd Edition, Row, Peterson and Co., Evanston, Harper and Row, New York.

Phelps, E. S. (2009). US monetary policy and the prospective structural slump. Whither Monetary Policy? Monetary Policy Challenges in the Decade Ahead, Seventh BIS Annual Conference, 26–27 June 2008, BIS Papers No 45, 5–16.

Posen, A. (2009). Finding the right tolls for dealing with asset price booms. Speech to the MPR Monetary Policy and the Markets Conference, London.

Poterba, J. M., & Rotemberg, J. J. (1986). Money in the utility function: An empirical implementation, NBER Working Paper No. w1796, National Bureau of Economic Research.

Roubini, N. (2006). Why central banks should burst bubble. *International Finance, 9*(1), 87–107.

Samuelson, P. (1948). Economics. McGraw-Hill.

Sidrauski, M. (1967). Inflation and economic growth. *Journal of Political Economy, 75*(6) (Dec), 796–810.

Tily, G. (2012). Keynes's monetary theory of interest. BIS Paper No. 65c, May

Chapter 4
Money in a Sequence Economy

Abstract This chapter considers how the money that is prevalently used in all economies (i.e., demand deposits issued by commercial banks) is injected in an economy with time as an essential factor and illustrates the approach derived from monetary circuit theory to analyze the integrated functions of banking and finance in a monetary production economy. The chapter employs a micro-founded, circuit-sequenced model of a decentralized economy, integrating production, exchange, and investment through money creation, with funds allocated by banks and non-bank financial intermediaries. The analysis focuses on the unique function of banks as money creators, the dynamics of saving and investment, and the mechanisms through which finance can disrupt the circuit process. Furthermore, the chapter explores how the circuit approach offers insights into economic and financial structural changes. It extends the model to illustrate how circuit theory explains the pivotal role of banks in contemporary "financialized" economies, where financial activities significantly overshadow traditional production. This topic has been of personal interest since my college days, highlighting the interconnectedness of banking and finance in a monetary production economy.

4.1 Preamble

The title of this chapter may sound tautological to an economics layperson: how can an economy be non-sequential—she would wonder—and why would anybody bother with money in a hypothetically timeless world?

Money exists because of time: we use and hold money because the future is unknown, markets are incomplete, and none can be fully trusted to always meet their future obligations. Money is essential for any real-world economy to operate since any real-world economy is inherently time-based.

Yet, as a long-established tradition in mainstream Economics, money is made to appear in macro-models in spite of time being assumed away from them, or its effects being neutralized (leaving no fundamental uncertainty in the agents' choice space), so that money's appearance requires specific assumptions in these models (such as

B. Bossone, *Trailblazing Visions of Money in Economic Theory*, Contributions to Economics, https://doi.org/10.1007/978-3-031-82544-6_4

that agents derive some (unspecified) utility from holding or they must use it in force of some (unmotivated) requirement), for it would not be justified otherwise.

In the previous chapter, I have shown that money delivers utility to its holders because of the essential role of time, and that a consistent money-in-the-utility function approach does bring to bear important implications for economic (dis)equilibria. In this chapter, I want to deep dive into how money works in a sequence economy—across its various stages from creation and injection into the economy to reflow (or reflux) and destruction—and what factors influence its circulation,potentially destabilizing the economy.

I, here, thus revisit (and expand) the work I did in the early 2000s, when I was hired for a new financial strategy and policy unit by the World Bank, fresh of my experience at the Bank of Italy with international financial markets and payment systems. In my new job, I was asked to look into how financial intermediation can cause economic instability. I then used the Circuit Theory of Money (CTM) as a conceptual underpinning, to analyze the special role of banks as money creators and initiators of economic activities in a production economy, represented as a circuit process, and I then extended the theory into what I called the Circuit Theory of Banking and Finance (CTBF). By re-establishing the CTM on microeconomic and financial foundations through the CTBF, I could visualize how financial intermediation can lead to circuit breakdowns, and hence to economic instability. Bossone (1999, 2000) were the outcomes of that work.

The reason today I am doubly proud of it is that, at the time, the money creation role of banks was not just ignored within mainstream economic environments like the World Bank (and the IMF, to where I next moved); it was outright rejected since, therein, banks were still strictly viewed as pure intermediaries. It was only well after the global financial crisis of 2008 that mainstream thinking started opening to the idea that banks create money—although notable exceptions persisted.[1]

This chapter illustrates the main points of the CTBF in the context of a monetary production capitalist economy—the typical context underpinning the CTM—and further shows how the theory can well explain the special role of banks as money creators also in contemporary "financialized" economies, where the financial dimension of capitalism far exceeds the sheer sphere of production.

Finally, a notation. The CBTF model I introduced in the early 2000s—illustrated in this chapter—incorporates two intertemporally optimizing and mutually interacting households (Bossone, 1998), thus anticipating by some two decades the Heterogeneous Agents New Keynesian literature.

[1] For references to works where banks are still considered as pure intermediaries to date, see Bossone (2020a). I wish to take this opportunity, however, to correct a mistake I did in that article, by erroneously including Adrian and Mancini-Griffoli (2019) among those works. In fact, these authors do recognize in their contribution the role of banks as money creators.

4.2 Introduction

The links between money, production, and finance have been studied systematically by the Circuit Theory of Money (CTM).[2] This nonorthodox strand of macroeconomics—methodologically closer to classical economics than to the modern neoclassical paradigm—analyzes the properties of monetary production capitalist economies modeled in the form of a circuit process.

Essentially, the circuit starts when money is advanced by the banks to firms that use it to buy goods and services as inputs for production. The process unfolds along a time sequence whereby production and exchange take place, incomes and savings are generated, and firms sell output and financial liabilities to income earners in their respective markets. The circuit closes when the firms that have embarked in production use the proceeds from output sales to pay back their bank debts.

Production in a circuit process can take place if and only if money is advanced by the banks to the enterprises through loans, and equilibrium holds if and only if all the money used in production re-flows back to the enterprises enabling them to pay off their debt, or if banks roll over any unrepaid loans.

The CTM studies how production, capital accumulation, and income distribution interrelate fundamentally with the creation and use of bank money—which today is still (by far) the most largely form of money used in all countries in the world.

Key to the CTM representation of the economy is the functional separation that the theory operates between banks and firms and their mutual relationship. The theory provides a powerful means to integrate the real and monetary dimensions of the economy and to analyze their relations through the interaction of macro-groups of agents. The theory also offers a consistent attempt to recognize (and rationalize) the role of banks, bank credit, and money in the functioning of a macroeconomy.[3]

---

[2] The CTM had its major proponents in Second Post-World War Europe—most notably France, Belgium, Italy, and Switzerland—where different groups of scholars are active under B. Schmitt, A. Parguez, and F. Poulon, J. Cartelier, A. Ceneini, M. De Vroey, A. Graziani, and M. Messori, to cite just some of the leading names. Today, the main defenders of the theory are R. Realfonzo, G. Fontana, and R. Bellofiore in Italy and M, Lavoie, L.P Rochon, and M. Seccareccia in Canda. Although the major contributions to the theory do not constitute a fully unified body of economic knowledge, and indeed considerable diversity exists across them, some basic and important common features are clearly distinguishable and provide foundations for an integrated theory of money and production. The literature on the CTM has grown rich since the pioneering work of Schmitt (1959); however, many publications are in languages other than English (for references, see Messori, 1988a and references in Rochon, 1999). Interested English-language readers should refer to Graziani (1990, 1996), Lavoie (1985), Rochon (1999) and Cencini (1995), and more recently Realfonzo (2012) and Gnos (2013).

[3] Graziani (1990) highlights that «the theory of the monetary circuit emerges as a reaction to the standard Neoclassical interpretation of economic equilibrium as the result of individual choices taken by isolated and independent agents. The model of the circuit is built instead so as to stress the existence of the relationships among macro-actors, going beyond individual choices. In this perspective, marginal theory of distribution is rejected, in favour of a theory stressing the power of banks, in that they provide the necessary means of payment, and the power of firms, in that they determine the allocation of productive resources. In this view, the level of employment (...) is determined by decisions taken jointly by banks and firms.» (p. 7).

However, while the CTM places great emphasis on the role of banks as money creators and circuit starters,[4] for a long time the theory has devoted no attention to the role of nonbank financial intermediaries in the circuit process, especially at closure,[5,6] Also, the macroeconomic focus of the theory (see ft. #2) and the aggregative nature of the circuit models have deliberately left the microeconomic aspects of finance out of the picture.[7]

As a result, although the theory grants ample latitude for understanding the relations between money banking, production, and economic equilibrium, it has left unexploited the analytical potential of studying money and its macroeconomic implications when banks and nonbank financial intermediaries act as core links between individual decisions and agent interactions. Thus, relevant areas of banking and finance—whose study would have benefited from circuit thinking—were unexplored by traditional circuit theory, such as the impact of money, banking, and finance on economic efficiency and stability and the role of finance as coordinator of individual choices in both the markets for funds and capital goods. Most importantly, the CTM has failed to identify the role that finance plays at end of the circuit process, where decisions on funds allocation may allow or inhibit the closure of the circuit and determine economy's multiple equilibria. Furthermore, more recently, the theory has been criticized for losing explanatory power in the reality of contemporary financial capitalism, where nonbank financial intermediaries seem to have taken a much more prominent role than banks and where production-related activities have lost relevance vis-à-vis financial activities. I will argue against this criticism, showing the continued validity of circuit theory (especially under its CBTF refoundation) in recognizing that banks maintain their special role as money creators even in "financialized" economies, where the financial dimension far exceeds the monetary production character of the circuit, and pointing to the new sources of fragility emerging from their role in the new context.

[4] The theory emphasizes the role of banks in sustaining the circuit process by providing fresh liquidity (through loan roll-overs) to firms that have failed to reappropriate money invested in unrealized production through output sales.

[5] Here and henceforth the expression "nonbank financial intermediaries" is used to indicate all financial intermediaries that cannot create money or whose liabilities are not accepted as money in the economy. In this sense, the expression could comprise also banks that do not issue demand deposit and only operate term financing acting as pure intermediaries. For a formal treatment of the separation within a bank between the money creation and financial intermediation functions and their impact on the bank's profit, see Chap.5.

[6] Cencini (1995) and Schmitt (1982) explored both the monetary and financial dimensions of the circuit, although they do not develop specific microeconomic behavioral assumptions (which I have shown to matter, as recounted in the Preamble, and as I will discuss later in the chapter). They also investigate the international monetary implications of the CTM. More recent contributions to the CTM consider specifically the nonbanking financial sector and will be referred to further on in the chapter.

[7] At the time of my work, cited in the Preamble, one notable exception on both counts was Messori (1988b). The role and the microeconomics of finance in a sequential monetary production economy with limited information and risk were further studied by Messori and Tamborini (1993, 1994).

This chapter revisits my efforts at re-establishing the CTM on microeconomic and financial foundations, extending it to what I called the Circuit Theory of Banking and Finance (CBTF).[8] Section 4.3 illustrates the essential monetary features of the economy's model underpinning the CTBF. Section 4.4 discusses the CTBF's implications for money, banking, finance, and the macroeconomy. Section 4.5 discusses how the CTBF approach can be used for an integrated analysis of economic and financial structural change. Section 4.6 concludes the chapter by showing that the CBTF can well explain the role of banks as money creators in today's "financialized" economies and the challenges deriving from money creation in such contexts. Appendix supplements the chapter's arguments by formally presenting the CTBF model in two articulations, one for a monetary production economy and the other for a financialized economy.

4.3 The Economy as a Circuit Process

4.3.1 The Model

This section offers a non-formal description of the CTBF model of the economy, referring the interested reader to the Appendix for the formal exposition.[9] The economy is closed and includes four classes (or macro-groups) of agents: firms, households, banks, and nonbank financial intermediaries (defined as above). For the purposes at hand, the model does not include the government sector and the central bank.

The circuit is represented as a one-period process with a beginning phase (circuit-start), an interim interval, and an ending phase (circuit-end). The circularity of the model is determined by the direction of the economy's flow of funds, which originate from the banking sector at circuit-start, spread through the economy in the interim interval, and return to the banking system at circuit-end, closing the circuit. The model describes the logical time sequence in which each class of agents operates within the one-period circuit (Box 4.1). The model is used to define more rigorously the role of banking and nonbanking intermediation in a production economy.

Box 4.1. Stylized Representation of the Monetary Circuit of Production

The sequence underpinning the circuit model is as follows:

1. At circuit-start (phase I in Chart 4.1), banks negotiate with firms the conditions for one-period loans. The banks credit the firms' deposit accounts with the negotiated loan amounts. At this stage, bank money is created and

---

[8] See references to my works in the Preamble to this chapter.

[9] Appendix presents two models: one for a monetary production economy, and the other for a "financialized" economy (see Sect. 4.5).

injected in the economy. The firms execute production using capital and labor. Loans are used to pay wages to household workers. Deposits are transferred from the firms' bank accounts to the accounts of wage earners.

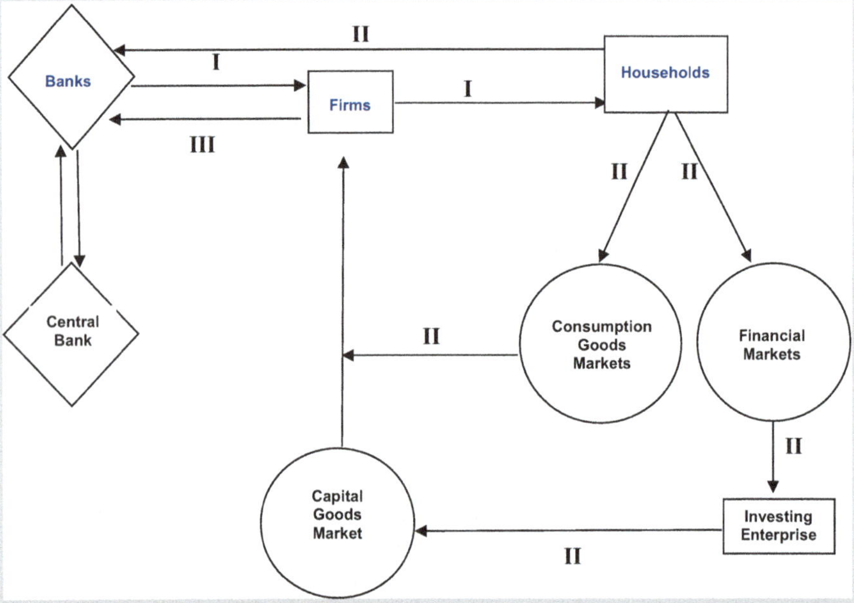

Chart 4.1 Circuit process of money and production

2. In the interim interval (phase II in Chart 4.1), household incomes are spent on consumption goods and/or saved). Savings go into bank deposits and/or into securities issued or traded by nonbank financial intermediaries. Firms wishing to add to their capital stock bid for funding from the intermediaries. The latter evaluate potential borrowers and allocate funds to the viable ones in exchange for securities. The financed enterprises buy the capital goods needed. All money payments for goods and securities take place through book entire on accounts held with banks.
3. At circuit-end (phase III in Chart 4.1), the firms use the process from output sales to pay off their bank debts. At this stage, the money originally created by the banks is destroyed and removed from the economy.

Agents in each group optimize their objective functions. Firms *produce* consumption commodities and capital goods and *invest* by purchasing capital goods. Two separate the two functions, when performing the former function, firms are defined as *producing* firms; when performing the latter, they are defined as *investing* firms.

Two types of households operate in the economy—one provides middleman services and the other supplies labor services to firms. The introduction of middlemen helps to frame households' interactions (and interdependencies) within a circuit process through interhousehold trade.[10] For clarity purposes, firms include *producing* and *investing* firms, as defined above.

At the beginning of the period, firms borrow commercial credit from the banks, employ labor services from one type of household, and use a constant-return technology embodied in capital to produce output in search for maximum profit. At the end of the period, they repay their bank debt out of their revenues from output sales. If firms are unable to sell their output, they seek to renew (or roll over) their credit from the banks.

Banks allow the circuit process to start. They possess technology and information to select and monitor loans.[11] At the beginning of the period, they provide firms with commercial loans to finance input acquisition and output sales, which must be paid off at the end of the period at negotiated interest rate. Since bank technology and information are specific to the bank-borrower relationship, loans are not liquid. The supply of loans to finance production and sales is positive in the loan interest rate and negative in the default risk of the borrowing firms. Other things being equal, the latter varies directly with the volume and price of credit to the firms. Thus, banks increase lending to the point where the marginal return from lending equals the marginal default risk.

The middleman households buy goods from (wholesale) from firms and sell (retail) to the other households, earning a price markup. The households' labor supply to firms is linear in leisure (i.e., it varies proportionately to the wage earnings). Households spend their income to purchase consumption goods and saving assets, based on the interest rate earned on such assets and the level of perceived uncertainty. Saving assets consist of bank demand deposits and financial investment instruments made available by nonbank financial intermediaries. The two household types maximize their intertemporal utility subject to their respective budget constraints.

Capital goods are purchased by firms wishing to add to their current productive capacity. Firms decide how much to invest based on cost-return considerations. They fund investments through long-term borrowings or equity issues in the financial market. Investment funds are intermediated by nonbank financial intermediaries that act on their own behalf or on behalf of individual savers to select best firms and

---

[10] Specifically, household interactions are modeled to reflect two basic (Keynesian) identities: (a) spending from one agent must result in the same amount of income for some others, and (b) all income must be either consumed or saved.

[11] There is no loss of generality or alteration of the model's results from taking the simplifying assumption that banks and nonbanks (see below) operate with no labor or capital inputs. One could think of households supplying them with labor services, similarly to what they do for the firms, and of banks and nonbanks investing in capital, as firms do, but this would not add any insights to the analysis, while overloading the model. With this assumption being made, the revenues earned by the banks and nonbanks are taken to go into the financial market and, through it, back into the circuit.

projects. Investment finance is characterized by the two moments of investment financing (or initial finance) and investment funding (or final finance), respectively.[12]

The supply of consumption and capital goods is based on expected demands and adjusts instantaneously to the latter, although credit rationing may cut supply short of expected demand (see below). With supply adjusting to demand and given relative prices, the interest rate determines the economy's equilibrium allocation of resources to current and future consumption (investment). The demand for capital goods increases with the difference between marginal capital efficiency and the cost of funds (discussed below) and is decreasing in aggregate capital, given by inherited capital plus new investment.

Corporate gross income is output sales minus total wages and investment costs. For simplicity, capital depreciation is set to zero. Actual sales of (consumption and investment) goods are the least of their respective market demands and supplies. Net corporate income equals gross income minus gross debt payments. If such income is negative, the circuit closes only if the firms borrow new money or manage to have their old loans rolled over by the banks. Any positive net corporate income is saved and invested in the financial market.[13]

The demand for capital goods is funded with long-term funds generated by savings. These are raised by nonbank financial intermediaries ("nonbanks") in the financial market and allocated to fund-users. Nonbanks base the volume of intermediate funds on the interest rate, which incorporates the interest rate on long-term saving instruments, a competitive fee for intermediation services, and is adjusted for default risk, which increases with both the volume of funds intermediated and their interest cost. Note that whereas the supply schedule of commercial loans is based on the borrower's expected cash-flow from output sales, the supply of nonbank funds is commensurate to the investors' capacity (as perceived by the nonbanks) to earn a future stream of positive net returns from their investment.

The supply of funds from nonbanks may not exceed their collection of long-term savings. This may result either from the intermediaries deliberately choosing not to raise additional funds than what they can (or want to) invest, or from savers preferring demand deposits to less liquid assets for their portfolios. In the former case, this might imply that nonbanks limit their demand for long-term funds from savers and thus

[12] Investment finance in the model features the following stylized sequence of steps (Davidson, 1991): (1) Companies wishing to add to their capital stock (investing firms) place orders of new equipment with capital goods producers and enter into contracts requiring them to issue cash payments to capital goods producers on delivery; (2) commercial banks extend short-term cash credit to capital goods producers to finance production (investment financing, or initial finance); (3) capital goods producers use cash credit to advance payments to workers and input suppliers; (4) savings accumulate in the economy as wage payments are issued and incomes are generated; (5) investing firms raise funding by issuing long-term securities (investment funding, or final finance) and use them to settle their contractual obligations with the capital goods producers; (6) capital goods producers use the cash proceeds from payments to pay out their bank debts; (7) the process starts anew with new bank credit being extended to capital goods producers to finance new production.

[13] Although profits could be retained and invested within the firm, nothing is lost by assuming that all firm profits are collected and intermediated by the financial market.

ration savers' supply of long-term funds. The investment funded is the least between the supply and demand for long-term funds.

Notice that banks, too, can act as intermediaries in the financial market through their financial departments, taking term deposits from the public and making long-term loans to firms or other forms of financial investments. As such, and only to the extent referred to this intermediation function, they would fall in the same category as the nonbank financial intermediaries.[14]

4.3.2 *Money*

Money is *created* and injected in the economy at circuit-start in the form of demand deposits issued by banks as borrowers' bank accounts are credited with the agreed loan amounts. Loans are thus liabilities of the borrowing firms and, at the same time, claims of the borrowers on the banks, which the banks promise to honor as borrowers draw funds from their accounts, out of the loans, to make payments relating to the activities funded with the loans. Deposits are *destroyed* and removed from the economy at circuit closure once loans are paid back to the banks.

No cash circulates in the economy and all payments are made through deposit transfers across bank accounts (within the same bank or across banks). All agents may hold deposits with banks for transaction and liquidity preference purposes. Banks extend unlimited credit to each other and at no charge as deposits are transferred from one bank. This assumption, which is later relieved, is accompanied by another simplifying assumption whereby the central bank (which is not explicitly included in the model) accommodates all reserve balances demanded by the banks for settlement purposes.

The introduction in the model of the central bank does not alter the mechanics of bank money creation and destruction. The central bank lends reserves to the banks, which they use to settle interbank obligations, to comply with reserve requirements, and as a precautionary (safe) asset. Each bank determines its own optimal level of reserve holdings (in addition to the regulatory requirements) vis à vis its future obligations deriving from money creation via lending. The central bank may alter the conditions for banks' optimal money creation/destruction (specifically, the cost for banks to achieve their optimal reserves ratios) by changing its reserves lending term and the reserve/ liquidity regulatory requirements, and by engaging in market purchases/sales of reserves from/to the banks. A bank's power to create money depends essentially on the bank having flexible access to credit from the other

[14] One could think of the bank as having two separate departments—a monetary department and a financial department—with the financial department holding a deposit account with the monetary department, call it FDA. When the bank raises term funds, it receives bank term deposits from depositors' accounts and credits them on the FDA. As the bank the extends term-loans and borrowers start making payments out of these loans to third parties, deposits move from the FDA to the accounts of these third parties. The distinction between the monetary and financial function of the bank serves to emphasize that the latter only intermediates bank liabilities issued under the former.

banks and from the central bank, and/or on it being in a position to clear a large share of interagent payments within its own books (see below, and also Chaps. 5 and 6, for a further discussion of this point this and of how the relative size of individual banks differently affects their money creation power). Here, it may suffice to say that the larger the bank (relative to the system), the greater its capacity to create money vis-à-vis the risk it faces to default on its own obligations.

The money supply and the flow of funds in the circuit are such that total bank deposits equal the stock of credit outstanding at all times of the circuit period: first, all deposits equal credit (by definition) at circuit-start. Second, if all deposits are used to purchase goods from the firms, the latter appropriate the money borrowed initially and can pay off their bank, so that the equality is satisfied. Third, if a positive stock of deposits is held idling on the bank accounts, corporate incomes are reduced equivalently, causing an equal stock of loans to default and to remain outstanding at circuit-end, and the equality is again satisfied.[15] Fourth and final, if households prefer to hold part of their savings in investment instruments alternative to bank deposits, funds will be diverted from banks to nonbanks, but the latter's deposits with banks will increase correspondingly (deposits are never destroyed until the original loans are repaid to the banks); as a result, the loans-deposits equality is once again satisfied.

4.3.3 Equilibrium

The general equilibrium of the economy is one where, at circuit-end: (i) all money incomes are spent in consumption and investment goods, so that all producing firms sell all their output; (ii) investing firms raise enough funds to settle their contract obligations with capital goods producing firms; and (iii) the latter pay off their debt with the banks. In equilibrium, all deposits that were originally created at circuit-start are destroyed at circuit-end.

The solution to the model shows that the interest rates on loans and long-term funds, the agents' level of perceived uncertainty, the firms' default risk and default rate, and the nonbanks' intermediation fees are crucial in determining the level of real aggregate production at which equilibrium is attained, the efficiency of resource allocation, and the conditions for successful circuit opening and closure. The circuit closes as producing firms use the proceeds from output sales to clear their debts with the banks.

Notice that while the model exemplifies reality through a one-round circuit process, a real-world economy consists of multiple, overlapping and not (necessarily) synchronous circuit rounds as bank loans are extended all the time, new production is carried out, and debts on old production are retired on an ongoing basis. But logical time is what matters for circuit theory, whose ultimate aims are to explain the role of money in transactions, the (hierarchical) relations between the various classes

[15] For an extensive discussion of the credit-deposit adjustment mechanisms in a circuit model with endogenous money, see Lavoie (1999).

of economic actors that money determines, and the condition for the economy to reproduce its production cycles over time.

4.4 Implications of the CTBF

Several implications can be drawn from the CTBF model, spanning from the macroeconomy to the nature of the banks.

4.4.1 Macroeconomic Implications

Saving and Investment

Having banks operating as circuit starters via money creation (through lending) affects the way in which aggregate saving is known to interrelate with investment. The dynamics of the circuit model springs from the agents' spending plans and build on spending decisions taken by agents placed upstream in the circuit sequence and influencing spending decisions by the agents placed downstream. It can be shown that, consistent with Keynes' *General Theory*, and unlike loanable-funds based theories (where investment and saving are mutually independent variables), the sequential and circular nature of the circuit makes aggregate saving behave as a residual variable that (passively) adjusts to aggregate investment, irrespective of individual agent plans and whether these plans are optimal. The following propositions are shown to hold in a circuit process[16]:

Proposition 1 *Far any given level of aggregate investment, changes in individual or sector savings do not affect the volume of aggregate saving, although they affect the economy's saving ratio.*

Proposition 2 *Changes in aggregate saving can only result from changes in the level of aggregate investment.*

Proposition 3 *Changes in the interest rate do not affect aggregate saving (independently of investment), although they may alter its composition.*

The first two propositions bear important implications for finance. They basically say that savings accumulated in a closed economy, as an aggregate, do not change autonomously and are always enough to fund the demand for capital goods produced and originally financed with short-term bank loans, even accounting for interactions between different agents. This means that with a given supply of capital goods, and even assuming away fund rationing, any excess demand for investment can only be

[16] These propositions are proved Bossone (2001a), Appendix.

financed through new bank credit, leading to asset-liability maturity mismatches in the balance sheet of either the banks or the firms and causing inflationary pressure.

According to Proposition 3, the interest rate does not have any independent effect on aggregate saving—it can only affect saving indirectly and to the extent that it influences investment (see Proposition 2). Compared to Classical, Neoclassical, and New Keynesian theories of saving, the CTBF changes the emphasis on saving in the economic process. In so far as the circuit sequence shows capital formation to fund itself at circuit-end, after bank credit has been made available to finance production, saving can no longer represent the source of capital accumulation. Since saving is determined as a residual to investment, what becomes crucial is both the way in which it is allocated to different uses and across different users and the mechanisms presiding over its reflow to the producing firms—a typical microeconomic problem and the one that prompted me to expand the CTM into CTBF.

The reversed saving-investment nexus and the role of nonbanks at circuit end offer important insights for studying an economy's equilibrium. Bankers supply credit to production and trade, based on the borrowers' capacity to service their debts. In the case of capital goods producing firms, this capacity ultimately depends on the firms' prospects to raise enough funds to pay for the capital goods on delivery. Therefore, large capital goods production finance requires a financial system that collects the funds generated by production, upstream in the circuit, and turns them over to the producing firms downstream, thereby linking the opening and closure of the circuit and making it financially self-sustainable. On the other hand, the lack—or poor functioning—of such linking mechanisms breaks the sequence and prevents banks from fully recovering their loans at circuit-end. This might lead them to ration lending, constraining income generation and eventually trapping the economy in a low-investment equilibrium, or it might push them to extend new loans to help keep the firms current but at the risk of exposing themselves to higher credit risk.

In an open-economy model, the economy could traverse to a high-investment equilibrium by opening the domestic financial sector to long-term foreign (non-speculative) capital inflows. By providing the missing circuit link, financial sector liberalization—if well governed—can improve bank prospects of recovering credits and catalyze new domestic bank lending to production.

Stability

The CTBF shows that the availability of aggregate saving per se can never be an issue, for investments always generate an equal amount of savings—whatever the behavior of individual agents. However, the theory points to the possibility that impediments along the circuit may preclude savings from fully funding investments, essentially barring the closure of the circuit—that is, causing the circuit to breakdown due to defaults—or determining closures at different levels of investment and resource use—that is, pushing the economy toward multiple equilibria events (something that is not recognized as a possibility in conventional theories, if not as a consequence of market imperfections or frictions). Thus, the conditions for economic (in)stability originate at the micro (not macro) level, although macroeconomic expectations affect agent choices (but that's why CTM needs CTBF).

Higher liquidity preference due to heightened uncertainty may induce households to lower their consumption. The consequent failure of producing firms to sell all their output would force them to either seek short-term debt renewal from banks or to default on their debt obligations. Circuit breakdowns may similarly occur when agents increase their share of bank deposits within their portfolio. This implies that an equivalent amount of funds fails to reach the firms through the financial markets. As above, the circuit breaks down if banks do not offset the leakage from the large demand for deposits by supplying new loans (or by rolling-over old loans) to the firms in need of liquidity: as deposits sit idle on bank accounts, some net liquidity is withdrawn from circulation and firms may find themselves unable to deliver on their obligations if liquidity support is not extended to them. Also, the nature of the circuit is such that if firms decided to settle bank debts by using their accumulated savings (that is, by liquidating part of their illiquid portfolio), this would subtract funds from the financial markets where they are invested and decrease the overall volume of term financing available for firms. This would feedback on capital goods producing firms, which would then be unable to appropriate the money needed to discharge their obligations. The original problem would still lie there unresolved.

Thus, if a positive stock of demand deposits is held in portfolios at circuit end, an equal stock of bank loans stands out unpaid, and the circuit's financial balance could be preserved only if banks refinanced their loans outstanding for as long as necessary. An increase in the demand for deposits, therefore, increases the liquidity needs of (and the loan demand from) the firms—a point made by Graziani (1988).

At the microeconomic level, the lack of information on individual fund-users, the weakening of borrowers' credit standing, and in general the perception of heightened risk, may discourage investment funding. Required risk premia on individual fund-users and the transaction costs involved in dealing with them may become so high as to make the expected returns on investable funds inadequate or, at best, uncertain. Under rising risk, nonbanks may at some point ration their supply of funds.

The integrated nature of the circuit is such that actions from agents upstream in the circuit affect the circuit functioning downstream the process. In the real world, with sequential circuit rounds, a circuit breakdown resulting in a round failure to close may impact upon the opening of subsequent rounds by altering agents' liquidity positions and expectations. A round failure to close would feed back on the banks' short-term loan supply schedules and lead them to revise their credit decisions at the next round-opening and constrain production. Similarly, evidence of round failures might induce firms to reconsider their production and investment plans and reduce their use of loans and term financing with resulting pressure on household incomes.

The CTBF shows that, despite the passive nature of aggregate saving, nonbanks are essential in a decentralized-decisions production economy to allow the circuit process to function smoothly, since they ultimately enable producing firms to appropriate the money initially spent on production and now needed to repay their bank debt. Their role is thus crucial for the economy to achieve financial equilibrium.

At the micro-level, nonbanks select fund-users. Their efficiency is therefore critical for selecting those with high likelihood to remain in intertemporal balance, contributing to generating flows of funds that are consistent with macroeconomic equilibrium and optimal use of resources, while their inefficiency would be critical for producing the opposite results. As it turns out, nonbanks play a key role for the overall consistency between the choices of different macro-groups of agents acting in their respective markets: firms and anonymous savers in the financial market; firms in the capital goods market; and firms and banks in the credit market.

In this respect, the financial system complements the price mechanism as a resource allocating device and supplements it in supporting the circuit process. For these reasons, a non-performing financial system can be the cause of severe instability issues. Notice that any form of instability would not alter the aggregate saving-investment balance, which—as the three Propositions above indicate—would only adjust residually to changes in the overall level of investment. Instabilities would only be the consequence of microeconomic inefficiencies and choices, which, as such, must be recognized by any circuit theories that aspire to a full comprehension of capitalist economies. Money issuance establishes (hierarchical) relations between macro-groups or classes of actors at circuit-start, but financial intermediation determines economic (dis)equilibria at circuit-end rooted in micro-choices, and while banks affect the level of economic activity at circuit-start, finance influences the unfolding of the circuit process and determines the level and efficiency of capital accumulation.

Examples of such possible disequilibria, despite a given aggregate saving-investment balance, would be those cases where financial intermediaries decline to fund (i.e., ration their funds supply to) firms that demand liquidity to stay current with their bank debt obligations and, instead, provide funding to other (productive or speculative) activities promising better risk-return combinations. These (micro) choices would impact circuit closure and overall economic equilibrium dynamics. These cases are especially likely to materialize in highly financialized economies (to be discussed in Sect. 4.5).

Micro-choices are relevant for banks at circuit-end, as banks may need to discriminate between illiquid but solvent firms, which deserve temporary credit support, and insolvent firms that should undergo restructuring or exit the market. In this realm, credit decisions by the banks bear on the trade-off between averting circuit breakdowns, on one side, and ensure short-term financial stability but at the cost of building higher risk in the system, and allowing circuit breakdowns to occur, on the other, which produces correct incentives to long-term efficiency as a byproduct, though at the cost of taking losses and potentially generating losses to the system.

The CTBF seeks to capture the essential features of real-world capitalist economies, where the "macro"-dimension of the aggregate variables continuously interacts with the "meso"-dimension involving the behavior of different groups (or classes) of agents, and with the "micro"-dimension of the choices made by individual agents using procedural rationality[17]—all of them progressing through historical time, in contexts of incessant change and radical ignorance of the future (Holtham,

[17] Procedural rationality is a concept introduced by Herbert A. Simon (1976), which emphasizes the processes and procedures involved in decision-making. Unlike classical theories of rationality, which assume that decision-makers have complete information and can make optimal choices,

2024). Later in the chapter, the realism of the interactions just recalled will be evaluated in the context of financialized economies.

4.4.2 Implications for Money and Banks

Banks are special because they create money

The CTBF marks the different role played in the circuit, respectively, by the credit market, where liquidity is created to finance production, and the financial market, where existing liquidity accumulated by savers is allocated to investments. This, in turn, implies a distinct role for banks and nonbank financial intermediaries (nonbanks), whereby:

a. **Banks operate upstream in the circuit process**. They allow the circuit to start by providing new liquidity to production. This liquidity is in the form of banks' own liabilities, or debt claims drawn on the banks themselves, which are made available to borrowers.[18] Banks do not intermediate existing liquidity but add to the system's liquidity every time they extend new credit to firms through deposit creation, while simultaneously maintaining full liquidity to depositors' claims. In other words, when banks issue claims that borrowers use as money for transactions, depositors do not part with the liquidity stored in their bank deposits and always retain the right to exercise their related liquidity option by mobilizing deposits on demand. This allows the deposits stock to grow with new lending (and to remain outstanding until the loans that originated them are retired).
b. **Nonbanks operate downstream the process**. They act as financial market intermediaries with longer-term horizons than banks, collect existing liquidity (bank deposits) from savers with long positions (who in this case do part with liquidity), in exchange for liabilities with longer-term maturity and riskier features, and allocate it to investors with short positions. As any other agents in the economy, nonbanks may as well invest their own money directly into firms' financial obligations. Unlike banks, the money intermediated or invested by them does not represent claims drawn on themselves. This money always consists of claims on banks (i.e., deposits) and, as such, it can only move across bank accounts. Thus,

procedural rationality acknowledges the limitations and constraints faced by individuals in real-world scenarios. It is based on the concept of bounded rationality, which suggests that people aim for satisfactory solutions (satisficing) rather than optimal ones due to constraints like limited information and time. The approach focuses on adaptive decision-making, where individuals learn and adjust their strategies over time, and considers the context and environment as crucial factors influencing rationality. This perspective offers a more realistic view of human decision-making compared to classical theories that assume perfect information and optimal choices.

[18] According to the Accounting View of Money (AVM), discussed in Chap. 2, bank deposits are hybrid financial instruments featuring a dual nature, being partly a liability and partly equity of the issuing bank. Yet this property does not need to detain us here, and we can therefore talk of deposits as bank liabilities or toward depositors or debt claims of depositors on the banks where they hold their deposits.

while nonbanks can transfer money across agents with different liquidity preferences, in no case can they create liquidity.[19] By funding investment, they enable firms at circuit-end to appropriate the money spent in production and service their short-term debt obligations to banks.[20]

What, thus, characterizes banks as "special" is that—unlike nonbanks—they can issue and lend claims on themselves that are accepted by the public as money. The function of banks in a circuit process implies a forward-looking vision whereby money creation precedes (and makes possible) the generation of real value through production. The latter (and only the latter) gives money its real purchasing power. Inherent in this vision is the inflationary risk that derives from money creation if it is not followed by proportionate output production. In this case, too much money would chase too few goods, with a negative effect on the value of money and the price level of goods and services.[21]

Banks and nonbanks perform functions that are complementary in originating money and making it circulate and reflow to its point of origin in the circuit process. These functions may be carried out either by different entities (as in the model above) or jointly under more "universal" type of entities that combine multiple banking and nonbanking activities. However, this should not shade their distinct role in the context of the circuit process. In a market economy, however, both banks and nonbanks share the task of having to select and finance firms that can add real value to the economy.

The complementarity of banking and nonbanking functions in a monetary production economy is reflected in the information specialization that the two entail. Whereas banks—in the sense under item a. above—build up knowledge of their borrowers' day-to-day operations, liquidity needs, payment flows, as well as of short-term factor and product market developments, nonbanks develop knowledge of longer-term business prospects, investment potential and prospects, market trends, and changes in economic fundamentals affecting fund-users. However, as the economy shifts from production to finance, the information horizon of banks and nonbanks changes accordingly, from factors relating to the real economy to those relating to the financial sphere.

The CTBF presents several dimensions from which to look at the specificity of banks.[22] It shows that their power to create money, and to advance it at an interest, characterizes them as special entities vis-à-vis nonbanks and bears several significant

[19] In principle, agents could conventionally accept a nonbank's liquid liabilities as money for transaction purposes. As to the capacity of the nonbank to create new liabilities and inject them in the economy, as banks do, this depends on whether they would be allowed by regulation to lend their liabilities to third parties (or issue them in exchange for securities or other forms of value), as banks do in fractional reserve regimes. In such a case, the nonbank would de facto be a bank as understood in circuit theories.

[20] This function was well recognized already in the 1930s by Bresciani Turroni (1936).

[21] This stands in stark contrast with the conclusion by Fama (1980) whereby the pure intermediary function of banks precludes them from exerting any autonomous effect on price determination.

[22] The special nature of banks has been a subject of considerable importance in the theory of finance. A comprehensive review of the literature until the turn of the millennium is presented in Bossone (2000).

implications. First, in a circuit process, banks command net real resource transfers from firms—they extract seigniorage from the economy.[23]

Since banks create deposits by lending and in so far as loans do not originate from transfers of savings, the interest charged on loans may not be conceptualized as a compensation to foregone consumption or intermediation services. In the circuit process, the interest rate (net of the resource costs involved in lending, comprising the cost of selecting monitoring and administering loans, and including the remuneration of deposits and the cost of interbank credit, when these apply) is a pure rent that banks extract from borrowers by virtue of their exclusive power to create money at a cost that is lower than its value.[24]

Such exclusivity rests fundamentally on both government and society restricting the acceptance of money only to financial liabilities issued by selected types of agents. No rent would in fact be involved if, hypothetically, all agents could issue their own liabilities and have them accepted as money by everybody else. This same argument explains why different market structures of the banking sector, resulting in different market entry rules and in stronger or weaker competition among banks, alter the seigniorage power of banks.

Seigniorage is not extracted by nonbanks, since they only intermediate pre-existing liquidity. Unlike commercial loan interests and like payments for inputs, interest payments on long-term obligations to financial investors represent a production cost item against the company's revenues. Correspondingly, they are a compensation to investors for temporarily parting with the liquidity they own and/or to nonbanks for providing intermediation services. Such payments, therefore, do not involve any net real resource transfers from firms to savers and to intermediaries: they are one side of *quid pro quo* transactions.

This issue of seigniorage, already discussed from the accounting point of view in Chap. 2, will be treated analytically from the economics standpoint in Chaps. 5 and 6.

4.5 The Circuit Process and Financial Sector Development

Depending on the development of banking and financial institutions in the economy, the circuit process can produce different economic efficiency/stability configurations. This section shows how the circuit approach can be used for an integrated analysis of economic and financial structural change. Consider the following stylized description of an evolutionary circuit process.

---

[23] In real-world economics, with central banks, seigniorage is extracted by both the banks and the central bank.

[24] As noted, banks may temporarily and deliberately postpone the borrowers' obligations by refinancing them, but, at some point, repayment borrowers will have to relinquish real resources to the lending banks since their debts will not be postponed indefinitely. The net real resource transfer involved in loan interest payments is recognized by Graziani (1988).

4.5.1 *Early Industrialism*[25]

Early in the process of industrialization—as in XVIII-century Europe—the circuit process is dominated by manufacturing firms. Family-owned firms specialize in profit-oriented production and commercialization of commodities. Production and trade are financed through issues of bank-guaranteed commercial paper. While the acquisition of the capital goods used in production is funded with the owners' own funds and business internally generated surpluses, capital goods producers finance their inventories through commercial credit from input suppliers and contract sales.

Firms determine the total level of resource employment for the given production technology. Since they finance the acquisition of capital goods internally, they (as a group) also determine the share of the economy's resources allocated to consumption and investment. To the extent that labor market negotiations set nominal wages and trading involves commodities already produced (that is, no forward contracts exist or are allowed), firms (as a group) also determine the volume of output that they appropriate at circuit-end.[26]

Workers' saving decisions that turn out to be inconsistent with firms' production plans prompt commodity price adjustments to the point where all the money spent by the firms is reappropriated by them at circuit-end.

The circuit process of the early industrial economies is rudimentary and relatively stable overall (to the extent that, and for as long as, its distributional effects are accepted by the society). The limited role of banks as money suppliers constrains production and saving generation, while capital accumulation is limited by the lack of organized finance for long-term investment and depends almost exclusively on the capitalists' sources of personal wealth.

Bank seigniorage is low or non-existent and thus there is no net transfer of resources ownership from firms to banks.

---

[25] This subsection draws on Graziani (1988), Minsky (1990), and Chernow (1997).

[26] Following Graziani (1988), aggregate output is produced by N workers with productivity λ and earning unit wage w and sells at market-determined price p. Assuming workers' propensity to consume equal to one, the demand from workers is given by wN. If I is the amount of output that firms purchase and l is the share of total labor resources necessary to produce it, then $I = l\,\lambda\,Np$. Equilibrium requires $\lambda Np = wN + l\lambda Np$. Output price is thus $p = \left(\frac{1}{1-l}\right)w/\lambda.$. Defining the profit ratio as the ratio between net output and the money spent on production (i.e., the total wage bill) $\pi = \frac{(\lambda p - w)N}{wN} = \frac{1}{1-\lambda}$. Total nominal profit is thus $\Pi = \pi wN = \frac{1}{1-\lambda}wN$, yielding real profit $\frac{\Pi}{p} = \frac{\lambda}{N}$. With flexible prices, this result holds even if workers have a positive propensity to save. Note that the real profit equals the output share that firms have decided to purchase. This validates Kalecki's well-known proposition whereby "workers spend what they earn, while capitalists earn what they spend".

4.5.2 Banking Finance

The integrated role of banking and finance in the circuit process evolves when the demand for capital equipment and labor inputs intensifies and financial needs exceed personal wealth—as in Europe and America of late 1800s-early 1900s. Banks finance growing production with money creation and provide funding for firms to stay current with their debts. To do so, they develop investment banking and financial intermediation functions. With capital markets in their infancy and relatively few (as well as unsophisticated and not well informed) large investors, banks are well positioned to collect term funds from savers and transfer them to investing firms on acceptable terms. As more bank loans are injected into production, financial intermediation provides investing firms with "patient money." Once used to fund investments, such money enables producing firms to stay current on their bank debt service obligations. Essentially, finance serves production, financial markets are comparatively small, stable, and passive, and the net real resource transfer from firms to banks (through seigniorage) increases.

Banks and firms grow a strong common interest to protect the latter's cash-flow generation and develop exclusive mutual relationships whereby firms gain through the banks stable access to long-term capital—even at times of adverse contingencies—in exchange for privileged information that banks receive from firms. Exclusive relationships give then to the banks considerable rent-extraction power over the firms being financed. Universal banks even emerge in some countries, which acquire strong control of enterprises and manage to clump firms operating at different vertical levels of the same commodity sectors under single parent entities, with the purpose to stabilize the flow of funds from savers to end-users and to ensure regular bank credit recovery at circuit-end.

The system may become more stable overall as firms face lower risk of not appropriating the full money at circuit-end, and circuit closure is therefore more safeguarded. In the long run, however, exclusive relationships lead to market information opaqueness, illiquid investment positions, restrictions on competition in both the real and financial sectors, and lesser reliability of the price system as allocation device. Eventually, exclusive relationships weaken the incentives to efficiency, technological innovation, and new industry creation (Rajan and Zingales 1999).

4.5.3 State Finance

To a large extent, the expanding role of the public sector in finance—as experienced by the industrial counties in the 1930s and in the aftermath of the Second World War until the 1980s—replaces investment banking at the core of the financial side of the circuit of capitalist economies, both by directly absorbing savings and by centrally managing funds allocation through financial repression, directed and subsidized lending, public money transfers, and control of financial institutions. This was greatly facilitated by an international world economic order (established at Bretton Woods in 1944) whereby the expansion of international trade was to be supported by finance had to remain strongly national.

With the state acting as a financial intermediary, or largely affecting private-sector financial intermediation, savers become less concerned with the reputation of private-sector financial institutions and place their savings with banks (many of them state-owned or state-controlled) under the implicit or explicit guarantee of the (perceived) unlimited solvency of the public sector. On the broader economy's side, the large share of public spending on aggregate output stabilizes the flow of funds that firms need to appropriate at circuit-end to keep with their bank loan repayments.

In terms of the CTBF model above, the expanding role of the state in finance is reflected in a flatter and further-out-to-the-right long-term fund supply schedule, with equilibria occurring at higher levels of investment than with less state involvement, where the shadow cost of funds may far exceed the marginal efficiency of capital. In fact, under state finance, the actual cost of funds is typically below its shadow equivalent and bears little or no relation to risk- and information-related factors. Funds allocation is heavily influenced by the government, based on macroeconomic or political policy objectives, and irrespective of risk consideration factors, and overall economic efficiency is compromised.

In the extreme forms of state finance, no seigniorage is extracted by the banks from the enterprises. In fact, as the state advances money to firms at below-equilibrium (possibly negative) real interest rates (directly, or indirectly through subsidization or repressed finance) aimed at pushing production, investment, and resource employment above their market equilibrium, the net real resource transfer from the firms to the banks is nihil (or even negative). No market for corporate control emerges since the state guarantees the firms (especially the large ones) against the risk of insolvency and circuit breakdowns.

By directing the mobilization and allocation of funds, state-controlled finance ensures greater stability of fund supply to firms but, for the same reason, it causes less efficient selection of investing firms and higher moral hazard from borrowers. The state role as a financial intermediary severs producers' and investors' decisions from the profit motive. This results in a highly leveraged corporate sector and in large and inefficient investments with poor output performances.

In more extreme forms, this situation is typical of centrally planned economics, where the circuit operates under state control. Liquidity for production is created at will by a centralized banking system, funds are funneled back to the state through forced savings and taxation, and from there, they are then allocated to firms to finance capital goods purchases and ensure circuit closure. Historically, these economies have at most proven effective in delivering the required output for limited periods of time. Their success is possible when the meta-economic objectives of the society (such as preparing for war, restoring order after periods of economic upheaval, or affirming the supremacy of the central plan) are strong enough to mobilize the necessary individual efforts beyond commensurate individual economic rewards, and when the output required from the collective effort addresses specific needs (e.g., building up heavy industries) that are imposed on (and even accepted by) the collectivity as absolute national priorities. However, as the meta-incentives weaken, these systems become unable to preserve the necessary steam to production: the circuit is deprived of the capacity to allocate funds to best uses, and circuit closure can only be achieved at the cost of larger fiscal deficits and higher inflation.

4.5.4 Private Finance

Starting in the 1980s, the economic efficiency and welfare losses attributed to the large role that the state had taken in capitalist economies in the West called for a major correction of the incentive structure of the economy toward decentralization. Such route was followed as well, from the 1990s, by a growing number of emerging economies, and the same logic applied at a much bigger scale for guiding the transition of the formerly communist countries of the East from the central plan to the market. The change was felt necessary by the reform architects to give way to decentralized, private-sector finance as a resource allocator device that would better succeed in aligning efforts, risks, and rewards in market contexts. The process of change accelerated at the turn of the century, facilitated by the unprecedented pace of technology developments and their application to finance (with implications that will be discussed in the next section).

Essentially, the change amounted to repositioning the circuit on decentralized-decisions settings where the perimeter of finance is no longer constrained within domestic border, access is open to nonbank financial intermediaries, and financial markets attract investors of all sizes (from very small to very large), with variegated risk-return preferences, and interested in diversifying their investment portfolios.

In the new context, banks are led to compete more intensely in the traditional markets for deposits and loans and are allowed to operate into new markets and to expand their range of services to clients. Financial markets are promoted through infrastructure development and entry of nonbank financial intermediaries. Competition drives the latter to calibrate their investment strategies on savers' risk-return preferences, while the development of the financial infrastructure facilitates the entry of savers of all sizes (from middle-class individuals to mega corporates) into the financial market as investors. The latter are well placed to influence, with their preferences, the intermediaries' strategies due to strong competition and investor-oriented laws and benefit from innovative technologies to mobilize funds at declining transaction costs and from the expanding mass of data and information made available on investment opportunities and risks.

As captured by the CTBF model above, financial decentralization implies that investors' proactivity toward risk and sensitivity to uncertainty increase and gain influence on the financial resource allocation process. Information disclosure from market participants and regulation and supervision of their behavior take hold as individual investors' supply of investible funds become more sensitive to profit opportunities and risk factors. This and the transparency made possible by the development of financial infrastructure complicates the survival of exclusive bank-firm relationships and, as financial market efficiency grows, informational advantages by individual agents are competed away and no longer ensure them the permanent appropriation of extra-rents (Bossone et al., 2003). Competition between banks and nonbanks increases. Also, synergies between banking and nonbanking financial intermediation functions increasingly lead to conglomeration or mergers of banks and nonbanks.

In a decentralized financial environment, funds can be more easily withdrawn from fund-users that are perceived to be riskier, bringing them under stronger market discipline. On the other hand, markets become subject to large price and flow volatility due to higher sensitivity of financing decisions to shifts in risk perceptions, new information, changes in market opinion and sentiment, and imitation and bandwagon behavior effects. Thus, while financial resource allocation under nonbank finance may be more efficient than under alternative regimes, the circuit process is more vulnerable to risks of breakdown due to a less stable supply of funds. Also, although the quality of both capital and output is higher, real investments may turn out to be more volatile, circuit closure more at risk, and the spread out of disturbances across sequential circuit rounds more likely to occur. Greater uncertainty may weaken long-term investment funding, tighten credit to production, and reduce bank flexibility in assisting those firms that fail at circuit end to appropriate the money needed to service their debt. The banking system becomes more exposed to risks of instability.

Finally, in private finance-based systems, liberalized banking markets allow banks as a group, or class, to regain greater seigniorage power than under state finance, although most of the seigniorage extracted accrues to the larger banks.[27] Banks have thus strong incentives to expand their scale and broaden their activities. Consolidation becomes a way for leading banks to increase their seigniorage. Confronting developed capital markets and being exposed to stronger competition for raising funds than under state finance, producing firms need to raise equity funds to preserve long-term solvency. Corporate ownership and control tend to be marketed to a much broader public of investors.

However, while—as recalled—these developments have characterized the world economy from the 1980s onward, the financial securities sold to a wider array of investors have typically tended to be held till maturity through most of the twentieth century.[28] It is only in the first quarter of the new century that institutional asset management has become a mass industry, catering to vast sectors of country populations, and financial securities have eventually been commoditized through the explosive growth of securities trading worldwide (Lysandrou, 2020). This opened most of the economies across the globe to the era of "financialization," the topic of the next section.

---

[27] On seigniorage and bank size, see Chap. 4.

[28] This not only happened in the bank-centered corporatist networks of continental Europe and East Asia, but also in the capital market-based Anglo-Saxon economies.

4.6 Circuit Theory and "Financialization"

Do banks continue to play their special role of money creators in financialized economies?[29] I approached this question soon after I had completed my work on the CTBF in the early 2000s, considering the evolution of finance taking place at that time and trying to envision the future of it (Bossone, 2001b). My interest was essentially on how money creation would be performed, and by whom, in the ever fast-changing world of finance where material production was becoming less and less relevant to the advanced economies. By looking today at what I wrote then, I am pleased to realize that my vision of the future turned out to be on the mark. Several years after my article was written, several contributions were made on the topic, which, while overlooking my work and benefiting of more information, arrived at its same conclusions.

The analyses by Seccareccia (2012), Sawyer (2013), and Passarella (2014), for example, reverse the sectoral balances assumed in the CTM and cast the corporate sector (the firms) as the main creditor and the household sector as the main debtor in today's financialized economies, depicting the former as having switched from productive to rentier activities. And yet, while the counterparties to credit transactions may have switched positions under contemporary capitalism, the CTM's logic still stands, and the power of commercial banks to create money via lending remains intact.

Michell, cit., moves further on by noting that the modern circuit operates in a perverse and mutated form vis-à-vis the original circuit representation, as it opens with lending to households and closes when household debts are moved off banks' balance sheets and into "shadow banks"—the counterpart assets to these off-balance sheet debts being the short-term liquid assets of corporations and high-net-worth individuals. The new forms of credit relationships mediated by "shadow banks" bear characteristics of both banking and market-based finance; yet, from a circuit perspective, their issued claims are not money because they cannot be used for payment settlements and the accumulation of claims in the "shadow banking" sector relies on the prior creation of money claims by the traditional banking sector. Banks, thus, keep their special role as money creators even in highly financialized economies.

More broadly, in financialized economies, banks create money through different channels and instruments. They may lend to firms to finance production, as they have done traditionally, but they can also finance production by purchasing firms' short-term securities. Banks, as well, lend to households to finance their extra consumption, and lend to rentier households and firms earning extra profits to finance their portfolio investment activities. Moreover, banks increasingly lend to, or preferably purchase securities from, nonbanks to support their intermediation activities. Finally, banks may extend guarantees by issuing contingent liabilities to entities wishing to limit their risk exposure on securities or derivative products. Notice that much of these

[29] As noted by Michell (2016), the CTM had been considered for a world less complex than today's financialized capitalism, and the assumption that bank credit is mainly used by capitalists for the financing of production, while true for the past, is no longer defensible today.

financial activities involve securities trading in the secondary markets or transactions on already existing real-estate property.

In fact, it is quite common for banks to prefer financing nonbanks for the purchase and resale of financial products than financing long-term industrial investments. This preference is driven by the high liquidity of financial products like bonds, stocks, and derivatives or securitized assets, which can be bought and sold quickly, generating the necessary cash-flow for the nonbanks to repay the short-term loans. The ability to quickly refinance through profitable trades reduces the risk for banks since nonbanks can repay loans before or as they mature. Furthermore, these financial products often serve as collateral for additional loans, maintaining liquidity without the need to sell assets immediately. This arrangement also provides banks with greater security, as they can claim rights to these assets, and the existence of active secondary markets ensures that assets can be quickly liquidated, reducing the risk of holding illiquid investments.

As Chap. 2 has clarified, bank money creation takes place as banks lend or sell deposit claims drawn on themselves. These claims, which the public accepts as means of settlement and stores of value, continue to exist and to circulate in the economy until the original loans are repaid or the original securities are extinguished.

Some of the bank money issued support production activities at circuit-start, as in a traditional monetary production circuit; other issuances support purely financial activities, giving origin to financial circuits, which, too, require longer-term financing to ensure successful closure at circuit-end (Box 4.2).[30]

Box 4.2. The Extended Circuit

A detailed representation of the circuit model extended to financialized economies is offered by Botta et al. (2015). As Chart 4.2 shows, there are some differences vis-à-vis the monetary circuit of production model with regard to both the demand and supply sides of financial assets and services. Regarding demand, financialized economies tend to feature different net deficit and surplus financial positions between non-financial firms (large corporations in particular) and households. In the case of non-financial firms, profits may remain "liquid" and take the form of money market mutual funds (MMMFs) shares rather than being used to finance productive investment. MMMFs will in turn use these funds to acquire liquid assets such as asset-backed commercial papers (ABCPs) or to take part in repurchase (REPO) agreements vis-à-vis investment banks. MMMFs, together with investment banks, are relevant buyers of ABCPs and asset-backed securities (ABSs).

[30] Appendix 1.B formalizes the CTBF model in the case of a financialized economy. A comprehensive analysis of the workings of the financial circuit is presented by Botta et al. (2015), form which Box 4.2 largely draws.

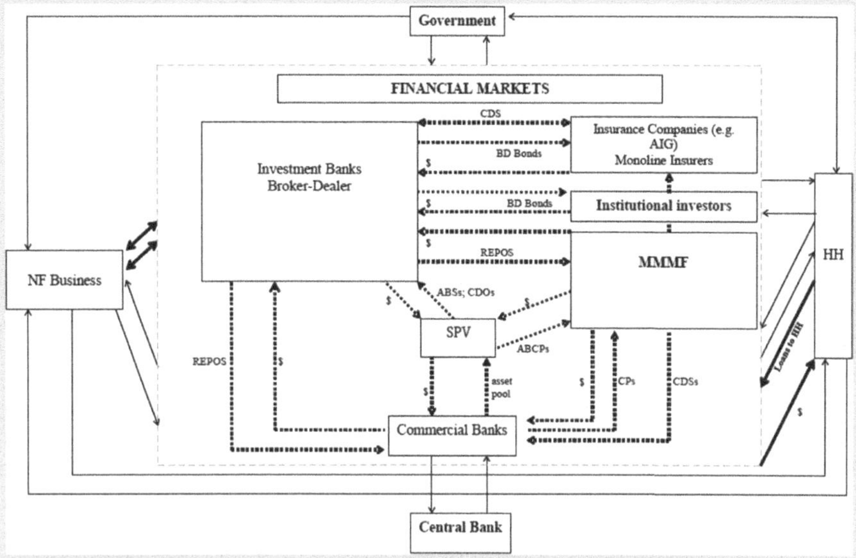

Chart 4.2 Circuit process of a financialized economy *Source* Botta et al. (cit.)

On the supply side, the supply of ABSs, ABCPs, and collateralized-debt-obligations (CDOs) rests fundamentally on the securitization of loans or mortgages by commercial banks. These replace their traditional "originate and hold" practice with the "originate, repackage and distribute" practice, so that part of their assets is moved off their own balance sheets and into legally separate special purpose vehicles (SPVs). The SPVs buy bank assets using the proceeds from the sale of ABSs and ABCPs to MMMFs, investment banks, and broker-dealers (BDs).

Securitization allows banks to transform illiquid assets into marketable ones and to sell them in the financial markets in exchange for liquidity. It also allows banks to open new financial positions while profiting from previously created and then sold assets. When banks sell assets to SPVs, they downsize the asset side of their balance sheet and liquid liabilities (i.e., SPV deposits) are correspondingly destroyed. The banks' equity-asset ratio improves and leverage decreases as a result.

Investment banks and BDs finance ABSs purchases by issuing bonds to investment funds and insurance companies. As well, they use REPOs as short-term means of financing and credit default swaps (CDSs) for protection against default risks on insured assets. Self-feeding inner-finance cycles emerge whereby banks provide investment banks and BDs with fresh money through REPOs, and investment banks and BDs use the money to buy ABSs supplied by the banks themselves through securitization.

Interestingly, these circuits coexist in contemporary capitalist economies and, resembling Palley's (1998) "twin circuits" of exchange, they may mutually interact so that money flows can pass from the production to the financial circuit and vice versa, depending on agent choices.

As the CTBF suggests, these interactions may create circuit breakdowns. For example, heightened agent preferences for financial investments, accommodated with money creation by the banks upstream in the process, would cause growing money flows transiting from the production to the financial circuit, possibly generating asset price inflation and bubble formation. This would hamper the closure of the production circuit downstream in the process—with negative balance sheet consequences for producing firms and their loan-originating banks, as earlier discussed.

On the other hand, a persistently accommodating stance by the banks toward financial investments might keep the cost of money artificially low for long and incentivize the formation of excessive debt exposures within the economy, which could lead into debt default events if (or as) agent expectations become pessimistic or if money becomes suddenly costlier, or is rationed, due to banks' changed risk perceptions or restrictive policy decisions by the monetary authorities.

Concrete manifestations of these tendencies characterized the long period preceding the global financial crisis of 2008, when commercial banks supplied ABSs, sold them to investment banks, and at the same time provided the latter with the money needed to buy the ABSs. These, in turn, were used by the investment banks as collateral to access bank money through REPOs. All this stimulated ABS demand and led to explosive circuit dynamics (Botta et al. cit.).

In financialized economies, money destruction is decoupled from asset destruction and debt repayment by initial borrowers. While borrowers' initial liabilities remain outstanding, they do no longer appear in the commercial banks' balance sheets and are recorded, instead, in the balance sheet of nonbank financial intermediaries.

Also, unlike in monetary production economies, the link between money and output is attenuated. With securitization, bank money is continuously created and destroyed without entering in contact with any real side institutions. To the extent that money is created to support the financial circuit, the money itself and the assets that its creation enables investors to purchase get de-linked from the output produced by the economy, with the ratio between the asset stocks and the flow of output produced growing manifold over time. As a result, the real value of the assets (in terms of output) declines (especially if their convertibility at par in foreign currencies is uncertain) and their nominal value is exposed to the risk that their demand will fall at some point.

Investigating how micro-choices influence the behaviors of different groups or classes of agents in a financialized circuit, using the CTBF approach, can help understand and potentially predict their impact on the macroeconomy. This understanding can inform the development of appropriate policy responses. This is particularly important when certain (classes of) agents dominate the financial markets, causing substantial flows of money into or out of domestic economies, which can either reward or penalize policy choices, amplifying or diminishing their effectiveness. Chapters 13 and 14 will explore this topic in detail.

Having discussed how money circulates in the economy, and the role of banks in the process, let us now examine how banks create money and the related implications—the topics of Chap. 6.

Appendix: The CTBF Model

This appendix consists of two sections. Section 4.7.1 reports and explains the CTBF model equations for a monetary production economy (with some corrections on the original version in Bossone (2001a)). Section B adapts the model to a financialized economy. The economy is closed and includes four classes (or macro-groups) of agents: firms, households, banks, and nonbank financial intermediaries. The variables are expressed in real terms.

The Formal Model of a Monetary Production Economy

Households

$$y_i = c_k - c_w \tag{4.1}$$

$$c_w = \alpha c_k \qquad 0 < \alpha < 1 \tag{4.2}$$

$$y_k = w_k \tag{4.3}$$

$$c_{j=i,k} = c\left(y_j^e, rs\right) \qquad c'_y > 0, c'_r < 0 \tag{4.4}$$

$$s_j = y_j - c_j \qquad j = i, k \tag{4.5}$$

$$s_j = s_j\left[z_j + \left(1 - z_j\right)\right] \qquad 0 \leq z_j\left(\leq z_j^-\right) \leq 1, \tag{4.6}$$

$$z_j = z_j\left(r_{s,}\sigma_j\right) \qquad z'_r > 0, z'_\sigma < 0 \tag{4.7}$$

The income of household i—the middleman—is given by its revenues minus costs, Eq. (4.). Household interactions are captured by i's income being determined by k's consumption and i's costs correspond to its wholesale purchases of c_w, as a fixed proportion of sales c_k after incorporating the value added from distribution services, Eq. (4.2). Household k's income is given by its wage earnings, Eq. 4.3). Household consumption is a function of permanent income y_e and the return on assets r_s, Eq. (4.3). Households are rational and forward looking and include their interactions in their plans; their consumption is derived from solving optimal intertemporal plans (see subsection B, below). Household saving is the difference between current income and optimal consumption, Eq. (4.5). Households invest a share z of their savings in longer-term, less liquid financial assets and hold the remaining share in non-interest-bearing bank demand deposits, Eq. (4.6). Share z is positive in the rate of interest r_s and negative in the agent's perceived uncertainty σ_j on her future income, Eq. (4.7). However, z can be bounded from above, z^-, by nonbank financial intermediaries limiting their collection of funds; in other words, the demand for funds from nonbanks may constrain the supply of long-term funds from households below its notional level.

Firms

$$w_k = v(c + I) \qquad 0 < v \leq 1 \tag{4.8}$$

$$c = E\left[\sum_{j=i,k} c_j\right] \tag{4.9}$$

$$I = I(\mu - r_{FI}) \leq LF \qquad I' > 0 \tag{4.10}$$

$$\mu = \mu K = \mu(K_0 + I) \qquad \mu' < 0 \tag{4.11}$$

$$\sum_f y_f^n = (1 - v)(c + I) - LFr_{FI} - CR(1 + r_l) \tag{4.12}$$

Production (wage) costs are a share v of total production value, Eq. (4.8), where v can be thought of either as a distributional parameter determined exogenously to the model, or as reflecting the value added from production. The supply of consumption and capital goods adjust instantaneously to demands, Eqs. (4.9)–(4.10). In Eq. (4.10), the demand for capital good I increases with the difference between the marginal efficiency of capital μ and the cost of funds r_{FI} (see below) and is bound above by the long-term finances made available by the financial intermediaries (see below); μ is decreasing in aggregate capital K, given by inherited capital K_0 plus new investment I, Eq. (4.11). Net corporate income y_f^n is gross income minus debt repayments, Eq. (4.12). If y_f^n is negative, the circuit closes only if firms borrow new money or manage to have their old loans rolled over by the banks. Any positive y_f^n is saved (see below) and invested in the financial market.

Banks

$$CR^s = \sum_b CR_b = \sum_b CR_b(r_L, \psi), \qquad CR'_r > 0, CR'_\psi < 0 \tag{4.13}$$

$$CR^d = CR^d(r_L) \qquad CR' < 0 \tag{4.14}$$

$$\psi = \psi(CR, r_L) \qquad \psi'_{CR} > 0, \psi'_r > 0 \tag{4.15}$$

$$CR = \min(CR^s, CR^d) \tag{4.16}$$

$$CR = D = \sum_b D_b \tag{4.17}$$

$$CR_{bB} = D_{Bb} - D_{bB} \tag{4.18}$$

$$\sum_b y_b = (1 - \psi^-)CRr_L \tag{4.19}$$

Banks allow the circuit process to start. At the beginning of the period, they provide firms with commercial loans to finance input acquisition and output production, which must be paid off at the end of the period at negotiated interest rate r_L. The supply of loans CR^s is positive in the interest rate and negative in the firms' default risk ψ, Eq. (4.13), and the demand for loans is negative in the interest rate r_L, Eq. (4.14). The default risk is a positive function of the volume of loans extended to firms CR and of the interest cost r_L, Eq. (4.15). Banks increase lending to the point where their marginal return from lending equals the marginal default risk of the borrowers. The loans extended to firms are thus the minimum between the amount supplied and the amount demanded, Eq. (4.16).

Money is created by the banks in the form of bank demand deposits D as borrowers' bank accounts are credited with the total amount of loans extended to firms, Eq. (4.17). Loans are thus liabilities of the borrowing firms and, at the same time, claims of the borrowers on the banks, which the banks promise to honor as borrowers draw funds from their accounts, out of the loans, to make payments relating to the activities funded with the loans. No cash circulates in the economy and all payments are made through deposit transfers across bank accounts (within the same bank or across banks). All agents may hold deposits with banks for transaction and liquidity preference purposes. Banks extend unlimited credit to each other and at no charge as deposits are transferred from one bank to another: bank b supplies credit to bank B to finance net deposit transfers from the latter to itself, Eq. (4.18).[31]

[31] This is, arguably, a very strong assumption and one that certainly does not hold, as crisis experience shows, when risk perceptions and uncertainty increase, leading banks to limit, reduce, and eventually stop lending to each other altogether, with severe circuit breakdowns or even collapse.

Deposits are destroyed only when loans are paid back to the banks. Bank income consists of the capital and interest shares of loans that are repaid by borrowers, Eq. (4.23), where ψ^- indicates the ex-post rate of default on bank debts.

Nonbank Financial Intermediaries

$$LF^d = I^d \tag{4.20}$$

$$LF^S \le \sum_{h=i,k,f,b,F} z_h s_h \le \sum_{h=i,k,f,b,F} s_h = S = \sum_{j=i,k} s_j + \sum_f y_f^n + \sum_b y_b + \sum_F y_F \tag{4.21}$$

$$LF^S = LF^S(r_{FI}, \phi) \qquad LF_r' > 0, LF_\phi' < 0 \tag{4.22}$$

$$r_{FI} = r_S + q \tag{4.23}$$

$$\phi = \phi(LF, r_{FI}) \qquad \phi_{LF}' > 0, \phi_r' > 0 \tag{4.24}$$

$$LF = \min(LF^s, LF^d) \tag{4.25}$$

$$\sum_F y_F = (1 - \phi^-) LF r_{FI} \tag{4.26}$$

Nonbank financial intermediaries, or nonbanks, operate in the financial market, aggregate savings from several sources, and allocate them to fund-users. The demand for capital good I^d is funded with long-term funds LF, Eq. (4.24) generated by aggregate saving, Eq. (4.25). Nonbanks' supply of fund LF^s varies positively with the interest on financial intermediation r_{FI} net of default risk ϕ, Eq. (4.26). Interest rate r_{FI}, in turn, is based on asset return r_S and incorporates a competitive fee for intermediation services q, Eq. (4.27). Default risk ϕ is positive in the amount of long-term funds effectively invested LF and their cost r_{FI}, Eq. (4.28). Funds are supplied until their marginal return equals the marginal default risk of the investing firms, and the amount invested is the minimum between the amount supplied and the amount demanded, Eq. (4.29). Nonbank income consists of the actual flow of returns on the invested funds.

Notice from Eq. (4.25) that the supply of funds from nonbanks to investing firms may not exceed their collection of long-term savings. This may result either from the intermediaries deliberately choosing not to raise more funds than what they can (or want to) invest, or from savers preferring to hold deposits with banks than riskier assets. Thus, as the equation indicates, the supply of long-term funds may be less than the aggregate saving available, with the implications that were earlier discussed. In an open-economy model, the nonbanks could invest a share of domestic savings into foreign markets, with similar implications for the domestic economy.

Interacting Households

In the above model, the households interact and adopt the following plans:

$$\max_{c>0} U_j = E\left[\sum_j^{\infty} \beta^t u_j(c_j)\right], j = i,\ k \tag{4.27}$$

s. t.

$$A_{jt}(1 + r_S) - A_{jt} = s_{jt} \tag{4.28}$$

and to transversality condition

$$\lim_{t\to\infty} A_{jt} = 0, \tag{4.29}$$

where A is non-human wealth, $u(\cdot)$ is a well-behaved utility function, and $0 < \beta < 1$ is the time discount factor. Solving the household plans with dynamic programming and noting from Eqs. (4.27) and (4.28) that $y_j = \gamma c_k$, where $\gamma = 1 - \alpha$, yield the Euler conditions for interacting households i and k:

$$i : \phi_i\left[\gamma(w_{kt} - s_{kt}) - s_{it}\right] = (1 + r_S)E\beta\left\{\phi_i\left[\gamma(w_{kt+1} - s_{kt+1}) - s_{it+1}\right]\right\} \tag{4.30}$$

$$k : \phi_k(w_{kt} - s_{kt}) = (1 + r_S)E\beta\left[\phi_i(w_{kt+1} - s_{kt+1})\right], \tag{4.31}$$

where $\phi(\cdot) = u'(\cdot)$ is the instantaneous marginal utility of consumption. Notice that the influence of household k on household i is direct, immediate (within the same circuit round), and visible from Euler equation (4.30) as it originates from the consumption decisions of k, which becomes the income of i. On the other hand, the influence of household i on household k is indirect, not immediate (it takes place over subsequent circuit rounds), and it is not visible from Euler equation (4.31), since it is due to i's consumption decisions and their impact on the firms' decisions to change production and, hence, wage bill w_k.

The Formal Model of a Financialized Economy

The monetary production model described in Section 4.7.1 is modified as follows:

Households

$$y_i = c_k - c_w + inv_i r_S \tag{4.32}$$

$$c_w = \alpha c_k \tag{4.33}$$

$$y_k = w_k \tag{4.34}$$

$$c_{j=i,k} = c\left(y_j^e, r_s\right) + CR_j^c \tag{4.35}$$

$$inv_j = y_j - c_j - r_l CR_j^C + (1 - r_L)CR_j^{inv} \tag{4.36}$$

$$s_j = s_j\left[z_j + \left(1 - z_j\right)\right] \tag{4.37}$$

$$z_j = z_j\left(\sigma_j\right). \tag{4.38}$$

Here, the differences with the monetary production economy's model are that households' income include returns on portfolio investment, Eq. (4.32), and that households can borrow from banks to support both consumption, Eq. (4.35), and financial investment, Eq. (4.36).

Firms

$$w_k = v(c + I) \tag{4.39}$$

$$c = E\left[\sum_{j=i,k} c_j\right] \tag{4.40}$$

$$I = I(\mu - r_{FI}) \leq LF \tag{4.41}$$

$$\mu = \mu K = \mu(K_0 + I) \tag{4.42}$$

$$\sum_f y_f^n = (c + I)(1 - v(1 - r_L) + CR_f^{inv}(r_S - r_L) - LFr_{FI}. \tag{4.43}$$

Here, the difference with the monetary production model is that firms can borrow from banks also to finance portfolio investments, with their net income reflecting the flows of investment returns and debt payments to banks, Eq. (4.43).

Banks

$$CR^s = \sum_b CR_b = \sum_b \left\{CR_{bf}^w(r_L, \psi_f) + CR_{bf}^{inv}(r_L, \psi_f) + CR_{bj}^c(r_L, \psi_j) + CR_{bFI}^{inv}(r_L, \psi_{FI})\right\} \tag{4.44}$$

$$CR^d = CR^d(r_L) \tag{4.45}$$

$$\psi = \psi(CR, r_L) \tag{4.46}$$

$$CR = \min(CR^s, CR^d) \tag{4.47}$$

$$CR = D = \sum_b D_b \tag{4.48}$$

$$CR_{bB} = D_{Bb} - D_{bB} \tag{4.49}$$

$$\sum_b y_b = (1 - \psi^-)CRr_L \tag{4.50}$$

Here, the differences are that banks can extend loans to households, firms, and financial intermediaries to support their portfolio investments, Eq. (4.44). Notice that $\sum_b (CR^w_{bf}) = CR^w = v(c + I) = w_k$, that is, banks finance firms' production with loans.

Nonbank Financial Intermediaries

$$LF^d = I^d \tag{4.51}$$

$$LF^S \leq \sum_{h=i,k,f,b,F} z_h s_h \leq \sum_{h=i,k,f,b,F} s_h = S = \sum_{j=i,k} s_j + \sum_f y^n_f + \sum_b y_b + \sum_F y_F \tag{4.52}$$

$$LF^S = LF^S(r_{FI}, \phi) \tag{4.53}$$

$$r_{FI} = r_S + q \tag{4.54}$$

$$\phi = \phi(LF, r_{FI}) \tag{4.55}$$

$$LF = \min(LF^s, LF^d) \tag{4.56}$$

$$\sum_F y_F = (1 - \phi^-)LFr_{FI} + CR^{inv}_{FI}(r_S - r_L) \tag{4.57}$$

Here, the difference is that nonbank financial intermediaries can borrow from banks, with their net income reflecting the flow of investment returns and debt service, Eq. (4.57).

Interacting Households

$$\max_{c>0} U_j = E\left[\sum_{j}^{\infty} \beta^t u_j(c_j)\right], \qquad j = i,\, k \tag{4.58}$$

s.t.

$$A_{jt} + CR_j^{inv}(r_S - r_L) - CR_j^C r_L - A_{jt} = s_{jt} \tag{4.60}$$

and transversality condition

$$\lim_{t\to\infty} A_{jt} + CR_{jt} = 0. \tag{4.60}$$

Here, the difference is that households can borrow from banks to finance extra consumption and/or portfolio investments, Eq. (4.59), and the transversality condition must comprise bank debt as well, Eq. (4.60). The Euler conditions for interacting households i and k correspondingly change, respectively, into:

$$i : \phi_i\left[\gamma(w_{kt} - s_{kt}) - s_{it}\right] = (1 + r_s)(1 - r_l)E\beta\left\{\phi_i\left[\gamma(w_{kt+1} - s_{kt+1}) - s_{it+1}\right]\right\} \tag{4.61}$$

$$k : \phi_k(w_{kt} - s_{kt}) = (1 + r_s)(1 - r_L)E\beta\left[\phi_i(w_{kt+1} - s_{kt+1})\right]. \tag{4.62}$$

References

Adrian, T., & Mancini-Griffoli, T. (2019). *The rise of digital money. FinTech Notes, Note/19/01.* International Monetary Fund.

Bossone, B. (2020). Money and customer funds in the world of digital finance: Who really owns what? *Journal of Payments Strategy and Systems, 15*(1), 37–53.

Bossone, B., Mahajan, S., & Zahir, F. (2003). Financial infrastructure, group interests, and capital accumulation: theory, evidence, and policy. IMF Working Paper, WP/03/24, International Monetary Fund, Washington D.C.

Bossone, B. (1998), "Can saving be scarce? *International Review of Economics and Business 45*(1), 1–26.

Bossone, B. (1999). The role of trust in financial sector development. mimeo, The World Bank, Washington, DC, October, available at SSRN: https://ssrn.com/abstract=623953

Bossone, B. (2000). What makes banks special? A study on banking, finance, and economic development, Policy Research Working Paper, WPS2408, The World Bank.

Bossone, B. (2001a). Circuit theory of banking and finance. *Journal of Banking and Finance, 25*(5), 857–890.

Bossone, B. (2001b). Do banks have a future? A study on banking and finance as we move into the third millennium. *Journal of Banking and Finance, 25*(12), 2239–2276.

Botta, A., Caverzasi, E., & Tori, D. (2015). Financial{real-side interactions in an extended monetary circuit with shadow banking: Loving or dangerous hugs? *International Journal of Political Economy, 44*(3), 196–227.
Bresciani, T. C. (1936). *The theory of saving*. Economica.
Cencini, A. (1995), *Monetary theory, national and international*. Routledge, New York.
Chernow R. (1997), *The death of the banker: The decline and the fall of the great financial Dynasties*. The Triumph of the Small Investor, Vintage Books, a Division of Random House, New York.
Davidson, P. (1991). Finance, funding, saving and investment. In Davidson, L. (ed.), The collected writings of Paul Davidson, vol. l, University Press, New York, pp. 365–372.
Fama, E. (1980). Banking in the theory of finance. *Journal of Monetary Economics, 6*, 39–57.
Graziani, A. (1990). The theory of the monetary circuit. *Économies Et Sociétés, 24*(6), 7–36.
Graziani, A. (1988a). Le teorie del circuito e la teoria generale di Keynes. In *Messori*, pp. 285–330.
Graziani, A. (1996). Money as purchasing power and money as stock of wealth in Keynesian economics. In E. Neill, & G. Deleplace, (Eds.), *Money in Motion*, Macmillan, London.
Gnos, C. (2013). "A historical perspective on the theory of the monetary circuit: from Schumpeter to Parguez," Chapters. In: Louis-Philippe Rochon & Mario Seccareccia (Ed.), Monetary Economies of Production, Chapter 3, pp. 23–32, Edward Elgar Publishing.
Hotham, G. (2024). Fabulous macroeconomics. *Real-World Economics Review, 108*, 33–39.
Lavoie, M. (1985). Credit and money: The dynamic circuit, overdraft economics and post-Keynesian economics. In M. Jarsulic (Ed.), *Money and Macro Policy* (pp. 63–84). Kluwer-Nijhoff.
Lavoie, M. (1999). The credit-led supply of deposits and the demand for money: Kaldor's reflux mechanism as previously endorsed by Joan Robinson. *Cambridge Journal of Economics, 23*, 103–113.
Lysandrou, P. (2020). Financialisation and the limits of circuit theory. *Finance and Society, 6*(1), 1–18.
Messori, M. (Ed.). (1988). *Moneta e Produzione*. Einaudi.
Messori, M. (ed.) (1988b). Agenti e mercati in uno schema periodale. In *Moneta e Produzione*.
Messori, M., & Tamborini, R. (1993). *Money, credit, and finance in a sequence economy", Foundations of a macroeconomic model* (p. 20). Dipartimento di Scienze Economiche, Università di Roma La Sapienza.
Messori, M., & Tamborini, R. (1994). Moneta, finanza e credito in un'economia sequenziale". In G. Vaciago (Ed.), *Moneta e Finanza* (pp. 55–100). Il Mulino.
Michell, J. (2016). Do shadow banks create money? 'Financialisation' and the monetary circuit," Working Papers PKWP1605, Post Keynesian Economics Society (PKES).
Minsky, H. P. (1990). Schumpeter e la Finanza. In S. Biasco, A. Roncaglia, M. Salvati (Eds.), Istituzioni e Mercato nello Sviluppo Economico. Saggi in Onore di Paolo Sylos Labini, La Terza, Bari.
Palley, T. I. (1998). The twin circuits: aggregate demand and the expenditure multiplier in a monetary economy. *Review of Radical Political Economics, 30*, 3.
Passarella, M. (2014). Financialisation and the monetary circuit: A macroaccounting heterodox approach. *Review of Political Economy 26*(1), 128–148.
Rajan, R. G., & Zingales, L. (1999). Financial systems, industrial structure, and growth. In *Symposium on the International Competitiveness of the Swedish Financial Industry, Organized by the Bank of Sweden Tercentenary Foundation.*
Realfonzo, R. (2012). Circuit Theory.In J. E. King (ed.) *The Elgar companion to post Keynesian economics*, Edward Elgar, pp. 87–92.
Rochon, L. P. (1999). The creation and circulation of endogenous money: A circuit dynamic approach. *Journal of Economic Issues, 33*(1).
Sawyer, M. (2013). Endogenous money, circuits and financialization. *Review of Keynesian Economics, 1*, 230–241.
Schmitt, B. (1959). L'Équilibre de la Monnaie," Revue d'Économie Politique, novembre-décembre
Schmitt, B. (1982). Théorie Unitaire de la Monnaie, Nationale et Internationale, Castella, Albeuve.

Seccareccia, M. (2012). Financialization and the transformation of commercial banking: Understanding the recent Canadian experience before and during the international financial crisis. *Journal of Post Keynesian Economics, 35*(2), 277–300.

Simon, H. A. (1976). From substantive to procedural rationality. In T. J. Kastelein, S. K. Kuipers, W. A. Nijenhuis, & G. R. Wagenaar (Eds.), *25 years of economic theory*, Springer, Boston, MA.

Chapter 5
Money Creation by Banks

Abstract This chapter further elaborates on the role of banks as money creators and focuses on two aspects of bank money: its creation process and the extraction of seigniorage by banks being able to create money at a lower cost than its value. The chapter reviews the growing body of literature surrounding banks as money creators, while recognizing the notable lack of research focused specifically on bank seigniorage. It delves into how banks generate money and the constraints they encounter through the payment systems where they operate, alongside the rules and technologies they must adhere to within their operational frameworks. Additionally, seigniorage is scrutinized in light of its differences from profits gained through traditional financial intermediation. The chapter reflects on the broader implications of these mechanisms, asserting the critical nature of bank seigniorage in understanding the economic landscape, ultimately linking these dynamics to broader concepts of material and financial productivity within contemporary economies. The chapter concludes by discussing policy measures to eliminate, mitigate, or redistribute seigniorage across the economy.

5.1 Preamble

Studying the "circuit" approach to monetary theory—the subject of Chap. 4—made me explore deeply the idea that banks create money. By combining the theory with the policy of payment systems and the practice with their operation, which I had acquired as a central banker earlier on, and as a commercial banker more recently, I could understand from firsthand experience how bank money creation power is affected (and constrained) by payment system operations and settlement rules. This helped me to be very cautious about the conclusion, which many economists (especially heterodox ones) often tend to reach, that banks create money "out of thin air," as if the process of money creation was free from costs and entirely driven by the banks themselves.

In this chapter, based on my earlier work (Bossone, 2020), I discuss how the theory of bank money creation originated, how it has evolved, and how it has eventually entered mainstream Economics. The chapter, then, illustrates how bank money

B. Bossone, *Trailblazing Visions of Money in Economic Theory*, Contributions to Economics, https://doi.org/10.1007/978-3-031-82544-6_5

creation is influenced (and constrained) by payment settlement rules and technologies. Further on, elaborating on Chap. 4, this chapter also argues that, in so far as banks create money at a cost that is less than what is worth, they essentially extract seigniorage from the economy—just like any "sovereign" does by issuing the country's money—and how this differs from banks exercising monopolistic power on the deposit and credit markets where they operate.

5.2 Introduction

Today, the largest share of the monies circulating in countries worldwide—even including the fast-growing incidence of digital currencies—are bank deposits (Ryan-Collins et al., 2012).[1] These are claims on commercial banks, issued by the commercial banks when they lend money to their clients or when they use them to buy securities. These claims are transferable to third parties, they are accepted as means of payments in the economy's exchange process, and they are redeemable in cash at par by their holders on demand.[2]

For a century or more, starting in the early 1900s, the creation of money by commercial banks (henceforth, "banks") had been recognized by economists. Some scholars even held that banks create money *ex nihilo* (out of nothing), while others thought this option would be feasible only for the banks acting collectively, as a system, and would not be possible for individual banks acting alone. The theory remained prominent until the early post-war years, when it disappeared altogether from the research literature and textbooks and adherents continued to thrive only within heterodox schools.[3]

In most contemporary academic literature (see below), banks are in fact represented as pure financial intermediaries.[4] They have no power to create money; they can only buy assets with funds they have previously acquired in the form of deposits or through issuance of shares or bonds. This view is the counterpart—on the finance side—to what loanable funds theory is on the macroeconomics side, whereby, simply

---

[1] Buiter et al. (2022) argue persuasively that, in spite of the current (in some cases, successful) growth of private-sector e-monies, these will prove only a temporary phenomenon, while commercial bank money with enhanced technical functionalities will remain the dominant form of money. Despite the many structural changes in finance and financial services, a similar conclusion was reached some twenty-odd years earlier by focusing on the unique bank money creation process under fractional reserve regimes (Bossone, 2001).

[2] *Commercial* banks (henceforth also referred to simply as "banks") are here and throughout defined as institutions that accept demand deposits from the public *and* lend money to borrowers by issuing demand deposit claims to them, that is, claims that give their owners the right to convert them in cash or to transfer them to third parties either for settling payment obligations or for value transferring purposes.

[3] For a detailed review of the theories of banks as money creators and their historic evolution, see Werner (2016).

[4] A comprehensive historical reconstruction of the evolution of economic thinking on banks as pure financial intermediaries vs. banks as money creators is contained in Bossone (2020).

put, new investments can only be funded with accumulated (pre-existing) savings. Financial intermediaries (banks among them) help the two to match each other at the "right" price (i.e., the equilibrium interest rate).

As the next section discusses, the money creation power of banks has once again been recognized recently within the economics discipline, including by its "mainstream." Since the early 2000s, I have tried to contribute to this issue arguing that the banks' power to create money must fundamentally consider the role that banks play in the payments system and, therefore, the impact that payment system rules and technologies exert on the banks' money creation power, limiting it differently, depending on the banks' relative size and share of the payments market, and affecting their profitability accordingly.

This chapter considers the role of banks as money creators and focuses on two dimensions of the banks' money creation process: how banks create money and under what limitations, and the extent to which banks extract seigniorage from the economy by being able to create money at a lower cost than its value.[5] Section 5.3 revisits the literature on bank money creation and discusses recent theoretical progress. Section 5.4 analyzes how banks create money and the constraints on their money creation deriving from the banks' payments activity and the rules and technologies of the payment system(s) where they operate. Section 5.5 studies analytically that banks extract seigniorage through money creation and that bank seigniorage differs from profits derived from pure financial intermediation. Section 5.6 closes the chapter with considerations on the nature of bank seigniorage. Three appendixes complete the chapter: the first analyzes the differences in lending operations carried out by banks and nonbank financial intermediaries, respectively; the second shows how different types of payment settlement system technologies and rules affect banks' money creation power; and the third and final appendix delves into the relationship between bank money, central bank reserves, and seigniorage.

5.3 The Literature on Bank Money Creation[6]

Three different theories have taken hold on the role of commercial banks as creators of money, spanning the full stretch of the twentieth century (Werner, 2016.) until today. The first theory is that banks create money out of nothing, simply by extending new loans. The second theory is that banks cannot create money individually, but they can do so collectively as they operate in fractional reserve regimes.[7] The third theory is

[5] Being a form of rent (or unearned income), seigniorage will be associated with the capacity of the banks to gain extra profits from their money creation process, that is, profits that are in excess of their "normal" level, commonly defined as the minimum profit level that a company can achieve to support its continued operation in the market where there is competition.

[6] This section, taken from Bossone (2020), draws on and integrates the reviews of the literature on bank money creation by Werner (2016) and Morelli (2018).

[7] Here and throughout this chapter, a "fractional reserves regime" is any regulatory regime that do not require banks to back up with reserves the totality of all their (demand) deposit claims issued.

that banks cannot possibly create money since they are only financial intermediaries. These theories are discussed in turn.

5.3.1 Banks Create Money

The oldest theory holds that each bank creates money literally "out of thin air" every time it executes a loan contract or buys assets in exchange for demand deposit claims, which it itself issues and the economy accepts as money. To do so, as the theory goes, banks do not need to collect deposits or to raise reserves to fund their lending or purchasing transactions, and, as they issue new deposits, an increase in total balances occurs since no proportional decrease takes place elsewhere.

One of the first and most authoritative scholars who supported this theory was Macleod (1856), an expert on banks and a lawyer. His influential work, published in many editions up to the twentieth century, underlines the importance of considering the accounting, legal, and financial aspects of banks together. Money creation through credit was investigated by Wicksell (1898),[8] who, while not explicitly using the term "money creation" in the modern sense, emphasized the pivotal role of banks in influencing the market rate of interest through their ability to issue loans by creating deposits in the accounts of borrowers, effectively increasing the money supply. This message was spread out wide open by Hartley Withers (1918), a prolific writer on this subject and for many years a director of the Economist, who argued that when a customer goes to a banker for a loan, the banker gives him a credit in his books and thus adds to the deposits on the liability side of the bank's balance sheet. Around those same years, influential supporters of the theory were Schumpeter (1912), Davenport (1913), Howe (1915), Hawtrey (1919), Cassel (1923), and the Keynes (1924) of the *Tract on Monetary Reform.* The theory was reflected in the highly influential Macmillan Report,[9] which identified the creation of bank credit as the central point of its investigation and noted that banks create deposits by granting loans, allowing money to be drawn on an overdraft, or by purchasing securities.

By 1920, the theory had gained prominence in macroeconomics textbooks, and one of the leading economists of the 1930s, Irving Fisher, insisted on money creation via bank lending. The theory remained prominent until the early post-war years, when it altogether disappeared from the research literature and textbooks, though

[8] Translated in English language in Wicksell (1936).

[9] Macmillan Committee (1931), "British parliamentary reports on international finance: The report of the Macmillan Committee," London: H.M. Stationery Office. The report was issued by the Committee on Finance and Industry, led by Hugh Macmillan and commonly known as the Macmillan Committee (1931) and established in the UK, in 1929, by Royal command to determine whether the contemporary banking and financial system was helping or hindering British trade and industry.

adherents continued to thrive among the so-called Austrian economists (e.g., Hoppe et al., 1998) and scholars from the post-Keynesian school.[10]

5.3.2 *Bank Money Expansion Under Fractional Reserves*

The fractional reserve theory maintains that banks are financial intermediaries and can only lend out money that was previously deposited with them. It is only at the system level—where the mechanical, cumulative aggregation of all bank deposit and lending operations takes place—that money creation becomes possible through the process of multiple deposit expansion.

The first supporter of the fractional reserve theory of bank money creation was Alfred Marshall, who, in the recount by Yohe (1995), considered what part of its deposits a bank can lend and what part of its loans would be redeposited with it and with other banks and, vice versa, what part of the loans made by other banks would be received by it as deposits, which would thereby feed the process in a geometrical progression until exhaustion. The theory was advanced by Phillips (1920), who argued that credit creation theory was predicated upon the contention that a bank would be able to make loans to the extent of several times the amount of additional cash newly acquired and held at the time the loans were made, whereas a representative bank in a system is actually able ordinarily to lend an amount only roughly equal to such cash. Accordingly, individual commercial banks cannot create credit or money, but they can do so collectively, as new reserves split into small fragments, become dispersed among the banks of the system, and come to constitute the basis of a manifold loan expansion through the process of dispersion. Each bank is thus deemed to be a financial intermediary and each banker is thought of as handling chiefly the funds lent by others and thus holds no power to create money. Banks can create money only in the aggregate, a point emphasized by Crick (1927) and eventually shared also by Keynes (1930) who in the meantime had changed his mind on the topic. The role of commercial banks as money creators remained at the center of the economic debate during the 1920–1930 decade.

Fractional reserve theory became dominant in the 1950s and 1960s, influencing the description of the money process in the academic textbooks on macroeconomics and monetary economics of the time. The major example is Samuelson (1948)'s best-selling economics textbook, which notes that banks must first raise funds from depositors to be able to lend but shows the iterative process whereby the loans from

[10] See, for instance, Moore (1979, 1983) and the literature on monetary circuit theory. As this literature is too vast to be cited here and to do justice to its many contributors, we refer only to Augusto Graziani, one of the theory's most authoritative exponents. In fact, a survey into the history of economic ideas reveals important antecedents (see Graziani, 2003). I have myself contributed to circuit theory, in particular by introducing in the theory the role of banks at the initial—*financing*—stage of the circuit, where money is advanced to firms for getting production started, and the role of financial intermediaries at the closing—*funding*—of the circuit, where savings need to be allocated to investment (Bossone, 2000, 2001); the latter is reprinted in Rossi and Rochon (eds.) (2017).

one bank become deposits of another bank (assuming no "cash spill") and so on, until the resulting chain of deposit creation leads to the formation across the whole banking system of an amount of total deposits that are a multiple of the initial amount: the "money multiplier." The banking system as a whole can thus do what each small bank is not able to do on its own. What Samuelson calls "expansion of multiple deposits" still appears in the fifteenth edition of his book half a century later (Samuelson & Nordhaus, 1995), which points that each depository institution can create loans (and deposits) to the extent that it holds excess reserves. The fractional reserve theory of money creation attracted many followers, including Von Hayek (1929).[11] In recent times it has resurfaced in the widely read textbook by Stiglitz (1997).

5.3.3 Banks Cannot Create Money

In most contemporary academic textbooks and research papers (see below), banks are represented as pure financial intermediaries. They have no power to create credit and money; they can only buy assets with funds they have previously acquired through deposits by customers or the issuance of shares or bonds to investors. This view is the counterpart—on the finance side—to what loanable funds theory is on the macroeconomics side, whereby, simply put, new investments can only be funded with accumulated (pre-existing) savings; accordingly, financial intermediaries (banks among them) help the two to match each other at the "right" price (i.e., the equilibrium interest rate).

The view of banks as mere financial intermediaries is at least as old as Von Mises (1912), which noted that the activity of the banks as negotiators of credit is characterized by the lending of other people's money (that is, money that the banks had borrowed from people). Several decades later, the view was articulated in the seminal works by Gurley and Shaw (1955, 1960), which rejected the idea that banks hold the power to create money and explained instead that banks engage in multiple creation of particular liabilities, in relation to the class of assets they hold, which enable them to collect deposits and lend them out to clients. Tobin (1963), too, refused the idea that banks create money and credit, and Sealey and Lindley (1977) modeled banks as financial firms specialized in a transformation process that involves the borrowing of funds from surplus spending units and the lending of those funds to deficit spending units and consists of a multistage activity requiring intermediate outputs, where loanable funds, borrowed from depositors and used by enterprises to purchase capital, labor, and material inputs are employed them in the production of earning assets. Since then, this theory has prevailed, with contributions from Baltensperger (1980) to Fama (1980) Diamond and Dybvig (1983), Bernanke and Blinder (1988), Riordan (1993), Bernanke and Gertler (1995), Kashyap et al. (2002),

[11] See Werner (2016) for references to the several authors belonging to this camp.

and more recently Brunnermeier and Sanniko (2016), and IMF's Adrian and Mancini-Griffoli (2019), just to cite some of the most relevant ones. The theory of financial intermediation encompasses also the so-called credit view, which has become an important pillar in monetary macroeconomics. The view proposes a banking credit channel of monetary transmission, whereby banks are financial intermediaries that transform liabilities into assets with different characteristics, in terms of maturity and liquidity, and monitor debtors' repayment capacity.[12] Widely read books on money and banking (e.g., Cecchetti, 2008; Casu et al., 2006; Matthew and Thompson, 2005), and the latest edition of one of the most popular macroeconomic textbooks (Mankiw, 2019), all feature banks as mere conduits for the transfer of funds from savers to investors.

5.3.4 Banks Create Money: A Comeback

Perhaps as a reflection of their belonging to the family of mainstream financial institutions *par excellence*—the central banks—the message from Bank of England's et al. (2014a, b), whereby commercial banks create money in the form of bank deposits by making new loans (only constrained by market forces and risk consideration), has been heard loud and clear, reverberating throughout the international economic and financial community to an extent that the *bank-create-money* theory has once again gained prominence.[13]

Still, from the Bank of England, Jakab and Kumhof (2015) hold that, in the real world, banks provide financing through money creation through lending, being

[12] As a leading proponent of the credit view, Bernanke (1993) frequently refers to "credit creation," clarifying that: "...By credit creation process I mean the process by which, in exchange for paper claims, the savings of specific individuals or firms are made available for the use of other individuals or firms (for example to make capital investments or simply to consume). Note that I am drawing a strong distinction between credit creation, which is the process by which saving is channeled to alternative uses, and the act of saving itself... In my broad conception of the credit creation process I include most of the value added of the financial industry, including the information-gathering, screening, and monitoring activities required to make sound loans or investments, as well as much of the risk-sharing, maturity transformation, and liquidity provision services that attract savers and thus support the basic lending and investment functions. I also want to include in my definition of the credit creation process activities undertaken by potential borrowers to transmit information about themselves to lenders: for example, for firms, these activities include provision of data to the public, internal or external auditing, capital structure decisions, and some aspects of corporate governance." (p. 50).

[13] That such message originated from the world of central banking, however, should not be much of a surprise, after all. In a post titled *Central Bankers: "We're all Post-Keynesians now,"* Jesse Frederik suggests that central bankers may have grasped the reality of commercial bank money creation somewhat earlier than academics, who in their textbooks still to this day, as noted, continue to subscribe to the conventional "money multiplier" story. See also the related post *Who is right? Krugman or Keen or/and 9 Central Bank economists?* A full section of statements by leading central bankers acknowledging that banks create their own funds through lending is reported in Jakab and Kumhof (2015).

mainly constrained by profitability and solvency considerations. They incorporate this view into a dynamic stochastic general equilibrium (DSGE) model and compare its predictions with those obtained from an otherwise identical DSGE model that incorporates the conventional intermediation of loanable funds, concluding that predictions from the former model are much more in line with stylized facts.

Interestingly, a few years earlier BIS's Borio and Disyatat (2011)—they themselves from the international community of central banking—had criticized the loanable funds theory's failure to understand global current account imbalances without distinguishing between saving (a national account concept) and financing (a cash-flow concept) and thus focusing on net rather than gross capital flows. In their view, the theory neglects the monetary character of contemporary economies, where bank credit creation plays a fundamental role and the banking system endogenously generates financing means, regardless of the underlying real resources backing them.

A decisive contribution to the *banks-create-money* theory is Werner (2014), as further elaborated in Werner (2016), whose analysis goes at the very heart of what uniquely enables banks to create money and whose empirical tests reject the financial intermediation and fractional reserve theories.

Two non-academic contributions deserve mentioning in this camp. One is Fullwiler (2012), which provides a rigorous reprisal to Krugman's rearguard defense of banks as pure intermediaries, arguing that banks are not limited by their deposits either individually or in the aggregate. The second is Sheard (2013), which explains analytically that banks do not lend out deposits or reserves but lend by creating deposits. Both contributions take into consideration banks' payment obligations, but neither recognizes their constraining role on bank money creation, which is discussed next.

Whereas the literature on banks as money creators has become substantial, the related issue regarding the seigniorage associated with bank money creation has not received particular attention from research, so far. As a result, the literature on the subject is still quite limited. Early references on the origin of commercial bank seigniorage are Baltensperger and Jordan (1997) and Bossone (2000, 2001), and empirical studies have been done by Cardoso (2003), Arby (2006), Soldatos and Varelas (2015), and recently Bjerg et al. (2017) and Macfarlane et al. (2017). Not much more can be found in the literature, except the recent work on the Accounting View of Money and its implications for bank seigniorage, discussed in Chap. 2.

5.4 Bank Money Creation: The Process

The theories of banks as money creators, including the most recent versions just cited, ignore a crucial aspect that is strictly inherent in banking: the role that banks play in the payments system and the constraints that derive for their money creation power from their payment obligations and from the structures and rules of the payment system(s) where they operate.

Indeed, banks create the money they lend by fiat, in the form of newly issued demand deposits, and do not need central bank reserves to do that. They simply create their own demand deposit liabilities by crediting borrowers' accounts with the funds loaned to them; by such an act of creation, new liabilities and assets are simultaneously recorded on the bank's balance sheet. In fact, banks create money not only when they lend but also when they sell deposits, for instance, in securities (re)purchase operations. Deposit lending features very close analogies to deposit selling: as banks issue deposits to customers in exchange for money, banks become owners of the money received and acquire the rights to use it as they wish, subject to existing laws and regulations (Bossone, 2021).

Money creation via lending is unique to commercial banking, in as much as banks only are allowed by regulation to (i) hold customers' demand deposits *and* issue loans to customers in the form of demand deposits and (ii) carry both operations through customer accounts held in their own books. On the other hand, these features are not shared by pure financial intermediaries, which may (a) intermediate only pre-existing funds and (b) perform lending functions only by ordering transfers of pre-existing funds to take place across bank accounts (Appendix 1).

As was noted and empirically tested by Werner in several contributions,[14] and as recently emphasized by Borio and Disyatat (2011), the distinction between lending claims on pre-existing real resources (savings) by financial intermediaries and lending claims on not yet created real resources is possible only when monetary factors are considered. In "non-monetary" (real) models, investments can only be carried out by transferring pre-existing real resources from saving units to investment units: pre-existing savings (or "endowments") are necessary to carry out investment, and when financial intermediaries are present, they perform no other functions than allocating purchasing power that already exists in the economy and is backed by output already produced. In a "monetary" economy, on the other hand, some special intermediaries—banks—do create additional purchasing power.

5.4.1 The Role of "Funding"

When banks create money by extending new loans, they need to avail themselves of the resources required (by interbank conventions, payment system rules, or central bank regulations) to settle the mutual obligations that are triggered when the newly created deposits are mobilized by borrowers to make payments or when they are redeemed by their holders against cash; otherwise they would default on their obligations and incur the related costs and penalties, including market punishments and regulatory sanctions. Indeed, contemporary payment systems in most jurisdictions across the world require that settlement takes place in central bank money since this is the safest and most liquid asset that an economy can use to settle transactions

[14] See references in Werner (2014).

(CPSS-IOSCO, 2012). The other key reason for so requiring is that, as long as banks demand reserve balances to pay each other, the central bank can set the marginal price of reserves, thus determining the opportunity cost for banks to lend funds to each other and thereby influencing interest rates in the money markets and further on across all assets markets.

Notice that the principle of settling obligations using a liquid and safe asset has been adopted by payment systems even before central banks were created and is adopted today in payment systems where the use of central bank reserves is not a feasible option. Where this is the case, settlement happens using the liability issued by one of the participating banks, typically the one bank that is most highly reputed, financially solid, and sufficiently large, which acts as a central institution providing clearinghouse and settlement services to all other banks participating in the system. All these other banks must hold enough balances of such liability for them to be able to fulfill their settlement obligations in due time. Loans may be extended by the central institution to participants that need liquidity to complete settlement, but eventually all such loans must be retired and settled in the liability issued by the central institution and which no other bank can issue (as it would not be acceptable to the others as settlement asset).[15]

Where settlement takes place in central bank money (reserves), the reserves that banks need to raise (funding) for settlement purposes consist of:

i. Cash reserves and reserves deposited with the central bank (held in response to regulatory requirements, for payment and cash-out purposes, or as part of general pool of liquid resources);
ii. Reserves from settlement of incoming payments or transfers from other banks (net of the reserves for settling outgoing payments and transfers);
iii. Borrowings from the interbank market;
iv. Borrowings from the central bank;
v. Unencumbered assets in the balance sheet that can be liquidated immediately; and
vi. New deposits of cash from (old and new) customers (new non-cash deposits may consist only of deposits transferred from other banks, which as such fall under item ii).

Thus, while banks may in principle create all the money the economy is willing to absorb, in practice their money creation power (or, more precisely, their ability to support the payments activity associated with their money creation) is constrained by their own ability to raise the required funding and the cost of doing so.

True, reserves are not a binding constraint on lending in so far as central banks do not choose to determine a specific level of reserves that bring about the desired short-term interest rate, which then ration bank demand for reserves at that rate. Instead, central banks set a policy interest rate and at that rate stand ready to supply all the

[15] This solution was the norm in the clearinghouse arrangements adopted in the USA and UK in the past centuries (Norman et al., 2011) and is still today the case for several payment systems, especially for cross-border transactions (CPSS, 2013).

reserves that banks demand—the supply of reserves is thus endogenous. However, although the supply of reserves accommodates fully the demand from banks, banks do not have an infinitely elastic capacity to acquire reserves.

The capacity of each bank to raise funding (reserves) is constrained by two scale factors: (i) the size of the bank itself, as proxied by its share of the payment market(s) where it operates and (ii) the bank's level of capital (i.e., equity plus accumulated reserves). A bank's share of the payment market(s) where it operates reflects its capacity to receive funding through incoming payments from other banks, which should on balance be adequate for settling outgoing payments. The level of capital of a bank, on the other hand, reflects (ceteris paribus) its capacity to access (borrow) external funding to ensure settlement of its obligations under adverse contingencies, such as temporary liquidity shortages.

On the other hand, three factors allow banks to economize on the use (and cost) of reserves (funding):

a. ***The economy's desire to hold commercial bank deposits that pay less interest than bonds.*** Such preference, noted by Baltensperger and Jordan (1997), is due to the "moneyness" of demand deposits, as supported by the whole complex of institutional, technical, and policy solutions that support public trust in their use as money (which includes inter alia payment infrastructures, banking supervision, central bank liquidity support, deposit insurance, etc.). This factor allows banks to save on the cost of funding relative to non-bank financial intermediaries.
b. ***The payments market share of each individual banks.*** In a fractional reserve regime, banks hold only a fraction of reserves against their total deposit liabilities out of which payments take place. Similarly, the volume of reserves they use for settling interbank obligations and for cash withdrawal from customers are only a fraction of the total transactions settled. Economies of scale related to the share of the payments market captured by a bank allow the bank to economize on the use of reserves. Such economies specifically relate to i) the share of total payment transactions that a bank intermediates: the larger the share of incoming payments (and, hence, of settlement reserves received) the bank receives from the others, the less it needs to raise and hold reserves to settle outgoing payments, and ii) the number of depositors: this allows the bank to settle a larger share of payments in its own books ("on us" payments), to expand its sources of reserves through incoming transfers and payment, and to benefit from asynchronous withdrawals of deposits from depositors. Consolidation generates increasing returns for banks, enabling them to create liabilities (by lending or selling deposits) with decreasing reserve margins needed for coverage. Here, economies of scale in the use of reserves combine with scale economies in bank production, which empirical research shows to be significant.[16]

[16] See Anolli et al. (2015) and Wheelock and Wilson (2015), and the ample literature therein referred, which show that banks (especially large ones) operate under increasing returns to scale in production. Also, value-maximizing financial intermediaries benefit from "systemic scale economies" effects, whereby intermediaries operating in large systems are expected to have lower costs of production,

c. ***Rules and technologies for payment settlement.*** While the payments market share of individual banks affects, as discussed above, each bank's optimal demand for reserves at the margin, the rules and technologies for settling payments determine the structural demand for reserves of the whole system. Payment system rules determine such demand via two channels: the settlement modality (typically netting or gross) and the technology adopted for transferring value at settlement. As discussed below, each of the two modalities has a drastically different effect on the system's demand for reserves, with netting requiring much less reserves than the gross modality (at the cost of higher settlement risk). Similarly, by re-introducing elements of netting into the gross modality, modern technologies (such as liquidity-saving mechanisms in hybrid real-time gross settlement systems) do increase the velocity of reserves circulation in the payments system and allow banks to economize on the use of reserves for any given volume and value of payments to be settled. Both factors interact with payment system scale economies.[17] Appendix 2 shows how different types of payment settlement system technologies and rules affect banks' money creation power.

As an exemplification of the above factors, take the hypothetical case of a cashless economy with a fully consolidated banking system where all agents hold accounts with only one bank. In this case, all payments and money transfers would be "on us" for the single bank. The bank would need no reserves for settling transactions, it would be under no debt obligation toward its customers, and it might in fact create all the money the economy would be willing to absorb at a given interest rate without having to hold (costly) reserves. The single bank's deposit liabilities would become the accepted instrument to settle debts within the economy and would de facto be irredeemable, much as legal tender is in any economy.[18] On the other hand, in the opposite extreme case of an atomistic banking sector (with zero-dimensional banks), every single bank could still issue new deposits as loans to borrowers; yet, they would have to cover all newly issued deposits with central bank reserves.[19]

In the real world, systems are populated by pluralities of banks. Yet, in highly consolidated systems, the largest banks (and the systems as a whole) feature significant economies of scale in reserves use and can thus extract the extra seigniorage that such economies make possible vis-à-vis less consolidated systems.

---

risk absorption, and reputation signaling than intermediaries operating in small systems (Bossone and Lee, 2004).

[17] Significant scale economies in payment systems are found by Beijnen and Bolt (2007) and Humphrey (2009).

[18] This situation would be identical to that of a central bank settling all interbank payments on its books. Precisely because all payments and transfers happen on its own books, and because they take place in the money instrument that the central bank itself issues, the central bank does not need any external funding to complete the settlement process of interbank obligations.

[19] With atomistic banks, the fractional reserve regime would de facto be equivalent to a regime where the fraction is 100% and every deposit unit created by a bank must be backed with a unit of central bank reserves.

5.4.2 Optimal Bank Money Creation

The limited capacity of a bank to satisfy its funding needs acts as a constraint on the bank's power to create money by lending deposit claims issued on itself. At the margin, the cost of funding for each bank may be higher than the expected return from creating money or may become prohibitive and even unavailable at whatever price. A bank's idiosyncratic decision to, say, double at once its total lending by issuing new deposit claims would run against the bank's capacity to support the new lending with adequate funding. The bank would always be able—in principle—to create money by signing off new loans with a stroke of a pen (or, in our times, with a click on a computer pad). Yet, the new money created would not be sustainable under the bank's normal funding structure: as most of the payments generated by the new loans would go to payees holding accounts with other banks, the bank would not be able to settle its obligations since it would not be able to raise the needed funds, even if reserves in the system were not in shortage. The bank would not be able to expand at once its deposit base as needed or to capture a larger payments market share overnight; it would not have all the collateral needed to borrow from the central bank; and borrowing so much extra funds from the market might be perceived as being too risky or even suspicious by investors and bank creditors, with borrowing becoming too expensive or even being rationed and the bank's market valuation and rating being penalized as a result. Even a deep money market and a fully accommodating central bank's monetary policy stance would not help if the bank's funding structure and capital were unchanged: the marginal cost of the extra funding could become unsustainable to the bank.

The conclusion is that a bank can create money by lending or selling deposits only within an overall resource envelope that is determined by the bank's capacity to raise funds (reserves) at costs that are consistent with the sustainability of its business as a going concern. Banks do create money but they can do so within the limits of their funding plan, which must take into account their in- and out-payments (as adjusted for growth and risk factors), their borrowing capacity, and the cost of raising and holding funds vis-à-vis the prospective return from lending or investing the money created.[20] It does not matter whether the funding is in place prior or after the act of money creation: creating deposit claims, per se, does not require any funding, and central bank reserves (and even less deposits) are not what banks lend out when they extend credit to their clients. What matters, though, is that (i) funding is in place when the bank's new financial obligations to other banks (or other payment system

[20] Setting aside ethical considerations, not even gimmicks used by banks to raise capital fictitiously (see Werner, 2016, for the case of Credit Suisse) would do the trick, precisely because of the fictitious nature of the extra capital raised. Gimmicks would work only if a bank used the extra (fictitious) capital to (falsely) project the image of a larger and financially healthier institution and, hence, expand its depositor base. The additional funding only, not the larger capital per se (which is fictitious), would enable the bank to support a larger payments activity and, thus, to expand its money creation.

participants) fall due and are to be settled, and that (ii) funding can be obtained without impairing the bank's financial equilibrium and business objectives.

The bank extends loans (or sells deposit claims) within its planned funding envelope and associated costs. The bank continues this process until the marginal returns from lending and investing, adjusted for risks and administrative costs, no longer exceed the marginal cost of raising and holding funds (Tobin, 1963).[21] On this very price mechanism rests ultimately the power of central banks to govern monetary conditions in contemporary economies, where sophisticated markets make the use of direct control instruments (e.g., required reserve ratios or credit ceilings) inefficient and ineffective. Central banks operate indirectly by changing the policy interest rates and by publicly communicating their policy strategy in view of achieving their low-inflation objective. These indirect instruments are intended to affect the current and expected costs of funding to the banks, thus influencing their risk-return prospects and ultimately their money creation decisions. Other regulatory tools (such as capital, liquidity, and leverage ratios) may act as constraints on the overall power of banks to create money; they do not intervene directly on deposit issuances but influence the cost factors that banks consider when extending new credit. Importantly, also, they link the money creation power of each bank to the size of the bank, as discussed next.

It must be noted, however, that in a context where most or all banks were to decide conjointly to expand their lending activity, the funding constrains of each bank would be simultaneously relieved as payments in the system would (be expected to) increase and, hence, generate larger funding flows from incoming payments triggered by new loans: this would by itself enhance the banks' money creation power (all else equal). Such circumstance would be typical of expansionary phases of the business or financial cycle, where positive anticipations of future higher activity levels, supported by an accommodative stance of monetary policy, encourage and coordinate individual bank decisions toward more lending. Obviously, the opposite would happen during contractionary phases and following central bank signals of monetary policy tightening.

Notice that what precedes assumes a monetary policy operating framework that is based on scarce reserves to set a "corridor" of policy rates, as has been (and still is) typically the case in most jurisdictions worldwide. Different conclusions would derive in those systems (today only a handful) that adopt frameworks with abundant reserves to see a "floor" policy interest rate (Borio, 2023). In the latter, obviously, bank money creation through lending would be unconstrained by reserves and would only be limited by the demand for loans, or for bank money, and by supply limitations (e.g., rationing) determined by bank's internal decisions.

All considered, it can be concluded that under the fractional reserve regimes that characterize all contemporary capitalist economies, bank money is endogenous in the sense that the amount of bank money that exists at any point in time is determined within the system and by the system, based on its needs and the terms and conditions, and ultimately the price, at which the money is demanded and supplied. The central

[21] Before achieving such equality, lending may be limited by the bank's decision to ration it or by regulatory (administrative) restrictions that limit its supply.

bank governs the process from outside by influencing the price through its policy rates but being willing to accommodate all the reserves demanded at the set price.

5.4.3 *The Costs of Creating Bank Money*

The earlier discussion clarifies that there are costs involved in money creation by banks. While banks can issue deposits at (virtually) zero cost, supporting the payments activity triggered by deposit issuances require them to face the costs of raising and managing adequate liquidity. As noted, this constrains their money creation power and the associated seigniorage extraction.

Looking more broadly, there are other fundamental cost elements that need to be considered when evaluating bank money creation. Following Rendahl and Freund (2019), not only adequate liquidity is necessary, as noted; solvency as well is a fundamental precondition for bank money to be supported by public trust and trade at par with central bank issued money, either in the form of currency (which individuals and businesses can use to settle transactions) or reserves (which commercial banks use for the same purpose), including for having access to liquidity under normal condition or when necessary under extraordinary circumstances. That is, bank deposits can be accepted in society as money only to the extent that the issuing banks are trusted to hold sufficient and healthy assets.

This, in turn, requires banks to invest significant resources in activities, organizational structure, and infrastructure for them to be able to select the right assets (loans, securities, commercial activities) and monitor their performance, as well as to earn enough revenues to maintain profitability, accumulate financial and reputational capital over time, and build robustness and resilience against potential adversities. All this involves costs that diminish banks' seigniorage extraction.

5.5 Bank Seigniorage

If banks create money by fiat and extract from it a value that exceeds the cost of producing it and the cost of providing services relating to its use (typically, monetary and payment services), then they do receive a rent that, as such, represents unearned income that goes to the exclusive benefit of the bank owners. Following Macfarlane et al., cit., bank seigniorage is operationally understood as the additional costs a bank would have had to incur if, rather than being able to create, it was instead forced to first borrow the money it itself then lends out in the market. This net saving (made possible by the bank's money creation power) allows for the bank to gain an extra profit (i.e., a profit level exceeding its normal level), which corresponds to a form of unearned income (rent).

5.5.1 Conditions for Bank Seigniorage

This section shows the conditions under which commercial banks extract seigniorage from the economy through money creation. Bank B operates as a profit-maximizing firm in a fractional reserve regime. It is authorized both to offer its customers demand deposit (DD_B) accounts earning interest i_{DD} and to lend money to borrowers by crediting their accounts with funds L_B (and by issuing to them equivalent deposit claims) at interest i_{L}, where, for simplicity, the bank faces no costs other than deposit remuneration and the cost of raising central bank reserves RES needed to back its deposits liabilities.

Bank B's payments market share is proxied by $\sigma_B = \frac{\mathrm{DD}_B}{\mathrm{DD}}$, the ratio of the bank's demand deposit liabilities over total demand deposits outstanding in the system, DD.[22] Scale effects are such that at zero-dimensional share, $\sigma_B = 0$, bank B operates in a perfectly competitive environment and enjoys no economies of scale in liabilities management, whereas at maximum share, $\sigma_B = 1$, the bank enjoys the largest economies of scale in liabilities management possible; it is a monopolist in the lending market and a monopsonist in the deposits market.

Bank B's cost structure, thus, is given by:

$$[(1 - \mu_B)i_{\mathrm{DD}} + \mu_B i_{\mathrm{RES}}]\mathrm{DD}_B = \phi_{\mathrm{DD}}\mathrm{DD}_B,$$

where $\mu_B = \frac{\mathrm{RES}_B}{\mathrm{DD}_B}$, with $0 \leq \mu_B \leq 1$, where i_{RES} is the interest rate at which the central bank lends reserves and is a policy instrument controlled by the central bank, and where $\mu_B = 0$ for $\sigma_B = 1$ and $\mu_B = 1$ for $\sigma_B = 0$, that is, in principle, parameter μ_B may vary from 0 to 1, taking the extreme value of zero in the (hypothetical) case of a cashless economy with only one bank, where all payments are all "on us" and their settlement does not require central reserves, and taking the extreme value of 1 in a perfectly competitive economy with atomistic banks. Parameter μ_B could also be set by central bank regulation or, else, it could be set by each bank as part of its liquidity management policy. In this last case, and assuming a fractional reserves regime, the parameter would also be a function of the structure, rules, and procedures of the payment system(s) where each bank operates.

Note that $\phi_{\mathrm{DD}} = \phi_{\mathrm{DD}}(i_{\mathrm{DD}}, \mu_B, i_{\mathrm{RES}})$ is the cost of raising and holding reserves RES as a fraction of demand deposit liabilities and includes both the remuneration of bank B's demand deposit liabilities and the cost of accessing reserves through alternative sources. At i_{RES}, the central bank supplies all the reserves that banks demand. One may therefore posit:

i. $i_L = i_L(\sigma_B)$, with $\frac{\partial i_L}{\partial \sigma_B} > 0$ and $i_L = i_L^*$ for $\sigma_B = 0$,

   where i_L^* is the equilibrium loan interest rate under perfect competition,

ii. $i_{\mathrm{DD}} = i_{\mathrm{DD}}(\sigma_B)$, with $\frac{\partial i_{\mathrm{DD}}}{\partial \sigma_B} < 0$ and $i_{\mathrm{DD}} = i_{\mathrm{DD}}^*$ for $\sigma_B = 0$,

[22] The payments market share could obviously be proxied by alternative and more accurate indicators; however, this issue does not need to detain us here.

where i^*_{DD} is the equilibrium deposit interest rate under perfect competition, and

iii. $\mu_B = \mu(\sigma_B)$, with $\mu' > 0$ and $\begin{cases} \lim\limits_{\sigma \to 0} \mu_B = 1 \\ \lim\limits_{\sigma \to 1} \mu_B = 0 \end{cases}$

Item (iii) implies that, as the bank's payments market share grows, the bank economizes on the reserves held at the central bank.

Bank B's loan supply function is:

$$L^S_B = L^S_B(i_L - \phi_{\text{DD}}) = L^S_B(i_L, \phi_{\text{DD}}(i_{\text{DD}})) \leq L^S_B(\rho) \text{ for given } \mu_B \text{ and } i_{\text{Res}},$$

$$\text{with } i_L > \phi_{\text{DD}} \text{ and } \begin{cases} L^{S'}_B > 0 \text{ for } i_L \leq \rho \\ L^{S'}_B = 0 \text{ for } i_L > \rho \end{cases},$$

where ρ is the critical credit risk threshold, beyond which bank B no longer lends (i.e., the bank rations the supply of loans), and where the demand functions for bank B's loans is:

$$L^D_B = L^D_B(i_L) \quad \text{with } L^{D'}_B < 0,$$

On the deposits market side, while the supply is determined by the supply of loans, the demand for bank B's deposits is:

$$\text{DD}^D_B = \text{DD}^D_B(i_{\text{DD}}) \quad \text{with DD}^{D'}_B > 0$$

Under the above conditions, at the zero-dimensional market share ($\sigma_B = 0$), that is, with perfect competition, equilibrium attains at:

$$L^*_B = \min_L\left[L^*_B\left(i^*_L, i^*_{\text{DD}}\right), L^S_B(\rho)\right]$$

where bank B's maximum profit is normal profit:

$$(A1) \quad \text{Max } \Pi_B|_{\sigma_B=0} = i^*_L L^*_B\left(i^*_L,\ i^*_{\text{DD}}\right) - \phi_{\text{DD}}\left(i^*_{\text{DD}}\right) \text{DD}^*_B\left(i^*_{\text{DD}}\right)$$

for given μ_B and i_{RES} and $i^*_L \leq \rho$. Call π^*_B the unit normal profit rate, at which bank B extracts no seigniorage. As the market share of bank B's increases, the bank enjoys larger scale economies and greater monopolistic and/or monopsonistic powers; as a result, its profit grows above normal (or zero extra profit),

$$\text{Max } \Pi_B|_{\sigma_B=1} > \text{Max } \Pi_B|_{1>\sigma_B>0} > \text{Max } \Pi_B|_{\sigma_B=0},$$

and its unit seigniorage rent increases $s_B \equiv \pi_B - \pi^*_B > 0$. Notice that s does not reflect any value added created for the economy by bank B; it amounts to pure extraction of net resources from the economy by the bank and, unlike the seigniorage earned by the central bank (which is partly returned to the state budget after covering for the central bank's expenses and profit), commercial bank seigniorage is owned by the bank (net of any tax imposed by the state on the banks' income).

Notice that, in the real world, commercial banks provide various types of services in addition to lending (e.g., for account management and payments), typically against the charge of fees and commissions from customers. In this chapter, for reasons of simplicity, but without loss of generality for its results, it is assumed that banks only accept deposits from customers and lend money to borrowers in the form of newly issued deposits, and do not carry out any other value-adding activities.

5.5.2 Seigniorage from Money Creation Versus Profit from Financial Intermediation

This section clarifies the distinction between seigniorage from commercial bank money creation and profit from pure financial intermediation. A stripped-down-to-the-bone model is used that builds on two financial intermediaries, a commercial bank ("bank") and a pure intermediary, respectively. The two differ from each other precisely and only for the money creation power that characterizes the bank exclusively, while they are identical in all other respects.

Call the two financial intermediaries bank B and pure intermediary I. Bank B is the same as in previous subsection. Pure intermediary I is authorized to offer its customers (non-demand) term deposit (TD_I) accounts bearing interest i_{TD} and to lend long-term funds L_I at interest i_I. Both intermediaries operate in identical quasi-monopolistic market environments and at the same scale,$1 > \sigma_B = \sigma_I > 0$.

For purposes of comparison, the following additional assumptions apply. The two entities feature identical administrative and operational cost structures (including, inter alia, such items as the costs for screening, selecting, and monitoring borrowers, and those to enforce contract terms), which for simplicity are here set to zero. They charge on loans the same net-of-risk interest rate ($i_L = i_I$). Credit rationing is assumed away.

As in Sect. 5.4.1, bank B maximizes profits:

$$\Pi_B|_{1\geq\sigma_B\geq 0} = i_L L_B(i_L, i_{\mathrm{DD}}) - \phi_{\mathrm{DD}}(i_{\mathrm{DD}})\mathrm{DD}_B(i_{\mathrm{DD}}).$$

Similarly, pure intermediary I maximizes profits:

$$\Pi_I|_{1\geq\sigma_I\geq 0} = i_{\mathrm{TD}} L_I(i_I, i_{\mathrm{TD}}) - i_{\mathrm{TD}}\mathrm{TD}_I(i_{\mathrm{TD}}),$$

where $\Pi_{B,I}|_{\sigma_I=0}$ sets the normal (zero excess) profit of the two intermediaries under perfect competition. Now, looking at bank B's cost structure, notice that the variable RES consists of reserves from incoming payments (RINP) and borrowed reserves (BR), which include reserves borrowed (wholesale) from other banks (RW) and those borrowed from the central bank (RCB), which also reflect the cost of holding collateral (safe and liquid) assets against potential cash borrowing needs. Knowing that $i_{\text{DD}} < i_{\text{TD}}$, and noting that:

$$i_{\text{RES}} = \frac{i_{\text{RINP}}\text{RINP} + i_{\text{BR}}\text{BR}}{\text{RES}}$$

where $i_{\text{RINP}} = 0 < i_{\text{TD}}$,[23] and $i_{\text{BR}} = \frac{i_{\text{RW}}\text{RW}+i_{\text{CB}}\text{RCB}}{\text{BR}} < i_{\text{TD}}$, since the cost of borrowing reserves from the interbank market or from the central bank is lower than the interest rate on term deposits, the following strict inequality holds:

$$\phi_{\text{DD}} \equiv (1 - \mu_B)i_{\text{DD}} + \mu_B i_{\text{RES}} \ll i_{\text{TD}},$$

that is, all else equal, bank B's cost of liabilities management is strictly lower than for pure intermediary I. Moreover, since both are profit maximizers and the marginal cost of lending is lower for bank B than for pure intermediary I, the former will always be able to create money and expand equilibrium lending beyond what is feasible for the pure intermediary, that is, $L_B^* \gg L_I^*$, where L_B^* is the volume of loans that the economy is willing to borrow at i_L^*, where $i_L^* < i_I^*$ are equilibrium values. Thus, it will always be the case that:

$$\Pi_B|_{1>\sigma_B=\sigma_I>0} - \Pi_I|_{1>\sigma_I=\sigma_B>0} \gg 0.$$

It follows that, all else equal, money creation allows commercial banks to extract from the economy larger rents than is possible for pure financial intermediaries, under (hypothetically) identical market (and price) conditions. Importantly, in the above hypothetical case, monopolistic/monopsonistic powers affect both intermediaries identically; thus, the extra profit extracted by the bank (which goes into seigniorage) is due exclusively to its money creation power, which by construction is precluded to the pure financial intermediary. This would be apparent considering, for instance, the effect of an increase in scale σ_B on bank B's cost structure ϕ_{DD} through parameter μ_B (all else being equal), and hence on interest margin $i_I - \phi_{\text{DD}}$, given prices i_L and i_{DD}, and thus ruling our monopolistic and/or monopsonistic effects.

Consolidation increases seigniorage not (only) because it grants the consolidated banking institutions higher quasi-monopolistic and monopsonistic powers—over loans, deposits, and their prices (interest rates)—but because it enhances their power to expand their balance sheet by deposit creation while economizing on the resources (reserves) needed to back the deposits and to support the interbank payments activity associated with the deposits created.

One way of setting apart a bank's market power from its seigniorage power is to consider that the latter affects quantities (i.e., it enhances the bank's power to create

[23] Notice that the zero cost of reserves from incoming payments and transfers, as a cost of *funding*, should not be confused with the positive (opportunity) cost of *holding* reserves (that remunerate less than the best available investment alternative).

money by economizing on reserves) while the former works through prices (since it enables the bank to increase the loan-deposit interest rate spread).

5.6 Reflections on Bank Seigniorage and Conclusion

Seigniorage is rooted in the historical prerogative of governments to mint and issue currency. Etymologically understood as the "right of the lord to mint money," seigniorage has historically belonged to governments. Through the monopoly of coinage, governments could effectively extract resources from the economy, functioning as a form of implicit taxation (Buiter, 2007). This historical context underscores the significance of seigniorage as a mechanism for wealth transfer from the broader economy to the governing authority.

Over time, with the evolution of modern monetary systems, the role of money creation was more centralized, typically within the purview of central banks. These institutions have eventually become the guardians of monetary policy and currency issuance, assuming responsibility for generating seigniorage. However, the relationship between central banks and governments varies across different economic systems, with some central banks operating independently of direct government control, while others maintain closer ties or even function as government agencies.

In contemporary economies, seigniorage remains a crucial aspect of monetary policy and fiscal management. The revenues generated from seigniorage contribute to government finances, helping to fund public expenditures and service debt obligations. Moreover, seigniorage plays a role in influencing monetary policy decisions, as central banks navigate the delicate balance between price stability, economic growth, and financial stability.

Does it then make sense to talk about seigniorage in the case of banks? Is the concept correctly applicable to them? Some do raise their eyebrows at the notion of attributing seigniorage to banks, given their traditional portrayal as intermediaries rather than creators of money. This skepticism is deeply rooted in the longstanding belief that money creation is a prerogative of the state, a notion reinforced by mainstream economic theories. While there is a gradual shift in this perception within the economics community, entrenched historical perspectives continue to cast doubt on the association of seigniorage with banks.

Nevertheless, these reservations can be mitigated by acknowledging that seigniorage is fundamentally linked to the function of money creation, rather than the specific legal identity of the entity engaged in it. Although banks do not operate in isolation when creating money—their deposit liabilities must be backed by liquid assets, when accepted as money instruments in the payment process. These can take the form of central bank reserves or highly liquidable securities that can be easily converted into central bank reserves, or else peer bank liabilities when these act as settlement money. It is important to recognize, however, that this backing need only be partial, especially in fractional reserve banking systems. From this perspective, bank seigniorage emerges from leveraging fractional reserve systems to expand the money supply, as elaborated upon below.[24] Appendix 3 further delves into the relationship between bank money, central bank reserves, and seigniorage.

Before concluding, let us delve deeper into two possible counterarguments to bank seigniorage. The first is that the income earned by banks on the deposits issued as loans is not a rent but rather the compensation for the valuable resource allocation services that banks provide, inter alia, through the application of specialized resource-intensive screening and monitoring technologies. Here, it is essential to notice that while these services contribute to overall output and merit fair compensation, they are not inherently linked to the process of money creation by banks, as Part II of this book will show. These services can be provided through pure intermediation without necessitating the creation of money.

The second counterargument is that the rents generated from bank seigniorage ultimately benefit bank shareholders in the form of dividends, similar to how central bank profits from seigniorage are returned to the government. Here, some clear distinctions must be drawn between the different destinations of seigniorage. Unlike central banks, which extract resources from the economy but largely return them to the public through the government budget, commercial banks appropriate these resources for their owners. While owners may reinvest these resources into the economy, this reallocation does not fully compensate those who initially bore the burden of seigniorage.

In conclusion, this chapter has analyzed the money creation process of commercial banks and has emphasized the role that the payment system plays in limiting such process. In particular, the chapter has investigated how banks' payment obligations, and the payment system rules that govern settlement, influence the extent to which each bank can exercise the power to create money. Also, the chapter has studied how money creation enables banks to extract seigniorage from the economy and how bank seigniorage differs from the profits derived from pure financial intermediation. Finally, the chapter has drawn distinctions between central bank seigniorage and commercial bank seigniorage.

The next natural question now is, does bank seigniorage affect the economy and how? This is a very relevant and new issue, and it is the topic of this chapter.

[24] A critical argument against this conclusion is that commercial banks lack the same capacity as governments to extract seigniorage, since, unlike governments, they cannot as easily expand their balance sheets. In fact, historical trends challenge this notion, with examples such as US banks holding more reserve balances at the Federal Reserve in the past, despite significant growth in payment volumes. This highlights the disconnect between changes in central bank reserves and nominal economic variables like GDP or transaction values, contrasting with the strong correlation between bank money creation and associated transactions (payments). Thus, despite individual banks facing limitations, the power of banks collectively to extract seigniorage remains substantial relative to governments.

Appendix 1: Bank Lending Versus Lending from Nonbank Financial Intermediaries

When a nonbank financial intermediary intermediates funds, say, by accepting funds from savers against the issuance of term deposits or securities and by lending them as, say, mortgages to homebuyers, the intermediary typically receives the funds in an account that it holds with a bank and transfers those funds from that account to the bank accounts of the homebuyers.

In such a case of pure financial intermediation, there is no money creation and the funds on-lent to the homebuyers are the same funds that were originally saved by the intermediary's customers. As said, both the intermediary and its borrowers hold deposit accounts with banks and all fund transfers in the example (i.e., from the savers to the intermediary, and from the intermediary to the homebuyers) take place across deposit accounts held with banks.

The crucial difference between banks and pure financial intermediaries, as explained by Werner (2014) and as discussed above, is that only banks (not the intermediaries) may—by regulation—credit their borrowers' bank deposit accounts with newly issued deposit claims. It is this special account structure, permitted by regulation, that confers on the banks the power to "create" money by allowing them to originate new assets (loans) and equivalent new liabilities (deposits).

Thus, money creation by lending is unique to banking, in as much as banks only are allowed by regulation to (i) hold customers' demand deposit liabilities and issue loans to customers in the form of demand deposit claims and (ii) carry both operations through customer accounts held in their own books. On the other hand, as shown in Sect. 5.4, these features are not shared by pure financial intermediaries, which may (a) intermediate only pre-existing funds and (b) perform lending functions only by ordering fund transfers to take place across accounts held with banks. Unlike banks, pure intermediaries may not, and cannot, create money by issuing new deposit liabilities and originating corresponding loan assets.

Appendix 2: The Influence of Bank Money Creation and Payment System Structures and Rules

It is important to understand bank money creation in the context of different types of payment settlement systems. In this appendix, following current practice worldwide, it is assumed that settlement of interbank payments takes place in central bank money (reserves). Since holding reserves carries an opportunity cost for banks (unless such reserves are remunerated at the same level as their best possible alternative option), the cost from holding reserves detracts from commercial bank extra profit. As different payment settlement systems require banks (ceteris paribus) to mobilize different volumes of reserves, each type of system has a different impact on bank extra profits.

A simple numerical example makes the point. Take an economy with a central bank (CB), two banks (A, B), and four customers (a1, a2, b1, b2), where a1 and a2 are customers of bank A and b1 and b2 are customers of bank B. Banks A and B hold no reserves with CB initially. The case is analyzed where the same transactions are executed and settled in two different systems, respectively: (i) a real-time gross settlement (RTGS) system and (ii) a deferred netting settlement (DNS) system.

RTGS and DNS Systems

In RTGS systems transfer of money or securities takes place from one bank to another on a "real time" and on a "gross" basis. Settlement in "real time" means payment transaction is not subject to any waiting period: the transactions are settled as soon as they are received, accepted, and processed. Transactions are executed only if they are covered by sufficient liquidity. "Gross" settlement means that transactions are settled on a one-to-one basis, without bundling or netting them against any other transactions. Once executed, payments are settled with "finality" (funds transfers are irrevocable and unconditional). In DNS systems, credit and debit transactions are recorded on the clearinghouse books throughout the business day, and at the end of the operating day (in case of one netting cycle) or at the end of each netting cycle (in case of multiple cycles a day), the clearinghouse calculates the total "net" multilateral balances of all transactions and determines what each bank owes to/is due from all others. Settlement of such balances then takes place with finality.

Reserve Management in RTGS Systems

The following sequence takes place:

- A lends $100 to a1 (and creates an equal amount of deposits)
- a1 pays $100 to b1
- A borrows $100 from CB and transfers $100 to B: interbank settlement is done
- B lends $150 to b2 (and creates an equal amount of deposits)
- b2 pays $150 to a2
- B receives $100 from A (item 3 above) and borrows $50 from CB
- B pays $150 to A: interbank settlement is done
- A repays $100 to CB
- B borrows $50 from A and repays $50 to CB, or
- B renews its loan from CB
- At the end of the sequence, CB has issued $150 intraday.

Under item 9 all $150 reserves go to zero by end-of-day as A and B repay their loans to CB: no net central bank money (reserves) creation. Yet $250 commercial bank money (demand deposits) were created, which supported $250 worth of transactions.

Under alternative item 10, the $50 intraday loan converts into an overnight loan and becomes money supply: $50 net reserves creation. But, as above, $250 demand deposits were created by banks, which supported $250 worth of transactions.

Reserve Management in DNS Systems

Assuming the same transactions take place in a NSS, it can be immediately seen here that the end-of-day balance to be settled between A and B is $50, which B borrows from CB. Although this resembles item 10 above, netting in fact saves borrowing costs overall, since under RTGS total borrowing from CB is $150 while under netting it is only $50. Deposit creation and transactions are as above.

In both cases, commercial bank money has been created in excess of central bank money and has supported a correspondingly larger volume of (real and financial) transactions. As the demands for converting deposits into cash are limited, the greatest share of deposits created in excess of reserves remains in the system as such: this large mass of deposits outstanding (net of all conversions, destructions, and new deposit creations) earn an ongoing flow of net revenues. These net revenues originate from the banks' exclusive power to create money (in excess of central bank money) and represent their extra profits.

Money Creation, Reserve Requirements, and Extra Profits

Bank extra profits range between a maximum value when money issuance is not constrained by the demand for reserves and a minimum of zero when money issuance is subjected to full reserves requirements (e.g., currency board, 100% reserve, or narrow banking). In all intermediate cases, profits are above zero.

Appendix 3: Bank Money, Central Bank Reserves, and Seigniorage

Banks always need to hold adequate reserves to settle payments (BIS, 2013), and if they do not have enough of them (since reserves may be inadequate in the aggregate, or they may be adequate in the aggregate but inadequately distributed across banks), banks must borrow them. Banks normally attract reserves every day by receiving payments from other banks, which they need to settle their own payments in turn. Should they (hypothetically) not receive incoming payments, they would run out of reserve balances very soon, given the huge disproportion of reserve holdings vs. the value of payment settlements.

True, surplus banks may lend their reserve surpluses to deficit banks and thus allow them to settle. Yet, the latter will have to come up with extra reserves to pay their debts to the surplus banks and continue to operate. And if surplus banks were unwilling to lend, or if the total stock of reserves were inadequate vis-à-vis the extant settlement obligations, the central bank must be there to provide the extra reserves needed. Finally, if the central bank were (hypothetically) to deny the supply of extra reserves, the payments system would come to a gridlock, with potentially systemic consequences. As was explained in this chapter, since banks are in the business of extending loans, they must always pay attention to the availability and cost of reserves, if they want to keep their business sustainable.

Yet, for the banks operating in advanced economies the world of reserves management has changed since the global financial crisis, as central banks have responded to the crisis with ultra-accommodative monetary policy programs. The increase in the supply of reserves that followed those programs has confronted the same central banks with a new sensitive issue: how to compensate banks for the loss of seigniorage deriving from both the larger reserve holdings to which they would be forced under the programs, on one side, and the low demand for loans from the economy due to the crisis, on the other.

In the USA, the Federal Reserve (FED) started paying interest on reserves (IOR). As the FED explained, the purpose was to inject more money into the economy without lowering the federal funds rate below target (Summer, 2019). But behind the scenes the seigniorage story is evident, and the IOR has since been fiscal policy in disguise: an outright subsidy to the banks whereby the FED transfers part of its own seigniorage to the banks to support their balance sheet. This is eventually at the expense of the US Treasury, which is the ultimate beneficiary of the FED's seigniorage revenue (Haslag, 1998).

The same was not done in Europe and Japan, where even negative interest rates (NIR) were applied on bank reserves, under the expectation that the contraction of seigniorage would push banks to recover it by increasing lending to the economy. In fact, NIR acted as an extra tax on the European banks and two-tier systems for reserve remuneration were eventually introduced to reduce the NIR impact on their seigniorage (Tötterman, 2019).

References

Adrian, T., & Mancini-Griffoli, T. (2019). *The rise of digital money.* FinTech Notes, Note/19/01. International Monetary Fund.

Anolli, M., Beccalli, E., & Borello, G. (2015). Are European banks too big? Evidence on economies of scale. *Journal of Banking and Finance, 58*, 232–246.

Arby, M. F. (2006). Seigniorage Earnings of Commercial Banks and State Bank of Pakistan. Munich Personal RePEc Archive.

Baltensperger, E. (1980). Alternative approaches to the theory of the banking firm. *Journal of Monetary Economics, 6*, 1–37.

Baltensperger, E., & Jordan, T. J. (1997). Seigniorage, banking, and the optimal quantity of money. *Journal of Banking and Finance, 21*(6), 781–796.

Beijnen, C., & Bolt, W. (2007). Size matters: Economies of scale in European payments processing. DNB Working Paper, No. 155.

Bernanke, B. S. (1993). Credit in the macroeconomy. *FRBNY Quarterly Review*. Federal Reserve Bank of New York, New York, pp 50–70

Bernanke, B. S., & Blinder, A. S. (1988). Credit, Money, and Aggregate Demand. *The American Economic Review, 78*(2), 435–439.

Bernanke, B. S., & Gertler, M. (1995). Inside the black box: The credit channel of monetary policy transmission. *Journal of Economic Perspectives, 9*(4), 27–48.

Bjerg, O., McCann, D., Macfarlane, L., Nielsen, R. H., & Ryan-Collins, J. (2017), Seigniorage in the 21st Century: A study of the profits from money creation in the United Kingdom and Denmark. CBS Working Paper.

Borio, C., & Disyatat, P. (2011). *Global imbalances and the financial crisis: Link or no link?* BIS Working Papers No. 346. Bank for International Settlements.
Borio, C. (2023). Getting up from the floor. BIS Working Papers No. 1100.
Bossone, B. (2000). What Makes Banks Special? A study on banking, finance, and economic development. Policy Research Working Paper, WPS2408. The World Bank.
Bossone, B. (2001). Circuit theory of banking and finance. *Journal of Banking and Finance, 25*(5), 857–890.
Bossone, B. (2020). Bank create money (but only to a point): The 'payments perspective.' *Journal of Payments Strategy and Systems, 14*(3), 286–304.
Bossone, B. (2021). Commercial bank seigniorage and the macroeconomy. *International Review of Financial Analysis, 76*, 1–15.
Bossone, B., & Lee, J. K. (2004). In finance, size matters. *IMF Staff Papers, 51*(1), 19–46.
Brunnermeier, M., & Sannikov, Y. (2016). The i theory of money. Mimeo.
Buiter, W. H. (2007). Seigniorage. Discussion Paper, Economics, No. 2007-8.
Buiter, W. H., Sibert, A. C., Tollenaar, N. (2022). E-money tokens, tokenised money-market shares, and tokenised bank deposits. VoxEu.
Cardoso, E. (2003). Seigniorage, reserve requirements, and spreads in Brazil. In P. Honohan (Ed.), *Taxation of financial intermediation: Theory and practice for emerging economies* (pp. 241–267). Oxford University Press and World Bank.
Cassel, G. (1923). *The Theory of Social Economy*. T. Fisher Unwin.
Casu, B., Girardone, C., Molineux, P. (2006). *Introduction to Banking*. FT Prentice Hall, Pearson Education Ltd.
Cecchetti, S. G. (2008). *Money, banking and financial markets* (2nd ed.). McGraw-Hill Irwin.
CPSS. (2003). *The role of central bank money in payment systems, report by the Committee on Payment and Settlement Systems*. Bank for International Settlements, Basel.
CPSS-IOSCO. (2012). *Principles for financial market infrastructures*. Joint report by the Committee on Payment and Settlement Systems Technical Committee of the International Organization of Securities Commissions, Bank for International Settlements, Basel.
Crick, W. F. (1927). The genesis of bank deposits. *Economica, 7*(20), 191.
Davenport, H. J. (1913). *The economics of enterprise*. Augustus M. Kelley.
Diamond, D. W., & Dybvig, P. H. (1983). Bank runs, deposit insurance, and liquidity. *The Journal of Political Economy., 91*(3), 401–419.
Fama, E. (1980). Banking in the theory of finance. *Journal of Monetary Economics, 6*, 39–57.
Fullwiler, S. (2012). *Krugman's flashing Neon sign*. Naked Capitalism.
Graziani, A. (2003). *The monetary theory of production*. Cambridge University Press.
Gurley, J. G., & Shaw, E. S. (1955). Financial aspects of economic development. *American Economic Review, 45*, 515–528.
Gurley, J. G., & Shaw, E. S. (1960). *Money in a theory of finance*. The Brookings Institution.
Haslag, J. H. (1998). *Seigniorage revenue and monetary policy economic review*. Third Quarter, Federal Reserve Bank of Dallas.
Hawtrey, R. G. (1919). *Currency and credit*. Longmans, Green and Co.
Von Hayek, F. (1929). *Geldtheorie und Konjunkturtheorie*, Hölder-Pichler-Tempsky.
Hoppe, H. H., Hülsmann, J. G., & Block, W. (1998). Against fiduciary media. *Quarterly Journal of Austrian Economics, 1*(1), 19–50.
Howe, R. H. (1915). *The evolution of banking; A study of the development of the credit system*. C. H. Kerr & Company.
Humphrey, D. B. (2009). Retail payments: Integration and innovation payment scale economies, competition, and pricing. ECB Working Paper Series, No. 1136.
Jakab, Z., & Kumhof, M. (2015). Banks are not intermediaries of loanable funds—and why this matters. Working Paper No. 529, Bank of England.
Kashyap, A., Rajan, R. G., & Stein, J. (2002). Banks as liquidity providers: An explanation for the coexistence of lending and deposit-taking. *Journal of Finance, 57*, 33–73.
Keynes, J. M. (1924). *Tract on monetary reform*. Macmillan.

Keynes, J. M. (1930). *A treatise on money*. Macmillan.

Macfarlane, L., Ryan-Collins, J., Bjerg, O., Nielsen, R., & McCann, D. (2017). *Making money from making money. Seigniorage in the modern economy*. New Economics Foundation, Copenhagen Business School.

MacLeod, H. D. (1856). *The theory and practice of banking* (Vol. 2). Longman, Greens and Co.

Macmillan, H. (1931). Report of the Committee on Finance and Industry. CMD 3897, HMSO, London.

Mankiw, N. G. (2019). *Macroeconomics* (10th ed.). Worth Publishers.

Matthews, K., & Thompson, J. (2005). *The Economics of Banking*. John Wiley and Sons.

Moore, B. (1979). The endogenous money stock. *Journal of Post Keynesian Economics, 2*(1), 49–70.

Moore, B. (1983). Unpacking the post Keynesian black box: Bank lending and the money supply. *Journal of Post Keynesian Economics, 5*(4), 537–556.

Morelli, M. (2018). *Signoraggio Secondario, Banche e Creazione di Moneta: Un Sistema Insostenibile?* Università degli Studi di Macerata.

Norman, B., Shaw, R., & Speight, G. (2011). The history of interbank settlement arrangements: Exploring central banks' role in the payment system. Working Paper No. 412, Bank of England.

Phillips, C. A. (1920). *Bank credit*. Macmillan.

Rendahl, P., & Freund, L. B. (2019). Banks do not create money out of thin air. Vox.

Riordan, M. H. (1993). Chapter 11: Competition and bank performance: A theoretical perspective. In C. Mayer & X. Vives (Eds.), *Capital markets and financial intermediation*. Cambridge University Press.

Rossi, R., & Rochon, L. P. (eds.). (2017). *Post-Keynesian Economics*. The International Library of Critical Writings in Economics series, Edward Elgar Publishing.

Ryan-Collins, J., Greenham, T., Jackson, A., & Werner, R. A. (2012). *Where does money come from: A guide to the UK Monetary and Banking System*. New Economics Foundation.

Samuelson, P. (1948). *Economics*. McGraw-Hill.

Samuelson, P., & Nordhaus, W. (1995). *Economics*. McGraw-Hill.

Schumpeter, J. A. (1912). *Die Theorie der wirtschaftlichen Entwicklung*. Duncker und Humblot.

Sealey, C., & Lindley, J. T. (1977). Inputs, outputs and a theory of production and cost at depositary financial institutions. *Journal of Finance, 32*, 1251–1266.

Sheard, P. (2013). *Repeat after me: Banks cannot and do not 'lend out' reserves*. Standards & Poor's Rating Services, RatingsDirect, Economic Research.

Soldatos, G. T., & Varelas, E. (2015). On the quantity theory of money, credit, and seigniorage. *The International Journal of Business and Finance Research, 9*(5), 93–102.

Stiglitz, J. E. (1997). *Economics* (2nd ed.). W. W. Norton.

Summers, L. H. (2019). *The left's embrace of modern monetary theory is a recipe for disaster.* The Washington Post.

Tobin, J. (1963). Commercial banks as creators of 'money'. In: D. Carson (ed.), *Banking and Monetary Studies*. Cowles Foundation Paper 205. Irwin.

Tötterman, K. (2019). "The Eurosystem's two-tier system for remunerating excess liquidity holdings". *Bank of Finland Bulletin, 12* November.

Von Mises, L. (1912). *Theorie des Geldes und der Umlaufsmittel*. Duncker und Humblot.

Werner, R. A. (2014). How do banks create money, and why can other firms not do the same? An explanation for the coexistence of lending and deposit-taking. *International Review of Financial Analysis, 36*, 71–77.

Werner, R. A. (2016). A lost century in economics: Three theories of banking and the conclusive evidence. *International Review of Financial Analysis, 46*, 361–379.

Wheelock, D.C., & Wilson, P. W. (2015). The evolution of scale economies in U.S. banking. Economic Research. Federal Reserve Bank of Saint Louis, Working Paper 2015-021C.

Wicksell, K. (1936). *Interest and Prices: A Study of the Causes regulating the Value of Money.* MacMillan and Co., Translated by R. F. Kahn from the original Swedish (Wicksell, 1898)

Wicksell, K. (1898). *Geldzins und Guterpreise: Eine Studie über die den Tauschwert des Geldes bestimmenden Ursachen*. Gustav Fischer Verlag.

Withers, H. (1918). *The business of finance*. John Murray.

Yohe, W. P. (1995). *Interactive money and banking*. Blackwell.

Chapter 6
Money, Banks, and Seigniorage

Abstract This chapter offers an in-depth analysis of bank seigniorage, a subject that has received scant attention in existing literature, despite its significant implications for the economy. It highlights the insufficient examination of how banks, as money creators, derive seigniorage and the subsequent effects on aggregate output, price levels, and resource distribution. Utilizing both a general aggregate production function and a multi-sector model, the chapter analyzes how seigniorage extraction influences equilibrium prices and labor utilization, ultimately reshaping economic behavior and welfare distribution. The analysis reveals the intricate relationships among bank seigniorage, capital-labor dynamics, and income distribution between different sectors such as households, firms, and banks. Furthermore, the chapter aligns its findings with broader political-economy implications, offering policy recommendations aimed at ameliorating the adverse impacts of seigniorage. In doing so, it contributes to a more nuanced understanding of the complexities surrounding bank seigniorage, suggesting pathways for future empirical investigation and enhanced monetary policy frameworks.

6.1 Preamble

The last chapter discussed how commercial banks extract seigniorage from the economy by creating money through the credit channel or by selling deposit claims against securities. Strangely enough, reactions to such conclusion from reviewers of my previous works on the topic were skeptical on the very concept of bank seigniorage (as if only governments can extract seigniorage) or indifferent to the potential impact of seigniorage on the macroeconomy (as if it would be negligible, in any case).

In fact, given the widespread and important role of bank money in all contemporary economies, I hold that banks' seigniorage must not only be quantitatively significant; its nature as a form of rent must also have important effects on the macroeconomy. Specifically, it can be shown that bank seigniorage alters the economy's incentive structure and, hence, the use of labor and capital inputs in production, which in turn affects the level of aggregate output. I also hold that bank seigniorage impacts the

B. Bossone, *Trailblazing Visions of Money in Economic Theory*, Contributions to Economics, https://doi.org/10.1007/978-3-031-82544-6_6

general price level, which then changes the distribution of income among workers, firms, and banks, depending on their relative power to set their own prices and to secure their real value.

This chapter examines the economics of these relationships and illustrates the theoretical methods I have used to analyze them—notably a neoclassical model to study the aggregate output effects of bank seigniorage and a Kaleckian model (augmented with the banking sector) to study its effects on income distribution, under alternative assumptions on sector behaviors (Bossone, 2021). A natural prosecution of this strand of research would be to try to estimate the above relationships empirically and test their quantitative relevance.

6.2 Introduction

Thus far, the power of banks to extract seigniorage from the economy and the impact of seigniorage extraction on the economy (i.e., the economy's aggregate output, prices, and resource distribution) have not received attention from research,[1] although as discussed in the previous chapter, the power of banks to create money has long been recognized by important scholars (and has today been almost widely accepted even by mainstream economists).

Yet, and as seen earlier, not many contributions to the literature consider the seigniorage associated with bank money creation, and virtually none can be found that evaluates the impact of bank seigniorage on the economy. This chapter aims to fill this void.

The chapter delves into the implications of bank seigniorage, shedding light on its role in affecting aggregate output, shaping the general equilibrium price level within the economy, and influencing resource allocation across sectors. It analyzes the dynamics of bank seigniorage through the lens of an intertemporal general equilibrium model of a three-sector economy (with households, firms, and banks), where money—essential for facilitating transactions—is issued by banks in the form of demand deposits. The chapter investigates the impact of profit-maximizing banks on aggregate output both with and without seigniorage extraction.

The chapter also underscores the relationship between seigniorage, relative prices, and income distribution, and provides insights into the implications of bank seigniorage for resource allocation and economic welfare. Unlike in traditional theories of financial intermediation, where savings are leveraged, here banks finance

[1] In a post titled *Central Bankers: "We're all Post-Keynesians now,"* Jesse Frederik suggests that central bankers may have grasped the reality of commercial bank money creation somewhat earlier than academics, who in their textbooks still to this day continue to subscribe to the conventional "money multiplier" story. See also the related post *Who is right? Krugman or Keen or/and 9 Central Bank economists?*. Interestingly, among central bankers, Sir Mervyn King, former Governor of the Bank of England, addressing a conference of businesspeople once recognized that, "When banks extend loans to their customers, they create money by crediting their customers' accounts." (Speech to the South Wales Chamber of Commerce at The Millennium Centre, Cardiff on 23 October 2012).

production by issuing loans in the form of new claims on real resources, which must be repaid back to them at an interest when production is completed. This leads to net transfers of real output from the economy to the banks in the form of rents, which redistributes the economy's resources and potentially heightens tensions between capital and labor.

These findings hold implications for monetary policy, particularly in understanding how central bank interventions influence lending decisions and interest rate dynamics, and highlight the interplay between policy adjustments, inflationary pressures, and the sustainability of price adjustments, and point to potential policy measures aimed at mitigating the adverse effects of bank seigniorage.

The chapter is organized as follows. Section 6.2 reviews the existing literature on the subject and indicates the contribution of this chapter to the literature; Sect. 6.3 analyzes the effect of seigniorage on the economy's aggregate output and shows how equilibrium prices are determined when banks extract seigniorage; Sect. 6.4 studies the impact of seigniorage on resource distribution across the economy's sectors of activity and draws preliminary political-economy implications; and Sect. 6.5 discusses policies to eliminate or redistribute seigniorage. Section 6.6 closes the chapter with concluding remarks.

6.3 Bank Seigniorage and Aggregate Output

This section examines the impact of bank seigniorage on the overall output of the economy by employing an intertemporal general equilibrium model. This model encompasses various economic activities such as consumption, saving, investment, and production, alongside the presence of bank money. Within this framework, prices are determined competitively, ensuring that all factors of production receive compensation equal to their marginal productivity rate, without any agent accruing rents. Subsequently, this initial setup is utilized to observe alterations in equilibrium output and prices resulting from the extraction of seigniorage by banks, which refers to profits exceeding the norm or rents derived from the economy.

The economy consists of three sectors, households, firms, and banks. H households supply labor services N to firms, and firms are owned by entrepreneurs who organize production by employing labor and capital K through a given technology. Money is necessary to relieve the financing (cash-in-advance) constraint and to make exchange activities possible. In order for an instrument to be accepted as money in transactions, it must be a liability of reputable third parties. Banks play such role and issue money in the form of demand deposits by extending loans to firms.

Using standard notations and functional forms, as in Ravenna and Walsh (2006), household preferences are defined over a consumption good C and leisure $1 - n$, where $n = \frac{N}{H}$, and N is total supply of labor services. Thus, households maximize the expected present discounted value of utility

$$\text{Max } U = E_t\beta^i \sum_{i=0}^{\infty}\left(\frac{(c_t)^{1-\sigma}}{1-\sigma} - \chi\frac{n_{t+i}^{1-\eta}}{1+\eta}\right) \tag{6.1}$$

s.t.

$$E_t\left[\sum_{i=0}^{\infty} C_{t+i}\frac{1}{(1+r)^i}\right] = E_t\left[\sum_{i=0}^{\infty} Y_{t+i}\frac{1}{(1+i_{\mathrm{DD}})^i}\right], \tag{6.2}$$

where E_t is the expectation operator at time t, $c_t = \frac{C_t}{P_t}$, real consumption; r is the rate of time preference; and i_{DD} is the rate of demand deposit remuneration, assumed to be the only saving asset in the economy. According to Eq. (6.1), lifetime consumption must equal lifetime income. The following first-order conditions, on consumption and labor supply, respectively, hold in equilibrium:

$$c_t^{-\sigma} = \beta E_t\left[\frac{(1+i_{\mathrm{DD}t})P_{t+1}}{P_t}c_{t+1}^{-\sigma}\right] \tag{6.3}$$

$$\frac{\chi n_t^{\eta}}{c_t^{-\sigma}} = \frac{W_t}{P_t(1+i_{\mathrm{DD}t})}. \tag{6.4}$$

Banks are thought of as providing a technology that creates deposit claims. For reasons of formal tractability of the model, but without loss of generality for the purpose at hand, banks are assumed not to employ capital or labor inputs.[2] They issue and lend deposit claims $L = \mathrm{DD}$ to firms, which firms use to advance wage payments wN to households as suppliers of labor services and get production started, and which are used by households to purchase goods and to store savings. Banks are owned by a special type of entrepreneurs—bankers—who act as households in the market for goods. As from Sect. 5.5.1 of Chap. 5, banks maximize profits by supplying loans $L = wN$ demanded by firms at interest rate i_L and funding cost ϕ_{DD}:

$$\text{Max } \Pi_{Bt} = E_t\delta^j \sum_{j=0}^{\infty}\left[i_{L_{t+j}}L_B\left(i_{L_{t+j}}, i_{\mathrm{DD}_{t+j}}\right) - \phi_{\mathrm{DD}t+j}\left(i_{\mathrm{DD}_{t+j}}\right)\mathrm{DD}_B\left(i_{\mathrm{DD}_{t+j}}\right)\right], \tag{6.5}$$

Under perfect competition, the lending and funding cost rates are such that bank B earns normal profit rate π_B^* and extracts no seigniorage ($s_B = 0$). In the more general case where banks enjoy a larger payments market share, the interest margin is above its perfectly competitive equivalent and seigniorage is positive ($s_B = \pi_B - \pi_B^* > 0$).

The economy's real output is produced through a Cobb–Douglas technology with constant returns to scale, $Y_t = AK_t^{\alpha}N_t^{\beta}$, $\alpha + \beta = 1$, where A is total factor productivity, and K and N are, capital and labor inputs, respectively. Firms E own capital K and borrow

[2] The use (and compensation) of capital and labor inputs would obviously detract from seigniorage but would not alter the nexus between seigniorage and output, which is the purpose of the analysis.

$$L_B = wN \tag{6.6}$$

from the banks to hire labor services at wage w and start production of output Y.[3] Without capital adjustment cost and depreciations, they maximize expected intertemporal profits:

$$\text{Max } \Pi_{Et} = E_t\delta^j \sum_{j=0}^{\infty}\left[AK_{t+j}^{\alpha}N_{t+j}^{\beta}P_{t+j} - K_{t+j}p_{t+j}^{K} - K_{t+j-1}p_{t+j-1}^{K} - w_{t+j}N_{t+j}\left(1+i_{L_{t+j}}\right)\right] \tag{6.7}$$

where P is output price and p^K is the price of capital. The following first-order conditions follow in equilibrium:

$$\alpha AK_{t+j}^{\alpha-1}N_{t+j}^{\beta} = \frac{p_{t+j}^{K}}{P_{t+j}} \tag{6.8}$$

$$\beta AK_{t+j}^{\alpha}N_{t+j}^{\beta} = \frac{W_{t+i}}{P_{t+j}}\left(1+i_{L_{t+j}}\right) \tag{6.9}$$

Using Eq.'s. (6.5), (6.8), and (6.9), replacing them in the production function, and dropping the time subscript, equilibrium is attained at those values of the variables (Y; w, p^K, P, i_L, i_{DD}), for given values of the parameters (σ, χ, n, α, β, η), where the demand for aggregate consumption C and investment ΔK equals aggregate output supply:

$$Y^* = C^* + \Delta K^* = \mathcal{A}\left[\frac{w^*}{P^*}\frac{c^{-\sigma *}}{\chi}\frac{\left(1+i_L^*\right)}{\left(1+i_{DD}^*\right)}\right]^{-\frac{\alpha\beta}{\eta^2}}\left(\frac{p^{K*}}{P^*}\right)^{-\frac{\alpha}{\beta}}, \tag{6.10}$$

where the aster indicates equilibrium variables under perfect competition, $\mathcal{A} = \left(\frac{H}{\alpha A^{\beta}}\right)^{-\frac{\alpha}{\beta}} > 0$, $-\frac{\alpha\beta}{\eta^2} < 0$ and $-\frac{\alpha}{\beta} < 0$, the latter two inequalities implying that an increase in the real relative price of each input factor decreases the contribution of that factor to aggregate output.

Equations (6.5), (6.8), and (6.9) are key to evaluate the impact of bank seigniorage on aggregate output. Equation (6.8) shows that if bank money is needed to advance wage payments, firms employ labor up to the point where the marginal return on labor services equals the real wage augmented by the real interest rate charged on

---

[3] Here, the assumption is that firms borrow money (on a short-term basis) from banks only to advance wage payments. In principle, one could extend the assumption from labor to other inputs of the production process, and in general to all forms of working capital. Yet, this generalization would only complicate the analysis while not adding to its basic results. To contemplate the case of longer-term borrowing from firms to finance the purchase of capital, a more complicated model would be necessary to incorporate the role of financial intermediation (in addition to money creation from commercial banks). See my work cited in Sect. 6.3. This generalization, too, however, would not add to the results of the analysis.

bank loans. Equation (6.5) shows, however, that workers change their supply of labor directly with the real wage they expect to receive; thus, the interest rate charged on the money created by the banks introduces a wedge within the relative price mechanism, between the wage earned by the worker and the wage bill effectively paid by the firm, which, for a given nominal wage w would translate into a lower demand for labor services than would obtain in the hypothetical case of interest-free loans, since $N^S = \left(\frac{w^*}{P^*}\frac{c^{-\sigma *}}{\chi}\right)^{\frac{1}{\eta}} < \left(\frac{w^*(1+i_L)K_{t+i}^{-\alpha}}{(1+i_{DD})A\beta P^*}\right)^{\frac{1}{\beta}} = N^D$, for any $i_L > 0$, where superscript S and D stand for supply and demand, respectively, and output would settle at a level of labor services used that corresponds to the minimum between their demand and supply.

To analyze the effect of seigniorage, assume under *ceteris paribus* conditions an increase in the interest rate margin beyond the level consistent with normal bank profit, reflected in the model as an increase in the $\frac{1+i_L}{1+i_{\mathrm{DD}}}$ ratio, following, say, greater consolidation in the banking sector (see Chap. 5). From Eq. (6.10), such an increase would trigger a range of different possible price and output responses depending on the flexibility of factor prices:

i. Under *fully flexible nominal factor prices* w and p^K, wage w drops proportionally to the increase in the interest rate and so allows first-order condition (6.8) to be fulfilled at an unchanged level of employment, capital, and output price. In this case, a larger share of aggregate output goes from the workers to the banks.
ii. Under *fixed nominal factor prices* w and p^K, two cases are possible:
    a. Firms do not adjust prices (i.e., output price P does not change); in this case, from Eq. (6.9), the demand for labor services and, hence, equilibrium aggregate output declines, $\left[\frac{w^*}{P^*}\frac{c^{-\sigma *}}{\chi}\frac{(1+i_L)}{(1+i_{\mathrm{DD}})}\right]^{-\frac{\alpha\beta}{\eta^2}} < \left[\frac{w^*}{P^*}\frac{c^{-\sigma *}}{\chi}\frac{(1+i_L^*)}{(1+i_{\mathrm{DD}}^*)}\right]^{-\frac{\alpha\beta}{\eta^2}}$, where $i_L > i_L^*$, and $i_{\mathrm{DD}} < i_{\mathrm{DD}}^*$, and a larger share of the output produced goes from the firms and workers to the banks.
    b. Firms adjust prices (i.e., output price increases to $P' > P$) in order to absorb the higher (gross) cost of labor services, so that $\frac{w^*}{P'}\frac{(1+i_L^*)}{(1+i_{DD}^*)}) = \frac{w^*}{P^*}$. As a result, first-order conditions (6.8), (6.9) are restored at a lower level of employment N and a larger stock of capital K (since the drop in the relative price of capital requires the marginal productivity of the latter to decrease). Aggregate output is thus subject to opposite forces: from first-order condition (6.8), the real wage reduction causes workers to reduce the labor supply and, thus, to reduce output (as in the case above); on the other hand, from first-order condition (6.8), the larger use of capital leads to higher output. However, from Eq. (6.10), the net effect of the price change on aggregate output is positive:

$$\frac{\partial Y}{\partial P} = \frac{\partial \mathcal{A}\left[\frac{w}{P}\frac{c^{-\sigma}}{\chi}\frac{(1+i_L)}{(1+i_{DD})}\right]^{-\frac{\alpha\beta}{\eta^2}}\left(\frac{P^K}{P}\right)^{-\frac{\alpha}{\beta}}}{\partial P}$$

$$= \mathcal{A}\left(\frac{\alpha\beta}{\eta^2} + \frac{\alpha}{\beta}\right)\left[\frac{wc^{-\sigma}}{P\chi}\frac{(1+i_L)}{(1+(i_{DD})})\right]^{-\frac{\alpha\beta}{\eta^2}}\left(\frac{P^K}{P}\right)^{-\frac{\alpha}{\beta}}(P)^{-1} > 0 \tag{6.11}$$

Notice, however, that, at the new level of output, real wages are lower and, as a consequence, a greater share of the output produced accrues to the firms and the banks, at the expense of labor.

This result is quite interesting, considering of the realism of the price assumption that underlies it (i.e., flexible prices by firms and sticky nominal wages).

6.4 Bank Seigniorage and Resource Distribution

Consider an "augmented" Kaleckian distribution model of an economy with three sectors; firms, households, and banks—where the latter represents the model's "augmentation."[4] Define bank seigniorage as $s_B \equiv \pi_B - \pi_B^* > 0$, that is, a form of unearned income (rent) that originated from profits beyond normal rate. How does seigniorage affect this economy's price level and resource distribution?

In the case of no seigniorage, where the banking sector is perfectly competitive, the economy's real output is distributed across the three sectors of the economy as

$$Y^* = \frac{w^*N^*}{P*} + \frac{\pi_E^*K^*}{P*} + \frac{\pi_B^*L_B^*}{P*}, \tag{6.12}$$

where for π_E is the firms' unit profit rate the aster refers to perfectly competitive equilibrium values. On the other hand, where the banking sector exploits larger than atomistic shares of the payments market, bank seigniorage is positive, $s_B = \pi_B - \pi_B^* > 0$.[5] In this case, the given aggregate output produced is not enough to satisfy all sector claims that materialize at the original equilibrium price level; nor can additional output can be produced if and as the factors employed are unchanged; thus,

$$Y^* < \frac{w^*N^*}{P*} + \frac{\pi_E^*K^*}{P*} + \frac{\pi_B L_B^*}{P*}, \tag{6.13}$$

[4] The model is qualified as "Kaleckian" since it incorporates distributional dynamics (i.e., the functional income distribution between wages and profits) and assumes the interest rate to be exogenously determined as a markup over the unit cost of funds.

[5] For the reasons discussed earlier, this is not the result of banks exploiting their market power and applying a higher interest rate on their loans, but of banks exploiting scale or technology to save on the reserves used to back up their loans (or, more precisely, the payments activity deriving from their lending). At given interest rates, this would generate higher (beyond-normal) profits or rents. These rents are the seigniorage originating from bank money creation.

where $\pi_B > \pi_B^*$. To restore balance, and to accommodate the higher claims (rents) from the banks, the price level must adjust upward in order both to increase output and to redistribute it across the three sectors. While various possible price adjustment dynamics could be set in motion depending on the relative price flexibility, all dynamics bear distributional implications. Thus, in the real world, the emerging adjustment process would be determined by the bargaining power of each affected sector.

Abstracting momentarily from how the distributional tensions would be resolved between the firm and household sectors (to be discussed later), the aggregate real resource balance under seigniorage requires using some share of the output produced to pay for the higher claims (rents) extracted by the banks from the economy. One way to achieve this new balance is through a higher general price level that transfers resources across sectors, such that,

$$Y^* = \left[\frac{w^*N^*}{P^*} + \frac{\pi_E^*K^*}{P^*} + \frac{\pi_B L_B^*}{P^*}\right]\left(1 + p'\right)^{-1}, \tag{6.14}$$

yielding

$$Y^* = \left[\frac{w^*N^*}{P'} + \frac{\pi_E^*K^*}{P'} + \frac{\pi_B L_B^*}{P'}\right], \tag{6.15}$$

where $P' = \left(1 + p'\right)P^*$ is the new price level required to restore real resource balance, and p' is the implicit rate of price adjustment. Thus, by generating surplus from the economy's output beyond their initial contribution, banks gradually erode the real value of money, as detailed in Eq. (6.13). This erosion prompts an overall uptick in the price level, serving as a corrective measure to neutralize the surplus claims on the economy's output at the original equilibrium price level. It is essential to recognize that while this erosion chips away at banks' normal real profits to some extent, it fails to entirely counterbalance the rent they derive from money creation through lending.

An alternative route to restoring equilibrium in real resources could entail the adjustment being wholly absorbed by the firm and/or household sectors, leading to reduced nominal profits and/or wages at the prevailing general price level. However, the practicality of this approach remains uncertain and hinges on various factors, including the relative bargaining power of these sectors and their willingness to accept unfavorable relative prices. Notably, any incomplete adjustment in prices, allowing the imbalance delineated in Eq. (6.13) to persist, would necessitate firms to negotiate with banks for refinancing original loans they are unable to repay or face default on their obligations to banks, potentially resulting in asset seizure by the latter.

To analyze the distributional implications of bank seigniorage in greater detail, divide Eq. (6.14) by Y^* to get:

$$1 = \frac{w^*N^*}{Y^*P'} + \frac{\pi_E^*K^*}{Y^*P'} + \frac{\pi_B L_B^*}{Y^*P'} = \phi_N + \phi_E + \phi_B, \tag{6.16}$$

where the ϕ's are the shares of total real income accruing to labor, firms, and banks, respectively. Assume, then, that the price level adjusts fully, and divide the terms in the last expression of the RHS of Eq. (4.4) by the total of labor services employed N. Recalling that $wN = L_B$ and that $\pi_B = s_B + \pi_B^*$, and positing

$s_B = l_B - \pi_B^*$

any level of aggregate output per unit of labor can be decomposed as:

$$\frac{Y}{N} = \frac{w}{P} + \frac{\pi_E K}{PN} + \frac{\pi_B L_B}{PN} = \frac{w}{P}(1 + \pi_B) + \frac{\pi_E K}{PN} = \frac{w}{P}(1 + l_B) + \frac{\pi_E K}{PN}. \tag{6.17}$$

Using natural log transformations, applying Taylor's expansion to derive the equality $\ln(1 + s_B) \approx s_B$, for small s_B,[6] taking income shares into account from Eq. (6.16), and solving Eq. (6.17) for the change in real seigniorage s_B yield:

$$s_B - p \approx \frac{1}{2}\left[\frac{\lambda}{\phi_B} - \frac{\phi_N}{\phi_B}(w - p) - \frac{\phi_E}{\phi_B}(\pi_E - p + k - n) + n\right], \tag{6.18}$$

where $\lambda \equiv y - n$ is labor productivity growth and normal rate of profit π_B^* is constant. Treating (6.18) as an equation expresses bank seigniorage as the share of productivity growth that is extracted by the banking sector from the household and firm sectors (the real economy), and its underlying algebra makes explicit the growth accounting relationships between the different economic sectors that are considered in the model and are implicit in the expression. Equation (6.18) highlights the relationships between changes in bank seigniorage and changes in labor productivity, inflation, wages and profits, capital endowment, and bank lending.[7]

These relationships should be understood in the context of the distributional dynamics characterizing any given economy. Equation (6.18) identifies the constituent elements of bank seigniorage (in real terms). It indicates that such form of seigniorage depends on the political-economy context in which banks and the other economic agents operate, including their power to affect the economy's resource distribution process. For instance, all else equal, more consolidate is the banking sector, the higher is the banks' capacity to extract rents from the economy, and the higher is the growth of labor productivity required for the firms to be able to repay their bank debt. In point of political-economy considerations, most notable is the indication from Eq. (6.18) of a negative relationship between the seigniorage power of banks and the share of national output going to workers and/or to firms.

---

[6] From Taylor's expansion, and dropping subscript B, $\ln(1 + s) = s - \frac{s^2}{2} + \frac{s^3}{3} - \frac{s^4}{4} + \frac{s^5}{5} - \cdots = \sum_{n=1}^{\infty} (-1)^{n+1} \frac{s^n}{n}$, $\forall s \subset (-1, 1]$, and $\lim_{n \to \infty} (R_n) = -\frac{s^2}{2} + \frac{s^3}{3} - \frac{s^4}{4} + \frac{s^5}{5} - \cdots = \frac{(-1)^n}{(1+\xi)^{n+1}} \frac{(s)^{n+1}}{(n+1)!} = 0$, $\forall \xi \in (0, s)$, and $\forall s \in (-1, 1]$. Thus, $\ln(1 + s) \approx s$.

[7] In Bossone (2021), where I developed this analysis, I omitted by mistake to consider the sector income shares, thereby deriving unweighted growth rate components. However, while the omission is an error, it does not alter the qualitative nature of the relationships therein analyzed and here replicated.

6.4.1 Three Relevant Cases

Three cases are of interest from the resource distribution standpoint and deserve consideration:

(a) The case where firms protect the value of their capital.
(b) The (neoclassical) case where the rate of change of marginal productivity of labor equals real wage growth.
(c) The case where nominal wage growth lags inflation.

Case A: Protecting the Real Value of Capital

The real value of the firms' capital is protected when $\pi_E \geq p$, For this to be possible under positive bank seigniorage in real terms, $s_B - p > 0$, and assuming stationarity of the capital endowment per worker, $k - n = 0$, it follows from Eq. (6.18) that inequality $\lambda/\phi_B - \phi_N/\phi_B(w - p) > (\pi_B^* - p + l_B - n)$ must hold whereby the output that firms extract from labor must be equal to or greater than the output absorbed by the banks. This requires that firms engineer an increase in labor productivity for given real wage dynamics or manage to compress real wage growth through internal devaluation and/or higher price growth.[8] Call "labor appropriation" the resources that accrue to the firms in excess of those that the firms transfer back to the banks, $\lambda/\phi_B - \phi_N/\phi_B(w - p) - [(\pi_B^* - p + l_B - n)] > 0$. Clearly, all else being equal, the larger the seigniorage (in real terms) extracted by the banks, $s_B - p$, the larger the labor appropriation needed by the firms; moreover, with a growing stock of capital per worker, $k - n > 0$, labor appropriation would have to be even larger. Notice that the capacity of the firms to sustain seigniorage payment via real wage compression, here, does not consider the feedback from lower real wage to household consumption and, hence, firms' revenue.

Case B: The Neoclassical Case

In this case, the economy follows the neoclassical rule whereby labor productivity and real wages grow at the same rate, $\lambda = w - p = 0$. Positive seigniorage in real terms, $s_B - p > 0$, requires that $\left(\pi_B^* - p + l_B - n\right) > \phi_E/\phi_B(\pi_E - p)$, meaning that the resources needed to secure extra profits to the banks can only come from the firms. This implies that firms' capital must progressively shift to the banking sector for the firms to be able to repay their debt obligations to the banks. Call "capital expropriation" the net resources $(\pi_B^* - p + l_B - n) - \phi_E/\phi_B(\pi_E - p) > 0$ that accrue to the banks in excess of firms' profits, reflecting banks' seigniorage power. Notice that, all else being equal, capital expropriation grows with the capital-to-labor ratio. Consequently, bank seigniorage disincentivizes capital accumulation since any resource newly accumulated is eventually appropriated by the banks. With a growing stock of capital per worker, $k - n > 0$, capital expropriation would have to grow even more.

---

[8] The incentive effect on productivity from a higher interest rate is discussed in Heinshom and Steiger (1983).

Case C: Wages Lag Inflation

Finally, the case when $w < p$, that is, real wages decline, which materializes when nominal wage dynamics lag price growth. According to Eq. (6.18), positive (real) bank seigniorage, $s_B - p > 0$, requires $\lambda/\phi_B - \left[\phi_N/\phi_B(w-p) + \phi_E/\phi_B(\pi_E - p + k - n) + \left(\pi_B^* - p + l_B - n\right)\right] > 0$. Assuming no productivity growth and stationary capital endowment per worker (that is, $\lambda = 0$ and $k - n = 0$), the condition can be re-written as $\phi_B\left(\pi_B^* - p + l_B - n\right) > \phi_N w - \phi_E \pi_E$, implying that firms enjoy some flexibility, in that they can service their bank debt even if wages grow faster than profits, at least up to a limit. This flexibility would be heightened by positive productivity growth, $\lambda > 0$, while it would be eroded by a positive growth of the capital stock per worker, $k - n > 0$: productivity growth would generate extra resources that could be transferred to the banks at no cost to the firms (in terms of profit losses); a growing capital stock per worker, on the other hand, would increase the firms' claims on any given level of the economy's output and thus require lower nominal wages and/or higher nominal profits for them to secure higher claims to themselves and to the banks.

Under the three cases just evaluated, the very existence of bank seigniorage affects resource distribution between firms and labor. Moreover, given the sanctity of debt, seigniorage raises tensions between the two classes of agents and determines a zero-sum game type of situation, for any given level of output, where one class may gain only at the expense of the other and where the firms' inability to protect the real value of their capital causes part of their capital to be appropriated by the banks.

6.5 Policy Implications

The preceding findings underscore the impact of bank seigniorage on the economy's general equilibrium price level, thereby underscoring the pivotal role of commercial banks in resource allocation across sectors.

As delineated in the analysis, heightened prices constitute firms' reaction to bank seigniorage, as they endeavor to recuperate the resources necessary for servicing their bank obligations. Notably, such indebtedness does not stem from traditional financial intermediation of preexisting savings but rather from the creation of claims on real resources—exchange value—by banks, exceeding their actual contributions to the economy by supplying money. These claims precipitate net positive transfers of real output from the economy to banks in the form of rents. Should firms falter in their resource recovery efforts—be it by reducing their profits or compressing real wages—they may be compelled to seek fresh bank loans. Should banks opt to prolong existing debts, this could lead to a gradual accumulation of new loans until firms manage to secure the necessary resources to meet their obligations. Conversely, if banks refrain from extending further credit, firms may face insolvency, potentially resulting in asset seizure by creditor banks. Bank seigniorage thus redirects resources from the real economy to the banking sector, fostering distributive tensions between capital and labor. The significance of seigniorage ultimately hinges on the dominance of banks in the payments market and their scale.

These findings bear notable implications for monetary policy and prompts preliminary reflections on potential measures to eliminate (or mitigate) seigniorage.

6.5.1 Monetary Policy

The model presented above abstracts from the consideration of costs incurred by commercial banks in holding or attracting reserves from central banks. Introducing this cost element into the model serves to diminish bank seigniorage. Expanding the model to incorporate the demand of commercial banks for central bank reserves opens up avenues for monetary policy intervention. Specifically, the policy interest rate(s) set by the central bank would impose a cost on commercial banks, thereby influencing their lending decisions and the interest rates they charge on loans.

Adhering to a Taylor monetary policy rule, the central bank would adjust the policy interest rates upwards in response to inflation surpassing the target level. Consistent with the model outlined above, such an increase in policy interest rates would prompt banks to raise their lending rates, leading firms to adjust their prices accordingly. This outcome aligns with the findings of the monetary policy "cost channel" literature and conforms to Neo-Fisherian predictions (Cochrane, 2016). However, as elucidated in the preceding analysis, if nominal wages and/or firm profits fail to keep pace with inflation, there exists a critical threshold beyond which further price adjustments become unsustainable. This could occur due to resistance from workers and firms against additional value extraction, or as a consequence of declining real compensation for labor and capital, resulting in diminished output.

While central bank intervention through policy rate adjustments may initially curb inflation, the effectiveness of such measures could be undermined if commercial banks opt to extend or renew loans to firms. Should firms choose to borrow from banks, raise sale prices, or accommodate demands for higher wages, it would spur an increase in money circulation and velocity. This, in turn, would lead to heightened borrowing of central bank reserves by banks at elevated rates, potentially fueling a spiral of interest-price-wage dynamics and exacerbating inflationary pressures. Effective monetary restraint would necessitate a departure from interest rate policies in favor of quantity targeting, whereby the central bank restricts the supply of reserves to commercial banks. However, such a shift could disrupt debt repayment dynamics and overall payment activity across the economy.

6.5.2 How to Deal with Seigniorage?

Given that bank seigniorage imposes an unjustified cost—or dead-weight loss—on society, the focus shifts to exploring potential policies that could reduce or mitigate, or else redistribute it within the economy.

Taxation emerges as a natural consideration, presenting a means to reintegrate the extracted rents back into the economy through the fiscal budget. However, accurately estimating seigniorage poses challenges, including determining the threshold at which earnings transition into rents (see Bossone et al., cit.). Moreover, there is a risk that higher taxes could be passed on by banks to their borrowers and depositors, leading to adverse effects on lending, output, and resource allocation.

Alternative remedies involve financial policies aimed at eliminating the generation of seigniorage. One approach is to enhance competition within the banking sector and deconsolidate banking institutions, thereby reducing the average size of banks, their market share in payments, and their overall market influence—all factors influencing bank seigniorage. However, the benefits of this policy must be weighed against the potential for increased risk-taking by banks due to lower earnings, which could heighten financial instability.

Another avenue is to abolish the fractional reserve system that underpins modern commercial banking and transition to a "narrow banking" model.[9] Here, banks would be mandated to fully back their demand deposit liabilities with reserves held at the central bank or with safe, liquid assets like high-quality government bonds. This would eliminate money creation, transitioning all lending to pure intermediation and consequently eradicating seigniorage. However, the societal costs of depriving the economy of the money supply elasticity facilitated by the fractional reserve system must be carefully considered. Notably, this shift could elevate the cost of credit to the economy (Bossone, 2001).

Considering the complexities and potential trade-offs associated with policies targeting seigniorage reduction, careful deliberation is warranted. An alternative approach could involve incentivizing forms of bank ownership, such as not-for-profit community or cooperative banks. These entities mitigate seigniorage extraction by offering credit at low rates or reinvesting profits into the local economy, thereby potentially counteracting its negative effects. Such banks, including local savings and mutual cooperative banks, already exist in significant numbers in many countries but have yet to dominate their domestic banking sectors in terms of market share. A similar option would be for banks to be owned by the state and operate under an obligation to reinvesting their profits.

Other, more radical ways to eliminate seigniorage by introducing entirely new forms of money and financial intermediation, while preserving the incentives for sound processes of money creation and distribution, will be discussed in Part III of this book.

[9] Here and throughout this chapter, a "fractional reserves regime" is any regulatory regime that do not require banks to back up with reserves the totality of all their (demand) deposit claims issued.

6.6 Concluding Remarks

This chapter has explored the ability of commercial banks as money creators to extract rents from the economy through seigniorage. Specifically, it has elucidated how bank seigniorage affects the economy's aggregate output, relative prices, and the general price level, shedding light on its potential political-economy implications concerning resource distribution, notably by exacerbating tensions between labor and capital. Lastly, preliminary economic-policy implications have been outlined in this chapter, addressing conflicts over resource distribution raised by seigniorage and proposing policy measures to mitigate or eliminate its adverse effects.

The special role of banks as money creators and the impact of bank money on the economy raise important economic and financial policy issues. But before moving into the policy dimension, I want to dedicate some space to a new analytical approach to bank money, which I have introduced recently working with an expert of a completely different scientific discipline—quantum physics—and which is the topic of this chapter.

References

Bossone, B. (2001). Do banks have a future: A study on banking and finance as we move into the third millennium. *Journal of Banking Finance, 25*(12), 2239–2276.

Bossone, B. (2021). Commercial bank seigniorage and the macroeconomy. *International Review of Financial Analysis, 76*, 1–15.

Cochrane, J. (2016). Do higher interest rates raise or lower inflation? Mimeo. http://faculty.chicagobooth.edu/john.cochrane/research/papers/fisher.pdf.

Heinshom, G., & O. Steiger (1983). Private properly, debts and interest or: The origin of money and the rise and fall of monetary economies. *Studi Economici 21*, 3-56.

Ravenna, F., & Walsh, C. E. (2006). Optimal monetary policy with the cost channel. *Journal of Monetary Economics., 53*(2), 199–216.

Chapter 7
Money Quanta

Abstract This chapter focuses on the hybrid nature of bank money as it emerges from the Accounting View of Money (AVM) introduced in Chap. 2. With demand deposits being shown by the AVM to encompass both debt and equity components (in a mix that depends on factors that relate to the issuing banks and the environment where they operate and interact), the idea is explored that they can be treated as objects of Quantum Physics—which typically feature a dual nature—and therefore be subject to quantum analysis. The chapter evaluates the merits of the idea and illustrates the work done using a quantum model to describe how the banks' power to create money is affected by the interactions taking place among the banks and between the banks and their environments. The chapter reports the main conclusions of numerical simulations run based on the afore-mentioned interactions and discusses how the information extracted through this process can be used for drawing financial stability considerations.

7.1 Preamble

Before falling for economics as my university major (and then as my lifelong occupation), physics had originally been my passion in high school. In fact, in the months after graduating and just a few weeks before application day, I was convinced that I would become a physicist. That was until I discovered Economics, which struck me as a sort of "physics of society" that combines scientific and humanistic elements. It soon became my first choice. Yet, my fascination with physics has never faded over the years. In particular, the world of quantum physics has exerted a profound intellectual impact on me, extending beyond its specific scientific aspects.

It is therefore only natural that when the "hybrid" ("dual") nature of bank money emerged as one of the main outcomes of the Accounting View of Money (see Chap. 2), I thought of that hybrid entity as a quantum physics object existing in a superposition of different states—debt and equity.

I was then curious of digging into that analogy and so I started looking for a quantum physicist who would be interested to collaborate with me on exploring

B. Bossone, *Trailblazing Visions of Money in Economic Theory*, Contributions to Economics, https://doi.org/10.1007/978-3-031-82544-6_7

the idea. I eventually run into Fabio Bagarello, an eminent academician with great experience in Econophysics,[1] who had already experimented with the application of quantum physics methodologies to social sciences, and economics in particular. We embarked on this intellectual journey, wondering whether it would lead us anywhere. The results of our work were published in Bagarello and Bossone (2024). This chapter reports a short illustration of the work done and its main results. One thing I am particularly proud of is the "translation" I did (with Fabio's help) from quantum physics to economics of the key variables used in the model and reported in the appendix to the chapter.

As is obvious, I could not have done this work without Fabio's involvement, and I am still grateful to him agreeing to join me in the effort.

7.2 Introduction

As discussed in Chap. 2, the Accounting View of Money (AVM) of Bossone and Costa (2021) shows that, in fractional reserve regimes, bank deposits take a hybrid form, whereby only a share of them is debt of the banks issuing there, while the remaining non-debt share represents net worth (equity) of the same banks.[2] The AVM also shows the nature of deposit-issuing banks as hybrid institutions (part creators of money and part pure financial intermediaries).

This chapter illustrates how these important results were used in Bossone and Bagarello (2024) to explore the association of the "hybrid" nature of bank deposits with the "dual" nature that typifies the objects of quantum physics and to investigate whether and how the application of quantum analytical methods to money with dualistic features can be used to extract valuable economic information.

In other words, this chapter is about the exploration of bank deposits—the largely prevailing form of money in all modern economies—as a possible form of "quantum money," which can be analyzed through the methods of quantum mechanics.[3] Its purpose is to see what informational benefits can be gained from the new approach. The chapter describes, in its essentials, the quantum mechanical model used to this purpose and some of its results.

---

[1] For those who are interested, see *Econophysics and Policy—Understanding the Economy*, Organization for Economic Co-operation and Development (OECD), available at https://www.oecd.org/naec/events/understanding-the-economy/econophysics-and-policy.htm#:~:text=Econophysics%20is%20an%20interdisciplinary%20research,stochastic%20processes%20and%20nonlinear%20dynamics.

[2] Here and throughout this chapter, a "fractional reserves regime" is any regulatory regime that do not require banks to back up with central bank reserves (or other similarly liquid assets) the totality of all their (demand) deposit claims issued.

[3] In fact, while using the expression "quantum money" to define bank money would be perfectly correct, Fabio and I decided to avoid it, since it has already been used in the money literature with reference to the quantum cryptographic protocol that is utilized to create and verify banknotes that are resistant to forgery. We thus preferred to use the word "quanta" and refer it to bank deposits as quantum objects, and this is the term that will be used henceforth in this chapter.

The chapter, which summarizes (in a highly simplified form) the original work done with Fabio Bagarello, is organized as follows. Section 7.3 briefly recalls the AVM, its analysis of the process of money creation by commercial banks, and its theoretical findings about the dual nature of bank deposits. Section 7.4 investigates the analogies between bank deposits and quantum objects and discusses the merits of analyzing bank money through quantum mechanics tools; the section also describes a simple quantum model for readers who are not familiar with quantum systems. Section 7.5 illustrates the quantum model of a two-bank system. Section 7.6 reports the main conclusions of the numerical simulations carried out in the original work, describing different situations: banks interacting with their environments, but not between them; banks mutually interacting, but not interacting with their environments and, finally, a *richer* situation in which all interactions are active. Section 7.7 concludes the article. Appendix 1 reports the "translator" I developed (with Fabio Bagarello's help), which maps the quantum mechanical quantities (e.g., parameters and operators) to economic variables, juxtaposes their physic and economic interpretations, and facilitates the comprehension of the application of quantum mechanics modeling to the banks' money creation process.

7.3 The Hybrid Nature of Bank Deposits

Let's recap the main lines of Chap. 5. Deposits are claims that depositors hold on the banks that issue them in exchange for cash or funds received from other banks. Such claims entitle a depositor to get cash on demand from her bank or to instruct her bank to make transfers or payments on her behalf in favor of a third party. Technically, this entails the bank debiting her deposit account and crediting the deposit accounts of the receiving party. When this movement of claims happens between clients of different banks, the payor's bank must deliver funds (that is, central bank reserves) to the payee's bank at settlement time. Bank deposits are considered money in the economy because they are exchanged at the same value as reserves and are used as a medium of exchange by all participants.

Banks create money in the economy by issuing deposit claims and exchanging them with clients against securities or promises to repay equivalent funds (at an interest) at some future dates. Banks may in principle do so without getting deposits first, and they can lend or sell the deposits so created (Werner, 2014). Yet they still need cash and funds (reserves) as clients take out cash or use deposits for payments or transfers. Notice that reserves matter only for payments between clients of different banks are relevant, because payments between clients of the same bank (or "on us" payments) do not need reserves from the central bank and just involve changing account records within the books of the same bank. For cash withdrawals and interbank payments, every bank must figure out the best amount of cash and reserves to cover deposits. In broad terms, these reserves consist of: (i) cash reserves and reserves deposited with the central bank; (ii) reserves from settlement of incoming payments from other banks; (iii) borrowings from the interbank market; (iv) borrowings from the central bank; (v) immediate liquidation of unencumbered assets in the balance sheet, and (vi) new deposits of cash from old and new clients. The new non-cash deposits from clients can only consist of deposits transferred from other banks, which fall under item (ii) above.

Bank deposits constitute a debt liability for the issuing banks, since, as noted, the latter are under an obligation to convert deposits into cash on demand from their clients or to settle payments in reserves on request by their clients.

In fractional reserve systems, banks need to cover with reserves only a fraction of their deposit liabilities and normally use only a fraction of their reserves base for interbank payment settlements. To the extent that they can economize on the use of reserves, banks can create new deposits with fewer reserves. Thus, all else being equal, large banks (which intermediate large shares of the payments executed in the economy) can economize on reserve holdings vis-à-vis their total deposit liabilities and vice versa for small banks.

The use of reserves by banks is influenced by two factors: the way payments are settled (either by netting or gross settlement) and the technology used. Modern technologies introduce (or reintroduce) elements of netting into gross settlement processes and make reserves circulate faster, which allow banks to use less reserves for the same value of payments settled. In the hypothetical case of a cashless economy with only one bank that holds all accounts of all participants in the economy, there would be no need for reserves for settling transactions and would be able to create all the money that the economy would demand without holding reserves. In such case, bank money would be equivalent to central bank money as settlement instrument.

In the real-world economies, on the other hand, there are many banks that make payments and create interbank debts all the time. But because of the rules of the payment system and the different timings of deposit mobilization by clients, banks can still hold less reserves to back up their deposit liabilities and, dynamically, they can issue more deposit liabilities with less reserves needed to back them up. This means that, if everything else is the same, a banking system with fewer banks can cover its deposit liabilities more easily and cheaply than a system with many banks.

More generally, unless there is a severe crisis that makes depositors withdraw all their money at once or move all their deposits to other banks, not all deposit liabilities outstanding at any time date represent debt obligations that require coverage with reserves. In fractional reserve regimes, banks can create this free resource by issuing deposit liabilities that exceed their reserve holdings. This free resource can be used by them to acquire claims on real resources (for example, loans that generate capital and interest payments). This free resource is thus a source of income for the issuing banks. If this income is accumulated and not distributed, it is equivalent to equity. Deposits, therefore, consist of "debt-deposits" and "equity-deposits"—one of the main AVM's propositions that were examined in Chap. 2.

The hybrid (dual) nature of deposits is stochastic in as much as when a bank issues a deposit claim, the latter can act like either a debt or an equity, depending on the probability that the bank will have to pay cash or settle with another bank. The bank only keeps enough cash and reserves to cover the expected amount of debt, plus some margin for variation, not the whole value of the deposit—the origin of the concept of "fractional reserve banking."

"Stochastic" means that a bank that makes one unit of deposit expects only part of that unit to become debt, while the rest will not be subject to requests to turn it into cash or reserves. How much debt-deposits (or equity-deposit, the other part) depends on things like people's habits, rules, and events. When markets are stressed, debt-deposits go up, but when people trust the economy (and banks especially), they go down, and equity-deposits go symmetrically up. Thus, things that boost such trust (like the central bank giving liquidity when needed, or deposit insurance) make equity-deposits bigger.

The same logic applies to the whole banking system and to each bank in it, though the effect may vary for different banks depending on their size (where size means how much and how valuable the payment transactions that the bank mediates are compared to the total payment transactions in the system). This means that, if everything else is the same, small banks have a higher random portion of debt-deposits than large banks. On the other hand, the bigger the bank is, the higher the portion of equity in its deposit liabilities is. To sum up, whereas the conventional view says that bank deposits are a liability (debt) of the banks that issue them, the AVM says that, in a fractional reserve regime, they are only partly debt obligations of the issuing bank, while the rest is equity of the same bank in the form of retained and undistributed income.

7.4 Bank Deposits as "Money Quanta": The Concept

As discussed, bank deposits can take two different forms. They stand (stochastically) to be converted into cash or to be used for payments (and require reserves for settlement) or to be untouched. In the former case, they are liabilities of the issuing bank[4]; in the latter case, they are equity of the issuing bank. Ex ante, one unit of deposit could take both forms and the two forms would overlap (in a kind of superposition of states in quantum physics) until some external events cause the deposit unit to collapse in one form or the other.[5]

[4] While economists consider the balance sheet as consisting of "assets" and "liabilities," accountants correctly consider the balance sheet as consisting of "resources" and "claims," with the latter including "liabilities" (i.e., debts) and "equity."

[5] Also, the non-happening of events requiring the conversion of deposits into cash or reserves would be an event.

7.4.1 Bank Money and Quantum Mechanics

This looks very much the same to what happens in quantum mechanics, when a given system is in a state that is (usually) a superposition of states (spin up and spin down, first or second energetic level, and so on), but when some measurement is performed on the system, which leads to its collapse in a specific state that corresponds to the result of the measurement.

The hybrid nature of bank deposits may be subject to different dynamics, depending on the characteristics of the issuing banks, their interactions with the environment where they operate, and their mutual interactions within the payments system.

The role of bank size has been discussed already, with large banks enjoying a larger potential for issuing equity-deposits and smaller banks being more constrained to rely on debt-deposits. Yet, all else equal, the debt/equity mix of the deposits issued by the same banks can change due to changes in, say, the risk attitude of banks. A bank (of any size) showing greater risk tolerance, and therefore wanting to take a more aggressive stance on lending, would issue more deposits for any given volume of its cash and central bank reserve holdings, thus raising the relative share of equity-deposits over the total deposits issued, and vice versa for lower risk tolerance and a more conservative lending policy. This is important from the financial stability standpoint: whereas high money creation power can be the sign of a soundly managed bank that achieves efficiency in use of reserve and manages liquidity effectively, the same power may be abused if the bank behaves unsoundly, exposing itself to poor asset quality and large (uncovered) liabilities.

Similar effects would follow from changes in the public sentiment characterizing the economic environment where the banks operate. The diffusion of positive news and related rise of optimism within a banking business community might induce banks (of all sizes) to extend more loans for given cash and reserve levels, again, raising their relative share of equity-deposits over their total deposits.[6] An important additional effect, in this case, would derive from the (positive or negative) spillovers generated by the banks' strategic interactions within the payments system: if, under optimism, each bank expects the others to expand their lending, all will figure that reserves will circulate more rapidly within the payments system, with more reserves accruing to them as they receive more payments. This means that more deposits can be issued for a given volume of reserves circulating in the payments system, which will increase the share of equity-deposits over total deposits. Obviously, the reverse would happen under pessimistic expectations and negative spillovers from bank interactions. Finally, the payments system, too, may have an impact on the debt/equity deposit mix. As an example, the adoption of liquidity-saving automated solutions within payment systems (which reintroduce some degree of netting within real-time gross settlement systems) allows banks to economize on the reserves needed

[6] In all the above examples, nothing ensures that the ex-ante (expected) mix of debt/equity deposits would coincide with its ex-post (actual) value, since the payments activity of banks may require them to demand more reserves for settlement purposes than they had initially planned.

to settle given volumes and values of payment transactions. All else being equal, this raises the (optimal) equity-deposits over debt-deposits ratio that banks can target.

Having shown the hybrid (dual) nature of bank deposits and their stochastic underpinning, as well as the superposition of states that they embody and the possible dynamic evolution of their associated states, it is more than tempting to think of deposits as quantum-like objects—that is, as a form of "money quanta"—which would therefore be susceptible of being treated analytically with the mathematical apparatus of quantum mechanics. What advantages, if any, would such an approach bring to bear for economic analysis, such as for instance for financial stability and policy purposes?[7]

For readers who are not familiar with quantum physics, it might be useful to know that at the beginning of the twentieth century, scientists were unveiling one of the most well-kept natural mysteries—the dual wave particles or the dual nature of matter and energy. Initially, and for a long time, the properties of a material object or light were defined by their respective particle or wave structure. It was then discovered by experiments that matter has wave characteristics, much as light shows behaviors that can only be associated with a particle structure. Therefore, both were said to have a "dual" nature, that is, a nature that features both particle and wavelength characteristics.

The concept of wave-particle duality of matter and energy is the essence of quantum mechanics, the branch of physics that studies microscopic objects. Quantum mechanics refers to the physical properties of matter at the scale of an atom or subatomic particles. It differs from classical physics in that energy, momentum, and other quantities of a system are usually restricted to discrete values (quantization); objects, as said, have characteristics of both particles and waves; and there are limits to how accurately the value of two physical (conjugate) quantities, like the position and the momentum of a given particle, can be efficiently measured, given a complete set of initial conditions (the so-called uncertainty principle).

A fundamental feature of the quantum mechanics is that it usually cannot predict with certainty what will happen, but only assign probabilities to different events. For example, a quantum particle like an electron can be described by a wave function, which associates to each point in space a probability amplitude to find the electron in a given position in space. One consequence of the mathematical rules of quantum mechanics is a tradeoff in predictability between different measurable (again, conjugate) quantities. The most well-known version of the uncertainty principle says that no matter how a quantum system is prepared, or how carefully experiments upon it are arranged, it is impossible to have a precise prediction for the measurement of its position and, at the same time, for the measurement of its momentum. This is a consequence of the properties of the position $\hat{x}$ and momentum $\hat{p}$ not to commute:

---

[7] This exercise would still be worth doing even if only under an "as if" assumption. That is, considering that the AVM idea of bank deposits as hybrid financial instruments (partly debt, partly equity) may still encounter resistance (despite the AVM being grounded on extra solid principles, with scholars and experts moving in its direction), it would still be useful for the "resistants" to suspend their judgment and accept the quantum exercise assuming for a moment that the AVM holds true, and see what the results would be.

$\hat{x}\hat{p} \neq \hat{p}\hat{x}$. This is necessary since quantum variables are time-dependent *operators* rather than *functions*. A consequence of this non-commutativity of the observables of quantum systems is that, if we try to measure the position of the quantum particle, we lose information about its momentum, and vice versa. This feature, which is intrinsic with quantum mechanics, is easily met in other, and completely different, contexts. For instance, decision making under uncertainty is one of such a context: we have to decide on some specific problem, but we have some uncertainty (like noise, rumors, external inputs, etc.) which makes it difficult to come out with a clear and unique decision.

This is just one of the many appearances of some quantum-like features outside quantum mechanics. Bagarello (2012, 2019) illustrates how quantum mechanics can be applied to classical problems in finance, biology, economics, and elsewhere, and how quantum tools. The original driving idea was that the interrelated lowering and raising operators can be used in the description of processes where some relevant quantities change discontinuously. To cite a few examples, these processes include stock markets, where shares are exchanged; migration flows, whereby peoples move from one place to another; and biological systems, where one cell duplicates producing two cells and so on. This suggests that objects labeled by natural numbers are important. More technically, nonnegative integers can be seen as eigenvalues of some suitable number operator constructed using ladder operators, and ladder operators can be efficiently used to describe systems where discrete quantities of some kind are exchanged between different agents (Box 7.1; Appendix 1). Hence, ladder operators, and some combinations of them, can be used in the description of specific systems and will be seen below. To clarify, the simple so-called predator–prey model is described below that shows the logic of applying quantum mechanics to economic systems.

Box 7.1. Number operator and ladder operators in quantum physics

Number Operator

In quantum mechanics, the number operator N counts the number of particles, such as electrons or photons, in a given quantum state. It is defined by a set of creation and annihilation operators (see below) as $N = a^{\dagger}a$, and it quantifies the energy level in a system

Ladder operators

Ladder operators are tools that help move between different energy states in the quantum system. Ladder operators are of two types:

Creation operator ($a^{\dagger}$): It is an operator that adds one quantum of energy to the system. If it applies to a state with n quanta of energy, it increases the energy quanta by one, moving the system to the state with $n + 1$ quanta. Think of it as stepping up a ladder

Annihilation operator (a): It is operator that removes one quantum of energy from the system. If it applies to a state with n quanta of energy, it decreases the energy quanta by one, moving the system to the state with $n - 1$ quanta. This is like stepping down a ladder

How they work together

Imagine being on a ladder where each step represents a different energy level. The creation operator allows to move up to a higher step (higher energy), and the annihilation operator allows to move down to a lower step (lower energy). The number operator tells what the current step is (how many energy quanta you have). In mathematical terms, if $|n\rangle|n\rangle$ is a state with n quanta:

Annihilation operator $a|n\rangle = n|n-1\rangle$

- Removes one quantum, taking the system from n to $n - 1$.

Creation operator $a^{\dagger}|n\rangle = n + 1|n + 1\rangle$

- Adds one quantum, taking the system from n to $n + 1$.

Number operator $n|n\rangle = n|n\rangle$

- Simply returns n, the number of quanta in the state.

Visualizing the concept

Think of a simple analogy:

- Number operator is like a label on a box that tells you how many items are inside.
- Creation operator is like putting an extra item in the box.
- Annihilation operator is like taking an item out of the box.

In summary, these operators are crucial in quantum mechanics because they help understand and manipulate the quantum states of systems, allowing to predict and explain various physical phenomena

7.4.2 A Simple "Predator–Prey" Model

Imagine an economy with two interacting agents. These agents could be thought of as different economic entities or sectors, like firms and consumers or two competing firms. The economy's behavior is governed by a mathematical construct called a Hamiltonian, which in this context is:

$$H = H_0 + \lambda H_1, \;\; H = \omega_1 a_1^{\dagger} a_1 + \omega_2 a_2^{\dagger} a_2, \;\;\; H_{I=} a_1^{\dagger} a_2 + a_2^{\dagger} a_1.$$

where in economic terms:

- ω_j represents some inherent characteristics of each agent (like their natural growth or decline rate).
- λ represents the strength of interaction between the agents.
- $a_j^\dagger$ can be seen as a mechanism that increases the agent's activity level.
- a_j decreases it.

In the economy, interactions between agents are crucial:

- If $\lambda = 0$, there is no interaction; each agent operates independently.
- When $\lambda \neq 0$, the agents influence each other. For example, if one agent (say, a bank) increases its loans $\left(a_1^\dagger\right)$, it may increase the deposits available for the other agent (say, a firm, represented by a_2). Conversely, if the bank reduces its loans (a_2), the resources for the firm would decrease $(a_2^\dagger)$.

The system's state is described by a set of possible states (like different economic conditions). The fundamental states of the system form a basis, representing different combinations of agent activities:

- $\phi_{0,0}$: both agents are inactive.
- $\phi_{1,0}$: the first agent is active, the second is inactive.
- $\phi_{0,1}$: the first agent is inactive, the second is active.
- $\phi_{1,1}$: both agents are active.

The economic interactions evolve over time, described by the differential equations:

$$\dot{a}_1(t) = -i\omega(t)a_1(t) - i\lambda a_2(t)$$

$$\dot{a}_2(t) = -i\omega(t)a_2(t) - i\lambda a_1(t).$$

Solving these equations shows that the agents' activities oscillate over time, reflecting cycles of economic activity. For instance, in a boom period, increased bank lending increases firms' activities, possibly inducing oversupply; this may cause a slowdown in bank lending and firms' activities to a point where resource unemployment might follow.

7.5 Bank Deposits as "Money Quanta": The Model

Before describing the model, readers should know that Appendix 1 lists the main variables and parameters of the model (both their denomination and formal—symbolic—representations), explains their meaning in physics, and interprets them in terms of economics.

The economy's banking system consists of two banks, bank 1 and bank 2, and two related sets of information, B_1 and B_2, each reflecting the "environment" where each bank operates, comprising factors that are external to the bank and influence its operations, such as inter alia, the systemwide and local (or sectoral) macro-financial conditions underpinning the bank's activity, market expectations, bank reputation with the public, the size of the market where the bank operates relative to the whole economy, the supervisory and regulatory regime under which the bank operates, and the payment system rules that shape the its money creation power, as discussed in Chap. 5. The model centers around the dynamics of the ratio between the *debt-deposits, DD*, and the total deposits issued by the bank: $r^{\mathrm{D}} = \frac{\mathrm{DD}}{\mathrm{D}}$, where $D = \mathrm{DD} + \mathrm{DE}$ and DE is *equity-deposits*, Hence $r^D \in [0, 1]$. In particular, $r^D \approx 0$ for very large banks and $r^D \approx 1$ for smaller banks, as discussed in Sect. 7.3.

At time $t = 0$, each bank could be in two possible states, 0 and 1. The intermediate states are simply linear combinations of these. Hence, there are four different possibilities, to which, following Bagarello (2015) and Bagarello et al. (2017), four different and mutually orthogonal vectors can be associated in a four-dimensional Hilbert space H_B. These vectors are $\phi_{0,0}$, $\phi_{1,0}$, $\phi_{0,1}$ and $\phi_{1,1}$. The first vector, $\phi_{0,0}$, describes the fact that, at $t = 0$, the two banks hold no reserves, that is, $r_1^D = r_2^D = 0$. This choice can change during the time evolution of the economy. Analogously, $\phi_{0,1}$ describes the circumstance that, at $t = 0$, the first bank has a $r_1^D = 0$, while the second has $r_2^D = 1$. And so on. The general vector of the economy's banking system $B = B_1 \cup B_2$ (i.e., the two banks), for $t = 0$, is a linear combination.

$$\Psi_0 = \sum_{k,l=0}^{1} \alpha_{k,l} \varphi_{k,l},$$

where it is natural to assume $\sum_{k,l=0}^{1} \left|\alpha_{k,l}\right|^2 = 1$ to normalize the total probability. For clarity, $|\alpha_{0,0}|^2$ should be interpreted as the probability that, at $t = 0$, the system is in state $\phi_{0,0}$. Analogous interpretations can be given to the other coefficients. In summary, the given expression for Ψ_0 describes a quantum state as a superposition of four basis states—specifically, in this case, a linear combination of basis states $\varphi_{k,l}$.

Construct now the states $\phi_{k,l}$, using two fermionic operators, that is, two operators b_1 and b_2 that satisfy the following *canonical anti-commutation rules* (CAR).[8] Take

[8] In quantum physics, a "fermionic operator" is a mathematical tool used to describe the behavior of fermions, which are particles like electrons, protons, and neutrons. Fermions follow specific rules called anticommutation relations (CAR), which ensure that no two fermions can occupy the same state simultaneously (Pauli exclusion principle). This means that applying a creation or annihilation operator in a different order can result in a negative sign, reflecting the unique properties of fermions. For a simple analogy, imagine a row of seats where each seat can either be empty or occupied by one person (representing a fermion): the creation operator is like seating a person in an empty chair; the annihilation operator is like removing a person from an occupied chair. These operators help us describe and predict how fermions behave in various physical systems, such as in atoms or solid materials.

$\phi_{0,0}$ as the vacuum of b_1 and b_2: $b_1\phi_{0,0} = b_2\phi_{0,0} = 0$, and construct form it the other vectors:

$$\varphi_{1,0} = b_1^\dagger \varphi_{0,0},\ \varphi_{0,1} = b_2^\dagger \varphi_{0,0},\ \varphi_{1,1} = b_1^\dagger b_2^\dagger \varphi_{0,0}.$$

The operators in this expression will be used to write down the Hamiltonian for the whole system.

Let $\hat{n}_j = b_j^\dagger b_j$ be the number operator of the j-th bank, which represents bank j's net money creation power as determined by the combined effects of the creation and annihilation operators defined above (see also Appendix 1). The $\hat{n}_j$ operator describes, at an operational level, the time-evolved version of r_j^D, whose optimal value is determined by the environment where bank j operates (as discussed below). Notice that if $\hat{n}_j$ increases (i.e., r_j^D increases), then the money creation power of bank j declines, and vice versa.

The Hamiltonian H must then be introduced to represent the dynamics of the number operators $\hat{n}_j(t) := e^{iHt}e^{-iHt}$ for the banks in the economy, and the mean values of these operators on some suitable state must be computed, which describe the status of the system at $t = 0$ (see below). Notice that H is the Hamiltonian of the system where the two banks interact, including with their environments B_1 and B_2. Changes in the interaction among the banks and between the banks and their environment can be used to analyze the effects of changes in the values of the r_j^D's, that is, on money creation by the banks.

The system's full Hamiltonian H is:

$$\begin{cases} H = H_0 + H_I + H_{\text{int}} \\ H_0 = \sum_{j=1}^{2} \omega_j b_j^\dagger b_j + \sum_{j=1}^{2} \omega_j \int_{\mathbb{R}} \Omega_j(k) B_j^\dagger(k) B_j(k) \mathrm{d}k \\ H_I = \sum_{j=1}^{2} \lambda_j \int_{\mathbb{R}} \left(b_j B_j^\dagger(k) + B_j(k) b_j^\dagger \right) \mathrm{d}k \\ H_{\text{int}} = \mu_{\text{acm}} \left(b_1^\dagger b_2 + b_2^\dagger b_1 \right) + \mu_{\text{cm}} \left(b_1^\dagger b_2^\dagger + b_2 b_1 \right) \end{cases}$$

Here, ω_j, λ_j, μ_{acm}, and μ_{cm} are real quantities, and $\Omega_j(k)$ are real functions, $k \in R$. In economic terms, ω_j measures the (marginal) cost that bank j sustains to change its money creation, with its value being lower the larger the bank, and vice versa[9]; λ_j measures the strength of the interaction between bank j and its own environment; μ_{cm} measures the tendency of the two banks' money creation powers to comove (that is, to increase or decrease together); μ_{acm} measures the tendency of the banks' money creation power to move in opposite directions; and $\Omega_j(k)$ measures the relative importance of bank j's environment relative to the system where the bank operates.

[9] A physical interpretation of this feature is the following: if we have a quantum system driven by an Hamiltonian $h = \omega b^\dagger b$, if ω is *small*, then it is easier to move from one energetic level to another, since ω is exactly the difference between the energy of the levels. On the other hand, if ω is large, then a larger amount of energy is needed to move from the ground to the excited level, and this transition is less probable.

In analogy with the b_j's, fermionic operators $B_j(k)$ and $B_j^\dagger(k)$ are used to describe the environments where banks operate.

The various terms of H describe the following effects: (i) H_0 is the *free* Hamiltonian, which produces no time evolution for the number-like operators $\hat{n}_j$,[10] since $[H_0, \hat{n}_j] = 0$; (ii) H_I describes the interaction between each bank and its own environment. The idea is that this interaction is one of the essential mechanisms driving the value of $r_j{}^D$; and (iii) H_{int} describes two different interactions between B_1 and B_2. Setting $\mu_{\text{cm}} = 0$, the surviving term in H_{int} describes an opposite behavior of the two banks: if the value of r_2^D decreases, because of b_2, that of r_1^D increases, due to the action of $b_1^\dagger$, and vice versa. This is the effect of $b_1^\dagger b_2$. On the other hand, setting $\mu_{\text{acm}} = 0$, what survives in H_{int} describes a comoving effect: both r_1^D and r_2^D either decrease or increase simultaneously. Of course, these two choices of μ's are extreme. Yet, they determine the range within which the system may evolve over time, as the banks' environment changes and the banks themselves may behave differently in the market. And it might easily happen that the values of μ_{acm} and μ_{cm} change during the time evolution of the system.

When $\mu_{\text{cm}} = 0$, that is, when there is no tendency for the banks' money creation powers to comove (i.e., increase or decrease together), the two r^D's change differently, while they change in the same way when $\mu_{\text{acm}} = 0$, that is, when there is no tendency for the banks' money creation powers to move in opposite directions. When both μ_{cm} and μ_{acm} are not zero, the dynamics can be even richer and include (realistically) cases where banks can change behavior over time, from comoving to moving in different directions and/or vice versa.

The Heisenberg equations of motion $\dot{X}(t) = i[H, X(t)]$ can now be used to deduce the following set of differential equations[11]:

$$\begin{cases} \dot{b}_1(t) = -i\omega_1 b_1(t) - i\lambda_1 \int\limits_{\mathbb{R}} B_1(k,t)dk - i\mu_{\text{acm}} b_2(t) - i\mu_{\text{cm}} b_2^\dagger(t) \\ \dot{b}_1(t) = -i\omega_2 b_2(t) - i\lambda_2 \int\limits_{\mathbb{R}} B_2(k,t)dk - i\mu_{\text{acm}} b_1(t) - i\mu_{\text{cm}} b_1^\dagger(t) \\ \dot{B}_j(k,t) - i\Omega_j B_j(k,t) - i\lambda_j b_j(t) \end{cases}$$

With $j = 1, 2$. The solution of this system of equations can be written as follows:

$$b(t) = e^{iUt} b(0) + i \int\limits_0^t e^{iU(t-t_1)} \beta(t_1)\, dt$$

where:

[10] Their time-evolved mean values produce the main object of study, the so-called quantum functions (see below), which represent the dynamics of the banks' money creation power—the time-evolved version of r_1^D's.

[11] The Heisenberg equations of motion describe how quantum operators evolve over time. They are the quantum analog of classical equations of motion, providing a way to track the time dependence of observables in a quantum system. Economically, the equation represents the dynamics of the money creation operators and the banks' environments (see Appendix 1).

$$b(t) = \begin{pmatrix} b_1(t) \\ b_2(t) \\ b_1^\dagger(t) \\ b_2^\dagger(t) \end{pmatrix}, \quad \beta(t) = \begin{pmatrix} \lambda_1\beta_1(t) \\ \lambda_2\beta_2(t) \\ \lambda_1\beta_1^\dagger(t) \\ \lambda_2\beta_2^\dagger(t) \end{pmatrix},$$

$$U = \begin{pmatrix} \lambda_1\beta_1(t) \\ \lambda_2\beta_2(t) \\ \lambda_1\beta_1^\dagger(t) \\ \lambda_2\beta_2^\dagger(t) \end{pmatrix} \begin{pmatrix} i\nu_1 & -\mu_{\text{acm}} & 0 & \mu_{\text{acm}} \\ -\mu_{\text{acm}} & i\nu_2 & \mu_{\text{cm}} & 0 \\ 0 & \mu_{\text{cm}} & \overline{i\nu_1} & \mu_{\text{acm}} \\ -\mu_{\text{cm}} & 0 & \mu_{\text{acm}} & \overline{i\nu_2} \end{pmatrix}$$

and where $\Omega_j(k) = \Omega_j k$, $\Omega_j > 0$, $\nu_j = i\omega_j + \pi\frac{\lambda^2}{\Omega_j}$, and $\beta_j(t) = \int_{\mathbb{R}} B_j(k)e^{-i\Omega_j t}\mathrm{d}k, j = 1, 2$.

Now, the average must be computed of the time evolution of operators $\hat{n}_j(t) = b_j^\dagger(t)b_j(t)$, and operator N_j is introduced. This can be considered as the optimal value of ${r_j}^D$ to which bank j's money creation, $\hat{n}_j$, tends to converge dynamically, if the banks do not interact among themselves. Note that N_j is determined by bank j's environment. Obviously, the actual realizations of ${r_j}^D$ over time may differ from the optimal value, N_j, due to the bank's choices (as influenced by its interactions with the environment and the other banks). Such differences expose the bank to changes in the (liquidity, credit, and settlement) risks that its faces during its business activities.

Skipping all technicalities (for which the interested reader is referred to the original work), the following general formulas for the *Quantum functions* (QFs) of banks 1 and 2, that is, the dynamics of their money creation power, can be derived as:

$$\begin{cases} n_1(t) = b_1^\dagger(t)b_1(t) = \mu_1^B(t) + \delta\mu_1^B(t) + n_1^B(t) \\ n_2(t) = b_2^\dagger(t)b_2(t) = \mu_2^B(t) + \delta\mu_2^B(t) + n_2^B(t) \end{cases}$$

which for each bank identify contributions from three different sources: the term $\mu_j^B(t)$ originates exclusively from bank j; the term $\delta\mu_j^B(t)$, too, depends on bank j only and it is an *interference term*, since it equals zero only if the initial state of the bank is known with certainty; finally, the term $n_j^B(t)$ originates from the interaction of bank j with its environment.

7.6 Some Numerical Simulations

While in the original work, several simulations were run by varying the various parameters of the model, this chapter only reports the three main scenarios that were analyzed in it and summarizes their results.[12] In the first scenario, the two banks interact with their environments, but not among themselves; this corresponds to

[12] The graphical representations of the simulations are not reported in this chapter and can be made available on request to the author.

assuming $H_{\text{int}} = 0$. The second scenario assumes that $H_I = 0$, implying that the two banks interact with one another but not with their environments. In the third scenario, all the interactions are active, that is, both H_{int} and H_I are nonzero.

A remark is in order on the choice of parameters that was made in the original exercise, especially for the benefit of economist-readers who might not be familiar with the application of quantum models and their use for economic simulations. The explicit numerical values of the parameters used in the original work were specifically chosen to adapt the quantum model to the problem at hand and to make it tractable in an economic context. Not their specific values are relevant for the purpose of the exercise as much as the relations between them. For instance, taking ω_1 and ω_2 to differ from one another (that is, the marginal cost for each bank to change its money creation) shows that $n_1(t)$ and $n_2(t)$ would have small oscillations around their mean values. The amplitude of these oscillations increases when the value of ω_1 approaches that of ω_2. As shown below, this is a central result of the quantum model as applied to bank money: the more divergent the money supply behavior of interacting banks, the more stable their debt/equity deposit mix over time and, thus, the lower their exposure to (liquidity, credit, and settlement) risk.

It should also be noted that, because of the fermionic nature of the operators used in the model, there are natural constraints which must be satisfied (e.g., no two fermions can occupy the same state simultaneously). Thus, in what follows, N_1 and N_2 take values in the interval [0,1]. In economic terms, this corresponds to the optimal values of each bank's debt/equity deposit mix, r_j^D, taking values only within that interval (as the case should be in the real world).

Scenario 1: No Interactions Between the Banks

This scenario assumes $\mu_{\text{cm}} = \mu_{\text{acm}} = 0$, that is, there are no systematic patterns of how the money creation (deposit issuance) by the two banks evolve, that is, they are mutually uncorrelated. Hence $H_{\text{int}} = 0$, and the system is decoupled into two separate subsystems, one, S_1, with environment B_1 and bank B_1, and the other, S_2, with environment B_2 and bank B_2. For this reason, it is sufficient to change the parameters of, say S_2, while keeping fixed those of S_1, to analyze their role and implications for the economy.

The QFs of the banks, $n_1(t)$ and $n_2(t)$, are derived for the following set of parameters and initial conditions, and the simulations relate to different levels of the bank-environment interaction and to different average levels of money creation power. In the absence of interactions between the banks, the model produces the following outcomes:

1. The QFs behave monotonically. They always decrease, or stay constant, and the limit is always the value of N_1 and N_2.
2. The role of the other parameters in H is relevant to determine the *speed of reaction* of the banks. While the functions $n_1(t)$ decay to their limiting value always with the same speed, the functions $n_2(t)$ decay to their limiting value at faster paces, and even faster as Ω_2 and/or λ_2 increase. That is, when the contribution of each bank's environment to the bank's money creation power and/or each bank's

interaction with its own environment increases, the convergence of the related QF to environment-determined $N_2 = 1$ is more rapid. On the other hand, increasing ω_2 would, in general, slower this procedure, that is, as the bank's marginal cost of money creation rises, the QF's dynamics slow down.

Scenario 2: No Interactions Between Banks and Their Environments

The second scenario assumes put $\lambda_1 = \lambda_2 = 0$, implying $H_I = 0$. In this case, the two banks do not entertain any interaction with their environments. This scenario, which is unrealistic, is nonetheless useful to examine how other factors affect bank behavior, after controlling for their environments.

Under these assumptions, the QFs keep oscillating (or stay constant), which means that their r_j^D changes all the time. This is because the environment-determined N_j's do not exert any attractive force on the QFs. Of course, if other than having $\lambda_1 = \lambda_2 = 0$, one were also to set $\mu_{\text{cm}} = \mu_{\text{acm}} = 0$, the situation would trivialize since H would only consist of the free component: no interactions and, therefore, no interesting dynamics. On the other hand, considering cases where μ_{cm} or μ_{acm}, or both, are different from zero leads to interesting results. The model indicates that the role of the comovement between the banks' money creation, μ_{cm}, is more relevant than their tendency to move opposite directions (anti-comovement), μ_{acm}: it is sufficient to have $\mu_{\text{cm}} \neq 0$ for the system to show oscillations independently of the choice of its quantum state Ψ_0. This suggests that, all else being equal, banks increasing or decreasing their money creation together cause the debt/equity deposit mix to oscillate over time, exposing them to higher (liquidity, credit, and settlement) risks. On the other hand, setting $\mu_{\text{cm}} = 0$ and $\mu_{\text{acm}} \neq 0$ leaves the system in a stationary state. This is because the comovement term in H_{int} amplifies the effect of the interactions between banks 1 and 2, with potential negative consequences for financial instability, while the anti-comovement term tends to cancel this effect out, due to the joint presence of a raising and a lowering operator.

It should be noted that, in these simulations, the functions $n_1(t)$ and $n_2(t)$ overlap. Also, the choice of Ω_1, Ω_2, N_1, and N_2 is unessential, since the fact that $\lambda_1 = \lambda_2 = 0$ implies that the environments do not contribute to the dynamics. The oscillations are only connected to the presence of a nonzero μ_{cm}, and their frequencies increase with μ_{cm}, but not with μ_{acm}, as noted.

Scenario 3: Full Interactions

This third and final scenario shows what happens when all the terms of H are nonzero, that is, when all interactions are at play in the system, and when both μ_{acm} and μ_{cm} are nonzero, which is what typically occurs in the real world as banks may change behavior over time, i.e., their money creation dynamics may at times comove at times or may move in opposite directions, or independently of one another.

Four different choices of Ψ_0 are assumed for this scenario (for the specifics, readers are referred to the original work by Bagarello and Bossone (2024). All simulations relating to this scenario are obtained under the assumption that the larger bank B_2, benefits from larger scale economies.

Summarizing the results obtained, an important finding is that, unlike what happens when $\mu_{\rm acm} = \mu_{\rm cm} = 0$, the asymptotic values of the QFs do not coincide with N_1 and N_2, and their values are never zero or one, showing that mutually incoherent bank behaviors—whereby banks behave in ways that are mutually uncorrelated—prevent the debt/equity deposit mix of individual banks from taking extreme values, which is in general a better feature from the standpoint of financial stability.

Some of the simulations show that, during their time evolution, one of the QFs (the one relating to the largest bank) gets closer to the zero value of ${r_j}^D$ (that is, maximum money creation power), and even more so as the marginal cost of money creation declines.

Another important result is that the width of the oscillations of the QFs is much smaller for values of $\mu_{\rm acm}$ larger than for $\mu_{\rm cm}$, suggesting that the destabilizing effects of $\mu_{\rm cm}$ are much stronger than those of $\mu_{\rm acm}$, as already observed in the second scenario. Again, when the banks behave similarly, their QFs oscillate more, and vice versa.

In conclusion, the model indicates that the most efficient [i.e., with lower long-time value of $n_j(t)$] and stable (i.e., with smaller variations) system configuration is achieved for large values of the ratio $\frac{\mu_{\rm acm}}{\mu_{\rm cm}}$ and for $N_1 = N_2 = 0$. However, for different values of the parameters, one bank is more efficient than the other, showing the relevance of the environments in which the banks operate: the smaller the value of the environment-determined N_j, the lower the asymptotic value of $n_j(t)$, and vice versa. In other words, the environment affects the banks and the whole system by strengthening or weakening their efficiency.

The relevance of the banks' interactions is also visible: the comovement of their money creation (deposit issuance) raises their exposure to risks both by making their dynamics more volatile and by widening the gap between each bank's actual value of their debt/equity deposit mix and its optimal value. While less impactful, the anti-comovement too raises the banks' exposure to risks. From the financial stability standpoint, a better configuration is one where the money supplies from banks are mutually uncorrelated or diversified. This conclusion resonates with Danielsson (2024), which argues that a diverse financial system, characterized by many small and varied institutions, minimizes systemic risk by preventing collective risk-taking; it effectively dissipates economic shocks by ensuring different institutions react in opposing ways and reduces the need for large systemic risk buffers.

7.7 Conclusions

According to the Accounting View of Money (AVM), discussed in Chap. 2, the money issued by commercial banks in the form of demand deposits is shown to feature a hybrid nature: one share of a bank deposit bears the typical characteristics of debt obligations (debt-deposits) and the complementary share of the same bank deposit bears the characteristics of an atypical equity instrument (equity-deposits). The mix of the two shares depends on factors that relate specifically to the issuing banks and to the environments where they operate and interact. Such a mix may change over time, following the evolution of the conditions relating to the banks and their environments. In light of this important finding, it is consequential to associate the hybrid nature of bank deposits with the dual nature of the objects of quantum physics.

This chapter has presented the results of the work I have done with physicist Fabio Bagarello to investigate whether and how the application of quantum analytical methods to money showing dualistic features (as discussed, bank deposits) can be used to extract valuable economic information. The work has used a quantum model to describe how banks' power to create money (i.e., issue deposits typically via the credit channel or against securities) is affected by the interactions taking place among the banks and between the banks and their environments.

The main general conclusion that can be drawn from the exercise is that efficient and stable banking systems are highly diversified, that is, they are populated by banks of different sizes, operating in different environments, and behaving differently in the market. Diversification is conducive to non-extreme debt/equity deposit combinations that reduce banks' exposure to financial risks.

Another important conclusion is that systems where all banks' money supplies comove, that is, change their deposit issuance behavior in the same direction (i.e., either increasing or decreasing it) are less stable than systems where banks change it in less correlated—more diversified—patterns.

The results obtained through the application of quantum mechanics to bank money are only preliminary and suggest that important knowledge gains can be attained through this new approach in terms of system behaviors and properties.

After this chapter, which concludes Part I of this book on "Money," let us return to the policy issues raised by bank money and the issues of instability: how can monetary systems be designed to ensure that bank money is sound? This is the topic of Part II of the book.

Appendix 1: The Model's Variables and Parameters: A Synoptic Table

This appendix reports the "translator" I developed (with Fabio Bagarello's help) and used in the original work, whose purposes are to (i) map the quantum mechanical quantities (e.g., parameters and operators) into economic variables, (ii) juxtapose their physic and economic interpretations, and (iii) facilitate the comprehension of the application of quantum mechanics modeling to the banks' money creation process.

Name of the model's variables and parameters	Symbols of the model's variables and parameters	Meaning in physics	Meaning in economics
Vector	φ_{k}, l $k, l = (0,1)$	This vector describes a two-mode system, each mode with two possible levels: $k = l = 0$ is the ground state (the state which minimizes the energy), $k = 1, l = 0$ and $k = 0, l = 1$ are states with one excited mode, $k = l = 1$ is the vector with both excited modes	The money creation (deposit issuance) power of each bank at a given moment in time, e.g., where k, $l = (0, 1)$ and only two banks, $\varphi_{0,0}$ indicates that a certain date both banks are characterized by deposit ratio$r^D = 0$, i.e., high money creation power **MEMO**: $r_j^D = \frac{\mathrm{DD}_j}{D_j}$, where $D_j = \mathrm{DD}_j + \mathrm{ED}_j$, DD_j is debt-deposits; ED_j is equity-deposits; and D_j is the total deposits issued by bank j
Probability amplitude	$\alpha k,l$	If a system is described by the vector Ψ_0 (see below), $\lvert\alpha_{0,0}\rvert^2$is the probability that the first mode of the system is in level k, and the second is in level l	The probability amplitude that, in a system with two banks, at a certain time, is in the state $\varphi_{k,}$. For instance, $\lvert\alpha_{0,0}\rvert$ is the probability that $\Psi_0 = \varphi_{0,0}$
Vector	$\Psi_0 = \sum_{k,l=0}^{1} \alpha_{k,l}\varphi_{k,l}$	Different choices of the coefficients $\alpha_{k,}$ correspond to different vectors of the Hilbert space $\mathcal{H}_{\mathcal{B}}$ (see below). With suitable choices of the coefficients, it describes the system at $t = 0$	Linear combination of the states $\varphi_{k,}$ used to describe the most general expected money creation powers of the banks
Hilbert space	$\mathcal{H}_{\mathcal{B}}$	The vector space of the two fermionic modes: the set of all the $\varphi_{k,}$ is a particularly useful orthogonal basis of $\mathcal{H}_{\mathcal{B}}$	The space on which the interactions of banks with one another can be efficiently described
Fermionic raising operator	$b_j^\dagger$	This operator increases by one unit the level of the j-th mode, if this is zero. Otherwise, it destroys the state (this is the Pauli principle for fermions)	*Creation* operator: it operates counterintuitively; it increases the value of the r_j^D ratio, thus decreasing bank j's money creation power. An example could be bank j's decision to hold a higher reserves ratio for prudential purposes

(continued)

(continued)

Name of the model's variables and parameters	Symbols of the model's variables and parameters	Meaning in physics	Meaning in economics
Fermionic lowering operator	b_j	This operator decreases by one unit the level of the j-th mode, if this is one. Otherwise, it destroys the state	*Annihilation* operator. It operates counterintuitively; it decreases the value of the r_j^D ratio, thus, increasing bank j's money creation power. An example could be an increase in bank j's share of the market for payments
Number operator	$\hat{n}_j = b_j^\dagger b_j$	Returns the explicit value of the level of the j-th mode of the vector $\varphi_{k,}$, when acting on it. In optical systems, it is often used to compute the energy of the system	Bank j's net money creation power, after factoring in the combined effects of the creation and annihilation operators. If $\hat{n}_j$ increases (i.e., r_j^D decreases), and thus the money creation power declines, and vice versa
	$n_j(t)$	The mean value of the time evolution of $\hat{n}_j$, on a state which represents the whole system at initial time, $t = 0$	The quantum function of bank j. It represents the dynamics of the bank's money creation power. It is the time-evolved version of r_j^D
	N_j	A global parameter of the reservoir of the j-th mode: it is often connected with the density of this reservoir	An overall "measure" of the information of the "environment" of bank j. It is the asymptote of $n(t)$, which tends precisely to N_j if the banks interact with their environment only and do not interact among themselves. On the other hand, $n(t)$ moves closer to N_j but may not equal it if banks also interact among themselves
Fermionic reservoir	B_j		The set of information that reflects the "environment" where bank j operates, which is characterized by factors that are external to the bank
Fermionic operator	$B_j^\dagger(k)$		Operator that improves the environment of bank j
Fermionic operator	$B_J(k)$		Operator that weakens the environment of bank j

(continued)

(continued)

Name of the model's variables and parameters	Symbols of the model's variables and parameters	Meaning in physics	Meaning in economics
Interaction	$b_j^{\dagger} B_J(k)$	Typical quadratic creation-annihilation interaction	Interaction between bank *j* and its own environment, which brings the bank to shrink its money creation power
Interaction	$B_j^{\dagger}(k) b_j$	Typical quadratic annihilation-creation interaction	Interaction between bank *j* and its own environment, which brings the bank to expand its money creation power
Real quantity	ω_j	Measure of the difference between different energetic levels of mode *j*	The marginal cost incurred by bank *j* for changing its money creation. It is lower, the larger the bank (and vice versa)
Real function	$\Omega_j(k)$	Continuous version of ω_j: measures the energy of the *j*-th mode of the environment	Measure of the contribution of bank *j*'s environment to the bank's money creation power
Interaction parameter	λ_j	Strength of the interaction strength between the *j*-th mode of the system and its environment	Strength of the interaction between bank *j* and its own environment
Interaction parameter	μ_{cm}	Strength of the interaction between two modes, forcing the same changes in their energetic levels	Measure of the tendency of the banks' money creation powers to comove, that is, to increase or decrease together
Interaction parameter	μ_{acm}	Interaction strength between two modes, forcing opposite changes in their energetic levels	Measure of the tendency of the banks' money creation powers to move in opposite directions
Hamiltonian	$H = H_0 + H_I + H_{\text{int}}$	Hamiltonian	The money creation power of the economy, including both actual and potential money creation. It derives from the sum of three components:
	H_0	Free Hamiltonian	• The money creation power of the economy when the money creation power of each bank is given, and no interactions take place

(continued)

(continued)

Name of the model's variables and parameters	Symbols of the model's variables and parameters	Meaning in physics	Meaning in economics
	H_I	Interaction Hamiltonian between the system and its environment	• The total money creation power of the economy as the money creation power of each bank changes by interacting with its environment
	H_{int}	Interaction Hamiltonian between the modes, describing two opposite effects: co-motion and motion in opposite directions	• The overall money creation power of the economy deriving from the interactions among banks. The change in the economy's total money creation power is higher, the higher is the money creation power of each of the interacting banks. H_{int} is sensitive to whether the money creation powers of the interacting banks increase or decrease together (i.e., $\mu_{\text{cm}} > 0$ and $\mu_{\text{acm}} = 0$) or whether they change differently (i.e., $\mu_{\text{cm}} = 0$ and $\mu_{\text{acm}} > 0$)
Canonical anti-commutation rule (CAR)	$\{b_k, b_l^\dagger\} = \delta_{k}, l_1$ $\{b_k, b_l\} = 0$	Algebraic rules used in the description of fermions	A mathematical way to describe the changes of the money creation power with an algebraic simple approach. From these rules, our interpretation of the operators b_k and $b_l^\dagger$ above follows
Heisenberg equation of motion	$\dot{X}(t) = i[H, X(t)]$	The equation of motion of the operator $X(t)$ when the physical system is described by the Hamiltonian H, which is not explicitly time dependent	The equation represents the dynamics of the money creation operators and the banks' environments

References

Bagarello, F. (2012). *Quantum dynamics for classical systems: With applications of the Number operator*. Wiley.

Bagarello, F. (2015). A quantum-like view to a generalized two players game. *International Journal of Theoretical Physics, 54*(10), 3612–3627.

Bagarello, F. (2019). *Quantum concepts in the social.* Cambridge University Press.

Bagarello, F., & Bossone, B. (2024). Bank deposits as money quanta. *Quantum Economics and Finance, 1*(1), 1–30.

Bagarello, F., Haven, E., & Khrennikov, A. (2017). A model of adaptive decision making from representation of information environment by quantum fields. *Philosophical Transactions A, 375*, 20170162.

Bossone, B., & Costa, M. (2021). Money for the issuer: Liability or equity? *Economics, 15*(1), 43–59.

Danielsson, J. (2024). Why so many crises happen when we know why they happen and how to prevent them. Vox/CEPR.

Werner, R. A. (2014). How do banks create money, and why can other firms not do the same? An explanation for the coexistence of lending and deposit-taking. *International Review of Financial Analysis, 36*, 71–77.

Part II
On "Sound" Money

Part II explores how monetary instruments and their supporting systems can be (re)designed to reduce the financial instability risks associated with credit-based monies.

Chapter 8
Preventing Banks from Creating Money

> Competition delivers autos in the popular colors. So why has it never delivered [safe transactions] balances? My answer is that because owners of transactions account and other bank balances have, generation after generation, mistakenly relied on governments for protection, there has been nothing for competition to deliver. It would seem to follow that under laissez faire banking policy there would be no fractional reserve banking. (Kareken, 1985)
>
> … using narrow banking to cope with the potential problems of banking illiquidity is analogous to reducing automobile accidents by limiting automobile speeds to zero. (Wallace, 1996)

Abstract This chapter presents, with minimal alterations, an early study conducted by the author of this book that investigates the longstanding proposal to restrict the scope of banking activities. The narrow-banking proposal, aimed at enhancing financial stability, would prohibit commercial banks from lending to the private sector and would bar non-bank intermediaries from funding investments with demand deposits. The chapter examines the existing literature, comparing narrow banking with contemporary banking theories, assessing its potential ramifications on finance and the real economy, and drawing relevant policy insights. The chapter reports the author's early attempt to run empirical estimates of the economic costs of bank narrowness. The chapter ultimately argues against the adoption of narrow banking by highlighting its potential to restrict the fundamental money-creation capabilities of banks, which could lead to adverse effects on credit availability and economic growth.

8.1 Preamble

At the World Bank, and then at the IMF, in the late 1990s–early 2000s—as I recounted earlier—I was exposed to all the most interesting debates of the time on financial system risks, financial crises, and policy options to try to prevent them or to mitigate their impact, if things went bad. My special interest in bank money creation

B. Bossone, *Trailblazing Visions of Money in Economic Theory*, Contributions to Economics, https://doi.org/10.1007/978-3-031-82544-6_8

had led me to focus attention on the idea, once again proposed by several highly respected scholars, of removing fractional reserves from banking through regulations that would prohibit banks from lending and require them, instead, to only hold reserves or safe securities against their sight deposit liabilities. This was the idea of transforming commercial banks into so-called narrow banks, which would then supposedly be perceived to be maximally secure by their client depositors.

It is to this topic that I was devoting my attention when I moved across 16th Street, NW Washington DC, from the "Bank" to the "Fund," and here is where I wrote two articles on whether "narrowing" banks was indeed such a good idea, after all. The first article was (Bossone, 2001c) and the other was eventually accepted in the IMF Working Paper Series (Bossone, 2001d) and it was widely circulated as such. I also published a summary version of the latter article with the Levy Economics Institute (Bossone, 2002). This chapter reproduces the text of the IMF working paper almost entirely in its original form, with only a few changes and integrations. I believe, perhaps immodestly, that it still appears fresh and contemporary, and it continues to represent a valuable contribution to a topic that periodically resurfaces, especially in the aftermath of significant banking crises.[1]

If I were to summarize my opinion on "narrow banking" before delving deeper into the subject, I would refer to the second of the two epigraphs that opened my IMF working paper and that also precede this chapter: people are aware that driving cars carry risks, and yet do not even think of giving up on it; instead, they buy insurance against the risks and bear the cost of the uninsured ones, because they still like (or need) to drive cars. The same goes for banking: the elasticity that banks provide to the economy through their power to create money is taken by the economy to be worth the risks and costs associated with it. Yes, societies do take extra steps to mitigate them, but they never "narrow" the banks to the point of suppressing their money creation power. A clear illustration of this can be seen in Switzerland, a financially conservative country that held a national referendum on June 10, 2018, regarding a narrow banking proposal. The initiative faced significant opposition, with approximately 76% of Swiss voters ultimately rejecting it.[2]

8.2 Introduction

The idea of preventing banks from creating money by "narrowing" their activity of deposit-issuing banks to the funding of fully safe assets would rid depositors of the risk of issuer default. This idea has been championed over time by eminent financial regulatory experts and well-known academics, including at least three Nobel

[1] See, for instance, the review by Cohen-Setton (2014), and CEPR (2023) ten years later.

[2] See, *Popular initiative "For crisis-safe money: Money creation by the National Bank only! (Sovereign Money Initiative),"* The Federal Council, The portal of the Swiss government, https://www.admin.ch/gov/en/start/documentation/votes/20180610/Sovereign-Money-Initiative.html?utm_source=chatgpt.com.

Prize winners (Box 8.1). In some industrialized countries, proposals to adopt narrow banking regimes have been given very serious consideration by policymakers, especially in the aftermath of major banking crises. Surprisingly, such proposals have often received support from prominent bankers. Narrow banking proposals have been recently considered for emerging countries, as well, while policy advisors within international financial institutions and governments have not been immune to the appeal of narrow banking as a way out of bank weaknesses in post-crisis countries.

Box 8.1. Nobel Laureates in Economics and Narrow Banking

One Nobel laureate in economics who has championed the idea of narrow banking is Tobin (1985, 1987). Tobin proposed the concept of "narrow banking" as part of his broader work on financial systems. He suggested that banks should separate their riskier activities (such as lending and investment) from the safer task of safeguarding deposits. Narrow banks, according to Tobin's concept, would focus solely on holding deposits in safe, liquid assets, such as government securities, reducing the risk of bank runs and improving financial stability. As an alternative, the Federal Reserve banks could offer deposit accounts, termed "Federal Funds," through conveniently located agencies in private banks or post offices. In no case, overdrafts would not be permitted. Milton Friedman was another Nobel laureate in economics who supported ideas related to narrow banking. Friedman advocated for a banking system in which deposits would be fully backed by reserves (also called 100% reserve banking). This proposal aligns closely with the narrow banking concept, where banks would only hold liquid, safe assets, such as government bonds, to match their liabilities (deposits), thereby minimizing the risk of bank failures. Friedman's view was that separating deposit-taking from riskier banking activities could help reduce the instability inherent in the financial system. A third Nobel laureate in economics who supported ideas related to narrow banking is Merton Miller. While Miller was not an outspoken advocate of narrow banking in the same way as Milton Friedman or James Tobin, he was concerned with the risks of traditional banking structures and supported reforms to make the system more resilient, including proposals like full-reserve banking, which align with the narrow banking concept. His emphasis on minimizing systemic risk is consistent with the ideas behind narrow banking, where riskier banking activities would be insulated from deposit-taking functions

No country has ever experimented with narrow banking so far, and thus, no insights have been gained from experience. In the absence of unsupportive evidence, the idea remains attractive to many, perhaps owing to its direct call on common sense. It periodically resurfaces in academic journals and the media, as well as in the policy debates on banking system reforms. With only one notable exception, to be recalled later in this chapter, narrow banking has never been challenged on rigorous theoretical grounds; it has not been evaluated against contemporary banking theories, nor has it been the object of attempts to estimate its potential effects on the economy.

By submitting a comprehensive reflection on the pros and cons of narrow banking, and the results from a simple empirical exercise, the study reported in this chapter concludes against narrow banking and provides a yardstick against which to measure the consistency of narrow banking proposals.

8.3 Scope of the Study

A core factor to achieve monetary and financial stability in the economy is that banks, generally understood to be institutions involved in supplying monetary assets, are sound and shock resilient. Banking systems virtually everywhere, throughout history, have evolved into fractional reserve regimes specialized in creating private money by lending to individuals and businesses.[3] However, as theory shows and history confirms, banks operating under a fractional reserve regime are vulnerable to runs from depositors. Contagion of depositor runs across banks, in turn, makes the banking system at large exposed to public panics and to risk of collapse.

Since private arrangements to cope with such risks suffer from free-rider and coordination failure problems, governments typically intervene through regulatory instruments and safety nets (such as prudential rules, deposit insurance, and lending-of-last resort facilities), with the aim to reduce the likelihood of shocks to banks (and of systemic transmission of shocks) as well as to mitigate the financial cost of crises, once they have occurred.

Yet, the fundamental mismatch which characterizes banking between demand deposit liabilities (often implicitly or explicitly insured by the government) on one side and the illiquid, risky, and opaque loans used as collateral to those liabilities, on the other side, remains at the heart of potential crises. It keeps the implicit cost of the public safety nets high and tends to be widened by the very presence of the safety nets.

As the public's demand for safe assets (such as short-term government paper) usually exceeds that for banks' demand deposits manifold, some view this as evidence of a large unsatisfied demand for risk-free assets that banks do not match because of the distortive effects of the safety nets, which tilt the bank preferences toward illiquid portfolios (Kareken, 1985). By implication, absent government interference, a laissez-faire regime would induce banks to compete in trying to satisfy the public's demand for safe money by fully matching their liquid liabilities with risk-free assets Enabling the banks to cope with any future runs on deposits would in fact eliminate the likelihood of runs themselves.

With this purpose in mind, more and more frequently in the scientific and financial policy literature proposals have been formulated to "break the Gordian knot

[3] Here and throughout this chapter, a "fractional reserves regime" is any regulatory regime that do not require banks to back up with reserves the totality of all their (demand) deposit claims issued.

between deposit-taking and commercial lending" (Litan, 1987, p. 145). This would be accomplished by introducing "narrow banking" regulations. Narrow banks are banks that specialize in deposit-taking and payment activities. They are prohibited, or restricted, from lending to the private sector, and invest all their deposit liabilities in assets of very high quality.[4] If public insurance further protects narrow-bank deposits from bank fraudulent behavior, narrow banking does indeed offer to the public a highly safe type of money in that it provides ready funds to meet deposit withdrawals, making narrow-bank deposits the equivalent of currency.

The advocates of narrow banking hold that safety nets and bank prudential regulations would have no reason to exist under narrow banking. The nonbank intermediaries could operate under securities firm regulations, they should be free to engage in all types of non-monetary financial activities using non-guaranteed funds and should be allowed to fail. Under narrow banking, market discipline would be more effective in leading to prudent investment behavior while the financial system could be deregulated significantly, thereby achieving higher levels of efficiency.

There are no real-world examples of narrow banking regimes that could be used to assess their actual costs and benefits. Therefore, evaluating narrow banking necessarily entails some kinds of mental experiment, which, in the best of circumstances, can only lead to conjectural conclusions. However, taking stock of the considerable wealth of informed views accumulated on the subject over the years, and assessing the potential consequences of narrow banking against the backdrop of contemporary banking theory, may at least help correctly identify the various aspects and implications of the proposals. It would also provide policy insights for developing countries, at a time when their financial integration in the world economy renders the development of stable and efficient domestic financial systems an objective of international concern.

This study offers an evaluation of the theory and policy of narrow banking. The study will answer such questions as: would narrow banking deliver greater financial stability, as it promises to do? At which costs would that happen, if at all? Is narrow banking recommendable for developing economies?

The study rejects the validity of narrow banking on conceptual and empirical grounds, concluding that it would deprive the economy of the key functions and benefits of conventional banking. The study also finds no convincing elements in support of the practicability of the narrow banking proposals.

The rest of the study is organized as follows. Section 8.3 reviews the existing literature on narrow banking. Section 8.4 contrasts the narrow banking concept with contemporary theories of banking; it evaluates the potential consequences of narrow banking on finance and the real economy and derives empirical evidence on the costs of bank narrowness. Section 8.5 concludes the chapter by drawing policy implications.

---

[4] Boot and Greembaum (1992) characterize narrow banking as a form of direct regulation that proscribes specific types of activities, as opposed to indirect regulation which aims to induce (socially) optimal choices by altering the firms' incentive structure through rules (such as for minimum capital and liquidity, loan loss provisions, exit/entry, accounting and disclosure, and the like).

8.4 Narrow Banking Proposals: Origins and Contents[5]

8.4.1 Historical Antecedents

Narrow banking is the modern and more elaborated equivalent of the "100% reserve banking " principle, invoked by early economists to correct the inadequacy of money reserves against the stock of banknotes in circulation.[6] Aside from the examples of the goldsmiths and first deposit banks of centuries ago, historical precedents of such principle can be traced to the early monetary system of the American colonies in the eighteenth century and to the National Banking Acts of the US Government of 1863 and 1864. These can all be built on the notion that the primary forms of means of payment be backed with federal government securities (Phillips, 1995).

Perhaps, it is Sir Robert Peel's decision at the Bank of England, in 1844, to revert to the 100% reserve regime and to divide the Bank of England into a lending department and an issuing department, which constitutes the very first antecedent of a narrow banking regime.

The 100% reserve regime progressively came to be seen as a remedy to banking system instability problems, when new proposals were articulated to the effect that commercial banks be narrowed in scope, that is, restricted to accept only demand deposits and to invest funds only into safe assets.

Ideas to reform the banking system accordingly were debated in the USA since 1933, prompted by a series of memoranda to the Roosevelt administration from a group of economists of the University of Chicago, among whom the most prominent were Frank Knight, Henry Simons, and Lloyd Mints.[7] At a time when a major overhaul of the banking industry was deemed necessary, what since became known as the "Chicago Plan" propounded the abolition of the fractional reserve regime, the adoption of a 100% reserve requirement on demand deposits, and the displacement of existing deposit banks by at least two distinct types of institutions: deposit banks holding 100% reserves, and investment trusts performing lending funded by securities. These measures would prevent new banking panics, restore full government

---

[5] With only one exception, the review in this section draws exclusively on the Anglo-Saxon financial literature.

[6] In the Wealth of Nations, Adam Smith warned that "The whole paper money of every kind which can easily circulate in any country never can exceed the value of gold and silver... which would circulate there, if there was no paper money. Should the circulating paper at any time exceed that sum, [m]any people would immediately perceive that they had more of this paper than was necessary for transacting, and... they would immediately demand payment of it from the banks." (Bk. [I, II: 361-62). Later, David Ricardo would write: "To secure the public against any other variations in the value of the currency than those to be brought, and we should possess all the advantages by subjecting the [blank to the delivery of uncoined gold or silver at the Mint standard and price, in exchange for their notes." (From The Works of David Ricardo, Vol. I, Principles of Political Economy, edited by P. Sraffa, Cambridge University Press, 1951: 358).

[7] For an historical reconstruction of these contributions and their political fate, see Phillips (1992a). On the Chicago Plan see also the references in Friedman (1959), Chap. 3, footnote 8: 108.

control of the money supply process, and reduce economic fluctuations (Simons, 1934).

The first (and still the most comprehensive) study of the structure and implications of 100% reserve banking is Fisher (1935) "100% Money," written to show how such a regime would keep bank checking deposits fully liquid and prevent business cyclical instability. Fisher did not go much into the institutional issues of how best to segregate the deposit-taking and loan-making functions of a bank; he was more interested in the underlying economics and assumed that each function be carried out by a distinct department within the same bank.[8]

The idea of 100% reserve banking would be revived years later by Allais (1948), who strongly criticized fractional banking,[9] and it was further articulated by Friedman (1959) as a way to remedy the money supply instability and to reduce government regulatory intrusion into lending and investing activities. Friedman's proposal would make all the money stock in the system—whether currency or deposits—a government liability issued under uniform arrangements. Drawing from the Chicago Plan, all banks would hold 100% reserves, in Federal Reserve notes or deposits, against all outstanding deposit liabilities payable on demand or transferable by check. In this way, the stocks of money and high-powered money would coincide, and the instability in the money supply originating from the randomness of the money multiplier would be removed, thereby suppressing the need for deposit insurance. Friedman would break the commercial banks in two separate types of institution: on the one side, a pure depository that would have one dollar of central bank reserve for each dollar of demand deposits and the owners' capital available for lending; on the other, an investment trust that would acquire capital by selling shares or securities and use capital to fund loans and to acquire investments. This second type of institution was not to engage in money creation or destruction and would not require any special regulatory control. Friedman's proposal differed from the Chicago Plan in that it recommended interest to be paid on the 100% reserves.[10]

8.4.2 Modern Narrow Banking

Narrow banking proposals resurfaced in the USA in the 1980s, when tumultuous financial innovation and financial crisis episodes called for a reassessment of the extant banking regulatory regime. Before the issue became the object of more extensive policy analysis, some highly reputed scholars voiced their support for

[8] See, for instance, Fisher (1935), Chap. V, Part II.

[9] For a reappraisal of Allais' theory, see Phillips (1992b).

[10] Friedman justified this measure on three grounds. First, it would allow banks to pay interest on deposits and thus avert unproductive real resource investments by individuals to economize on cash balances. Second, it would lessen the incentive for banks to evade the 100% requirement. Third, it would redistribute back to the economy the government's monopolistic rents from money issue.

100% reserve banking, but without giving much emphasis to institutional aspects.[11] Various proposals have been formulated since [Even the World Bank (2001) has suggested that narrow banking could be used in some countries as a response to crises]. Proposals differ in terms of restrictions to be placed on bank asset portfolios and feature different institutional designs.

As regards the asset-portfolio dimension, proposals differ in the degree of restriction placed on the types of assets that narrow banks should be permitted to hold. Proposals vary from introducing a 100% reserve requirement that bound banks to fully back transaction accounts with marketable short-term treasury debt (Kareken, 1986; Mishkin, 1999; Spong, 1991; Thomas, 2000; Tobin, 1985), to requiring banks to invest (fully insured) deposits only in high-grade securities including government paper or government-guaranteed securities of various maturity (Herring & Litan, 1995; Litan, 1987), to allowing banks the use of insured checkable deposits for short-term lending to consumers and businesses (against securitized instruments), including securities issued by non-affiliated financial services companies (Pierce, 1991).

Some proponents argue that if the demand for highly liquid, riskless transaction deposits exceeds the supply of government paper, then the class of collateral assets should be broadened to include a well-diversified portfolio of traded short-term, high-grade corporate debt (Merton & Bodie, 1993; Spong, 1993). Such broadening, however, is controversial as it obviously reintroduces default risk into narrow banking (Litan, cit.).[12]

Some advocates of the more restrictive versions of narrow banking also propose that narrow banks marked to market the debt held in their portfolio frequently (Kareken, 1986; Mishkin, 1999). This provision would force them to adjust the value of their liabilities to that of their assets, much as mutual funds do. As a result, while the nominal value of the transaction account balances outstanding would not be guaranteed, the taxpayers would not be called upon to rescue insolvent institutions.[13]

---

[11] See, for instance, Black (1985), Tobin (1985), and Kareken (1985). Tobin (1987) elaborates on his earlier proposal, moving away from narrow banking strictly and proposing a redefinition of commercial banking that preserves the link between deposit money and commercial lending. This idea is close to Bryan's (1991) "core banking " model, whereby the scope of banking is narrowed down to a core of activities where banks have a demonstrated comparative advantage: issuance of checking, savings, and money market deposit accounts; provision of payment, trust, and custody services; and loans to individuals, small businesses, and medium-sized companies. A core bank, on the other hand, would not lend to large corporations and developing countries; it would not engage in high-leveraged transactions and in large commercial real estate projects; it would not undertake global money market activities of large money center banks or large regional banks; and it would not underwrite securities. According to Bryan, a core bank is a "safe place to keep your money," and the core banking functions he refers to are those where banks reportedly make the overwhelming bulk of their profits.

[12] Litan discusses the consequences of broadening the class and term-structure of the securities available to narrow banks for investments, and the regulatory actions that would have to be associated with those changes.

[13] As Kareken points out, there is a clear tradeoff here between a contract of certain value but carrying the risk of not being honored and a contract of uncertain value, but which is going to be

The narrow banking proposals vary also with respect to institutional factors. Noting that technology and bookkeeping techniques allow banks wanting to offer risky balances to evade such regulation by switching funds across different types of accounts at high speed and low costs, Kareken (1986) suggests that banks offering transaction balances be prevented from issuing other types of services,[14] although he remains agnostic as to whether this should be accomplished by splitting banks into distinct subsidiaries or by allowing two separate industries to emerge (one made up of narrow banks and the other, broader and more inclusive, made up of lending companies).

Others see the functional segregation of banking from nonbanking activities as the optimal regulatory response to the risks associated with financial deregulation and innovation, and with the increasing power of banks. Litan and Pierce, in the two studies cited above, propose that highly diversified (financial or non-financial) firms offering both insured depository services and lending services be transformed into financial holding companies that engage in different activities through separate subsidiaries. In particular, depository functions would be carried out by subsidiaries operating under narrow banking restrictions, while other subsidiaries would have to be used to extend loans funded by uninsured liabilities and equity. Only narrow banks would have access to the payment system, and nonbank corporations would not be allowed to hold accounts at their affiliated narrow banks.

Functional segregation (which neither Litan nor Pierce envision for smaller banks[15]) would prevent financial holding companies from using the resources of their depositories to bail out risky nonbank affiliates or to finance connected lending. It would also serve to limit the high concentration of economic power in the hands of a few large financial organizations. Functional segregation has been advocated by market specialists, as well, in that securitization and competition allow banks to be unbundled into their component functions, so that each can be performed by whichever players are most capable of delivering the best service at the best price.

Mishkin (1999) proposes regulation that would permit banks to issue both insured narrow-bank deposits collateralized by high-grade securities and uninsured deposits to finance private-sector lending. This solution would preserve banks' economies of scope between deposit issuance and bank lending, which would otherwise be lost under restrictive functional segregation rules. Furthermore, this solution would

---

honored with certainty. Goodhart (1988) evaluates (and supports) the idea of introducing such type of mutual-funds money.

[14] Through sweep accounts, banks can handle large volumes of transaction balances throughout each business day but record only a small amount at the end of the day. While recorded balances would be insured, the unrecorded ones would be unprotected by insurance and bear full risk to their holders.

[15] The exemption of smaller banks recognizes that narrow banks need some minimum scale to operate efficiently. The exemption would also help to counteract any contraction of credit supply to small businesses, without imperiling systemic stability. As importantly, the exemption would facilitate the access to funds from small organizations that lack direct access to major credit markets (Spong, 1993).

leave to the banks the decision to combine narrow banking and conventional banking activities, based only on profit considerations.[16]

Recent theoretical contributions have revisited the issue of narrow banking from the standpoint of informational efficiency. Peters and Thakor (1995) show that it is not feasible for a single bank to provide optimal incentives for depositors to monitor asset allocation from bank managers, and for bank managers to monitor borrowers. They thus prescribe to separate banks along functional lines whereby some narrow-bank types of institutions offer insured deposits against assets whose value is invariant to bank monitoring, while nonbanks issue uninsured liabilities to fund riskier assets.

In a different context, Craine (1995) studies an environment with two types of intermediaries, one investing in non-traded private-information assets and the other holding traded public-information assets, and calls "banks " those intermediaries that choose to issue insured transaction accounts. Craine shows that, when regulation restricts the issue of transaction accounts to private-information intermediaries, an inefficient equilibrium is achieved where these intermediaries have an incentive to over-invest in risky portfolios and earn rents on insured accounts. He further shows that, when regulation is relaxed and all intermediaries are given access to bank status (i.e., they are authorized to issue insured transaction accounts), a voluntary efficient separating equilibrium ensues whereby all public-information intermediaries issue insured accounts and do not extract rents from them, and all private-information intermediaries fund assets with private sources.

8.5 Evaluation of Narrow Banking

The benefits of narrow banking seem straightforward and immediately evident. First, by locking bank assets in high-quality instruments, narrow banking regulation would minimize banks' liquidity and credit risks. Second, as narrow banks would be precluded from supplying loans and collateralizing deposits with high-quality assets, the confidence in the value of their claims used to make payments could not be weakened by changes in the value of loans. Third, with payment system access restricted to narrow banks, payments would be fully secure since payment system participants would be protected against liquidity, credit, and settlement risks, and any shock to nonbanks would be isolated, with no systemic fallout (Burnham,

[16] As Mishkin notes, eventual reduction of insured deposits would be consistent with no loss of efficiency since the deposits that disappear would have been issued in larger amounts only because of the deposit insurance subsidy.

1990; Thomas, 2000).[17] Fourth, narrow banking improves the central bank's ability to control the money supply process.

As a result, capital requirements for narrow banks could be reduced substantially, the potential recourse to the taxpayer for depositor protection would become infrequent, and the inequitable too-large-to-fail bailout clause would be removed by making the failure of large narrow banks less likely. There would thus be a much lesser need for subjecting narrow banks to special regulation and supervision (Bruni, 1995; Thomas, 2000). Also, since narrow banks would be protected from nonbank activities, a broader range of activities and a wider ownership structure might be possible for their nonbank affiliates than under current banking regulations in many countries (Spong, 1993).

Other important benefits are associated with narrow banking. Short of a (socially costly) deposit insurance mechanism, the availability of narrow-bank deposits would eliminate any discrimination between well-informed and uninformed depositors, and it would instead leave the investors free to choose among alternative asset risk/return configurations on the basis on non-subsidized terms, while it would protect all depositors, reduce moral hazard, and prevent expensive bank runs. As well, the delegation of lending decisions to uninsured and market-disciplined institutions would halt the inequitable practice, induced by deposit insurance, of granting equal access to funds to both weak and sound lenders.

Furthermore, a narrow banking regime would afford greater shock resiliency to the whole financial system: a failure of the market to elicit enough sound behavior from nonbanks would still leave the economy's monetary sector unexposed to shocks. While the market would/should eventually punish (ex-post) the untoward behavior from individual institutions or investors, both money and the payment system would be unaffected by such behavior.

On the developmental side, narrow banking is expected to spur the relevant financial system structural changes already underway in the advanced economies. Commercial banks having to switch to narrow banking regulation could be expected to transfer their credit exposures to existing or newly established finance companies, which typically operate with higher capital ratios and fund themselves with relatively larger volumes of long-term debt. Banks would remove loans from the portfolio of prospective narrow banks through securitization, packaging similar types of credit into new securities and selling them to a host of institutional investors. Furthermore, as commercial banks would progressively move out of the long-term stretch of the

[17] The concerns expressed by some on the risks raised by interbank overdrafts (see for instance (Phillips, 1995; Pierce, 1991; Spong, 1993) are overstated. In a narrow banking regime, the exchange of fully covered deposits through the payment system would make payment settlement by netting safer than under fractional reserve banking, since all the interbank intraday lending implicit in the netting process would be fully collateralized (by construction): banks could not create mutual debit/credit positions that exceeded their deposit cover, since no uncovered deposits would be allowed in the system. Adopting a gross settlement rule would therefore add only protection against the risk of some participants deliberately refusing to settle their outstanding debit balances, when required, or against the (even more remote) risk of some participants losing access to the means necessary to settle interbank payments.

market, insurance companies, pension funds, and non-financial companies interested to assume bank-like functions would fill the gap and expand their lending activity.

As to the viability of the narrow banking model, its advocates cite the successful experience of the US money market mutual funds industry. The increasing demand for mutual funds products shows the potential attractiveness of narrow-bank deposits and transaction services.

Not the least important, at times of disorderly market conditions the industry has proven capable to weather depositor runs (Kareken, 1985; Kareken, 1986; McCulloch, 1987; Phillips, 1995).

However, the downsides to narrow banking do not appear to be any less substantial than the advantages. Some of them in fact challenge the benefits just discussed. This section assesses narrow banking against contemporary theories of banking and shows that narrow banking regulations would dissipate the benefits associated with the specialness of conventional banks. This section also evaluates the potential consequences of narrow banking on finance and the economy and estimates the effects of narrow banking on the cost and availability of credit in the economy.

8.5.1 Narrow Banking Versus Banking: Insights from Theory[18]

Strong reservations to narrow banking emerge from contrasting its notion with recent theories of banking. In this subsection, the narrow banking concept is evaluated against contemporary theories of banking as a mechanism for: liquidity generation, optimal contract design, efficient joint-production of deposit-taking and lending, and money creation.

Banks as Liquidity Generators

An important strand of research, following Diamond and Dybvig (1983), stresses the role of banks as insurers against liquidity shocks. In a setting where all individuals are initially identical but learn only subsequently to have different intertemporal consumption preferences, banks are shown to generate liquidity to help individuals who discover to be "patient" consumers to satisfy their needs. They do so by transforming illiquid assets into liquid deposits. This is possible because the averaging out of the withdrawal demands from many depositors allows banks to stabilize their deposit base and transfer deposit ownership without liquidating the assets. From this angle, the social benefit of banking derives from an improvement in risk-sharing, i.e., the increased flexibility of those who have an urgent need to withdraw their funds before the assets mature (Diamond & Dybvig, 1986).

In fact, the benefit of banking cannot be fully appreciated if the asset and the liability side of the bank balance sheet are not considered connectedly. The benefit

[18] The approach here used expands on Kobayakawa and Nakamura (2000).

derives from the banks using their stable deposit base to finance production technologies that increase output over time. The output effect enables banks to provide a pattern of returns to depositors which is superior to what they could obtain by holding the illiquid assets and/or a perfectly (non-interest bearing) asset such as cash.[19]

In such light, banks generate liquidity to depositors and simultaneously assure patient money to producing enterprises in a way that would not be feasible without the special intermediation of banks (a point hinted at by Gorton and Pennacchi, 1990, but surprisingly not emphasized by Diamond and Dybvig themselves).

This crucial link between liquidity and production is explicitly recognized in Diamond and Rajan (1998, 1999), where banks are regarded as superior devices to tie human capital with real (illiquid) assets, and where the sequential service constraint ordering the way in which banks service withdrawal demands (up to when they become illiquid) work as an incentive for bankers to behave prudently. As Wallace (1996) elegantly demonstrates, narrow banking would break that link, thereby eliminating the social benefit of banking.

Merton and Bodie (1993) argue that asset and liquidity transformation services are performed whenever a collection of assets is repackaged, and the resulting liabilities created have a smaller bid-ask spread than the original assets. They conclude that, to generate liquidity, banks need not invest in highly illiquid assets with large bid-ask spreads. Instead, they support the use of "next-nearest" asset for transformation, underpinning narrow banking, to support safe demand deposits.

The point remains, however, that production requires patient money and involves risks, while agents with money may not be as patient and risk-inclined to lend it to firms: banks do provide a mechanism to reconcile both sets of preferences by generating liquidity. Narrow banks are designed precisely not to do so.

Banks as Providers of Optimal Contracts for Transforming Liquidity and Maturity

Without specially designed contracts, uninformed parties would be reluctant to provide credit for fear of being exploited by better-informed parties. Depositors would not lend their funds to banks, and banks would not lend their funds to firms. But while bank loan agreements incorporate features that permit banks to protect the bank's interests, depositors are typically less informed that bank managers and face much higher costs of protection from acts against their interests. Demandable debt (i.e., the demand deposit contract) is for the depositors a particularly potent and economical means of avoiding bank exploitation. By requiring banks to make good on deposits at fixed nominal value on demand and with low transaction costs, depositors can easily withdraw their investment in a poorly managed bank and thus exert discipline on bank behavior (Calomiris & Kahn, 1991; Diamond & Rajan, 1998, 1999).

[19] In other words, if depositors hold the illiquid assets, they may have to forego immediate consumption needs. If they hold the perfectly liquid asset, they forego higher future consumption possibilities.

This property of deposits allows banks to expand the volume of resources that they can make available to their borrowers for illiquid investments. Although alternative forms of liabilities can be used to finance illiquid investment, they would not be as widely accepted as deposits by uninformed investors and would thereby reduce the funds for such investments and raise their cost. Equity is more costly than debt in a setting of asymmetric information about the value of a bank's assets, since uninformed equity holders are reluctant to agree to the issuance of new equity against unknown new assets and cause new issues to depress share values (Myers & Majluf, 1984). On the other hand, in an environment of asymmetric information long-term debt is more costly than demandable debt to depositors as control on banks would involve longer lags and higher transaction costs. The use of demand deposits, therefore, occurs precisely because bank assets are of uncertain value and because depositors are less informed than bankers (Pozdena, 1991).

Banks as Efficient Joint-Producers of Deposit-Taking and Lending

The provision of lending and deposit-taking services is more efficient if processed by the same institution (Kashyap et al., 1999). Deposits, like loan commitments, provide liquidity on demand. Since liquidity commitments need to be supported by a buffer stock of cash and safe securities, banks can economize on such stock by combining the two types of services (provided that deposit and loan withdrawals are not strongly mutually correlated). Banks can thus hold a smaller buffer than would be required by two intermediaries offering the same services separately. Such economies allow banks to offer liquidity services to their customers at lower prices than other intermediaries. Saidenberg and Strahan (1999) corroborate this theory with evidence showing that banks maintain a very important role as reliable suppliers of liquidity to the corporate sector, especially at times of securities market distress. Since at such time investors revert to bank deposits, banks do not have to run down their buffer stock of liquid assets to provide liquidity to borrower.

By separating deposit and lending services, narrow banking would suppress the synergetic effect and generate inefficiency in the supply of liquidity to the private sector, with the level of inefficiency varying with the type of asset portfolio allowed to narrow banks.

Banks as Creators of Money

Even when banks are modeled as generators of liquidity, still they act as intermediaries who ultimately draw (accumulated) real resources from one side of the market, against the issue of liquid claims, and transfer them to the other side of the market, against the issue of longer-term claims. Intermediaries presuppose the existence of real resources, or of claims thereof, which can be deposited with them in exchange for promissory notes. Such promissory notes are therefore claims on some output already produced and accumulated in the economy.

But banks and bank money do more than that. As deposits represent debt claims on banks that the public accepts as money, banks can mobilize production factors by lending to producers newly issued debt claims. The new money is to be backed by the output coming out of the new production financed with it, and this can only happen ex-post, once the output is produced and sold. Ultimately, the money is as good as the banks can select good borrowers.

Banks stand at the inception of the production cycle, as the theory of the monetary circuit holds (Bossone, 2001a, b), and conveniently create money and allocate it to the firms that need it to carry out their activity. This process is evident in the hypothetical case of an economy with only one bank and only one type of money, where all agents hold their deposit accounts with the same bank. Aside from inflationary and risk considerations, the bank would be able to create all the deposits it so wished (to the extent that depositors would continue to accept them), since the re-depositing automatically following payments would prevent the bank from running into illiquidity or insolvency.[20] In a multi-bank environment, the money creation power of banks needs to be supported by interbank (non-reserve) credit arrangements (such as overdraft and netting facilities) to supplement the re-depositing mechanism. The cost of creating money thus depends on the (explicit and implicit) cost of interbank credit and the cost of holding higher-powered reserves against liabilities.

Narrow banking would suppress the money creation feature of banking. As a result, credit to the economy would become scarcer and more costly. To see why, let's analyze how money would be supplied under narrow banking. If the nonbanks fund their assets with short-term non-deposit debt, overall lending to the economy can be maintained only if the investors are willing to replace bank deposits with nonbank debt in their portfolio. Yet, all else equal, this would require a higher remuneration of the nonbank debt, which would make lending costlier and reduce the liquidity in the system (since, by regulation, the nonbank debt cannot be used as money).

Alternatively, the nonbanks could borrow or purchase money from the central bank, against collateral or in exchange for securities, and on-lend it to the business sector. But the nonbanks' cost of lending would be larger than for conventional banks since the latter can fund their loans by creating deposits. Still, the central bank could lend uncollateralized reserves to the nonbanks, but this would come at a risk for the central bank. In this case, either the central bank would be capable to determine the optimal interest rate risk-premium for each borrower or it would misprice risk, with system-wide distortions. In the end, assuming away money-substitution phenomena, narrow banking brings the whole money creation process back to the central bank, therefore maximizing the central bank's control of the money supply, but it would so at a considerable efficiency loss to the economy.[21]

Finally, since it relies heavily on reserve money, a narrow banking regime is vulnerable to a serious potential failure: in the event of a net overall reserve shortage, the nonbanks would need eligible paper to raise reserves, but they might not be able to buy or to borrow the paper precisely because they don't have enough reserves! To be sure, the class of eligible securities could be broadened as to allow wider access to reserve money, but in most cases, the units in the economy with surplus holdings

---

[20] Even in this special case, the depositors' potential demand for convertibility would require the bank to hold a fraction of its liabilities in the form of some higher-powered claim.

[21] For a very recent and insightful theoretical analysis of the (in)efficiencies associated with private and public money regimes, see Azariadis et al. (2001).

of eligible securities would have to either lend securities directly to the deficit units, or use their securities to raise cash from the central bank and lend it to the deficit units, in both cases bearing the related credit risk. Once more, there is a natural need for somebody in the system to get the power to create liquidity (money or securities, as necessary) at a risk.[22]

The importance of the money creation feature of banking survives to today's financial market transformation and to the banks' lesser involvement in direct lending to production. Aside from the continuing relevance of bank lending to small and medium sized businesses, it is undoubtedly the case that in the advanced economies, nonbank quasi-money and financing products are taking increasing business shares away from banks, while nonbanks manage to offer products which allow investors and consumers to economize on less remunerative bank deposits. Yet, money transactions take place by deposit transfers across bank accounts, and the acceptance by the public of nonbank products owes to these products' convertibility into bank deposits. This presupposes the existence of banks and their readiness to supply deposits to refinance such products when necessary?.[23] Narrow banking would hamper the development of the nonbank financial sector, contrary to what its advocates assert.

Today, banks increasingly specialize in retail services or in wholesale businesses. Through both channels, they continue to use lending and loan commitments to supply the economy with the money needed to effect transactions. Narrow banking, at least in its more conservative versions, would abort those channels at a major loss to the society.

In conclusion, as one judges from theory, forcing a synchronization of maturity between bank assets and liabilities, and eliminating potential bank difficulties by removing conventional banks, would dissipate the significant benefits associated with conventional banking systems, which stem from issuing demandable deposits to finance other than government liabilities.

8.5.2 Potential Consequences of Narrow Banking

Aside from the theoretical considerations above, there are important, more operational issues concerning the impact of narrow banking on finance and the real economy, which need discussing. These include:

---

[22] Note that the *liquidity creation* in this example rests on the regulatory fiat broadening the class of papers eligible for conversion into reserve money.

[23] As confidence in the nonbank products grows, nothing prevents the public from accepting nonbank quasi-monies as money at some point. The issuing nonbanks would then no longer need to rely on bank deposits to effect transactions. At that point, they would have an incentive to start lending their own-produced money, precisely like banks do.

The Supply of High-Quality Assets

All narrow banking proposals must confront the question of whether there is in the economy enough of the instruments eligible to be used as collateral for transaction deposits. If narrow banks were required to hold government paper only, the supply of such paper would depend on the government's debt management strategy. To the extent that a country runs large debt-financed deficits, the stock of public securities outstanding might be enough to serve the economy's monetary needs.[24] But this need not be the case, especially when the country decides to cut its public deficits and reduce its stock of debt (see Schinasi and Smith, 2001; IMF, 2001, Ch. IV).

More importantly, tying the provision of monetary services to public debt management and assigning it to the government might not be a good policy. Similarly, tying public debt management to monetary and payment system objectives does not look sensible either. (By construction, such a link would become the strongest once the flexibility afforded by conventional banking as a creator of private money would be suppressed by narrow banking, and all the stock of money available to the public would have to be fully backed with government paper).

The alternative is to extend the admissible narrow-bank portfolios to a broader class of assets, including private-sector securities. This, obviously, would reflect on the creditworthiness of the narrow banks and on the costs of monitoring more diversified portfolios. In particular, if narrow banks were permitted to hold high-grade corporate bonds, one would have to question whether the quality of such bonds would still be the same in the absence of bank commitments to provide contingent liquidity to corporations when needed.

Narrow Banks and the Safety Nets (I)

Can narrow banks do without safety nets? Insuring narrow-bank deposits is usually predicated for the only purpose of protecting depositors against the residual risk of bank fraud (Mishkin, 1999). For narrow banks to be able to do without safety nets, they must obviously be perceived by the public as being financially viable and fully safe. I shall deal with the viability issue further below. On the safety issue, narrow banks are clearly as good as their assets. Now, even under regulation requiring narrow banks to hold only short-term government paper, full safety cannot be achieved in the absence of a credible commitment from the issuing banks to convert on request into cash, at par, all deposit holdings. To the extent that the narrow-bank collateral is not accepted in the economy as money, there is always a chance that depositors would rush to their banks if they perceived their collateral to be losing value or to become illiquid, and if they fear that other depositors might do the same at the same time.

Perceptions of less than full safety may become significant when fluctuations in the market value of government paper are marked, and when sovereign risk is not

[24] Add to this that, as the system shifted to the narrow banking mode, the public might want to economize on transaction deposits and invest elsewhere their wealth—say in uninsured short-term paper—so that the overall stock of transaction deposits would shrink, thus making collateralization easier.

negligible.[25] Developing countries may suffer from both these problems. Ghosh and Saggar (1998) discuss the significant market and capital loss risks that narrow banks would likely confront in developing economies. In particular, they point to the many historical cases of governments and central banks deliberately inflicting capital losses on public debt holders through inflation, repudiation, and outright manipulation of yields. Since a large exposure to a single borrower (i.e., the government) might not be advisable in some countries, an alternative could be to permit narrow banks to hold foreign assets (although this would introduce the foreign exchange risk dimension).

Narrow banks would likely take huge capital losses in the process of massive stock selling, even if they could liquidate the collateral in a large, deep, and well-developed secondary market. They might still be unable to face withdrawal demands unless they held enough extra capital.

In the end, like under conventional banking, only an "insurer" (in the form of a deposit insurance mechanism, or a lender of last resort) would remove the risk of default from narrow banks altogether. Alternatively, narrow banks could be (even more stringently) required to hold only central bank notes or deposits, although not even this option could protect them from runs on the currency (unless the central bank held a 100% foreign reserve collateral).

Narrow Banks and the Safety Nets (II)

Does narrow banking eliminate the need of safety nets for nonbank intermediaries? As discussed, one of the most strongly held expectations by narrow banking advocates is that, once transaction money is fully protected, the rest of the financial system can be left to operate outside of any public protection mechanism. Their belief is that, without the distortive effect of public protection that subsidizes liquidity transformation, there would be no real incentives for banks to operate as such (Kareken, 1985). Accordingly, if safety nets were to be removed from under fractional reserve deposits, banks would cease to finance loans with transaction deposits, they would transform themselves into some other types of nonbank intermediary and try to match their asset/liability term structure to resolve their fragility.

However, this stands in stark contrast against the historical evolution of banking, which shows that earliest banks developed without safety nets, let alone regulation, by conducting maturity and liquidity transformation, and by issuing banknotes in excess of reserves.

History thus shows the existence of a natural incentive for some firms to finance dynamic portfolios of opaque assets with relatively short-term liabilities (Flannery, 1994), leading to the establishment of intermediaries specialized in the supply of liquidity and asset transformation services (Mussa, 1986), and to the emergence of special intermediaries ("banks") capable of financing loans by creating money (see

---

[25] In countries where government securities are free of default risk, a regulation that would permit narrow banks to hold long-term government paper (following, for example, Litan, 1987) could subject them to a considerable interest rate risk. McCulloch (1987) notes that at the time he wrote the Macaulay duration (and thus the interest rate sensitivity) of 30-year US Treasury bonds was greater than that of 30-year amortized mortgage loans.

below). Under narrow banking, such natural incentive would lead some intermediaries to compete for the provision of conventional banking services, eventually replicating the world before narrow banking. The public would again demand safety nets for their short-term liabilities, and government guarantees would tend to along with depositor funds to the new intermediaries.[26]

Also, runs are not confined to narrowly defined transaction accounts within the narrow banks but can occur on non-transaction deposits (CD accounts, bankers acceptances, and time deposits) that are not covered by narrow-bank deposit insurance (Calomiris, 1999), and no-bailout commitments are not credible, especially when the issuers of such instruments are large institutions.

In conclusion, government appears unable to credibly commit to not insuring bank deposits, as well as to not extending insurance to other types of financial sector liability, under public pressure. Limiting insurance to narrow-bank deposits might fail to add to market discipline, and narrowing the scope of banking might not do much to repeal deposit insurance.[27]

The Cost of Restructuring

A practical concern on narrow banking regards the cost of breaking long-standing multifunction banks into specialized, legally, and physically separate corporations (Benston & Kaufman, 1993). New structures would have to be built, or old structures redesigned; employees would have to be reassigned to each organization; and information costs to and for customers might be significant.

As a least-cost alternative, some propose that the institutions that wished to offer depository services (even in addition to other nonbank riskier services) be simply required to keep a 100% reserve in government securities against their transaction deposit liabilities.[28] The proponents of this option believe that such constraint would be enough to protect transaction deposits from the other activities of the depository institution and would not eliminate bank scale or scope economies from "one-stop" consumer shopping.

Though appealing, this solution must be proven to be able to raise a tight enough "firewall" between the monetary and the non-monetary financial activities. This is deemed necessary to prevent that narrow-bank assets were used to bail out the non-monetary financial activities in the event of some liquidity or solvency problems. For

[26] Caprio and Summers (1993) and Caprio (1996) note that under narrow banking, the rise in the price of safe assets will lead investors to want to hold some less secure paper than narrow-bank deposits, motivating nonbanks to offer deposit accounts backed by higher yielding assets which could be subject to default. This would induce a demand for safety nets to be extended to such accounts.

[27] As Calomiris (1999) notes, politically, the absence of de jure protection on bank liabilities outside the narrow bank does not imply the absence of de facto protection by the government. Absent the government's credible commitment to not intervene to prop up banks during a crisis, narrow banking may only end up substituting ad hoc bailouts for explicit insurance coverage.

[28] See Benston et al. (1989), Merton and Bodie (1993), and Benston and Kaufman (1993).

this reason, narrow banking proposals usually recommend that narrow-bank assets be segregated and unreachable.[29]

The Viability of Narrow Banks

How attractive is the narrow banking business? Based on the experience of money market mutual funds, Spong (1993) argues that, once freed from major regulatory burdens, narrow banks should be able to offer depositors a return competitive with other low-risk investment alternatives. Narrow banks would earn interest income from their assets and non-interest income from the fees charged on transaction services. Also, because of their minimal capital needs, narrow banks could operate on low margins and still be able to earn satisfactory returns on equity.

From the opposite stance, Ely (1991) sees the restrictions in the range of investment activity to result in a reduction of narrow banks' size and income. This tendency, he contends, would be accentuated by the small bank exemption clause (see the proposals by Pierce and Litan above), which would prompt the formation of many small banks, especially in urban areas.[30] In fact, the income losses associated with the smaller scale might turn out to be significant in light of the recent findings on scale economies in the banking industry.[31]

Moreover, in countries where banks are not free to close branches as they see fit, a reduction in activity would face would-be narrow banks with increasing unit operating expenses, possibly leading them to depress the interest rate paid on deposits and causing outflows of funds toward nonbanks.

The reduction in size anticipated by Ely is consistent with country evidence indicating a small demand deposit base in relation to overall banking activity. Using 1995 survey data on India, Ghosh and Saggar (1998) conclude that the imposition of narrow banking would squeeze the country's banking sector. They also argue that requiring banks to invest only in government paper may lower their income substantially (even after adjusting for the gains from lower non-performing loans) and note that such gains could be easily wiped out by a single interest rate shock similar to those experienced in India in the late 1990s.

Separating lending from deposit-taking activities may also cause intermediaries to miss the efficiency gains from the joint-production of the two services (see above).

Finally, in the case of developing economies with large price volatility in the government securities markets, it is less than certain that the after-risk rate of return on narrow-bank portfolios would be competitive with the return on well-diversified and well-managed conventional bank portfolios.

---

[29] See the discussion on this point in Phillips (1995).

[30] Considering the high standardization of the narrow banking products and the need for achieving economies of scale, one could make the case that the narrow banking business is a natural monopoly, In this case, narrow banking services could be provided directly by the central bank, or by one single banking entity with a large geographical presence across the country. The Postal Office could be an example of such an entity.

[31] For an extensive review of the literature on scale economies in banking and the nonbanking financial sector, see Bossone et al. (2001).

Private-Sector Credit Availability

Opponents of narrow banking argue that not enough credit would flow to the private sector if commercial banks were to turn into narrow banks. Credit would become relatively scarcer and costlier, most notably for smaller (firm and consumer) borrowers, since noninsured financial companies would be motivated to invest in larger enterprises.

With the exception of Wallace (1996) and the above discussion, this issue has usually been debated outside of well-defined theoretical frameworks. The following are the typical arguments used by narrow banking proponents to dismiss the concern on short credit supply.

Proponents of narrow banking trust that the incentives prompted by narrow banking would further the ongoing transformation of the financial system away from traditional banking and into nonbanking intermediation. They hold that experience so far shows that nonbanks in the advanced economies attract more and more business away from banks. Thus, new entry into the market of finance companies, investment banks, and institutional investors, as well as the increasing use of financing instruments alternative to deposits (e.g., securitization, equities, and junks bonds), it is asserted, should supplement the supply of credit as needed.

On the other hand, the exemption of small banks from narrow banking regulation would help protect the flow of credit supply to the small business sector. However, if the cost of credit did increase overall, this would be the (explicit) price that society would have to pay to achieve higher financial stability in a system that does not subsidize risk taking through public guarantees (Burnham, 1991). Finally, if credit to small borrowers remains a concern, then some form of explicit public support mechanism would be preferable than the continued use of distortive indirect subsidy schemes such as deposit insurance.

8.5.3 *In Search of Evidence*

In the absence of historical experience with narrow banking, this section looks for indicative empirical evidence out of a simple proxy experiment. This consists of estimating through OLS method the impact of bank narrowness on the cost and availability of lending to the private sector over a large sample of countries and across an extended period.

The results are reported in Appendix 1, Bank narrowness is proxied by the liquidity-to-asset ratio of the domestic banking sector, where liquidity is defined to include total claims on the central bank and government bonds held by the banks. Note that tables bearing identical caption use alternative definitions of (one or more) of the same variables. If predictions from contemporary banking theories are correct, all else equal, narrow banking should reduce the supply of credit to the private sector and raise its cost to borrowers.

The data used in the exercise are from the IMF's International Financial Statistics and cover 46 industrial and developing countries, each reporting for different years ranging variously from 1966 to 2000. The bank market concentration indicator included in one equation is from Beck et al. (1999).

For the purpose at hand, identifying structural equations to explain the variability of the lending rate was considered less important than finding a simple, straightforward relationship with a large statistical predictive power, to which the bank narrowness indicator could be added to get a sense of its relative impact on private-sector credit. A good candidate for a simple model was a cost-based relationship, in the assumption that the lending rate would be strongly correlated with the deposit interest rate.

The results (Table 8.1 in Appendix 1) show bank narrowness to have a positive, statistically significant effect on the cost of lending to the private sector. The equation, however, may hide the effect of reserve requirements in that they impose an implicit tax on banks (if they are not adequately remunerated), which banks eventually recover through lower deposit rates and higher lending rates. In this case, it would not be clear if a change in reserve requirements would affect lending rates because of their effect on bank cost structure, or because they make credit scarcer through the bank narrowness effect.

A simple regression was thus tested to measure the dependence of the spread between lending and deposit rates on the reserves-to-asset ratio and on banking concentration, showing the reserve ratio effect to be significant (Table 8.2).[32] Considering this result, the lending rate equation was rerun eliminating reserves from the bank narrowness indicator. The equation proved to be more than robust, in that the statistics for (re-defined) bank narrowness all improved (Table 8.3).

Narrow banking should make bank credit to the private sector relatively scarcer. To show this, credit to the private sector was regressed against the lending rate and the bank narrowness indicator. The results (Table 8.4) support the prediction showing a significant, negative effect of bank narrowness on bank credit to the private sector (in percent of GDP). In fact, the marginal impact of bank narrowness is significantly larger than that of the price variable.

The advocates of narrow banking argue that the restriction of credit would be offset dynamically through alternative supplies of funds. The effect of bank narrowness was then measured on a credit aggregate which includes credit to the private sector financed with instruments other than demand deposits: if the substitution effect is in place, it must be captured by the estimated coefficient of bank narrowness, which should turn out to be significantly lower (in absolute value) than under the narrower credit aggregate, or statistically not different from zero. In fact, the results (Table 8.5) show a significant, negative coefficient (even larger in absolute value than under the narrower credit aggregate), suggesting that, as bank narrowness increases, no alternative forms of credit emerge enough to offset the reduction of bank credit.

[32] It must be noted that the reserves variable used in the equation includes all bank claims with the central bank, with no distinction between required and free reserves. It is therefore likely that the obtained regression coefficient overestimates the required reserves effect discussed above.

Running the same regression on the sample including only developing countries confirms this result (Table 8.6).

This simple model does not explicitly control for other factors like sovereign risk. Often, one finds high lending rates and little private-sector credit in countries with high sovereign risk, where banks just invest in government bonds. In part, this phenomenon reflects adverse selection issues in which any party willing to borrow at high rates (perhaps because of sovereign risk) is a poor credit risk and the only alternative for lenders is to invest in government paper. The model, however, uses nominal lending rates. In so far as they are market-determined, such rates incorporate various risk factors. Unsurprisingly, all model regressions in the exercise show a negative coefficient of the lending rate, perhaps suggesting that the adverse selection effect is controlled for in the equations, and that the estimate of bank narrowness is orthogonal to it.

To improve on these results, an equation was run where the lending rate is corrected for inflation and inflation is included separately as a proxy for country macroeconomic risk. The results are even stronger than in the alternative formulation and confirm the negative effect of all the three variables considered (Tables 8.7 and 8.8). Based on the full country sample, it turns that on average a I percent increase in bank narrowness reduces the availability of credit to the private sector by 0.73%.

8.6 Policy Discussion and Conclusion

From the above analysis, it seems fair to conclude that narrowing the scope of banking would, at best, bear less than certain benefits in terms of greater financial stability, while it would exact some heavy costs in terms of efficiency and credit availability.

Narrow banking would severe the link between liquidity, money, credit, and economic activity, which banking has a natural incentive to establish efficiently (under stable macroeconomic conditions). By suppressing bank money as an instrument to finance lending to the private sector, narrow banking would create serious market incompleteness. The consequent economic losses might generate incentives for other financial firms to fill in the gap left by undertaking conventional banking activities. While this would forswear the very purpose of narrow banking, it would eventually replicate the world before narrow banking, engendering the same risks that were supposed to be removed in the first place through limiting the scope of banks.

The economic costs of narrow banking could be particularly significant for developing countries, where the need is vital for an efficient banking system both as an engine of economic growth and a support for the development of a strong nonbank financial sector. Also, in many developing countries, propositions to move to narrow banking should be resisted given the absence of a well-developed secondary market for government securities, a highly volatile environment for securities prices, the existence of sovereign risk, and a non-credible government commitment not to insure deposits or financial instruments of large public use.

Better alternatives to narrow banking would be Bryan's core banking model (footnote 9, Section Ill), or those regulatory regimes that separate commercial (short term) banking from investment (longer-term) banking activities, even within the same financial holding companies.

There is some favor to the idea that narrow banking could be used in some countries as a response to crises (World Bank, 2001). In particular, weak banks could be required to operate as narrow banks with a view to fixing their balance sheets. Whereas selective intervention on individual banks could be justified, policymakers should be aware that the banks required to operate as narrow banks would rapidly dissipate their banking knowledge capital.[33]

While mandatory narrow banking regulations should be rejected, nothing should stand in the way of individual institutions wanting to offer narrow banking services to their customers on a voluntary basis or to create narrow-bank subsidiaries that would be segregated from other businesses within the same bank holding companies.

An efficient, free-choice regulatory solution would be that prospected by Mishkin (1999) and discussed earlier. While not suppressing the risks inherent in conventional banking, such solution would retain the money creation power of conventional banks, avail risk-averse investors of a full risk-proof money instrument and let the financial institutions and their customers free to opt for conventional and/or narrow banking instruments based on their own convenience.

There are two additional (not mutually exclusive) alternatives that would improve the incentives to prudence for both banks and depositors while preserving conventional banking. Banks could issue uninsured deposits bearing an option clause whereby, in the event of liquidity problems, a bank could suspend deposit convertibility up to a predetermined time interval while it liquidates its assets in an orderly fashion. In the meantime, the bank's deposits would continue to circulate in the payment system. To induce depositors to accept such provision, the bank would commit to pay an interest penalty in the event it invoked the option or to pay a premium on the deposit interest rate.[34]

On the other hand, banks could issue uninsured subordinated debt, as proposed by Keehn (1989) and Wall (1989), and recently by Calomiris (1999). The subordinated debt would produce a signal to the market and the banking supervisors on the relative risk-ness of the issuing banks. By inducing debtholders to use information optimally,

[33] A few years ago, while visiting officially one major emerging economy where a long record of macroeconomic instability and disproportionately high interest rates on government securities had driven most banks to disengage from lending to the private sector and to invest in government paper, I was told by major local bankers that a transition to a stable environment and to less distorted financial prices would find most banks unprepared to return to their old banking business and to make profits by selecting good risks.

[34] In the early nineteenth century, Scottish banks adopted this solution for their notes (England 1991).

it would strengthen the incentive to prudence inherent in the banks' sequential service constraint and in the associated risk of runs.[35]

While contributing to increasing financial market completeness, the approaches recalled above, alternative to narrow banking, would spur competition within the banking sector and strengthen market discipline, without suppressing conventional banks: the patient's health would be restored through good medicines, not euthanasia.

However, other approaches can be contemplated, which more than others would ensure superior forms of stable money. This is the topic of the next two chapters.

Appendix 1: Results of Panel Regression

See Tables 8.1, 8.2, 8.3, 8.4, 8.5, 8.6, 8.7, and 8.8.

Table 8.1 Bank narrowness and the cost of lending

Variables	Dep. variable Lending rate*	*t*	*P*
Constant	1.67	4.35	0.0001
Deposit rate	1.31	43.38	0.0001
Bank narrowness	2.88	2.37	0.0179
No. of obs.	763		
R^2	0.73		

* Yearly average

Table 8.2 Bank reserves and the cost of lending

Variables	Dep. variable Lending–deposit rate	*t*	*P*
Constant	4.38	2.58	0.0106
Banking sector concentration	– 0.84	– 0.38	0.7060
Reserves/asset	33.81	5.20	0.0001
No. of obs.	181		
R^2	0.13		

[35] Evanoff and Wall (2001) show that, while some measures such as capital ratios have no predictive power and, therefore, are not good candidates to trigger prompt corrective actions from supervisors, subordinated-debt yield spreads (on a riskless rate) perform better in this regard. See also the recent supportive evidence by Hancock and Kwast (2001).

Table 8.3 Bank narrowness and the cost of lending

Variables	Dep. variable Lending rate*	*t*	*P*
Constant	1.56	3.95	0.0001
Deposit rate	1.33	45.38	0.0001
Bank narrowness**	4.49	2.71	0.0068
No. of obs.	762		
R^2	0.73		

* Yearly average
** Redefined by eliminating reserves

Table 8.4 Bank narrowness and credit availability

Variables	Dep. variable Credit to private sector/GDP	*t*	*P*
Constant	0.78	42.53	0.0001
Deposit rate	– 0.01	– 7.90	0.0001
Bank narrowness	– 1.02	– 17.59	0.0001
No. of obs.	763		
R^2	0.38		

Table 8.5 Bank narrowness and credit availability

Variables	Dep. variable Credit to private sector*/GDP	*t*	*P*
Constant	1.17	43.45	0.0001
Lending rate	– 0.01	– 8.42	0.0001
Bank narrowness	– 1.56		0.0001
No. of obs.	763		
R^2	0.41		

* Includes credit financed with instruments other than demand deposits

Table 8.6 Bank narrowness and credit availability (Developing countries only)

Variables	Dep. variable credit to private sector*/GDP	*T*	*P*
Constant	0.87	31.00	0.0001
Lending rate	– 0.01	– 6.03	0.0001
Bank narrowness	– 1.06	– 14.60	0.0001
No. of obs.	537		
R^2	0.41		

* Includes credit financed with instruments other than demand deposits

Table 8.7 Bank narrowness and credit availability

Variables	Dep. variable Credit to private sector*/GDP	*t*	*P*
Constant	1.42	26.77	0.0001
Lend rate–inflation	– 0.01	– 4.76	0.0001
Inflation	– 0.02	– 6.17	0.0001
Bank narrowness	– 1.73	– 6.46	0.0001
No. of obs.	763		
R^2	0.50		

* Includes credit financed with instruments other than demand deposits

Table 8.8 Bank narrowness and credit availability (Developing countries only)

Variables	Dep. variable Credit to private sector*/GDP	*t*	*P*
Constant	1.16	20.17	0.0001
Lend rate–inflation	– 0.01	– 3.85	0.0002
Inflation	– 0.01	– 5.78	0.0001
Bank narrowness	– 1.27	– 5.66	0.0001
No. of obs.	537		
R^2	0.49		

* Includes credit financed with instruments other than demand deposits

References

Allais, M. (1948). *Economie et Intérêt: Exposition Nouvelle des Problèmes Fondamentaux, Relatifs au Rôle Economique du Taux de l'Intérêt et de leurs Solutions*. Librairie des Publications Officielles.

Azariadis, C., Bullard, J., & Smith, B. D. (2001). Private and public circulating liabilities. *Journal of Economic Theory, 99*, 59–116.

Beck, T., Demirgüç-Kunt, A., & Levine, R. (1999). *A new database on financial development and structure*. Financial Sector Discussion Paper No. 2. The World Bank.

Benston, G. J., R. Dan Brumbaugh, Jr., J. M. Guttentag, R. J. Herring, G. G. Kaufman, R. E. Litan, & Scott K. E. (1989). *Blueprint for Restructuring America's Financial Institutions*. Report of a Task Force, Washington D.C.: The Brookings Institution.

Benston, G. J., & Kaufman, G. G. (1993). Deposit Insurance Reform: A Functional Approach. A Comment. In *Carnagie-Rochester Conference Series on Public Policy* (Vol. 38, pp. 41–50).

Black, F. (1985). The future of financial services. In R. P. Inman (ed.), *Managing the service economy, prospects and problems* (pp. 223–231). Cambridge University Press.

Boot, A. W., & Greembaum, S. (1992). Bak regulation, reputation and rents: Theory and policy implications. In C. Mayer, & X. Vives (eds). *Capitat markets and financial intermediation* (pp. 262–285). Cambridge University Press.

Bossone, B. (2001a). Circuit theory of banking and finance. *Journal of Banking and Finance, 25*(5), 857–890.

Bossone, B. (2001b). Do banks have a future? A study on banking and finance as we move into the third millennium. *Journal of Banking & Finance, 25*(12), 2239–2276.
Bossone, B. (2001c). A proposal to deregulate banking: Comment on Thomas. *Cato Journal, 21*(2), 333–339.
Bossone, B. (2001d). *Should banks be narrowed?* IMF Working Paper, WP/01/159.
Bossone, B. (2002). Should banks be 'Narrowed'? Public Policy Brief Highlights No. 69A. Levy Economics Institute of Bard College.
Bossone, B., Honohan, P., Long, M. (2001). *Policy for small financial systems.* Financial Sector Discussion Paper No. 6. The World Bank.
Bruni, F. (1995). Prudential regulation in an integrated financial market: Issues of optimality and credibility. In G. Ferrarini (ed.), *Prudential regulation of banks and securities firms: European and international aspects.* Kluwer Law International.
Bryan, L. (1991). Core banking. *The McKinsey Quarterly, 1*, 61–74.
Burnham, J. B. (1990). *A financial system for the year 2000—The case for narrow banking.* CSAB Formal Publication No. 97. Washington University, Center for the Study of American Business.
Calomiris, C. W., & Kahn, C. M. (1991). The role of demandable debt in structuring optimal banking arrangements. *The American Economic Review, 81*(3), 497–513.
Calomiris, C. W. (1999). Building an incentive-compatible safety nets. *Journal of Banking and Finance, 23*(10), 1457–1555.
Caprio, G., Jr., & Summers L. H. (1993). "Finance and its reform: Beyond Laissez Faire". Policy Research Working Papers 1171, August, Washington D.C.: The World Bank.
Caprio, G. Jr., (1996). "Bank regulation: the case of the missing model". Policy Research Working Paper Series 1574, Washington D.C.: The World Bank.
CEPR. (2023). *VoxEU debate: Lessons from recent stress in the financial system.* Centre for Economic Policy Research.
Cohen-Setton, J. (2014). *Blogs review: The return of narrow banking.* Bruguel.
Craine, R. (1995). Fairly priced deposit insurance and bank charter policy. *Journal of Finance, 50*, 1735–1746.
Diamond, D. W., & Dybvig, P. H. (1983). Bank runs, deposit insurance, and liquidity. *The Journal of Political Economy, 91*(3), 401–419.
Diamond, D. W., & Rajan, R. G. (1998). "Liquidity risk, liquidity creation and financial fragility: A theory of banking". NBER Working Paper No. W7430, December (Cambridge, Mass: National Bureau of Economic Research).
Diamond, D. W., & Rajan, R. G. (1999). *A theory of bank capital.* NBER Working Paper No. W7431. National Bureau of Economic Research.
Diamond, D. W., & Dybvig, P. H. (1986). "Banking theory, deposit insurance", and bank regulation. *Journal of Business, 59*(1), 55–68.
Ely, B. (1991). The narrow bank: a flawed response to the failings of Federal Deposit Insurance. *Regulation, 14*(2)
England, C. (1991). Are banks special? *Regulation, 14*(2).
Evanoff, D. D., & Wall, L. D. (2001). Sub-debt yield spreads as bank risk measures. Working Paper 2001-11. Federal Reserve Bank.
Fisher, I. (1935). *100% money.* Adelphi Company.
Flannery, M., Jr. (1994). Debt maturity and the deadweight cost of leverage: Optimally financing banking firms. *The American Economic Review, 84*(1), 320–331.
Friedman, M. (1959). *A Program for Monetary Stability*, The Millar Lectures Number Three (New York City: Fordham University Press).
Goodhart, C. A. (1988). *The evolution of central banks.* The MIT Press.
Gorton, G., & Pennacchi, G. (1990). Financial intermediation and liquidity creation. *Journal of Finance, 45*(1), 49.
Gosh, S., & Saggar, M. (1998). Narrow banking: Theory, evidence and prospects in India. *Economic and Political Weekly, 9*, 1091–103.

Hancock, D., & Kwast, M. L. (2001), Using subordinated debt to monitor bank holding companies: Is it feasible? Finance and Economics Discussion Series 2000-21. Federal Reserve Board.

Herring, R. J., & Litan, R. E. (1995). *Financial regulation in the global economy*. Brookings Institution.

IMF. (2001). *International capital markets: Developments, prospects, and key policy issues* International Monetary Fund.

Kareken, J. H. (1985). *Ensuring financial stability, in the search for financial stability. The past fifty years* (pp. 53–77). Federal Reserve Bank.

Kareken, J. H. (1986). Federal bank regulatory policy: A description and some observations. *Journal of Business, 59*(1), 3–48.

Kashyap, A. K., R. Rajan., & Stein, J. C. (1999). "Banks as liquidity providers: An explanation or the co-existence of lending and deposit-taking", NBER Working Paper 6962 (Cambridge, Mass.: National Bureau of Economic Research).

Keehn, S. (1989). Banking on the balance: Powers and the safety net, a proposal. Working Paper. Federal Reserve Bank.

Kobayakawa, S., & Nakamura, H. (2000). *A theoretical analysis of narrow banking proposals*. IMES Discussion Paper Series, No. 99-E-19. Bank of Japan, Institute for Monetary and Economic Studies.

Litan, R. E. (1987). *What should banks do?* Brookings Institution.

McCulloch, J. H. (1987). Bank Regulation and Deposit Insurance. *Journal of Business, 59*(1), 79–85.

Merton, R., & Bodie, Z. (1993). Deposit insurance reform: A functional approach. In *Carnagie-Rochester Conference Series on Public Policy* (Vol. 38, pp. 1–34).

Mishkin, F. (1999). Financial consolidation: Dangers and opportunities. *Journal of Banking and Finance, 23*, 675–691.

Mussa, M. (1986). Safety and soundness as an objective of regulation of depository. *The Journal of Business, 59*(1), 97–117.

Myers, S. C., & Majluf, N. S. (1984). Corporate financing and investment decisions when firms have information that investors do not have. *Journal of Financial Economics, 13*(2), 187–221.

Peters, S. R., & Thakor, A. V. (1995). *A rationale for the functional separation of qualitative asset transformation services in banking*. Working Paper. Indiana University.

Phillips, R. J. (1992). *The 'Chicago Plan' and new deal banking reform*. The Jerome Levy Economics Institute Working Paper No. 76. The Jerome Levy Economics Institute of Bard College.

Phillips, R. J. (1992). *Credit markets and narrow banking*. The Jerome Levy Economics Institute Working Paper No. 77. The Jerome Levy Economics Institute of Bard College.

Phillips, R. J. (1995). *Narrow banking reconsidered—The functional approach to financial reform*. The Jerome Levy Economics Institute Public Policy Brief No. 17. The Jerome Levy Economics Institute of Bard College.

Pierce, J. I. (1991). *The future of banking*. Yale University Press.

Pozdena, R. J. (1991). The false hope of the narrow bank. FRBSF Weekly Letter No. 91–39. Federal Reserve Bank.

Saidenberg, M. R. & Strahan, P. E. (1999). Are banks still important for financing large businesses. *Current Issues in Economics and Finance, 5*(12).

Schinasi, G., & Smith, T. (2001). "Financial Implications of the Shrinking Supply of U.S. Treasury Securities". IMF Working Paper No. 2001/061, May.

Simons, H. A. (1934). A positive program for Laissez Faire: Some proposals for a liberal economic policy. In H. D. Gideonse (ed.), *Public Policy Pamphlet No.* 15.

Spong, K. (1991). *A narrow banking proposal*. Federal Reserve Bank of Kansas City.

Spong, K. (1993). *Narrow banks: an alternative approach to banking reform*. The Jerome Levy Economics Institute Working Paper No. 90. The Jerome Levy Economics Institute of Bard College.

Thomas, H. (2000). A proposal to deregulate banking. *The Cato Journal, 20*(2), 237–253.

Tobin, J. (1987). The case for preserving regulatory distinctions. In *Restructuring the Financial System* (pp. 167–183). Federal Reserve Bank of Kansas City.
Tobin, J. (1985). Financial innovation and deregulation in perspective. *Bank of Japan Monetary and Economic Studies, 3*(2), 19–29.
Wall, L. D. (1989). A plan for reducing future deposit insurance losses: puttable subordinated debt. *Economic Review*, 2–17.
Wallace, N. (1996). Narrow banking meets the Diamond-Dybvig model. *Federal Reserve Bank of Minneapolis Quarterly Review, 20*(1), 3–13.
World Bank. (2001). *Finance for growth: Policy choices in a volatile world.*

Chapter 9
Superstable Money (I): Separating Bank Money Creation from Lending

Abstract This chapter introduces the first "superstable" system design. It begins by highlighting that financial crises typically prompt demands for reforming financial systems that have either demonstrated vulnerability to shocks or have contributed to the crises themselves. The chapter contends that a fundamental issue with the current systems is that bank money is generated through the process of lending. It then illustrates the advantages of an alternative system where money creation occurs through specialized commercial institutions that issue money on a non-lending basis and free of charge (rather than lending at an interest) and supply payment services to customers. The chapter shows that the operation of these institutions, supported by an appropriate financial system policy framework, generates non-inflationary purchasing power without raising private-sector debt, allows broader access to purchasing power, fuels domestic output growth through higher domestic demand, reduces the economy's financial risks, and preserves the flow of money to the economy during crises.

9.1 Preamble

When, in 2001, I once again crossed 19th Street, NW, Washington DC, this time to move back from the World Bank to the IMF, my main research interest was still on the Circuit Theory of Money (CTM), extended to incorporate finance, and on its implications for general economic (dis)equilibrium, as discussed in Chap. 4. At that time, my understanding of a monetary economy of production was entirely centered on the role of commercial banks as money creators and on credit as the channel for bank money creation.

Once at the Fund, I was approached by a young and bright colleague from Senegal, Abdou Sarr. He had come across my recently published articles on CTM (Bossone, 2000; 2001a, 2001b) and was eager to discuss his innovative idea for a new monetary model. Abdou passionately expressed his belief that CTM could serve as an effective foundation for his concept. In his model, money creation would be the responsibility of specialized liquidity management entities known as Deposit Creating Institutions

B. Bossone, *Trailblazing Visions of Money in Economic Theory*, Contributions to Economics, https://doi.org/10.1007/978-3-031-82544-6_9

(DCIs). Unlike commercial banks, these organizations would inject funds into the economy without extending loans or charging interest. The recipients of funds would not have any obligations to the issuing DCIs, allowing the DCIs to generate revenue from their payment activities and other services provided to their deposit customers.

Abdou and I collaborated on an article advocating for a new circuit-based monetary system that separates money creation from lending. We argued that this innovative approach would generate non-inflationary purchasing power without increasing private-sector debt. The system we proposed aimed to enhance access to purchasing power, stimulate domestic output growth by bolstering domestic demand, mitigate financial risks, and ensure a steady flow of money into the economy during times of crisis.

The article was initially distributed as an IMF working paper and garnered significant attention. Following this, we were invited to present our theory at a conference in Italy in honor of Professor Augusto Graziani, one of the fathers of the Theory of Monetary Circuit (CTM). We were also asked to contribute an article on the topic, which became a chapter in a book published after the conference (Bossone & Sarr, 2005).

The IMF expressed great interest in our innovative work, leading Abdou and me to collaborate on an article for the IMF Survey, the fund's widely read magazine. Just as we finalized the draft and sent it to the printers, senior management intervened, concerned that our unconventional proposal might be misconstrued as an official endorsement from the IMF. It was truly unfortunate…

PS: After completing the draft of this chapter in April 2024, I stumbled upon the news that Abdou had just been appointed Minister of the Economy of Senegal. It had been a while since we last spoke, so I reached out to congratulate him. This achievement is well-deserved, and I believe he is an excellent choice for his country. I have no doubt he will excel in his new role. Best of luck, my friend!

9.2 Introduction

As discussed in Part I of this book, contemporary capitalist economies are largely based on the use of bank money or demand deposits (henceforth, "deposits"), that is, claims that banks are allowed to issue on themselves and provide to other parties under loan contract terms, or sell to other parties in exchange for securities. The title on these claims is such that the issuing banks are obliged to exchange them back for cash on demand by their holders or to execute transfers or payments to third parties on request by their holders. For this reason, these claims are accepted and used by the people in their transactions as means of payments and debt settlement instruments.

To the extent that banks are permitted to operate under a fractional reserve regime,[1] accept funds in exchange for deposit claims, and extend loans or purchase securities

[1] That is, they are not required to fully back their demand deposits outstanding with central banks reserves.

in the form of deposit claims made available on accounts open in their books, they effectively create money,[2] and they do so at a cost that is lower than their face value.

Since bank money, once created, is used for payments, preserving consistency between credit issuances and bank reserves (with a view to ensuring payment finality and to protect the banks' capacity to meet deposit withdrawals) is essential for the proper functioning and stability of both the financial system and the real economy. The link between credit money creation, the payment system, bank liquidity, and the economy is one of the reasons why governments have traditionally been so heavily involved in regulating banking much more than other financial market segments. Indeed, the risk that a bank in difficulty may rapidly pass its problems on to others through the payment system, or that it may lead claim-holders suddenly to fear that other banks may run into the same difficulties, explains why governments are so willing to step in and rescue banks (at least those that are deemed to be too large to fail) in such events. This risk provides the rationale for governments to extend deposit insurance protection to depositors, the aim being to avoid that banking sector problems spill over to the real economy via payment system disruptions.

The policy to preserve financial stability typically includes measures to ensure that banks select good credit risks, maintain adequate liquidity throughout their activity, and have access to sufficient liquidity in case of temporary liquidity shortfalls. A good financial policy also needs to include rigorous market entry/exit criteria as well as strong and prompt corrective actions to be taken when banks run excessive risk positions.

Experience shows, however, that striking the right balance between efficiency and stability in the banking sector is no easy task, not even in the most advanced economies with well-developed regulatory and supervisory institutions. Pushing banks to compete in the market for new risks is essential to keep the real economy vital and innovative, but may lead up to excessive risk-taking behavior. On the other hand, over-regulating banks can prevent failures and crises but at the cost of limiting firms' access to capital beyond reasonable need, thereby hampering business activity and development opportunities. One way for banks to circumvent tight regulation has been to originate loans by creating money and to repackage them to be sold to investors. The loans are thus taken off the banks' balance sheets and the liquidity the banks gave away through the original loans is recaptured, thus giving them the capacity to originate new loans.

Proposals to narrow the scope of banking have long been debated in the literature to resolve the efficiency/stability tradeoff, especially in the aftermath of banking crises. Proposals have typically ranged, just to cite a few, from reducing the size of banks to eliminate the "too big to fail" systemic risk, to separating commercial banks from investment banks, prohibiting credit relations between commercial banks and investment banks, eradicating speculation (e.g., derivatives, high-frequency trading) and separating consulting activities from market activities, and to even socializing the banking sector. None of these has been implemented in any jurisdiction so far,

[2] Throughout the text, the term "deposits" will be used to refer exclusively to demand or sight deposits.

and actual remedies have generally included tightened regulations and supervisory practices. A radical proposal to remove the endemic fragility of banks, that has cyclically resurfaced after major banking crisis episodes, consists of changing banking legislation from fractional reserves to so-called narrow banking. This would require banks to fully back their deposit liabilities with high-quality and liquid assets. The most extreme version of this proposal is the "100% reserve banking" regime, invoked by early economists, whereby banks would be required to keep 100% of the funds deposited with them by customers as reserves balances held at the central bank, which carry zero liquidity and credit risks. All other bank lending functions would be transferred to mutual-fund-like institutions that would not be insured by government. This arrangement would prevent bank money creation (via lending) and allow government or the industry to scale back costly deposit insurance programs without jeopardizing the safety of the banks and their depositors. In addition, as the proponents argue, the institutions that inherited the banks' role in commercial lending would be loath to take excessive risks, because their own capital and that of their investors would be at stake.

On the other hand, while bearing less than certain benefits in terms of greater financial stability, narrowing the scope of banking might exact some heavy costs in terms of efficiency and credit availability. By severing the link between liquidity, money, credit, and economic activity, which banking has a natural incentive to establish efficiently (under stable macroeconomic conditions), narrow banking would dissipate the significant benefits associated with conventional banking systems, which stem from issuing demandable deposits to finance other than government liabilities. Better alternatives to narrow banking would be (Bryan, 1991) "core banking" model, or those regulatory regimes that separate commercial (short term) banking from investment (longer-term) banking activities, even within the same financial holding companies.

In narrow banking proposals—such as Milton (Friedman, 1960) 100% reserve variant—deposit-taking banks would be prohibited from creating money through lending activities to the private sector and would instead be required to place all their demand liabilities into safe and fully liquid government securities. The payment system would thus be insulated from the intermediation process. However, while narrow banking might succeed in reducing credit and liquidity risks that conventional banking brings into the payment system, it would deprive the banks of their power to create money and to allocate it to the private sector (Bossone, 2001a, 2001b; 2002).

In this chapter, I illustrate the alternative system proposed by Bossone and Sarr, cit., whereby the banks' function to create and allocate money to the private sector is separated from their lending and financial intermediation activities. The system is characterized by a new type of financial institutions that are specialized in supplying payment services and are separated from institutions that intermediate between savers and borrowers. These new institutions may not lend money, but are allowed to distribute the money they create to depositors on a non-lending basis (that is, under no restitution obligation). Each depositor's share of distributed liquidity is determined by the new institutions, according to their own assessment of the liquidity risk (see below).

The alternative system separates money creation from lending, building on the recognition that there is no intrinsic need for the two functions to be carried out jointly by the same institution. With an appropriate redesign of the financial sector and its policy framework, the noncredit money system would considerably increase financial sector stability and efficiency and have the same positive real-sector effects of conventional commercial banking.

The plan of the chapter is the following. Section 9.3 describes the alternative system, explaining how a noncredit money creation system would work, and under which policy rules it should work. Section 9.4 assesses the implications of a noncredit money creation system, showing how it would overcome some crucial limitations of conventional banking. Section 9.5 discusses the key practical transitional issues involved in moving from conventional banking to the noncredit money creation system. Section 9.6 concludes the chapter.

9.3 Noncredit Money

To gain a clear understanding of how noncredit money system discussed in this chapter would operate, it is useful to recapitulate how conventional credit money comes into being. A bank creates money any time it *credits* a borrower's deposit account with a new loan amount or in exchange for securities. As a credit, the amount lent originates an obligation of the borrower to the bank (i.e., it constitutes an asset of the bank). As a debit, the amount deposited on the borrower's account originates an obligation of the bank to the borrower (i.e., it constitutes a liability for the bank). Credit money (or a demand deposit) thus is both an asset and a liability for the bank issuing it.

Note that no money creation is possible for a nonbank financial institution that may not entertain deposit account relationships with customers: the nonbank cannot *issue* new deposits and lend them to borrowers; it can only *transfer* existing funds from those who save them to those who borrow them. The nonbank may only act as an *intermediary* between the two sides.

Also note that, unlike the traditional story of the deposit multiplier, deposit multiplication does not require the pre-existence of reserve money (i.e., cash and bank deposits with the central bank). Assuming for simplicity that no agents in the system wish to hold cash or use it for payments, and that no requirements compel banks to hold deposits with the central bank (against the deposits of their clientele or to settle payments), banks can create deposits at will (through lending) without mobilizing reserves. Whereas this can be immediately visualized in a system with a single bank, in a system with more than one bank it would require that banks permanently roll over their net payment balances with no settlement. However, while reserves are not necessary for banks to create deposits, the demand for reserves is necessary to limit deposit creation: if the demand for reserves were not induced by the market, it would have to be imposed through regulation.

Inherent in the process thus far described is the interlink between deposits, payments, and the bank lending function. In the noncredit money system here envisages, however, deposit creation and payments are separated from bank lending. This is achieved by creating specialized payment service providers, which—like conventional banks—will only need to keep a fraction of their deposit liabilities as reserves with the central bank to settle net deposit outflows. Unlike banks, these institutions will not be allowed to take advantage of fractional reserves to become lenders, since they will never receive funds intended for that purpose. They will be allowed to create and distribute money to depositors; yet, unlike in conventional banking, their money creation will not occur through lending, but through *giving*. Call them Deposit Creating Institutions (DCIs). While DCIs specialize in providing payment services, all other financial intermediaries are allowed to fund their assets exclusively by issuing nondemandable debt or non-debt instruments. The latter are intermediaries only.

In conventional banking, money creation through lending is socially desirable because. If credit risk selection is sound, banks will lend to productive firms, and the new funds will generate a new stream of real goods and services, thereby avoiding price inflation: the new money will be backed by new output. In the noncredit money system, the same result can be achieved when funds are distributed as gifts to depositors who, through consumption or investment spending decisions, select the firms that will capture the new money created. Consumption demand will select the recipients deserving the new money created by bidding up the relative price of their output, while the higher relative price of the goods purchased will drive the allocation of real resources toward their production (see below for a model reflecting this feature). The efficiency of the distribution mechanism of noncredit money is thus assured by market forces and the power of the "invisible hand."

Below, the technical aspects of the system are discussed, including the operations of the DCIs in the real world, the exit of insolvent DCIs, the underlying monetary and financial policy framework, and some of the core issues involved in making the transition from conventional banking to a noncredit money creation system.

9.3.1 Operation of the DCIs

The DCIs create deposits and provide deposit safekeeping and payment services but are not allowed to extend credit. As illustrated below, and like conventional banks, the DCIs create deposits by crediting the account of their depositors under no restitution obligation. Depositors may use deposits for payments of all kinds. Like in conventional banking, payments between individual agents consist of deposit transfers across the agents' accounts held at DCIs, through the instruments usually available for the purpose (checks, money orders, debit/credit cards, etc.). The DCIs ensure payment finality through settlement at the central bank where they (like banks) hold reserve deposit accounts.

The DCIs earn revenues from the fees charged to customers for the services rendered to them. Since depositors can pay the fees out of the new money they receive, it can be argued that the DCIs distribute liquidity on a net-of-fee basis. However, the fee portion is the income of the DCI and needs to be transparently charged and shown in the income statement. This fee income is the reason investors would want to start a DCI. The DCIs may provide other services, such as consulting services in cash management to enterprises. For the purpose at hand, however, they can be taken as only providing payment and liquidity management services.

The proportion of average deposit balances a DCI distributes—equivalent to the amount of loans a conventional banking can safely make (the loan-to-deposit ratio)—is a market strategy variable determined by the DCI itself. In competing with one another, different DCIs may apply different rates to different types of depositors. The DCIs decide whether and when to distribute liquidity. If deposits are unstable or decrease, and the DCI determines that it would be unsafe to distribute liquidity, then liquidity distribution would not take place, just like in conventional banking where under the same circumstances loans would not be extended. For instance, DCIs aiming to achieve large market shares may prefer to attract many small depositors rather than few large ones. On the other hand, intermediaries wishing to offer DCI payment services within broader financial service packages (e.g., cash management services to corporations) may aim at fewer but larger customers. As in conventional banking, each DCI would use statistical techniques, depositors' payment/receipt records, and information on factors affecting net deposit outflows, to determine the amount of noncredit money that can be distributed without running into liquidity problems. In the absence of an interest rate mechanism, the deposit distribution rate is one of the instruments available to the DCIs to compete in the market for transaction deposits.[3]

To minimize liquidity risk, a ceiling on distributing funds to single depositors can be imposed on the DCIs, just like conventional banks are regulated on their exposure to individual borrowers. This might induce large depositors to invest their surplus funds in the capital market for a return, which would end up being deposited back with the DCIs since these have the monopoly of the payment services provision. This liquidity distribution regulatory issue is not explored any further in this chapter. The DCIs determine their liquidity distribution policy, much like conventional banks do to determine their lending subject to central bank's reserve or liquidity requirements for monetary policy or financial regulatory purposes. Monetary policy and reserve requirement regulation would ensure that the stock of noncredit money grew in line with potential output and desired inflation, thereby preventing pyramid schemes.

As indicated, the liquidity distributed takes the form of deposits issued on the accounts of depositors and is additional to the deposits outstanding at the time of distribution—just like loans. Deposits are convertible into cash and foreign exchange

[3] A depositor's share in a given amount that would have been available for lending by a conventional bank could be based on her average deposit balance during a reference period (say, a month) relative to other depositors. DCIs, however, would be free to determine money distribution as part of their market strategy.

on demand by their holders. Depositors can use the available balances (including existing deposit holdings and distributed deposits) to finance all types of real and financial transactions (see below).

The liquidity created and distributed by a DCI is reported on the asset side of the DCI's balance sheet for record-keeping purposes only but gives rise to new deposit liabilities as loans of conventional banks do (see Box 9.1, below). The difference is that a DCI is effectively insolvent with respect to the deposits it is allowed to create. Yet *solvency* ceases to be a criterion for DCI soundness, since the DCI system builds on a no-restitution-obligation of the money created; *liquidity* takes its place as the key criterion for systemic stability.

Box 9.1. The balance sheet of a DCI

Assets		Liabilities	
RR	10	DD	100
LA	20	Dept	20
DL	90	Equity	20
FA	20		
Total	140	Total	140

RR = reserve requirements (10%)

LA = Liquid assets

DL = Distributed liquidity (loans, in a conventional bank)

DD = Demand deposits

FA = Fixed assets.

Debt + Equity = LA + FA= capital

RR + LA = primary liquidity

Note that liquid assets other than reserve requirements and free reserves can only be held against nondemand deposit liabilities. In other words, fixed and other non-reserve assets cannot exceed equity and debt capital.

The capital of a DCI equals its fixed assets plus its own liquid funds. Hereafter, call *primary liquidity* the aggregate including the funds that the DCIs are required to hold as cash, central bank reserves, and liquid securities, and any funds in excess of requirements that the DCIs deliberately hold in any or all of such forms. The DCIs may purchase government securities on their own behalf and only with their own capital, not with the public's deposits (see note in Box 9.1). Given the asset structure of a DCI, its primary liquidity coincides with its total assets net of physical assets.

The DCIs need primary liquidity to comply with regulatory requirements, to settle payments to other DCIs, and to meet demands for cash from customers. Primary liquidity is a key factor of competition in the noncredit money system.[4] The DCIs that are more capitalized can take more liquidity risk and distribute more inside money, thereby attracting depositors from other DCIs. In turn, by expanding its capacity to attract deposits, a DCI economizes on the use of (costly) primary liquidity since its share of "*on us*" payments increases relative to its competitors. A larger deposit capacity also enables a DCI to distribute new deposits with a higher probability to attract them back to its own books.

In sum, the DCIs compete in the market for primary liquidity with a view to increasing their capacity to provide their main output: payment services. To this end, the DCIs seek to enhance their deposit creation capacity and to attract more depositors. Winning over a larger share of the deposit market increases their profitability by increasing their fee revenues and, simultaneously, by reducing their optimal level of primary liquidity relative to liabilities. In fact, a DCI market would most likely tend to consolidate into a system with a small set of very large operators.

9.3.2 Exit of a Failed DCI

A DCI fails when it runs out of primary liquidity and is unable to settle its payment obligations. Since DCIs are subject to a reserve requirement (see next section), a payment settlement failure happens when a DCI has lost primary liquidity to the point where it cannot comply with its requirement.

This situation may result from competitive pressure or from depositor runs. Competition may be such that deposits are attracted to the DCIs that offer better services and thus move out of a less competitive DCI. The process may be gradual, but there is a point where the losing DCI becomes unable to settle deposit outflows with its reserves.

More generally, like in conventional banking, a run may follow a crisis of public confidence. However, since the DCIs are not subject to solvency problems in relation to their deposit liabilities, as noted above in Section A, they are much less exposed than banks to the risk of runs. This is a seemingly paradoxical yet major implication of a system that creates and distributes claims on real resources through *acts of giving*, rather than lending.

The risk of runs is reduced by the way DCI failures are handled. Once a DCI has run out of primary liquidity and has exploited all options to raise the needed reserve balances, it is allowed to fail and thus exits the system. A DCI exiting the system is left with its fixed assets since, as indicated, the liquidity distributed to depositors does not bear DCI claims attached and does not give rise to DCI demandable debt obligations. Thus, only the fixed assets of a failed DCI can be liquidated to repay its (nondeposit) debts. Upon failure, the deposit liabilities of the failed DCI, along

[4] Like in conventional banking systems, DCIs can economize on primary liquidity, for a given stock of deposits distributed, by setting up mutual (intra-settlement) liquidity facilities and payment netting arrangements.

with its physical assets (including its branch network) and distributed liquidity, are allocated on a pro-rata basis to the surviving DCIs that have net open credit positions outstanding vis-à-vis the failed institution. Alternatively, the allocation can be done on a pro-rata basis relative to the primary liquidity of each surviving DCI. Obviously, in the post-allocation period, depositors are free to transfer their deposits to other DCIs, or to use them when and as they wish. As in the case of liquidity risk regulation discussed above, this issue is not explored any further.

Since DCI liabilities are not matched by real claims on the DCIs' books, their allocation to other DCIs does not require their full collateralization with performing assets (restructuring bonds). The only necessary and sufficient condition for the allocation not to undermine public confidence in the receiving DCIs and their stability is that these have enough primary liquidity margins to maintain their required ratios, given their higher level of post-allocation liabilities. Now, if there are no leakages in the system into currency, this condition is satisfied by construction. Any net deposit outflow from a DCI A to a DCI B requires an equal net reserve flow in the same direction. As the deposit outflow carries on, A loses all its reserves in favor of B and fails. To the extent that A and B were both reserve compliant before A's failure, all residual deposits of A can be allocated to B, who will then have enough reserves to remain compliant even after the deposit allocation. DCI A can exit the market while depositors are as well off as before the failure. A central bank reserve requirement (discussed later) prevents DCIs from "evergreening" their way out of competitive pressures by distributing extra liquidity, since they would no longer be reserve compliant and would be considered for foreclosure by the central bank if they did not correct their position immediately. This rule fosters good liquidity risk management and minimizes the risk of runs.

In the event of leakages to currency, however, the actual reserve ratio of the leaking DCIs can drop below the required level, and they may find themselves unable to settle their payment obligations. In the case of failure(s), the allocation of the liabilities to surviving DCIs would cause their actual reserve ratio to drop below the required level: a portion of the allocated liabilities would be uncovered by existing reserves. Any such reserve shortage would have to be supplemented through recapitalization. The needed injection of funds, however, would likely cost less than under a comparable case of bank failure, where all the bank's uncovered liabilities would have to be written off, or matched with restructuring bonds, or refunded with deposit insurance funds—the scenario that has been witnessed with the bailout of major banks in the USA following the sub-prime crisis and which is typical of all banking crises.[5]

The exit of a failed DCI, however large, would not trigger systemic reactions since depositors would have their deposits immediately transferred to surviving DCIs that

[5] Note that, in a DCI system, US banks that are liquid or nonbanks that transform into commercial banks but are liquid would not have to be bailed out, since solvency with respect to the money created would not be a criterion to remain operational. The key criteria would in fact be liquidity and compliance with the central bank's reserve requirement. The discussion in Sect. 9.6, explaining how the loans of a conventional bank can be unwound to create a DCI and nonDCI departments in transitioning from conventional banking to a DCI system, provides a roadmap that can be used by the USA to transform failed banks under existing capital regulatory requirements.

either would be able to honor their liabilities or could be recapitalized to that effect. In the event of a run on all DCIs simultaneously, the public sector could in principle let all DCIs fail, order the transfer of all deposits to a central institution, and keep the payment system alive allowing deposit transfers to be executed with only a fractional reserve base. This outcome is unlikely to occur, however, since depositors have no incentive to run on the system in its entirety if deposits are guaranteed by the state. This guarantee does not create moral hazard—as it does, instead, in conventional banking—since the DCIs do not lend funds and their deposit distribution capacity is constrained by reserve requirements.

Finally, the system would not be sustainable in the case of a run on the currency, but the consequences would not be different than under conventional banking.

9.3.3 Monetary and Financial Policies in the Noncredit Money System

Throughout their operation, the DCIs are required to hold a minimum reserve-to-deposit ratio with the central bank. Prudentially, the DCIs can also be required to hold a minimum ratio of liquidable securities. Note, again, that this liquidity requirement is equivalent to a capital requirement, since DCIs cannot purchase securities with the public's deposits (see Box 9.1, above). Individual DCIs could exceed the required ratio(s) based on their own prudential criteria and preferences.

Like in conventional banking, a minimum reserve requirement determines the maximum possible deposit creation by the DCIs. Thus, through the required reserve ratio, the central bank sets a ceiling on the liquidity distribution by individual DCIs and, hence, on aggregate money supply.

The central bank issues reserve money periodically and determines the reserve stock consistently with its output growth forecasts and its inflation objectives. (Box 9.2 discusses the risk of inflation and money over-issuance associated with the DCI system.) Issuance and withdrawals of reserves take place through open market operations (OMO) with DCIs and financial intermediaries. To avoid distorting competition in the DCI market, the central bank may not provide reserves to support the expansion of individual DCI balance sheets or to rescue DCIs from liquidity pressures resulting from market competition. Recall that liquidity is a key factor of competition in the system. To facilitate payment settlements, however, the central bank may sell reserves to DCIs against securities they bought using their own capital or can make reserves available overnight or for very short time windows on a collateralized basis (against DCIs securities purchased with their own capital) and at penalizing interest rates. The DCIs can raise liquidity in the money market using their own assets and the headroom provided by reserve requirement averaging. It is to be reminded that all financial intermediaries hold accounts with the DCIs, so that OMO with financial intermediaries are reflected immediately on the reserve balances held at the DCIs and, indirectly, on the supply of deposits.

The central bank thus controls the overall liquidity of the economy through the reserve requirement and the supply of reserves to the financial market. The central bank does not have an interest rate policy since this would interfere with DCI market competition for primary liquidity.[6] The interest rates at which liquidity is provided to support the payment system follow market interest rates, rather than determining them. Interest rates are determined in the financial market and, as such, they also reflect monetary policy decisions and credibility. In turn, the central bank may use market interest rates as indicators of the economy's liquidity conditions, but the long-term expansion of the money supply will essentially be driven by potential output growth. The monetary policy operating target will therefore be quantitative, specifically aiming at base money, to achieve an inflation target.

DCI activities and balance sheets must be kept separate from the activities and the balance sheets of other financial intermediaries. To this purpose, DCIs can either be dedicated entities, or specialized subsidiaries of financial holding companies, or else specialized fire-walled departments within financial companies offering a range of different products.

Box 9.2. A New "John Law" Scheme?

One of the reviewers of the original article by Bossone and Sarr, cit., was concerned that our proposal would turn to be the blunder into which John Law fell three centuries ago, referring to the spectacular inflationary spiral and stock price bubble bursting in France after John Law's financial experiment ended with the collapse of his Compagnie des Indes, in 1720. (For a recount, see Bordo, 1988, and the references therein contained, and Clough & Rapp, 1975).

In fact, the incentives structure of the noncredit money creation system works in the direction of monetary stability. Yet: how can a system that creates and distributes inside money be non-inflationary?

This question can be answered, first, by comparing the noncredit money system with conventional banking. Any fractional reserve system operates—by construction—on a partially covered money basis, whereby money is created that is not backed by existing output, but is supported by real resources only ex-post, when the production it has financed has come on stream and is available on the market. This implies that the non-inflationary nature of the new money

[6] An interest rate target is operationally achieved by the central bank standing ready to intervene in the money market daily, at the banks' initiative, to limit interest rate volatility and periodically through OMO at its own initiative, to meet banks' demand for reserves. This implies that a failing DCI is to be granted access to reserves if the central bank aims at its target. Note, however, that, unlike a conventional bank, a DCI cannot be *temporarily* illiquid since illiquidity indicates that it is being competed out of the market by more efficient DCIs. Therefore, in a noncredit money creation system, the central bank is never confronted with the option of extending financing to an illiquid but otherwise solvent DCI. Any lending of last resort to an illiquid DCI would necessarily alter competition. An interest rate target policy would not be consistent with a DCI competitive market.

rests on the banks' capacity to select good risks (that is, businesses that generate output that is effectively on demand) as much as on the overall macroeconomic policy stance. In the noncredit money system, money creation is separated from lending, but the financial intermediaries involved in production finance remain responsible for selecting good businesses. The system enables the economy to generate demand more easily than conventional banking; but if firms meet the new demand profitably, banks and other intermediaries can lend to them safely. DCIs, moreover, can generate demand through new money issue only within the limits set by regulatory and prudential requirements.

John Law's experiment with a private bank of issue (the Banque Générale, established in 1716 and then renamed Banque Royale), while being initially successful, resulting in output and employment growth, eventually turned into money over-issue to finance the speculative activities of the Compagnie des Indes: delinking note issuance from specie convertibility, encouraging speculation on the company stock by declaring dividends unrelated to the company's true prospects, and monetizing the company stock by pegging its price inevitably, all led to financial disaster. (Freeman, 1996, shows the unsustainability of unconstrained private money issue).

The DCIs, on the other hand, are envisaged to operate under a strong central bank, in a reserve-based money regime, and in competition with one another (with no recourse to central bank refinancing of created and distributed liquidity as is done with loans); also, illiquid DCIs are allowed to exit the market. An environment like this would hardly be prone to inflation and speculation. The very difference between the noncredit money system and conventional banking, and in general all noncommodity-based money regimes, does not lie on money creation, but rather on how money is distributed, and to whom, as it gets created. To use Milton Friedman's words, in the DCI system the government–through the central–would "set an external limit to the amount of money and prevent the economic equivalent of counterfeiting, broadly conceived." (Friedman, 1960, p. 66).

9.4 Effects of Noncredit Money

A system based on noncredit money may overcome many of the important pitfalls of credit money in conventional banking. In particular, the system would increase financial stability and the efficiency of financial intermediation and would also have the same real-sector effects of conventional banking, if not superior.

9.4.1 Effects on the Real Economy

The noncredit money system has two key advantages relative to conventional banking, which relate respectively to supporting real-sector production and to managing aggregate demand in situations of resource underemployment that are typical of economies undergoing stagnation or deflation. First, in a noncredit money system, depositors select through their consumption decisions the enterprises that stand to capture the liquidity created by the DCIs. As this happens, the price of these enterprises' products is driven up relative to that of other products and to the cost of unused labor (leisure). Higher relative prices (and profits), in turn, attract production factors into the production of these goods. Higher productivity, larger employment, and more output follow from DCI liquidity creation, as is shown analytically in Annex I. Sophisticated credit-risk analysis by banks providing payment services would not be necessary to create money and to get it allocated to successful entrepreneurs. The money created by the DCIs is allocated across the economy by the "invisible hand" of the market and the price mechanism. This feature turns out to be particularly important during credit crises, since a boost in aggregate demand could be engineered through DCIs money, without resorting to fiscal measures that are necessarily selective and fall upon taxpayer pockets. Moreover, noncredit money creation does not raise the moral hazard (excessive lending due to banks' deposit insurance) and adverse selection (lending to too risky borrowers), problems that are inherent in the money creation process based on lending.

The proportion of DCI distributed liquidity that depositors decide to hold as savings with financial intermediaries could also fund investments in enterprises whose output is in higher demand. If the lack of credit-risk management infrastructure, or a credit crunch, prevents such investments from being funded by intermediaries, enterprises may be able to fund their investments through the larger retained earnings coming from higher relative prices and consumer direct demand. Stimulating the economy could also be done more directly and easily through supply of central bank liquidity to the market and deposit distribution through the DCIs. This would avoid large government expenditures and debt, the benefits of which may not be assured. Through the DCIs, growth would be fostered when excess capacity exists, but weak effective (monetary) demand, poor credit-risk management infrastructure, or a credit crunch prevents the economy from getting out of a depression or stagnation.

Second, since conventional banks represent the transmission channel for central bank demand management policies, structural constraints to the provision of credit can prevent monetary policy from being an effective demand management tool. For instance, protracted bank restructuring problems, weak bank balance sheets, or tightened prudential regulations can weaken the banking channel of liquidity provision aimed to fuel demand. This situation can lead to a central bank lowering interest rates and injecting liquidity in the market with no effect on credit and aggregate demand (that is, a liquidity trap).

This disconnect between the micro-dynamics within the banking sector and the macroeconomic objectives of the central bank can be responsible for the ineffectiveness of monetary easing, whereby expanding the money supply would fail to reverse the decline in credit and sluggish demand. If this situation also coincides with a lack of fiscal flexibility, a prolonged recession may ensue. A situation has been observed in Japan during the 1990s and, more recently, in the USA due to the financial turmoil.

In the noncredit money system, the DCIs would not be confronted with such problems, since liquidity distribution would fuel demand with no need for credit intermediation and would translate directly into household disposable income. The quantity of liquidity made available would increase demand permanently, while lower interest rates could induce formation of production capacity to match the expected permanent increase in demand. The effect would be permanent since DCI money is created and distributed on a non-lending basis, and thus, it carries no restitution obligation. In conventional banking, on the other hand, the money created via lending is destroyed as loans are repaid, as explained earlier. This requires banks to create more money on a gross basis than is destroyed if the money stock is to grow in line with nominal GDP growth; otherwise, deflation and depression would set in. This latter scenario has been hunting the USA.

9.4.2 *Effects on the Financial System*

The expansion of noncredit money would have important effects on financial stability and deepening. In a noncredit money system, important financial stability effects would be achieved through the separation of money creation from lending. These effects would even be superior to those claimed by the proponents of narrow banking. (Box 9.3 discusses the efficiency of noncredit money creation relative to a narrow banking regime). Like narrow banks, the DCIs would run no credit risk and take liquidity risk responsibly, since they put their own capital at risk in the market for liquidity and face competition on that market alone.[7] Also, like in narrow banking, in a noncredit money system the illiquidity or insolvency of financial intermediaries would not affect the liquidity of deposits. Yet, unlike narrow banking, a noncredit money system would have the power to create inside money and distribute it to the private sector. In other words, while the separation of lending from money creation would avert the risks involved in collateralizing money liabilities with illiquid assets (as narrow banking does), the DCIs would still allow new money to be issued to the private sector, thus overcoming one of the major shortcomings of narrow banking.

Also, in a noncredit money system, no financial intermediary could rely on insured demand liabilities. Thus, all such liabilities would be priced at levels that

---

[7] More precisely, credit risk would be zero for DCIs and low but nonzero for narrow banks (since they extend loans). On the other hand, DCIs would run a higher liquidity risk than narrow banks since, by construction, they are based on fractional reserves while narrow banks operate on a 100 percent collateral basis.

reflect the true asset riskiness of the liability issuer. Moreover, since no failure of any intermediary would affect the payment system, or would have systemic ripples through deposit runs, public intervention would be unnecessary to protect financial liabilities or to salvage failing institutions, as is being done in the current financial turmoil. Also, the separation of the payment system from lending would eliminate the need for bank capital requirements based on complex credit-risk evaluations of overly complex bank products that make rules-based regulation virtually impossible. All financial intermediaries (including those that provide bank-like credit services) would be regulated under capital markets supervision based on disclosure and market self-regulation.

The DCIs would be much easier to monitor than banks in a credit money system, since primary liquidity ratios could be observed immediately, and the failure of DCIs can be resolved seamlessly overnight. Such high transparency would enable financial supervisors and market players (depositors, DCI shareholders, and investors in DCI shares) to monitor the DCIs and their market efficiently. This would subject the DCI sector to strong discipline from both the market and the financial authorities.

Box 9.3. NonCredit Money and Friedman's "100% Reserve" Banking

In developing a plan for monetary stability, Milton (Friedman, 1960) revived the 100% reserve banking idea that would later evolve into the narrow banking proposals referred to in the text. The whole money in the system (whether currency or deposits) would become a government liability, as the government reclaimed the monopoly to create money it had partly relinquished to banks through the fractional reserve system. Accordingly, all banks would hold 100% reserves in Federal Reserve notes or deposits, against all outstanding deposit liabilities payable on demand or transferable by check. As a result, the stocks of money and high-powered money would coincide, and the instability in the money supply originating from the randomness of the money multiplier would be removed. Friedman proposed that commercial banks be separated in two types of institutions: a pure depository that would hold one dollar of central bank reserve for each dollar of demand deposits, and an investment trust that would acquire capital by selling shares or securities and use it to fund loans and investments. Investment trusts were not to engage in money creation or destruction. Banks would charge fees for their services to depositors, earn interest on central bank reserve holdings, and pay interest on deposits. Interest payment on deposits would induce an optimal stock of money holding and reduce the incentive for nonbanks to create money substitutes.

The noncredit money system is superior to Friedman's proposal in several respects. First, in Friedman's proposal, money (not just reserves, but also what banks themselves would create in a fractional reserve regime) would be supplied to the economy either through government budget spending or through private-sector asset purchases by the central bank. Friedman himself deemed both solutions not particularly appealing since they would place the government into the banking business, something his 100% reserve proposal was in fact purported to eliminate. In the noncredit money system, on the other hand, money is supplied to the private sector by private-sector entities (the DCIs) via a competitive market mechanism, thus overcoming Friedman's legitimate concern on government involvement. Second, assuming that money grows annually at the rate of nominal GDP, for a given velocity of circulation, and that all depositors have the same average deposit balance over the year, noncredit money creation would amount to deposits paying interest equal to nominal GDP growth. This interest-like, market-determined distribution mechanism would allow the DCIs to attract deposits and make their deposit base more stable, thus reducing their liquidity risk.

By competing to win more customers through improvements in service quality and pricing, and by distributing liquidity to depositors, the DCIs would likely have a stronger and more rapid impact than banks on financial deepening and broader access to financial services and bank liquidity. Agents who typically are unable to participate in the financial system would increase their purchasing power by converting cash into deposits and by using the (formal) payment systems run by the DCIs. Through liquidity distribution, more individuals would reach sooner the threshold level of wealth beyond which they can afford to participate in the broader financial system. Indeed, since the DCIs would be net fund providers, they would foster the formation of a larger depositor base and a broader distribution of wealth.

Since average deposit balances would be used to determine depositor shares in the liquidity to be distributed, individuals would want to be paid in deposits rather than cash, as this would allow them to maximize their average deposit balances. Similarly, individuals would tend to prefer businesses that offer noncash means of payments so as to minimize their cash holdings. A DCI network would feature considerable externalities; its expansion would generate scale economies in the payment system that would translate into lower transaction costs and further increase participation.

By distributing liquidity, the DCIs would enable depositors to pay for resource-intensive payment services and would foster an increase in the real demand for transactions balances. They also would make liquidity available to depositors without collateral requirements and with no need for credit risk analysis. This would circumvent the obstacle to money circulation that underdeveloped credit risk management infrastructure imposes on developing economies by forcing banks to hold excess reserves and/or foreign assets (Bossone & Sarr, 2002).

9.5 Transition to a Noncredit Money System

In moving from conventional banking to a DCI system of noncredit money—where each bank has to choose between being either a DCI or a nonbank—banks willing to transform themselves into DCIs can sell their loans to nonbank financial institutions. Other banks can transform themselves into financial companies that either control separate DCI and NonDCI subsidiaries or run separate (fire-walled) DCI and NonDCI departments. Every NonDCI subsidiary (department) is allocated the assets of the transforming bank and issues nondemandable debt liabilities to investors or offers depositors to voluntarily swap nondemandable debt instruments for demand deposits at market conditions.

In the absence of nonbank financial institutions willing to buy conventional bank loans, or in the event that the market would not finance the NonDCI subsidiaries (departments), a process of bank debt unwinding can be put in place. This may be done by letting old loans mature and by allowing DCI depositors to use the free allocated liquidity to accelerate bank debt repayment. This alternative would imply that conventional banks become institutions with separate fire-walled departments. A numerical example below illustrates the transition process.

Assume an economy with a single bank, no currency in circulation, and no financial assets other than demand deposits used for payments. In such a system, no surplus funds are available, and therefore the bank cannot convert itself into a NonDCI by selling loans to nonbanks or individual depositors. The bank will need to separate its loan business from its payment services business by creating two separate (DCI and NonDCI) departments, as explained in the following steps.

Step 1. The Original Bank is Transformed into Two Departments

The bank only has demand deposits (DD) in liabilities and loans (L) in assets. It does not have reserves since there is no currency in circulation, implying that all payments net out on its books. When the bank is split into a DCI and a NonDCI department, the DCI department inherits the demand deposits while the NonDCI inherits the loans. Since the loans were the assets backing the demand deposits, the DCI now holds an asset against the NonDCI department (Capital K) (Table 9.1).

Step 2. Depositors Repay Loans by 10

When depositors repay their loans by 10, they make a transfer from their accounts to the account of the NonDCI department at the DCI department (recall that all transaction accounts are held at the DCIs). The loan stock at the NonDCI declines by

Table 9.1 Step 1

Original bank		New financial institution			
		DCI department		NonDCI department	
Assets	Liabilities	Assets	Liabilities	Assets	Liabilities
100 L	100 DD	100 K	100 DD	100 L	100 K

Table 9.2 Step 2

New financial institution			
DCI department		NonDCI department	
Assets	Liabilities	Assets	Liabilities
90 K	90 DD	90 L	90 K

10 and the NonDCI now holds 10 in liquid assets (LA) in the form of DCI demand deposits. At this point if the NonDCI were expected to continue its operations, it could use the 10 units to lend funds again. That way, the balance sheet remains as it is above. The NonDCI is essentially identical to a conventional nonbank institution intermediating investment funds, while the DCI only deals with the payment system.

If, instead, the bank is transitioning to a specialized DCI, the DCI department offsets the NonDCI liability by 10 when the loan is reimbursed. The balance sheets shrink to 90 as a result (Table 9.2).

In the absence of new deposits created by the DCI, the balance sheets shrink to zero as loans are repaid, with deflationary effects: new money needs to be created to fill in the deflationary gap.

Step 3. The DCI Department Creates and Distributes Money on a Non-lending Basis

To avoid deflation, the DCI department needs to create money (distributed liquidity DL) both to offset the deposit destruction that occurs as loans are repaid (10 in the above example) and to accommodate expected nominal GDP growth. Assuming a nominal GDP growth of 10%, the DCI needs to distribute $20 = (10 + 0.10 \cdot 100)$. This represents a 20% distribution rate. Assuming all the loans were repaid in this period, then the DCI would need to replace 100 in deposits and create 10 to accommodate GDP growth. The balance sheet of the new institutions would be as shown below. When the loan repayment process is completed, new money distributed would equal nominal GDP growth every year (unless the velocity of money decreases because of an increased demand for inside money for transactions purposes) (Table 9.3).

In the context of a crisis, for instance, the described transition to a DCI system would be beneficial to consumers and facilitate an exit from the credit crunch. The transition would allow consumers to unwind their debt by contributing to repaying the mortgages through which money creation has been taking place (the home equity loans, cash-out refinancing, and sub-prime mortgages). This would release their own income to consume goods that they desire, and would be preferable to higher government spending and tax cuts that increase public debt, create a future tax burden,

Table 9.3 Step 3

New financial institution			
DCI department		NonDCI department	
Assets	Liabilities	Assets	Liabilities
110 K	110 DD	0	0

and perpetuate credit money creation. As discussed, the transition system would also provide a framework for dealing with failed banks under existing banking regulations.

Finally, another important issue worth noting is the impact of the transition on the exchange rate in countries where the extension of credit is constrained by lack of adequate credit-risk management infrastructure. For a given marginal propensity to import, part of the demand generated by the distributed DCI liquidity could translate into a larger demand for imports and could affect balance of payments equilibrium. The demand for foreign exchange could lead to a loss of reserves under a fixed exchange rate regime and reduce the impact of the distributed liquidity on domestic output if the exchange rate were out of line with the new equilibrium dictated by a better money distribution system. This leakage could be attenuated by currency devaluation, or exchange rate depreciation under a flexible exchange rate regime, to a level consistent with the higher deposit creation and income growth. The relative price of the tradable goods in demand would increase, thereby fostering their production and encouraging efficient market-based import substitution.

9.6 Concluding Remarks

Contemporary economies are based on the use of credit money, that is, claims that banks are allowed to issue on themselves under loan contract or securities sale terms, and that people accept and use to execute payments and settle debt obligations. To the extent that banks are permitted to operate under a fractional reserve regime, they conveniently create the bulk of the economy's money.

Since credit money, once created, is used for payments, preserving consistency between credit creation and reserves (to ensure payment finality and to protect the banks' capacity to meet deposit withdrawals) is essential for the proper functioning of the real economy. The link between credit money creation, the payment system, bank liquidity, and the economy is one of the reasons why governments have traditionally been so heavily involved in regulating banking much more than other financial market segments, and why they are so hard pressed to protect deposits.

Experience shows, however, that striking the right balance between efficiency and stability in the banking sector is no easy task, not even in the most advanced economies with well-developed regulatory and supervisory institutions. Pushing banks to compete in the market for new risks is essential to keep the real economy vital and innovative but may lead up to excessive risk taking as it has observed with the housing market crisis in the USA in 2008. On the other hand, over-regulating banks can prevent failures and crises but at the cost of limiting firms' access to capital, thereby hampering business activity and development opportunities.

In this chapter, drawing on my cited work with Abdou Sarr, I have illustrated an alternative system that separates the banks' ability to create and to allocate money to the private sector from their lending activity. Accordingly, a new type of financial institutions specialized in liquidity management and supplying payment services (called Deposit Creating Institutions, DCIs) would not be allowed to lend money but could issue deposits and distribute them to their depositor customers on a non-lending basis (under no restitution obligation). The system builds on the recognition that there is no intrinsic need for the two functions to be carried out jointly by the same institutions. The operation of the DCIs, accompanied by an appropriate redesign of the financial system and its policy framework, would generate non-inflationary purchasing power without raising private-sector debt, allow for broader access to purchasing power, fuel domestic output growth through domestic demand, reduce the economy's financial risks, and preserve the flow of money to the economy during crises.

Chapter 10 will discuss an alternative model for "superstable" money system, which I have developed more recently in cooperation with another researcher.

Appendix: Money Creation, Payment Services, and Output Effects: A Formal Analysis

This appendix shows analytically the output, price, and financial deepening effects of the DCI system illustrated in the chapter. The exercise draws on Freeman (1996) model, inter alia by integrating production in it.

Freeman (1996) illustrates the check clearing role of banks and the role of a central bank in limiting the over-issue of bank liquidity that may arise owing to less than full redemption of fiat money by depositors. His model is set up so that both cash and private debt (in the form of checks as promises to pay, or IOUs) are demanded by nonbank agents to finance their trades. Agents are spatially separated and travel through a common area (the bank) where check settlement takes place against cash.

The key feature of the model is that agents do not arrive at the bank at the same time. If holders of checks arrive before check issuers who bring in cash for settlement, settlement cannot take place. Trade would therefore not occur, thus reducing welfare. Freeman shows that, if the bank is allowed to use float to provide holders of checks with check privileges against the funds owed to them, trade can take place. At the end of the trading period, check issuers deposit the cash at the bank to clear the float. To the extent that agents accept bank float, there is no need for cash recipients to withdraw cash for their expenditures after the settlement process is completed: they may well go on using checks. As the bank realizes that the float issued is never redeemed for cash, it may decide to issue new check privileges as money for its own consumption or for investment. (It may as well distribute cash to clients, in a DCI-like fashion.) If the new money is used for consumption or is distributed to clients, the price of the goods consumed increases each time the bank adds money in the system. Freeman shows that bank reserve requirements can limit the over-issue of check privileges.

In the noncredit money system, agents use cash M (issued by the central bank) and cash-substitute B as means for payments. Cash-substitute B consists of deposits issued and allocated by DCIs to individuals (as illustrated in the main text), which can be transferred electronically via, say, debit cards and can be exchanged for M on demand at DCIs. DCIs use M to settle payments at the central bank and to satisfy cash withdrawals from depositors. Agents accept B and may hold them indefinitely, because of their immediate convertibility into cash and because they trust that the DCIs would honor such convertibility.

The model assumes that there is an even number of islands arranged in a circle around a central island. These peripheral islands are equally split in two (paired for trade) groups: agricultural islands and services islands. The central island hosts the DCIs and the central bank; the latter is responsible for settling payments. The key to the noncredit model is that (like in a conventional banking system) not all depositors withdraw cash, and not all of them do so simultaneously.

In the agricultural islands live $N/2$ identical, three-period (t, $t+1$, and $t+2$) lived agents. At time t, each of them may inherit stocks of M and B from the previous generation, receives new distributions of B from DCIs, and is endowed with 1 unit of labor and technology $A = \alpha_a p(1-\Lambda_a) 0 \leq \Lambda \leq 1$, to produce agriculture goods A. Λ stands for leisure and p is the price of A. Condition $\alpha_a p > 0$ implies that the marginal cost of leisure in terms of output forgone is negative ($-\alpha_a p < 0$). It is assumed that $\alpha_a' p < 0$ and $\alpha_a' p \geq 0$. The assumption $\alpha_a' p < 0$ implies that, as the price of good A increases, the marginal cost of leisure increases $\left(-\alpha_a' p > 0\right)$ or, equivalently, that the marginal product of labor increases thereby inducing more work, better work, and more output A. Furthermore, $\alpha_a'' p \geq 0$ implies that $-\alpha_a' p \leq 0$ or that the marginal product of labor (the marginal cost of leisure) increases at a decreasing rate as the price of A increases. This ensures an equilibrium price level beyond which any increase in the price of A would not justify an increase in labor supply because it would not be worth the leisure forgone.

When young, agricultural islanders produce for their own (present and future) consumption as well as for the (present and future) consumption of old service islanders in exchange for M or B. When old, they consume the amount of A produced earlier, and use M or B to purchase and consume S. Their utility function can be written as $V(A_{at}, \Lambda_{at})$ whereby they choose between present consumption of A and leisure Λ (which co-determine the level of A available for future consumption and for market sales to support future consumption of S). In other words, the utility of leisure today reflects the opportunity cost of foregone utility from consumption tomorrow. At the end of $t+2$, the old agricultural islanders may leave holdings of B and M for their future generation and finally die. A new generation of agricultural islanders starts off a new cycle in the subsequent period.

In the service, islands live $N/2$ identical, three-period lived agents. At time t, each service islander: inherit stocks of M and B from the previous generation, may receive allocations of B from DCIs; and specializes in applying up to 1 unit of her labor endowment to produce services S at $t+1$, at price x, using technology $S = \sigma_s x(1-\Lambda_s)$. Production function S shares identical mathematical properties of those assumed above for the production function of good A. Service islanders consume A when young and old, which they purchase using their holdings of M and B, sell S to old agricultural islanders in exchange for M or B and consume S when old. In analogy with agricultural islanders, the utility function of service islanders is

$U(A_{st}, \Lambda_{st+1})$. At the end of $t+2$, the old service islanders may leave their holdings of M and B for their future generation and finally die. A new generation of service islanders starts off a new cycle in the subsequent period.

The DCIs have no endowment of goods. They are endowed with cash M that they hold as reserves with the central bank and use to settle payments and satisfy request of cash withdrawals from depositors at $t+1$. They may issue and distribute deposits B at t and $t+1$.

A compact representation of the exchange sequence is reported in Table 9.4, at the end of this appendix.

From the exchange sequence described in the table, notice that the agricultural islanders can mobilize their holdings of M and B only at time $t+1$, since services S will not be available on the market for them to purchase until then. On the other hand, service islanders need to consume A from date t and, therefore, have to use their holdings of M and B to finance their initial consumption since they are not immediately productive and will not earn money until $t+1$ when they will sell services to old agricultural islanders.

The plan of the young agricultural islander is

$$\text{Max } V(A_{at}, \Lambda_{at}) \tag{9.1}$$

$$\text{s.t. } A_{at}p_t + A_{at+1}p_{t+1} + S_{at+1}x_{t+1} = a_a p_t(1-\Lambda_{at}) - A_{st}p_t$$

Table 9.4 Exchange sequence

Islanders	Period		
	T	$t+1$	$t+2$
Agricultural (a)	Inherit M and B from previous generation and receive new B from (d) Sell A to (s) for M or B Consume A	Buy S from (s) with M or B May either sell B for M via (d) or hold it at (d)	Consume A and S Hold M and B at (d)
Service (s)	Inherit M and B from previous generation and receive new B from (d) Consume A	Sell S to (a) for M or B Buy A from (a) with M or B Cash B for M via (d) or hold B at (d)	Consume A and S Hold M and B deposits at (d)
DCIs (d)	Hold M deposits with (c) Distribute B to (a) and (s)	Accept B from (a) and (s) for M Deliver M to (c) to settle payments	Keep B held by (a) and (s)
Central bank (c)	Sells M to (d) Keep M deposits held by (d) Holds settlement accounts of (d)	Settles payments on the accounts of (d)	Keep M held by (d)

$$-A_{st+1}p_{t+1} + \Delta(b_{at+1} + m_{at+1}) \quad (9.2)$$

where $b = B/N$ and $m = M/N$ denote holdings of B and M, respectively, b includes the new deposits distributed by the DCIs, and the Δ operator indicates changes in stock from the last period. Note that since production decisions for A are taken and executed at time t, and condition consumption at $t + 1$, budget constraint (9.2) is intertemporal. Noting that the nominal amount of S consumed at $t + 2$ is purchased at $t + 1$ at the ongoing price, condition (9.2) requires that consumption equal surplus agricultural production plus any net (positive or negative). accumulation of M and B holdings needed to purchase services S. For a given level of production, an increase in consumption of S requires a decrease in current and future consumption of A (and, correspondingly, a larger sale of A to service islanders) and/or a greater decumulation of B and M holdings at $t + 1$. Denoting subscripts a and λ as partial derivatives, the solution to plan (9.1)–(9.2) is

$$V_a/V_l = -1/ap_t$$

that is, the staple producer's equilibrium marginal rate of substitution of good S for good A.

The plan of the young service islander is

$$\text{Max } U(A_{st}, \Lambda_{st+1}) \quad (9.3)$$

$$\text{s.t. } A_{st}p_t = \Delta(b_{st} + m_{st}) \quad (9.4)$$

$$A_{st+1}p_{t+1} = S_{at+1}x_{t+1} = \sigma_s p_{t+1}(1 - \Lambda_{st+1})x_{t+1} - S_{st+1}x_{t+1} + \Delta(b_{st+1} + m_{st+1}) \quad (9.5)$$

In this case, there are two separate budget constraints for each period of consumption. Condition (9.4) indicates that service islanders can finance consumption of A at t only by decumulating their initial holdings of M and B. Here, the advantage of a DCI system is immediately visible over a system where agents are liquidity constrained by the absence of facilities to extent credit to them against their future income: allocations of B from DCIs would release those constraints, thus supporting higher demand and production in the economy. Noting that the nominal amounts of A and S consumed at $t + 2$ are purchased at $t + 1$ at the ongoing prices, condition (9.5) requires that consumption at $t + 2$ equal total earnings plus any net (positive or negative) accumulation of M and B holdings. The solution to plan (9.3)–(9.5) is

$$U_a/U_\lambda = -(p_t/\sigma_s p_{t+1})x_{t+1}$$

The golden rule of exchange between islanders, requiring $V_a/V_\lambda = U_a/U_\lambda$, yields.

$$\sigma_s x_{t+1}/\alpha_a p_t = p_t/x_{t+1} \tag{9.6}$$

From conditions (9.2) and (9.5), one derives

$$p_t = \Delta(b_{st} + m_{st})/A_{st} \tag{9.7}$$

$$x_{t+1} = \Delta(b_{at+1} + m_{at+1})/S_{at+1} \tag{9.8}$$

that is, the price of each good varies directly with the monetary demand for the good and inversely with its market supply. Recalling that $\alpha'_a p < 0$ and $\sigma'_s x < 0$, and that $\alpha''_a p \geq 0$ and $\sigma''_s x \geq 0$, equations (9.6)–(9.8) imply that optimal changes in prices p and x can be induced that maximize the incentive for all producers to forgo leisure for labor, thus raising productivity and labor use across the economy.

The point of essence of the model is that an increase in B engineered by the DCIs at times t and $t + 1$ leads to lower values of α_a and σ_s, through (9.6)–(9.8), which in turn push the production of A and S to grow until conditions (9.2) and (9.4)–(9.5) are satisfied. The demand for goods financed with DCI distributed liquidity increases the goods' prices relative to leisure, thus raising the incentive for producers to increase their supply. By charging a fee for the use of B for payments, the DCIs would share in the output growth they make possible.

If B were never redeemed for cash (say, it is perceived by the islanders as a perfect substitute of it), the DCIs would have the option to issue B permanently and to use it actively (holding a less than 100% M reserve requirement at the central bank). They could use it to purchase goods (counterfeiting), invest it for a return (such as purchasing government securities as conventional banks do), lend it at an interest (as conventional banks also do), or distribute it to islanders and allow them to use it for payments for a fee (in a DCI fashion).[8] Note that, under a no redemption assumption, the DCIs would not need to back B with cash reserves. A cash reserve (regulatory or prudential) requirement would be necessary only to limit the risk of B over-issue.

The results of the model show that a DCI system would well apply to economies with significant resource underemployment, such as developing economies or advanced economies under stagnation or deflation.[9]

References

Bordo, M. D. (1988). Law, John in the new Palgrave. In: J. Eatwell, M. Milgate, & P. Newman (Eds.), *A dictionary of economics*, (p. 143). Palgrave Macmillan.

[8] Note that the use of B for lending or investment purposes would not require any prior act of saving, and simply derives from the existence of a stable float.

[9] For an analysis of how a noncredit money system can fight poverty in developing economies, see Bossone and Sarr (2002).

Bossone, B. (2000). *What Makes Banks Special? A Study on Banking, Finance, and Economic Development*. Policy research working paper, WPS2408, The World Bank.

Bossone, B. (2001a). Circuit theory of banking and finance. *Journal of Banking and Finance, 25*(5), 857–890.

Bossone, B. (2001b). Do banks have a future? A study on banking and finance as we move into the third millennium. *Journal of Banking and Finance, Elsevier*, *25*(12), 2239–2276.

Bossone, B. (2002). *Should Banks Be Narrowed?*. Public Policy Brief Highlights No. 69A, Levy Economics Institute of Bard College, November 2002.

Bossone, B., & Sarr, A. (2002). *A new financial system for poverty reduction and growth*. IMF Working Paper, WP/02/178, International Monetary Fund.

Bossone, B., & Sarr, A. (2005). In: G. Fontana, & R. Bellofiore (Eds.), *The monetary theory of production tradition and perspectives*, (pp. 187–201). Palgrave Macmillan.

Bryan, L. (1991). Core banking. *The McKinsey Quarterly*, (1), 61–74.

Clough, S. B., & Rapp, R. T. (1975). *European economic history. The economic development of western civilization*. McGraw Hill Book Company.

Freeman, S. (1996). Clearing house banks and banknote over-issue. *Journal of Monetary Economics, 38*, 101–115.

Friedman, M. (1960). *A program for monetary stability*. Fordham University Press.

Chapter 10
Superstable Money (II): Separating Money Creation from Banks

Abstract This chapter explores a different "superstable" system design, contrasting fractional reserve banking's inherent instability with full reserve systems like narrow banking, which promote stability at the expense of lending capacity. The chapter discusses the potential of a Central Bank Digital Currency (CBDC) to create a secure domestic currency. However, introducing a CBDC could disrupt traditional bank lending and intermediation. To address these challenges, the chapter presents the "CBDC next-level model," wherein the central bank lends money to banks, which then allocates these funds to the economy according to their criteria. This model ensures that deposits move from banks to the central bank, mitigating the risk of bank runs while maintaining banks' lending functions. It shields the central bank's capital and depositors from individual bank defaults. Moreover, the chapter outlines the transition from conventional banking to the CBDC-based system, promoting enhanced financial stability compared to current models.

10.1 Preamble

I got interested in central bank digital currency (CBDC) ever since it started to gain attention from researchers and policymakers in 2020. Eventually, I was asked to join World Bank's and IMF's expert groups that advised emerging market economies' central banks on this new topic and co-led the writing of World Bank (2021) main publication on CBDC.

While working on the topic, I got an email from Michael Heines, an intellectually and socially committed Australian entrepreneur who was member of a group that wanted to use Sovereign Money for a Universal Basic Income in his country. Michael had read my article on commercial bank seigniorage and noted the example I had given in that article to show that if the economy was cashless and had only one bank, all payments in the economy would happen in the bank's books and no central bank reserves would be needed as settlement money. In fact, the money created by the single bank would be the settlement tool for the economy.

B. Bossone, *Trailblazing Visions of Money in Economic Theory*, Contributions to Economics, https://doi.org/10.1007/978-3-031-82544-6_10

Michael noted that example because he had envisioned a system where the central bank would buy all the bank deposits in circulation and require that the money used to pay the depositors would be put back into central bank accounts. In Michael's system, all the money in the economy would in fact become CBDC and commercial banks would act as agents of the central bank, managing customer accounts, dealing with deposits and loans for interest and fees (with all transactions being recorded by the central bank), and monitoring and ensuring loan repayments to the central bank. Crucially, in Michael's system, banks would still make new loans, but these would be entirely financed with borrowings from the central bank that commercial banks would have to pay back. This would separate bank lending from money creation.

We then decided to collaborate and write a paper, which later the Levy Economics Institute accepted in its working papers series (see below). This chapter illustrates our proposal for a different kind of CBDC than the one usually examined in the existing literature. The characteristics of our proposed CBDC model, and the banking structure that would build around it, would result in a "super-stable" financial system.

10.2 Introduction[1]

In a market economy, any two economic agents are free to agree on the means of payment to be used to settle a transaction. Yet, the acceptance of any form of money depends on the receiver's confidence that, subsequently, a third party will accept that money in trade. And since fiat money is intrinsically worthless, its acceptance must rest on the trust that the community accepts it in the exchange process—and will always do so for the foreseeable future.

Maintaining trust in money, and facilitating its circulation, represents a major public interest. Currently, in most countries, this responsibility is entrusted with the central bank, which looks after the safety and efficiency of the payment systems and seeks to preserve the stability of the (real) value of money in the economy. In discharging this responsibility, the central bank issues a claim on itself for use as money (central bank money).

However, in most market economies, other forms of money—typically issued by commercial banks, and increasingly today by nonbank entities—are used in everyday transactions. Confidence in these forms of money lies in the ability of their issuers to convert them at par value into central bank money, or fiat money, upon demand by their clients, which in turn depends on the extent to which these monies are supported ("covered" or "backed up") with enough central bank money. Should this coverage prove inadequate, parity would not be sustainable without some form of government guarantee.

[1] This chapter draws from Bossone and Haines (2023).

Importantly, still to date commercial banks (henceforth, "banks")[2] are the primary issuers of money, and their sight (demand deposit) liabilities represent most of the stock of money in circulation (henceforth, "bank money"). Banks create money by lending to borrowers (as discussed in Chap. 5) and the economies draw significant benefits from this unique form of decentralized money creation process. Yet (as it also has been discussed in Chap. 5), banks can conveniently create money only to the extent that they can economize on the use of the central bank money required to settle their mutual obligations to repay deposits and other loans. This implies that bank money creation essentially rests on an inherent type of instability ("fragility") whereby, on one side, banks must minimize their demand for central bank money if they want to maximize their money creation power but, on the other, they must maximize their holdings of central bank money to give enough coverage to their money liabilities.

This chapter proposes a system that while preserving the advantages of decentralized lending through banking, removes the inherent fragility of banking. Building on the recent (rapidly evolving) literature on Central Bank Digital Currencies (CBDCs), this chapter proposes a CBDC-based system (the "CBDC next-level model") whereby the central bank creates money by lending to banks, and banks on-lend the proceeds to the economy, thus inducing a degree of financial stability that would be unparalleled by conventional banking systems—what we, perhaps unimaginatively but effectively, call "superstability."

While the overarching aim is to ensure system stability, the CBDC next-level model we propose would also protect the real value of deposits and loans through the introduction of new tools that would improve the central bank's ability to limit inflation and unemployment, and mitigate asset booms and busts, without sending the economy into recession.

The chapter is organized as follows. Section 10.3 illustrates the main components of the bank money creation process, analyzed in detail and at length elsewhere in the literature; considers the claims and counterclaims regarding the seigniorage that banks extract as rent from the economy, thanks to their money creation power; identifies the constraints limiting bank money creation; evaluates the pros and cons of bank money creation; and recalls the radical proposals that have been submitted until the recent past to reform the banking sector. Section 10.4 summarizes the basic CBDC architectures that have emerged so far from research and central bank practice, upon which the CBDC next-level model proposed in this chapter develops. It also discusses the relative advantages and disadvantages of each type of architecture. Section 10.5 describes the CBDC next-level model as the basis for a new financial architecture. The section explains how the new system would change current banking and identifies the roles of its actors and its major features and impacts. Section 10.6 focuses on the implications of the CBDC next-level model for monetary policy, showing how

[2] As earlier in this book, "commercial banks" are here and throughout this chapter defined as institutions that accept demand deposits from the public *and* lend money to borrowers by issuing demand deposit claims to them, that is, claims that give their owners the right to convert them in cash or to transfer them to third parties either for settling payment obligations or for transferring value.

it enriches the policy toolkit of the central bank, highlighting its advantages for effective policy. Section 10.7 concludes with some final remarks. The chapter is supplemented with two appendixes. Appendix 1 suggests "carrots and sticks" that could be employed to ensure the banks support adoption of the CBDC next-level model, and Appendix 2 compares the key elements of current banking systems with the CBDC next-level model.

10.3 Money in Today's Banking Systems

Chapter 5 has extensively dealt with the process of money creation by banks. This section summarizes its main lines, as this is useful for the purpose of this chapter. Through the issuance of loans and the creation of demand deposits ("deposits"), banks play a central role in expanding the money supply and influencing economic activity. This recognition has gradually permeated mainstream economics, underscoring the importance of understanding the mechanisms through which banks create money and the implications thereof.

Economies of scale and the power of individual banks in the markets where they buy and offer deposits and supply payment services amplify their money creation capacity and enhance their profitability. Benefiting from scale efficiencies and network effects, banks can expand their depositor base (relative to others), capture a larger share of payment flows, and minimize reserve requirements, thereby maximizing their money creation potential.

At the heart of the discussion of money creation lies the concept of seigniorage, which refers to the ability of money creators, including banks, to extract economic rent from their power to create money at a cost that is lower than its value. Seigniorage represents a form of economic power wielded by money creators, enabling them to exert influence over real resources and command a share of the economy's output without necessarily contributing equivalent value in return. This phenomenon has profound implications for income distribution, resource allocation, and economic stability, and discussed in Chap. 6 of this book.

Regulatory frameworks shape banks' money creation behavior and mitigate the associated risks. Prudential regulations, such as capital adequacy requirements and liquidity ratios, are designed to ensure the stability and soundness of the banking system. These regulations impose constraints on banks' lending activities, limiting their ability to create money excessively and mitigating the potential for destabilizing financial crises.

In addition, central banks govern monetary conditions and influence banks' money creation decisions by utilizing a range of policy instruments, including interest rate adjustments and open market operations, to influence the cost and availability of credit in the economy. By manipulating the cost of funds and signaling their policy intentions, central banks seek to steer banks' lending behavior and manage macroeconomic variables such as inflation and economic growth.

The goal of central banks' policy instruments is to change the present and expected funding costs for the banks, which affect their prospects of risk and return and ultimately their money creation (lending) choices, which will have an impact on retail borrowers. They partly rely on psychology, as the central bank communicates ("forward guidance") its policy plans in the hope that lenders and borrowers adjust their behavior to match the central bank's goals. Actual changes are done through adjusting the rates of lending and borrowing among banks and through buying and selling securities. These actions either lower borrowing and spending (by increasing interest rates), which reduces demand, or raise borrowing and spending (by decreasing interest rates), which boosts demand.

However, these instruments are very coarse, often causing negative effects on the whole economy, especially when inflation is caused by supply shocks, not by a rise in demand from too much borrowing. The system also leads to unfair pricing when interest rates are lower than the inflation rate, harming savers and allocating resources poorly. Other financial regulatory tools (such as capital, liquidity, and leverage ratios) may limit the banks' ability to create money. These instruments do not directly affect deposit issuances but influence the cost factors that banks must consider when giving out new credit.

Pros and Cons of Bank Money Creation

The power of banks to create money by lending is a key factor in efficiently allocating society's resources. Rather than leaving it entirely in the hands of a centralized bureaucracy to decide where and on what "new money" ought to be allocated and spent, current banking systems distribute the decision-making process across the community by putting it in the hands of specialized institutions (banks), which compete for identifying opportunities to lend resources and/or for providing financial services that can match the demand. A centralized process would inevitably be less efficient and effective than a decentralized process taking place in an information-intensive environment; and would render the money supply process much less elastic, and less apt to meet the variegated and changing needs of the economy.

In carrying out this function, banks should ensure that the proceeds of the loans are used for lawful purposes, in line with societal objectives. Ideally, bank loans should be restricted to the "low-risk" end of the market, as they represent "new money" being injected into the economy at the lowest cost, while higher risk loans ought to be financed by investors putting their own money at risk in the expectation of higher returns. Banks should also manage liquidity prudently, with the aim always to be able to match their clients' demands for cash withdrawals and deposit mobilization, and to accomplish payments settlement in due time.

History shows that this is not always the case, and the financial literature explains why banks are inherently *fragile*. In the seminal work by Diamond and Dybvig (1983), banks can profitably intermediate liquidity between savers who want to deposit in liquid accounts and borrowers who need to take out long-maturity loans, only at the cost of exposing themselves to the risk of a run. That is, by aggregating funds from many different depositors with different time preferences for fund withdrawals, banks can commit to lending money on longer terms, counting on their ability to service depositors' immediate liquidity needs. Yet this makes banks inherently fragile, in the sense that if, for some reason, all depositors wanted to withdraw their money at the same time, banks would find themselves unable to honor their obligations. The inherent fragility is evident considering that if, hypothetically, banks wanted to guarantee themselves fully against the risk of runs, the liquidity they would have to hold as collateral would prevent them from lending to borrowers: banking, understood as deposit-taking *and* lending, would be impossible.

Diamond and Rajan (2001) further develop the essential role of *fragility* for banking. They argue that banks purposefully adopt a fragile structure as a commitment device, whereby a bank's refusal to deliver a depositor the amount requested would prompt all other depositors to try to withdraw as well and effectively cut off all lending to the bank. Thus, they voluntarily expose themselves to the risk of a run and commit to managing such risk to enable depositors to withdraw funds when needed while buffering borrowers from depositors' liquidity needs. If credible, this commitment induces depositors to trust banks with their money. A credible commitment also allows banks to deliver on their promises while economizing on costly central bank reserves.

As these studies show, and several other contributions corroborate,[3] the whole banking system is inherently fragile when the reserves base of the banks is fractional, which explains the institutional arrangements (e.g., access to central bank refinancing facilities, deposit insurance, public guarantee mechanisms, etc.) that most jurisdictions worldwide adopt to prevent risk of default and to mitigate its consequences.

Throughout modern history, including recently, governments worldwide have had to support banks to avoid system collapse. The problem occurs usually in rising markets: to stay competitive, banks (especially, but not exclusively, the large ones) are tempted, in competition with each other, to take on more risk than is prudent, in the expectation that they would be protected by government guarantees if the risk materializes (engendering "moral hazard"). The result is booms and busts in asset markets, and the broader economy, leading to recessions and, in the worst cases, depressions.

10.4 Proposals to Reform Banking

Chapter 9 has referred to the banking reform proposals that have been submitted over the years, especially in the aftermath of major banking crises, mostly involving the outright suppression of banks' power to create money. The chapter then illustrated the radical proposal by Abdou Sarr and myself, which would retain inside money creation by specialized payment service institutions but separate it from lending, as money is allocated on a non-lending basis. This solution was intended to preserve the advantages of decentralized money creation, which only conventional banking

---

[3] For a recent review of the literature on banking fragility, see Amador and Bianchi (2021).

can deliver, at the same time removing the rents that conventional banks extract from the economy through seigniorage.

In recent years, a new proposition has been made possible by technology progress: the issuance of retail CBDC (henceforth, "CBDC"), which would make available to the public the highest quality asset that a jurisdiction could possibly produce in digital form. CBDC has already become a reality in some countries and is being actively researched and experimented in many others.[4]

A CBDC system that replaced conventional banking would provide the ultimate solution to the quest for deposit safety, since CBDC would be a direct claim on the state (like physical cash is) and (like physical cash) it would be a perfectly safe and liquid asset since its issuer—the central bank—could not default on its own obligations and could always issue additional CBDC, when necessary.[5]

However, whereas the proposals discussed in Chap. 9, including the system proposed by Abdou Sarr and myself, have been thought of precisely for the purpose of changing the existing banking regime altogether, no central bank today considers CBDC as a game-changer aimed to replace conventional banking. On the contrary, one of the main concerns commonly shared by central banks is the fear that CBDC issuance would disrupt the deposit-taking and lending functions of banks and, hence, they do take extra care to consider how CBDC could be introduced in ways that do not destabilize the existing financial market structures. Just by way of example, the concern is such that, fearing the risk of destabilization from CBDC, the ECB is considering adopting design features that "would contain the circulation of digital euro while offering benefits to users" (Bindseil et al., 2024). In other words: while wanting to issue CBDC, on one side, central banks should limit its use, on the other…!

The CBDC next-level model does point, instead, to a CBDC system as a game-changer that replaces conventional banking while not losing its benefits. The model combines centralized money creation by the central bank with decentralized credit provision by banks. Such a CBDC system would provide money to society at lower costs and significantly lower risks than current banking systems do. The CBDC next-level model builds on one of the basic CBDC architectures that have emerged so far from research and central bank practice, as discussed next.

---

[4] For tracking CBDC progress around the world, see Central Bank Digital Currency Tracker (by the Atlantic Council), available at https://www.atlanticcouncil.org/cbdctracker/; CBDC Tracker, available at https://cbdctracker.org; Central Bank Digital Currency Tracker (by SME Finance Forum), available at https://www.smefinanceforum.org/post/central-bank-digital-currency-tracker; or Kiffmeister's Global Central Bank Digital Currency Monthly Monitor—The CBDC Think Tank, available at https://cbdctt.com.

[5] Of course, while this holds true in principle, in practice there is a limit beyond which additional CBDC issuance would affect the credibility of the central bank and compromise its macro-financial policy objectives.

Basic CBDC Architectures

Two models have been identified in the recent literature as the technical benchmarks for CBDC architectures[6]: the "direct" (or single-tier) modeland the "hybrid" (or two-tier) model (Chart 10.1). In both models, the central bank is the only issuer and redeemer of CBDC, and both models allow for either account- or token-based access to CBDC. In the direct model, the central bank offers direct access to CBDC from retail users, handles all payments in real time, keeps a record of all balances, and updates it with every transaction. In the hybrid model, retail users can access CBDC only indirectly via (bank or nonbank) payment service provides (PSPs).[7]

The direct model looks attractive for its simplicity, as it eliminates system dependence on intermediaries by doing away with them. Yet, for the very same reason, no central bank seems to show preference for it, since its adoption might seriously upset existing market structures and disrupt current businesses by disintermediating banks and payment institutions. Also, the model would require the central bank to fulfill some significant, new responsibilities such as, interalia, for handling customer relationships, engaging in dispute resolution, executing Know Your Customer (KYC) requirements, and providing all related retail services, raising central bank costs and risks, and involving the central bank in functions and tasks that transcend its perimeter and capacity.

The "hybrid" model is by far the preferred one by central banks. Accordingly, all banks and nonbank PSPs (not the central bank) handle all communications with retail users, clear payments, and send/receive payment messages to/from other PSPs and wholesale payment instructions to/from the central bank. The latter settles wholesale

---

[6] In only a few years the literature on CBDC has become simply too vast for being reflected in a list of references that would do justice to the huge effort made by the international community on the topic so far. Many central banks, academics, and macro-financial policy experts have produced reports, studies, simulations, and experiment results, which have enormously contributed to global knowledge on CBDC. Here, we only refer to select work by international organizations like the Bank for International Settlements (BIS), the International Monetary Fund, and the World Bank are the reports issued by seven central banks and the BIS, which investigate users' needs, technological design options, and financial stability implications of retail or general purpose CBDCs. The World Bank (2021) report considers CBDC from the perspective of payment systems and services and aims to provide central banks and other relevant public authorities with a decision-making framework to be used as they investigate the potential use of CBDC as an instrument to strengthen or modernize their national payments system. Finally, IMF (2022) studies six advanced CBDC projects, drawing on collaboration and exchanges with the respective central banks, to get insights beyond what has previously been published for the purpose of sharing lessons and open questions with countries that will embark on CBDC initiatives.

[7] A third type of architecture has been proposed by Kumhof and Noone (2018), under the name of "indirect" CBDC, and by Adrian and Mancini-Griffoli (2019), under the name of "synthetic CBDC," and appears on the original of Chart 1 taken from Auer and Böhme, cit. Accordingly, CBDC would originate from a public–private partnership whereby PSPs would issue a digital currency and be required by regulation to ensure that the value of the digital currency is always fully matched by funds held at the central bank. PSPs issuing this fully backed digital currency would act like narrow banks, and since the currency would be a claim on the issuing PSPs (not on the central bank), it would not qualify as CBDC. A discussion of what would be required for this currency to be a close replica of CBDC is provided in Bossone (2021b).

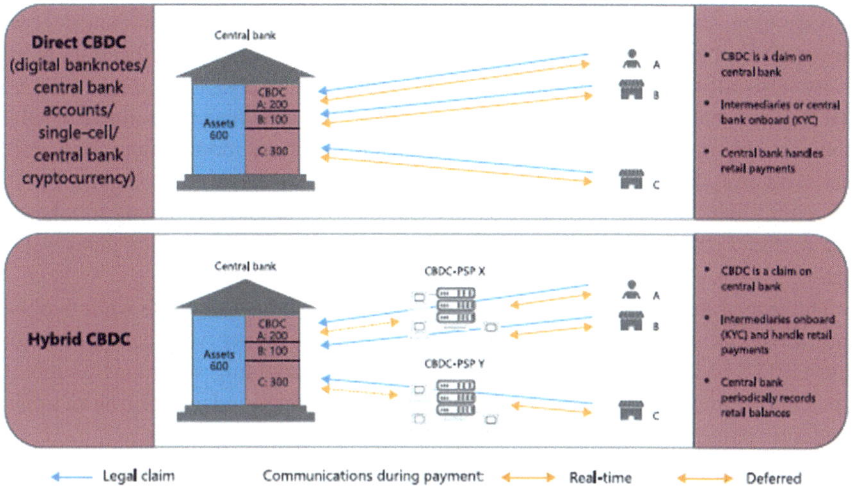

Chart 10.1 CBDC today's basic identified architectures. *Source* Auer and Böhme (2020)

CBDC transactions with finality and retains a copy of all CBDC holdings, allowing it to transfer holdings from one PSP to another in the event of a PSP's technical failure. As the central bank does not directly interact with retail users, it can concentrate on a limited number of core processes, while banks and nonbank PSPs deliver services for which they are specialized and over which they have a comparative advantage vis-à-vis the central bank.

While a full comparison of the two architecture solutions can be found in Auer and Böhme (2020), some important remarks are here in order on the implications of the hybrid model for the money supply process, which give justifications to the CBDC next-level model proposed in this chapter.

The potentially disruptive effects of CBDC on the money supply process arise from the substitution away from bank money that CBDC could trigger if it were to be preferred by the public as settlement asset and means of payment vis-à-vis currently existing instruments (typically, bank deposits). While a central bank would accommodate the demand for CBDC, flows into CBDC would drain reserves from the banking system in the same way as flows into banknotes and central bank deposits held by non-monetary counterparties (e.g., the treasury, foreign central banks, or financial market infrastructures) currently do. If banks found their reserve balance position to be below their preferred level, they would compete for funding to restore their original reserve position to their desired level, which would raise the level of short-term interest rates.

The central bank could intervene with compensatory measures, for instance, by expanding the availability of reserves to the banks. Yet, with massive portfolio shifts toward CBDC, banks would need to have large stocks of eligible assets to use as collateral in refinancing operations or as securities to trade in open market operations. This would add to bank costs.

Assuming strong public preferences for CBDC, and hence significant deposit substitutions, bank money creation via lending would decline and/or become more costly, also affecting the demand for bank loans negatively. The more attractive CBDC, the greater the disintermediation of banks and the greater the impact on the money supply process: CBDC issuance would shift the bank money supply schedule backward. As a result, the money supply process would become centralized, with the central bank and the national treasury (through fiscal budget) having to take on a more direct role in money provision to the economy, with the inefficiencies noted earlier.

The fear of disintermediating banks and disrupting their business is such that the central banks that today are engaged in CBDC initiatives are very cautious about their CBDC becoming "too successful" and consider adopting safeguards (such as caps or price mechanisms) that would limit CBDC holdings and use for transactions: a seeming paradox.

The remainder of the chapter focuses on how to replace bank money with CBDC without destroying the banks' basic business model, and in fact even improving the role of banks as lenders and their terms of lending provision to the economy. If, as discussed, fractional reserve regimes generate fragile banking, and if full reserve regimes remove fragility but at the cost of suppressing the role of banks as lenders, a CBDC could provide safe money but at the cost of potentially disrupting bank lending. Only allowing banks to on-lend CBDC borrowed from the central bank, as discussed next, would remove fragility, and preserve bank lending at the same time.

10.5 CBDC for a New Financial Architecture

The CBDC next-level model is essentially a two-tier model where, in the first tier, the central bank creates money and distributes it (wholesale) to banks which, in the second tier, on-lend it (retail) to borrowing enterprises and households (Chart 10.2).

All resident individuals, non-financial enterprises, and nonbank financial intermediaries (as well as select non-resident agents) would have access to CBDC through banks or nonbank PSPs, which would be responsible for mobilizing their CBDC holdings on demand. Unlike banks, nonbank PSPs would not be permitted under legislation to engage in lending operations.

To Start

With appropriate legislation, at an appointed time, the central bank would in a round robin issue and loan CBDC to each bank sufficient to pay out its depositors (including term deposits), as well as all loans from other banks, and bond holders who request their bonds to be paid out (see also below). Prior to the round robin, nonbank investors (bondholders) could choose to leave their money at risk with the banks. In this case, the corresponding bank liabilities would not be paid out. Instead, they would count toward the banks' "at-risk" capital. Alternatively, investors could choose to be paid out and have their money switched into CBDC holdings at the central bank.

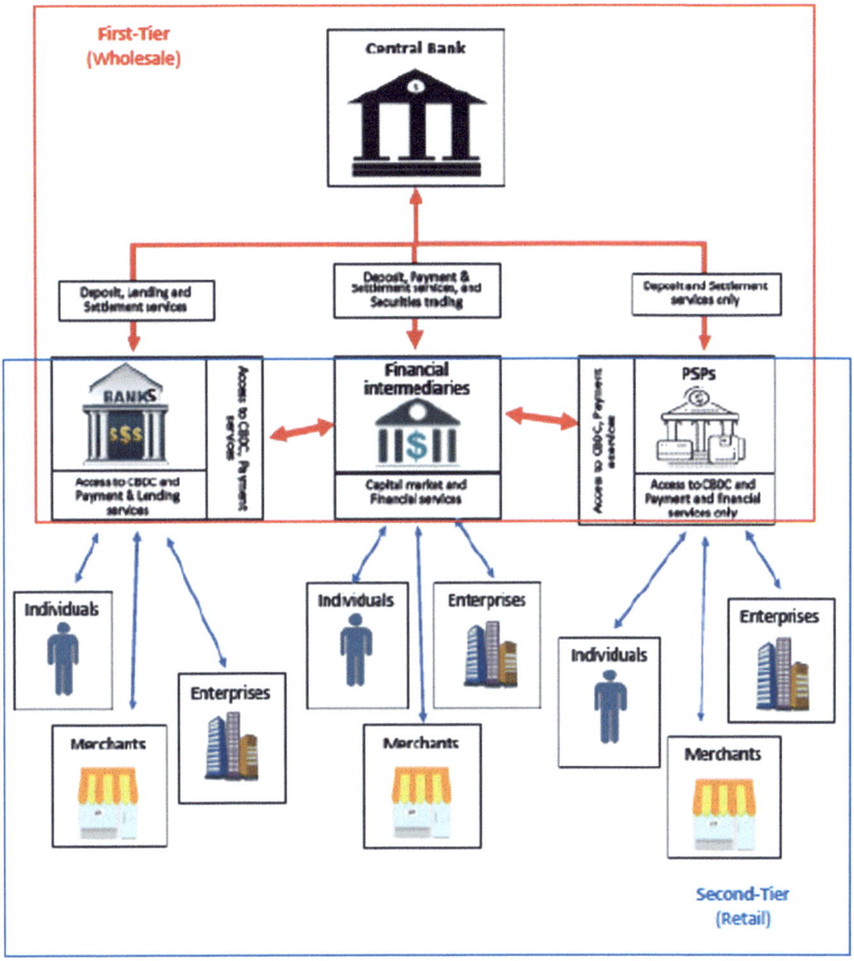

Chart 10.2 "CBDC next-level model" architecture

Each bank would then pay out each depositor, bank, and requested bonds by transferring the CBDC they received from the central bank to a new deposit account opened with the central bank in the name of the depositor/bank/bondholder. In this way, all deposits, and all loans from another bank, as well as any nonbank loans elected to be paid out would shift from the books of the bank to the books of the central bank where they would all appear as deposits.

Customers would at any time be free to transfer their money to any bank of their choice or to any nonbank PSP. Overseas banks that had their loan transferred from a bank to the central bank could elect to have the money paid out in a different currency at the current exchange rate. All local banks that had an interbank loan paid out would retain the payout in their own central bank account. This would leave each bank with its own loan (asset) book balanced on the liability side by the loan received from the central bank (rather than by deposits and third-party loans).

Deposits would never have to be repaid, other than in cash. They would get transferred from one central bank account to another. Or they could be paid out in physical cash or transferred as eCash to a device/wallet on demand by the customer (within specified limits to reduce illicit transactions). This would simply change the form of the claim on the central bank but would not alter the money supply or its legal nature.

The deposit accounts would sit on a ledger managed by the bank as "fiduciary" (i.e., agent of the central bank). The bank would have no liability to repay the deposits. While these would be off the books of the banks, and on the books of the central banks, the banks would continue to manage the deposits of their customers and the whole payments system in such fiduciary capacity for whatever fees they chose (in competition with other banks). To protect privacy, the central bank would have no direct access to the individual accounts; it would simply have a "real time" running total of deposits held by each bank and nonbank PSP.

Such deposits would be claims of their holders on the central bank and would thus constitute retail CBDC, equivalent to cash. Following the changeover, any CDBD holder would have the ability to access their CBDC account and withdraw funds to either get physical cash, or eCash, or to make payments and/or transfers into other accounts at any time, without any risk of loss or delay (i.e., virtually instantly). As will be explained, this would significantly reduce system risk and cost of money.

Existing loans made by banks to nonbank borrowers would remain standing, on the terms that are current at the time of changeover. Banks should find it convenient to join the new system, due to the advantages discussed below. Yet, if reluctance remains, incentives and penalties can be used to get all banks on board (Appendix 1).

Loans

Whenever a bank plans to make a loan to a borrower, it calls on the central bank to create the required volume of CBDC, which would be deposited into the bank's account with the central bank and recorded as a loan from the central bank to the bank. The central bank would provide the CBDC to the bank "on demand," without any need for oversight by the central bank. The central bank would record both the deposit and loan in its own ledger, keeping its books in balance.

The interest applied by the central bank on loan advances would be sufficient to meet its operating costs, plus a margin based on monetary policy considerations, which would act as a policy rate (this is discussed in the section on Monetary Policy).

The bank would then lend the CBDC to the borrower by transferring CBDC out of its central bank account and into the central bank account of the customer (which it would still manage, but now as fiduciary). In effect, the bank would replace the "cash on hand" in its own account with the central bank, with a "loan to a borrower," as the matching asset against the new loan from the central bank, thereby remaining in balance.

The loan interest rate would reflect the risk profile of the borrower, as appraised by the bank, the interest applied by the central bank on loan advances, as well as its own operating costs and profit margin, and the competition in the banking market for loans.

Importantly, the loan from the central bank to the bank would be repayable at the same time as the borrower is expected to repay the bank. No longer would the system record a mismatch between lending and borrowing schedules, and no longer would resources need to be devoted by the bank to managing funding. This alone would simplify the business of banking, reducing cost.

In making the loan to the borrower, the bank would transfer the money from its central bank account to the borrower's central bank account (managed by the bank), where it would appear as a new deposit. At any time, the borrower would instruct the bank to pay specific third-party accounts as the loan was spent. In each case, the money would go from the borrower's central bank account to the payee's central bank account (managed by the payee's bank), or to an eCash device held by the payee (subject to specified limits). As the borrower repaid her loan, the money would be transferred from her central bank account (managed by the bank) to the bank's central bank account.

To ensure the matching flow of funds, the bank would keep only the interest component of the loan repayment as compensation for its services, while it would pass on the principal component (adjusted for inflation) to the central bank, thus repaying its loan to the latter. The reversal of the entries in the books of the central bank would have the effect of destroying the money initially created when the loan was made.

Until it is destroyed through the repayment process, the money would never leave the central bank's accounts—unless taken in physical cash or eCash. Cash controls would continue to be required to limit the black market.

While from the borrower's perspective the interest is the "cost of money," from the bank's perspective, it is the revenue to cover the cost of its services, to provide for risks, and to generate profit.

Payment Services

Banks and nonbank PSPs would manage their customers' central bank accounts as fiduciaries and would manage the payments activity between their own customers and the customers of other banks and nonbank PSPs. These would be entitled to charge fees for their services. All payments would go from one central bank account to another, in real time, and these accounts would appear on central bank subsidiary ledgers managed by banks and nonbank PSPs (or to eCash devices, subject to limits).

As an example, as an enterprise received a bank loan and started spending the proceeds, for each payment it would direct its bank to pay a certain amount to another specific person or business accounts. If this other account were managed by another bank or nonbank PSP (as fiduciary), a message would be sent to the other bank or nonbank PSP that would credit the specific central bank account with CBDC, and the enterprise's CBDC holdings would be reduced equivalently. That is, immediately after the switch to the new system, CBDC would always go from one central bank account to another, regardless of which bank or nonbank PSP acted as fiduciary for which people or businesses. At no point, in any transaction, could the CBDC be lost or stolen (unless taken as cash or eCash[8]).

The central bank would play no part in any retail operations. It would have no access to individual accounts and would only see the running total of each subsidiary ledger, making overall reconciliation instantaneous.

Each account should continue to be subject to Know Your Customer (KYC) requirements to combat money laundering, tax evasion and terrorist financing, without breaching the privacy of CBDC holders who obey the law.

While all licensed banks and nonbank PSPs would be permitted to act as fiduciaries, only the entities licensed as banks could issue loans of new CBDC.

Inflation Adjustment

In an important change, the CBDC would be adjusted by the daily inflation rate[9] (tax-free) to keep their real value stable (unless taken as eCash). It would work as follows:

- The total outstanding amount advanced to each bank by the central bank would be adjusted by the daily rate of inflation,[10] to keep the real value of the advances stable. This is key to ensuring economic efficiency.
- The money collected from the banks in the form of the inflation adjustment would be returned to the community via a similar inflation adjustment on all deposits held with the central bank.
- The inflation adjustment would flow through to the bank's borrowers, increasing the amount of the outstanding principal, thus bearing no impact on the bank's costs, profit, or net worth.

However, each bank would be entitled to earn interest on the adjusted balance of the loans it makes. In this way, interest *income* would also keep pace with inflation, without any change in the interest *rate*.

---

[8] The term "eCash" refers to CBDC held on a separate device/wallet. The CBDC would be downloaded from the customers' central bank account (reducing the account by the amount of the download). The CBDC on the device could then be used to pay for goods and services anonymously, just like paper money. Specific limits would need to be imposed on the amount of cash that could be held on a device and the number of devices a person could have to the limit illicit use of cash. Once CBDC was downloaded to a device, it would no longer attract the inflation adjustment.

[9] In principle, where feasible, no adjustment should be made where a drop in supply (e.g., due to a drought, supply chain disruption, etc.) were the cause of a spike in prices, as the prices themselves are the mechanism for re-balancing the market. Yet, it might be difficult to apply this principle in practice. A practical way to handle this issue would be for the adjustment to take place automatically based on an inflation index selected to match the cost base of most people (irrespective of the "true" nature of inflation), and for the central bank then to act on inflation through its various instruments (depending on the nature of inflation and the tools chosen to deal with it), based on the central bank's target envelope. Looking forward, however, one of the upsides of moving to CBDC is that the new and evolving technology supporting it would make it possible at some point to incorporate misidentified "meta data" along with every transaction, which would extract and aggregate real-time information that would better assist the central bank investigating and understanding the true nature of price dynamics.

[10] Excluding inflation due to supply shortages, where it can be identified, see previous footnote.

Thus, banks would not be put at a competitive disadvantage with other lenders. With all deposits adjusted by the inflation rate, all lenders would have to recover the real value of their loan as a minimum. Otherwise, the money would be better left on deposit. This alone will greatly improve economic efficiency, eliminating negative interest rates.

With these arrangements in place, funding and inflation would no longer be an issue for banks. Their focus would be on cost control, borrower risk mitigation, and provision for defaults, as well as service provision to maximize profits, in competition with other banks.

How interest on central bank deposits and bank loans would be managed is discussed below.

Actors, Features, and Impacts

Depositors

All the money issued and distributed by the banking system (including the central bank and the banks) would become legal tender (CBDC, Cash and eCash). As CBDC would only move across central bank accounts, no deposit could ever be at risk due to a bank failure. Nor could a depositor lose access to her account (unless in breach of the law). And even in the case of theft from a central bank account, if the depositor has followed the required procedures, any loss could be reinstated.[11]

Since CBDC would be held without risk, holding it would be no different than holding cash in a safe, so it would earn no interest, just like cash. Better than cash, however, CBDC need not be invested at risk for its holders to maintain the real value of their deposit. This is important not only for economic efficiency, but also for equity. If a person has added value through work or investment and received money in recognition of that value, the holder of the money ought to be able to take out from society the same amount of value when they come to spend it—no matter how long they wait to spend.

To give effect to this principle, depositors would receive a daily tax-free credit equal to the inflation rate applied to their deposit, to keep the real value of their deposit stable.

Borrowers

Borrowers would be required to repay the real value of their loans, with the outstanding balance adjusted by the daily inflation rate.[12] This adjustment would not be tax-deductible, and interest would be payable on the adjusted balance. Once the adjusted loans are repaid, the borrowers and society will be square. They will

[11] For a loss to be irretrievable, the thief would have to take the money in cash (with limits imposed to reduce the risk of crime) or transfer it overseas (subject to monitoring and control processes prior to the transfer).

[12] Again, where possible, no adjustment should be made for price rises due to supply shocks. See the previous footnote.

have put back in what they have taken out—*in real terms*. This will have a major positive impact on economic efficiency.

Borrowers who are not in default would no longer be at risk of having their loans called in to pay out depositors due to a bank failure, or of having their interest rate raised to cover bank losses on other loans. Why this would be so is discussed in the section Regulatory Oversight and Bank Failure.

The Central Bank

Unlike a bank's liability to depositors, CBDC would never have to be repaid by the central bank or redeemed in any form of value other than another claim on the central bank (i.e., physical cash or eCash).[13] Any withdrawal of cash would simply replace one form of central bank liability with another, which the central bank can similarly issue at will, and any CBDC transfer would simply go from one central bank account to another central bank account. Nor would the central bank ever run out of CBDC.

As such, it is more accurate to categorize the CBDC on issue as equity of the central bank, as it represents the collective claim of citizens on society's resources, like the collective claim that shareholders have on the resources of a company (see Chap. 2). This bears crucial implications for the stability of the CBDC next-level model.

Any bank loan that a borrower failed to repay would simply stay on the books of the central bank. The central bank would suffer no real loss as the money would not have disappeared. As the borrower spent their loan proceeds, the money would always end up in some other person's or entity's deposit account with the central bank. The central bank could simply change the entry in its books from "loan to bank A," to "money in permanent circulation." Excluding loss of cash, money disappears (or better, it gets destroyed) only as and when a loan is repaid, since the entries in the books of the bank and central bank are both reversed.

The central bank could agree to defer repayment of its loans, allowing the banks to defer repayment of principal by its borrowers. The interest would be repayable, so the bank had the income to go (on trading). This could be done, for example, if there is a big downturn in the property market (perhaps at the same time as higher inflation), so large sections of people are struggling to meet their higher payments and house prices are falling. As a result, the bank may be struggling to meet its obligations to the central bank. Yet, calling in the loans (both the banks and the borrowers) will only make the situation worse.

In exchange for deferring loan repayments, banks should be required not to increase the interest rate on the borrowers who are struggling, as that would make things worse. With the support of the central bank both the banks and their borrowers will weather the storm. However, if a bank has made loans to borrowers who cannot repay them, and there is little hope of recovery, it would be allowed to fail.

As explained in the section "Regulatory Oversight and Bank Failure" the deposit register, borrowers who are not in default, and those with good prospects of recovering

---

[13] Unless the central bank was operating under a currency board or was tied to a fixed exchange rate arrangement.

any shortfalls would be sold to a viable bank for the future income stream. The in-default borrowers with no prospects of full recovery would be pursued by the bank's administrator. Any security would be sold up with all recoveries, together with the proceeds of sale of the viable business, would go first to the central bank, with all losses put against the banks at-risk capital (equity and debt).

Once injected in the system, irrespective of however it is used, wherever it accumulates, and whoever holds and uses it, CBDC will always represent central bank equity, and no losses or defaults by individual banks or borrowers can ever dent it or weaken the central bank's capital position or hurt depositors. Individual borrowers and banks would still be required to honor their debt in full, lest they would be bound to exit the market or even be forced into bankruptcy.

No current banking system could possibly replicate this "superstability" property. The new system would also offer the opportunity to provide additional tools to help the central bank minimize inflation and unemployment, thereby mitigating booms and busts. How this can be done is discussed in the section on Monetary Policy Implications.

The central bank would have its operating costs met via a percentage levy on the total of its inflation adjusted loans to each bank.

Banks

In fractional reserve regimes, a banking license is literally a license to create money. This would change in the CBDC next-level model, where the purpose of banks is to manage CBDC deposits and payments as fiduciaries of the central bank and to lend newly issued CBDC as principal to third parties at low risk, with fees and interest charges to cover its operating costs, provisions for defaults, and profits.

Banks would be required to pay fees to the central bank (and other relevant regulators) to cover the authorities' operating costs. The fees would be a percentage of the total amount of CBDC on loan to each bank.

In the CBDC next-level model, banks would no longer extract seigniorage from the economy as they would no longer be permitted to create money out of fractional reserves. The bank's costs would also be lower as they would no longer need to borrow in the open market to fund their own loans. All else equal, this would lower the cost of money to borrowers, while the proposed inflation adjustment would ensure that they repaid the real value of their loan, enhancing economic efficiency.

After changeover to the new system, the central bank would become the sole creditor in the books of each bank, other than trade creditors (or bank shareholders and bondholders putting their money at risk as part of the bank's "at-risk" capital—see Regulatory Oversight and Bank Failure).

The main constraints on bank lending would be:

1. The demand for loans, which would be influenced by interest rates, economic conditions, and any levies imposed by the central bank to mitigate inflation (see section on Monetary Policy Implications).
2. The capital ratio that would limit a bank's total loan book to a multiple of the bank's "at-risk" capital (equity and debt).

3. Regulatory restrictions on the type/purpose of loans.

Thus, reserves (and their cost) would no longer affect the resource envelope of banks, as it happens in fractional reserve regimes.

Regulatory Oversight and Bank Failure

Banks would continue to be subject to regulatory oversight. However, regulatory frameworks could be simplified, since no deposits would be at risk, and the failure of any one bank would not impact other banks (because there would be no cross-investment among banks).

To ensure the banks have "skin in the game," each bank would only be permitted to lend a set multiple of its "at-risk" capital (equity and bonds).[14] Once a bank reached the limit of its capital ratio, it would have to raise more capital to lend more or increase its capital by retaining earnings.

For the bank to carry the risk of its lending decisions, just because the borrower defaults, the bank would not be freed from its obligation to repay the central bank, together with any interest due to the central bank on the pre-agreed schedule. This means the bank must enforce its default provisions against any borrower unless the central bank agreed to defer repayment of its loan to the bank to support the economy during a downturn (see section Monetary Policy Implications).

Bank Directors and Officers

With all loans funded through the central bank, the directors and officers of each bank would retain primary responsibility under corporate law to determine if, and when, their bank could no longer pay their debts as they fell due, and/or losses on their bank's loan book were likely to exceed their capital, forcing them to stop trading. Without depositors and other bank lenders on its books, this decision would not impact the banking system.

Bank directors and officers would thus be in the same boat as those of any other business. However, they would have one major advantage over the latter. They could seek dispensation from the central bank to go on supporting their bank to get them out of insolvency—if it appeared that the bank could ultimately recover its losses. Unlike normal creditors, the central bank can afford to take a long-term view of what is in the best interest of the economy overall.

In exchange for such support, the payment of bonuses should be restricted until the bank has recovered viability. This would also provide a unique benefit to bank shareholders and bondholders that no other entity would enjoy.

If a decision were eventually made to wind up a failed bank, the only ones impacted would be the shareholders and bondholders, perhaps some trade creditors, as well as the directors and senior staff, and possibly some other employees, who would lose their jobs. A bank failure would have zero impact on depositors and all borrowers whose repayments were up to date, or on any other bank, or any other financial institution.

---

[14] An optimal multiple would have to be identified, but a factor of 12 would seem prudent.

The central bank could continue to support the bank while an administrator (appointed by the central bank or any other authority under the law) would sell the loans not in default and the management rights to the central bank deposit register (together with any necessary operating assets and staff) as a going concern to a viable bank. The administrator would pursue the borrowers who were in default. The proceeds of sale, and any recoveries from delinquent borrowers, would go first to the central bank, then to other creditors, bondholders and finally shareholders, as per the normal bankruptcy provisions.

Bank Shareholders and Bondholders

Monies invested in a bank could only go toward providing its operating assets (including working capital) or held on deposit with the central bank as security. As with all deposits, these "security deposits" would be increased by the daily inflation rate to maintain their real value, tax-free. A bank's income would be restricted to the net return on the loans that it makes and any fees it charges for managing deposits and payments.

As the whole system should be far more stable, banks should have no trouble attracting investment (both equity and debt) to grow their "at-risk" capital to meet market demand for new loans. The investment of a bank's shareholders and bondholders would be lost entirely if the total losses due to loan defaults exceeded the total of the bank's at-risk capital (equity plus debt), after the bank had been liquidated—as with any other business.

On the positive side, if the bank remains solvent, it is assured of funding from the central bank, without any need to attract depositors or other lenders. Also, because the central bank (unlike depositors) can afford to carry banks and their borrowers through a downturn, only in the worst cases would the foreclosure of loans (and potentially bankruptcy of the bank) be required.

Payment Service Providers

These may only facilitate customer access to CBDC and offer customers payment services as well as any additional value-added services that could be associated with CBDC account or wallet. PSPs would not be permitted under legislation to enter the lending business.

Nonbank Financial Intermediaries

These intermediaries would operate under their own regulator and use savings to invest in higher risk projects and/or second-level financing (on top of bank lending), as well as to buy existing securities and financial assets. People would have to put their own money at risk for these markets to operate efficiently.

Banks would not be allowed to make loans to nonbank financial intermediaries. Nonbank financial intermediaries would hold their own central bank accounts, which would be managed by banks or nonbank PSPs. Alternatively, they could be granted by the central bank direct access to CBDC accounts. They would not be allowed to create money but could extend loans out of their own funds or by intermediating their clients' savings.

The Payments System

In the CBDC next-level model, as in all retail CBDC systems, CBDC would be the economy's digital cash. Payments made by any entity, either on its own behalf or on behalf of its customers (in the case the entity is an intermediary), would go from its central bank account (or device/wallet) to the payee's central bank account (or device/wallet). CBDC would be the settlement asset for all (wholesale and retail) transactions. The money would never leave the central bank's ledger unless taken in physical cash or eCash.

Other forms of money, issued by private-sector agents under regulation, would be possible and interoperability would allow agents to convert CBDC into any other currency instrument accepted in the economy, and vice versa. However, where feasible, settlement in all systems should take place in CBDC, which would be the only legal tender (along with traditional Cash and eCash).[15]

The Banking and Monetary Systems

With banks getting all their loan funds from the central bank, they would no longer have to attract money from depositors or other lenders. While loans should always be expected to be repaid, repayments would not be necessary to meet depositor demands

[15] Scam cryptocurrencies would be outlawed outright (as China and other countries have already done). These include currencies that are deflationary by design (which simply advantage the holder of the "money" over the holders of assets, the reverse of inflation—in both cases the antithesis of "sound money"), and which deliver nothing but a key to the code that holds a record of who owns the currency. Bitcoin would fall into this category: if I hold the key to a bitcoin and you are a "retail" buyer, (as an example) you must pay me $30,000 fiat (which I can then spend). All you get is a key to the code. You can only realize a profit, if someone else is prepared to pay you more than $30,000. This is the essence of a Ponzi scheme. Looked at from the viewpoint of a "miner," such currencies are like counterfeit money. The counterfeiter must incur cost, using society's resources, either in the form of energy, plates, paper, and ink in the case of fake notes, or energy and hardware in the case of crypto. The counterfeit money gives the counterfeiter/cryptominer access to society's resources without contributing anything of value in return. In the case of crypto it is worse, as the deflationary design enables the miner (and any subsequent holder) to accrue a rising benefit for doing nothing but holding the coin! Worse still, simulations run by Phillip Rosedale, founder of Second Life, show that most of this benefit accrues to the original promoters who retain most of the initial coins. He claims crypto wealth is more concentrated than wealth in the real world, so much for helping the "unbanked!" Bitcoin and its ilk are the ultimate counterfeiter's dream. They are run in the open without fear of goal. Large holders can use anonymous accounts to bid up the price without losing control of the tokens, and then sell out, watch the price fall, and buy back in again, rinse and repeat, turning their scam money into real money. While, in theory, the price of the coin could fall to zero (as it has zero backing), the world is a big place, so there will always be another "mark" (unless it is outlawed). Even then, it will be impossible to stop it completely, although it can be greatly constrained if people know that it can never be used in lawful exchanges. Last but by no means least, crypto is also used for illicit trade, to avoid taxes, money laundering, to finance terrorism, for extortion, and as scams. Of course, fiat money is too! However, regulating well-identified entities is much easier than trying to regulate thousands that cannot be held accountable due to the distributed global nature of cryptocurrencies. There are in fact valid uses for blockchain and crypto tokens that act more like "securities," where their value is based on some underlying good or service, and they should be regulated as such.

for liquidity, since all deposit claims outstanding would—by construction—be with the central bank.

Most importantly, the CBDC next-level model would eliminate the risk of bank runs and system failure due to bank insolvencies. By adjusting both outstanding loan balances and deposits to reflect inflation, it would also be a fairer and more efficient system overall.

Banks would not need to access wholesale funds from other banks (or other intermediaries), since all loans would be funded using CBDC. However, the money market might still operate, but on a more limited basis. Banks would no longer need to access it, but other private entities may need cash that they cannot get from a bank, due to the risks involved, while those with cash surpluses may look for higher returns by offering them in the money market. Trading in money market shares would be prohibited since it would be equivalent to creating new money (which under the new system may only be done by the central bank).

The competitive edge between banks would have nothing to do with their "cost of funds" (as that would be the same for every bank). It would be based solely on their operating costs, risk profile and provisions for defaults, and profit margin, together with the quality and variety of their service offering. This could put small banks on a more equal footing with large banks, thereby strengthening competition.

Banks would still vie for depositors as a future source of borrowers, as a source of fees for managing their deposits and payments, and as clients of their financial subsidiaries for investment services provision.

The market would ensure that all borrowers (not just bank borrowers) would have to repay the real value of their loans, plus a margin for putting the money at risk. Otherwise, there would be no incentive for anyone to lend, as opposed to leaving their money on deposit (where it would be adjusted at the daily inflation rate).

Under the CBDC next-level model, as the principal would be adjusted for inflation, interest rates would only need to reflect the operating costs of the banks, the banks' margin for default, and the banks' profit margin. This would make interest rates far more stable, though inflation would impact the principal.

Overall, permitting banks to continue their characteristic lending activity would maintain the benefits of decentralized money supply process much better than other radical alternatives.[16] The benefits include adapting local supply to a highly variegated and rapidly evolving demand, therefore making the whole system more efficient and effective.

Finally, no CDBC could be lost, stolen, or inadvertently destroyed (unless taken in cash or eCash); nor could it be counterfeited.

---

[16] As discussed, these alternatives include centralization of money supply or the use of term-financing instead of demand deposits to fund loans: the former alternative would be highly inefficient, the latter would be largely inadequate to match demand and significantly more costly.

Other Options to Mitigate System Risk and Enhance Efficiency and Effectiveness

The following provisions would be contentious. They are offered as options that the new system would permit. However, they are not critical to its implementation.

Banks are given a license to lend newly created money. This is a social license, so that it is proper for society to impose restrictions aimed at protecting the common good. To further mitigate systemic risk, banks should be prohibited from lending to, or investing in, other banks, or associated parties. Nor should they be allowed to create money to invest in any form of securities or property, as principal.

Ideally, to ensure each bank retained the risk of its lending decisions, no bank should be permitted to on-sell any of its loans. This ensures that the banks making decisions to lend bear the loss if any loan cannot be repaid, further improving economic efficiency.

If an individual bank has mispriced risk, this has nothing to do with existing borrowers who are making good on their loans. With funding and inflation out of the equation, once an interest rate is agreed, and borrowers are keeping up their payments, a bank should be prohibited from raising their rate to offset losses deriving from other borrowers who are not repaying their loans. Raising rates on "good" loans to compensate for losses on "bad;" loans is like a car manufacturer seeking a top up from buyers of previous models to pay for losses on a current model! If that is seen as a "step too far," at the very least, borrowers ought to have the option to refinance with other banks at no cost. That is, the bank should absorb any discharge costs and application costs.[17]

The biggest unknown is widespread defaults driven by changes in economic conditions. Even in this case, the new system offers several tools that can help to mitigate the impacts of a downturn on both the banks and borrowers. These are discussed in the next section.

10.6 Monetary Policy Implications

Monetary Policy Toolkit

Adjusting central bank deposits and bank loans to reflect inflation would, all else being equal, prevent any alteration to the outstanding stock of money in circulation. While depositors would earn more, borrowers would have to repay more, with the two flows offsetting each other.

Even so, the objective of the monetary policy authorities remains to minimize inflation and unemployment, with the aim to mitigate booms and busts. This is done conventionally by adjusting the policy rate or through quantitative (easing or tightening) measures.

---

[17] In all cases, the Ombudsman could be called upon to adjudicate if borrowers felt they have been treated unfairly.

With the new CBDC system, quantitative measures would no longer be required to "save the banks" in extreme conditions (see also below), thus removing a major distortion from the markets, since all money would be issued as CBDC by the central bank to the banks on demand to fund loans (and the payments activity deriving from them).[18]

The demand for bank loans could be managed via the interest rate charged by the central bank on CBDC balances advanced to each bank (for subsequent on-lending), which would act as a policy rate. Yet, this would remain a blunt instrument, since it would impact all bank lending equally, and it would take time for it to work its way through highly diversified asset markets. Aside from forward guidance—whose effects are transitory, if at all—a general increase in interest rates (via the rate charged by the central bank on its loan advances to banks,) would indeed suppress inflation at some point, but likely at the cost of throwing the economy into recession (Storm, 2022).

With CBDC the interest rate strategy could be refined to improve targeting. Instead of applying the interest to the whole outstanding balance of its advance to the bank, the central bank could limit the interest to only new loans, and further limit it to loans for specific purposes, in specific regions and/or specific sectors of the economy.

An alternative approach is to give the central bank a new power to levy an extra charge on select loans, by type, sector, and region. This levy would be payable by all borrowers whose loans fell under the designated category, and it would be collected by *any lender* (not just the banks) and remitted by them to the central bank. This mechanism would work much like the value-added tax (VAT), which is collected from customers by vendors and remitted to the tax department. It could be much better targeted than the policy rate, limiting undesired impacts.

For example, if the housing market is overheating in one region of an economy, while the rest of the economy is relatively calm, the objective should be to mitigate excessive house price rises in the specific market, without impacting the rest of the economy. In this case, the central bank could levy an extra charge on all *new* loans made for *existing* homes in the region. There would be no need to apply the same levy to *existing* loans and for *new* loans for *new* homes. As the levy was raised, this would dampen demand (and hence prices) for existing homes in the region, while lending for new homes would be untouched, encouraging supply (which would also tend to reduce prices).

All existing loans, and new lending across the rest of the economy would also be unaffected, which is consistent with the overall policy objectives.[19] This strategy

[18] A central bank with large securities holdings (for instance, because of past Quantitative Easing (QE) operations, could unwind its current position over time to "let the markets down slowly," at a rate that did not adversely impact the market. This would imply that, in future, equity markets would have to stand on their own feet: no more would they have the central bank "Put" to support them.

[19] The levy could be even better targeted. Housing is fundamental to improving health, happiness, and motivation, adding to social cohesion. If there is an acute shortage of low-cost housing while labor and materials are directed to providing high-end homes, it would be in the public's best interest to switch resources to the low end of the market. This could be done by adding a levy based on the

could be adapted to target specific types of loans in specific regions, or nation-wide, depending on the market stressors, for example to dampen consumer credit without impacting business loans.

While the central bank should refrain from engaging in Quantitative Easing (QE) operations as a way to support aggregate demand (with the severe distortions that QE causes), the central bank should retain the power to purchase and/or sell securities from/to nonbank financial intermediaries, both as an emergency measure to support markets under extreme stress conditions and as a policy tool to ensure asset price consistency across the full range of markets, from short-term bank loans to financial securities of different risk and maturity profiles.

As another tool, the central bank could agree to defer repayment of its loans, allowing the banks to defer repayment of principal by its borrowers. The interest would be repayable, so the bank had the income to go on trading). This could be done, for example, if there is a big downturn in the property market (perhaps at the same time as higher inflation), so large sections of people are struggling to meet their higher payments and house prices are falling. As a result, the bank may be struggling to meet its obligations to the central bank. Yet, calling in the loans (both the banks and the borrowers) will only make the situation worse.

Banks should not be permitted to increase the interest rate on the borrowers who are struggling, as that only makes things worse, and would simply increase their profits. Once the emergency has passed and the economy has recovered (and wages have caught up to inflation?), normal repayments may resume. It would be up to each bank to manage this process.

Say there has been a major fall in property prices that takes years to recover, so in some cases, the home no longer covers the loan. While the borrower maintains their repayments, they are the only ones out of pocket… but they still have a home. The alternative is what happened in the Global Financial Crisis—thousands made homeless, and the homes left to rot, or picked up by predatory investors at bargain prices, and later leased back to the people who once were the owners. By taking a longer-term view, people can stay in their homes, neighborhoods can be sustained, and there will be a lot less anger and fear in the community. As house prices recover, the owner's equity will rebuild over the decades during which the loan is repaid. At no point would the banks or central bank be "out of pocket" while the interest is paid.

Borrowers and the banks would still have to repay their inflation adjusted loans in full, with interest, but they would be given more time. The central bank could afford to do this at zero cost (unlike depositors and lenders under the current system). The aim should be to limit harm to the population.

With the support of the central bank, both the banks and their borrowers will weather the storm. However, if one bank has been making loans to people who simply cannot afford them, and there is little hope of recovery, it can be allowed to fail. As we've said, the deposit register and good borrowers and perhaps those with a good prospect of recovering any shortfalls are sold to a viable bank for the

value of the contract, dampening demand so that the resources would be freed to deliver houses for those in need.

future income stream. The remainder are pursued by the bank's administrator, with the security sold up with all recoveries and proceeds of sale of the viable business going first to the central bank, with all losses put against the banks at-risk capital (equity and debt).

Finally, to support aggregate demand more effectively, besides its intervention through the bank lending channel, under the CBDC next-level model proposed in this chapter, the central bank should consider using CBDC for carrying out "helicopter money" operations as a tool to affect spending decisions more directly than through the interest rate and its related portfolio effects (Buetzer, 2022).[20]

Advantages for the Conduct of Monetary Policy

The CBDC next-level model would bear significant advantages for the effectiveness of monetary policy. First, with competitive banking, changing the interest rate(s) on central bank loan advances to banks would shorten the transmission channel of monetary policy impulses and thus exert a direct and immediate impact on the cost of money to the real economy.

This would be especially evident in the case of effective lower bound on nominal interest rates since the application of negative rates on central bank loan advances to banks would swiftly be passed on by the banks to their borrowers and act as incentives on the latter to borrow and spend more.

Second, negative interest rates on bank loans need not impact interest rates on CBDC holdings; in fact, the former could be *decoupled* from the latter, thus giving more latitude to monetary policy. This is because, unlike in conventional banking systems (where, as experience shows, the transmission of negative rates from central bank reserves to bank deposits and, hence, to bank loans is neither automatic nor assured under banks' portfolio decisions, often weakening bank profits), in the CBDC next-level model negative interest rates would apply directly on the loans and would not affect bank profits.

Third, if needed, the central bank could exercise outright monetary control on demand by rationing the supply of loan advances to banks. This would act as a quantitative monetary policy tool and could be applied across the board (that is, on all new loans) or selectively (that is, only on certain types of loans or categories of borrowers, or by region).

Fourth, the ability to levy an additional charge on any loan by type, region and sector could provide a greatly enhanced capacity to target specific problems without causing adverse reactions in the wider economy.

Fifth, given the central bank's power, under the CBDC next-level model, to intervene directly and with sufficient precision on the loan market either by setting the policy rate on loan advances to banks or (in extreme cases) by rationing loan advances, the central bank can use its interventions in the securities market to influence the price

[20] We consider the judicious use of "helicopter money" in a forthcoming paper that examines how it can be used to not only eliminate systemic poverty, but as a tool to mitigate wage-push inflation, and to keep the labor market in dynamic balance as automation, virtualization, and demographics radically change it.

of assets with different maturities and risk profiles. As well, the central bank could agree to defer payment on its loans to each bank on condition the same privilege was extended to the banks' borrowers, to prevent the dislocation usually caused by a temporary downturn.

Finally, CBDC could facilitate the use "helicopter money" operations by the central bank as a tool to support aggregate demand.[21]

10.7 Concluding Remarks

This chapter has discussed a new monetary and banking system that while preserving the advantages of decentralized lending through commercial banks removes the inherent fragility of banking by suppressing their money creation power.

Building on the recent (rapidly evolving) literature on central bank digital currencies (CBDCs), this chapter has discussed a retail CBDC-based system (called "CBDC next-level model") whereby (i) the central bank creates money by lending to banks, and (ii) banks on-lend the proceeds to the economy, thus inducing a degree of financial stability that would be unparalleled by conventional banking systems (which we have called "superstability"). The chapter has also proposed how to transition the banking system from its current fractional reserves regime to the CBDC next-level model.

The CBDC next-level model is essentially a two-tier model where, in the first tier, the central bank creates money and distributes it (wholesale) to banks (on demand) which, in the second tier, on-lend it (retail) to borrowing enterprises and households. The loan from the central bank would be repayable at the same time as the loan made by the bank. The bank would act as principal in this case. The outstanding balance of the central bank loan and the bank's loan to the ultimate borrower would both be adjusted by the inflation rate, with the principal being repayable at the same rate and time. The central bank would charge a percentage to cover its operating costs.

All resident individuals, corporates enterprises, and nonfinancial intermediaries (as well as select non-resident agents) would have access to CBDC through banks or nonbank PSPs. In this case, the banks (and nonbank PSPs) would act as fiduciaries, managing the deposits on behalf of the central bank and their customers. Unlike banks, nonbank PSPs would not be permitted under legislation to engage in lending operations. CBDC would be adjusted tax-free to keep their real value stable, greatly improving economic efficiency.

[21] We recognize that all these new tools would need to be used with a great deal of care, and that in general the market should be allowed to function without interference. Yet, there will be times where action is required. In such cases, we urge a gradual approach, that allows time to understand the impact of any initiative. Over time, it would be hoped that data on their use could improve operation of the new tools. While modeling may provide some guidance, the expectation is that the complexities of the real world militate against accurate forecasting. Use of the new tools should mirror the way interest rates are changed: by "sucking and seeing" in small steps.

Significant risk would be removed from the banking system by taking deposits off the balance sheet of banks and into the balance sheet of the central bank, without adversely impacting their basic business model. This would eliminate the threat of bank runs and system collapse, as well as mitigate the risk of "moral hazard."

Essentially, the CBDC next-level model turns the liabilities of the banks (demand and term deposits, and bond obligations) into equity of the central bank (money on issue). This equity represents the community's collective claim on its resources (natural, built, human, technological, knowledge, organizational, legal, and cultural). The key is to ensure the amount of money on issue remains in balance with these resources as they constantly change (to avoid deflation or excessive inflation).

The central bank would no longer need to engage in QE, eliminating the distortion caused by the central bank "Put." Instead, it could use direct interest charges made on its advances to the banks and/or levies on all loans for specific purposes related to specific sectors or regions. Both these tools would have a much more immediate (and potentially targeted) impact on activity than simply moving the policy rate, which is the central bank's primary tool at present. Systemic risk would be further reduced due to the lack of any need for interbank lending, or indeed any lending from banks to nonbank financial institutions.

All nonbank financial institutions would have to raise money from people and organizations putting their own money at risk. As a result of these measures, the regulatory regime could be lightened, with the focus being on a simple multiple of the bank's at-risk capital (equity and debt).

Importantly, central bank's capital would never be at risk and the central bank could afford to weather any downturn by simply not calling in its loans in case of temporary breaches of the banks' capital ratios. This would give both the banks and their borrowers time to recover with the upturn in the economy, without calling in loans that would only worsen the downturn.

Of course, if a bank were too reckless in its lending and found itself beyond recovery, the central bank could let it fail, but this would have no impact on anyone but the bank's employees, officers, directors and shareholders, and the defaulting borrowers. Everyone else would be untouched, including all borrowers who were maintaining their payments. None would have their loans called in. These would simply be transferred to a viable bank on their existing terms. It would be up to the bank's directors to determine at what point the bank could no longer pay its debts (as in any bankrupt business). The change can be undertaken bank by bank overnight. As each bank moves to the new model, the system becomes more stable. Depositors would shift quickly to those banks offering 100% security plus tax-free adjustment equal to the inflation rate. At the same time, to encourage the shift, the government could, after a certain time, remove the deposit guarantee. It may also be in our interest to offer a "carrot" to limit opposition (see Appendix 1).

Overall, the system would become much more stable, resilient, and efficient, and much simpler. Competition between banks and nonbank PSPs would foster the development of new payment and financial services built on top of the banking network.

Concluding this second part of the book, on "sound money," we now proceed to Part III which considers money in the context of macroeconomic policy.

Appendix 1: "Inducements" for Banks to Join the New System

People are naturally resistant to change for fear of "unintended consequences." For this reason, banks may be reluctant to switch to the new system, although it would provide them with significant benefits. One way to get all banks on board would be to pay them a "carrot,"[22] another would be to use a stick.

Carrot

The cost of the carrot would be a one-time *investment,* amortized over the life of the change (effectively indefinitely!), and would represent a permanent injection of new money that the central bank could legitimately recognize as "equity" in the new system. The "carrot" could take one of two forms:

1. It could be set in a tender process where the aim would be to get most of the banks on board. Each bank would submit a bid to receive an extra payment over ten years. The central bank would then create a cut-off (say 80% of the sector by loan volume). Those banks asking more than the cut-off would then have to switch over without a carrot. This would not need to be compulsory. The central bank would simply withdraw its guarantee on the deposit liabilities of those banks that failed to meet the cut-off. No bank could afford to stay out of the new system, since they would then find themselves uncompetitive on deposits and would soon suffer a run. The alternative would be for them to sell their business to a successful bank.
2. Once the legislation is passed, no new banks would be permitted to register under the new scheme for (say) five years. The moratorium in granting new licenses would be an incentive for incumbent banks to switch over.

Stick

As the change can be made overnight bank by bank, it would be possible to simply use "market forces" to effect the change. The government could advise that on a certain date in the future (say 5 years) all bank guarantees and deposit insurance would be void. Banks that made the switch early would soon attract most depositors who would be keen one the 100% safety of CBDC and the payment of a tax-free inflation adjustment. To avoid system instability, the industry would be encouraged to work together so that all banks made the change at the same time.

[22] The idea of a "carrot" was suggested to us by Geoff Crocker based on the UK's experience when introducing the National Health Scheme (NHS). In that case, substantial inducements were offered to key participants to agree to the establishment of the NHS.

Appendix 2: Comparative Analysis

This appendix compares the key elements of current banking systems with the CBDC next-level model (Table 10.1).

Table 10.1 Banking regimes: a synoptic comparison

Features	Conventional	CBDC next level
Role of Central Bank	• Issuer of reserves • Governing the banking system to ensure it remains viable • Governing the monetary system to keep inflation and unemployment low • Not involved in retail customers	• Issuer of CBDC • Governing the banking system to ensure it remains viable • Governing the monetary system to keep inflation and unemployment low • Not involved in retail customers
Money on issue	• Liability of central bank	• Equity of central bank
Reserves regime	• Fractional coverage • Interest charged on reserves used as policy rate	• Full coverage • Interest charged to cover the central bank's operating costs, plus additional margin as required (see table entry "Monetary Policy Implications")
Role of banks	• Deposit takers, loan makers, money creators, and payment service providers • Sources and managers of funds • Managers of associated risks • Providers of ancillary financial and investment services	• Distributors of CBDC via lending • Managers of associated risks • Fiduciary for depositors • Payment service providers
Organization structure	• International branch offices permitted	• Every bank must set up as a separate company (which can be owned by another entity, which may be offshore), with its own local board and capital funding to ensure compliance
Funding	• Borrowings from retail and wholesale markets, as well as trading in Money Market Shares • Mismatch between deposit and loan maturities exposing the bank to risk	• CBDC from the central bank, with repayments timed to coincide with repayments by borrowers, removing liquidity risk—eliminating the need to manage funding

(continued)

Table 10.1 (continued)

Features	Conventional	CBDC next level
Wind up of banks	• Extremely complicated and disorderly • Sometimes taking decades to resolve. All bank borrowers and depositors severely impacted	• Very simple and orderly • Viable loans and the deposit register sold to a viable bank • Proceeds of sale and any recoveries from delinquent borrowers going first to the central bank, and then according to bankruptcy law • No impact on depositors or borrowers that are not in default
Seigniorage	• Banks extract seigniorage derived from their power to create money	• With all banks having equal access to CBDC, competition would be enhanced, reducing (if not eliminating) extraction of seigniorage
Inflation adjustment	• None	• All outstanding CBDC (other than eCash) balances adjusted daily
Interest on loans to the bank	• Set in the market	• Set to cover the central bank's costs, unless a higher rate is set by the central bank to damp demand
Interest rates on loans from the bank	• Set in the market • Highly variable rates	• Set in competition with other banks, based on the bank's operating cost, risk profile and profit margin. Paid on the inflation adjusted balance to maintain the real value of the interest without changing the rate • Highly stable rates
Share and bond subscriptions, and retained earnings	• No specific restrictions on use	• Can only be used to finance bank operations, or held in the banks' inflation adjusted CBDC accounts as collateral, underpinning the banks "capital ratio"
Know your customer	• Required	• Required
Regulatory lending constraints	• Closely regulated based on capital, liquidity, and leverage ratios x class of asset	• Lightly regulated based on single "capital" (equity and "at-risk" debt) ratio

(continued)

Table 10.1 (continued)

Features	Conventional	CBDC next level
Restrictions on bank operations	• Wide latitude to extend and manage loans, including to associated parties and to other banks and financial intermediaries, as well as for packaging and on-sale of loans into derivative securities	• Banks focus on low-risk loans • Loans to associates, other banks and financial intermediaries are prohibited and • Banks are prohibited from using central bank loan advances to spend on their own account and from on-selling loans (they must carry the risk of their own lending)
Types of public money	• Cash (coins and notes): legal tender) • Demand deposits (claims on bank: not legal tender)	• Cash (coins and notes: legal tender) • CBDC (claim on central bank: legal tender)
Account privacy	• Private, subject to due process	• Private, subject to due process
Payments	• Made by messaging between banks to effect changes to accounts and with the central bank to effect changes to reserves • Payments often delayed due to intermediate steps, though less so with new fast/instant payments systems	• Made by messaging between banks to effect changes to accounts and with the central bank to effect changes to total CBDC balance • Payments are "instant" • Given deposits are adjusted by inflation, it would be open to banks to charge the real costs of managing deposits, and of making payments
Account rectification	• May be frozen and/or reversed, and/or restored subject to due process	• May be frozen and/or reversed, and/or restored, subject to due process
Risk for Central Bank	• In worst cases (as over the last decade or more) central bank needs to increase its balance sheet massively to support the system	• As all CBDC would be on the central bank's balance sheet as equity, no bank failure could impact central bank capital. Any unrepaid loans remain as "money on issue"
Risks for banks	• Liquidity • (*Including risk of run*) • Credit	• Credit
Risks for shareholders and bondholders	• At risk in the event of insolvency or a run • Banks can increase interest rates on existing loans to recover losses • Shareholders and even bondholders could take a "haircut" even if rescued by the government	• Risk of run eliminated • No ability to increase interest rates on existing loans to recover losses • However, central bank able to take long-term view in the interests of the wider economy reducing insolvency risk

(continued)

Table 10.1 (continued)

Features	Conventional	CBDC next level
Risk for directors and officers	• Risks of insolvency mitigated by government guarantees and central bank liquidity support, which is seen as necessary to avoid system collapse, especially for bank's regarded as "too big to fail" • This induces banks to take on higher risk to keep pace with competitors knowing the government will pick up the tab	• Directors in same position as all other enterprise directors: it is their call when to stop trading. As this would have zero impact on depositors or other banks, there would be no pressure on the central bank to come to the rescue. This reduces the incentive for banks to take on undue risk • However, the bank could seek dispensation from the central bank to defer its loan repayments in line with any deferral granted to its borrowers where it was likely the borrowers and banks could recover their position in due course • Unlike other creditors, the central bank can afford to take a longer-term view and support a bank if it was likely the bank could recover
Risk for borrowers	• Interest rates highly variable and liable to be increased and/or principal called in to cover losses on non-performing loans	• Stable interest rates (though principal subject to inflation adjustment). Rates cannot be increased on existing loans (unless part of a general increase due to the bank's costs exceeding inflation and approved by the regulator, and the borrower can opt out) • Nor can the principal be called in early to cover losses on non-performing loans
Risk for depositors	• Liquidity • (*Except for share of insured deposits)* • Credit • Inflation	• None
Risk for system	• Inherently fragile • Systemic risk	• Inherently stable: • No systemic risk ("Superstability")
Systemic risk mitigation	• Government guarantees of retail deposits (to specified limits) plus QE to provide liquidity	• Not required • Removal of deposit guarantee

(continued)

Table 10.1 (continued)

Features	Conventional	CBDC next level
Monetary policy toolkit	• Policy rate and QE/QT • "Helicopter money" is possible	*To damp demand*: • Interest could be levied on central bank advances to banks. This would be passed through to borrowers (to discourage borrowings) • Interest could be applied to the whole outstanding central bank balances, or only on new loans (potentially targeted by type, sector, and region) • Or, (targeted) levies could instead be applied to all commercial loans (not just bank loans) • Or, there is the potential for direct control over, and rationing of, loan advances to banks in extreme circumstances *To stimulate the economy*: • While there would be potential for negative rates on loans (to encourage borrowings), decoupled from the inflation adjustment on deposits, we don't recommend this as it distorts resource allocation. We prefer the use of "helicopter money" as it provides equal benefit to all citizens • Also, it would be possible for the central bank to agree to delay principal repayments on condition the same forbearance was extended to the banks' borrowers if a downturn threatens stability of the system, where foreclosure would only make the problem worse • QE possible • "Helicopter money" is possible
Competition between banks	• Larger banks have greater pricing power through less need for reserves	• Increased competition as all banks have access to CBDC on the same terms • Competitive advantage is based solely on the bank's operating costs, risk profile and provisions for defaults, and profit margin, together with the quality and variety of service offering
Competition with cryptocurrencies	• While the landscape is still evolving, the potential for cryptocurrencies to disrupt the existing system is considerable	• Bank managed CBDC offers virtually all the advantages of a stable cryptocurrency without the drawbacks of having multiple currencies that require policing to protect against fraud or use in illicit dealings

(continued)

Table 10.1 (continued)

Features	Conventional	CBDC next level
Money market and interbank lending	• Essential to operation of system	• Not required. Trading in money market shares would be prohibited
Economic efficiency	• Negative real interest rates, inflation impact on savings and borrowings, & QE all distort markets and detract from economic efficiency and fairness • Decentralized allocation of newly created money ensures economic efficiency	• Both deposits and borrowings reflect real value (with inflation adjusted principals flowing across all forms of lending, not just bank lending) • Decentralized allocation of newly created money ensures economic efficiency and fairness

References

Adrian, T., & Mancini-Griffoli, T. (2019). *The rise of digital money*. FinTech Notes, Note/19/01. International Monetary Fund.

Amador, M., & Bianchi, J. (2021). *Bank runs, fragility, and credit easing*. Federal Reserve Bank of Minneapolis, Working Paper 785, 15 October.

Auer, R., & Böhme, R. (2020). *The technology of retail central bank digital currency*. BIS Quarterly Review, March.

Bindseil, U., Cipollone, P., & Schaaf, J. (2024). *The digital euro after the investigation phase: Demystifying fears about bank disintermediation*. VoxEu/CEPR, 19 February.

BIS. (2020). *Central bank digital currencies: Foundational principles and core features*. Joint report by the Bank of Canada, European Central Bank, Bank of Japan, Sveriges Riksbank, Swiss National Bank, Bank of England, Board of Governors of the Federal Reserve, and BIS Innovation Hub, 9 October.

Bossone, B. (2001). Do banks have a future? A study on banking and finance as we move into the third millennium. *Journal of Banking and Finance, Elsevier*, *25*(12), 2239–2276.

Bossone, B., & Haines, M. (2023). *CBDC next-level: A new architecture for financial super-stability*. Working Paper No. 1015, Levy Economics Institute of Bard College.

Buetzer, S. (2022). *Advancing the monetary policy toolkit through outright transfers*. IMF Working Paper, WP/22/87. International Monetary Fund, Washington D.C., May.

Diamond, D. W., & Dybvig, P. H. (1983). "Bank Runs, Deposit Insurance, and Liquidity". *Journal of Political Economy, 91*(3), 401–414.

Diamond, D. W., & Rajan, R. G. (2001). Liquidity risk, liquidity creation, and financial fragility: A theory of banking. *The Journal of Political Economy, 109*(2), 287–327.

IMF. (2022). Behind the scenes of Central Bank digital currency: Emerging trends, insights, and policy lessons, by G. Soderberg, M. Bechara, W. Bossu, N. Che, S. Davidovic, J. Kiff, I. Lukonga, T. Mancini-Griffoli, T. Sun, & A. Yoshinaga, Fintech Note/2022/004, International Monetary Fund, 9 February.

Kumhof, M., & Noone, C. (2018). *Central bank digital currencies—Design principles and balance sheet implications*. Bank of England Working Papers, no 725.

Storm, S. (2022). *Inflation in the time of corona and war*. Working Paper No. 185. Institute for New Economic Thinking, 30 May.

World Bank. (2021). *Central Bank digital currency: A payments perspective*. The World Bank Group, November.

Part III
On Money Effectiveness

Part III focuses on the efficacy of monetary and fiscal policies as instruments to use "public" money for macroeconomic stabilization purposes. It comprises six chapters.

Chapter 11
Beyond the Lucas Critique

Abstract This chapter discusses the author's early attempts to address the Lucas Critique. It argues that the effectiveness of a policy regime depends on the reference model that people believe accurately reflects the economy. If the reference model changes, people's expectations and behaviors will also change. This, in turn, alters the impact of new policy rules compared to those based on the old model. The chapter shows that in an economy agents do not only adjust their behavior in response to policy changes, thereby altering historical responses; they also modify their response to policy changes based on the model of the economy they believe correctly represents the economy. Consequently, monetary policy may or may not be effective depending on: (i) the economic model adopted (albeit conventionally) by the agents and (ii) the behaviors that agents consider rational (in accordance with the accepted convention) and consequently adopt. Importantly, in evaluating the effectiveness of monetary policy, understanding the prevailing conventions that lead agents to accept a model as "true" is more rimportant than pinpointing the ontologically "true" model of the economy.

11.1 Preamble

By the early 1990s, when I started researching into the issue of monetary policy effectiveness, the Lucas Critique had already come to dominate the mainstream macroeconomics of the time. Nonetheless, my conviction in the fundamental cogency of Keynes' liquidity preference theory and its underlying concept of "conventional beliefs," further developed in Prof. Frank Hahn's theory of "conjectural equilibria,"[1] led me to believe that the Lucas Critique could (and should) be superseded by elevating it to a new level. Let me explain.

I wanted to demonstrate that it is not only that the policy regime affects people's expectations and beliefs, so that both change when policy rules change as (Lucas, 1976) had famously shown. My point was that the effectiveness of any policy regime depends on the reference model that people consider to be the correct representation

[1] See Hahn (1977, 1978).

B. Bossone, *Trailblazing Visions of Money in Economic Theory*, Contributions to Economics, https://doi.org/10.1007/978-3-031-82544-6_11

of the economy. If the existing reference model changes, and is replaced by a new one, the way people's expectations and behaviors are shaped will also change, and the impact of new policy rules will differ from what it would be under the old model.

Consequently, while the Lucas' Critique suggested that economic relationships within a model remain stable despite policy changes—implying "policy invariance"—this invariance, I thought, breaks down when people shift their reference model. In such cases, the structural parameters of the economy change, leading to different outcomes even if the policy changes are hypothetically the same. In simple terms, if people believe the economy operates according to a Keynesian, monetarist, or rational expectations model, the effectiveness of government macro-policies will ultimately align with the predictions of their reference model.

This is essentially the conclusion of the article I later published (Bossone, 1996), which I want to repropose in this chapter. Its main message is captured by two thought-provoking quotes by Prof. Hahn, which I found highly inspirational when I began considering the article. In the first quote, Prof. Hahn states that «(...) that the monetarist objections to Keynesian policies must be based (...) on the unverified assertion that economic agents have monetarist expectations (...). Therefore, it might benefit society more to tax all monetarist writings and subsidize the Keynesian ones» (Hahn, 1984, p. 135).[2] In the second quote, Prof. Hahn notes that «(...) Mrs. Thatcher persuaded much of the British public of monetarist doctrine. The result was (and is) that increases in demand, which might well have led simply to increased output, instead led to self-confirming price rises» (Hahn, 1994, p. 256).[3]

Before moving on, I should emphasize—benefiting from my more recent research—that the relevance of the reference model for policy effectiveness is further enhanced when it influences the decisions of powerful market players who can bring the model's predictions to materialize through their investment decisions. In my view, this conclusion is particularly important for today's "globalized" economies. In later chapters, I will illustrate how I have arrived at it and the implications that follow from it.

11.2 Introduction

The effectiveness of monetary policy has been a central issue in macroeconomic thought, undergoing significant evolution as different economic paradigms have emerged and influenced both academic and policy-making circles. By the early 1990s, the Lucas Critique had firmly established itself within mainstream macroeconomics. Lucas (1976) insights demonstrated that policy changes could shift agents' expectations, leading to altered economic behaviors and, ultimately, different outcomes.

[2] This is my translation from the Italian version of the original book (Hahn 1983).

[3] Margaret Thatcher was Prime Minister of the United Kingdom from 1979 to 1990 and Leader of the Conservative Party from 1975 to 1990. She was the longest-serving British prime minister of the twentieth century and the first woman to hold the position.

This approach suggested that policy models needed to account for expectation adjustments, challenging Keynesian frameworks that emphasized the stabilizing role of government intervention without fully integrating dynamic expectations.

Despite the Lucas Critique's widespread acceptance, Keynes's theory of liquidity preference and the concept of "conventional beliefs" offered a fundamentally valuable perspective. Building on Keynes, Hahn (1977, 1978) notion of "conjectural equilibria" proposed that economic agents' expectations are shaped by commonly held beliefs, or conventions, about how the economy operates.[4] This suggested the idea that economic relationships within a model are inherently stable under different policy regimes, as Lucas argued. Instead, agents' reference models of the economy—understood as collective assumptions about the true nature of the economy—significantly impact how they interpret and respond to policy changes. If agents shift to a new reference model, their expectations and behaviors will change, affecting the outcomes of monetary policies in ways that differ from predictions based on the previous model.

This chapter discusses these ideas, arguing that the effectiveness of monetary policy hinges not only on agents' responses to policy rules but also on the prevailing conventions they hold about the economy's structure. The chapter shows that these conventions—whether based on Keynesian, monetarist, or rational expectations frameworks—shape agents' responses in profound ways. As such, the outcome of any policy intervention is likely to align with the predictions of the dominant reference model, suggesting that the "true" model of the economy is less influential than the convention accepted by agents at a given time. By exploring these insights, the chapter illustrates the importance of understanding prevailing economic conventions and their impact on macroeconomic policy, particularly in today's interconnected and globalized economy, where dominant beliefs among influential market players can significantly influence policy effectiveness.

This chapter is organized as follows: Sect. 11.3 provides an overview of the evolution of monetary policy thought, from Keynesian theories to the New Classical paradigm shaped by the Lucas Critique. Section 11.4 discusses the concept of "conventional" beliefs and how they influence economic equilibria. Section 11.5 illustrates how different economic conventions—such as Keynesian and monetarist models—affect the effectiveness of monetary policy by aligning or diverging from the expectations and behaviors of agents. Section 11.6 concludes the chapter,

[4] I want to make sure not to overlook the connection between Hahn's theory of conjectures and Guesnerie (1992) theory of "eductive" expectations, which is built on the rational expectations framework but introduces a higher level of iterative reasoning. Agents form expectations based not only on economic fundamentals but on what they believe other agents expect. This iterative process of deducing others' expectations can result in convergence toward or divergence from equilibrium, depending on how well agents coordinate their beliefs. Both Hahn and Guesnerie focus on the fragility of market equilibria, particularly when expectations play a central role. While Hahn's conjecture highlights the risks of expectations destabilizing markets, Guesnerie's eductive expectations framework provides a mechanism to understand how agents might fail to coordinate on an equilibrium, reinforcing Hahn's concerns about equilibrium instability. Guesnerie's work essentially formalizes and extends Hahn's insights by focusing on the strategic nature of expectation formation and the conditions necessary for equilibrium to be eductively stable.

emphasizing the importance of understanding prevailing economic conventions in evaluating policy outcomes.

11.3 True Models, False Models, Conventions

Imagine an economy that is not perfectly competitive where firms make their choices not only by looking at price signals, but also discounting quantity constraints. Assume that each firm forms its strategy by making conjectures about the possible choices it expects the other firms to make in the market. Assume, further, that due to a persistent weakness in aggregate demand, the economy is characterized, at current wages and prices, by the presence of unused resources. It is reasonable to expect that, in this circumstance, the wages and prices of unused resources will tend to adjust to rebalance the markets at a higher level of activity. How will firms react to this situation? The correct answer is: it depends...

In the absence of a mechanism to coordinate firms' choices, the conjectures formulated by them are relevant in this context: if all or most of them believe that low prices stimulate demand, they will resume production and investment, thus activating the strategic complementarities (Cooper & John, 1988) that will contribute to reviving the cycle (Roberts, 1987). If, on the contrary, firms believe that the income effect will prevail over the substitution effect, causing adjusting prices and wages to translate into a decline in aggregate demand and negative profits, they will refrain from taking risky turns and, by doing so, will effectively delay the recovery of the cycle (Tobin, 1975).

The new equilibrium position of the economy will not necessarily be dictated by the "true" model of the economy, as this might be understood by the firms, but rather by the model that firms collectively believe to be true. For this to occur, it is essential that a prevailing consensus develops among the firms regarding the assumed "true" model, which leads to convergent behaviours. In other words, it is both necessary and sufficient for the firms to agree upon a common reference model—as a share "convention"—even if it is not the actual "true" model. In fact, if a false model is widely accepted as the true model within the business community, based on a shared convention, it becomes entirely rational for the firms to form expectations that are consistent with that convention.[5]

[5] In this regard, it is worth noting the close connection between the concepts of truth, conviction, and utility or convenience found in the Pragmatism doctrine of C. S. Peirce and W. James (see White, 1983, Chaps. 10 and 11). Peirce defined truth as the opinion that is destined to prevail among those who pursue it in their inquiry (and reality as the object of that opinion), while James argued that what is true is what reality shows to be more advantageous for us to believe; in other words, according to James, what is true is that conviction which the facts confirm to be more useful or convenient for those who hold it. The reference to Pragmatism is not accidental. This school of thought has certainly had a strong influence on the North American culture of our century, aptly interpreting the spirit of confidence and optimism that has traditionally underpinned the practical action emanating from that culture. And although it is not intended here to draw easy connections between culture and practice, in a domain that furthermore falls outside the scope of this article, the hypothesis that

The choice of a convention by individual agents is based more on the convenient/not convenient dichotomy than on the true/false one. It occurs within a set of options constituted by rational beliefs and the degree of trust in those beliefs. Essential in guiding the choice, particularly for smaller agents in relation to the market, is knowing—or intuiting—the prevailing opinion in the market, that is, the opinion that is presumed to have the greatest likelihood of being established as such.

The strength of conventions is such that they can produce equilibria that confirm their validity. Breaking away from them can lead individual firms to incur losses or miss earnings. A convention thus acts as a model of reality that is taken up by a multitude of agents operating in the markets, pertaining to choices to be made under conditions of uncertainty and ignorance of the future. If, for example, agents share the belief that the long-term equilibrium real interest rate is determined by the interplay of supply and demand for savings, the spreading belief in the markets of a persistent shortage of savings supply will be sufficient to lead agents to consider that high real interest rates are the norm in the markets, and consequently, to demand high rates on their lendable funds.

It should be noted that two conventions are at play in this example: the first concerns the determination model of the equilibrium real interest rate, which is based on loanable-funds theory; the second—which, too, is grounded in neoclassical theory—relates to the idea that an actual shortage of aggregate savings can indeed occur in the economy ex ante. Now, even if one were to assume the theoretical inconsistency of such conventions and consider instead the Keynesian theory of liquidity preference as valid, combined with the (also Keynesian) idea that aggregate savings is merely a residual variable determined by autonomous spending, there is no doubt that conventions, however erroneous, would still lead the markets to maintain interest rates at high levels: an expansionary maneuver on liquidity supply, aimed at eliminating its shortfall and easing interest rates, would be perceived as inflationary and would, if anything, lead to an increase in the rates themselves, producing the opposite effect to that desired.

The choice of a convention by individual agents is guided by the prevailing opinion in the market, or the opinion that is presumed to have a greater likelihood of being established as such. The convention thus acts as a model of reality that is adopted by numerous subjects operating in markets when making choices under conditions of uncertainty and ignorance.

Conventions extend beyond merely selecting general economic models; within any specific model, they can encompass more focused aspects that, while perhaps narrower in scope, still wield significant influence over market trends. It is known, for example, that in efficient financial markets, interpretations of news related to events

---

the practical approach inspired by Pragmatism is congenial to the functioning of markets today—indeed largely shaped by North American economic and organizational culture—seems intriguing. On the other hand, reliance on rational conventions can be extremely useful in contexts such as modern financial markets, where the times for action and reaction imposed on agents by technology are very brief, and where revising dominant conventions is only advantageous when they prove to be clearly or persistently erroneous (false, precisely in pragmatist thought), and overturning them creates opportunities for profit.

that have occurred or are expected to occur in a country where investors hold large financial positions can lead, if converging, to divestment decisions that ultimately validate those interpretations, regardless of their truthfulness. In well-functioning, integrated, and efficient financial markets, news can significantly impact investor behavior. When investors with substantial financial stakes in a country share similar interpretations of the income news, their converging views may lead to divestment decisions that reinforce those interpretations, irrespective of their actual truthfulness.

The convergence of interpretations regarding events or data often stems from conventional responses to fears or rumors among agents who seek to align their actions with what they perceive others will do under similar circumstances. This phenomenon is particularly evident when numerous agents decide to open or close financial positions based on the actions of key players, who are viewed as having superior information or the capacity to sway the market through their ability to deploy significant capital swiftly. Under this assumption, it would be entirely rational for followers to follow the leaders (at least, up to a point), and it would be irrational to do otherwise. This dynamic can give rise to "herd behavior," where individuals collectively gravitate toward the decisions made by leaders. As a result, conventional prices may emerge in the markets, leading to equilibria that deviate from competitive equilibrium.

11.4 The New Classical Convention

Beginning in the 1970s, the Keynesian paradigm that had effectively supported post-war reconstruction and growth during the early years of the Bretton Woods era began to face significant challenges. This crisis prompted a resurgence of orthodox economic traditions, leading to a renewed evaluation of the true effectiveness of monetary policy in influencing the real economy over the long term. As early as the 1950s, monetarist theorists, notably Milton Friedman, highlighted the destabilizing effects of monetary policy in the short and medium term, while later positing the hypothesis that such policies are neutral in the long run (Friedman, 1953, 1968).

The monetarist paradigm pinpointed the causes of its initial effects in the lack of knowledge among monetary authorities about the channels and timing of monetary policy transmission. This critique significantly challenged the traditionally Keynesian belief in the State's superior knowledge and its ability to rectify the market's inefficiencies, often referred to as the failures of the "invisible hand." Furthermore, monetarism posited the long-term neutrality of money by proposing the concept of a "natural" rate of unemployment and suggesting a mechanism through which economic agents adjust their expectations in line with prevailing inflation rates.

The theory revealed that two key factors undermined the substitutability relationship between inflation and unemployment, a relationship that governments had previously believed they could leverage through carefully calibrated economic policy interventions. These hypotheses suggested that, if allowed to function without interference, markets could effectively guarantee full employment and an optimal allocation of resources. Indeed, proponents of the New Classical paradigm (Lucas, 1972, 1976; Sargent, 1973; Sargent & Wallace, 1976), based on the rational expectations theory, argued that in real markets, which are always in equilibrium, and where agents possess complete information and strive for maximum individual well-being, any announced monetary expansion would lead only to a corresponding rise in inflation. This would occur without affecting the supply and demand for goods or productive factors, ultimately resulting in a net loss of welfare for the economy.

In contrast to traditional monetarism, which regarded monetary policy as a powerful instrument that needed careful adjustments to mitigate its potentially destabilizing effects stemming from incomplete knowledge, New Classical theorists posited that economic agents possess a comprehensive and shared understanding of these consequences. As a result, they asserted that any tangible impacts on the economy can only stem from unexpected actions taken by monetary authorities. This perspective effectively dismissed the idea that a higher level of rationality exists in the management of the economy.

The New Classical paradigm delivered a clear, concise, and easily understood message that resonated with a diverse audience—economists, market participants, government officials, and commentators alike—cementing its place as the prevailing convention. By the late 1970s, it had established itself as the cornerstone of the conventional wisdom embraced by financial markets. Moreover, one could argue that the increasing influence of international financial markets—naturally inclined to conservatism—further paved the way for the New Classical approach to gain traction. This shift bolstered confidence in the market's capacity to achieve social optimality while simultaneously discouraging government intervention in the economy, which could potentially jeopardize the stability of wealth mediated by these markets.

On the other hand, it is not inappropriate to believe that financial stability is the primary objective of financial markets; for which, instead, the level of resource employment may not represent a decisive concern, except in terms of how it interferes with the conditions of social and political stability and, therefore, with the very conditions for the orderly functioning of market activities. It follows that the increasing role and greater influence of international financial markets on national economies have progressively oriented their functions of social welfare to reflect the preferences of the markets themselves, thus leading to the acceptance of economic models and economic policies that conform to those preferences.

According to the New Classical convention, a practice emerged among market participants that equates even high unemployment rates with "natural" equilibrium states in economies. These states were viewed as the result of optimal choices made by rational, well-informed agents who have the freedom to allocate their resources among various alternatives. This perspective held that high unemployment can either be a byproduct of voluntary choices or a consequence of market failures that demand-side policies cannot effectively address. The emergence of the New Classical convention fostered the prevailing belief that simply announcing monetary stimulus measures would lead to higher prices and nominal interest rates, which, in turn, reduce their quantitative impact—either partially or completely.

The New Classical convention gained significant traction in the 1980s through advancements in economic theory, particularly the concept of dynamic or temporal inconsistency, as introduced by Kydland and Prescott (1977). This led to the development of reputation models that describe an infinitely repeated "game" between central banks and the market. In this framework, a government that fails to credibly commit to its monetary policy may be tempted to exploit the trade-off between inflation and unemployment—using unexpected increases in the money supply to temporarily boost production and employment. Under the rational expectations assumption of these models, the public adapts its inflation expectations in response to government actions, which ultimately discourages any further attempts at monetary expansion. As a result, the economy can end up experiencing excessive price growth. To mitigate this risk, the implementation of rigid monetary constraints or the appointment of a conservative and independent central banker, as suggested by Rogoff (1985), is essential. Such measures help to insulate the control of the money supply from political pressures, thereby bolstering the central bank's anti-inflationary reputation and enhancing the credibility of its policy decisions.

The concept of reputation holds practical significance primarily in its relation to the anticipated behavior of the entity to which it is attributed—gains signaling value in the market due to the infinitely repeated nature of the game. This scenario enables agents to make informed decisions based on the strategies they believe the central bank will adopt in the future. Consequently, the level of trust the public has in a central bank's commitment to maintaining price stability, particularly one known for its strong anti-inflation reputation, motivates economic agents to engage in behaviors that align with this goal. As a result, a robust reputation not only lessens uncertainty for market participants but also enhances the effectiveness of monetary policy. In light of evolving economic models, critical concepts such as the reputation of monetary authorities, the credibility of economic policies, the independence and autonomy of central banks, and the establishment of rules and anchors for monetary policy have become widely accepted in contemporary discourse.

The concept of reputation is crucial, particularly regarding its influence on the anticipated behavior of the entity to which it is ascribed. In financial markets, reputation gains signaling value because of the infinitely repeated nature of interactions among agents. This framework enables individuals and organizations to make informed decisions based on their expectations of the strategies that a central bank will adopt in the future. Trust in a central bank's commitment to maintaining price stability, especially one recognized for a strong anti-inflationary stance, drives economic agents to adopt behaviors that support this objective. Consequently, a solid reputation not only reduces uncertainty for market participants but also enhances the effectiveness of monetary policy.

11.5 Conventions, Expectations, and the Effectiveness of Monetary Policy

To demonstrate the impact of "conventions" on the effectiveness of monetary policy, let's start from the model by Sargent and Wallace (1976), which underpins the New Classical paradigm. Sargent and Wallace (SW) start from the following structural equation for output:

$$y_t = \xi_0 + \xi_1(m_t - E_{t-1}m_t) + \xi_2 y_{t-1} + u_t, \tag{11.1}$$

and consider the feedback rule of monetary policy and the related agent expectations:

$$m_t = g_0 + g_1 y_{t-1} + \varepsilon_t, \tag{11.2}$$

and

$$E_{t-1}m_t = g_0 + g_1 y_{t-1}, \tag{11.3}$$

where the variables are expressed in logarithms, y is output, t is time, m is the money supply, E_{t-1} is the expectations operator conditioned on the information available at time $t-1$, and u and e are random errors that are serially and mutually independent and with mean zero. SW, then, derive

$$y_t = (\xi_0 - \xi_1 g_0) + (\xi_2 - \xi_1 g_1)y_{t-1} + \xi_1 m_t + u_t \tag{11.4}$$

and the corresponding reduced form

$$y_t = \xi_0 + \xi_2 y_{t-1} + u_t + \xi_1 \varepsilon_t, \tag{11.5}$$

after substituting $g_0 + g_1 y_{t-1}$ for m_t in (11.4). The independence of the stochastic process for y_t from the parameters g_0 and g_1 is evident from (11.5). Hence, the invariance of the economic structure, as represented by (11.1), to the behavior of the monetary authorities. SW concludes that monetary policy decisions, if appropriately anticipated by the public ($E_{t-1}m_t + \varepsilon_t = m_t$), do not have a stable influence on the output generation process.

As SW show, (11.4) takes the form:

$$y_t = \alpha + \lambda y_{t-1} + \beta m_t + u_t, \tag{11.6}$$

where $\alpha = \xi_0 - \xi_1 g_0$, $\lambda = \xi_2 - \xi_1 g_1$, and $\beta = \xi_1$. Given (11.6), the potential level of output y^*, and the objective of minimizing the variability of output around its potential level, the optimal values of the policy parameters are given by

$$g_0 = \frac{(y^* - \alpha)}{\beta}$$

and

$$g_1 = -\frac{\lambda}{\beta}.$$

Notice that, in the SW model, the independence of y_t from m_t derives from the assumptions that agents: (i) rationally use the information available at time $t - 1$; ; (ii) share the same informational set as the economic policy authorities; and (iii) know and share the same model (the "true" model) of the economy. The result of SW is valid if, for example, the classical quantitative relationship holds:

$$m_t + v_t = p_t + y_t, \quad (11.7)$$

where v is the velocity of money circulation and.

$$y_t = y^*. \quad (11.8)$$

If $v_t = 0 = p_t$, then

$$m_t = m^* = y^*, \quad (11.9)$$

where m^* is the optimal money supply rate, assuming that $p^* = 0$ is the optimal inflation rate. Under these conditions, any increase in the money supply relative to the optimal rate ($m_t\prime > m^*$) exclusively produces inflationary effects:

$$m_t\prime = y^* + p_t\prime, \quad (11.10)$$

where

$$m_t\prime - m^* = p_t\prime - p^* > 0 \quad (11.11)$$

and

$$m_t\prime = E_{t-1}m_t\prime + \varepsilon_t\prime. \quad (11.12)$$

Therefore,

$$y_t = y^* + f\left(m_t\prime - m^*\right), \quad \text{with} \quad f' = 0. \quad (11.13)$$

Define the New Classical Convention as the widespread opinion among agents that the economy behaves according to the model described by Equations (11.7)–(11.13). In this case, and under the SW assumptions expressed by relations (11.1)–(11.5), monetary policy has no power to influence y_t: agents believe that the output's progression is stochastically aligned with the trend corresponding to the economy's potential (or "natural" level), y^*, and that money cannot alter the real variables of the economy. In response to new quantity signals, each agent reacts by promptly adjusting prices, anticipating that others will do the same.

Under the New Classical Convention, if a negative shock to the velocity of circulation of money ($v_{t-1} < v^*$) occurs in the presence of the New Classical Convention—with flexible prices and wages—this leads to a proportional reduction in prices while output remains at its potential level: output is stationary at its potential level.

Suppose now that the public, instead, believes in a "Keynesian Convention," according to which: (a) wages and prices are downwardly rigid; (b) the marginal returns of production factors do not decrease at output levels significantly below the potential level and tend to decrease rapidly as one approaches this level; (c) the velocity of money circulation is unstable and reflects waves of optimism and pessimism that spread among the public based on available information and the expectations that agents form; (d) expansionary policies can stabilize output. Assume, furthermore, that the assumptions (i)–(iii) of the SW model are upheld.

If agents share the Keynesian Convention in situations of less than full resource employment, they react by adjusting quantities, anticipating that others will make similar adjustments. In this context, if agents behave consistently with the KC, it is then reasonable to expect that, if $v_{t-1} < v^*$, then.

$$p_{t-1} = p^* = 0 \quad \text{and} \quad y_{t-1} < y^*,$$

where $v^* - v_{t-1} = y^* - y_{t-1}$.. In this case, it is evident that the optimal money supply rate (which allows to reattain y^* given v_{t-1}, and which agents discount in their plans, is m^{**}, such that:

$$m^{**} + v_{t-1} = E_{t-1}m_t - v_{t-1} = m_{t-1} + \left(v^* - v_{t-1}\right) + v_{t-1} = y^*. \tag{11.14}$$

Notice that by subtracting v_{t-1} from (11.14) and replacing (11.3) in it, positing $g_0 = m_{t-1} + y^*$ and $g_1 = -1$, gives the optimal rate of money supply under the Keynesian Convention to restore potential output after the occurrence of shock $v^* - v_{t-1}$ to money velocity:

$$m^{**} = m_{t-1} + y^* - y_{t-1} - v_{t-1} - v_{t-1} = m_{t-1} + \left(v^* - v_{t-1}\right) = y^* - v_{t-1}. \tag{11.15}$$

The structural equation can then be expressed as:

$$y_t = \phi_0 + \phi_1(E_{t-1}m_t - m_{t-1}) + \phi_2 y_{t-1} + \eta_t, \tag{11.16}$$

where the expression in parentheses indicates that the public expects a monetary policy adjustment for the purpose of stabilizing the output, if output has turned out to be below potential, and where η_t has the same characteristics as u_t and e_t. Substituting (11.3) into (11.15) and rearranging the terms yield:

$$y_t = \phi_0 + \phi_1 y^* + (\phi_2 + \phi_1 g_1) y_{t-1} + \eta_t. \tag{11.17}$$

From (11.6), the parameter g_1 is given by:

$$g_1 = -\frac{\lambda}{\beta} = -\frac{(\phi_2 + \phi_1 g_1)}{\phi_1} = g_1 - \frac{\phi_2}{\phi_1},$$

which implies $\phi_2 = 0$. Equation (11.16) then becomes:

$$y_t = \phi_0 + \phi_1 y^* + \phi_1 g_1 y_{t-1} + \eta_t, \tag{11.18}$$

which, contrary to (11.5), is not independent of policy parameter g_1. In this case, even with rational expectations—and possibly because of them—policy invariance ceases to hold, monetary policy proves to be effective, and output is no longer stable at its potential.

Notice, however, that while derived from the Keynesian Convention, the form of (11.18) is general enough to capture the New Classical Convention and its effects. Consider two cases where the actual level of the previous period output has been observed by agents to be below potential: in the first case, the agents take this to be a signal of a transient phenomenon ($y_{t-1} = y^* - \eta_{t-1}$); in the second case, they take it as a signal of a permanent change to a new potential supply level ($y_{t-1} = y^{**} < y^*$). In the former case, substituting $y^* - \eta_{t-1}$ for y_{t-1} in (11.18) shows that y_t is independent of monetary policy. In the latter case, substituting the new potential output level y^{**} into (11.18) for y_{t-1}, yields:

$$y_t = \phi_0 + \phi_1 \left(y^* - y^{**}\right) + \eta_t. \tag{11.19}$$

Setting m^{***} as the optimal value of m consistent with y^{**}, given constant velocity $v_t = v_{t-1}$ and zero inflation $p_t = 0$ (so that $m^{***} = y^* - v_t$), and substituting in (11.19) the corresponding optimal values of m for y^* and y^{**}, respectively, yield:

$$y_t = \phi_0 + \phi_1 \left(m^{**} - m^{***}\right) + \eta_t, \tag{11.20}$$

which identically to (11.13), establishes the autonomy of y_t from m_t for $\phi_0 = y^{**}$ and $\phi_1 = 0$. In both cases, increases in the money supply generate proportional increases in prices and wages and thus keep the structure of supply invariant to policy parameters (as in SW), thus rendering monetary policy ineffective. Equation (11.18) is thus consistent with both conventions and generates output predictions that depend on the underlying conventions.

This conclusion moves us beyond the Lucas Critique: not only do agents adjust their behavior in response to policy changes, thereby altering historical responses; they also modify their response to policy changes based on the model they believe correctly represents the economy. As a result, monetary policy may or may not be effective depending on (i) the economic model adopted (albeit conventionally) by the agents and (ii) the behaviors that agents consider rational (in accordance with the accepted convention) and consequently adopt: output predictions, and thus the effectiveness of policy, change with the underlying conventions. A central corollary to this conclusion is that, in evaluating the effectiveness of monetary policy, understanding the prevailing conventions that lead agents to accept a model as "true" is more important than pinpointing the ontologically "true" model of the economy.

The conclusion above can be looked at from a different angle. Economic historian Michel De Vroey highlights a key distinction between the methodological approaches of Keynes and Lucas in their study of the economic process (DeVroey, 2012). Keynes, operating from a Marshallian perspective, conceptualized his theoretical work as functioning on two levels: the theoretical framework and the underlying model. In contrast, Lucas, adopting a Walrasian viewpoint, contended that the model and the theory are one and the same thing, and constitute a unified entity.

Lucas designed this unified entity to be consistent across different policy environments by building on individual behavior and expectations, and argued that traditional Keynesian models had failed to account for the lack of policy invariance, that is, the idea that agents will alter their behavior if they anticipate policy changes, thereby causing the model's parameters to shift and nullifying the predictable effects suggested by those models. Lucas claimed that without incorporating rational expectations, Keynesian models were unreliable for evaluating the long-term effects of policy changes, as their parameters are likely to shift in response to policy itself.

However, Lucas could only see a single-model theory that he believed represented the sole framework for understanding how rational (optimizing) agents fathom the effects of policy changes and adjust their behavior accordingly. The findings presented in this chapter stem from the observation that, in reality, agents may utilize a diverse array of models and theories when making decisions. These varying frameworks can provide distinct interpretations of the impacts of policy changes, potentially leading agents to exhibit different behaviors in response to the same policies. If the evolution of conventional beliefs prompts agents to adopt a model theory that diverges from Lucas's original framework, then a wider array of outcomes than Lucas anticipated will emerge.

11.6 Conclusion

The exercised illustrated in this chapter has shown that a market economy with rational agents allows for the existence of multiple "conventional" equilibria, defined as stable macroeconomic states shaped by the shared beliefs ("conventions") held by agents, which influence their expectations and decisions, leading to outcomes that align with these collective assumptions, regardless of the underlying "true" model of the economy. The exercise has shown that not only do the parameters of the economic model depend on the expectations of the agents—as the Lucas critique has held—but the parameters and the expectations of the agents also depend on the prevailing conventions in the economy. The exercise has demonstrated that, in addition to the parameters of the economic model being influenced by agents' expectations—as highlighted by the Lucas critique—both the parameters themselves and the agents' expectations are shaped by the prevailing conventions within the economy.

In the decades following the dominance of the New Classical convention, especially since the years of the Global Financial crises of 2008, that convention was replaced by the New Keynesian one, whereby informational imperfections, price rigidities, and various type of market frictions, present in the economy and stemming from the optimizing choices of agents, allow for a limited effectiveness to the stimulative action of monetary policy.

It would then be an important research topic to determine how and why conventions change, and under which conditions new conventions come to dominate agent beliefs, or which conventions may dominate depending on the different states of the economy. However, this topic transcends the scope of this chapter.

Considering the link between policy effectiveness and conventions, which emerges as the major conclusion of this chapter, an important question is how international financial integration and the conventions held by global investors affect the effectiveness of monetary policy (and in general macroeconomic policies) in countries with open and financially integrated economies. This topic will be investigated later in the book. The next chapter will discuss the effectiveness of monetary and fiscal policies in addressing Secular Stagnation.

References

Bossone, B. (1996). Quale ruolo per la politica monetaria oggi? Riflessioni keynesiane. Conclusioni ortodosse, Rivista di Politica Economica, Anno LXXXVI, Serie III, Fascicolo IV, (pp. 3–33).

Cooper, R., & John, A. (1988). "Coordinating coordination failures in keynesian models". *Quarterly Journal of Economics, 53*, 441–463.

DeVroey, M. (2012). Dead or alive? The ebbs and flows of keynesianism over the history of macroeconomics. Chapters, In: T. Cate (Ed.), *Keynes's general theory*. Chapter 4, Edward Elgar Publishing.

Friedman, M. (1953). The effects of full-employment policy on economic stabilization. In: *Essays in positive economics*. University of Chicago Press.

Friedman, M. (1968). The role of monetary policy. *American Economic Review, 58*(1), 1–17.

Guesnerie, R. (1992). An exploration of the eductive justifications of the rational-expectations hypothesis. *American Economic Review, 82*(5), 1254–1278.

Hahn, F. H. (1977). Keynesian economics and general equilibrium theory: Reflections on some current debates. In: G. C. Harcourt, (Eds.), *The microeconomic foundations of macroeconomics*. Other International Economic Association Publications Series, Palgrave Macmillan.

Hahn, F. H. (1978). On non-walrasian equilibria. In: E. S. Phelps (Eds.), *Microeconomic foundations of employment and inflation theory*.

Hahn, F. H. (1984). *Moneta e inflazione*. Il Saggiatore, Milano.

Hahn, F. H. (1994). *An intellectual retrospect*. BNL quarterly review, No. 190 (pp. 245–258). Banca Nazionale del Lavoro, Settembre.

Hahn, F. H. (1983). *Money and inflation*. MIT Press.

Kydland, F., & Prescott, E. C. (1977). "Rules Rather Than Discretion: The Inconsistency of Optimal Plans". *Journal of Political Economy, 85*(3), 473–491, University of Chicago Press.

Lucas, E. R., Jr. (1972). Expectations and the neutrality of money. *Journal of Economic Theory, 4*(2), 103–123.

Lucas, R. E., Jr. (1976). Econometric policy evaluation: A critique. In K. Brunner & A. H. Meltzer (Eds.), *The Phillips curve and labor markets, Carnegie-Rochester conference series on public policy* (Vol. 1, pp. 19–46). American Elsevier.

Roberts, J. (1987). "An equilibrium model with involuntary unemployment, competitive prices and fiexible wages". *American Economic Review, 77*(5), December, 856–874.

Rogoff, K. (1985). "The optimal degree of commitment to an intermediate monetary target". *The Quarterly Journal of Economics, 100*(4), 1169–1189.

Sargent, T. J. (1973). *Rational expectations, the real rare of interest, and the natural rate of unemployment* (pp. 2–2). Brookings Papers on Economic Activity.

Sargent, T. J., & Wallace, N. (1976). Rational expectations and the theory of economic policy. *Joumal of Monetary Economics*, (2).

Tobin, J. (1975). "Keynesian Models of Recession and Depression". *The American Economic Review, Papers and Proceedings of the Eighty-seventh Annual Meeting of the American Economic Association*, May, *65*(2), 195–202.

White, M. (1983). *The age of analysis: 20th century philosophers*. New American Library.

Chapter 12
Money and Secular Stagnation

Abstract This chapter reconsiders the root causes concept of secular stagnation, an idea that regained prominence following the 2008–09 financial crisis. It highlights how a strong preference for liquid assets over illiquid ones, fueled by persistent pessimism among economic agents, can entrap economies in stagnation. Utilizing the micro-founded model based on utility theory illustrated in Chap. 3, Secular Stagnation is shown to emerge from money and other asset stock dynamics ultimately driven by liquidity preference (in Keynes's tradition), rather than by investment-saving relations. The chapter discusses various demand-side policy strategies, including quantitative easing, negative interest rates, and "helicopter money," arguing that unconventional methods can better stimulate aggregate demand in the face of entrenched liquidity preferences. It emphasizes the importance of expectations and suggests that even slight increases in optimism can shift liquidity preferences and spur recovery. Ultimately, this work advocates for bold fiscal actions and integrated monetary policies to address the structural challenges of advanced economies and foster sustainable growth.

12.1 Preamble

The severity of the Great Recession in the 2010s persuaded several scholars to re-evaluate Keynes' teachings, which had for decades made disappear from mainstream economic theory and practice. Yet, while the economics profession found renewed interest in Keynes' demand management policy, it failed to recognize Keynes' liquidity preference theory (LPT) as the fundamental explanation of why a capitalist economy can feature permanent involuntary unemployment, and how effective can monetary and fiscal policies can be in driving the economic recovery.

Thus, when, at the peak of the crisis, Alvin Hansen's idea of Secular Stagnation was revived by such eminent economists as Larry Summers, Paul Krugman, and Robert Gordon, invoking factors like the falling relative price of capital goods, deleveraging, low population growth, sluggish technical progress, unequal income distribution, and poor human capital accumulation, I felt that something was missing

B. Bossone, *Trailblazing Visions of Money in Economic Theory*, Contributions to Economics, https://doi.org/10.1007/978-3-031-82544-6_12

from their picture: the fear of illiquidity and retraction from investment that Keynes had theorized as consequences of the deep and perduring state of uncertainty, widespread across the markets and the public.

Keynes had shown that saving is always residual to investment: it can never limit investment, nor exceed it—not even ex ante—since it is not what finances investment and only captures the contribution that expenditures other than consumption make to aggregate output (see Chap. 4). Thus, the root cause of economic recessions must be low investment (and, in general, low spending)—not low saving—and in situations of deep, perduring and widespread uncertainty, low investment (spending) is the result of high liquidity preference, not excess saving. When uncertainty is profound and pervasive, people avoid risks and stay more liquid, seek safe assets, consume less, and invest less. In such cases, reducing interest rates doesn't fix the problem; instead, it worsens market sentiment, causes even higher liquidity preference, kills the "animal spirits" and, if anything, it lowers investment even further.

With this persuasion, I went back to my utility-based model of money and assets (see Chap. 3) and used it to show the explanatory power of LPT and to identify the optimal policy response. This is the topic of this chapter.

12.2 Introduction

The financial crisis of 2008–09 and its protracted global economic consequences led to the re-emergence of the concept of Secular Stagnation, dating back from the 1930s. The expression refers to a steady state of underemployment equilibrium in which the advanced economies are "stuck," marked by a liquidity trap, low inflation rates, a decline in productivity, a long-term economic slowdown, and a drop in population. The difference from the last century is that now the financial markets play a bigger role, where leverage makes liquidity abundant and adds to a saving surplus.

The topic became highly debated, centering around two broad views about the causes of stagnation and the insufficient recovery. From the demand-side front, the argument was that the output gap was abnormally persistent because the economies were having difficulty absorbing demand deficits. From the supply-side front, the idea was that potential growth had been weakened.

The debate went on until world developments such as the Covid pandemic, first, and then Russia's invasion of Ukraine, and their economic impacts, caused inflation to regain center stage after being quiet for decades. Yet, continuing to think through the issue is not a sterile exercise. Not only are theorists and policymakers aware that major and prolonged recessions are very real possibilities that advanced economies may confront in future, but the world might not be at all out of stagnation despite the recovery after Covid. Some consider that Secular Stagnation is not over (Blanchard, 2023; Buiter, 2023) and might even evolve into some new form of Stagflation (Roubini, 2022).

The purpose of this chapter is twofold. The first purpose is to analyze the emergence of Secular Stagnation as the consequence of a rise of strong liquidity preference caused by the upsurge and persistence of pessimistic expectations, in an economy where rationality and emotionality are integral and mutually interrelated factors within the agent's decision-making processes (Lo, 2017; Pfister & Böhm, 2008). To this end, the model introduced in Chap. 3 is here used whereby: (i) agents derive utility from holding assets of different liquidity; (ii) the utility provided by each asset is explicitly (formally) derived; and (iii) rational expectations interact with market sentiment changing in response to changes in economic observables. As in Keynes' LPT, in the model used in this chapter equilibrium interest rates are not determined by the relationship between saving and investment flows (as in loanable funds theories) but by agents deciding how to allocate their stocks of wealth. In other words, LPT is about agents deciding the degree of liquidity at which their savings are held.,[1,2]

The second purpose of the chapter is to evaluate alternative policy options to address secular stagnation. The model is here used to assess the relative effectiveness of alternative demand management tools available for policymakers to deal with Secular Stagnation. Interestingly, the chapter shows, inter alia, the relative effectiveness of "helicopter money" as a policy to stimulate aggregate demand and finds that increasing interest rates on money balances stimulates inflation, consistently with the Neo-Fisherian predictions (Cochrane, 2016).

In this model, to the extent that agent expectations remain strongly pessimistic and induce strong liquidity preference (I will refer to this state as "*liquidity preference dominance*"), no policy measures can reverse moods and expectations effectively and rapidly, unless they stimulate demand. And if Secular Stagnation driven by pessimistic expectations determines a negative equilibrium interest rate, the rate will stay at that level until exogenous factors intervene and change those expectations by convincingly stimulating demand.

---

[1] Agent decisions concern the stock of accumulated savings—wealth—at any point in time, rather than any new flow of saving exclusively; therefore, the equilibrium rates of interest on assets are not determined by the supply of and demand for (flows of) saving, but by the supply of and demand for (stocks of) assets into which holdings of wealth can be placed, and are influenced by agents' expectations and states of confidence (Tily, 2012).

[2] I wish to reiterate a point I made in Chap. 2 on LPT. Several critiques of LPT stem from the erroneous conflation of "liquidity" with "money." This conflation leads to confusion between the demand for money and the demand for liquidity. The demand for money refers specifically to the market for the asset that an economy accepts as means of exchange and payment instrument. In contrast, liquidity is a characteristic that all existing assets—both real and financial—possess to different degrees (and bearing in mind that such degrees can change over time based on circumstances). Therefore, the demand for liquidity encompasses all asset markets and reflects agents' preferences for each asset relative to others regarding its liquidity. Notice that the demand for money aligns with a partial equilibrium approach, while the demand for liquidity corresponds to a general equilibrium approach. Thus understood, the demand for liquidity extends to all types of agents (households, firms, and financial intermediaries) and determines their spending and financing decisions.

The chapter is organized as follows: Sect. 12.3 reviews the recent literature on Secular Stagnation, it contrasts the analysis developed in the chapter against the relevant contributions in the literature, and identifies the innovations introduced by the analysis. Section 12.4 describes the model used in the chapter and its building blocks. Section 12.5 uses the model to analyze Secular Stagnation as the result of strong and persistent agent liquidity preference and to study asset market dynamics that may lead to Secular Stagnation. Section 12.6 evaluates alternative economic policy options to bring an economy out of Secular Stagnation. Section 12.7 considers what policies would be necessary for the economy to be stabilized at its full-employment potential. Concluding remarks follow in Sect. 12.7.

Readers should be aware that the model used in this chapter is drawn from Chap. 3 and will not be replicated in its entirety here. Interested readers should therefore be referred to Chap. 3 for a full illustration of the model.

12.3 Review of the Literature and Original Contributions

The idea of Secular Stagnation, first proposed by Hansen (1939), was brought back to the stage by Summers (2013). Summers's initial challenge sparked a big debate,[3] and led to his other publications and the work of various scholars propounding diverse arguments from various theoretical viewpoints. I refer the interested readers to Dufrenot and Rhouzlane (2018) and Di Bucchianico (2019) for references to these contributions and their comprehensive and analytical reviews.

Here, just for quick recap of the main strands of the relevant literature, it is worth recalling that the views expressed in the debate involved: Neo-Keynesian explanations of long-term market failures stress the importance of the differences in savings and investment behavior over the life span to explain why here are too many savings and not enough investments that cause low long-term interest rates; Post-Keynesian works that emphasized the role played by the financial sector in the sharing of national income and explain how this can generate crises (bubbles, over-indebtedness); Neo-classical opinions whereby Secular Stagnation mainly reflects a low long-term steady-state equilibrium caused by slower productivity growth and the demographic aging of the industrialized countries; Schumpeterian arguments considering Secular Stagnation as a transitional state reflecting a phenomenon of creative destruction; and, last but not least, New Keynesian analyses typically approaching prolonged stagnations as the outcome of price rigidities and imperfections in the financial markets. This last camp, in fact, received the most attention and was the most researched.

Using a New Keynesian overlapping generations model, Eggertsson and Mehrotra (2014, 2017) showed that a persistent slump is possible, triggered by shocks that create an oversupply of savings (typically, population aging, income inequality, a

[3] See *Blogs review: The secular stagnation hypothesis*, by Jérémie Cohen-Setton, Bruegel, 25 November 2013, and the collection of contributions edited by Teulings and Baldwin (2014).

decline in the relative price of investment, and a debt deleveraging shock), which reduce the equilibrium real interest rate indefinitely. The approach used in this chapter, which applies the utility-based framework presented in Chap. 3, focuses on liquidity preference—caused by the upsurge of pessimistic expectations—as the source of a persistent drop in aggregate demand and shows Secular Stagnation to emerge from asset stock dynamics that are ultimately driven by liquidity considerations, rather than by investment vs. saving imbalances. Its results complement those obtained from models based on deleveraging (such as Eggertsson & Krugman, 2012), since in the end it is the increased demand for liquidity (caused by heightened risk perceptions and negative market sentiment) that leads lenders to withdraw their loans and to limit credit: in the absence of higher liquidity preference, lenders would not deleverage or they could relend or invest elsewhere the resources withdrawn from borrowers, thereby keeping liquidity flowing in the economy and supporting aggregate demand (which would remain stable). In other words, deleveraging itself is a symptom, not the cause, of depression, and a state of higher liquidity preference is needed to explain it.

The approach used in this chapter features analogies with Farmer (2012), whereby unemployment is a potentially permanent feature of a market economy in a steady-state equilibrium, as determined by the beliefs of participants in the asset markets and their influence on economic activity. More specifically, in Farmer (2012) beliefs about the value of the stock market select one particular labor market equilibrium out of a continuum of possible equilibria. Like Farmer (2012), this chapter features steady-state indeterminacy; yet it does not assume sunspot beliefs to pin down specific steady states and considers, instead, the role of agent expectations as influenced by changes in market sentiment-driven, in turn, by information on the state of the economy.

The approach of this chapter also bears relations with Caballero and Farhi (2013), which analyzes situations of excess demand for safe assets where nominal interest rates are bound from below and cannot provide enough adjustment space. Accordingly, a "*safety trap*" follows, akin to the Keynesian liquidity trap, where recession kicks in to restore equilibrium in the asset markets by reducing the wealth of safe-savers and hence their asset demand. Unlike Caballero and Farhi (2013), the model used in this chapter shows that no additional provision of liquidity can lift the economy from secular stagnation if pessimistic expectations persist and no innovation triggers their reversal. The model's results point to specific forms or monetary and fiscal policy coordination as superior options.

The persistence of pessimistic expectations due to economic observables features similarities with Kozlowski et al. (2015), where the long-lasting effects of the "Great Recession" are understood as reflecting agent perceptions of an extremely unlikely event leading them to re-assess tail risks.

Finally, like Benhabib et al. (2001), the model used in this chapter, too, considers how agent expectations may precipitate the economy into a liquidity trap and a deflationary spiral when interest rates are at the effective lower bound (ELB). Unlike their work, however, the model incorporates a formation mechanism of expectations interacting with market sentiment, driven by economic observables, and draws inferences on policy options to shift the economy onto a socially superior equilibrium.

With respect to the exiting literature, the approach of this chapter presents several innovations. Unlike standard micro-founded macroeconomic methodologies, and as noted in Chap. 3, the model here used considers all assets as vehicles to immediate and/or future consumption; as such, money and assets enter agent utility and demand functions are explicitly derived drawing from first principles. Also, agents' intertemporal and intratemporal resource allocation choices are derived as solutions to a dynamic stochastic general equilibrium model modified (i) to incorporate rational expectations that can be "distorted" by (changes in) market sentiment, and (ii) to allow for the possibility of multiple steady-state equilibria to obtain, driven by agent expectations. The model uses the utility framework to analyze the micro-foundations of Secular Stagnation and to evaluate alternative policies to address it. As discussed below, the chapter investigates a purely demand-driven economy, where supply of goods and assets adjusts instantaneously to demand unless otherwise indicated and shows why price flexibility would not provide a re-equilibrating mechanism when rational expectations are distorted by market sentiment. Importantly, in the model used in this chapter, future the income of households does not just stochastically fluctuate around its full-employment equilibrium level: households incorporate within their plans the possibility of protracted periods of un(der)employment income.

12.4 The Model

12.4.1 The Economy

The model is the same as the one discussed in Chap. 3, but for reader's convenience this section recaps its essential elements.

For analyzing Secular Stagnation in the context of a purely demand-driven economy, a simplifying assumption on the supply side of the economy is adopted whereby the representative firm sells all the output demanded by the household at the going price, and output adjusts immediately to changes in demand. The model could be enriched by incorporating in it a standard New Keynesian price adjustment model. Yet, since this would add nothing substantial to the analysis for the purpose at hand, I use the simpler assumption of quantity adjustments. Similarly, it is assumed that the firms accumulate as much capital as households are willing to hold in the form of capital shares, while labor employment depends on the level of capital used. Therefore, household expectations—as influenced by the prevailing market sentiment—determine capital accumulation, output and employment thereby providing the closure of the model.

The economy consists of a representative infinitely lived, intertemporal utility-maximizing household, a representative firm, the government, the central bank, and four asset types: money M, which is used as a store of value and as the instrument for executing payment transactions, a short-term treasury bill T, a long-term government bond B, and non-liquid asset that can be thought of as a claim on the economy's productive capital stock K. Each asset trades at price $P^{Q(=M,T,B,K)}$, where $P^{M} = 1$ under normal conditions.

The Household

The household supplies the hours of work that are demanded by firms, at competitive nominal compensation rate, y, and receives from the government a non-pecuniary public good, G, in the form of a material and immaterial services (e.g., law & order, education, financial stability, etc). The household orders its preferences across consumption $C, M, T, B,$ and K, according to a strictly quasi-concave, time-separable, and well-behaved utility function $u(\cdot)$, with $u'''(\cdot) > 0$ (that is, decreasing absolute and relative risk aversion). All assets deliver utility to their holders, as discussed in Chap. 3. In this chapter, utility from money and other assets is not just assumed (as it is done in the money-in-the-utility-function literature[4]); it is derived and formalized (Sect. 12.4.2, below), and is used to make assets and consumption all mutually comparable in a general state-dependent equilibrium context driven by optimal microeconomic choices from rational agents. In the utility-based model used here, and as discussed below, asset liquidation costs are variable and agent expectations are rational but distortable by changes in the state of market sentiment that are ultimately driven by changes in economic observables.

In each period, the household earns asset nominal returns $r^{Q=(M,T,B,K)} = (1+\rho^{Q})(1+\pi^{Q})$, where ρ is the nominal interest rate or the dividend paid on the assets and π^{Q} is rate of change of asset price P^{Q}. The real rate of return on asset Q is $R^{Q=(M,T,B,K)} = (1+\rho^{Q})(1+\pi^{Q})(1-\pi^{C})$, where π^{C} is the rate of consumer price inflation. As discussed below, R^{Q} reflects the liquidity and riskiness characterizing each asset as determined by the market.

In calculating its intertemporal budget constraint, the household evaluates its future income perspectives by considering its job value, that is, the present discounted value of the future difference between a worker's productivity and the worker's current pay (Hall, 2013),

$$JV_t = E_t\left[\sum_{\tau=t+1}^{\infty}\prod_{i=t}^{\tau}\beta_i(p_\tau x_\tau - y_t)|\omega_\tau\right], \tag{12.1}$$

where x and y are, respectively, the household's output and remuneration, and ω reflects the combination of expectations and market sentiment, as discussed in Chap. 3; the job value declines with pessimistic prospects about future levels of remuneration and risk of unemployment (and vice versa with optimistic prospects). It is assumed that the household the same job value as estimated by the firm:

$$E_t[y_\tau|\omega_t] = E_t\left[y_\tau^{\{[JV_\tau(\omega_t)/\overline{\Pi}]\}}\right], \tag{12.2}$$

---

[4] See Blanchard and Fischer (1989), Chap. 4.

where $\overline{\Pi}$ is the normal rate of profit, $\frac{JV_t}{\overline{\Pi}} = 1$ holds under normal economic conditions, and $\frac{JV_t}{\overline{\Pi}} > 1 (< 1)$ under optimistic (pessimistic) expectations: the household expects a higher or lower future income level (or an interruption of income) depending on how the prevailing market sentiment affects its own expectations (and those of the enterprises) and reflects on the job value estimates. Equation (12.2) can be considered as an expression for household permanent income built on expectations and market sentiment. As already noted in Chap. 3, this equation provides an important channel to which uncertainty (and, specifically, idiosyncratic uninsurable risks) can be introduced in the model. Equations (12.1)–(12.2) introduce two very important features of the model:

- First, household future income does not just stochastically fluctuate around its full-employment level: households do factor into their plans the possibility of protracted periods of underemployment or unemployment income. This feature is consistent with the findings by Guvenen (2017) on income risk.
- Second, although (as discussed below) price responses to demand shocks are not considered in this chapter, Eqs. (12.1)–(12.2) suggest that, especially in deflationary environments, price adjustments might not provide simple equilibrating mechanisms since expected price (and wage) dynamics enter the job value estimates and reflect on the demand responses.

The Firm

The firm employs physical capital K and labor L to produce composite output Y, consisting of consumption and investment goods, through a standard neoclassical production function,

$$Y = C + k = Y(K, L).$$

The supply of C is an increasing function of consumption good price:

$$C_t = C\left(P_t^C\right), \quad \text{with } C' > 0$$

and the demand, which is derived from first principles below, can be written in a general form as a function of relative prices:

$$C_t = C\left(P_t^C, P_t^T, P_t^B, P_t^K\right), \quad \text{with } C'_C < 0, C'_T > 0, C'_B > 0, C'_K > 0.$$

Each period the firm adds investment k to its existing capital stock,

$$K = K_{-1} + k.$$

The firm finances investment k by selling shares of K to the households. In each period, capital K earns real return $r^K = \left(1 + y^K\right)\left(1 + \pi^K\right)\left(1 - \pi^C\right)$, where y^K is capital's unit output rate, and π^K is rate of change of capital price P^K. The firms hold the level of K that households are willing to finance based on the stream of future real rates of return that they expect to earn on K, as reflected by its current price,

$$K_t = K\left(P_t^K\right), \quad \text{with } K' > 0.$$

The demand function for K is derived from first principles below. Capital K embodies a technology that employs household labor at competitive nominal compensation rate y. Based on capital K, the firm hires household labor L

$$L_t = L(K_t) \quad \text{with } L' > 0.$$

A reduction in the demand for K would cause the demand for L to decline and output to shrink, and vice versa. Even admitting some degree of substitutability between the two inputs, any significant change in one would imply or require a same-directional change in the other.

The Government

The government produces a non-pecuniary public good G and finances production by issuing the earlier defined bills and bonds T and B, respectively, to match household portfolio preferences of different maturity and liquidity services),

$$G_\tau + r_{\tau-1}^T P_\tau^T T_\tau + r_{\tau-1}^B P_\tau^T B_\tau = P_\tau^T T_\tau + P_\tau^B B_\tau + Tax_\tau, \tag{12.3}$$

under an intertemporal constraint whereby all state expenditures must eventually be paid through tax revenues

$$\sum_{t=0}^{\infty} \beta^i \prod_{i=t}^{\tau-1} \left[(G_\tau + P_{\tau-1}^T T_{\tau-1} r_{\tau-1}^T + P_{\tau-1}^B B_{\tau-1} r_{\tau-1}^B) - Tax_\tau \right] = 0. \tag{12.4}$$

The government sells as many T and B as households wish to buy at and on their respective prices. The functional form of the household demand for government bonds is derived from first principles below, but they can be written here respectively in the general form:

$$T_t = T\left(P_t^T, P_t^C, P_\tau^B, P_t^K\right), \quad \text{with } T_T' < 0, T_C' > 0, T_B' > 0, T_K' > 0$$
$$B_t = T\left(P_t^B, P_t^C, P_\tau^T, P_t^K\right) \quad \text{with } B_B' < 0, B_C' > 0, B_T' > 0, B_K' > 0.$$

The Central Bank

The supply of M is governed by central bank's policy rule:

$$M_\tau = M\left(r^* - r_\tau^T\right), \quad \text{with } M\prime > 0 \text{ if } r^* - r_\tau^T < 0, \tag{12.5}$$

whereby the central bank governs the supply of M so as to minimize deviations over time between the nominal interest rate on (short-term and risk-less) treasury bill T and the neutral rate of interest r^*, which holds when real-sector supply and demand are in intertemporal equilibrium and consumer price inflation is constant $\left(\pi^C = 0\right)$. The central bank thus fully accommodates the demand for M.

For brevity, the features of the model concerning the utility derived by the households from their holding assets, the cost of liquidating assets, and the interaction process between household expectations and market sentiment are not repeated here. For a full illustration of these features, the reader is thus referred to Chap. 3. For convenience, however, Table 12.1 reports all relevant variables and equations used in the model.

12.4.2 Optimal Allocations

The household maximizes her intertemporal utility:

$$U = \text{Max}_{C,M,T,B,K}\beta^{\tau}E_t\left\{\left[\sum_{t=\tau}^{\infty}u(C_{\tau}, M_{\tau}, T_{\tau}, B_{\tau}, K_{\tau},)\right]|\omega_t\right\}, \tag{12.6}$$

subject to budget constraint

$$\begin{aligned} &P_{\tau}^{C}C_{\tau} + P_{\tau}^{T}T_{\tau} + P_{\tau}^{B}B_{\tau} + P_{\tau}^{K}K_{\tau} + M_{\tau} \\ &\quad = y_{\tau} - Tax_{\tau} + M_{\tau-1} + r_{\tau-1}^{T}P_{\tau}^{T}T_{\tau} + r_{\tau-1}^{B}P_{\tau}^{T}B_{\tau} + r_{\tau-1}^{K}P_{\tau}^{K}K_{\tau}, \end{aligned} \tag{12.7}$$

where

$$C_{\tau}, M_{\tau}, T_{\tau}, B_{\tau}, K_{\tau} \geq 0, \tag{12.8}$$

and subject to transversality condition

$$\sum_{t=0}^{\infty}\beta^{\tau}(P_{\tau}^{C}C_{\tau} + P_{\tau}^{T}T_{\tau} + P_{\tau}^{B}B_{\tau} + P_{\tau}^{K}K_{\tau} + M_{\tau} - y_{\tau}) = 0, \tag{12.9}$$

and where, as recalled from Chap. 3, the utility of any asset Q (=M, T, B, K) is defined as,

$$u(Q_t) = u(Q_t|\Omega_t) = E_t\left\{\beta R_{t+1}^{Q}\left\{u\left(\frac{P_{t+1}^{Q}Q_t}{P_{t+1}^{C}}\right)\vartheta_{t+1}(\omega_t)\right.\right.$$

Table 12.1 Summary of the model's relevant variables and equations[(*)]

Aggregate output	$Y = C + k = Y(K, L)$ $K_t = K\left(P_t^K\right)$ with $K\prime > 0$ $L_t = L(K_t)$ with $L\prime > 0$
Interaction between economic information and market sentiment	$\boldsymbol{D} : iD \in (I \times R) \rightarrow \Omega\prime > \Omega$ for $\Omega < 1$, or $\Omega\prime \langle \Omega$ for $\Omega \rangle 0$, with $\Omega\prime, \Omega \in (0, 1)$, so that $\omega = \frac{\Omega\prime}{\Omega} \in (0, \infty)$
Probability of having to finance consumption shock s_t	$\vartheta_t \in (\Theta, S, \Phi) \equiv Pr_\tau[(s_{t=\tau+\varepsilon}), \varepsilon \rightarrow 0] = \vartheta(\omega_\tau), \vartheta\prime < 0$ $\vartheta_t = \begin{cases} \lim\limits_{\omega \rightarrow 1} \vartheta(\omega_\tau) \\ \lim\limits_{\omega \rightarrow 0} \vartheta(\omega_\tau) \end{cases}, \quad \omega \in (0, \infty)$
Expected utility lost to the liquidation of asset Q (=M, T, B, K) as a fraction of the utility of asset Q	$\xi_T^Q = \left\{ \dfrac{E_t\left[u\left(\frac{q(\Omega_t)_T P_T^Q Q_t}{P_T^C}\right)\right]}{E_t\left[u\left(\frac{P_T^Q Q_t}{P_T^C}\right)\right]} \right\} = \xi^Q(\omega_t)_T, = t, \infty \quad$ with $\xi\prime > 0$
Expected utility lost to the price volatility of asset Q as a fraction of the utility of asset Q	$\sigma_T^Q = \left\{ \dfrac{\left\{u\left[E_t\left(\frac{P_\tau^Q Q_t}{P_\tau^C}\right)\right] - E_t\left[u\left(\frac{P_\tau^Q Q_t}{P_\tau^C}\right)\right] \mid \omega_t\right\}}{E_t\left[u\left(\frac{P_\tau^Q Q_t}{P_\tau^C}\right)\right]} \right\} = \sigma^Q(\omega_t)_T, = t, \infty$ with $\sigma\prime > 0$
Utility of asset Q	$u(Q_t) = u(Q_t \mid \omega_t) = E_t\left\{\beta R_{t+1}^Q \left\{u\left(\frac{P_{t+1}^Q Q_t}{P_{t+1}^C}\right)\vartheta_{t+1}(\omega_t) + \sum\limits_{\tau=t+1}^{T=\infty} \beta^\tau\right.\right.$ $\left.\left.\prod\limits_{\tau=t+1}^{T=\infty} u\left(\frac{P_\tau^Q Q_t}{P_\tau^C}\right) R_\tau^Q [1 - \vartheta_\tau(\omega_t)]\left[1 - \xi_\tau^Q(\omega_t)\right]\left[1 - \sigma_\tau^K(\omega_t)\right]\vartheta_T(\omega_t)\right\}\right\}$
Job value	$JV_t = JV_t(\omega_\tau) = E_t[\sum\limits_{\tau=t+1}^{\infty} \beta^i \prod\limits_{i=t}^{\tau} (\rho_\tau \lambda_\tau - y_\tau) \mid \omega_\tau]$,
Expected wage compensation	$E_t[y_\tau \mid \omega_t] = E_t\left[y_\tau^{\{[JV_\tau(\omega_t)/\overline{\Pi}]\}}\right]$
Government budget constraint	$G_\tau + r_{\tau-1}^T P_\tau^T T_\tau + r_{\tau-1}^B P_\tau^T B_\tau = P_\tau^T T_\tau + P_\tau^B B_\tau + Tax_\tau$
Government enhanced budget constraint	$G_\tau + r_{\tau-1}^T P_\tau^T T_\tau + r_{\tau-1}^B P_\tau^T B_\tau = P_\tau^T T_\tau + P_\tau^B B_\tau + Tax_\tau - DTax_\tau + DM_\tau$

(continued)

Table 12.1 (continued)

Central bank money supply	$M_\tau = M\left(\delta - r_\tau^T\right)$
Household objective	$U = \text{Max}_{C,M,T,B,K}\beta^\tau E_t\left\{\left[\sum_{t=\tau}^{\infty} u(C_\tau, M_\tau, T_\tau, B_\tau, K_\tau,)\right]\lvert\omega_t\right\}$
Household budget constraint	$P_\tau^C C_\tau + P_\tau^T T_\tau + P_\tau^B B_\tau + P_\tau^K K_\tau + M_\tau$ $= y_\tau - Tax_\tau + M_{\tau-1} + r_{\tau-1}^T P_\tau^T T_\tau + r_{\tau-1}^B P_\tau^T B_\tau + r_{\tau-1}^K P_\tau^K K_\tau$
Household enhanced budget constraint	$P_\tau^C C_\tau + P_\tau^T T_\tau + P_\tau^B B_\tau + P_\tau^K K_\tau + (M_\tau + DM_\tau)$ $= y_\tau - (Tax_\tau - DTax_\tau) + M_{\tau-1} + r_{\tau-1}^T P_\tau^T T_\tau$ $+ r_{\tau-1}^B P_\tau^T B_\tau + r_{\tau-1}^K P_\tau^K K_\tau$
General equilibrium condition	$\left[u\prime(C_\tau^*)\left(\frac{1}{P_\tau^{C*}}\right)\lvert\omega_t\right] = \left[u\prime(M_\tau^*)\lvert\omega_t\right] = \left[u\prime(T_\tau^*)\left(\frac{1}{P_\tau^{T*}}\right)\lvert\omega_t\right]$ $= \left[u'(B_\tau^*)\left(\frac{1}{P_\tau^{B*}}\right)\lvert\omega_t\right] = \left[u'(K_\tau^*)\left(\frac{1}{P_\tau^{K*}}\right)\lvert\omega_t\right]$
Key variables: State Control Endogenous	$\omega,\ K_{-1},\ \overline{\Pi}$ M, T, B $C_\tau^*, K_\tau^*, P_\tau^{T*}, P_\tau^{B*}, P_\tau^{K*}$

$$+\sum_{\tau=t+1}^{T=\infty}\beta^\tau\prod_{\tau=t+1}^{T=\infty}u\left(\frac{P_\tau^Q Q_t}{P_\tau^C}\right)R_\tau^Q[1-\vartheta_\tau(\omega_t)]\left[1-\xi_\tau^Q(\omega_t)\right]\left[1-\sigma_\tau^K(\omega_t)\right]\vartheta_T(\omega_t)\Bigg\}\Bigg\}, \tag{12.10}$$

with $\Delta\not{}_Q^* = \xi^Q = \rho^Q = 0$, and for $Q = M$, that is, money is the only asset that trades immediately and at no loss, and it bears a zero nominal interest rate.

Plan (12.6)–(12.9) is the household's program to allocate resources optimally between current consumption, money and non-money assets with a view to maximizing—both within each date and over time—the streams of utility derived from each, subject to the given resource constraint. The Bellman's equation to solve the plan is:

$$\begin{aligned} &V(y_t, C_t, M_t, T_t, B_t, K_t\lvert\omega_t) \\ &= \text{Max}_{(C,M,T,B,K)}[u(C_t, M_t, T_t, B_t, K_t\lvert\omega_t) \\ &\quad + \beta V(y_{t+1}, C_{t+1}, M_{t+1}, T_{t+1}, B_{t+1}, K_{t+1})\boldsymbol{R}'\lvert\omega_t\big]. \end{aligned}$$

The Euler equation is:

$$u'(C_t, M_t, T_t, B_t, K_t\lvert\omega_t) = \beta E_t\left[u'(C_{t+1}, M_{t+1}, T_{t+1}, B_{t+1}, K_{t+1})\boldsymbol{R}'\lvert\omega_t\right],$$

which determines the optimal intertemporal path for consumption and asset holdings, conditional on state variable Ω_t. The optimal intradate allocation across consumption and assets, conditional on ω_t, is derived as a solution to Eq. (12.6), subject to constraints (12.7)–(12.9), which yields the following first-order conditions:

$$U'(C_t) = \left\{ u'(C_t)\beta^i E_t \left[\left(\frac{1}{P_t^C} \right) \prod_{i=0}^{t} R_i \right] |\omega_t \right\} - \lambda_t = 0,$$

where R is the real gross rate of household wealth growth,

$$U'(M_t) = \left\{ u'(M_t)\beta^i E_t \left[\left(\frac{1}{P_t^C} \right) \prod_{i=0}^{t} R_i^M \right] |\omega_t \right\} - \lambda_t = 0$$

$$U'(T_t) = \left\{ u'(T_t)\beta^i E_t \left[\left(\frac{1}{P_t^C} \right) \prod_{i=0}^{t} R_i^T \right] |\omega_t \right\} - \lambda_t = 0$$

$$U'(B_t) = \left\{ u'(B_t)\beta^i E_t \left[\left(\frac{1}{P_t^C} \right) \prod_{i=0}^{t} R_i^B \right] |\omega_t \right\} - \lambda_t = 0$$

$$U'(K_t) = \left\{ u'(K_t)\beta^i E_t \left[\left[\left(\frac{1}{P_t^C} \right) \prod_{i=0}^{t} R_i^K \right] \right] |\omega_t \right\} - \lambda_t = 0$$

$$\begin{aligned} &\lambda_t E_t \{ [P_\tau^C C_\tau + P_\tau^T T_\tau + P_\tau^B B_\tau + P_\tau^K K_\tau + M_\tau + Tax_\tau \\ &[-M_{\tau-1} - r_{\tau-1}^T P_\tau^T T_\tau - r_{\tau-1}^B P_\tau^T B_\tau - r_{\tau-1}^K P_\tau^K K_\tau = y_\tau] |\omega_t \} \\ &\lambda_t \geq 0. \end{aligned}$$

These conditions, including the general and well-behaved functional forms assumed in the model, imply that at planning date *t*, and for expected real gross returns $(R_\tau^M, R_\tau^T, R_\tau^B, R_\tau^K)$ for all τ's, the household selects allocation $(C_\tau^*, M_\tau^*, T_\tau^*, B_\tau^*, K_\tau^*)$ and the economy determines the equilibrium price set $(P_\tau^{C*}, 1, P_\tau^{T*}, P_\tau^{B*}, P_\tau^{K*})$, which exists and is unique and clears the markets for goods and (money and non money) assets.

For future expected real rates of return on assets $(R_\tau^M, R_\tau^T, R_\tau^B, R_\tau^K)$, for all τ's, for agent expectations undistorted by market sentiment $(\omega = 1)$, and for the given resource constraints, the solution determines the path to optimal intertemporal consumption and a sequence of allocations $(C_\tau^*, M_\tau^*, T_\tau^*, B_\tau^*, K_\tau^*)$ that satisfy the optimal intradate rule of weighted marginal utility (w. m. u.) equality at each future date $\tau = t + 1, \ldots, \infty$, and clear the markets for the economy's goods and assets at prices $(P_\tau^{C*}, 1, P_\tau^{T*}, P_\tau^{B*}, P_\tau^{K*})$:

$$\left[u'(C_\tau^*) \left(\frac{1}{P_\tau^{C*}} \right) |\omega_t \right] = [u'(M_\tau^*)|\omega_t] = \left[u'(T_\tau^*) \left(\frac{1}{P_\tau^{T*}} \right) |\omega_t \right]$$

$$= \left[u'(B_\tau^*) \left(\frac{1}{P_\tau^{B*}} \right) | \omega_t \right]$$
$$= \left[u'(K_\tau^*) \left(\frac{1}{P_\tau^{K*}} \right) | \omega_t \right] = \lambda_\tau, \tag{12.11}$$

and

$$\lambda_\tau / \lambda_{\tau+1} = \beta E_t R_{\tau+1}^M = \beta E_t R_{t+1}^{B_D} = \beta E_t R_{\tau+1}^T = \beta E_t R_{\tau+1}^K. \tag{12.12}$$

Optimal rules (12.11)–(12.12) require that:

Proposition 12.1 *In equilibrium, at each date the household derives the same level of utility from each marginal unit of consumption and asset holdings, and all real rates of return on money and assets, in present (discounted) value, and net of default risk, are equalized at each date and intertemporally.*

Optimal rules (12.11)–(12.12) hold under expected real interest rates and asset returns conditional on the knowledge of, and information on, the economy and its prospects at the times expectations are formed. Full employment general equilibrium would require expectations to be rational and undistorted by market sentiment. Distorted expectations (by pessimistic or optimistic beliefs) lead the economy to suboptimal equilibria with less than full resource employment or higher than optimal inflation.

12.5 Secular Stagnation

From the household optimal plan, as it will be seen analytically below, a large and persistent deterioration of market sentiment $\omega_{t \in (t,\ldots,t^+)} < \omega_{t-1}$, where t^+ is an indefinite future date, causes the household's job value and expected income to fall, leading to lower optimal intertemporal consumption, and raises the household's demand for liquidity (in this model, money and short-term bills). Liquidity preference increases as a rational agent response to fears of future worsening of economic conditions and triggers a change in equilibrium asset returns.

This chapter analyzes the case where both the deterioration of market sentiment and its impact on agent expectations are such as to induce what is here referred to as "*liquidity preference dominance*," that is, a situation where, with nominal interest rates constrained from falling below the ELB, agents strongly prefer to hold liquid assets, engage in liquid asset purchases, and stand ready to exchange less liquid asset holdings for any amount of liquid ones at their going prices. With the ELB binding, the demand for liquid assets might not be satiated.

Importantly, and as noted above, under the liquidity preference theory (LPT) here adopted, equilibrium interest rates are not the equalizer of desired saving and investment at the aggregate level, but the balancing mechanism of the supply and demand for the assets into which agents wish to keep their wealth, as influenced by expectations and market sentiment.

A digression here is in order. Keynes' LPT helps to understand the nature of the fallacy. According to Keynes, liquidity preference is the decision about the degree of liquidity at which savings should be held, and it is determined by agents' expectations and state of mood: it is a decision concerning the stock of savings—wealth—at any point in time, rather than the flow of saving. In Keynes' LPT, the rate of interest is not determined by the supply and demand for saving flows, but by the supply and demand for assets into which holdings of the stocks of wealth can be placed. In other words, the interest rate depends not on the strength of the desire to hold wealth, but on the strengths of the desire to hold it in liquid and illiquid forms respectively, coupled with the amount of the supply of wealth in one form relatively to the other. In LPT terms, the low interest rates prevailing during the global crisis, and since then, can be explained by the extremely strong liquidity preference dominating all sectors of the economy (including the financial and the external sectors), rather than by a persistent tendency for planned savings to exceed planned investment. Strong liquidity preference means that agents want to stay liquid: consumption, investment, and investment finance all freeze, causing economic activity to come to a gridlock, and the economy falls into a liquidity trap where, contrary to mainstream predictions, any money injected into the system would be hoarded, with no effects on prices or output.

Assuming output adjusts instantaneously to demand and that goods prices remain constant so that $\pi = 0$ for a low enough level of $\omega_{t\in(t,\ldots,t^+)} \ll 1$ (strong pessimism) until a far distant date t^+, restoring optimal (equilibrium) allocation $(C_\tau^*, M_\tau^*, T_\tau^*, B_\tau^*, K_\tau^*)$ may require $\rho^{M**} < 0$, where the nominal interest rate adjustment $|D\rho^{M**}| = \left|\rho^{M**} - 0\right| \geq \rho^{K*} - 0$ equals the erosion in the liquidity premium on M that is needed to restore equilibrium, and where the negative interval $[\rho^{M**}, 0]$ defines the space where nominal interest rates on liquid assets would have to fall, in the absence of the ELB, for the economy to exit Secular Stagnation. In the model above, all else equal and drawing from the derivative signs in Eq. (12.10), both the rise and persistence of pessimistic expectations:

(a) Reduce the household's job value JV and tighten the household's budget constraint as a result, thereby lowering the optimal consumption time path;
(b) Raise probability ϑ_τ for τ's closer to the agent planning time t and thus increase the m. u. of liquid assets M and T relative to that of less liquid assets B and K;
(c) Raise expected utility losses ξ^B and ξ^K as well as σ^B and σ^K and thus lower the marginal utility of less liquid assets B and K;
(d) Reduce $(1 - \vartheta_\tau)$ and further compound the effect under c).

In words: the rise and persistence of pessimistic expectations lead the households to reduce intertemporal consumption, raise their probability chances of having to face immediate consumption shocks, and increase the liquidation costs of less liquid assets while reducing the present value of their expected returns. As a result, the households change preferences toward holding assets with higher access speed to consumption and sure nominal value (i.e., liquidity). In fact,

Proposition 12.2 *Strong and persistent liquidity preference driven by overly pessimistic expectations may cause a state of protracted under-consumption and under-investment, leading to Secular Stagnation.*

Process analysis is used here and in the following sections to demonstrate the propositions submitted. By focusing on the process, the causal mechanisms can be identified that drive changes in endogenous variables, as well as the sequence of changes occurring in these variables, and the interactions can be observed that occur between the different markets during the adjustment dynamics.

For Proposition 12.2, take for simplicity an economy with only two assets, M and K, where the ELB binds, and still for simplicity assume that the ELB coincides with $\rho^M = 0$. From plan (12.6)–(12.9), and the Euler equations for C, M and K, at equilibrium prices $(P_\tau^{C*}, 1, , P_\tau^{K*})$ a rise in pessimism $\omega_t < \omega_{t-1}$ yields the following inequality:

$$\begin{aligned} \left[u'(C_\tau^*)\left(\frac{1}{P_\tau^{C*}}\right)|\omega_t\right] &= \left[u'(C_\tau^*)\left(\frac{1}{P_\tau^{C*}}\right)|\omega_{t-1}\right] \\ \left[u'(C_{\tau+i}^*)\left(\frac{1}{P_{\tau+i}^{C*}}\right)|\omega_t\right] &> \left[u'(C_{\tau+i}^*)\left(\frac{1}{P_{\tau+i}^{C*}}\right)|\omega_{t-1}\right], i = 1, \ldots, \infty \\ \left[u'(M_\tau^*)|\omega_t\right] &> \left[u'(M_\tau^*)|\omega_{t-1}\right] \\ \left[u'(K_\tau^*)\left(\frac{1}{P_\tau^{K*}}\right)|\omega_t\right] &< \left[u'(K_\tau^*)\left(\frac{1}{P_\tau^{K*}}\right)|\omega_{t-1}\right]. \end{aligned} \tag{12.13}$$

Hence, importantly:

$$\left[u'(M_\tau^*)|\omega_t\right] > \left[u'(K_\tau^*)\left(\frac{1}{P_\tau^{K*}}\right)|\omega_t\right], \tag{12.13b}$$

where liquidity dominates agent preferences. As the ELB prevents the adjustment in the rates of return $R^{Q=M,K}$ from restoring equilibrium, Inequality (12.13b) leads to new equilibrium allocations where:

$$(C_\tau^{**}, C_{\tau+i}^{**}, M_\tau^{**}, K_\tau^{**}), \tag{12.14}$$

where $C_\tau^{**} = C_\tau^*$, $C_{\tau+i}^{**} < C_{\tau+i}^*$, $M_\tau^{**} > M_\tau^*$, $K_\tau^{**} < K_\tau^*$. Persistent pessimistic expectations cause households to anticipate lower levels of future wealth, which leads them to reduce future consumption. Also, the effects of persistent pessimistic expectations on the w. m. u. of, respectively, M and K, discussed under Proposition 12.1, push households to demand more money and less capital, thus causing aggregate employment and output to decline (see Sect. 12.4.1).

To the extent that pessimistic expectations persist in the absence of signals that induce changes in the prevailing market sentiment, and with the ELB binding, suboptimal equilibria such as $(C_\tau^{**}, C_{\tau+i}^{**}, M_\tau^{**}, K_\tau^{**})\forall i = 1, \infty$, may hold indefinitely. The demand for liquidity dominates agent preferences since the w. m. u. of liquidity exceeds that of capital, as in Inequality (12.7b), and the economy finds itself entangled in Secular Stagnation. For the economy to achieve this equilibrium position, key is the interaction between expectations and market sentiment as influenced by the underlying macroeconomic developments. However, considering the role of information in influencing market sentiment, it would be incorrect to interpret this model as assuming that sentiments are the primary and ultimate cause of economic conditions.

While the model used does not incorporate the financial sector, one can speculate that if agents had access to, say, bank credit, an uncertainty shock leading to pessimistic expectations, as assumed above, would exacerbate the negative outcomes by inducing banks to ration the supply of loans for fear of higher credit risk and to even accelerate loan repayments from borrowers, thus causing financial acceleration effects.

12.5.1 Relative Price Dynamics and Equilibrium

As noted, this chapter focuses on the impact of liquidity preference on aggregate demand and ignores supply-side adjustment effects driven by changes in relative prices. However, with distorted expectations price flexibility under falling prices and nominal wages may likely fail to restore full resource employment equilibrium. This is because pessimism induces a wedge between the expected real wages as evaluated by households and firms, respectively. To see this, let's consider equilibrium real wage compensation under full information and undistorted expectations $E_t\left[y_\tau|\omega_t = 1\right]$, $\tau > t$, as a benchmark for all agent types. Interestingly, the persistent state of pessimism $\omega_{t+} < 1$) leads the households, on the one hand, to expect nominal wage compensations to fall more rapidly than goods prices, but it also leads firms to hold the opposite expectations, on the other. That is,

$$E_t^F\left[y_\tau|\omega_t < 1\right] > E_t\left[y_\tau|\omega_t = 1\right] > E_t^H\left[y_\tau|\omega_t < 1\right],$$

where subscripts H and F stand for households and firms, respectively. That is, both forms and households would expect real wage compensation to evolve to their disadvantage, with the latter growing with the level of pessimism (and expectations distortion). Resource employment (and output) would thus be limited to the minimum between supply and demand, and the occurrence of unemployment would both confirm the pessimistic beliefs and contribute to further protracting economic stagnation. Although derived differently, the non-re-equilibrating effect of flexible prices is analogous to Eggertsson et al. (2017).

12.5.2 Secular Stagnation and Asset Deflation

Secular Stagnation can be studied also, dynamically, as the result of an asset price deflationary process set in motion by changes in expectations (as affected by negative market sentiment). Take the example of a significant critical event occurring at time t leading agents to re-assess downward the expected future stream of returns from corporate capital stock K. In the model above, based on the new information set available at t, ω_t, the anticipated decline in the price of K lowers the w. m. u. of the asset relative to that of consumption and the other (more liquid) assets. In terms of optimal rules (12.11)–(12.12), the situation at time t now looks like:

$$\left[u'(C_\tau^*)\left(\frac{1}{P_\tau^{C*}}\right)|\omega_t\right] = \left[u'(M_\tau^*)|\omega_t\right] > \left[u'(T_\tau^*)\left(\frac{1}{P_\tau^{T*}}\right)|\omega_t\right]$$
$$> \left[u'(B_\tau^*)\left(\frac{1}{P_\tau^{B*}}\right)|\omega_t\right]$$
$$> \left[u'(K_\tau^*)\left(\frac{1}{P_\tau^{K*}}\right)|\omega_t\right]. \tag{12.15}$$

Under undistorted rational expectations and a perfectly flexible supply of capital stock K, both price P_T^K and quantity K_T settle instantly at their undistorted rational expectations equivalents, leading to an equilibrium allocation consistent with optimal rules (12.11)–(12.12). On the other hand, with expectations distorted by market sentiment, $\omega_t\prime < \omega_t$, and a sluggish supply adjustment of physical capital K, the dynamics would be richer, leading to

Proposition 12.3 *With capital stock adjusting only gradually to demand shocks, persistent pessimistic expectations may trigger asset deflation—a process consisting of capital price fall and fire sales of shares—and lead to Secular Stagnation.*

Inspecting the m. u. expression for asset $Q = K$, using Eq. (12.10) above, yields

$$u'(K_t) = u'(K_t|\omega_t) = E_t\left\{\beta R_{t+1}^K\left\{u'\left(\frac{P_{t+1}^K K_t}{P_{t+1}^C}\right)\vartheta_{t+1}(\omega_t\prime)\right.\right.$$
$$\left.\left.+\sum_{\tau=t+1}^{T=\infty}\beta^\tau\prod_{\tau=t+1}^{T=\infty}u'\left(\frac{P_\tau^K K_t}{P_\tau^C}\right)R_\tau^K[1-\vartheta_\tau(\omega_t\prime)]\left[1-\xi_\tau^K(\omega_t\prime)\right]\left[1-\sigma_\tau^K(\omega_t\prime)\right]\vartheta_T(\omega_t\prime)\right\}\right\} \tag{12.10a}$$

Equation (12.10a) indicates that if a consistent stream of negative news leads households to expect a declining trend of P^K and unit output y^K, pessimistic expectations raise the values of both ξ^K and σ^K: as the households anticipate having to liquidate K ahead of time in order to buffer possible immediate consumption needs, they solve for optimal rules (12.11)–(12.12) expecting both $[1 - \vartheta_\tau(\omega_t\prime)] \approx 1$ to hold for all i's, and $\vartheta_T(\omega_t\prime) \approx 0$ to hold for later periods T. This raises the premium on liquidity and decreases the relative w. m. u. of K (and, hence, the demand for it), in particular relative to the more liquid assets.

If the supply of K responds only slowly to negative demand shocks, optimal rules (12.11)–(12.12) requires P^K to overshoot its undistorted rational expectations equivalent. Price overshooting feeds into lower values of Ω and causes P^K to stay below equilibrium (or to further decrease) even as the supply of K gradually adjusts to lower demand. Pessimistic expectations might induce a large decrease in the perceived m. u. of asset K; this

(a) gives rise to *investment disincentive* $\mathfrak{D}^K$

$$\mathfrak{D}^K = \mathfrak{D}(K_t, P_t^{\mathrm{K}}|\omega) = \left\{ \left[\frac{u^{'(K_\tau^*)}}{P_\tau^{K*}} |\omega_t{}' \right] - [\frac{u^{'(K_\tau^*)}}{P_\tau^{K*}} |\omega_t \right\} < 0,$$

which brings to a temporary equilibrium (or to a sequence of temporary equilibria) featuring values of K and P^K that are both below their undistorted rational expectations equivalents, and

(b) feeds into *asset deflation* $\mathbb{D}^K$

$$\mathbb{D}^K = \mathbb{D}(K_t, P_t^{\mathrm{K}}|\omega) = \left\{ \left(K_t^*, P_t^{K*}|\omega_t{}'\right) \ll \left(K_t^*, P_t^{K*}|\omega_t\right) \right\}.$$

Investment disincentive $\mathfrak{D}^K$ and asset deflation $\mathbb{D}^K$ both characterize the economy's transition to Secular Stagnation, such as under Inequality (12.15) above, where agents move increasingly into liquidity and stay liquid as long as expectations remain pessimistic.

12.6 Policy Evaluation

Six types of policy to drive the economy out of Secular Stagnation are evaluated in this section: (i) the expansion of the central bank balance sheet through quantitative easing (QE); (ii) the determination of the central bank to generate inflation expectations; (iii) forward guidance; (iv) the application of negative interest rates to money; (v), helicopter money drops; and (vi) fiscal policy. Let's take them in turn.

12.6.1 Quantitative Easing

Let us consider the economy with the full range of assets introduced earlier: money M, short-term treasury bills T and long-term government bonds TB, and capital K. The model shows that quantitative easing (QE)—whereby the central bank issues new money to buy specified amounts of financial assets from commercial banks and other private institutions, thus raising their prices and lowering their yield (contrary to anticipations of Wallace neutrality)—is ineffective in boosting aggregate demand.

Proposition 12.4 *While QE may succeed in raising asset prices, under liquidity preference dominance it would not be able to stimulate consumption and/or investment. If persistently applied, however it may, influence positively market mood and agent expectations.*

With Inequality (12.15) holding, the nominal rate on the short-term treasury bill approaching zero, $\rho^{T**} \approx 0$, and the household's high liquidity preference pushing the equilibrium (implicit) return on money toward $\rho^{M**} < 0$ but hitting against the ELB, QE amounts to the central bank buying B in exchange for M so as to align the w. m. u. of B with that of M by raising its price P^B. In the limit, QE pressurizes bill and bond prices until the rates of return on money and bonds approach zero, that is, $\rho^{M**} \approx \rho^{T**} \approx \rho^{B**} \approx 0$. Yet, under liquidity preference dominance and a binding ELB, agents would willingly absorb whatever amounts of M they can afford in exchange for bills and bonds and hold on to M without altering their demand for K since $\left|Dr^M\right| < \left|Dr^{M**}\right| \geq r^K - 0$; that is, the ELB constraints the adjustment of the nominal interest rates on M, T, and B and binds their respective w. m. u. from declining far enough to incentivize investment in (illiquid) asset K. In practice, QE may not do better than bringing Inequality (12.15) to:

$$\begin{aligned}\left[u'(C_\tau^*)\left(\frac{1}{P_\tau^{C*}}\right)|\omega_t\right] &= \left[u'(M_\tau^{**})|\omega_t\right] = \left[u'(T_\tau^{**})\left(\frac{1}{P_\tau^{T**}}\right)|\omega_t\right]\\ &= \left[u'(B_\tau^{**})\left(\frac{1}{P_\tau^{B**}}\right)|\omega_t\right]\\ &> \left[u'(K_\tau^*)\left(\frac{1}{P_\tau^{K*}}\right)|\omega_t\right];\end{aligned} \tag{12.16}$$

that is, while QE might be effective in restoring equality between the w. m. u. of M, T and B, respectively, it fails to equalize the w. m. u. of money and bills and bonds with that of capital and would thus fail to stimulate investment demand.

The only way to ensure QE success, as Nick Rowe has provocatively suggested, would be for the government-owned central bank to "move toward communism," where the public sector purchases and owns all the assets in the economy.[5] In other words, the central bank could—at least, in principle—purchase equity shares directly, ultimately supplanting (or largely supplementing) the role of the private sector. In so doing, obviously, the central bank would move away from its proper domain and enter the realm of fiscal policy.

For extremely pessimistic expectations, one could even conceive of the possibility that agents holding asset B would be willing to get all the M they can in exchange for

[5] See Nick Rowe, "Fractional reserves, capital, communism, and the optimum quantity of money", Worthwhile Canadian Initiative, 8 September 2014, available at http://worthwhile.typepad.com/worthwhile_canadian_initi/2014/09/fractional-reserves-and-the-optimum-quantity-of-money.html.

B at its going price, thus neutralizing any effect that the central bank seeks to exert on long-term interest rates via QE: a sort of "super liquidity trap" would emerge as the agents strongly separated the assets they consider to be liquid (typically, bonds issues by a credible government) from all the others (typically, risky productive capital). In this case, too, obviously, and *a fortiori*, QE would fail to affect demand, since the use of the interest rate channel would be totally precluded to the central bank.

There is, however, an indirect (and slow motion) channel through which QE may stimulate the economy (assuming a neutral fiscal policy stance). By committing to fighting deflation through persistently low future interest rates, the central bank signals its determination to backstop recessionary tendencies. This may work through agent expectations, feeding new (positive) information into market sentiment, which eventually leads agents toward less pessimistic expectations, gradually affecting demand. Due to the indirect transmission mechanism of the policy stimulus and the lagged structure underpinning the change in market sentiment based on economic observables, this channel is necessarily slower and less effective than some alternative policy options discussed below that impact aggregate demand directly.

12.6.2 Acting Irresponsibly

Assume the central bank is willing to "*commit to being irresponsible*," in Paul Krugman's (1998) words, and ready "*to do whatever it takes*," in Mario Draghi's ones,[6] to drive the economy out of Secular Stagnation by augmenting inflation expectations. Also, ruling out "super liquidity traps" as described above, and with the ELB constraint binding, assume the central bank executes QE to achieve $\rho^B = 0$ and continues to purchase outstanding volumes of B to inject additional doses of M into the economy with a view to increasing the w. m. u. of consumption C and capital asset K by raising inflation expectations. The point is, in fact, that,

Proposition 12.5 *Under liquidity preference dominance, the central bank does not have effective channels to influence inflation expectations consistently.*

To show this, consider the impact of central bank's interest rate (conventional and unconventional) policies on aggregate demand. Start from consumption: assuming nominal interest rates on M, T, and B to have reached their lower bound, $\rho^M \approx \rho^T \approx \rho^B \approx 0$, future consumption cannot be affected through the interest rates. Under household optimal intertemporal plan (12.6)–(12.9), and optimal rules (12.11)–(12.12), future consumption declines as interest rates move down toward the lower bound. The only way for interest rate policy consistently to increase future consumption would be for the central bank to pay a positive interest rate on M on money balances (see Sect. 12.6.4).

---

[6] See his famous speech as President of the European Central Bank, at the Global Investment Conference in London, 26 July 2012.

Short of this option, the only strategic variable the central bank might seek to influence is the household's job value (Eq. 12.1). However, this can increase only if firms and households expect aggregate demand to revive as a result of central bank action: a circular argument.

Consider then investment: under liquidity preference dominance—Inequality (12.15)—the drop of nominal interest rates close to zero equates the w. m. u. of T and B to that of M, but does nothing to increase the relative attractiveness of risky asset K. To stimulate the demand for K, the central bank should seek to raise the m. u. of K (Eq. 12.10a). Since Eq. (12.10a) is strictly increasing in P^C, the central bank should aim at raising its level for a sustained period, implying higher future output sales from firms and higher sale prices that would feed back into the marginal efficiency of capital asset K and stimulate the demand for it. The central bank should therefore seek to fuel consumption; yet, as discussed above, it is unable to do so under the circumstances.

The conclusion is that QE is not effective in pulling the economy out of Secular Stagnation by revamping aggregate demand. On the other hand, and asymmetrically, expectations of QE reversals (or "tapering") would negatively and persistently affect price level P^C and would instantly lower the m. u. of K as a result.

Finally, and importantly, in the circumstances where QE succeeds in ensuring $\left[u'(M_\tau)|\omega'\right] = \left[u'(T_\tau)E_t\left(\frac{1}{P_\tau^T}\right)|\omega_{t'}\right] = \left[u'(B_\tau)E_t\left(\frac{1}{P_\tau^B}\right)|\omega_t\right]$, with $\omega_{t'} < \omega_t$, but also where $\left|D\rho^B\right| < \rho^{Q*} - \rho^Q$ and thus offers no incentive to new investment in K, households may search for higher yields and may eventually identify risky assets that are in short supply, whose supply adjusts only slowly to demand, and whose earning profile shows prospects of rapid gains. Under such circumstances, the liquidation cost of such assets would drop as their markets become more liquid. Assuming an asset S with such characteristics exists, optimal rules (12.11)–(12.12) would be violated since

$$\begin{aligned}\left[u'(S_\tau)\left(\frac{1}{P_\tau^{S*}}\right)|\omega_{t'}\right] &> \left[u'(C_\tau)\left(\frac{1}{P_\tau^{C*}}\right)|\omega_{t'}\right] = \left[u'(M_\tau)|\omega_{t'}\right] \\ &= \left[u'(T_\tau)\left(\frac{1}{P_\tau^{T*}}\right)|\omega_{t'}\right] = \left[u'(B_\tau)\left(\frac{1}{P_\tau^{B*}}\right)|\omega_{t'}\right] \\ &> \left[u'(K_\tau)\left(\frac{1}{P_\tau^{K*}}\right)|\omega_{t'}\right],\end{aligned}$$

and if—as would likely be the case—return differential $r^S - r^K$ was sufficiently large and expected to further increase swiftly, the households might want to shift some of their illiquid portfolio into S. This could lead to the formation of speculative bubbles. That is, the price of asset S would tend to overshoot its undistorted rational expectations equivalent (and to stay above it) and households would want to hold shares of S in excess with respect to the undistorted rational expectations equivalent, until market sentiment on S remains upbeat. No discernible effects on real aggregate economic activity would follow, however.[7]

Such are the risks that QE policies raise for the economy. The willingness of the central bank to "act irresponsibly" via the bond price channel might end up engendering irresponsible consequences with none (or very little) of the desired outcomes being achieved.

12.6.3 Forward Guidance

From the above findings follows (trivially) the ineffectiveness of forward interest rate policy guidance, which the central bank may use to communicate its intention to keep the policy interest rates at a low level for an indefinite period, even beyond the point when normalizing rates would be in order, thereby signaling its willingness to tolerate higher future inflation rates. In terms of the model above, forward guidance amounts to the central bank committing to keeping $\rho_\tau^M \approx \rho_\tau^T \approx 0$, for $\tau \in [t, \ldots t^+]$ and t^+ being an indefinite date into the future. As it has been discussed already, and in line with Eggertsson et al. (2017), this policy measure has no effect on aggregate demand under liquidity preference dominance. Like QE, however (but even more feebly than QE), forward guidance might affect expectations only moderately, its feebleness owing to the fact that, unlike QE, forward guidance by itself cannot directly impact longer term interest rates. Consequently, both its scope and depth are less than QE.

12.6.4 Negative Interest Rates

Would breaching the ELB by charging negative interest rates (NIR) on money holdings help the economy out of Secular Stagnation? The following proposition addresses this question.

Proposition 12.6 *Negative interest rates on money may stimulate demand, but with limitations; on the other hand, positive interest rates on money balances might be more effective.*

Assuming that NIR can be applied to cash (Buiter, 2009; Kimball, 2012), or simply assuming an interest-bearing central bank digital currency (CBDC) under NIR, from Eq. (12.10) the m. u. of money becomes:

$$u'(M_t) = u'(M_t|\omega_t) = E_t\left\{\beta\left(1+r^M\right)\left(1-\pi_{t+1}^c\right)\left\{u'\left(\frac{(1+r^M)M_t}{P_{t+1}^C}\right)\vartheta_{t+1}(\omega_t)+\right.\right.$$

[7] This result is similar to that discussed by Cochrane (2002) under the "convenience yield" view.

$$\sum_{\tau=t+1}^{T=\infty} \beta^{\tau}\left(1+r^{M}\right)^{\tau} \prod_{\tau=t+1}^{T=\infty} u'\left(\frac{(1+r^{M})M_t}{P_{\tau}^{C}}\right)\left(1-\pi_{\tau}^{c}\right)\left[1-\vartheta_{\tau}\left(\omega_t\right)\right]\left[1-\sigma_{\tau}^{M}\left(\Omega_t\right)\right]\vartheta_T(\omega_t)\Big\}\Big\}, \quad (12.10b)$$

where $r^M < 0$ and the price of M is no longer equal to unity but $P^M = 1 + r^M < 1$: money is de facto *"taxed"* by the central bank. Note from Eq. (12.10b) that the m. u. of M co-varies directly with its nominal rate of return if $u''_{r^M}(M) < 0$, as future holdings of M bear losses to their holders. Based on optimal rules (12.11)–(12.12), in so far as money is the only asset that gives immediate and costless access to real resources, and once the nominal interest rate on short-term treasury bill T approaches zero $r^T \approx 0$, the application of NIR leads to the following inequality:

$$\begin{aligned}\left[u'(C_\tau)\left(\frac{1}{P_\tau^{C*}}\right)|\omega'\right] &= \left[u'(T_\tau)\left(\frac{1}{P_\tau^{T*}}\right)|\omega_t{}'\right] \\ &= \left[u'(B_\tau)\left(\frac{1}{P_\tau^{B*}}\right)|\omega_t{}'\right] = \left[u'(K_\tau)\left(\frac{1}{P_\tau^{K*}}\right)|\omega'\right] \\ &> \left[\frac{u'(M_\tau)}{\left(1+r^M\right)}|\omega'\right].\end{aligned}$$

As a result, the demand for M declines, in principle stimulating consumption and the demand for other assets including capital K, with the overall stimulus effect ultimately depending on the intensity of the NIR policy, that is, on how far the central bank pushes the interest rate into negative territory. Yet, a too intensive use of NIR might induce the households to search for assets alternative to cash or CBDC, which earn better returns than "taxed" money and serve as a safer store of value and can be used as means of payment. Assume an asset A with such features is found. In such case, with liquidity preference dominating agent attitudes, the NIR signals would fail to be transmitted across the full spectrum of interest rates as households absorb as much of asset A as they can. In fact, the growing demand for A would raise its price and deliver a positive return to its holders. As a result, a new liquidity trap would emerge, the NIR stimulus would not impact household decisions to go less liquid (that is, consume and/invest in productive capital), and the economy would remain in Secular Stagnation.

Conversely to NIR policy, if money were to pay a positive interest rate (PIR), its m. u. would increase (although at a decreasing rate) and households would demand more of it until optimal rules (12.11)–(12.12) were satisfied, thus withdrawing stimulus from demand. However, if the central bank were to credibly persevere in raising PIR, so as to accommodate all the increasing demand for M, and pushed the PIR farther up until the supply of M to households reaches their demand satiation, the income effect of PIR would start exceeding its price effect and the households would get rid of "excess" balances by spending them on consumption and other assets in an attempt to restore optimal rules (12.11)–(12.12).

The PIR policy option carries analogies with the case of the central bank acting "irresponsibly" discussed earlier, but with an important difference: for PIR to be effective, the central bank must not rely on bond prices and should instead: (i) remunerate the cash held by households and (ii) raise cash remuneration to whatever highs is necessary. In this respect, PIR policy would resemble the "helicopter money" option to be discussed next.

Interestingly, the result showing the potential effectiveness of PIR—derived from the utility-based model used in this chapter (and introduced in Chap. 3)—is consistent with the predictions of Neo-Fisherian theory (Cochrane, 2016), whereby higher nominal interests *raise* inflationary expectations. In fact, the result of this chapter suggests the existence of a transmission mechanism running from interest rates on money to aggregate demand, which Neo-Fisherian theory fails to make explicit. In such theory, the positive relationship between nominal interest rates and expected inflation emerges purely as an equilibrium condition.

12.6.5 Helicopter Money

The idea of helicopter money (HM)—originally evoked by Milton Friedman (1969)—refers to a policy whereby new money is created by the central bank and is provided (*"dropped from helicopter"*) directly to households and private businesses, without generating new (public or private) debt, with a view to stimulating spending when the economy is in deep recession. Since central banks have generally no mandate to give money away (they can only exchange one asset for another) and to distribute it to select entities or the public, HM drops need to be backed by the budget-approval process and must essentially involve fiscal policymaking decisions (Grenville, 2013). In other words, HM requires a form of coordination between fiscal and monetary policies. The advantage of this *monetary cum fiscal* policy tool is to provide newly created purchasing power directly and at no cost to those (private and public sector) agents who can more immediately spend it (Bossone, 2016). In fact,

Proposition 12.7 *HM would directly affect aggregate demand.*

Today, the concept of HM extends to refer to the overt monetary financing of fiscal deficits, whereby central bank money creation supports aggregate demand by financing public spending or tax reduction programs. Buiter (2014) evaluates HM analytically through a formal model and identifies the conditions under which it boosts aggregate demand most effectively. One of these conditions is the irreversibility of the new money base stock creation, which constitutes a permanent addition to the total net wealth of the economy.

The impact of HM and the importance of the irreversibility condition can both be appreciated by considering the intertemporal budget constraints of the government and the household, respectively, Eqs. (12.3) and (12.7). As the government budget is partly and irreversibly funded by new central bank money, the fiscal budget constraint is permanently relaxed by an equivalent amount, implying that taxation can in turn be equally reduced and disposable income symmetrically increased. In this case, Eqs. (12.3) and (12.7) become, respectively,

$$G_\tau + r^T_{\tau-1}P^T_\tau T_\tau + r^B_{\tau-1}P^T_\tau B_\tau = P^T_\tau T_\tau + P^B_\tau B_\tau + Tax_\tau - Dtax_\tau + DM_\tau, \quad (12.3b)$$

where D $M_\tau = DTax_\tau$, and

$$\begin{aligned} P^C_\tau C_\tau + P^T_\tau T_\tau + P^B_\tau B_\tau + P^K_\tau K_\tau + (M_\tau + DM_\tau) \\ = y_\tau - (tax_\tau - Dtax_\tau) + M_{\tau-1} + r^T_{\tau-1}P^T_\tau T_\tau \\ + r^B_{\tau-1}P^T_\tau B_\tau + r^K_{\tau-1}P^K_\tau K_\tau. \end{aligned} \quad (12.7b)$$

Since irreversibility removes possible Ricardian Equivalence effects, consumption spending increases permanently. In fact, in the model of this paper HM acts also through the expectations channel: a large and sustained stimulus combining monetary and fiscal levers through Eq. (12.3b) increases the household's job value, Eqs. (12.1) and (12.2), and hence consumption through a less stringent budget constraint (Eq. (12.7b)) and raises the m. u. of both C and K (the latter via Eq. (12.10a)) by increasing output Y and consumption good price P^C: HM reverses pessimistic expectations and pushes the economy out of Secular Stagnation.

Irreversibility

A comment on irreversibility, contrary to what one could be led to believe,[8] the irreversibility condition does not imply that the central bank is to surrender the use of monetary policy forever. Irrespective of how the central bank engineers HM drops,[9] the newly created money would increase the economy's nominal financial wealth permanently and affect aggregate demand always (Turner, 2013, 2015). However, in all cases and at any point in time, the central bank could tighten monetary conditions if circumstances so require, for instance, by selling bonds held in its portfolio via open market operations,[10] or by issuing its own non-money debt liabilities. Such operations would change the composition and market value of the new financial wealth, depending on asset price changes and agent liquidity preference, but not the

[8] See, for, instance White (2013). See also, more recently Borio (2017), and my counterarguments (Bossone 2016).

[9] HM could be effect either by financing the government budget, with the central bank issuing reserves to purchase government debt, or by financing the private sector directly, with the central bank crediting the accounts of selected categories of individual economic agents with newly created reserves.

[10] In the case of HM drops injected through budget deficit monetization, a central bank wanting to undertake open market operations to offset HM injections would have to use debt instruments held in its possession other than those purchased under the HM and permanently monetized: once purchased, those debt instruments are effectively canceled.

amount of the new financial wealth created through HM. Only taxation could undo the financial wealth so created.[11]

Ricardian Equivalence

Utility analysis suggests that, even if agents were to expect an HM injection at present, to be followed by an equivalent tax increase at some future date, Ricardian Equivalence would not neutralize the HM stimulus since

$$\left[\frac{u'(DM_t)}{P_t^C}||\omega_t\prime\right] > \beta^{(\tau-t)}R^{(\tau-t)}E_t\left[\frac{u'(-Dtax_\tau)}{P_\tau^C}|\omega_\tau\right], \tag{12.17}$$

where $\omega_t\prime < \omega_\tau$, and $\tau > t$, even if $DM_t = -Dtax_\tau \beta^{(\tau-t)}R^{(\tau-t)}\frac{P_\tau^C}{P_t^C}$.

The rationale underpinning Inequality (12.17) is that any addition to the money stock *DM*, under an HM operation and a symmetric tax increase *DTax,* which would be intended to "undo" *DM* at some future dates, are both state-contingent policy decisions that take place under different economic conditions. Whereas HM would be executed in situations of economic depression and would be highly valued by people suffering from current unemployment and uncertain income prospects, a future symmetric tax increase would be expected to take place at a time of better employment and economic prospects, that is, in a situation where people would be better placed to absorb (and accept) higher taxes. Different underlying expectations and market sentiments would affect the utility calculation and the net welfare effects of the two symmetric policies and lead to the inequality above.

12.6.6 Fiscal Policy

By comparison with the HM policy just discussed, the fundamental factor characterizing fiscal policy is that the government can use only debt and taxation to finance its budget: relaxing the budget constraint now to allow for current lower taxation (or higher public spending) requires larger government indebtedness, which in turn implies higher taxation and/or lower public spending at some future dates. Whether, and to what extent, this is going to weigh negatively on current consumption decisions from rational households in actual (as opposed to theoretical) circumstances depends on various factors, such as, inter alia, their relevant time-horizon and the factors binding their rationality, as well as the conditions and sustainability of public finances and the credibility of the fiscal and monetary authorities.

It should be noted that, at times when $\rho_\tau^T = \rho_\tau^B = 0$, and real interest rates are negative, running a front-loaded expansionary budget with a view to back-loading the needed fiscal adjustment to some future date may seem to be a winning strategy to help the economy out of stagnation. However, the question is how the issuance of

[11] Taxation could take the form of government general taxation on the economy or the form of quasi-fiscal taxation like a higher reserve requirement by the central bank.

new public debt obligations would affect the current equilibrium interest rate. The answer ultimately depends on debt sustainability assessments. For a largely indebted country, for instance, the success of the fiscal stimulus would depend on the markets trusting the positive impact of the larger fiscal deficit on output growth and future debt sustainability. This would allow interest rates on the public debt to remain low as the government stretches its budget to finance the stimulus. Expectations would be self-fulfilling, and the fiscal stimulus would be effective.

Yet, since multiple equilibria are always possible—as influenced by market beliefs—an element of uncertainty would be inherent in the exclusive use of fiscal policy as a way out of Secular Stagnation. Just to stay with the above example, if markets were not to trust the effectiveness of the stimulus and were instead to anticipate a negative impact on debt and its servicing cost, the fiscal stimulus would lose effectiveness. Similarly, in largely indebted economies (especially those with no resort to the monetary policy lever) agents would expect any budgetary stimulus to be followed by corrective measures to neutralize the overall impact on the debt, thus setting in Ricardian Equivalence effects. Much deeper analysis of the effect of credibility on policy effectiveness is developed in the next two chapters.

For the above reasons, fiscal policy ranks second to HM as an effective tool to lift the economy from Secular Stagnation, since only HM can add to the economy's net financial wealth and boost demand directly and without altering the economy's debt profile by relaxing both the budget constraints of the government and households permanently in a way that fiscal policy, alone, cannot do.

12.7 Would Helicopter Money Be Enough?

Helicopter money can be effective to deliver a quick expansionary shock to an economy that would otherwise mire persistently into depression, and to send a strong public signal of the government's determination toward recovery. Yet, HM could not (and should not) provide a steady solution to keep the economy at full employment, especially in a situation where output potential has been permanently lowered by stagnant demand. Here is where the shock therapy must be complemented (and supplemented) by structural changes and where, again, Keynes' vision of the economy comes to the rescue. Noting that Keynes did never advocate the creation of chronic public deficits, he was for a much greater role of "social investments" to stabilize a capitalist economy at its full-employment potential and make it prosper in the longer term.[12]

Keynes proposed the definition of an "ordinary balance sheet" and a "capital account balance," providing for a separation that reflects the separation between

[12] In fact, he argued that public spending should generate effective benefits over time (Brown-Collier and Collier, 1995; Dwyer, 2011) and be able to repay itself.

public consumption and investment.[13] The ordinary budget reports current expenses and revenues and records the amortization of public debt, while the capital account balance shows the investment expenses. The distinction between the two budget definitions makes it possible to distinguish, in turn, two types of fiscal policy: deficit fiscal interventions and investment interventions. The former are a means to cure cyclical imbalances; the latter are a way to maintain a structural level of full employment.

Keynes opposed the use of the ordinary budget to stabilize the cycle, as well as the financing of public works and the use of taxation to affect the level of private consumption. Rather, he argued that, under normal conditions, the ordinary budget must have surpluses which, from time to time, must be transferred to the capital account to expand investments that generate a positive return. He admitted the use of debt, but to support investments that generate positive financial or economic returns that allow the government to repay the initial debt.

Keynes viewed with concern the accumulation of public debt issued to finance current spending (what he called "dead-weight debt") and believed that the ordinary budget should not be in deficit, while investment spending must be partly financed by debt and for the rest from taxes. This, again, implied that there should be no debt issuance to meet recurring expenses.

Keynes never argued that current or investment spending must be unconditionally deficit-financed,[14] and a careful reading of his contribution shows that he was generally against short-term fiscal activism. For Keynes, reliance on debt-financed government spending during a recession was a "second best" remedy, which can only be used temporarily if the capital account proves insufficient to maintain full employment. Instead, his basic vision was in favor of a permanent enlargement of the public sector, aimed at supporting the level of output and preventing fluctuations. High and stable public spending ensures full employment, while allowing the ordinary budget to remain balanced or in surplus. In this way, the economy minimizes output fluctuations around the full-employment potential, and prevents stagnation, through a high *socialization of investments*, preserving fiscal balance and ensuring the provision of the public goods necessary to support the economy's long-term development. In Keynes' own words, strongly doubting that the influence of monetary policy on the rate of interest would be sufficient by itself to determine an optimum rate of investment, he held that «...a somewhat comprehensive socialization of investment will prove the only means of securing an approximation to full employment; though

---

[13] Keynes defined the capital account budget as "a regular survey and analysis of the relationship between sources of savings and different types of investment and a balance sheet showing how they have been brought into equality for the past year, and a forecast of the same for the year to come" (see The Collected Writings of John Maynard Keynes, Volume 27: Activities 1940–1946: Shaping the Post-War World: Employment and Commodities, Moggridge, 1980, p. 368). Hence, on the capital account balance, the government predicts the private demand deficit and sets a level of public investment spending that meets the savings-investment requirements for full employment.

[14] As to why he did not give an unreservedly negative judgment on Abba Lerner's functional finance, despite his own LPT being with in flagrant contradiction with it, I suggest an opinion in Bossone (2020).

this need not exclude all manner of compromises and of devices by which public authority will co-operate with private initiative» (Keynes, 1936, p. 378).[15]

It is to be noted, however, that socializing investment did not necessarily imply an expansion of state ownership of assets, as in fact «...no obvious case is made out for a system of State Socialism which would embrace most of the economic life of the community. It is not the ownership of the instruments of production which it is important for the State to assume. If the State is able to determine the aggregate amount of resources devoted to augmenting the instruments and the basic rate of reward to those who own them, it will have accomplished all that is necessary» (Keynes, 1936, p. 378).

12.8 Concluding Remarks

This chapter has analyzed the emergence of Secular Stagnation as the consequence of a rise of strong liquidity preference caused by the upsurge and persistence of pessimistic expectations. The chapter has used a model where: (i) agents derive utility from holding assets of different liquidity, (ii) the utility provided by each asset is explicitly derived, and (iii) rational expectations interact with changes in market sentiment driven by variations in economic observables. Also, in the model future household income does not just stochastically fluctuate around its full-employment equilibrium level: households incorporate within their plans the possibility of protracted periods of underemployment or unemployment income.

In the model, Secular Stagnation emerges from the asset stock dynamics ultimately generated by liquidity considerations, rather than by investment vs. saving relations. The chapter has also investigated the effectiveness of a broad range of demand management policies in dealing with Secular Stagnation, concluding that "helicopter money" and fiscal policy (in that order of effectiveness) can boost aggregate demand and output in an economy in Secular Stagnation, whereas other unconventional forms of monetary policy are very likely to prove ineffective under pessimistic expectations and when liquidity preference strongly dominates agent attitudes, or they might even provoke undesirable consequences (as it could be the case with quantitative easing and, even worse, with negative interest rates on money). The model has shown why raising interest rates on money balances may yield Neo-Fisherian outcomes. The model has also shown why flexible prices may not provide a re-equilibrating mechanism to help the economy out of Secular Stagnation when rational expectations are distorted by market sentiment (indeed, the reverse would hold). Finally, in addition to re-evaluating LPT, this chapter has drawn further lessons from Keynes' view of how to stabilize a capitalist economy at its full-employment potential.

But besides all this, a key question is whether money is always and everywhere effective when it trades as an asset in the international financial markets. This question lies at the core of Chap. 13.

---

[15] For further development of the concept of socialization of investment, see Bellofiore (2014).

References

Bellofiore, R. (2014), The socialization of investment, from keynes to minsky and beyond. Levy Economics Institute Working Paper No. 822 , December.

Benhabib, J., Schmitt-Grohé, S., & Uribe, M. (2001). The perils of Taylor rules. *Journal of Economic Theory, 96*(1), 40–69.

Blanchard, O. (2023). *Secular stagnation is not over.* Published on the Peterson Institute for International Economics (PIIE), 24 January 24.

Blanchard, O. J., & Fischer, S. (1989). *Lectures on macroeconomics.* MIT Press.

Borio, C. (2017). Secular stagnation or financial cycle drag?. *Business Economics, Palgrave Macmillan; National Association for Business Economics, 52*(2), 87–98, April.

Bossone, B. (2016). *The true costs of helicopter money.* VoxEu, 5 September

Bossone, B. (2020). Global finance and effectiveness of macro-policies. *World Economics, 21*(2), 135–164.

Brown-Collier, E. K., & Collier, B. E. (1995). What Keynes really said about deficit spending. *Journal of Post Keynesian Economics, 17*(3) (Spring), 341–355.

Buiter, W. H. (2009). *Negative interest rates: When are they coming to a Central Bank Near You?.* Financial Times, Willem Buiter's Mavercon, 7 May.

Buiter, W. H. (2014). The simple analytics of helicopter money: why it works – always. *Economics, 8,* 2014–28.

Buiter, W. H. (2023). *Secular stagnation, not secular stagflation.* Project Syndicate, 6 January.

Caballero, R. J., Farhi, E. (2013). *A model of the safe asset mechanism (SAM): Safety traps and economic policy, mimeo.*

Cochrane, J. H. (2002). *Stocks as money: Convenience yield and the tech-stock bubble, presented at the Chicago Fed Conference on asset price bubbles*, April 2002.

Cochrane, J. (2016). *Do higher interest rates raise or lower inflation?.* Mimeo (Available at http://faculty.chicagobooth.edu/john.cochrane/research/papers/fisher.pdf).

Di Bucchianico, S. (2019). A critical analysis of the secular stagnation theory. Departmental Working Papers of Economics - University 'Roma Tre' 0245, Department of Economics - University Roma Tre.

Dufrenot, G. & Rhouzlane, M. (2018). Secular stagnation: new challenges for the industrialized countries in the 21st century. AMSE Working Papers 1818, Aix-Marseille School of Economics, France.

Dwyer, J. (2011). *Keynes's economics and the question of public debt.* The University of Sydney, 28 October.

Eggertsson, G. B., & Mehotra, N. R. (2014). *A model of secular stagnation, mimeo.* Brown University.

Eggertsson, G. B., Mehrotra, N. R., & Robbins, J. A. (2017). *A model of secular stagnation: theory and quantitative evaluation.* NBER Working Paper No. 23093, January

Eggertsson, G. B., & Krugman, P. (2012), Debt, deleveraging, and the liquidity trap: a Fisher-Minsky-Koo approach. *The Quarterly Journal of Economics, 127*(3), August, 1469–1513.

Farmer, R. E. A. (2012). Confidence, crashes and animal spirits. *The Economic Journal, 122*(559), 155–172.

Friedman, M. (1969). *Optimum quantity of money.* Aldine Publishing Company.

Grenville, S. (2013). *Helicopter money.* VoxEu, 24 February.

Guvenen, F. (2017). *Understanding income risk: New insights from big data—Large data sets reveal new insights into the risks individuals face from fluctuating incomes.* Federal reserve Bank of Minneapolis, June 26.

Hall, R. E. (2013). *The routes into and out of the zero lower bound, prepared for the Federal Reserve Bank of Kansas City's Jackson Hole symposium.* Global Dimensions of Unconventional Monetary Policy, August 23, 2013.

Hansen, A. (1939). Economic progress and declining population growth. *American Economic Review, 29*(1), 1–15.

Keynes, J. M. (1936). *The general theory of employment, interest and money*. Macmillan.

Kimball, M. (2012). *Getting the biggest bang for the buck in fiscal policy*. Confessions of a supply-side liberal, May 29, 2012.

Kozlowski, J., Veldkamp, L., & Venkateswaran, V. (2015). *The tail that wags the economy: Belief-driven business cycles and persistent stagnation*. NBER Working Paper No. 21719.

Krugman, P. (1998). It's Baaack! Japan's slump and the return of the liquidity trap. *Brookings Papers on Economic Activity, 2*, 1998.

Lo, A. (2017). *Adaptive markets*. Princeton University Press.

Pfister, H. R., & Böhm, G. (2008). The multiplicity of emotions: A framework of emotional functions in decision making. *Judgment and Decision Making, 3*(1), 5–17.

Roubini, N. (2022). The return of high inflation and stagflation. Project Syndicate, 13 June.

Summers, L. H. (2013). *Speech at the IMF fourteenth annual economic research conference in honor of Stanley Fischer*.

Teulings, C., & Baldwin, R. (eds.) (2014). *Secular stagnation: Facts, causes, and cures*. VoxEU.org eBook, CEPR Press.

Tily, G. (2012). *Keynes's monetary theory of interest*. BIS Paper No. 65c, May.

Turner, A. (2013). *Debt, money and Mephistopheles: How do we get out of this mess*. Cass business school lecture, 6 February.

Turner, A. (2015). *The case for monetary finance—an essentially political issue*. Paper presented at the 16th Jacques Polak Annual Research Conference Hosted by the International Monetary Fund Washington, DC, November 5–6.

White, W. (2013). *Overt monetary financing (OMF) and crisis management*. June 12, Project Syndicate.

Chapter 13
The Portfolio Theory of Inflation and Money (In)Effectiveness

Abstract This chapter investigates the pivotal role that Global Investors play in the valuation of currency and various financial instruments within economically integrated markets, emphasizing their international trading dynamics. Grounded in the innovative Portfolio Theory of Inflation (PTI), it delves into the complex interplay between capital allocation decisions made by these investors and the domestic monetary and fiscal policies employed by countries. By focusing on how Global Investors respond to country-specific attributes, particularly credibility, the chapter outlines the limited policy space available for national authorities. It highlights the circumstance that countries with perceived low credibility face significant constraints on implementing active macroeconomic policies, leading to adverse outcomes such as currency depreciation and heightened inflation rather than desired economic growth. This analysis ultimately reveals that the effectiveness of fiscal and monetary policies is inherently tied to the perceptions of Global Investors, thus reshaping our understanding of economic sovereignty and the intricate mechanisms of macroeconomic policy effectiveness in a globalized landscape.

13.1 Preamble

In the years of the EU debt crisis, as I discussed policy issues with French economist Charles Wyplosz, one thing he said made me think. He claimed that the effectiveness of macroeconomic policies cannot be unaffected by the credibility of the country enacting the policies. This idea, as I thought, suggested that a country undertaking an expansionary policy program would achieve different outcomes depending on how credible the markets consider it to be. Yet, for this to work, I thought, the financial markets where financial claims on governments (like money and public debt) are traded should be large and deep enough to affect the governments' policy options, so that if the credibility of a country is perceived to be low, issuing more claims to stimulate the economy would only lead to nominal effects (i.e., currency depreciation and higher inflation), rather than to more output and employment: with global financial markets, the policy space available to countries would be endogenous

B. Bossone, *Trailblazing Visions of Money in Economic Theory*, Contributions to Economics, https://doi.org/10.1007/978-3-031-82544-6_13

to investor decisions. Moreover, if markets form a given belief on a country's policy performance, they can make it happen—not because they make the right choices, but because they can (re)orient their investments to the point where they choices are proven right. This further reinforces the conclusion drawn in Chap. 11 regarding the Lucas Critique. It highlights that markets are increasingly driven by actors who possess the power to actualize the predictions of the model they view as the correct representation of the economy in which they are invested.

A fundamental, and admittedly radical, implication of this conclusion is that what matters for making valid economic predictions is not having knowledge of the right model of the economy, but rather understanding the model that the markets believe to be right, since they possess the power to enforce it. It follows that for sound policy making, it is necessary for a country to either conform to the good conduct criteria set by the markets or minimize its reliance on the markets.

I tried to study these relationships and discovered in the process that, to do so successfully, I had first to build a micro–macro model centered on a representative class of "Global investors," which would allow to analyze how the portfolio choices of this class of agents would impact the effectiveness of monetary and fiscal policies. This model eventually led me to establish what I called the "Portfolio Theory of Inflation, the subject of this chapter.

13.2 Introduction

From the very outset of this book, I have firmly asserted my belief in the non-neutrality of money. However, can we unequivocally claim that money non-neutrality is always and everywhere applicable? Isn't its effectiveness potentially influenced by how agents adjust their expectations in response to new policy shocks? If that is the case, wouldn't the credibility that agents confer upon policymakers significantly shape those expectations? Additionally, how might the expectations of agents with substantial influence over the value of money affect its effectiveness?

I have come to believe that answering these questions is what ultimately explains why, in Japan, expansionary fiscal and monetary policies of unprecedented duration and intensity achieved high employment at virtually zero inflation, during Abenomics, while considerably lesser stimuli in Turkey caused the lira to collapse and inflation dangerously to rise, in recent years; or why in the United States, the Federal Reserve and Treasury succeeded in bringing unemployment down to historic record lows without overheating the economy, after to the Great Recession of the late 2000s, whereas in the same period anti-recessionary fiscal and monetary expansion in Mexico only resulted in currency depreciation and higher inflation (Ahumada, 2009).

While these questions broadly stem from the inquiry posed by Obstfeld and Taylor (2004) regarding the true autonomy of monetary policy in financially open economies, they extend further in that they aim to explore whether (hypothetically) identical policy decisions, made within the constraints of financial globalization, can yield different outcomes based on country-specific characteristics as perceived by financial markets. As discussed in this chapter, answering these questions entails investigating the micro-foundations of global investment choices and their aggregate impact on the domestic policy space.

Interestingly, as I was closing this chapter, I run by chance into a working paper Philip Arestis and Malcolm Sawyer, who in the late nineties had alluded to the constraining role of financial markets on macroeconomic policy from a by post-Keynesian perspective (Arestis and Sawyer, 1997). I wish to quote two key passages from their paper. They argue that,

> Even if the actions of the financial markets are based on bubbles, fads etc. they may nevertheless influence the economic fundamentals. Clearly, if the fad raises interest rates, investment may be thereby effected and hence the fundamentals of the economy changed. Similarly, a falling exchange rate would stimulate domestic inflation which would change the fundamental value of the (nominal) exchange rate. Even when financial asset prices reflect fundamentals, the operation of financial markets may still pose a constraint on the economic policies pursued. (p. 6),

and continue by raising a question and sketching out the answer,

> In a world of uncertainty where knowledge of the economic fundamentals is given to few, it is perhaps inevitable that asset prices will fluctuate and follow fads and fashions. The significant question here is whether the adoption of a Keynesian demand reflation would set off adverse reactions in the financial markets, and whether those reactions undermine the reflation. The reactions are likely to create an air of crisis and strong political pressures to abort the reflation. (p.6).

The answer suggested by Arestis and Sawyer is demonstrated by the PTI discussed in this chapter. As I have several times emphasized in recent years,[1] despite the history of trade and financial globalization the world has gone through over several decades, the economic models that are typically employed to analyze the impacts of monetary and fiscal policies fail to acknowledge explicitly the influence wielded by Global investors on the market price of public sector financial claims, encompassing both money and debt, causing theory to fail comprehending the limitations that financial markets may pose to macro-policy effectiveness.

This holds true for conventional orthodox (mainstream) modeling, where local agents—families, businesses, and institutions—are depicted as sovereign entities making optimal allocative decisions within a set of possible options, as well as for heterodox approaches,[2] whereby governments are assumed to possess the capacity to issue all necessary money to finance public spending. Both paradigms, in fact, start from presuming that local agents have full sovereignty over their economic choices and (can) make optimal choices.

Especially in open and internationally highly financially integrated ("globalized") economies, the valuation of the financial claims on the public sector and the available space for expansionary monetary and fiscal policies are determined by the expectations and trading activities of a special class of economic actors—here called "Global

---

[1] See Bossone (2018, 2019, 2020c, 2020d, 2021b, 2022a, 2023a).

[2] See, for instance, the case of Modern Money Theory (MMT) as discussed in Chap. 14.

investors"—to be defined later,[3,4] Consequently, a comprehensive macro-analysis must bring Global investors to the forefront to comprehend how policies operate in the global financial context and to assess their impact on the real economy. This becomes even more imperative with the growing significance of the international bond market as a substantial source of external finance for numerous countries, coupled with a noteworthy surge in debt issuance following an extended period of low interest rates before the resurgence of inflation caused by the supply shocks caused by the COVID19 pandemic, first, and the Russian invasion of Ukraine, subsequently.

This chapter is about the Portfolio Theory of Inflation (PTI), which I have developed using the above arguments (as discussed in my cited works) and its implications. In the following sections, the micro- and macro-foundations of the PTI model are illustrated, which offer a rigorous framework for the analysis of Global investors' portfolio choices and their impact on the effectiveness of monetary and fiscal policies. The PTI analyzes how capital allocations by Global investors interact with monetary and fiscal policies.[5] Specifically, it examines how a country's level of policy credibility factors into the international capital allocation decisions of Global investors and how these decisions shape the country's policy space.

In the following, Sect. 13.4 reviews the literature on which the PTI builds; Sect. 13.5 discusses the role of Global investors in today's globalized economies, and how this role shapes the policy space available to countries; Sect. 13.6 reconsiders economic sovereignty in the context of globalized economies; Sect. 13.7 describes the economic model underpinning the PTI and the results from the application of the PTI model to the dynamics of exchange rate, inflation and output following macro-policy shocks. Section 13.8 appraises the policy implications of the results; Sect. 13.9 discusses the innovative aspect of the PTI as a new theory of inflation; and Sect. 13.10 concludes the chapter. Four appendices supplements the contents of the article: the first appendix shows that countries with higher (lower) policy credibility enjoy larger (narrower) policy space, using a "Allais-Baumol-Tobin" demand-for-money function modified to incorporate country credibility; the second appendix discusses the analytical foundations of country policy credibility; the third appendix derives analytically the utility delivered by money and other financial assets to their holders (following Chap. 3); and the fourth appendix describes narratively the transmission mechanisms of fiscal and monetary policy impulses in globalized economies and evaluates their effectiveness; the fourth and last appendix.

[3] The expression "policy space" denotes the leeway available to policymakers for implementing expansionary monetary and fiscal policies without jeopardizing the viability of public sector claims. It also implies the threshold at which measures may become imperative to guarantee long-term sustainability, potentially leading to the reconsideration or reversal of the initial policy measures.

[4] From Chap. 2, and the correct accounting terminology therein discussed, money and public debt in this chapter will be referred to as government "claims" (not "liabilities") or claims that the public sector issues on itself and are held by third parties.

[5] In this context, some corrections are made (and noted in the text) to some of the formal results I derived in previous works.

13.3 Review of the Literature

The PTI-based arguments discussed in this article overlap to some extent with those of Fritz et al. (2018), which show from a Keynesian-structuralist perspective that the international monetary asymmetry related to currency hierarchy imposes major constraints on the adoption of Keynesian policies in globalized economies. These constraints, accordingly, vary over time and space and depend on certain structures, including the global monetary regime and the specific domestic institutions and policy variables in place.

While consistent with the currency-hierarchy arguments, and possibly complementing them, the PTI differs from their underpinning theory. First, in PTI analysis, country credibility—not currency hierarchy—is the factor that ultimately shapes an economy's policy space[6]: a country may be (geo-economically) peripheral, and its currency low-hierarchy (in terms of international acceptance), but if it is perceived (by Global investors) to be highly credible, it enjoys a large policy space.[7] Second, whereas in the structuralist tradition the adjective "peripheral" is typically referred to "emerging market economies," in PTI analysis peripheral countries can include advanced economies that are attributed (by Global investors) different levels of credibility even though they share the same high-hierarchy currency: in this case, the policy space of each of these countries would be differently constrained.[8] In fact, a country could be peripheral in the structuralist sense, and thus belong to the group of emerging market economies, and yet be reputed as more credible than advanced economies.[9] Finally, PTI analysis is centered on a special class of market players—the Global investors—who hold the power to affect the policy space of the countries where they invest their manage wealth; PTI models the portfolio choice process adopted by Global investors and shows analytically how this choice process shapes the policy space of globalized economies and how the asset price dynamics in markets dominated by Global investors causes the real effects of Keynesian policies in weakly credible countries to dissipate in currency depreciation and higher inflation.

As regards the PTI specifically and the related literature, reference is made here to the research that is pertinent to each of the two pillars upon which the theory rests: i) the portfolio balance approach (PBA) to exchange rate determination, as modified to incorporate intertemporal choices by Global investors, and ii) the relationship between policy credibility, exchange rate and inflation.

---

[6] Undeniably, country credibility and currency hierarchy are closely interrelated, the former being a necessary (though not sufficient) condition for the currency of a country to achieve and maintain high-hierarchy status. Appendix 1 uses a modified version of the Allais-Baumol-Tobin inventory model for transaction money demand to show the relation between the demand for a currency and country credibility.

[7] Examples would include Abu Dhabi, Denmark, Hong Kong, New Zealand, Norway, Qatar, Singapore, South Korea, Taiwan, UAE.

[8] Examples are the EU countries.

[9] Using credit ratings as a proxy for country credibility, see the list at https://tradingeconomics.com/country-list/rating.

First pillar. In the PTI, the exchange rate is determined as in the PBA.[10] Here, financial markets create demand for predetermined stock supplies of domestic and foreign assets (e.g., money and bonds) and assets are imperfect substitutes. As in the PBA the PTI assumes that assets are part of the investor portfolios and changes in asset supplies induce investors to re-balance their portfolios based on risk-return considerations, setting in motion an adjustment process that influences, inter alia, the exchange rate via changes in the demand for assets denominated in different currencies. However, the PTI also goes beyond the PBA in that it assumes a highly integrated world capital market driven by investors who act globally and allocate resources across countries based on intertemporal optimization criteria (to be discussed below). Furthermore, the PTI gives prominence to governments' intertemporal budget constraint as an essential component in the market process to determine the value of national public debts. Finally, the PTI model encompasses a central role for money both as a monetary policy tool and as one of the economy's assets.

The PTI relies on a micro-founded model with intertemporal decisions, which draws inspiration on the Modern Open Economy Macroeconomics (MOEM).[11] Yet, it also diverges significantly from it. Rather than focusing on individual countries as intertemporally optimizing agents, as MOEM does, the PTI places emphasis on investors making critical cross-country resource allocation decisions from a global perspective and studies how such decisions choices affect the effectiveness of monetary and fiscal policies in countries with different policy credibility.

Distinctively, and to summarize, while the analysis of macro policy effectiveness typically assumes implicitly (as in the case of the PBA) or explicitly (as in the case of MOEM) that resource allocation decisions are taken by domestic agents, the PTI assumes that critical resource allocation decisions in globalized economies are taken by Global investors and uses this assumption to show that these decisions affect the effectiveness of monetary and fiscal policies at the country level.

Second pillar. The PTI falls within the strand of research on credibility initiated by Agénor (1994) and Calvo and Végh (1991), and further developed by Calvo and Reinhart (2002) under their "fear of floating" concept. In the literature, most research related to this topic is empirical and covers both the analysis of the pass-through effect from the exchange rate to inflation and the relationship between policy credibility and the intensity of the exchange rate pass-through (ERPT). On the ERPT effect, a relevant reference is the work by Benigno and Faia (2016), which uses US data to evaluate the channels through which globalization (especially in trade) has raised the degree of ERPT due to trade openness, greater competition, and the growing share of foreign products sold domestically. Furthermore, in 2016 the central bank of Sweden found that, since 2014, domestic inflation had shown a rising trend mostly led by krona depreciation (Riksbank, 2016). More generally, as a study from the Bank for International Settlements has found, while the ERPT effect in emerging market economies has decreased following the 2008–09 financial crisis, the effect in advanced economies has remained relatively low and stable

[10] See references in Branson (1985) and Wang (2009).

[11] See Obstfeld and Rogoff (1995, 1996).

over time (Jašová et al., 2016).[12] These findings suggest that policy credibility—all else being equal—weakens the link between the exchange rate and inflation. In Canada, for example, where exchange rate movements have historically had a material impact on the prices of consumer goods, the ERPT effect has recently been shown to have only a transitory influence over the rate of inflation, which is explained by long-run inflation expectations having being anchored near the Bank of Canada's inflation target, thereby playing a mitigating role on the ERPT (Savoie-Chabot & Khan, 2015). This causal relationship seems to be supported by several studies. Aleem and Lahiani (2014) show that a lower ERPT is associated with a credible monetary policy aiming at controlling inflation and find evidence that the EPRT is higher in Latin American countries than in East Asian countries, where it has declined since the adoption of an inflation targeting monetary policy.[13] A similar result was observed by Edwards (2006) examining emerging market economies, and by Takhtamanova (2008) analyzing OECD countries. Carrière-Swallow et al. (2016) and Lopez-Villavicencio and Mignon (2016) identify strong links between the ERPT and the monetary policy regime's performance in delivering price stability in several emerging economies. This result is further corroborated by Kabundi and Mlachila (2018) for South Africa and by Winkelried (2014) for Peru. Looking at the Brazilian experience, Ferreira de Mendonça and Tostes (2014) find that not only monetary but also fiscal policy credibility matters for reducing the pass-through on inflation of market prices and inflation expectations.

Finally, the PTI results discussed in this article, on the effectiveness of macroeconomic policies in relation to the credibility of the countries undertaking them, are in line with the empirical findings by Calderón et al. (2004) based on a panel of 11 emerging market economies and time-series data for Chile. These findings show that the cyclical properties of macroeconomic policies depend critically on policy credibility and support the conclusion that countries with higher credibility (as reflected by lower country risk levels) can conduct countercyclical fiscal and monetary policies, while countries with less credible policies fail to do so.

More recently, a growing literature has shown that investment funds are the most active investors and the most responsive to price signals in the debt markets, resembling very closely the role played by the Global investors according to the PTI.[14] Recent empirical findings will be discussed in Sect. 13.7.2.

---

[12] As regards emerging market economies, the following country studies on the ERPT effect are worth mentioning. Zelealem and Musila (2018) examine the temporal relationships between inflation and exchange rate changes, and their implications for the trade balance, and find that in the long run a real depreciation leads to an increase in inflation. Suleiman et al. (2018) estimate the quantitative effects of exchange rate depreciation on budget deficit and inflation in Nigeria and find that the impact of the exchange rate on inflation is positive, although it is not statistically significant. Also, a substantial ERPT effect, although incomplete and slow, has been found for Egypt by Helmy et al. (2018), who attribute the reason for the incompleteness and slowness to the circumstance that the consumer price index in Egypt include a relatively large number of subsidized commodities and goods with administered prices.

[13] In other words, the more credible the central bank, the quicker inflation returns to its steady-state level from before it suffered a shock.

[14] See Faia et al. (2024) and references therein, and see Fang et al. (2024).

13.4 The Relevance of Global Investors

In a globalized economy, local investors typically act as price takers and route their investments through Global investors (or through local intermediaries which then operate through Global investors), even if they hold a substantial share of the economy's wealth and engage in foreign investments. The pricing of internationally traded assets is in fact determined by Global investors, which act as "marginal" investors due to their size, interconnectedness, and comparative advantage.[15]

These global players may include various types of entities, ranging from international banks to institutional investors, broker-dealers, money market funds, private equity companies, hedge funds, asset managers, and special purpose entities. While not necessarily foreign entities, Global investors encompass a diverse range, including resident individuals, domestic subsidiaries of foreign entities, and foreign entities collaborating with local agents. With access to substantial resources and information processing capabilities, Global investors operate with significantly lower trading costs compared to local agents. Unlike local agents, they are not subject to "home bias" and allocate only a modest fraction of their managed wealth to local consumption. Alternatively, those Global investors residing in major global financial centers may indeed feature home bias (Subramanian et al. 2009); yet they are indifferent to the "home interests" that relate to the other countries where they invest, which then amplifies the effects of their portfolio reallocation decisions away from these countries when their risk perception of these countries deteriorates. In all cases, the primary objective pursued by Global investors is to maximize the net returns from the financial wealth they manage, prioritizing the protection and growth of their investments. They are not interested in the stability of the countries where they invest, until and unless expectations of instability put the value of their investments at risk. In such cases, Global investors may deem the financial claims on a country's public sector as less safe and swiftly reallocate their investments elsewhere. And since they determine the value of these claims at the margin, the demand for these same claims from local agents might not be enough to prevent its depreciation.

13.5 Global Investors and Economic Sovereignty

Although debt contracts are commonly denominated in nominal terms, investors acquire them as claims on real resources, anticipating the recovery of the full real value of their investment along with interest. Contracts expressed in domestic currency are expected to yield returns, net of risk, at least equivalent to those expressed in foreign reference currencies, typically high-hierarchy reserve currencies that serve as benchmarks for world real resources. Repayments in depreciating

---

[15] Bartholdy and Kate (2004) and more recently Chen and Zhang (2018) study the role of marginal investors in finance.

currencies, not adequately compensated by extra returns, may not legally constitute default but are economically equivalent to it. To prevent governments from exploiting the potential "free lunch" by borrowing in their domestic currency while having unlimited money printing capabilities, contracts should be structured to make subscribers indifferent between different currencies.

In globalized economies where public debt is traded in international financial markets, Global investors assess a government's capacity to repay its debt in real resources and determine the market value of that debt based on this capacity, independent of the currency in which it is denominated.

While allowing governments to print infinite amounts of domestic currency, monetary sovereignty does not reduce the risk of real losses investors may incur on debt contracts denominated in the local currency. Contracts in international financial markets are written so that investors would be equally protected from risks of future losses, whether these originate from government failures to repay their debts or from repaying their debts with a depreciated (and depreciating) currency.

Losses, if any were to be realized, would influence the terms of future contracts, incorporating extra protection for investors. Lower credibility of an issuing government may lead to a higher risk of currency depreciation, prompting investors to demand a higher interest rate premium on its financial obligations.

Thus, in a globalized world, no government is truly sovereign, and all governments are subject to an intertemporal budget constraint (IBC). The IBC requires governments to commit to generating the real resources needed to fulfill financial obligations to investors. Governments with monetary sovereignty are not exempt from the IBC, as Global investors consider the credibility of issuing governments. Anticipations of undisciplined fiscal and monetary policies erode a government's credibility, affecting the demand for its financial obligations, and thereby influencing the IBC.

Every government faces an IBC with endogenous elasticity to Global investor decisions. The concept of "elasticity" reflects the range within which the constraint may expand without compromising financial stability (in the eyes of the markets). Different levels of credibility attributed to a country result in varying constraints on government policy action. Countries with stronger credibility benefit from more flexible IBCs, allowing them greater latitude in policy actions, while countries with weaker credibility face tighter constraints.

More specifically, a government that is reputed to be capable to satisfy its IBC would be perceived as credible by the markets, and vice versa. The stronger its credibility, the higher the elasticity of its IBC and the greater the market's readiness to absorb larger amounts of money and/or debt at the given (or a growing) price.[16] Conversely, with weaker credibility, the prospects of the government raising sufficient resources to repay its future financial obligations or to back up its money stock would be perceived as uncertain, and the resulting tighter IBC would cause the value of such claims to fall. Further erosion of credibility might lead Global investors to no longer

[16] The price of money would be its exchange rate vis-à-vis foreign reference currencies.

buy or hold claims on the public sector and to shift their portfolios toward foreign assets, thus limiting the space available for active macro-policies.[17]

13.6 The Model of the Economy

The model of the economy discussed in this article includes two open economies and has two sides—a micro and a macro side—that are inter-linked by a representative Global investor. The two sides of the economy are considered in turn.

The Macro Side

The PTI model's macro section consists of two globalized country economies D and F, where F is large ("central") and D is small ("peripheral"). Country F acts as price setter in the international markets for goods and services, and D is price taker. The issuance of government debt bonds B_j in country j, where $j = D, F$, and their market value are tied to the country government's IBC:

$$P^B_{j,t}B_{j,t} = P_t\delta^t_j\beta^t_{j,t}|_{\omega_t}\sum_{\tau=t}^{\infty}\left[E_\tau\left(s_{j,\tau} + \Delta m_{j,\tau}\right)|\omega_t\right] \quad \text{with } 0 \leq \beta_j \leq 1 \tag{13.1}$$

$$B_{j,t} = B_{j,t-1} + \Delta B_{j,t} = B_{H,j,t} + B_{CB,j,t} \tag{13.2}$$

$$P_t = P^\alpha_{D,t}\left(e_tP_{F,t}\right)^{1-\alpha} \quad \text{with } 0 \leq \alpha \leq 1 \tag{13.3}$$

$$P_{D,t} = \Phi_D\left(e_tP_{F,t}\right)^\eta \Pi\left(X_{j,t} - X^*_{j,t}\right)^{1-\eta} \quad \text{with } 0 \leq \eta \leq 1;\ \Pi_X > 0 \tag{13.4}$$

$$\Phi_{D,t} = \Phi\left(\eta, \beta_{D,t}\right) \qquad \text{with } \Phi_\eta > 0;\ \Phi_\beta < 0 \tag{13.5}$$

$$\Delta B_{CB,j,t} = \Delta M_{j,t} = \mathrm{M}\left(i^{B_j}_t\right) \quad \text{with } M_i < 0 \tag{13.6}$$

$$i^{B_j}_t - i^{B_j}_N = \gamma\left(p_{D,t} - p^*_{D,t}\right) + (1-\gamma)\left(X_{j,t} - X^*_{j,t}\right) \quad \text{with } 0 \leq \gamma \leq 1 \tag{13.7}$$

$$X_{j,t} - X^*_{j,t} = X_{j,t} - X^*_{j,t-1}(1 + \mathrm{x})$$

[17] The terms "tighter" and "less stringent" should not be conflated with "harder" and "softer" when applied to the concept of a budget constraint. "Harder" and "softer" denote the degree to which a budget constraint genuinely constrains an agent, while "tighter" and "less stringent" have a more specific quantitative connotation and refer to how high or low the limit on the budget deficit is set relative to metrics like GDP.

$$= \mathrm{X}\left(i_t^{B_j} - i_N^{B_j}, \frac{e_{j,t}}{P_{Dj,t}}, \Delta g_{j,t}\right) \quad \text{with} \quad \mathrm{X}_i < 0, \mathrm{X}_{e/P_D} > 0, \mathrm{X}_g > 0 \tag{13.8}$$

$$\Delta g_{j,t} = \frac{\Delta(G_{j,t} - T_{j,t})}{P_{D,t}} = \frac{\left(-S_{j,t} + i_{t-1}^{B_j} B_{j,t-1}\right)}{P_{D,t}} = \frac{\Delta B_{j,t}}{P_{D,t}} = \Delta b_{j,t} \tag{13.9}$$

Equation (13.1) is the IBC of country *j*'s government and requires that the current market value of government bonds *B* equal the present discounted value of the future expected streams of government primary surpluses s_t and monetary financings Δm_t by the central bank (if any), based on information set ω_t available to the investors at time *t*. In the equation: δ is the time discount rate; *P* is the world price deflator used by Global investors to gauge at any time the real value of their wealth; *E* is the expectations operator; *B* is the number of nominal (interest-bearing) bonds issued by the government at a contractual value that is equal to 1 unit of money, and their market value is expressed as a ratio P^B to the bond's contractual value.[18] All else being equal, this ratio changes directly with credibility factor $\beta_{j,t}|_{\omega_t}$, a time-varying factor, conditional on information set ω_t, which acts as a scale factor that *corrects* the value of the IBC in the perception of the markets, based on the credibility that investors attribute to country *j*'s policy. This factor is key in the PTI context and is discussed in Appendix 2: it reflects the Global investor views of a country's credibility and recognizes country credibility as a core aspect of international capital allocation in global financial markets; it plays a special role in linking the macro and micro dimensions of such allocations; and it is a realistic feature, since establishing *ex ante* the credibility of a government to determine its debt repayment capacity is an ordinary practice of international finance.

According to Eq. (13.2), total public debt, which equals the stock of government bonds inherited from the previous period plus any current new bond issuance, is held by representative Global investor *H* and the central bank *CB* of the issuing country.

World price index *P* in Eq. (13.3) is used by Global investors to calculate the real value of relevant financial variables and is calculated as the weighted geometric mean of the general price level attaining in individual countries, P_D and P_F, with weights proxying the relative size of each country investment within the Global investor's portfolio, and P_F taken as exogenous. Country *D*'s price level P_D is determined from the cost side by foreign price level P_F via the nominal exchange rate *e*, and the exchange rate pass-through (ERPT) factor Φ, and from the demand side by the output gap (Eq. (13.4)), each with weight characterized by the openness of the economy to foreign trade. According to Eq. (13.5), ERPT factor Φ raises (structurally) with the degree of openness of the economy, η, and declines with country credibility as

[18] This ratio generally varies between 0 and a value less than 1. Following the Global Financial Crises, however, cases were observed where the value of the ratio exceeded 1. These are cases where some assets (typically bonds issued by highly credible governments) are considered by the markets to be especially safe, and trade at prices above their contractual value, thereby earning negative yields (see *Why do investors buy negative yield bonds?*, Financial Times, April 12, 2006). In such cases, private creditors of the issuing governments are de facto turned into private debtors.

higher credibility anchors inflation expectations and attenuates the impact on inflation caused by the ERPT effect (as discussed in Sect. 13.3).

Equation (13.6) reflects the central bank's decision to purchase or sell government bonds (and thus to issue money M or to withdraw it from circulation) following the Taylor rule of Eq. (13.7): the higher the target interest rate vis-à-vis the neutral level $i_N^{B_j}$, the larger the amount of bonds purchased and, thus, the larger the amount of money withdrawn from the economy.

Reduced form Eq. (13.8) posits a demand-driven real output gap (i.e., the difference between actual and potential output) to change (a) negatively with the deviation of current interest rate from its neutral level, (b) positively with the real exchange rate (assuming Marshall-Lerner condition), and (c) positively with the fiscal deficit (assuming away full Ricardian equivalence), and assumes potential output to grow at gross rate $(1 + x)$.[19] Debt-financed fiscal deficits (under a non-accommodative monetary policy) also affect the real output gap negatively due to their impact on the interest rate, as captured under relation a) above. It is assumed, however, that the net effect of fiscal deficits on output is generally positive. Finally, Eq. (13.9) is the debt-financed fiscal deficit expressed in real terms where S is the nominal primary surplus.

The Micro Side

The PTI model's micro side draws from the conventional portfolio balance approach to the exchange rate determination, reframed in the context of optimal intertemporal allocation choices by a representative Global investor acting in internationally integrated financial markets and perceived by the representative "marginal" Global investor (see above). This agent maximizes financial wealth intertemporally (in utility terms), with a view to consuming it all at "the end of time" (if she is infinitely lived) or to pass it on to future Global investors (if she is finitely lived), who will behave similarly across the infinite time horizon, as if they all worked for a company with the same company purpose. Global investors, thus, act collectively as an intertemporal class of agents, which treat the assets in their portfolios as "vehicles" to the utility associated with the future streams of real resources to which they give access. These agents may act in their own interest and/or they may intermediate financial resources intertemporally from surplus agents to deficit agents demanding resources for investment or consumption-smoothing purposes.[20]

Formally, representative Global investor H maximizes the intertemporal utility generated through wealth portfolio W:

---

[19] This simplifying assumption is justified by the model's focus on aggregate demand and not on the supply-side sources of output growth. Incorporating a properly structured dynamic supply function is a possible extension of PTI analysis.

[20] While including the modelling of deficit and surplus agents would enrich the model, it would not change its results. What is being studied here is the allocation decisions of Global investors, while the behavior of deficit/surplus units is not germane to the analysis.

$$U(\mathbf{W}_{H,t}) = \mathrm{Max}_W E_t\left[\sum_{t=\tau}^{\infty} \delta_H^t u(\mathbf{W}_{H,t})\right] \tag{13.10}$$

s. t.

$$W_{H,t} = M_{H,D,t} + e_t M_{H,F,t} + P^B_{D,t} B_{H,D,t} + e_t P^B_{F,t} B_{H,F,t} = M_{H,D,t-1} R^{M_D}_{t-1} + e_t M_{H,F,t-1} R^{M_F}_{t-1} + P^B_{D,t-1} B_{H,D,t-1} R^{B_D}_{t-1} + e_t P^B_{F,t-1} B_{H,F,t-1} R^{B_F}_{t-1} + \Delta W_{H,t-1} \tag{13.11}$$

$$M_{H,D}, M_{H,F}, B_{H,D}, B_{H,F} \geq 0;\ \Delta W_H \gtreqless 0 \tag{13.12}$$

$$\sum_H P^B_{j,t} B_{H,j,t} + P^B_{j,t} B_{CB,j,t} = P^B_{j,t} B_{j,t} = P_t \delta^t_j \beta^t_{j,t} |_{\omega_t} \sum_{\tau=t}^{\infty} E_t\left[\left(s_{j,t} + \Delta m_{j,t}\right)\right] \tag{13.13}$$

and transversality condition

$$\lim_{t\to\infty} W_{H,t} = 0 \tag{13.14}$$

In Eq. (13.10), $u(\cdot)$ is a standard strictly quasi concave, time-separable, and well-behaved utility function; ΔW_H is net additional investment or divestment taking place through Global investor H, where net divestments correspond to consumption decisions taken by agents who had previously invested in the portfolio of Global investor H[21]; and R is the real gross rate of return on any asset Q (here money M or bonds B), which includes the risk of loss and is calculated as $R^Q = \left(1 + i^Q\right)\left(1 + p^Q\right)(1 - p)\left(1 - l^Q\right)$, where i^Q is the nominal own rate of return on asset Q; p^Q is the rate of change of asset Q price, P^Q[22]; p is the rate of world price inflation, which also reflects the exchange rate variation between the currency of denomination of asset Q and the currency chosen as benchmark; and l^Q is the risk of loss from default on asset Q, as perceived by Global investors, which reflects the credibility that investors attribute to the issuer of the asset (i.e., it increases as credibility factor β declines), and while any functional form could be assumed to link the two variables, the simplest possible form used here for convenience and without loss of generality is $l_j^Q = 1 - \beta_j$, with maximum loss (i.e., $l_j^Q = 1$) for $\beta_j = 0$ and no loss (i.e., $l_j^Q = 0$) for $\beta_j = 1$.[23]

---

[21] In other words, these agents liquidate (part of) their investment to finance current consumption. If they divest funds to re-invest them, their net effect on Global investor H's portfolio is zero ($\Delta W_H = 0$). On the other hand, if agents invest more money, then this adds to the Global investor H's portfolio ($\Delta W_H > 0$).

[22] If P^Q is the price of a bond or a given stock, changes in P^Q correspond to capital gains or losses on asset Q.

[23] The introduction of the risk of loss is an shock on my original assets-in-the-utility function approach.

Equation (13.11) is the investor's instantaneous budget constraint, where only wealth inherited from the previous period and any new net investment can be allocated to domestic and/or foreign assets; notice that the term $\Delta W_{H,t-1}$ also incorporates any losses that may have materialized on past investments. According to conditions (13.12), the investor may hold non-negative quantities of each asset and net changes to the investor's wealth portfolio can be positive (due to investments), negative (due to divestments or losses from defaults), or zero (due to offsetting investments and divestments or to no investment and divestment activities taking place). Equation (13.13) requires that the aggregate demand of government bonds by investors and the central bank equal supply under the impending government IBC; this determines the policy space available to the central bank: given an expansionary monetary policy stance, if Global investors deem it consistent with the stability of the external value of the debt they hold (based on the world price deflator *P*, defined in Eq. (13.3)), they will allow for the policy to run its course, thus making it effective; otherwise, they will penalize it by bidding down the price of the debt and neutralizing the policy impact on real output (see below).[24] Finally, Eq. (13.14) is the transversality condition consistent with the role of the Global investor discussed at the outset of this section.

In this model, where assets are vehicles to future consumption, each characterized by its own "speed" (readiness and cost to be liquidated) and "power" (capacity to store value and to accumulate wealth over time), the utility of any asset *Q*, as shown in Appendix 3, is given by:

$$u(Q_t) = E_t\left\{\delta^T \sum_{T=t+1}^{\infty} u\left(\frac{P_T^Q Q_t}{P_T}\right)\prod_{n=1}^{t-1} R_n^Q \vartheta_T(1-\vartheta_{T-1})\left(1-\xi_T^Q\right)\right\} \tag{13.15}$$

where ϑ_{t+1} is the probability of *Q*'s holder having to converting the asset into consumption at the next date $t + 1$, and ξ^Q is the variable liquidation cost of asset *Q*.

[24] Equation (13.13) contains a degree of indetermination, which can only be resolved within each specific country context once investor expectations are formed based on investor perceptions of country policy credibility. This reflects the non-mechanistic nature of the PTI, in that it derives the nominal and real output consequences of specific policy actions according to country circumstances: the very same policy actions would have different impacts depending on the different levels of country policy credibility (as perceived by Global investors). Here, the adjustment mechanism is implicit in the ongoing revision of the information available to investors at each date, ω_t. While there is no guarantee that the arrival of new information would per se be enough to correct eventual bias factors, the detection ex post of systematic errors (and losses thereof) due to bias factors would generate incentives for investors to correct any bias factor.

13.7 Effects of Monetary and Fiscal Policies

13.7.1 Model's Solution

Using Bellman's equation to solve plan (13.10)–(13.15),

$$U(\boldsymbol{W}_{H,t}) = \mathrm{Max}_W E_t\left[\sum_{t=\tau}^{\infty} \delta_H^t u(\boldsymbol{W}_{H,t})\right] = V(\boldsymbol{W}_{H,t})$$
$$= \mathrm{Max}\left[u(\boldsymbol{W}_{H,t}) + \delta V(\boldsymbol{W}_{H,t+1})\boldsymbol{R}'_{t+1}\right] \quad (13.16)$$

where $\boldsymbol{R}'$ is the vector of the real returns (net of the risk of losses) on the assets held in portfolio $\boldsymbol{W}$, leads to the Euler equation:

$$u'(\boldsymbol{W}_{H,t}) = \delta^n E_t\left[u'(\boldsymbol{W}_{H,t+n})\boldsymbol{R}'_{t+n}\right], \quad (13.17)$$

which determines the optimal intertemporal path for wealth W managed by Global investor H, and where, using Eq. (13.15), the LHS of Eq. (13.17) can be expressed as:

$$u'(\boldsymbol{W}_{H,t}) = E_{H,t}\left\{\delta^T \sum_{T=t+1}^{\infty} u'\left(\frac{\boldsymbol{Q}_{H,t}\boldsymbol{P}^Q_{H,T'}}{P_T}\right)\prod_{n=1}^{t-1} R^Q_n \vartheta_T(1-\vartheta_{T-1})\left(1-\xi^Q_T\right)|\omega_t\right\}$$
$$= u'(\boldsymbol{Q}_{H,t}),$$

With vector $\boldsymbol{Q} = M, B$. Given the optimal time path of managed wealth W, as determined by Eq. (13.17), the optimal portfolio composition of Global investor H at each date of the relevant time horizon must reflect optimal intra-date allocations of the wealth portfolio across the range of available assets. These allocations are derived by fulfilling the following two f.o.c.'s:

$$u'(M_{H,D,t})R_t^{M_D} = \frac{1}{e_t}u'(M_{H,F,t})R_t^{M_F} = \frac{1}{P^B_{D,t}}u'(B_{H,D,t})R_t^{B_D}$$
$$= \frac{1}{e_t P^B_{F,t}}u'(B_{H,F,t})R_t^{B_F} = \lambda_t, \quad (13.18)$$

which requires equating the marginal utilities of M and B holdings, each weighted with its own price, and

$$\lambda_t/\lambda_{t+1} = \delta E_{H,t}R_{t+1}^{M_D} = \delta E_{H,t}R_{t+1}^{B_F} = \delta E_{H,t}R_{t+1}^{B_D} = \delta E_{H,t}R_{t+1}^{B_F}, \quad (13.19)$$

which requires equalizing all real rates of return on assets, in present (discounted) value and net of (default) risk, both at each date and intertemporally.[25]

Incidentally, but not irrelevantly, Eq. (13.18) embodies John Maynard Keynes's liquidity preference theory, whereby the rate of interest is not determined by the supply of and demand for (flows of) saving, but by the supply of and demand for assets into which holdings of (stocks of) wealth can be placed (Tily 2012).[26]

Solving the model simultaneously for all demand and supply relations, under well-behaved investor preferences and optimal fiscal and monetary policies (that is, policies that are consistent with the government IBC), as well as with complete ERPT, and a given world price deflator P, optimal portfolio allocations $\left(M^*_{H,D,t}, M^*_{H,F,t} B^*_{H,F,t}, B^*_{H,F,t}\right)$ attain at equilibrium asset prices $P^{B*}_{D,t}$ and $P^{B*}_{F,t}$, neutral interest rates $R_t^{M^*_D}$ and $R_t^{M^*_F}$,[27] and nominal exchange rate e^*_t consistent with a balanced (zero) real output gap. Critical to the existence of such general equilibrium position of the economy is that the stocks of money and debt required to ensure zero output gap are consistent with the government IBC. This reveals the relevance of the credibility factor β_j and its central role in linking the macro and micro sides of economies where capital resource allocations are determined by Global investors. For simplicity, but without loss of generality, assume utility to be $u(W) = \ln(W)$. Then, dropping subscript H and solving Eq. (13.18) for the equilibrium nominal exchange rate at date t obtain:

$$e^*_t = \frac{\dfrac{1}{M^*_{F,t} R_t^{M^*_F}} + \dfrac{1}{P^{B*}_{F,t} B^*_{F,t} R_t^{B^*_F}}}{\dfrac{1}{M^*_{D,t} R_t^{M^*_D}} + \dfrac{1}{P^{B*}_{D,t} B^*_{D,t} R_t^{B^*_D}}}. \tag{13.20}$$

This solution allows us to determine and evaluate the nominal and real effects of macro-policy shocks.

[25] For completion, since the Global investor acts on behalf of its client wealth holders, optimality requires that the periodical divestments from its portfolio to finance consumption activities (discussed earlier) generate, at the margin, the same utility that is generated by the assets held or acquired by the Global investor.

[26] To quote from Keynes's (1936) *General Theory*, "The current rate of interest depends…not on the strength of the desire to hold wealth, but on the strengths of the desire to hold it in liquid and illiquid forms respectively, coupled with the amount of the supply of wealth in the one form relatively to the supply of it in the other." (p. 213).

[27] In force of the inverse relationship between bond prices and the interest rate on bonds, equilibrium bond returns $R_t^{B^*_D}$ and $R_t^{B^*_F}$ are simultaneously determined with bond prices $P^{B*}_{D,t}$ and $P^{B*}_{F,t}$.

13.7.2 Nominal and Real Effects of Macro-Policies

Transforming Eq. (13.20) using natural logarithms, assuming $R_t^{M_j^*} = 0$, and noting that $\ln R_t^{B_j} = \ln\{(1 + i^{B_j})(1 - p)[1 + (1 - \beta_j)]\} \approx i^{B_j} - p + (1 - \beta_j)$,[28,29] yield:

$$\varepsilon_t = (m_{D,t} - m_{F,t}) + (b_{D,t} - b_{F,t}) + \left(p_t^{B_D} - p_t^{B_F}\right) + (\beta_{F,t} - \beta_{D,t}) \tag{13.21}$$

Equation (13.21) shows that, for a given demand for (domestic and foreign) money and bonds, the nominal exchange rate of domestic vs foreign assets, all else being equal, varies positively (i.e., depreciates) with:

i. The growth of domestic (relative to foreign) supply of money and bonds;
ii. The growth of domestic (relative to foreign) bond prices; and
iii. The risk of losses on domestic (relative to foreign) bonds as proxied by the credibility gap between the issuing countries.

Importantly, any persistent difference in country credibility has a persistent, and hence cumulative, effect on the exchange rate.

Log-linearizing around steady-states Eqs. (13.6), (13.8), (13.9), and (13.21) and replacing them into the log-linearized form of Eq. (13.4), assuming a fully accommodating monetary policy stance (i.e., $i_t^{B_j} = i_N^{B_j}$, from Eq. (13.7)), and solving for domestic inflation yield[30]:

$$\begin{aligned} p_{D,t} = &\frac{1}{1 + (1 - \eta)\Pi_X\left(X_{\frac{e}{P_D}} - X_G\right)} \\ &\Big\{\eta\phi + (1 - \eta)\Pi_X X_{\frac{e}{P_D}}\Big[(m_{D,t} - m_{F,t}) + (b_{D,t} - b_{F,t}) + \left(p_t^{B_D} - p_t^{B_F}\right)\Big\} \\ &+(\beta_{F,t} - \beta_{D,t}) + \eta\phi p_{F,t} + (1 - \eta)\, \Pi_X X_G g_{D,t}\Big]\Big\}, \end{aligned} \tag{13.22}$$

where small-case letters indicate logarithmic values. Notice that in Eq. (13.22), it is (realistically) assumed that $(1 - \eta)\Pi_X\left(X_{\frac{e}{P_D}} - X_G\right) \geq -1$, where $\Pi_X X_{\frac{e}{P_D}} \leq 0$ and $\Pi_X X_G \geq 0$, and the ERPT term has negative sign, except when the pass-through is complete (see Eq. (13.5)) and, therefore, $\phi(\cdot) = ln 1 = 0$). The equation shows that, all else being equal, domestic inflation varies:

---

[28] Applying Taylor's expansion, $\ln(1 + \chi) = \chi - \frac{\chi^2}{2} + \frac{\chi^3}{3} - \frac{\chi^4}{4} + \frac{\chi^5}{5} - \ldots = \sum_{n=1}^{\infty}(-1)^{n+1}\frac{\chi^n}{n}$, $\forall \chi \in (-1, 1]$, and $\lim_{n\to\infty}(R_n) = -\frac{\chi^2}{2} + \frac{\chi^3}{3} - \frac{\chi^4}{4} + \frac{\chi^5}{5} - \ldots = \frac{(-1)^n}{(1+\zeta)^{n+1}}\frac{(\beta)^{n+1}}{(n+1)!} = 0, \zeta \in (0, \chi)$. Thus, $\ln(1 + \chi) \approx \chi$.

[29] The rate of change of bond prices has been dropped from the calculation of the rate of return on the bonds since the inverse relationship between the price of a bond and the interest rate on the bond makes one of the two variables redundant.

[30] This version of Eq. (13.22) corrects its previous derivation in Bossone (2022).

a. Positively with changes in the domestic monetary and financial stocks relative to foreign benchmarks;
b. Positively with changes in domestic (relative to foreign) bond prices;
c. Negatively with country credibility;
d. Positively with foreign inflation; and
e. Positively with fiscal policy shocks.

Due to the persistent effect of credibility on the exchange rate, noted above, a lower level of country credibility (relative to a benchmark country) puts permanent pressure on inflation. In other words, less credible countries tend to have, on average, a higher rate of inflation (all else being equal).

Global investor choices and the country's macro-policies interact with each other, since changes in the budget and budget financing modalities bear changes in the stocks of M and B and trigger allocative responses by Global investors, based on country credibility as perceived by the latter. Such responses may change as new information arrives.[31]

Regarding the effects of monetary and fiscal policy shocks on real output (Eqs. (13.6) and (13.9)), log-linearizing Eq. (13.8), and solving for output yield:

$$x_{D,t} = x_{D,t}^{*} + X_i \delta i_t^{B_D} + X_e \varepsilon_{D,t}(\cdot|\beta_D) - X_P p_{D,t}(\cdot|\beta_D) + X_g \delta g_{D,t}. \tag{13.23}$$

Equation (13.23) incorporates, inter alia, Eqs. (13.21) and (13.22) and is dual to them: it shows that, all else being equal, policy shocks that do not dissipate into higher inflation do add to real output (and vice versa)—the dissipation effect being a consequence of credibility factor β, as already discussed. As a result, lower (higher) credibility makes macro-policies less (more) effective. Also, there is a critical level of credibility factor β at which there is no real output effect, since currency depreciation and inflation dynamics are such as to induce an interest rate adjustment, which depresses output through the $X_i \delta i_t^{B_D}$ term. This follows from the market pressure on the value of government debt (Eq. 13.1) and the concomitant action of the central bank that raises the target interest rate consistent with the Taylor rule (Eq. 13.7). At high rates of depreciation and inflation, it is also likely that the weight γ attributed by the central bank to the inflation objective (that is, the sensitivity of the central bank to mitigating inflation as a policy objective) moves closer to 1, at the expense of the output gap weight, $1 - \gamma$, which becomes relatively less important. Appendix 3 describes narratively how macro policy shocks reverberate through the economy under the PTI model.

[31] As an application of Eq. (13.22), take the case of highly credible reserve currencies, like the US, the Eurozone, and Japan, following such critical events as the global financial crisis of 2007–9 and the Covid19 pandemic more recently. In all these cases, the demand for assets denominated in their currencies exceeded even their fast-growing supply, causing $m < 0$ and $b < 0$ and thus weakening domestic inflation. This, in turn, has caused inflation to be low also in other (smaller) countries via Eq. (13.3). Notice that, from the perspective of each reserve-issuing country the subscripts D and F in Eq. (13.22) would be inverted, with the reserve-currency country being domestic (D) and the other countries being foreign (F).

Integrating and correcting, but also strengthening, the results derived in Bossone (2022), the term $\frac{1}{1+(1-\eta)\Pi_X\left(X_{\frac{e}{P_D}}-X_G\right)}$ of Eq. (13.22), which is implicit in Eq. (13.23), suggests two considerations. First, the higher is the sensitivity of aggregate demand-drive output to fiscal shocks (Eq. 13.8), the larger is its dampening effect on the inflation response to shocks from the variable on the RHS of Eq. (13.22), and hence the larger is the real output effect (Eq. 13.23), and vice versa. Second, even with no dampening effect and a large negative output gap, such that $\Pi_X X_{\frac{e}{P_D}} = \Pi_X X_G = 0$, demand policy shocks would still impact inflation through capital re-allocations by Global investors and their effect on the exchange rate: under a large country credibility gap and a high ERPT effect (i.e., ϕ close to zero), the occurrence of positive and fully accommodated fiscal shocks would cause the nominal exchange rate to depreciate and to feed fully into domestic inflation even at less than full employment output, and would thus weaken the real effect of the shocks. Recalling that less credible economies (especially the more open ones) feature higher ERPT effects, it follows that in the case of similar policy shocks occurring in such countries, the impact on domestic inflation would be larger and the impact on output would correspondingly be weakened. The more so as the country credibility gap grows larger.

Related to credibility is an important additional factor, which specifically affect the terms $m_{D,t} - m_{F,t}$ and $b_{D,t} - b_{F,t}$ and their impact on Eqs. (13.22) and (13.23). The policy space that more credible countries (especially those issuing international reserve currencies) can leverage is larger also because the demand for their currencies is much more elastic than in the case of less credible countries. Analytically, as Appendix 1 shows, if a country were to expand its money supply either to accommodate a fiscal stimulus or to lower interest rates and stimulate demand-driven output, a higher level of credibility would give it more space before the money supply exceeds its demand, since both supply and demand grow in tandem and the demand absorbs the supply, thereby averting inflationary pressures.[32] Conversely, a lower level of credibility would lead the country soon to run into excess money supply issues: in terms of Eq. (13.22), if $b_{D,t} > b_{F,t}$, as the country expands its money supply it would soon be the case that $m_{D,t} > m_{F,t} \cong 0$, with inflationary consequences and lower (or no) output gains as a result. Following Appendix 1, the term "soon" used above means that, all else being equal, the money stock in country D would start exceeding its own optimal level at a smaller ratio to output than country F. Low-credibility countries would therefore have less space available for expansionary fiscal and monetary policies than high-credibility countries.

Similarly, if the money supply did not accommodate the fiscal expansion, the country's low credibility would require government bonds to pay relatively higher (equilibrium) interest rates, limiting the real output effect of the expansion. On the other hand, things would not work better even in the absence of the interest rate adjustment since the supply of bonds would then exceed the demand. This would cause the nominal exchange rate to depreciate, followed by higher inflation (Eqs. 13.21–13.22), and the output response to be smaller (Eq. 13.23).

[32] This is another way to look at the "elasticity" of a country's IBC discussed earlier in this article.

In summary, according to Eq. (13.20), expansionary policies that undermine a country's credibility, particularly by jeopardizing the sustainability of its public sector financial obligations, lead to currency devaluation and to higher inflation as a result (Eq. 13.22). Any positive impact of exchange rate depreciation on real output would be offset, or worse reversed, if interest rates were adjusted to a point where they reduce real output (Eq. 13.23). Equation (13.1) determines how the weaker credibility affects the sustainability of public sector financial obligations and necessitates policy reversals.

The effectiveness of the same policy program can thus range from being fully effective to being fully ineffective (in terms of output), depending on the perceived credibility of the country by Global investors and on the expected impact of the policy program on the country's credibility. Ineffectiveness leads to the dissipation of policy effects through currency depreciation, causing higher inflation and further credibility loss.

In this context, Global investors play a crucial role in determining the relative effectiveness of macro-policies at the country level, which could be characterize as follows: ***A country with weaker credibility faces a narrower policy space, as determined by Global investors, and this space contracts further due to policy choices believed by Global investors to weaken the country's credibility.***

Turning to the exchange rate, the PTI suggests that in the presence of high international financial integration and Global investors as asset price setters, persistently growing stocks of money and/or public sector debt are expected to exceed their optimal level, sooner or later. This is especially true for countries with relatively weaker policy credibility, where the demand for instruments denominated in foreign currencies dominates over those denominated in domestic currency.

The PTI model predicts that the growth of excess claims on government is more likely to happen in countries with lower credibility, where the growth of money supply and debt cannot be easily absorbed by increasing demand. With expectations being incorporated in the PTI model, anticipations of future nominal exchange rate devaluation would accelerate actual devaluation, and, in the limit, rational expectations would fulfill themselves instantaneously.

Finally, the PTI model suggests that in countries with weak credibility, the nominal exchange rate depreciates even at less than full employment output. This depreciation is driven by the expected growth of public sector claims and is independent of their impact on inflation, as shown by the fact that inflation follows even if the negative output gap renders the economy's real resource constraint unbinding. In contrast to monetary theories of the exchange rate, the PTI shows that inflation follows, rather than cause, exchange rate depreciation due to the exchange rate pass-through (ERPT) effect, and that inflation is independent of resource employment levels.

Consistent with the PTI, recent evidence has shown the increased importance of investment funds in generating international capital flows in response to information changes. Specifically, in their study of three groups of investors—insurance companies and pension funds, banks and money market funds, and investment and mutual funds—Faia et al. (2024) find that the first two groups are slower to adjust and tend to hold securities from more credible countries with stable monetary regimes or inflation targeting; in contrast, investment funds are more willing to invest in riskier bonds from less credible countries that offer higher returns. These funds are less constrained by prudential policies and can better serve clients who require active rebalancing or have more flexible investment mandates. They play the role of marginal investors, and their choices influence, if not determine, market dynamics. The evidence by Faia et al., cit., and its relevance for the PTI are corroborated by the granular analysis by Fang et al. (2024), which finds that investment funds absorb substantially more of the variation in the outstanding debt of issuing governments than other investor groups, they are more responsive to reductions in the price of debt, and their behavior is crucial for understanding sovereign debt sustainability.

13.8 Policy Implications of the PTI

When the stocks of central bank money or public debts increase, it is essential that there are willing holders for them to maintain their value stable over time. In the case of a highly credible country, especially one that issues an international reserve currency, the public generally desires to hold its liabilities. This results in an elastic government's IBC, and the value of public debt or the money stock remains relatively unaffected. In fact, in crisis situations, those stocks happen to be even in higher demand than under normal times, from both resident and non-resident agents, and their price would thus increase. Conversely, in poorly credible countries, where the public may not want to hold such assets, the IBC becomes more rigid, leading to a decline in the relative price of the debt and money stocks.

While a *temporary* surge in both money and debt can serve as a short-term solution, particularly in poorly credible countries facing recessions (as discussed in the earlier case of helicopter money), a *permanent* increase in debt to finance ongoing state deficit spending will impact its value. In globalized economies, the prospect of indefinite or disorderly growth in money and debt stocks prompts portfolio adjustments away from these assets, causing their prices to drop and pushing the economy away from full employment. This critique is directed at theories neglecting stock variables in favor of flow variables, particularly in highly financialized economies.

In line with this critique, the PTI delves into the inflation generation process. If a government consistently run permanent deficits at a given level of aggregate output and the money created was not loaned out, this would cause the total stock of money to grow indefinitely, relative to output, since there would be no loan repayments and destruction of the originally created money (i.e., the "reflow" effect). Eventually, people would shift out of the money stock and into alternative assets, including foreign assets. Depending on various factors such as the level of the money stock, the issuing country's credibility, and their dynamics over time, this process could unfold either gradually or abruptly but leading in all cases to currency devaluation and to higher inflation as a result. Notice that the smaller and more open and financially integrated the economy, the more rapid the pace of devaluation and inflation. Likewise, if the country was largely indebted (either in foreign or domestic currency). Here, not only are openness and financial integration relevant, but also, as noted, wealth inequality and the institutionalization of savings would matter. Under both, the impact of ongoing money growth would be felt, first, on asset prices and the nominal exchange rate, and then on domestic inflation via the ERPT effect.

No economy is immune to the outlined narrative, but highly credible countries, especially those issuing international reserve currencies, have more significant policy space than less credible ones. The elasticity of their IBC, as perceived by financial markets, allows these countries to confront sustainability issues much later than less credible counterparts with similar initial conditions, after it has been possible leveraging effective expansionary policies. The elasticity of the IBC is influenced not only by domestic circumstances but also by global developments. In the case of non-idiosyncratic shocks impacting the global economy, the world demand for assets denominated in international reserve currencies is likely to increase, providing even more policy space for their countries of issue, while the opposite holds for less credible nations.

The PTI offers a rationale for understanding how global factors influence the value of the claims on a country's public sector (money and debt) in the context of high international financial integration. In essence, the PTI incorporates a global perspective into the analysis of a domestic economy, emphasizing that the factors affecting the value of its public sector claims are driven by global dynamics.

13.9 Why a New Theory of Inflation?

Current macroeconomic theories have not been successful in explaining inflation in modern economies. Theories such as the Old Monetarism and the New Classical school have not been able to explain why the large and persistent injections of money into advanced economies during and after the Great Recession did not result in a resurgence of inflation (except that caused by supply-side disruptions following the events of the last few years, from the Covid pandemic to the geopolitical crises). Similarly, New Keynesianism has not been able to account for the slow progress of low-interest rate policies in achieving their inflation targets (Palley, 2019), and its policy recommendations have been contradicted by its own theoretical Neo-Fisherian version (Cochrane, 2017).[33]

More recently, the Fiscal Theory of the Price Level (FTPL) has emerged as a theory to explain the general price level. The FTPL is based on government debt and fiscal policy alone (while monetary policy has at most an indirect effect), since the real contractual value of the outstanding stock of nominal (non-monetary) public debt

[33] See also the discussions by J. Hendrickson in In Defense of Neo-Fisherism The Everyday Economist, October 17, 2014, and in New Keynesian Failure, The Everyday Economist, August 20, 2015.

always matches the present discounted value of the current and future real primary surpluses and monetary financings of the state budget. However, the theory has been shown to be internally flawed.[34]

The above theories overlook how policy effectiveness may vary and impact inflation differently depending on investors' views of the countries where they invest. In countries suffering from weak credibility, their portfolio decisions are such that the scope for domestic policymakers using active demand management policies is constrained and the most probable outcome of such policies is currency devaluation and inflation, with little or no benefits on real output and resource employment. Vice versa in countries enjoying strong credibility. Therefore, there is a demand for a theory that can account for the (in)effectiveness of macroeconomic policies and their (non)inflationary effects in the context of globalized national economies. The PTI offers an explanation based on four features that make it especially fit as a theory of inflation:

1. ***No mechanical link***. According to the PTI, the transmission channel from financial claims on the government (money and/or public debt) to inflation dynamics does not depend on any mechanical factor. The transmission is based on the role of financial market expectations, perceptions, and conventional beliefs—as shown by Global investors through their portfolio choices—regarding the policy credibility of a country and the future sustainability of the claims on it. To illustrate the point with an example, a country that would issue money or debt to finance new output and employment creation, holding everything else constant, would either succeed in its attempt (and thus end up with higher output and low inflation) or fail (and thus end up with higher inflation and little or no change in the real variables), depending on how the market perceives the credibility of the country's authorities and policy institutions. Growing financial claims on the country's public sector would be seen as intertemporally sustainable in a highly credible country, but they would be seen as unsustainable in a poorly credible one, leading investors to very different portfolio allocation choices in each case. According to the PTI, in both cases the market is central in determining the elasticity of the country's IBC, and while investors may be assumed to act rationally (basing their portfolio choices on the best knowledge available), the theory does not need them to be necessarily correct—the theory simply predicts that whatever investors decide does ultimately determine the outcome of the country's policies.
2. ***The exchange rate as an asset price***. According to the PTI, financial claims on the public sector affect inflation indirectly through the exchange rate as an asset price. Investor portfolio preferences affect, first, the exchange rate of the domestic currency as a relative price of the assets that are traded globally and influence domestic inflation when the changes in the exchange rate are passed on to domestic prices via the pass-through and relative price adjustment mechanisms. Note that in the PTI framework, the pass-through effect also depends on country credibility and how it anchors inflation expectations, as evidence

[34] For a comprehensive review and radical analytical critique of the FTPL, see Buiter (2017) and Buiter and Sibert (2017).

supports. In the PTI, therefore, the financial and trade sectors, both internal and external, interact strongly with each other, reflecting the level of integration of the economies into the global (real and financial) markets and putting (perceived) credibility at the heart of signal transmission and resource allocation. The different speeds at which financial and trade markets process the information are important for the transmission of the price signals from financial assets to goods and services and back into the real value of the assets. As the model above showed, the PTI does not exclude direct effects of output changes on inflation, and the case is illustrated in Appendix 4 of expansionary fiscal policy triggering portfolio effects that cause output to fall, inflation to decrease, and the real exchange rate to increase.

3. ***A different theory of inflation (I).*** The PTI is different from the usual "demand-pull" theories of inflation. The idea of the theory is that inflation comes from the optimal (re)composition of country claims in Global investor portfolios: changes in local prices are the result of changes in the quality of those claims as they are seen by Global investors. If the quality of a country currency or government bonds (compared to other countries) is expected to worsen, due to their expected unstable dynamics, the demand for the currency or the bonds will drop and their relative price will decrease, causing the price of other assets, commodities, and goods to rise.
4. ***A different view of inflation (II).*** A key consequence of the above characteristics is that the PTI shows how the same policies can have different effects in different countries. For example, active demand management policies in countries with low credibility may not boost output and may instead increase inflation (even when there are large output gaps) and cause capital to leave the economy, due to a rigid IBC and unsteady inflation expectations. On the other hand, in highly credible countries with more flexible IBC (as determined by Global investors) and firmly anchored expectations, the same policy shocks may get the intended outcomes in terms of output and real resource use, with little or no adverse effect on the exchange rate and inflation. The PTI can thus account for the different shapes that the Phillips curve has in different countries, with credible countries having flatter curves and less credible countries having more steep ones in, and with flatter curves in highly credible countries becoming even flatter in times of global crisis.[35]

To avoid confusion, three possible misunderstandings about the PTI should be clarified:

i. ***The PTI is just another way to present the old argument that a "largely indebted" economy is vulnerable to capital outflows and, therefore, currency depreciation and higher inflation.*** This is not true: the PTI internalizes IBC elasticity and explains inflation as a possible (not inevitable) result of investor

[35] During times of crisis, when inflationary pressures in the goods and labor markets are subdued, the high-credibility premium results in low interest rates, which in turn leads to a lower cost of money as a production factor, as per Barth and Ramey (2000). This allows for the implementation of expansionary macro-policies to a greater degree before causing price inflation responses.

portfolio decisions. Even for a country with a large debt, if investors trust that the country is very credible, they will tolerate (and finance) even high levels of its indebtedness (i.e., the IBC would be more elastic). Policies would affect output and would not vanish into higher inflation through exchange rate devaluation. The opposite would apply, other things being equal, for countries with low credibility.

ii. ***The PTI recycles the old idea that currency devaluations are the main source of inflation***. No, the transmission from currency devaluation to inflation is key to the PTI, but the PTI goes much further than this mechanism. The theory shows how macro-policy ineffectiveness may turn into higher inflation in countries that suffer from low policy credibility, but also identifies the conditions under which policy ineffectiveness does not lead to higher inflation, despite currency devaluation. In fact, according to the PTI, the link between exchange rate devaluation and inflation is influenced by country credibility, since it depends on the anchoring of inflation expectations: the stronger the anchoring, the lower the ERPT effect.

iii. ***The PTI is just another way to say that policies are neutral, and money is always a veil***. Not at all: the PTI shows that monetary and fiscal policies are "ineffective" or less effective (as different from "neutral") in countries with low credibility, and vice versa in highly credible countries—where "effectiveness" refers specifically to the policy impact on output. Regarding prices, even when policies are ineffective, it would not necessarily imply that higher money growth or a larger fiscal deficit translate into higher inflation. The PTI shows that, depending on country credibility, investor portfolio choices might even cause output to fall and inflation to decrease, as a response to expansionary policies (see, for example, illustrations in Appendix 4). All these outcomes are far from neutrality as traditionally understood in the context of macroeconomic policies.

13.10 Conclusion

Globalization requires that each country realistically assesses how well its macro-policies can work, given its own features and conditions. This is especially (though not only) relevant for developing and emerging market economies. In fact, current macroeconomic policy modeling still depends on domestic representative agents reacting to state-driven policy shocks and does not acknowledge the influence financial investors acting globally (heretofore called "Global investors") have in determining the market value of public sector claims (money and debt). This influence may affect the nature of policy innovations or chocks, changing policy effectiveness.

Fixing this problem is what I have aimed to do with my work on the Portfolio Theory of Inflation heretofore "PTI"), through which I examine how financial globalization affects the policy options available at the national level—in many cases limiting them to the point of making expansionary macro-policies ineffective or even destabilizing.

This chapter has illustrated the PTI and how, according to the theory, capital allocations by Global investors interact with government macro-policies and affect nominal exchange rate and inflation. The chapter has discussed the role of Global investors in today's highly financially integrated economies. Through the PTI, it has shown how this role restricts or expands the policy options of the national authorities, depending on the credibility that Global investors assign to them.

Showing that the level of credibility assigned by Global investors to a country's policy making ability determines the policy options available to the country's authorities, the PTI can be used to derive and evaluate the impact of macro-policy shocks or innovation on the dynamics of exchange rate, inflation, and output following. Country credibility, as perceived by the markets, plays a crucial role in determining the effectiveness of its macroeconomic policies in terms of output and resource employment. Government policy choices influence Global investor allocation decisions, which in turn determine the value and sustainability of the financial claims on the public sector (money and debt).

The PTI contributes to the literature on grounds of methodology and economic and policy theory. On methodology, the PTI substitutes the conventional representative domestic household with a representative Global investor. With this important change, perceived country credibility becomes a key factor for intertemporal, cross-country, resource allocation decisions. Also, the PTI endogenizes government IBCs, making them dependent on the credibility of each country as it is perceived by the Global investors. On grounds of economic and policy theory, the PTI shows that the effectiveness of macro-policies is not influenced by the currency of denomination of the country's public sector claims (money and public debt): macro-policy effectiveness, equilibrium exchange rate and inflation are all the outcomes of portfolio choices by Global investors. Furthermore, the PTI explains why ineffective policies may dissipate into currency devaluation and higher inflation or they may not, and it also explains why monetary financing of public deficits may be effective (at most) as a short-term stopgap policy but is not sustainable in the longer run (a point that will be analyzed in Chap. 15 of this book, on Modern Money Theory, MMT). Finally, the PTI explains why and how (hypothetically) identical macro-policies adopted by countries featuring different levels of (perceived) credibility would lead to different outcomes.

Having developed the PTI in the context of globalized finance, a relevant question that arises in the same context is whether it makes any real difference for a government (of a globalized economy) to finance its budget by issuing debt denominated in the national currency, or in a currency issued by another country, or even by printing money. The question is answered by Chap. 14.

Appendix 1: The Optimal Demand for Money and Country Credibility

By analyzing the dynamics of money demand with respect to (nominal) output as a scale variable, this appendix shows that countries with higher policy credibility enjoys larger policy space, using a modified version of the Allais-Baumol-Tobin (ABT) inventory model for transaction money demand. The original ABT model is here modified to include the convenience yield that money delivers to its holders and the effect of expected exchange rate changes on the demand for money. The ABT approach is here selected as a simple and yet effective method to incorporate an optimal demand-for-money framework in the economy's model used in this article.

Suppose households receive nominal income PY at the beginning of each period and spend it evenly during the period. Average wealth is $PY/2$ and, according to the model assumptions, it is held in the form of money balances, M, issued by the domestic country d and delivering convenience yield i_M, and domestic and foreign assets, B_j, and yielding return i_j, with $j = D, F$.

To finance transactions, households must first hold M balances. To spend wealth that is not in the form of M balances, it must first be converted into M at transaction costs c_j. Suppose each household divides the period into n subperiods initially placing PY/n in money balances and the rest in bonds. Suppose also that the share of balances kept in foreign assets increases if the household expects the domestic currency to depreciate, so that money balances for each subperiod are $PY[1 - E(\varepsilon)]/n$, where $E(\varepsilon) = \varepsilon$ is the expected rate of currency depreciation. At the end of each subperiod, bonds and FX balances are converted into M balances in $n - 1$ transactions of equal size $PY(1 - \varepsilon)/n$. Thus, average money holdings over n subperiods will be $M = \frac{1}{n}\frac{PY(1-\varepsilon)}{2}$ and average holdings of bonds and FX balances will be $B_d + B_f = \frac{n-1}{n}\left(s_d + s_f\right)\frac{PY}{2}$, where $s_j = \frac{B_j}{PY}$, is the share of bond j over nominal income. The net gain, Γ, from holding wealth in all asset forms available, considering the need to finance transactions, is given by:

$$\Gamma = \frac{1}{n}\frac{PY(1-\varepsilon)i_M}{2} + \frac{n-1}{n}\sum_j s_j \frac{PYi_j}{2} - (n-1)\sum_j s_j c_j \qquad \text{with } j - d, f.$$

Maximizing Γ with respect to n requires:

$$\frac{\partial \Gamma}{\partial n} = \frac{-2n^2 \sum_j s_j c_j + \sum_j s_j PYi_j}{2n^2} - \sum_j s_j \frac{PY(1-\varepsilon)i_M}{2n^2} = 0$$

Therefore, the optimal choice for n is

$$n^* = \sqrt{\frac{PY\sum_j s_j\left[i_j - i_M(1-\varepsilon)\right]}{2\sum_j s_j c_j}} \tag{13.24}$$

and the optimal demand-for-money equation is

$$\frac{M^*}{P} \equiv m^* = Y\frac{1}{n^*} = Y\sqrt{\frac{2\sum_j s_j c_j}{PY\sum_j s_j\left[i_j - i_M(1-\varepsilon)\right]}},$$

which shows that the demand for money varies positively with real income, asset transaction costs, and the convenience yield on money balances, and varies negatively with the rate of return on alternative assets, nominal income, and the nominal exchange rate (currency depreciation). Notice that, because of the square root factor, the overall (net) effect of real income on money demand is positive.

Consider now that country D has lower policy credibility than country F, as proxied by a lower credibility factor β (see Appendix 2) and analyze the consequences of monetary policy mismanagement (although the same arguments would hold for fiscal policy mismanagement). Expectations that the government mismanages the money supply over the relevant future time horizon induce wealth holders, all else equal, to hold larger shares of their wealth held in foreign bonds, as they factor into their portfolio choices the future expected losses on the (internal and external) value of money. They may fear the risk of excess money supply creation and government's inadequacy or unwillingness to react to threats of currency depreciation and inflation through appropriate policy action. This implies that $n_D^* > D$ and, hence, $m_F^* < m_F^*$. Thus, in order to induce wealth holders in the country d and f, respectively, to hold the same level of excess real money $m - m_D^* = e\left(m - m_F^*\right)$, all else equal, it must be that $i_D(\cdot)|\beta_D > i_F(\cdot)|\beta_F$, that is, the required (equilibrium) convenience yield on county d's money must be greater than its equivalent on country f's money. Similarly, the change in the convenience rate required by a given rise of excess money balances will be larger in country d than in country f, and the difference will grow larger with the rise of excess money balances, that is, $i'_D(\cdot)|\beta_D > i'_F(\cdot)|\beta_F$. These relative differences in the yield adjustment will vary inversely with the difference in the level of policy credibility of the economies being compared, that is, the policy space available would be higher, the higher the level of policy credibility of the economy concerned). Formally, all these features are formally captured by the following equation for the convenience yield on money:

$$i = i\left(m_j - m_j^*;\, \beta_j\right), \text{ with } j = D, F \text{ and } i_D|\beta_D > i_F|\beta_F > 0;\ i''_D\big|\beta_D > i''_F\big|\beta_F > 0;\ i'''_D\big|\beta_D > i'''_F\big|\beta_F > 0, \tag{13.25}$$

where $m_j - m_j^*$ measures "excess" money in country j. Eq. (13.25) defines the position and shape of the optimal demand-for-money function and indicates that i) the required yield on money rises with excess money balances and ii) the height and steepness of the demand schedule in the $(i, m;\, \beta)$ space is conditional on the economy's level of policy credibility, all else being equal (Chart 13.1).

Considering Eq. (13.25), the optimal demand-for-money function can be written in implicit form as:

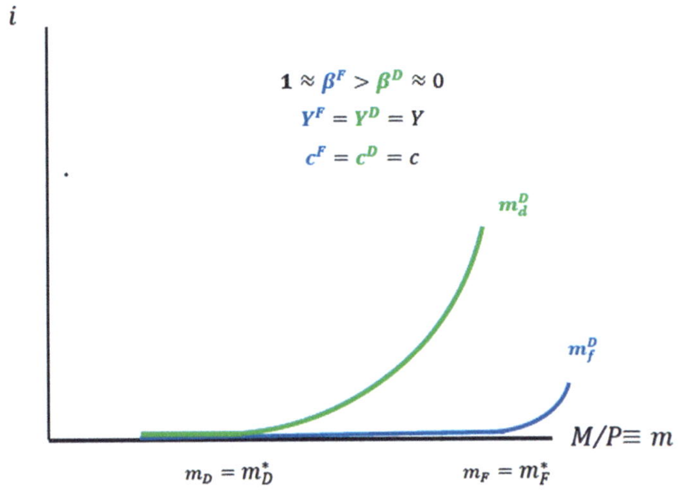

Chart 13.1 Stylized demand-for-money schedules in economies with different policy credibility

$$\frac{M_D}{P_D} = m(Y, i_M|\beta_D, c, i_F, \varepsilon_D|\beta_d), \tag{13.26}$$

where the exchange rate term within the parentheses is explained below. With c and i_f being set exogenously and assumed to be constant (for reasons of simplicity but at no loss of generality), Eq. (13.26) reduces to:

$$\frac{M_D}{P_D} = m(Y, i_M|\beta_D, \varepsilon_D|\beta_D), \qquad \text{with } m'_Y, m'_i > 0;\ m'_\varepsilon < 0.$$

which says that for any given stock of M, and all else being equal, a higher transaction demand for M driven by an increase in output Y requires a decrease in the convenience yield on M balances, i, and/or an increase in the expected rate of currency depreciation, ε, needed to keep the money market in equilibrium.

Appendix 2: The Credibility Factor "β"

Credibility factor "β" condenses Global investor views on the policy credibility of individual country economies. This factor can indifferently be thought of as an index that investors apply to the government IBC, which scales its value up or down correspondingly, or as a probability measure that generates an expected value of the IBC, or else as a risk factor that adjusts the value of the IBC. All else equal, a lower β_j reflects larger expected losses on government debt (either via higher inflation or default) and translates into a tighter IBC for j's government, thus requiring larger (and possibly more frontloaded) fiscal efforts to sustain a given debt stock.

The information set ω_t, at any time t, comprises all relevant information that Global investors deem relevant to their decision-making process, including to assess the policy credibility of a country government (e.g., economic, political, and social factors, both internal and external to the country, which influence the achievability and sustainability of government's specific policy commitments). New factors or events that raised the investors' concerns that country j's government might face future economic, political and social challenges (which would eventually induce the government to take such actions as defaulting on its future financial obligations, inflating its debt away, or even repudiating it) would be incorporated in a new information set ω_t^1 and cause β_j to fall ($\beta_{j,t}|_{\omega_t^{\prime}} < \beta_{j,t}|_{\omega_t}$), thus reducing the IBC elasticity accordingly. A fall of credibility might result in such a tightening of the IBC elasticity that investors would doubt the sustainability of the future primary surpluses and/or debt monetization required by the tightened IBC, until such a point where they might even stop buying and holding the country's debt altogether. This would cause the price of debt to collapse and, correspondingly, domestic interest rates to rise abnormally to levels where fiscal dominance would put pressure on the monetary authorities to monetize and inflate the debt away.

The relevant information set would also capture those developments (including, for instance, the evolution of local and/or global risks) that may induce investors to shift capital from lower-credible to higher-credible countries considered to be safer places for investment or issuers of safer financial instruments. In such instances, the credibility gap between countries (as perceived by the markets) may change and cause different dynamics of credibility factors β_j and, hence, different IBC elasticities in different countries over time. All else equal, different IBC elasticities across countries are sufficient to make otherwise identical bonds imperfect substitutes of one another.

Appendix 3: The Utility of Money and Other Financial Assets

This appendix offers a quick derivation of the utility function of money and financial assets (for a more extensive treatment of the topic, see Chap. 3). At each point in time and across its life, any asset Q delivers to its holder a level of utility that reflects the opportunity for the holder to liquidate the asset and to use the proceeds from liquidation to finance consumption needs C occurring with probability ϑ at any future date. The utility of asset Q at date t is calculated by summing over two terms: i) the utility directly derived from converting the asset into consumption at the next date $t + 1$ with probability ϑ_{t+1}, and ii) the utility indirectly derived from holding the asset further on with residual probability $(1 - \vartheta_{t+1})$, which in turn can be further decomposed as above at each future date. Notice that probabilities ϑ_τ, $\tau \in (1, \infty)$ are based on subjective judgments of asset holders and can change over time, also based on new information and changes in market sentiment.

Substituting iteratively for $u(Q)$ at each forward date yields across the time horizon, the process generates the following series of expressions:

$$
\begin{aligned}
u(Q_t) &= \delta E_t\left[u\left(\frac{P^Q_{t+1}Q_t}{P_{t+1}}\right)R^Q_{t+1}\vartheta_{t+1} + u(Q_t)(1-\vartheta_{t+1})\right] \\
&= E_t\left\{u\left(\frac{P^Q_{t+1}Q_t}{P_{t+1}}\right)\delta R^Q_{t+1}\vartheta_{t+1}\right. \\
&\quad \left.+\left[u\left(\frac{P^Q_{t+2}Q_t}{P_{t+2}}\right)\delta^2 R^Q_{t+1}R^Q_{t+2}\vartheta_{t+2} + u(Q_t)(1-\vartheta_{t+2})\right](1-\vartheta_{t+1})\right\} \\
&= E_t\left\{\left[\left(\frac{P^Q_{t+1}Q_t}{P_{t+1}}\right)\delta R^Q_{t+1}\vartheta_{t+1} + \left[u\left(\frac{P^Q_{t+2}Q_t}{P_{t+2}}\right)\delta^2 R^Q_{t+1}R^Q_{t+2}\vartheta_{t+2}(1-\vartheta_{t+1})\right]\right.\right. \\
&\quad + u\left(\frac{P^Q_{t+3}Q_t}{P_{t+3}}\right)\delta^3 R^Q_{t+1}R^Q_{t+2}R^Q_{t+3}\vartheta_{t+3}(1-\vartheta_{t+2})(1-\vartheta_{t+1}) \\
&\quad \left.+u(Q_t)(1-\vartheta_{t+3})(1-\vartheta_{t+2})(1-\vartheta_{t+1})]\right\} \\
&[\ldots] \\
&= E_t\left\{\delta^T\sum_{T=t+1}^{\infty}u\left(\frac{P^Q_T Q_t}{P_T}\right)\prod\nolimits_{n=t+1}^{T}R^Q_n\vartheta_T(1-\vartheta_{T-1}) + u(Q_t)\prod\nolimits_{T=t+1}^{\infty}(1-\vartheta_T)\right\},
\end{aligned}
\tag{13.27}
$$

And so on for each subsequent substitution of $u(Q_t)$, for each date until the end of the time horizon. Notice that, as in the macro side of the model, expectations are based on information set ω_t available to the investors at each date t, which has been dropped for ease of exposition. Since wealth (and, therefore, every asset held in the portfolio) must be converted into consumption by the end of the time horizon, holdings of Q vanish in the limit as $\lim\limits_{T\to\infty}(1-\vartheta_T) = 0$. Thus, summing over the agent's infinite time.

horizon gives the utility of asset Q at date t as

$$
u(Q_t) = E_t\left\{\delta^T\sum_{T=t+1}^{\infty}u\left(\frac{P^Q_T Q_t}{P_T}\right)\prod_{n=1}^{t-1}R^Q_n\vartheta_T(1-\vartheta_{T-1})\right\} \tag{13.28}
$$

The cost of asset liquidation

Liquidating assets may involve resource costs such as for information acquisition, search, evaluation and verification, legal and administrative requirements, bargaining and negotiations, etc. Depending on the efficiency of the financial system where asset trading takes place, as well as on the state of market mood, each asset Q requires its own minimum amount of time τ_Q^* (to be defined more precisely below) for its holder to be able to sell it at the ongoing market price P^Q, net of unit liquidation cost $q^* \in (0, 1)$. If the agent is compelled to realize the asset within a time interval $\tau_Q < t_Q^*$, then she must be willing to accept a sale price lower than $\left(1 - q_Q^*\right)P^Q$, that is, the asset must sell at a price discount larger than the unit liquidation transaction cost under optimal timing $\left(q > q_Q^*\right)$. The liquidity of asset Q is therefore variable and endogenously determined, and can be modeled in terms of the following structure for asset liquidation cost

$$q = q\left(t_Q^*/\tau\right),$$

where

(a) if $0 < t_Q^* < \tau$, then, $q_Q = q_Q^* > 0$: the seller has enough time to liquidate Q and pays only q_Q^* for the transaction;
(b) if $t_Q^* > \tau \geq 0$ then, $q_Q > q_Q^*$: the seller has not enough time and must sell Q at a discount larger than the optimal unit transaction cost;
(c) $\lim_{\substack{t_Q^* > \tau \\ \tau \to 0}} q_Q = 1$: the discount increases with the time pressure on the seller to sell Q; and
(d) if $t_Q^* = 0$, then, $q_Q^* = 0$: Q is perfectly liquid (cash),

and where

$$t_Q^* = \tau\left(\Psi^Q, s_Q\right), \text{ with } \tau_\Psi < 0 \ \tau_s < 0$$

that is, the minimum time interval required to sell Q optimally decreases with structural variable Ψ^Q, which reflects the level of financial system efficiency in the trading of asset Q (including such features as technology; market platform, legal, regulatory and supervisory infrastructure; etc.,), and increases with s_Q, which captures the prevailing market sentiment for trading Q, with a high (low) s_Q indicating the state of exuberance (pessimism) in the market for Q as perceived by the agents (which is not discussed in this appendix, but is illustrated at length in Bossone (2014)).Thus, greater (lower) efficiency of the financial infrastructure where Q is traded and a "seller" ("buyer") market would shorten (lengthen) t_Q^* and lower (raise) q.

Since, at any time $T > t$, the expected utility lost to the liquidation of asset Q, inherited from time t, is a fraction ξ^Q of the expected utility from the consumption financed through the proceeds of Q,

$$\xi_T^Q = E_t\left[u\left(q_{Q_T} P_T^Q Q_t / P_T^C\right)\right] / E_t\left[u\left(P_T^Q Q_t / P_T^C\right)\right],$$

where $\xi^Q = \xi\left(q_Q\right)$, $\xi' > 0$, $\xi(0) = 0$, $\xi(1) = 1$.

Then, Eq. (13.28) can then be rewritten as

$$u(Q_t) = E_t\left\{\delta^T \sum_{T=t+1}^{\infty} u\left(\frac{P_T^Q Q_t}{P_T}\right)\prod_{n=1}^{t-1} R_n^Q \vartheta_T(1-\vartheta_{T-1})\left(1-\xi_T^Q\right)\right\}, \tag{13.29}$$

which appears as Eq. (13.15) in the text.

Note that if asset Q is cash, or M, then $P^M = 1$, $i^M = 0$, $l^M = 0$, $\xi^M = 0$, and $R^M = -p$, although if cash were digital, this would allow for $i^M \gtreqless 0$ since the issuing central bank would be able to apply positive or negative interest rates on it.

The model above can be extended to show how asset utility changes with the variability of asset prices and with changes in market sentiment (see Chap. 3 of this book).

Appendix 4: Credibility and Macro-Policies

The PTI model allows to evaluate the effects of active fiscal and monetary policies of a government by analyzing how policy stimuli are financed and how the government's financing strategy is judged by the financial markets. In this appendix, the transmission mechanisms are described in a narrative form.

Assume that a largely indebted government engineers a persistent fiscal stimulus through the issuance of new domestic debt for an indefinite period to keep the real output gap down at zero. If the government's credibility is low, investors determine an inelastic IBC and require government to commit to attaining larger primary surpluses over the immediate future to keep bond prices from falling. In fact, for economies that already suffer from low credibility, especially those already carrying large debt positions, the very intention of relaxing macro-policies might be perceived by the markets as further weakening credibility, thus tightening the government IBC. A tight(er) IBC makes the effect of the stimulus small(er) and short-lived, if at all. Moreover, if the government does not (credibly) commit to attaining larger future primary surpluses, based on the new information set, bond prices fall as investors sell domestic bonds for foreign assets, leading to higher interest rates and a contraction in the supply of money supply engineered by the central bank to accommodate higher rates, which would stymie currency depreciation. Under such conditions, the country's credibility could drop to a critical level that neutralizes the positive effect on real output of both the fiscal stimulus and real exchange rate depreciation (Fig. 13.1a).

Consider now the central bank's decision to stimulate the economy by lowering the domestic policy rate and committing to keep it low for a protracted period by supplying more money through periodic purchases of government bonds. The share of domestic bonds held by the central bank increases (at an unchanged level of total outstanding government debt) and, correspondingly, Global investors reallocate their portfolio toward foreign bonds since the marginal utility of the money balances they have received in exchange for selling bonds to the central banks has declined. This is because they now hold domestic money balances in excess to optimal balances. Therefore, ceteris paribus, portfolio compositions would feature higher shares of

(a)

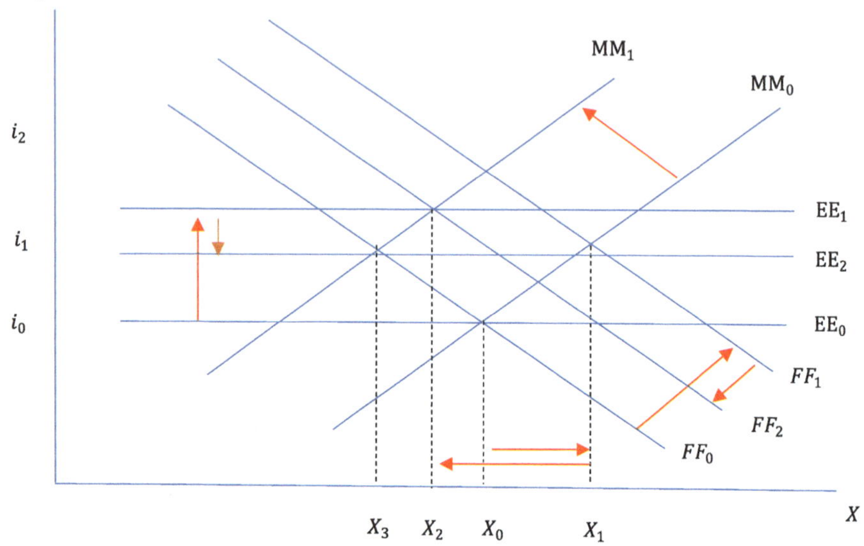

i
MM$_1$
MM$_0$
i_2
EE$_1$
i_1
EE$_2$
i_0
EE$_0$
FF_1
FF_2
FF_0
X
X_3
X_2
X_0
X_1

(b)

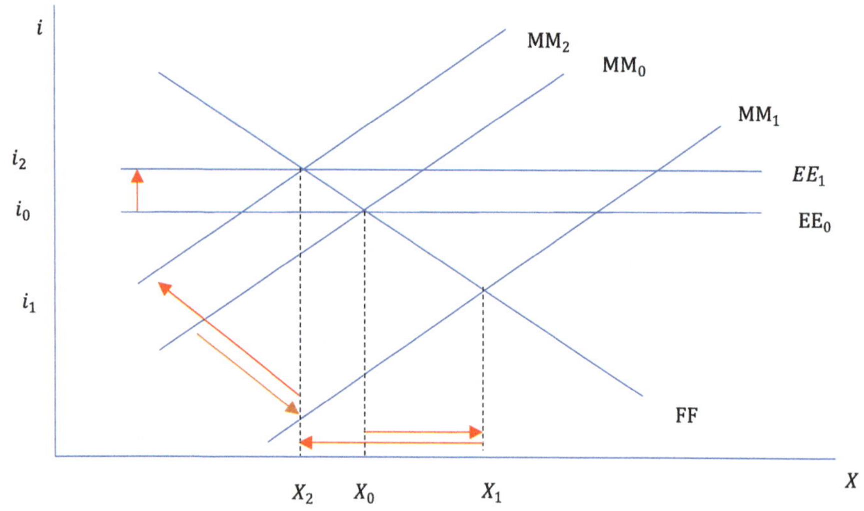

i
MM$_2$
MM$_0$
MM$_1$
i_2
EE_1
i_0
EE$_0$
i_1
FF
X
X_2
X_0
X_1

◄**Fig. 13.1** **a** Fiscal Impulse. **b** Monetary Impulse *Note* The curve MM is the locus of (i, X) pairs at which $\Delta b = 0$; the curve FF is the locus of (i, X) pairs at which $\Delta m = 0$; and the schedule EE is the locus of (i, X) pairs at which the real exchange rate does not change $\Delta\left(\frac{e}{P}\right) = 0$. Figure 13.1a portrays the case where the expansionary fiscal stimulus $\Delta b > 0$ is more than offset by the effects of the drop in the level of policy credibility as perceived by the market. The fiscal authorities initially shift the FF schedule rightward from FF_0 to FF_1 to a higher level of output, which is only partially dampened by a higher interest rate. However, the lack of credibility causes investors to sell off domestic bonds in exchange for foreign assets, and the monetary and fiscal authorities to adjust, respectively, the money and bond supply to keep balance in the bond and foreign exchange markets. As a result, the EE and MM schedules shift, respectively, from EE_0 up to EE_1 and from MM_0 backward to MM_1, and the FF schedule moves somewhat backward to FF_2, all crossing each other at an interest rate that more than offsets the initial stimulus. As noted in the text, the adjustment process might be such as to eventually lead to an appreciation of the exchange rate, lower output, and lower inflation, with the schedule EE shifting backward to EE_2. Figure 13.1b represents the case where the expansionary output effect of the monetary impulse $\Delta m > 0$ is more than offset by the effects of the drop in the level of policy credibility as perceived by the market. The monetary policy authorities initially shift the MM schedule from MM_0 to MM_1 to a lower interest and exchange rate levels. The lack of credibility, however, causes investors to sell domestic bonds for foreign assets, causing the interest rate to rise and the currency to weaken. The EE schedule shifts upward from EE_0 to EE_1 and the monetary authorities must shrink the money supply as necessary to restore equilibrium in the bond and foreign exchange markets. As a result, the adjustment might be such as to even more than offset the initial stimulus

foreign assets relative to domestic assets determine a higher nominal exchange rate. While nominal exchange rate depreciation may in principle amplify the stimulus, the intensity and duration of its effect ultimately depend on the amplitude and speed of the real exchange rate adjustment process (Fig. 13.1b).

The policy authorities should be mindful of the impact of credibility on the country's IBC. While high credibility raises the effectiveness of monetary policy, low credibility, or the erosion of credibility in the eyes of the markets, reduces it. A country's credibility might drop to such a critical level that neutralizes the effect of monetary stimulus on the nominal interest rate, and hence on real output, while the largest part of the effect would dissipate into nominal exchange rate depreciation and higher inflation.

If the central bank and government coordinate their acts and engineer a monetary financing of new debt issuance aimed to support fiscal stimulus large enough to stabilize the interest rate (a.k.a. "helicopter money"), no negative effects retrofit on real output. As a result, the fiscal-monetary impulse is unencumbered, and the policy program can be calibrated to stabilize real output at full capacity without causing inflationary pressure. This result is consistent with Buiter's (2016) conclusion that "helicopter money always works."

The monetary authorities should always consider the impact of their action on the exchange rate. If the stimulus is temporary, and the pass-through less than complete, the nominal exchange depreciation that follows the temporary excess supply of money amplifies the stimulus. However, under a persistent monetary financing of the fiscal deficits, the ongoing excess money creation affects the nominal exchange rate and the inflation rate, causing credibility to drop, the ERPT effect to increase, and the exchange rate and inflation to further rise. Thus, while policy coordination may achieve the best result possible, it is not by itself sufficient for the country to gain credibility in the eyes of the market.

Thus, as discussed in Sect. 13.9, there is no mechanical correspondence between changes in the financial claims on the government (money and/or public debt), the exchange rate, inflation, and real output. The correspondence is country-specific, it depends on the country's credibility as perceived by the markets (Fig. 13.2) and may change with government efforts (or lack thereof) to gain credibility.

Finally, consider situations where critical international developments (e.g., political turmoil, financial crises, major calamities) induce investors to shift capital to countries with high credibility, which are generally regarded as safe havens. In such situations, as the PTI suggests, the credibility gap may widen with the consequences

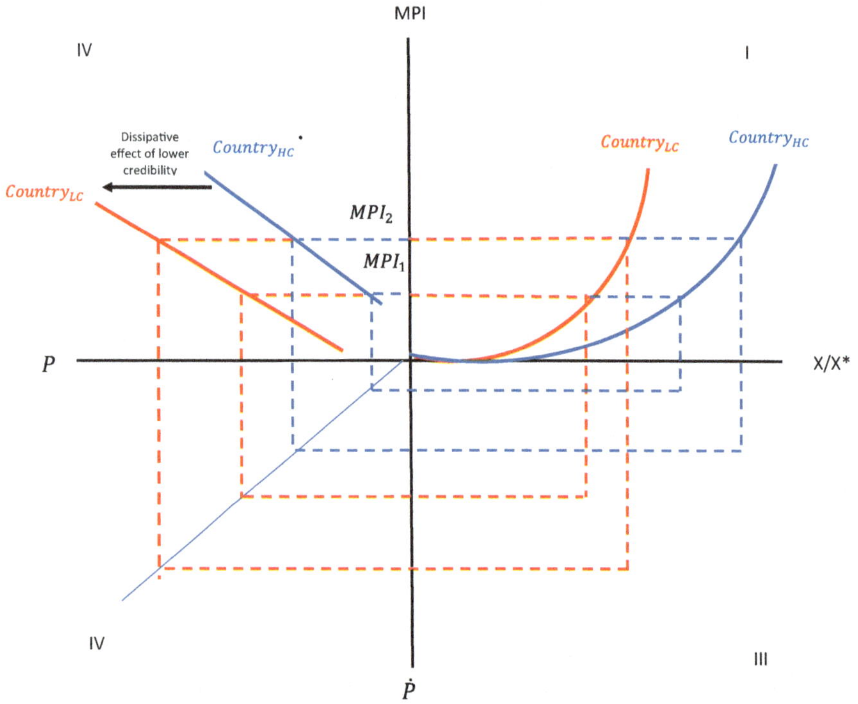

Fig. 13.2 Policy shocks and credibility *Note* The responses of real output (as a proportion to potential output) X/X* to policy shocks MPI_1 and MPI_2 are represented by the two schedules charted in quadrant I of Fig. 13.2 for high-credibility $Country_{HC}$ and low-credibility $Country_{LC}$, respectively. As discussed in Sect. 13.7, the variable MPI reflects the combined monetary and fiscal policy shocks to aggregate demand. The position of the two schedules indicates the higher effectiveness of policy shocks (in terms of output changes) in the high-credibility country. Symmetrically, policy shocks are relatively less effective (in terms of output changes) in the low-credibility country, where they dissipate instead into higher rates of inflation. The inflation response $\dot{P}$ to changes in MPI are represented by the two schedules charted in quadrant IV of Fig. 13.1 for high-credibility $Country_{HC}$ and low-credibility $Country_{LC}$, respectively. The position of the two schedules indicates the higher dissipation of the policy shocks (in terms of higher inflation) in the low-credibility country. The different colors used for the two countries are used to track their respective output and inflation responses to policy shocks, through the quadrants

that the IBC of the highest-credible countries becomes even more elastic, the policy space available to these countries for expansionary action increases further and, all else equal, their rate of inflation declines, while the opposite happens to the lowest-credible countries. In such cases, the credibility gap widens not because the authorities of the highest-credible countries have tightened their policy commitments, but because investors searching for asset protection value their credibility relatively more at times of stress.

References

Agénor, P. R. (1994). Credibility and exchange rate management in developing countries. *Journal of Development Economics, 45*(1), 1–16.

Ahumada, V. M. C. (2009). The short-term effects of fiscal policy in mexico: an empirical study. *Estudios Económicos, El Colegio De México, Centro De Estudios Económicos, 24*(1), 109–144.

Aleem, A., & Lahiani, A. (2014). Monetary policy credibility and exchange rate pass-through: Some evidence from emerging countries. *Economic Modelling 43*(C), 21–29.

Arestis, P., & Sawyer, M. (1997). Reasserting the role of keynesian policies for the new millennium. Levy Economic Institute of Bard College, Working Paper No. 207.

Barth, M. J. III, & Ramey, V. A. (2000). The cost channel of monetary transmission. NBER Working Papers 7675, National Bureau of Economic Research, Inc.

Bartholdy, J., & Kate, B. (2004). Testing for multiple types of marginal investor in ex-day pricing. *Multinational Finance Journal, 8*(3/4), 173–209.

Benigno, P., & Faia, E. (2016). Globalization, pass-through, and inflation dynamics. *International Journal of Central Banking, International Journal of Central Banking, 12*(4), 263–306.

Bossone, B. (2014), "Liquidity and capital under uncertainty and changing market sentiment: A simple analysis". *Review of Financial Economics 23*, 98–105.

Bossone, B. (2018). Exchange rates as a 'Veil.' *World Economics, 19*(2), 105–119.

Bossone, B. (2019). The portfolio theory of inflation and policy (in)effectiveness. *Economics Journal Article No., 2019–33*, 1–25.

Bossone, B. (2020a). Bringing global finance into macro-policy analysis. *World Economics, 21*(4), 89–110.

Bossone, B. (2020b). Global Finance and Effectiveness of Macro-Policies. *World Economics, 21*(2), 135–164.

Bossone, B. (2021). The portfolio theory of inflation and policy (in)effectiveness: A revisitation. *Macroeconomics and Finance in Emerging Market Economies, 14*, 2–19.

Bossone, B. (2022). The portfolio theory of inflation and policy (in)effectiveness: Exploring it further and righting the wrongs. *Economics, 16*(1), 257–275.

Bossone, B. (2023a). The *devils*: From real life to movie fiction, and economic theory and practice. *World Economics, 24*(1).

Branson, W. H. (1985). The dynamic interaction of exchange rates and trade flows. NBER Working Paper Series, Working Paper No. 1780, National Bureau of Economic Research, Cambridge, Mass.

Buiter, W. H. (2016). The simple analytics of helicopter money: why it works—Always. *Economics, 8*, 2014–2028.

Buiter, W. H., Sibert, A. C. (2017). The fallacy of the fiscal theory of the price level—One last time. Economics, Discussion Paper No. 2017–84.

Buiter, W. H. (2017). "The Fallacy of the Fiscal Theory of the Price Level – Once More," Columbia/SIPA, Center for Development Economics and Policy, CDEPCGEG Working Paper Series, No. 37, March.

Calderón, C., Duncan, R., & Schmidt-Hebbel, K. (2004). The role of credibility in the cyclical properties of macroeconomic policies in emerging economies. *Review of World Economics, 140*(4), 613–633.

Calvo, C., & Végh, C. (1991). Exchange-rate-based stabilization under imperfect credibility. IMF Working Papers, WP 1991/77, International Monetary Fund.

Calvo, G., & Reinhart, C. M. (2002). Fear of floating. *The Quarterly Journal of Economics 117*(2), 379–408.

Carrière-Swallow, Y., Gruss, B., Magud, N. E., Valencia, F. (2016). Monetary policy credibility and exchange rate pass-through, IMF Working Paper WP/16/240, International Monetary Fund.

Chen, Z., & Zhang L. (2018). Back to the beginning: does investor diversification affect the firm's cost of equity? 9 October. https://chenzhanhui.people.ust.hk/Chen_Zhang_2020.pdf.

Cochrane, J. H. (2017). Michelson-morley, fisher, and occam: the radical implications of stable quiet inflation at the Zero Bound. *NBER Macroeconomics Annual, 32*.

Edwards, S. (2006). The relationship between exchange rates and inflation targeting revisited. NBER Working Paper Series, Working Paper 12163, National Bureau of Economic Research.

Faia, E., Lewis, K. K., & Zhou, H. (2024). Do investor differences impact monetary policy spillovers to emerging markets?. CEPR Discussion Paper 19389.

Fang, X., Hardy, B., & Lewis K. K. (2024). Who holds sovereign debt and why it matters. CEPR Discussion Paper 17338.

Ferreira de Mendonça. H., & Tostes, F. (2014). The effect of monetary and fiscal credibility on exchange rate pass-through in an emerging economy. *Open Economies Review, 26*(4), 787–816.

Fritz, B., de Paula, L. F., & Magalhães Prates, D. (2018). Global currency hierarchy and national policy space: A framework for peripheral economies. *European Journal of Economics and Economic Policies: Intervention, 15*(2), 208–218.

Helmy, O., Fayed, M., & Hussien, K. (2018). Exchange rate pass-through to inflation in Egypt: A structural VAR approach. *Review of Economics and Political Science, 3*(2), 2–19.

Jašová, M., Moessner, R., & Takáts, E. (2016). Exchange rate passthrough: What has changed since the crisis? BIS Working Papers No 583, Bank for International Settlements.

Keynes, J. M. (1936). *The general theory of employment, interest and money*. Macmillan.

Lopez-Villavicencio, A., & Mignon, V. (2016). Exchange rate pass-through in emerging countries: Do the inflation environment, monetary policy regime and institutional quality matter? CEPII Working Paper No 2016-07.

Obstfeld, M., & Rogoff, K. (1995). Exchange rate dynamics redux. *Journal of Political Economy, 103*(June), 624–660.

Obstfeld, M., & Rogoff, K. (1996). *Foundations of international macroeconomics*. MIT Press.

Obstfeld, M., & Taylor, A. M. (2004). *Global capital markets: Integration, crisis, and growth*. Cambridge University Press.

Palley, T. I. (2019). The fallacy of the natural rate of interest and zero lower bound economics: why negative interest rates may not remedy Keynesian unemployment. *Review of Keynesian Economics*, 151–170.

Riksbank, S. (2016). The impact of the exchange rate on inflation. Monetary Policy Report.

Savoie-Chabot, L., & Khan, M. (2015). Exchange rate pass-through to consumer prices: Theory and recent evidence. Bank of Canada Discussion Paper 2015–9.

Subramanian, R. A., F. Nielsen, & Fachinotti, G. (2009). "Globalization of equity policy portfolios: A fresh look at strategic asset allocation from a U.S. institutional investor perspective". *Research Insight*, MSCI, October.

Suleiman, S., Alexander, A., & Olure-Bank, M. (2018). An econometric analysis of the nexus of exchange rate, inflation and budget deficit: Case of Nigeria 1981–2016. *Journal of World Economic Research, 7*(1), 1–13.

Takhtamanova, Y. (2008). Understanding changes in exchange rate pass-through. *Journal of Macroeconomics, 32*(4), 1118–1130.

Tily, G. (2012), "Keynes's Monetary Theory of Interest". BIS Paper No. 65c, May.

Wang, P. (2009). The portfolio balance approach to exchange rate determination. In *The economics of foreign exchange and global finance*, Springer, Berlin, Heidelberg.

Winkelried, D. (2014). Exchange rate pass-through and inflation targeting in Peru. *Empirical Economics, 46*(4), 1181–1196.

Zelealem, Y., & Musila, J. (2018). The dynamics of inflation, exchange rates and the trade balance in a small economy: The case of Uganda. *International Journal of Development Issues, 17*(2), 246–264.

Chapter 14
Indifference Between State Money and Public Debt

Abstract This chapter further dwells on the value of money and other instruments issued by the public sector when they are traded in globalized markets and its reflections on macro-policy effectiveness. The famous capital structure irrelevance principle of Modigliani and Miller, American Economic Review 48:261–297, (1958) is used to show that when international capital allocation choices are determined by well-informed, deep-pocketed Global investors, there are no net gains a government of a financially integrated economy can consistently extract from resorting to one type of deficit financing (say, debt) versus another (say, money) or by issuing debt in one form versus another. In particular, the approach is used to show that the cost of the capital needed by governments to finance their deficits is independent of whether: (i) financing originates from debt or money, (ii) debt is denominated in domestic or foreign currency, and (iii) money and debt are issued under floating or fixed exchange rates. The theorem's two corollaries show that governments seeking to monetize their deficits must remunerate money holdings with a real return that varies inversely with credibility and directly with the stock of money.

14.1 Preamble

The financial power of Global investors, discussed in the previous chapter, triggered my interest in another dimension of macroeconomic policies, in addition to their (in)effectiveness in globalized economies. Once the Portfolio Theory of Inflation (PTI) was developed, I started wondering whether it would make any real difference for a government (of a globalized economy) to finance its budget by issuing debt denominated in the national currency or in a currency issued by another country, or even by printing money (assuming, obviously, monetary sovereignty and setting aside the issue of an independent monetary authority having control over the money supply), as many believe that financing the debt domestically is less costly and can be shielded from the risk of default by monetizing it, if necessary.

My intuition was that the (real) value of different types of financial claims issued by a government on itself—if they are traded in the global markets—would be the

B. Bossone, *Trailblazing Visions of Money in Economic Theory*, Contributions to Economics, https://doi.org/10.1007/978-3-031-82544-6_14

same, since the government's debt repayment capacity (in real terms) is the same for all claims and since money, while not defaultable, still stands to lose (real) value if its issuances are not backed by real output (or by the capacity to produce real output in future). Besides, paying back using depreciated (or depreciating) money is a form of economic default anyway. In other words, I thought, in the eyes of global markets all claims on the same debtor must look the same, ex ante, since the expected real losses on them are the same, irrespective of their different nature or currency of denomination.

This consideration alerted me to the possibility that I could prove the validity of these arguments using the Modigliani–Miller theorem, after adapting and transposing it from the corporate world to the world of public finances. After all, using Merton Miller's colorful metaphor, a pizza eater would look at a "pizza" and not expect her appetite to be satisfied more by slicing the pizza into, say, eight rather than four pieces,[1] much like an investor would not expect the government's capacity to repay its obligations (in real terms) to change if the obligations were denominated in domestic or foreign currency, or if they consisted of money in alternative to debt securities.

The PTI further suggested that I could also use the theorem to show that governments perceived by the Global investors as having different credibility would belong to different "risk classes" (which Modigliani and Miller introduced in their original contribution), so that if governments sought to monetize their budget deficits, they would have to pay nonnegative (real) rates of interest on money holdings, whose level (in equilibrium) would vary inversely with the government's level of credibility. An important implication of the PTI is that, while the assumptions required for the Modigliani–Miller theorem to hold in the corporate world are restrictive and scarcely realistic, these are not so in financial contexts dominated by actors (i.e., the Global investors) who have the power to enforce their expectations on market outcomes (Chap. 13).

I first established these arguments in a working paper (Bossone, 2022), which I eventually published (after significant corrections and refinements) (Bossone, 2024). This chapter retraces the development of the Neutrality Theorem as I have applied it to the public finances of globalized economies and illustrates its results.

[1] Merton Miller literally said, "I have a simple explanation [for the first Modigliani–Miller proposition]. It's after the ball game, and the pizza man comes up to Yogi Berra and he says, 'Yogi, how do you want me to cut this pizza, into quarters?' Yogi says, 'No, cut it into eight pieces, I'm feeling hungry tonight.' Now when I tell that story the usual reaction is, 'And you mean to say that they gave you a [Nobel] prize for that?'" From the testimony of Merton H. Miller in Glendale Federal Bank's lawsuit against the U.S. government, December 1997, reported by Gifford (1998).

14.2 Introduction

By the 1990s, rating agencies had started to give a higher rating to domestic than foreign sovereign debt, based on the assumed greater ability and willingness of governments to pay back debt when this was denominated in their own currency. However, data analysis at that time did not find a consistent link between the currency of debt and the probability of issuer default (Packer, 2003), and a study of the cases of Argentina, Brazil, and Colombia even found that bonds issued in the international market tended to be cheaper than similar bonds issued in the domestic market (Borensztein et al., 2006).

The idea that local currency debt is less risky has become less common over time, and recent research covering large samples of emerging market economies has found little to no difference between local currency ratings and their foreign equivalents (Amstad et al., 2018). This may be partly due to the increased awareness that sovereigns can default in local as well as in foreign currencies (Reinhart & Rogoff, 2009), especially if default is broadly defined as not only stopping debt payments but also paying back domestic debt obligations in devalued (or devaluing) currencies, which lead to losses for debtholders in a similar way to default.

When financial markets are internationally integrated, and Global investors are able to exploit any price differences across markets (see Chap. 13), the irrelevance of debt composition becomes evident, as changing the type of debt does not affect a government's capacity to pay back what it owes: the government's capacity to repay (real) resources does not change regardless of the type of debt it chooses to issue. If this is true, one might also wonder why other types of differences should matter for the (real) cost of public finances, for example, differences in the underlying exchange rate regime (floating vs. fixed rates) or differences in deficit financing (debt vs. money). Could the government benefit by picking one type of funding over another (for instance, in terms of lower borrowing costs or greater policy space)?

Following my earlier studies, this chapter shows how I have applied the theorem of Modigliani and Miller (1958)—whereby the capital structure does not affect the value of a firm—to the public sector claims (money and debt) of highly financially integrated economies ("globalized"). The Modigliani–Miller (M&M) approach is adapted to public finances and proves what I have termed the Neutrality Theorem for Public Finances of globalized economies (the "Neutrality Theorem"), which states that in a globalized economy the cost of capital required by government to finance the fiscal deficits does not depend on whether (i) financing comes from debt or money, (ii) debt is denominated in domestic or foreign currency, and (iii) money and debt are issued under floating or fixed exchange rates. Two corollaries are also proven, which indicate that governments with low credibility that monetize their deficits (instead of using debt) need to offer a higher return on money holdings that increases (i) inversely with credibility and (ii) directly with the stock of money created.

The Neutrality Theorem builds on two blocks. First, like the original M&M corporate finance approach, where firms issue debt and equity, and following the Accounting View of Money (AVM) discussed in Chap. 2, the Neutrality Theorem assumes that fiat and irredeemable money issued by the state is equity (not debt) of the issuing state. Second, central to the theorem is the role of Global investors, who decide how to invest in a way that affects the value of government claims of globalized economies (see Chap. 13).[2]

This chapter is organized has follows. Section 14.3 reviews the previous studies on neutrality results in macroeconomics; Sect. 14.4 shows how the Neutrality Theorem contributes to the literature. Section 14.5 describes the main elements of the Neutrality Theorem, sets up the model of the economy, and derives its equilibrium conditions; Sect. 14.6 establishes the Neutrality Theorem and its two corollaries on the equilibrium return on money; Sect. 14.7 concludes the chapter by summarizing its findings and suggesting areas for future research.

14.3 Relevant Literature

This section reviews the literature that is relevant to the two tools that are used to prove the Neutrality Theorem. The first tool is the portfolio theory that explains the international capital allocation decisions made by the Global investors who buy and sell public sector claims issued by "globalized" economies—i.e., economies that have high international financial integration. The second tool is the M&M approach as applied to money and debt claims issued by the public sector of such economies.

The first instrument draws on the literature of the portfolio balance approach (PBA) to open economies (Branson, 1985; Backus & Kehoe 1989; Dornbusch, 1975; and references therein; Wang, 2009), which assumes that financial markets generate demand for predetermined stocks of domestic and foreign assets (such as money and bonds), depending on current wealth, and that assets are not perfect substitutes. It should be noted that while traditional PBA ignores the consequences of government budget constraints (Backus and Kehoe, cit.), the PBA underpinning Global investor choices in the Neutrality Theorem context emphasizes the pivotal role of governments' intertemporal budget constraint (IBC), as discussed below. In particular, the PBA used here goes beyond the traditional approach in that it assumes that investors have access to global capital markets and allocate resources across countries considering government IBCs as key factors for pricing their claims (money and debt).

The second instrument, namely the M&M approach, is a key tool in corporate finance (Pagano, 2005). It represents a milestone in the financial theory that helps to comprehend when and how the capital structure of a firm does not affect its value. By using the no-arbitrage condition, the M&M approach proves especially suitable

---

[2] In point of terminology, money and debt issued by the state are classified as "claims" on the issuing state, in compliance with international accounting principles and practices. While economists often mistakenly view balance sheets as being composed of Assets and Liabilities, the correct components of a balance sheet are Resources and Claims. Claims include Liabilities, such as debt, and Equity (see Chap. 2). Thus, in this chapter, money and public debt will be considered as government claims or claims issued by the public sector on itself and held by third parties.

for studying how the equilibrium market value of public sector claims (money and debt) is determined in frictionless global capital markets.

Furthermore, the extensions of the M&M approach used in this chapter and the assumptions underpinning its application (i.e., global competitive capital markets, negligible transaction costs, tax irrelevance for Global investors, full access to market funding from Global investors, and non-zero default risk of states as claim issuers) make the theorem robust against the weaknesses of its original formulation (Ahmeti & Prenaj, 2015; Stiglitz, 1967, 1988) and suitable to investigate the reality of today's financially globalized economies, as discussed below. Specifically, Stiglitz (1988) notices that the skepticism of the critics of the M&M approach focus on four assumptions underlying the model: firms are identified by risk classes; individuals and firms have same access to credit markets; investors have full information about the returns of firms; and there are no taxes (or, at least, tax policy does not treat debt and equity differently. Ahmeti and Prenaj (2015) criticize the lack of realism of the assumptions underpinning the M&M approach: no taxes, no transaction costs, perfect competition, and no bankruptcy.

Against this criticism, it should be noted that the Neutrality Theorem is based on Proposition I of the M&M approach (i.e., the firm's capital structure does not affect its cost of capital: among the three M&M propositions, it is the most robust to criticism, it is widely accepted by the mainstream, and its no-arbitrage proof has become a standard practice in finance (Miller, 1988).

The Neutrality Theorem holds even in the face of Ross's (1977) challenge to the M&M approach, later reiterated by Myers and Majluf (1984), whereby firm managers (who usually have access to better information than external investors) can signal to that their firm's prospects have improved by raising the firm's debt-to-equity ratio, and vice versa. In the Neutrality Theorem context, Global investors are not only enough informed to extract correct signals from changes in government finances (especially to infer whether they truly reflect the underlying economic fundamentals); they also play a key role in determining the market prices of government claims, even if the government sends inconsistent signals (see Chap. 13).

Similarly, the Neutrality Theorem is consistent with the results by Gersbach et al. (2015), which applies the M&M approach to the banking sector (that is, the value of banks) in a general equilibrium model and shows that while neutrality does not hold under certain frictions and distortions (e.g., moral hazard; deposit guarantee by government; and government rescue of banks in case of default, funded by taxes), it does hold when minimum equity capital requirements are imposed, which mitigate those frictions and distortions.

Indeed, the global context that supports the Neutrality Theorem allows more robustness to the M&M approach than the domestic context adopted by Gerbash et al., cit., since in the former neutrality can be maintained (even despite similar frictions and distortions) through minimum liquidity requirements (including foreign exchange reserves), which Global investors can compel governments to keep against their issued claims. More specifically, in the set of bad equilibria described by Gersbach et al., cit., bank debt-equity ratios are higher than in the set of good equilibria. Banks attract more funds than in the good equilibria, take excess risk in lending, and are financed largely by debt. They generate high returns on equity in the good states and default in the bad states. In the case of default, banks receive funds from the government to pay out their debt holders. Those government expenditures are financed by taxes levied on households and thus on the debt holders themselves. Ex post, the bailout is neutral for households as they essentially finance their deposit claims with their own taxes. Ex ante, however, households are willing to hold large amounts of deposits due to the deposit guarantee and have no influence on bank risk taking, the implied riskiness of bank equity, and the ensuing tax burden when banks default. The fundamental differences with the Neutrality Theorem context are that, unlike households in a domestic context, Global investors are not taxed in the case of bailout of a defaulting government; also, they might not be willing to hold large amounts of claims on certain governments (or under certain contingencies) in the absence of foreign guarantees; and, finally, they stand ready to exit their investment positions if they perceive excess risk taking by the governments in which they are invested. Importantly, in addition, Global investors (unlike households with banks) do influence governments' risk taking and the implied riskiness of their currencies. All these differences militate in favor of strengthening the neutrality result.

An extensive review of the relevant literature should also consider other neutrality theorems for public finances. The most relevant ones are the Ricardian Equivalence Theorem (RET) by Barro (1974) and the Wallace Irrelevance Proposition (WIP) by Wallace (1981). However, both theorems have important differences from the M&M application, which need to be discussed. As is widely known, the RET says that fiscal policy does not work as a way to boost aggregate demand and output, because rational households understand that the tax cuts or deficit spending done by the government today will have to be repaid in future: anticipating these payments, they increase their current savings and thus cancel out the fiscal stimulus.[3] Unlike the M&M, whose rationality and infinite life assumptions pertain more realistically to a special class of actors (i.e., the Global investors), the RET rests fundamentally on households being experts and fully informed, and planning ahead based on permanent income expectations over an infinite lifetime horizon (or being intergenerationally connected through income transfers motivated by altruistic behavior).

On the other hand, the WIP states that, under some conditions and holding fiscal policy constant, alternative paths of the monetary policies have no effect on the sequences of the price level and resource allocations in the economy. The proposition rests on a no-arbitrage argument like that of the M&M approach but, unlike the latter, it requires that all agents in the economy be expert, well-informed, and infinitely lived optimizers.

The neutrality results discussed in this chapter are similar to those obtained by Cunha (2006), though using a different methodology.[4] The application of the M&M approach to public finances lies at its core and is used to investigate its implications

[3] For a review of the RET-related literature, see Kooij (2011).

[4] Cunha, cit., offers a comprehensive review of the many works that have applied the reasoning of the M&Miller Theorem to analyze macroeconomic questions.

for the study of exchange rate policies. The study demonstrates that, in a deterministic model, the structure of government liabilities is undetermined in any competitive equilibrium, that is, every implementable allocation and price sequence can be decentralized by a floating regime, as well as by a regime in which the exchange rate never floats. It shows also that if the government can issue nominal bonds of several maturities, the same results can hold in a stochastic economy. The study finally concludes that the link between exchange rate policy and the M&M Theorem implies that a standard macroeconomic model with complete information and a passive government is ill suited to the study of exchange rate regimes.

Aside from the different analytical methods used,[5] the major difference between my approach and Cunha's rests on the global market configuration I have used, which renders the M&M assumptions non-restrictive and realistic (as discussed next). Also, the global market configuration of my approach lead to a conclusion that complements Cunha's, whereby (i) complete information is unnecessary to obtain neutrality—it is only necessary that Global investors are granted access to information by governments (which is the case if governments want access to international capital), and (ii) governments are not passive, yet their policy choices are judged by the markets and market judgments are reflected in the prices of public sector claims (i.e., money and all types of debts).

14.4 Contribution to the Literature

The Neutrality Theorem examined in this chapter demonstrates that the way a government pays for the budget with money or (domestic or foreign) debt does not affect the cost of capital it faces, and this is true for both fixed and floating exchange rate regimes (and any arrangements in the between). The theorem is based on more realistic assumptions than those that support the RET and WIP: whereas the latter require (unrealistically) that *many* (unexpert) households behave consistently with a model of the economy where all future generation plans are correctly retroflected within their current decisions (and are not robust to changes in assumptions[6]), the Neutrality Theorem only requires (realistically) that no more than a *relatively small number* of (expert) Global investors determine asset prices that fulfill their own beliefs on how the economies work in the global markets. However, this should be seen as a minimum condition, in the sense that the larger is the number of investors who share the same views, the stronger is their price setting power in the market. In

---

[5] To exploit the strengths of the M&M approach treating balance-sheet claims as variables subject to the valuation of competitive markets, I tried to stick as closely as possible to the original M&M methodology when dealing with claims issued by the state.

[6] For instance, the RET can be shown not to hold (and, hence, Keynesian multiplier effects to obtain) in dynamic optimizing models where one combines price rigidities and the birth of new agents (Bénassy, 2006), while the WIP ceases to be valid when the allocation of risk in the economy changes due to reallocations of assets holdings between private and public sectors (Benigno and Nisticò, 2020).

practice, also, it might happen that a small group of influential investors set the trend in the market that will be followed by a multitude of other smaller and less influential investors.[7]

In general, while the proof of the Neutrality Theorem relies on a very simplified setting (as do all other neutrality theorems in the literature), the method used in this chapter introduces an important element of reality in replacing the small domestic representative agent that is usually assumed in common modeling approaches with a big player (the Global investor) who holds the power to influence the market.

Another major benefit of the method used in this chapter, besides using a well-known approach (the M&M approach) drawn from the finance literature, is that it can produce several neutrality results at the same time—for different types of government claims (i.e., money vs. debt), for different exchange rate regimes (i.e., floating vs. fixed) under which they are traded, and for different currencies in which they are issued (foreign vs. domestic)—with a simple aggregate model of the economy, under assumptions that are more realistic than in standard M&M analysis due to Global investors' ability to set market prices. The factors that make the M&M assumptions and its core principle of no-arbitrage more realistic than other models using the M&M approach, based on local agents and segmented markets, are the global integration of financial markets, the rising inequality of wealth within countries, the institutionalization of savings management in many countries, and the prominent role of Global investors (especially their market power).

The Neutrality Theorem becomes important for the public finance decisions of governments of globalized economies precisely because it makes more realistic assumptions. Its underlying perspective is different from the one that underlies the original M&M approach (and the literature on "invariance propositions" in general): whereas the M&M approach uses a high abstraction (perfect competition) to show how things work when competition is imperfect, the Neutrality Theorem explores how things change in a world that is very competitive and some actors have the power to use competition to their advantage: the former ignores—unrealistically—the existence of market frictions; the latter assumes—realistically—their absence. In other words, adding to the analysis the assumption of frictions (for example, for arbitrage) would not make it more realistic; it would rather go against its aim, which is to study the impact of financial markets dominated by global players on public finances.

[7] Along with sharing beliefs that may lead Global investors to coordinate their investment decisions in the marketplace, the mechanisms should be noted through which Global investors obtain and maintain their authority as a group (or class) of transnational stakeholders by organizing themselves in a club-like fashion, where the "club" serves as the tool through which self-selected elite members of the community gain influence and reproduce their power (Tsingou, 2014).

14.5 The Building Blocks of the Neutrality Theorem

14.5.1 Money as Equity of the Issuing State

As increasingly emerging in the Economics literature and as the international accounting standards setting community is recognizing, state-issued fiat money that cannot be redeemed for anything else (i.e., a representation of value created out of nothing) creates a specific kind of revenue income that matches the real resources that the issuing state can obtain with fiat money (see Chap. 2). In other words, when the state exchanges its money for real resources or for promises to get real resources later, its value is an income source for the money issuing state. From the accounting rules perspective, this income is "equity" of the issuing state if it is not distributed, and it cannot be seen as debt anymore, as it would be if money could be redeemed for commodities or others' claims (e.g., under fixed exchange rate agreements, dollarization of the economy, and currency boards).[8]

The idea of money as equity of the state that issues it is very helpful to apply the M&M approach from its usual area of corporate finance to the area of public finances. However, while the "money-is-equity" idea makes the Neutrality Theorem and the original M&M approach look the same, since in both cases investors are indifferent between equity and debt, the traditional idea of "money-is-liability" would make them look different but would not change the theorem's outcomes and would show investor indifference between money and debt as between two kinds of public sector claims—the first one being unpayable but exposed to loss of value (through inflation and/or currency devaluation) and the second one being payable and exposed to default risk.

14.5.2 The Central Role of Global Investors

In this chapter, the Global investors are understood exactly as in Chap. 13 and their features will not be repeated here. It is only worth emphasizing their market power and influence over the price setting process of the securities and currencies issued by countries, with their power and influence being magnified where wealth is highly concentrated, savings are largely institutionalized, and wealth is managed professionally.

[8] Notice that when money is accounted for as equity of the state that issues it, it implies the recognition of certain ownership rights. However, these rights differ from those associated with corporate shares. While corporate shares grant their holders residual claims on the net assets of the issuing company, money as equity does not grant its holders residual claims on the net assets of the issuing state. Instead, the rights associated with money as equity consist of claims on the marketable national wealth or accumulated output. This means that money holders can exercise their claims at any time, acquiring generalized purchasing power on national wealth.

This section only elaborates on the realism that the role of Global investors adds to the Neutrality Theorem as applied to public finances, in contrast to the criticism of unrealism to which the original M&M approach has been subjected as applying to the corporate world.

The original M&M approach assumed perfect competition, which in modern equilibrium analysis terminology implies complete markets and symmetric information. These assumptions, while commonly used, are unrealistic and overly constrictive when assessing the connection between investors and invested entities. One could contend that while the model utilized for the Neutrality Theorem allows for a distinct category of actors (i.e., the Global investors) with enhanced information and extensive information-processing capability, and operating with ample diversification options, these actors would still never possess equal information to governments and would be unable to fully safeguard themselves against all contingencies and risks, due to market incompleteness.

Would neutrality apply under the less than "ideal" conditions? The answer is, "yes."[9] Neutrality of public finances in globalized economies does not need to rely on such extreme assumptions as the original M&M approach for it to be valid. Even with asymmetric information, the realistic traits that characterize Global investors place them in a powerful position, dissuading governments from concealing information on a consistent basis, for fear of losing market access and facing significant repercussions. It should be noted that given the pivotal role of credibility in driving Global investor decisions, any perceived or observed lack of transparency from governments promptly influences investment choices and market values, penalizing governmental opacity.

Ultimately, the Neutrality Theorem signifies that "sound policy," as judged by the markets, is what makes an economy attractive for investment. Consequently, policymakers of globalized economies must ensure their actions align with market preferences. Thus, incentives promote information symmetry and expectations alignment in the market. Moreover, neutrality only necessitates that Global investors can engage in arbitrage across various investments and markets at minimal cost and can demobilize investments instantly when they so wish. In conclusion, the presence of Global investors with the capability to enforce their own expectations in market outcomes mitigates some of the unrealistic aspects of the M&M assumptions, and even make them realistic. Additionally, the unrestricted access of Global investors to financial resources and their exemption from local investment taxes (except in their domiciles) further bolsters the realism of the frictionless nature of economy's model assumed.

---

[9] Notice that Cunha, cit., too, shares this conclusion, though using a different approach (as discussed in Sect. 14.2).

14.5.3 The Economy

The following analysis uses a simple and basic multi-economy model with general equilibrium, where each economy has two kinds of agents: the state and a representative Global investor. The model does not include other relationships (e.g., consumption, investment, external trade, etc.) that are not central to the problem at hand, but only focuses on the portfolio allocation decisions of the representative Global investor under different government budget financing options.

Each economy consists of two sectors and produces over time a stream of aggregate output X (see below). One sector—the state—finances production by taxing the private sector and issuing claims in the form of equity (money), M, and debt, D, which are held by the private sector, including both domestic and foreign entities, and notably Global investors among the latter. Global investors do not pay taxes within the domestic economy on their holdings of government claims. The private sector finances production by creating inside money, typically in the form of commercial bank demand deposits, DD, and by issuing equity, Q, on itself. Public and private sector claims are supported by the economy's capitalized output and their capacity to mobilize output to fulfill the obligations arising from those claims.

Each economy is characterized by credibility, $\beta \in [0, 1]$, attributed to it by the Global investors. Credibility factor β has a value range that goes from the lowest point of $\beta = 0$, which means no credibility at all, to the highest point of $\beta = 1$, which means complete trust.

Each economy generates a stream of future aggregate output levels $X(1), X(2), \ldots, X(t), \ldots, X(T)$, which extend indefinitely into the future; these levels are not constant, and they are uncertain. It is assumed that the mean value of the stream over time, or the average output-return per unit of time, is finite and represents a random variable subject to a (subjective) probability distribution. Specifically, the economy's output X is itself a random variable with probability distribution $\phi(X)$, whose form is uniquely determined by function $x(X) = x[X(1), X(2), Xt), \ldots, X(T)]$, and the expected aggregate output-return, $\overline{X}$, is defined as $\overline{X} \equiv E(X) = \int x(X)\phi(X)dX$, with $Var(X) = \int (x(X) - E(x))^2\phi(X)dX$.

The State

In this chapter, the term "state" means a single public entity, with a combined balance sheet of the central bank and the treasury, which decides the amount (or the price) and the type of the public sector claims. In each economy, the state in each economy creates money and debt claims. Debt consists of bonds denominated in either the domestic currency or a foreign (typically reserve) currency, which trade at prices P_{Dd} and P_{Df}, where subscripts d and f stand for domestic and foreign, respectively.

The assumption is that the government spends public sector debt at each date to close any possible gap between actual and potential output:

$$G_t - T_r = \Delta M_t + P_{D,t}\Delta D_t = \chi\left(X^E - X_t\right) \quad \text{with } \chi' > 0, \tag{14.1}$$

where T is taxes, and X^E is full-employment output, given the government's IBC:

$$P_{D,t}D_t = \sum_{\tau=t}^{\infty} \gamma^t \beta^t (T_t - G_t + \Delta M_t), \tag{14.2}$$

which requires that the government debt's current market value must be equal to the future streams of government primary surpluses, $T - G$, and monetary fundings, ΔM, discounted to their present value.

Equation (14.1) shows the policy reason for a government to intentionally run fiscal deficits and decide how to fund them. The value given by Eq. (14.2) shows government credibility as seen by Global investors and expressed in factor β (explained in Chap. 13), which summarizes the Global investors' opinions on the policy trustworthiness of different country economies. This factor can be equally understood as an index that investors use to adjust the government IBC, which increases or decreases its value accordingly, or as a probability measure that creates an expected value of the IBC, or else as a risk factor that changes the value of the IBC. All else equal, a lower β means bigger expected losses on government debt (either via higher inflation or default) and leads to a stricter IBC for the government, thus requiring bigger (and possibly more immediate) fiscal actions to support a given debt level.

Money and bonds are used by the domestic agents for consumption and saving-investment purposes and can be intermediated in foreign exchange and financial markets largely dominated by Global investors.

Money claims give their holders a real rate of return, r_M, and government debt offers to its holders real rate, r_D. As will be shown later, the return on money depends positively on the expected stock of money claims and negatively on the stock of debt existing as well as on the economy's credibility. The return on debt, too, varies inversely with the economy's credibility, but positively with ratio $\frac{P_{Dd}D_d + e_{df}P_{Df}D_f}{PX} \equiv \mathcal{D}$ (for a given demand for debt), where P is the economy's output general price level, and the ratio measures the market value of debt (in real terms) relative to the economy's output-return. Thus,

$$r_D = r(\mathcal{D}, \beta), \quad \text{with } r'_{\mathcal{D}} > 0 \text{ and } r'_{\beta} < 0 \tag{14.3}$$

that is, as the ratio $\mathcal{D}$ grows, and the economy's credibility weakens, the rate r_D increases until the government may reach a point where it cannot (or does not want to) continue to pay its debt in real terms; at this point, either it will stop its payments causing a technical default, or it will pay with domestic currency whose external value would (all else being equal) decline, thus making holders lose value (in real terms), which will from now on be called "economic" default. Specifically, denoting θ the probability of government default, this is determined by the following relationships:

$$\theta \in [0, 1] : \begin{cases} \approx 1, & \text{if } D \gg \mathcal{D}^C \\ = \theta_\beta \ll 1, & \text{if } \beta \gg 0, D \leq \mathcal{D}^c, \text{ and } \mu_d \leq \mu_f \end{cases} \quad \text{where } \mathcal{D}^c = \delta(\beta), \delta' > 0 \tag{14.4}$$

and

$$\theta = \theta(\mu_d - \mu_f), \quad \text{with } \theta' > 0, \tag{14.5}$$

that is, the default probability reflects the economy's credibility β and equals its minimum value θ_β, strictly lower than 1, if the debt ratio stays within its critical threshold and the rate of growth of the stock of domestic currency μ_d does not exceed that of the foreign currency μ_f taken as benchmark. If the debt ratio goes beyond the critical threshold, the default probability is higher, and it is at its maximum level when the latter condition is not met. Therefore, the more credible the economy, the more room its government has for proactive macroeconomic policies. Later, for analytical convenience, the default probability will be posited as $\theta_\beta = 1 - \beta$.

The Global Investor

The representative Global investor—acting on its own behalf and/or behalf of its clients—maximizes the intertemporal utility generated by wealth portfolio W[10]:

$$U(W_t) = \text{Max}_W E_t\left[\sum_{t=\tau}^{\infty} \gamma^t u(W_t)\right] \tag{14.6}$$

s.t.

$$\begin{aligned} W_t &= M_{d,t} + e_{df,t}M_{f,t} + P_{Dd,t}D_{d,t} + e_{df,t}P_{Df,t}D_{f,t} - \Delta W'_{t-1} \\ &= M_{t-1}R_{M,t-1} + e_t M_{f,t-1}R_{M,t-1} + P_{Dd,t}D_{d,t}R_{D,t-1} \\ &\quad + e_{df,t}R_{Df,t-1}P_{Df,t}D_{f,t} + \Delta W_{t-1} + (1 - r_W)\Delta W'_{t-1}, \end{aligned} \tag{14.7}$$

$$M_d, M_f, D_d, D_f \geq 0; \quad \Delta W \gtreqless 0 \Delta W' \geq 0, \quad \text{and} \tag{14.8}$$

$$\sum_{n=d,f} \frac{P_{n,t}X_{n,t}}{\rho_{\beta n}} = W_t \tag{14.9}$$

where e_{df} is the market exchange rate between domestic currency d and foreign currency f and is expressed as the number of units of the former per unit of the latter, and the summation term in Eq. (14.9) is the sum of capitalized output across the economies where Global investors invest and represents the source of real wealth (see the market valuation of public sector claims relative to the economy's output, below). Finally, the optimization plan is closed by transversality condition:

$$\lim_{t \to \infty} W_t = 0. \tag{14.10}$$

[10] This model follows the asset utility approach discussed in Chaps. 3 and 12.

In the above model, function $u(\cdot)$ is a standard strictly quasi concave, time-separable, and well-behaved utility function; ΔW is net additional investment or divestment taking place through Global investors, where net divestments correspond to consumption decisions taken by agents who had previously invested in the portfolio of the Global investor (in other words, these agents liquidate (part of) their investment to finance current consumption; if they divest funds to re-invest them, their net effect on the Global investor's portfolio is zero, $\Delta W = 0$. Conversely, if agents invest more money, then this adds to the Global investor's portfolio, $\Delta W > 0$; $\Delta W'$ is borrowing from the market that the Global investor might want to access in order to fund extra current investments; R is the real gross rate of return on assets and incorporates the risk of loss from government (technical or economic) default, $1 - \beta$.

Equilibrium (Not Necessarily at Full Employment)

Considering the potential for unemployment and the government's choice to use active macro policies to deal with it, as shown in Eq. (14.1), considering the government's choice to create money and/or debt claims of certain amounts and (or at certain prices) and in certain combinations to reach the policy goal under Eq. (14.1) given the constraint of Eq. (14.2), and given the economy's expected aggregate output, $\overline{X}$, in equilibrium the total real market value of the economy is

$$V^* = \frac{M^* + P_D^* D_d^* + e_{df}^* P_{Df}^* D_f^* + DD_D^* + P_Q^* Q_d^*}{P^*} = \frac{\overline{X}}{\rho^*}, \tag{14.11}$$

where ρ is the anticipated level of output-return for the economy-back to the market value of all claims and matches the average cost of capital. Equation (14.11) is the adaptation (after adjustments) of Modigliani and Miller's (1958) basic equation (Eq. (14.3) in their text) that supports their Proposition I. Applied to the economy, Eq. (14.11) means that in equilibrium the value of the economy, shown in the middle term of the equation as the real value of the total amount of (real and financial) wealth is equal to the capitalized value of the economy's output on the right-hand side of the equation. Another way to say this is that real output is what ultimately supports (and gives value to) the claims owned by wealth holders.

By including the economy's credibility factor β in Eq. (14.11), removing the aster, and assuming private sector money and equity claims are zero, which does not affect the analysis, since they are not important for it,[11] the equation can be rewritten in a more general form as:

[11] Including private sector claims in a non-trivial way would introduce unnecessary complications for the demonstration of the theorem, since the role of Global investors as market price setters would be much less relevant for private sector claims than for public sector ones: many private sector companies raise funds locally and do not need Global investors as defined in this chapter. The diversified set of heterogenous investors that would have to be contemplated, many of them small and local, would imply distortions and frictions that would forswear neutrality with public finances and add nothing to their better understanding.

$$V_\beta = \frac{\beta(+P_D D_d + e_{df} P_D D_d)}{P} = \frac{\overline{X}}{\rho_\beta}, \tag{14.11a}$$

where credibility β acts as a discount factor and can be interpreted as the expected value of the public sector claims outstanding that would be recovered—through the output generated by the economy—in the event of government (technical and economic) default, and $\rho_{\beta_1} > \rho_{\beta_2}$, if $\beta_1 < \beta_2$. Its complement, $1 - \beta$, is thus the expected value loss (as posited earlier). Also, ρ_β is the economy's expected rate of output-return on public sector claims, which reflects the government's credibility and, hence, its risk of default.

For given levels of the economies' output and given sequences of expected returns and exchange rate changes conditional on the economies' level of credibility $\left[(R_{M_d,t}, R_{M_f,t}, R_{D_d,t}, R_{D_f,t}, \varepsilon_{df,t})|\beta_d, \beta_f\right]$, for $t = T, \ldots, \infty$, solving plan (14.6–14.10) yields the optimal portfolio composition $\left(M^*_{d,t}, M^*_{f,t}, D^*_{d,t}, , D^*_{f,t}\right)$ of the Global Investor at equilibrium prices $\left(P^*_t, P^*_{Dd,t}, P^*_{Df,t}, , e^*_{df,t}\right)$ at each date of the relevant time horizon, as determined by the following two first order conditions; the first f.o.c. is:

$$u'(M_{d,t})R_{M_d,t} = \frac{1}{e_t}u'(M_{f,t})R_{M_f,t} = \frac{1}{P_{Dd,t}}u'(D_{d,t})R_{D_d,t} = \frac{1}{e_{df,t}P_{Df,t}}u'(D_{f,t})R_{D_f,t} = \lambda_t, \tag{14.12}$$

which requires equating the marginal utilities of domestic and foreign M and D holdings, each weighted with its own price, and the second f.o.c. is:

$$\lambda_t = \gamma E_t R_{Md,t+1}\lambda_{t+1} = \gamma E_t R_{Mf,t+1}\lambda_{t+1} = \gamma E_t R_{Dd,t+1}\lambda_{t+1} = \gamma E_t R_{Df,t+1}\lambda_{t+1}. \tag{14.13}$$

Equation (14.13) means that all returns on assets, after adjusting for inflation and default risk, should be equalized at any given time and over time. To make it complete, and even though consumption choices are not part of the model, it can be added that optimality implies that the marginal utility of selling some assets from its portfolio to pay for consumption activities (as mentioned before) is the same as the marginal utility of keeping or buying other assets.

Equation (14.11) shows that this model does not have any way to guarantee that equilibrium is reached when all resources are fully used. The expected output return of the economy can settle at any level and this level would reflect the portfolio decisions of Global investors. Thus, in situations of underemployment or unemployment of resources, governments may legitimately adopt active macro policies. How neutrality affects them is explored next.

14.6 The Neutrality Theorem for Public Finances

The Neutrality Theorem and the two Corollaries on the Equilibrium Return on Money are presented and analyzed here.

14.6.1 *Neutrality Theorem*

From Eq. (14.11a) in equilibrium, and in the vein of Modigliani and Miller, follows:

$$\frac{\overline{X}}{\beta\left(M + P_{Dd}D_d + e_{df}P_{Df}D_f\right)\frac{1}{P}} = \frac{\overline{X}}{V_\beta} = \rho_\beta, \tag{14.14}$$

which is the fundamental equation of the **Neutrality Theorem for Public Finances**: *In equilibrium, the average cost of capital to a government (i) is independent of the capital structure of the government finances and (ii) is equal to the capitalization rate of the output stream expected to be generated by the economy.*

The Neutrality Theorem can be demonstrated by showing that if Eqs. (14.11a) or (14.14) are violated for any pair of financially globalized economies with the same credibility level, then arbitrage will occur in the global capital market and restore the equalities. The term arbitrage is used deliberately. Because, if the theorem were false, Global investors could trade currencies and bonds and swap one income stream for another that is identical in all relevant aspects except that it has a lower price. This would be beneficial to Global investors regardless of their risk preferences,[12] and as they take advantage of these arbitrage opportunities, the value of the overvalued securities (currencies and bonds) drops and the value of the undervalued securities (currencies and bonds) increases, eventually removing any value differences.

Proof Consider two identical economies (i, j), featuring the same level of credibility, $\beta_i = \beta_j$, which generate equal output-returns, $\overline{X}_i = \overline{X}_j = \overline{X}$. Let the government of economy i finance itself entirely by printing money, M_i, and call it for brevity the "money-financed" economy, and let the government of economy j finance itself partly through money printing, M_j, and partly through issuing debt alternatively denominated either in the domestic currency, $P_{Ddj}D_{dj}$, or in a foreign (typically) reserve currency, $P_{Dfj}D_{fj}$, and call it the "debt-financed" economy.

The proof will consist of four scenarios: (i) high credibility and fixed exchange rates; (ii) high credibility and floating exchange rates; (iii) low credibility and fixed exchange rates; and (iv) low credibility and floating exchange rates. Before going

[12] In choice theory, exchanges are movements from inefficient points in the interior to efficient points on the boundary of the investor's opportunity set – not movements between efficient points along the boundary. Hence, in this chapter's analysis there is no implications for investor attitudes or behaviors other than they act consistently and always prefer more income to less income, ceteris paribus.

on with the proof, a remark is needed on the currency of debt denomination. The situations of domestic and foreign currency of public debt will be handled separately and under the assumptions of fixed and floating exchange rates, respectively. The two situations, however, are the same in the case of highly credible economies, where the chance of (technical or economic default) is zero and Global investors do not care about the currency of otherwise identical bonds that only differ for their currency, and thus consider them as perfect substitutes of each other. (The risk indifference issue will be discussed later.) In this case, as shown next, the analysis can be done in terms of one single currency of debt denomination only, since one case also covers exactly the other. The following analysis will only use the foreign currency except for the case of economies with low credibility, where the two different currencies may not be considered equally.

(i) ***High Credibility and Fixed Exchange Rates***

Economies i and j are both highly credible, $\beta_i = \beta_j = 1$, and economy j adopts a fixed exchange rate regime, with the exchange rate being set exogenously and is posited as $e_{jf} = 1$ for expositional convenience. Credibility is such that $E(\varepsilon_{jf}) = 0$, where ε_{if} is the rate of change of the exchange rate. This implies, as noted, that one unit of D^d is identical to, and perfectly interchangeable with, one unit of D^f and trades at the same price in the market. As an additional assumption, the debt ratio of both economies is well within the critical threshold corresponding to the economies' identical level of credibility, $\mathcal{D}_i, \mathcal{D}_j \ll \mathcal{D}^c_\beta$, so that no risk of default is considered for either government.

Following Modigliani and Miller, suppose the value of the debt-financed economy is conjectured to be larger than that of the money-financed economy, $V_j > V_i$, as it is the case when markets believe that deficit monetization is inflationary. Consider Global investors holding m_j unit of currency j, representing a fraction α of M_j. The return from this portfolio, denoted by Y_j, will thus be a fraction α of the income available for the holders of currency j, which is equal to the total output-return X_j less the interest charge,$r_{Dj}P_{Df}D_{fj}$. By the above assumption $\overline{X}_i = \overline{X}_i = \overline{X}$, the return from the initial portfolio can be written as:

$$Y_j = \alpha\left(\overline{X} - r_{Dj}P_{Df}D_{fj}\right). \tag{14.15}$$

Positing in the following $P = 1$ for convenience, suppose now that Global investors sold αM_j worth of currency j and acquired instead an amount $m_i = \alpha\left(M_j + P_{Df}D_{fj}\right)$ of currency i. They could do so by utilizing the amount αM_j realized from the sale of their initial holdings and by borrowing an additional amount $\alpha P_{Df}D_{fj}$ on their own credit and investing it in economy i, or by reducing the amount of bonds and other securities they already hold. They would thus secure for themselves a fraction $\frac{m_i}{M_i} = \frac{\alpha(M_j+P_{Df}D_{fj})}{M_i}$ of currency i. Making allowance for the interest payments on their debt $\alpha r_{Dj}P_{Df}D_{fj}$ or for the incomes forgone by selling bonds or other securities, the return from the new portfolio, V_i, is given by:

$$Y_i = \frac{\alpha\left(M_j + P_{Df}D_{fj}\right)}{M_i}\overline{X} - \alpha r_{Dj}P_{Df}D_{fj} = \alpha\frac{V_j}{V_i}\overline{X} - \alpha r_{Dj}P_{Df}D_{fj}. \tag{14.16}$$

Comparing Eqs. (14.15) and (14.16), it can be observed that if $V_j > V_i$, then it must be that $Y_i > Y_j$. Thus, it pays holders of currency j to sell it, thereby depressing its value and, hence V_j, and to acquire instead currency i, thereby raising its value, and hence V_i. The implication is that economies that rely on debt do not have an advantage over (hypothetically identical) economies that rely on money, because Global investors can achieve the same leverage in their portfolio by borrowing the required liquidity from the market.

Consider now the other possibility, namely that the value of debt-financed economy j is conjectured to be less than money-financed economy i, $V_i > V_j$, as for instance would be the case under expectations consistent with Modern Money Theory (see Chapter 14). Suppose that Global investors hold initially an amount m_i of currency i, representing a fraction α of the total outstanding stock of money, M_i. The return from this holding is:

$$Y_i = \frac{m_i}{M_i}\overline{X} = \alpha\overline{X} \tag{14.17}$$

Suppose now that Global investors exchange their initial holdings for an alternative portfolio, also worth m_i, but consisting of m_j units of currency j and d_j^f units of bonds j, where m_j and d_j^f are given respectively by:

$$m_j = \frac{M_j}{V_j}m_i,\ \text{and}\ d_j^f = \frac{P_{Df}D_{fj}}{V_j}m_i. \tag{14.18}$$

In other words, the new portfolio includes economy j's currency and bonds in the proportions $\frac{M_j}{V_j}$ and $\frac{P_{Df}D_{fj}}{V_j}$, respectively. The return from the currency in the new portfolio will be the fraction $\frac{m_j}{M_j}$ of the total return to economy j, which is $\left(\overline{X} - r_{Dj}P_{Df}D_{fj}\right)$, and the return from the bonds will be $r_{Dj}P_{Df}d_j^f$. Using Eq. (14.17), and since $m_i = \alpha M_i$, the total return from the portfolio, Y_j, is:

$$\begin{aligned} Y_j &= \frac{m_j}{M_j}\left(\overline{X} - r_{Dj}P_{Df}D_{fj}\right) + r_{Dj}d_j^f \\ &= \frac{m_j}{V_j}\left(\overline{X} - r_{Dj}P_{Df}D_{fj}\right) + \frac{r_{Dj}P_{Df}D_{fj}}{V_j}m_j = \frac{m_j}{V_j}\overline{X} = \alpha\frac{M_j}{V_j}\overline{X}. \end{aligned} \tag{14.19}$$

Comparing Eqs. (14.17) and (14.19), it can be observed that if $V_j < M_j \equiv V_i$, then it must also be that $Y_j > Y_i$. Thus, it pays the holders of currency i to sell it, thereby depressing its value and hence V_j, and to acquire instead the optimal mixed portfolio seen earlier, which includes a fraction of the currency and bonds of issued by debt-financed economy j. This raises their value, and hence V_i, and affords Global investors' access to a larger share of economy j's return $\overline{X}$.

The possibility of portfolio readjustments by Global investors prevents the value of debt-financed economies from being systematically less than those of monetized economies: readjustments "undo" the monetization and prevent the average cost of capital, $\frac{\overline{X}}{V_j} = \rho_j$, from being systematically higher for debt-financed than for money-financed economies, for a given level of credibility. This will be further clarified below.

Finally, since it has been shown that arbitrage will also prevent $V_j > V_i$, it can be concluded that, in equilibrium, it must be that $V_j = V_i$, in accordance with the Neutrality Theorem.

(ii) ***High Credibility and Floating Exchange Rates***

With floating rates, Eq. (14.19) is rewritten replacing the exogenously set exchange rate, $\hat{e}_{jf}$, with market-determined rate, e_{jf}. Under floating, the exchange rate affects how much the government has to pay for financial capital (although highly credible economies usually follow policies that reduce the fluctuations and increase the predictability of the exchange rate and make it easier and cheaper for investors to protect their portfolio against exchange rate risk). However, the Neutrality Theorem still applies in the sense that Global investors use their almost unlimited access to market funding and keep changing their portfolios until they reach equilibrium; moreover, since they work directly in the relevant foreign currencies, they protect their investments from exchange rate risk.

(iii) ***Low Credibility and Fixed Exchange Rates***

The case of low credibility with fixed exchange rates does not differ significantly from the case just discussed of high credibility if (and to the extent that) the economy's debt ratio stays well within the critical threshold, $\mathcal{D} \ll \mathcal{D}^c$, and domestic money growth does not exceed that of the reserve (benchmark) currency, $\mu_d \leq \mu_f$, thereby implying that the default probability is low $\theta = \theta_\beta \ll 1$ and signaling that the government intends to build credibility by pursuing a conservative policy stance.

Conversely, if the government sets to expand its deficits and either of the two conditions above, or both, are violated, the risk of (technical or economic) default on public sector claims is perceived by Global investors to increase. Similarly, the government's commitment to pegging the exchange rate at $e_{jf} = \hat{e}_{jf}$ is no longer credible, $E(\varepsilon_{jf}) \neq 0$, and the domestic currency is expected to depreciate.

The case of interest, which is analyzed next, is when the economy's credibility is low, the exchange rate is floating, and public sector claims grow inordinately (that is, beyond the levels that would be consistent with financial sustainability).

(iv) ***Low Credibility and Floating Exchange Rates***

Assume an output gap emerges in low-credibility, debt-financed economy j, and the government decides to stimulate aggregate demand by expanding public deficit. Since the risk of technical default rises, the government commits to printing new money that it would use to pay future debt obligations and so avert default. Specifically, the government promises to print future flows of new money claims, such that:

$$\overline{\Delta M}_j \equiv \lim_{T\to\infty} \frac{1}{T} \sum_{t=1}^{T} r_{Dj}\left[P_{Dd} D_j^d + e_{jf}\left(1 + E\left(\varepsilon_{jf}\right)\right) P_{Df} D_{fj}\right]. \tag{14.20}$$

However, from Eq. (14.19) the return on the portfolio is now

$$Y_j = \alpha \frac{\frac{M_j + \lim_{T\to\infty} \frac{1}{T} \sum_{t=1}^{T} r_{Dj}\left\{P_{Dd} D_{dj} + e_{jf}\left(1+E\left(\varepsilon_{jf}\right)\right) P_{Df} D_{fj}\right\}}{\lim_{T\to\infty} \frac{1}{T} \sum_{t=1}^{T} e_{jf}\left(1+E\left(\varepsilon_{jf}\right)\right)} - \lim_{T\to\infty} \frac{1}{T} \sum_{t=1}^{T} r_{Dj}\left\{P_{Dd} D_{dj} + e_{jf}\left(1 + E\left(\varepsilon_{jf}\right)\right) P_{Df} D_{fj}\right\}}{V_j}$$

$$\overline{X} < Y_i, \tag{14.21}$$

and hence $V_i > V_j$, since the money stock is now subject to expected depreciation, $E\left(\varepsilon_{jf}\right) > 0$. To further use the corporate analogy, it would be as if an enterprise started paying its obligations by issuing new shares, which, all else being equal, would dilute the value of the enterprise's whole stock of outstanding shares. Debt repayments with depreciated currency causes Global investors to lose value (in real terms) on their debt holdings (i.e., economic default). On such expectations, it then pays them to sell currency j. Yet this further depreciates the currency, unless and until an adequate return is paid on the currency (see below).

However, paying more interest on money claims would go against the initial policy goal, indicating that the government cannot benefit from using the printing press to pay off its debt obligations. Furthermore, if monetization is continued and sustained afterward, expectations of uncontrolled currency devaluation (and ultimately currency breakdown) would eventually make Global investors stop lending to the government (*sudden stop*) or even "leave the country" and move their capital somewhere else (*capital reversals*).

This case violates the Neutrality Theorem and reveals that the Emperor is naked: printing money only creates the false impression of being an alternative for limited foreign exchange (limited in the sense of the domestic government not having power over its creation). As new money is created that is not supported by new production, it causes value losses to all Global investors (and the domestic agents) holding it, all else being equal, and it worsens government j's finances.

Granted, it might seem less painful to pay debt with cheaper currency than to stop payments altogether; but the expected losses from either situation cannot be any different from each other: rational investors must assume that the same borrower will cause them the same losses in real value terms, no matter what kind of default events (technical or economic) may happen, since the borrower's ability to produce the real output needed to repay the debt is the same in all cases. Of course, differences between value losses can occur ex post, after different technical and economic default events; but ex ante, investors demand the same protection against their happening because the expected losses are the same. Should Global investors accept to be repaid in domestic currency, they would require the government to pay an adequate return on their money claims (see next section). This return should be high enough to reestablish equilibrium, where $Y_i = Y_j$ and $V_i = V_j$, restoring neutrality.

This concludes the proof of *Proposition 1*. Observe that the results just obtained are very similar (although in a more extended and general way) to those of Modigliani and Miller for their Proposition I on debt financing and its effects on securities prices.

A comment is needed on the neutrality result in relation to the equilibrium of the economy given by Eq. (14.14). Such an equilibrium could be compatible with the economy's fundamentals, but it could also be a random ("sunspot" equilibrium) phenomenon that bears no connection to the economic fundamentals (Woodford, 1987). In fact, this might well be the case under incomplete markets and with powerful Global investors that can influence, at the margin, price equilibria that are based on (self-fulfilling) expectations and beliefs that may not align with economic fundamentals (as derived, for example, from rational expectations equilibrium models). However, this would not invalidate the neutrality result, which relates to investor indifference between different government claims at any equilibrium that would be determined, at the margin, by the Global investors. On the contrary, the latter's arbitrage activity would determine prices that ultimately establish neutrality.

A more serious issue could be the heterogeneity of agents. In this case, Global investors with different expectations and beliefs, or different perceptions (e.g., of risks and country credibility), would not make neutral allocation choices, unless market information changed in a way that made them agree and converge on a common view. Yet, it only needs a small group of big global players sharing the same views and acting as key investors, for equilibrium prices to be set at levels that reflect neutrality between government claims. However, more work is needed in this area, as noted below.

14.6.2 The Equilibrium Return on Money

From the Neutrality Theorem follows:

Corollary 1 *In equilibrium, a nonnegative real rate of return must be paid on money holdings for Global investors to be induced to hold the money claims that the government issues to monetize its deficits,*

and

Corollary 2 *The equilibrium real rate of return on money claims would (ceteris paribus) varies inversely with the credibility of the economy and directly with the expected stock of money claims.*

Proof Considering money as equity, and its value being therefore determined as a claim on the economy's residual aggregate output (that is, the output that is left once interests have been paid out to the debt holders), the value loss that the investors expect to bear, $E(\mathcal{L})$, is given by the government default probability from Eq. (14.2), θ_β, as applied to the residual output on which the investors hold claims.

Positing for convenience $\theta_\beta = 1 - \beta$ and denoting $P_{Dd}D_d + e_{df}P_{Df}D_f \equiv P_dD$, the expected loss in real value terms is:

$$E(\mathcal{L}) = -(1-\beta)\left[\overline{X} - \frac{r_D P_d D}{P}\right]. \tag{14.22}$$

In equilibrium, the real rate of return on money issued in an economy with credibility β must therefore be large enough to protect investors from the above risk of real value loss by paying them a spread $\mathcal{S}$ on the rate of output capitalization for the given level of the economy's credibility, such that:

$$r_M = \rho_\beta + \mathcal{S} = \rho_\beta - \frac{E(\mathcal{L})}{M}. \tag{14.23}$$

Recalling Eq. (14.14) and augmenting it with government's deficit monetization plans given by Eq. (14.19) to obtain $\overline{X} = \rho_\beta \beta\left(\frac{M+\overline{\Delta M}+P_dD}{P}\right)$, noting that $\rho_\beta = \rho\beta$, substituting in Eqs. (14.22) and (14.23), and simplifying, yields:

$$r_M = \rho_\beta + (1-\beta)\left[\rho\frac{M+\overline{\Delta M}}{M} + (\rho - r_D)\frac{P_dD}{M}\right], \tag{14.24}$$

which proves both corollaries: in equilibrium money must pay a nonnegative real return (Corollary 1) and the equilibrium real return on money varies inversely with credibility (Corollary 2). This completes the demonstration of the two Corollaries.

Equation (14.24) is similar to (but in a broader and more general way) one of Modigliani–Miller's main findings under their Proposition II of debt financing and its effects on security prices. Significantly, Eq. (14.24) incorporates John Maynard Keynes's liquidity preference theory, which states that the interest rate is not set by the supply of and demand for (flows of) saving, but by the supply of and demand for assets that can hold (stocks of) wealth (Tily, 2012). To quote from Keynes' General Theory, "The current rate of interest depends…not on the strength of the desire to hold wealth, but on the strengths of the desire to hold it in liquid and illiquid forms respectively, coupled with the amount of the supply of wealth in the one form relatively to the supply of it in the other." (p. 213).

Noting from Eq. (14.3) that $\rho - r_D < 0$ for rising levels of debt and/or for declining levels of credibility, Eq. (14.24) also shows that if the government were to monetize its future deficits fully and never raised (domestic or external) debt, $P_DD = 0$, the dampening effect of debt interests on spread $\mathcal{S}$ would be nihil, and the equilibrium return on money would (ceteris paribus) be permanently higher and growing with the expected stock of money claims.

Finally, assuming hypothetically that a country had full credibility, $\beta = 1.$, then the money in equilibrium would have the same return as the economy's output capitalization rate, $r_M = \frac{\overline{X}}{V} = \rho$, which is the minimum possible average cost of capital for the government. The money's return, in this case, would be the convenience (implicit) return from holding an asset that is completely liquid and can be turned into real output (or claims on it) right away and at no cost.

14.7 Concluding Remarks and Future Research

The Neutrality Theorem for public finances illustrated in this chapter shows that when international capital allocation choices are determined by Global investors, there are no net gains ("free lunch") a government of a globalized economy can consistently extract from resorting to one type of deficit financing (say, debt) versus another (say, money) or by issuing debt in one form versus another, and that governments with weaker credibility will face higher cost of capital uniformly across all forms of financing they will seek to tap. This is essentially due to the Global investors' unique capability for arbitraging (which is so central to the M&M approach) and their role as "marginal investors" in internationally integrated markets.

Especially in the case of largely indebted countries with low credibility, issuing domestic rather than foreign denominated debt would not give the economy any cost advantage: the risk of real losses, as perceived by the markets, is the same and it is priced identically across all type of (issuable and issued) claims. Nor would an economy with monetary sovereignty benefit from its government financing public expenditures with printing assumedly cost-free money: money is not cost free, and its cost rises with its stock. And neither would the choice of floating exchange rates grant governments any sustained benefits vis-à-vis fixed rates: the risk of currency depreciation would require higher interest rates to be paid on public sector claims or cause investors to turn their money elsewhere.

In this sense, the Neutrality Theorem challenges some well-established arguments in the literature and the economic debate, such that issuing domestic denominated debt may prove a superior option to raising external debt (Bua et al., 2014),[13] or the arguments popularized by Modern Money Theory (MMT) whereby governments with monetary sovereignty (and the societies they govern) would be better off doing away altogether with (costly) debt and, instead, finance fiscal expenditures with (cost-free) money, resorting to taxation only if the economy shows sign of inflation due to overheating (as output exceeds its full employment level)—the topic of Chapter 14.

Finally, given the centrality of credibility to the Neutrality Theorem context, the theorem rediscovers the importance of the "risk classes" introduced by Modigliani and Miller in their original contribution and applies them to governments as issuers of claims and their credibility as perceived by the markets. The theorem finds that while neutrality ensures the irrelevance of the structure of public finances for the cost of capital faced by governments (i.e., the cost doesn't change if the structure changes), credibility matters for the determination of the cost of capital (i.e., the higher the credibility, the lower the cost, and vice versa).

[13] For a comprehensive analysis of domestic vs foreign sovereign debt in developing economies, see the excellent work by Panizza (2008).

Credibility is costly to build and easy to lose. As Garen and Clark (2015) stress, credibility—in terms of confidence in government—not only vanishes fast, but its comeback demands a rising cost and restoring it needs a substantial effort from the government. Beyond a certain point, getting back to the initial state is not easy. Also, no country that is integrated in the global economy can long maintain high credibility (and extract its attendant benefits) if it pushes inordinately and persistently on domestic indebtedness or on money printing (even under large resource unemployment) to finance its public deficits. Exceptions are countries with exceptional geostrategic, military, and/or economic prowess that make their currencies accepted as world reserve assets. As for other globalized economies, weak (or weakening) credibility does constrain the space available to their governments for conducting effective macroeconomic policies and raises their cost of financial capital. The Neutrality Theorem bears important policy implications that I have explored elsewhere (Bossone, 2022) but have not repeated here.

For future research on the theorem, one important direction would be to test the theorem's results and predictions empirically, looking for evidence of price convergence within countries across public sector claims of countries classified by credibility and degree of international financial integration, and possibly also considering the level of income distribution and the proportion of savings managed by institutions within countries. This empirical research agenda could be supplemented by exploring better ways of measuring the credibility factor, for example, by developing credibility indicators based on fiscal projections or forecasting errors of investor expectations from official targets, following the examples of Afonso et al. (2020) and End and Hong (2022), which have examined the effects of communication and expectations on fiscal credibility.

More generally, on the topic of credibility, research should try to estimate how much the credibility factor influences the price formation of public sector claims. By extending the theorem's results, and based on the arguments presented in Chap. 13, another area of research could study how the capital allocation decisions of Global investors affect the policy space of governments with different levels of credibility, with less space (and a higher cost of capital) for less credible governments that adopt expansionary policies, and the opposite for more credible governments. Lastly, research could aim to evaluate whether, and how much, neutrality varies with different stages of the financial cycle, with investors views becoming more similar during periods of growing optimism (or pessimism) and more diverse during calm times. These are only some suggestions; other readers, if they find this work interesting, might think of others.

Let's now turn to MMT.

References

Afonso, A., Jalles, J. T., & Kazemi, M. (2020). The effects of macroeconomic, fiscal and monetary policy announcements on sovereign bond spreads. *International Review of Law and Economics, 63*(C).

Ahmeti, F., & Prenaj, B. (2015), A critical review of Modigliani and Miller's theorem of capital structure. International *Journal of Economics, Commerce and Management, III*(6), 914–924.

Amstad, M., Packer, F., & Shek, J. (2018). *Does sovereign risk in local and foreign currency differ?* BIS Working Papers No. 709, March.

Backus, D. K., & Kehoe, P. J. (1989). On the denomination of government debt: A critique of the portfolio balance approach. *Journal of Monetary Economics, 23*(3), 359–376.

Barro, R. J. (1974). Are government bonds net wealth? *Journal of Political Economy, 82*(6), 1095–1117.

Bénassy, J. P. (2006). *Ricardian equivalence and the intertemporal Keynesian multiplier*. PSE Working Papers halshs-00590509, HAL.

Benigno, P., & Nisticò, S. (2020). Non-neutrality of open-market operations. *American Economic Journal: Macroeconomics, 12*(3), 175–226.

Borensztein, E., Levy Yeyati, E., & Panizza, U. (2006). *Living with debt, inter-American development bank report on economic and social progress in Latin America*. Harvard University Press and Inter-American Development Bank.

Bossone, B. (2022). *A Modigliani-Miller theorem for the public finances of globalized economies: Theory, policy implications, and Keynesian reflections*. PKES Working Paper 2202, January.

Bossone, B. (2024). A Modigliani-Miller theorem for the public finances of globalized economies. *International Review of Financial Analysis, 94*, 103257.

Branson, W. H. (1985). *The dynamic interaction of exchange rates and trade flows*. NBER Working Paper Series, Working Paper No. 1780. National Bureau of Economic Research.

Bua, G., Pradelli, J., & Presbitero, A. (2014). Domestic public debt in low-income countries: trends and structure. *Review of Development Finance, 4*(1), 1–19.

Cunha, A. B. (2006). *Implications of the Modigliani-Miller theorem for the study of exchange rate regimes*. IBMEC RJ Economics Discussion Papers 2006-03, Economics Research Group, IBMEC Business School, Rio de Janeiro.

Dornbusch, R. (1975). "A portfolio balance model of the open economy," originally printed in *Journal of Monetary Economics, 1*, 3–20, and reprinted in 2019 in *Credit and Capital Markets, 52*(4), 457–476.

End, M. N., & Hong, M. G. H. (2022). *Trust what you hear: policy communication, expectations, and fiscal credibility*. Working Paper No. 2022/036, International Monetary Fund.

Garen, J., & Clark, J. R. (2015). Trust and the growth of government. *Cato Journal, 35*(3), 549–580.

Gersbach, H., Haller, H., & Müller, J. (2015). The macroeconomics of Modigliani-Miller. *Journal of Economic Theory, 157*, 1081–1113.

Gifford, D. (1998). "After the revolution: forty years ago, the Modigliani-Miller propositions started a new era in corporate finance. How does M&M hold up today?". CFO Magazine, 1 July.

Kooij, A. J. (2011, August). Ricardian equivalence in the 21st century (a European experience). *Business Economics*, 1–27.

Miller, M. H. (1988). The Modigliani-Miller propositions after thirty years. *Journal of Economic Perspectives, 2*(4), 99–120.

Modigliani, F., & Miller, M. (1958). The cost of capital, corporation finance and the theory of investment. *American Economic Review, 48*(3), 261–297.

Myers, S. C., & Majluf, N. S. (1984). Corporate financing and investment decisions when firms have information that investors do not have. *Journal of Financial Economics, 13*(2), 187–221.

Packer, F. (2003). Mind the gap: Domestic versus foreign currency sovereign ratings. *BIS Quarterly Review, Bank for International Settlements*, 55–63.

Pagano, M. (2005). *The Modigliani-Miller theorems: A cornerstone of finance*. CSEF Working Papers 139, Centre for Studies in Economics and Finance (CSEF), University of Naples.

Panizza, U. (2008). *Domestic and external public debt in developing countries* (No. 188). UNCTAD.

Reinhart, C. M., & Rogoff, K. S. (2009). "The aftermath of financial crises". *American Economic Review 99*(2), 466–472.

Ross, S. A. (1977). The determination of financial structure: The incentive-signalling approach. *The Bell Journal of Economics, 8*(1), 23–40.

Stiglitz, J. E. (1988). Why financial structure matters. *Journal of Economic Perspectives, 2*(4), 121–126.

Stiglitz, J. E. (1967). *A re-examination of Modigliani-Miller theorem*. Cowles Foundation Discussion Paper No. 242, Cowles Foundation for Research in Economics at Yale University.

Tily, G. (2012). *Keynes's monetary theory of interest*. BIS Paper No. 65c.

Tsingou, E. (2014). Power elites and club-model governance in global finance. *International Political Sociology, 8*(3), 340–342.

Wallace, N. (1981). A Modigliani-Miller theorem for open-market operations. *American Economic Review, 71*(3), 267–274.

Wang, P. (2009). The portfolio balance approach to exchange rate determination. In *The economics of foreign exchange and global finance*. Springer.

Woodford, M. (1987). Three questions about sunspot equilibria as an explanation of economic fluctuations. *The American Economic Review, 77*(2), 93–98. Papers and Proceedings of the Ninety-Ninth Annual Meeting of the American Economic Association.

Chapter 15
The Fatal Flaws of Modern Money Theory

Abstract This chapter considers international financial integration as key to evaluate the effectiveness of the macroeconomic policy propounded by the supporters of Modern Money Theory (MMT)—a theory that has recently attracted the sympathy of a growing share of heterodox economists. The chapter shows that when the value of the domestic currency is determined by markets that are dominated by Global Investors, the monetization of fiscal deficits—which is central to MMT—cannot work as an effective and sustainable macroeconomic policy program aimed to achieve and maintain full-employment output in economies suffering from Keynesian unemployment or underemployment (unless very special and country-specific circumstances hold). Financially integrated economies that implemented MMT policies would either see their money stock grow unsustainably large, or they would have to adjust domestic interest rates to levels that would be inconsistent with the policy objective, leading to economic and financial instability instead.

15.1 Preamble

For years, I have been a true believer of Abba Lerner's "functional finance," which today lays at the core of Modern Money Theory (MMT).[1] But as my acquaintance with the functioning of international financial markets has grown through over time, I have eventually become convinced of the unsustainability of the macro-policies prescriptions based on it. So, while each chapter of this book blazes new trails in

---

[1] Notice the distinction between the terminology "Modern *Money* Theory," which will be used here throughout, and "Modern *Monetary* Theory," often referred to in the literature and in commentaries on the subject. In the words of one of the leading MMT theorists and proponents, L. Randall Wray, «I will note here that I use the terminology Modern Money Theory—and have seen that usage as following on from the title of my 1998 book (*Understanding Modern Money*). We also used this terminology in our textbook. However, many of my colleagues had used the other terminology Modern Monetary Theory. I object to that as it draws attention to the word "monetary" and leads many to believe it is all about monetary policy—while in reality much of the focus is on fiscal policy (and we argue that the traditional division between the two is highly misleading in any case). Further, it seems to conjure in some minds a similarity to Monetarism.» (Wray, 2019).

B. Bossone, *Trailblazing Visions of Money in Economic Theory*, Contributions to Economics, https://doi.org/10.1007/978-3-031-82544-6_15

monetary economics, this is the only chapter that warns against walking one trail: that of MMT.

In contemporary highly internationally integrated economies, the price of the money and debt instruments issued by governments is determined in the global markets where they are traded, and their price valuations have a major impact on key domestic macroeconomic variables of these economies, including total output, resource use, price inflation, and interest and exchange rates. Either in the form of "promises to pay" to their holders at some future dates (debt), or in the form of nonredeemable representations of value available to their holders for making transactions (fiat money), these instruments represent claims on real resources, whose value depends on how credible the governments issuing them are in the eyes of the markets where they are traded. Under these conditions, even full monetary sovereignty does not shield governments from the limits that market valuation places on the effectiveness of money and debt used as policy tools, as I have shown in Chaps. 13 and 14. Any good macroeconomic theory must consider these limits: MMT doesn't.

Yet, after the Global Financial Crisis, MMT convinced many economists (especially on the heterodox front) that governments could achieve full employment by creating money, using taxes to regulate inflation, and that this would not have negative effects. The circle of converts grew larger, even within my own surroundings, and at some point, I felt I had to voice my criticism.

My first article to do so used formal analysis (Bossone, 2021). In a subsequent contribution, considering MMTers' rejection of formalism, I articulated the same criticism without formal modeling (Bossone, 2023). In this chapter I show the flaws of MMT resorting to my original, more rigorous method.

15.2 Introduction

MMT claims that in any country where the public sector has one (consolidated) agency that issues the national currency, combining the central bank and the Treasury, the government is not limited by a budget constraint: it can always pay for spending to ensure full use of resources by printing the money required, and it can never fail to meet its obligations since money is irredeemable and thus non-defaultable. Also, MMT says that taxes and bond offerings are not necessary to pay for the budget but can be used to withdraw money from the economy to avoid that total demand exceeds aggregate output and causes inflation (Wray, 1998). As a related proposition, MMT rejects the use of the interest rate as a tool of stabilization policy and the government should use bond offerings to fix the overnight rate at (what MMT theorists think is) its natural or normal rate of zero, allowing markets to determine credit spreads based on risk (Forstater & Mosler, 2005). As another related proposition, MMT considers floating exchange rates essential to remove constraints on policy that compromise the government's ability to maintain full employment (Mitchell, 2018a). Under these assumptions, MMTers believe that in economies with Keynesian unemployment or underemployment governments can achieve and maintain full-employment output by using money-financed fiscal deficits persistently and using taxes as an inflation control devise when demand–supply imbalances occur.

This chapter argues that, in most country situations, MMT full-employment policy would not be viable and even if it were viable, it would not be sustainable, the exceptions being those few cases where the economy enjoys very high market credibility or issues an international reserve currency; in these cases, the negative effects of MMT policy can be prevented and expansionary policies can be successful.

While MMT has faced various criticisms (see Sect. 15.2), this chapter focuses on one specific (and very important) weakness of MMT: if MMT policy is used systematically in economies other than those that have very high policy credibility or issue international reserve currencies, there is a twofold risk that (i) either not all the (increasing) stock of money issued by the government is absorbed by the economy at a constant zero interest rate, which would fail to achieve the MMT main objective of full-employment output, or (ii) the uptake of the growing money stock requires such a high interest rate to be paid on money balances, which would eventually undermine the achievement of full employment.

This twofold risk raises a fundamental question that is often ignored when evaluating MMT: the theory claims that, in order to ensure full-employment output in an economy with structural private sector net (desired) saving surpluses, a future stream of fiscal deficits would have to be permanently financed by the state issuing a non-repayable (non-defaultable) zero-interest bearing instrument—i.e., money—instead of selling repayable (defaultable) positive interesting-bearing instruments—i.e., debt. However, the theory does not explain why, especially in the context of globalized economies, wealth holders should choose to hold money rather than debt, and what would happen to output and resource employment if wealth holders were in fact to prefer debt to money.[2]

Mosler (2018) claims that the government first spends money and then borrows from the economy, because deficit spending without borrowing would make the money market interest rate drop. As government spending went on indefinitely, public debt would have to keep growing as new debt is issued to cover new money injections, and all the existing debt would have to be rolled over (otherwise, the money stock would start growing again). Yet, every new debt issuance would add to the amount of debt outstanding and would inevitably lower its price (assuming everything else

[2] This point is made by Aspromourgos (2018): «in a world of inconvertible fiat currencies, public investment as a driver of aggregate demand faces little financial constraint. In the first instance, such a constraint would exist only to the extent that the suppliers of goods and services that government wishes to purchase are resistant to accepting payment in outside money or "cash" (including electronic or "book entry" outside money). But the willingness of private sector agents to accept payment in cash is one thing; their willingness to then *hold* money, as a desired asset, is another. If there results excess money balances for the private sector as a whole, then it is possible that the excess can be drained from the private sector via its purchasing government securities of various maturities…[I]f, at prevailing yields on government securities, the private sector as a whole is unwilling to substitute government securities for the entirety of any such excess money balances (net of taxation), then that money will find its way into other channels (expenditure on other assets or on goods and services) until it ceases to be an excess—unless government yields become more attractive.» (p. 510).

is constant). Therefore, the interest rate that the market demands to hold the growing debt would also have to increase indefinitely, with obvious negative effects on the real economy. In other words, if fiscal deficits are financed by money creation and are permanent, then either the money supply must grow without limit, or the debt must do so in its place. In both cases, and keeping everything else the same, the price of the growing stock of money or debt would go down (its return would go up).

Another way to look at the same issue is that a theory that, like MMT, relies on the unlimited power of the state to create money must assume that the state can maintain stable over time the domestic and external value of the money it creates. This raises the question of the credibility of the money issuing state: the lower such credibility, the less willing wealth holders are to hold the increasing stock of money at zero interest rate (because of the increasing risk of money losing value in future). This issue is especially important, and has significant implications for economic policy, in globalized economies, and even more so where wealth is largely concentrated and managed by investors who can easily move funds across different assets through financial markets across borders.

This chapter deals with the MMT's contradictions that were just mentioned. The chapter is structured as follows: Sect. 15.3 refers to the relevant literature; Sect. 15.4 explains why ISLM analysis can be used to assess the MMT's main contradictions and describes the economy's model used for the analysis; Sect. 15.5 applies the model to two hypothetically identical economies that only differ in the level of policy credibility that the markets attribute to them and evaluates the results of the model. Section 15.6 concludes the chapter.

15.3 Review of the Literature

Wray (2015), Mosler (2018) and Mitchell (2019) provide comprehensive illustrations of MMT. The theory has faced strong criticisms from several mainstream economists (such as Krugman (2019) and Summers (2019)) and from economists with the same Post Keynesian background as MMT theorists (such as Davidson (2019) and Sawyer (2019)). In a series of papers by Palley (2013), which are summarized in Palley (2020), these various critical arguments are examined analytically, covering topics such as the macroeconomics of money financed budgets, the choice of optimal targets and instruments,[3] existing macroeconomic constraints on MMT policy and negative policy feedbacks, the dishonesty about the role and necessity of taxes, the US centric thinking behind MMT, its unwarranted rejection of high inflation and default, and the drawbacks of its proposed Employer of Last Resort or Job Guarantee Program. The main point is that MMT overstates the benefits and downplays the drawbacks of

[3] Jayadev and Mason (2018) have recently discussed the issue and argue that MMT and orthodox macroeconomics share many of the same fundamental principles. The key difference is that mainstream economists believe monetary policy should be the primary tool for achieving full employment and price stability, while MMT economists believe fiscal policy should take precedence. However, Mitchell (2018b) strongly disagrees with this conclusion and the methodology used to arrive at it.

fiscal policy financed by money creation. MMT advocates have responded to these critiques in Tymoigne and Wray (2013), and PERI (2012) and RWER (2019) have published works from both supporters and critics of MMT.

The debates in these sources cover all major aspects of MMT. They are too many to be succinctly reported here, and doing so would go beyond the aim of this chapter, which is to focus on one specific—but fundamental—aspect of MMT as presented in Sect. 15.3: the effectiveness and feasibility of MMT policies to achieve and maintain full employment in the context of asset market (dis)equilibria, conditional upon the credibility of the governments that issue money.

15.4 Modeling MMT

In this chapter MMT's contradictions are shown to arise from the way macro policy shocks affect the basic economic relationships that the theory assumes. The model used to this purpose is built to reflect those relationships as accurately as possible, without adding elements that are not part of the theory, and yet having enough structure to assess the theory's consistency against stock-flow and price equilibrium conditions.

MMT is based on the Post Keynesian tradition where the economy does not naturally tend to full employment, even without market flaws and inflexibilities. Also, unlike mainstream (New Keynesian) macroeconomics, the idea of a natural interest rate makes no sense in MMT, and the theory does not agree that interest-rate changes set by policy can achieve full employment, even when the economy is not at its effective lower bound. MMT rejects the loanable funds theory that supports mainstream macroeconomics (Kelton, 2020), it does not account for optimal intertemporal choices by households and firms, and it does not assign any role to (rational) expectations in such decisions; it also dismisses the concept of government budget constraint as false, since governments (with monetary sovereignty) can always create the money they need. The theory predicts mechanically that changes in money-financed fiscal deficits increase aggregate output without any inflation cost when output is below full employment. Lastly, while MMT theorists have never formally expressed their theory using mathematical modeling, MMT relies on resource flow identities that ignore the prices at which (financial and nonfinancial) assets must be traded for their demand and supply to match, or the effect that equilibrium prices have on the real economy.[4]

[4] The relationship between expenses in one sector of the economy becoming income for other sectors, with savings being the result of investment, does not guarantee that savers will always be willing to hold all supplied asset stocks unless prices adjust to their satisfaction. When equilibrium prices fail to match the demand for asset stocks, savers may avoid adding to those stocks in their portfolios or even shift their investments elsewhere, leading to a decline in value. Even if equilibrium prices are reached, they may not support full employment, particularly in imperfect markets lacking mechanisms to ensure such equilibrium. The key lies not in the adequacy of aggregate savings but in the optimal composition of portfolios based on wealth-holder preferences. Equilibrium prices

Thus, there is no need to use dynamic stochastic general equilibrium (DSGE) models (even the New Keynesian ones) to show the basic economic relations of MMT[5]: the MMT's problems mentioned above show up without using rules that optimize how agents allocate resources over time. Moreover, no models should be used to represent MMT, which assume the independence of aggregate saving from investment. Yet, since money is by definition central to MMT, the theory's basic economic relations must be consistent with three key conditions: (i) money has a positive price, (ii) the value of money (like the price of any financial instrument) must reflect the credibility of its issuer, and (iii) there is always an optimal stock of money in the economy that people are willing to hold, based on money's streams of pecuniary and non-pecuniary returns and its associated opportunity cost; optimality implies the possibility that money supply exceeds its optimal demand.

15.4.1 Adapting the ISLM Model to MMT

The ISLM model is suitable for capturing the fundamental economic relations of MMT without using optimal rules like those in DSGE analysis, which MMT theorists reject. The adoption of the ISLM model allows for a direct comparison between the anticipated effects of MMT policy and the actual outcomes when considering stock and price dynamics. The ISLM model can serve as a foundation for interpreting MMT and for highlighting its differences from mainstream models. The flexibility of the ISLM model accommodates MMT's rejection of loanable fund theory and considers money demand in terms of transactional services and asset opportunity costs. The choice to use ISLM analysis in this context is driven by its ability to mirror MMT's economic relations and provide consistency checks, offering a framework that theorists can use to identify the assumptions underpinning MMT, draw implications from them, and isolate the points of agreement and disagreement on the theory.

15.4.2 A Stylized MMT Model

The model here used represents an open and internationally highly financially integrated economy (in the sense to be defined below). The economy has three markets: the market for real domestic output, Y, which can be used for consumption C and investment I; the market for money M, which supports domestic transactions; and the forex market where net export, $NX = X - IM$, is the difference between export and import. In a less than full employment economy, without public debt and taxation as noted above, money M is supplied through the fiscal expenses of a consolidated

should balance the supply and demand of money and other assets, aligning with holders' desires for liquidity and preferred forms of investment.

[5] Mitchell (2018b) rejects DSGE modeling as irreconcilable with MMT.

public sector, $\frac{\Delta M}{P} \equiv m = G$, where P is the general price level and G is government spending. Note that any taxes and public debt issuances would detract from the stock of money in circulation, while public debt repayments and interest payments would add to it.[6] M is injected in the economy to offset private sector net (desired) saving surpluses, $S - I$, causing actual output to be below the level of output, Y_f, corresponding to the full employment of the economy's resources. With inflation "off," both taxes and public debt in the model are set to zero and the government can determine monetary policy so that $G = \frac{\Delta M}{P} = g(Y_f - Y)$, where feedback response $g' > 0$ leads the government to issue and spend additional money to eliminate the output gap.

In line with MMT principles, price inflation is typically assumed to be zero when the economy is below full employment, with expansionary measures not impacting inflation until full employment is attained. This theory employs a simplified "on–off" inflation model: below full employment, any increase in demand leads solely to output growth without inflation, while at full employment, demand boosts result only in price spikes without affecting real output (Palley, 2013). Despite this theoretical framework, recent findings challenge this model's validity, revealing instances of inflation arising from expansionary policies even when the economy is operating below full employment.

In a deeply interconnected global financial system, a country's public financial obligations, comprising currency and any debt in circulation, are traded on the international financial stage. The prices of these assets are set by the decisions made by select "marginal investors." These investors (the "Global investors" of Chaps. 13 and 14) represent wealth owners or managers and possess the ability to swiftly move capital across borders at negligible transaction costs. They exhibit a global outlook in their investment management, unaffected by biases toward domestic markets.[7] Wealth holders have a vested interest in safeguarding and potentially enhancing the actual value of their wealth holdings. These holders, who encompass various entities like households, businesses accruing savings and profits, and financial intermediaries managing wealth either for clients or themselves, play a crucial role in deciding where money is allocated within the economy and beyond. The more easily they can access financial markets and move funds within them, and the greater the concentration of wealth they hold, the more significant and rapid the transfer of surplus funds into foreign assets becomes. This process results in the devaluation of the domestic currency.

Two identical hypothetical economies are subject to the model described below, with the sole distinction being the level of trust in policy attributed to them by the

---

[6] Thus, with non-zero tax and public debt, the complete expression for the money supply would be $\frac{\Delta M}{P} = G + B_{-1} i_{B_{-1}} - T - \frac{\Delta B}{P}$.

[7] See Chap. 13. Even in poorly internationally financially integrated economies, large wealth holders can find ways to move their money abroad (sometimes through illegal means, depending on the jurisdictions). In such situations, governments can depend on captive markets to issue their liabilities at subsidized rates, without facing the scrutiny and limitations imposed by the markets. However, this approach can result in significant economic distortions and limited access to valuable foreign investment resources.

markets: one with high credibility (HC) and the other with low credibility (LC). The term "policy credibility" in this context relates to the degree to which economic actors trust that the government will implement the macroeconomic policies it has pledged to follow (Backus & Driffill, 1985a; 1985b; Kreps & Wilson, 1982). This concept pertains to the government's capacity and willingness to fulfill its policy promises. Market assessments of policy credibility are influenced by a country's historical policy performance, the country's determination to uphold stated policy commitments and objectives, and how closely its policy framework aligns with criteria for prudent economic management and financial stability, as set by markets. In the specific context of the model here used, the policy credibility factor is captured by the parameter $\beta_j \in (0, 1), j = LC, HC$, which reflects the credibility that markets attribute to a country j's policy regime, institutions and conduct, and ranges from extremely poor ($\beta \cong 0$) to very high ($\beta \cong 1$) (see Chap. 13). Section 15.5 will show this factor to play a key role in determining the demand for money.

Model Specifications

The structure of total output and the functional makeup of its constituent factors are defined by the standard relationships below, all presented in real values and demonstrating traditional differentials:

$$\begin{aligned} Y &= C(Y, w(Y)) + I(\mu, i_M + s) + G - T + NX\left(Y^{RW}, Y, \varepsilon\right) \\ &\times \text{ with } \; 1 < c'_Y, c'_w > 0; I_{\mu'} > 0, I'_{i_M} < 0; NX'_{Y^{RW}} > 0, NX'_Y < 0, NX'_\varepsilon > 0, \end{aligned} \tag{15.1}$$

where:

- In line with MMT, aggregate output adjusts fully and seamlessly to demand, until it reaches its resource full employment level (see also the above discussion on inflation).
- Consumption behaves in a typical Keynesian fashion with respect to income and is positive in real wealth, w, defined below (see Eq. (15.5)).
- Investment is positive in the marginal efficiency of capital, μ, which in a typical Keynesian fashion responds to entrepreneurs' long-term expectations as influenced by psychological factors, and negative in the real cost of funding defined as $i_M + s$, where s reflects the cost of intermediation and risk factors and is conveniently assumed to be constant.[8] Notice that, in line with MMT, saving is a residual to investment (i.e., no loanable funds theory is assumed), which, however, does not rule out ex-ante saving-investment inequalities.

[8] The marginal efficiency of capital, denoted as μ in a standard Keynesian approach, is determined as the point where the price at which capital is supplied matches the current worth of the anticipated profits spanning an appropriate future timeframe, $P_K = \sum_{t=1}^{n} \pi_t (1 + \mu)^{-1}$ (Chick, 1983). MMT proponents like Bill (Mitchell 2012) and Warren Mosler (referenced in Rowe, cit.) adhere to Michal Kalecki's idea that the possibility of escalating debt levels leads to a scenario where the marginal efficiency of capital decreases as the market interest rate rises. Consequently, elevated interest rates make numerous projects unprofitable that would otherwise be viable under different circumstances.

- Net export is given by $\mathrm{NX}\big(Y^{\mathrm{RW}}, Y, \varepsilon \mathrm{EP}^{\mathrm{RW}}/P\big) = X\left(Y^{\mathrm{RW}}, \varepsilon\right) - \varepsilon \mathrm{IM}(Y, \varepsilon)$, where Y^{RW} is the output of the rest of the world, RW, and $\varepsilon = EP^{RW}/P$ is the real exchange rate, where E is the nominal exchange rate. $\mathrm{NX}(\cdot)$ is assumed to satisfy the Marshall-Lerner condition;
- Net export and the capital account, K, determine the changes in the foreign asset position of the economy, $\mathrm{NX}\big(Y^{\mathrm{RW}}, Y, \varepsilon\big) + \varepsilon K(i_M - i_{\mathrm{RW}}) = \varepsilon \Delta \mathrm{FX}$, with $K' > 0$, that is, the capital account is uniquely determined by the interest rate differential between the domestic and rest-of-the-world economy. For simplicity, but with no loss of generality, the interest rate on foreign asset, i_{RW}, is exogenous to the model and conveniently assumed to be constant.

From the above assumptions, the following three relations yield:

a. The **IS schedule** for the goods market

$$Y = \frac{1}{1 - c'_Y}\left[c'_W \frac{W}{P}(Y) + I(\mu, i_M + s) + G + NX\left(Y^{\mathrm{RW}}, Y, \varepsilon\right)\right], \tag{15.2}$$

where taxes are set to zero.

b. The **MM schedule** for the money market

$$\frac{M}{P} \equiv m = \frac{M_{-1}}{P} + \frac{\Delta M}{P} = m(Y, i_M | \beta), \quad \text{with} \quad m'_Y > 0, m'_{i_M} > 0, \tag{15.3}$$

where the optimal demand for money is derived as in Chap. 13, Appendix 1, and where the money supply grows by additions to the stock of money inherited from the previous period through government spending, $\frac{\Delta M}{P} = G$, when taxation is set to zero and no public debt is issued. In line with MMT, money is demanded for its services as a means of payment and taking the interest rate as its opportunity cost. Notice that, unlike the conventional LM schedule in ISLM analysis, the MM schedule has a negative slope: for a given stock of M and all else being equal, a higher transaction demand for M driven by Y requires a decrease in interest rate paid on M balances, i_M, required to keep the money market in equilibrium.

c. The **BP schedule** for the forex market

$$\mathrm{NX}\big(Y^{\mathrm{RW}}, Y, \varepsilon\big) = -\varepsilon K(i_M - i_{\mathrm{RW}}), \tag{15.4}$$

that is, trade deficits must be financed by capital account surpluses, which are determined by the differential between the interest rate on M and FX, where the latter is constant, as noted.

d. Finally, stock-flow consistency requires that:

$$\frac{W}{P} = \left(\frac{W}{P}\right)_{-1} + \left(1 - c'_Y\right)Y = m(Y, i_M | \beta), + \varepsilon\big[FX_{-1} + \varepsilon K(i_M - i_{\mathrm{RW}})\big], \tag{15.5}$$

where real wealth, W/P, is the sum of preexisting wealth and current savings and must equal the real stocks of money and foreign assets inherited from the past plus any current net additions to them. Equation (15.5) indicates that if an imbalance were to materialize in the money market (say, the supply of money exceeds demand) and was not followed by an interest rate adjustment, then wealth holders would transform excess money balance into additional FX holdings, that is, $\frac{\Delta M}{P} = -\varepsilon \Delta \text{FX}$, causing the value of the former to fall. On the other hand, if the imbalance were followed by the interest (and exchange) rate adjustment, then there would be no change in *FX* holdings, that is $\Delta \text{FX} = 0$, the excess money balances would be absorbed and become part of the optimal demand for money, and the value of money would not change.

Optimal Demand for Money and "Excess" Money Supply

MMT overlooks a crucial aspect: unlike credit money, the money injected into the economy through deficit spending doesn't adhere to the law of reflux. This means that the money infused into the economy can only be taken out through taxation or bond issuances. Consequently, under stable nominal output and other constant factors, continuous injections of money into the economy lead to a perpetual accumulation of excess money unless the private sector is willing to absorb all additional money flows as desired savings.[9] Wealth holders who are unwilling to hold surplus amounts of non-interest-bearing asset *M* invest them in foreign assets FX. This action reduces the external value of *M*, consequently elevating domestic prices of goods and services.[10]

If MMT policy is consistently applied to maintain full-employment output over the long term, the real money supply will continuously increase compared to real output. Consequently, a real interest rate would be necessary on money holdings as the money supply exceeds its optimal level to incentivize wealth holders to retain it without devaluing it. One can liken interest-bearing *M* to the concept of "Treasury electronic money" suggested by Cochrane (2015) as a US Federal debt instrument or to the more recent idea of an interest-bearing central bank digital currency (CBDC). This interest rate on money is termed the "required" real interest rate and is a government's prerogative whether to offer it or not. Failing to provide an interest rate on *M*-holdings would force the government to furnish their holders with an alternative financial

[9] As Palley (2013) observes, «In a no growth economy, having the fiscal authority run persistent money financed deficits will cause the money supply to increase relative to GDP…» (p. 8), and dynamically the same would hold under MMT as the stock of money would grow at a rate not lower than GDP (all else being equal).

[10] In an economy where there are other types of assets besides *FX*, wealth holders would also buy speculative assets (usually with very low output elasticity), and money would change hands faster among certain groups of (domestic and foreign) wealth holders, who would be hoping to gain more from higher asset prices, restricting money circulation in the economy, and eventually increasing the chance of bubble bursts. In the model above, this sequence of events would cancel out the wealth effect on consumption. At disequilibrium interest rates, some wealth holders could get rid of their extra money balances, but not all of them could do so at the same time. If an equilibrium price is not reached, some wealth holders would have to keep (some of) their extra balances temporarily, until new opportunities arise to restore normal (optimal) holdings.

instrument that yields a suitable return, like debt, as excess balances of an asset incurring increasing costs would be rejected.

The optimal demand-for-money function derived in Chap. 13, Appendix 1, and reported in Eq. (15.3) above allows for determining "excess" money holdings. The required real interest rate on money tends to be higher in economies with lower market credibility. In highly credible economies, governments can provide necessary money during recessions without constraints, as per Modern Monetary Theory (MMT). Conversely, in low credibility economies, money supply is limited by the interest rates demanded by wealth holders. Countries with very low credibility may encounter steep or even vertical money demand schedules. Chart 15.1 illustrates the differences in money demand between high credibility (HC) and low credibility (LC) economies at a specific output level.

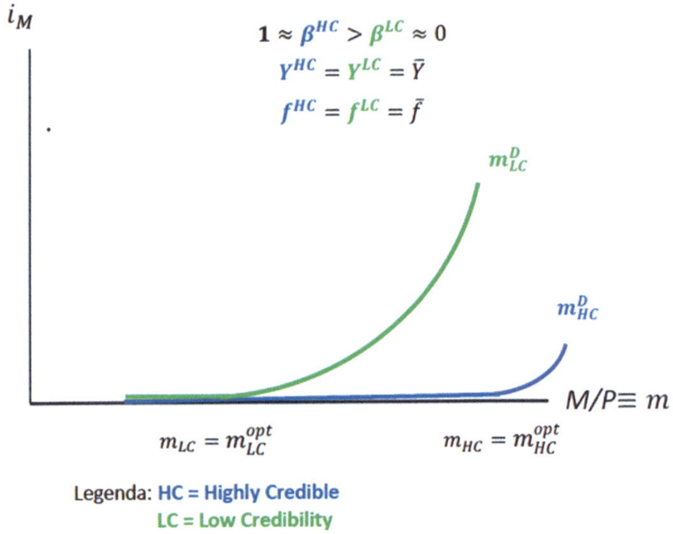

Chart 15.1 Stylized demand-for-money schedules in economies with different policy credibility. **Note to** Chart 15.1. The money issued by the highly credible (HC) economy is always in high demand (especially at times of market stress), and there is always a large share of unsatisfied demand for it. Thus, a very low or even zero real rate of interest is required at which the supply of money is absorbed by demand: it would take extremely large issuances of money before markets worried about "excess" balances, at which point the equilibrium interest rate would start rising. In the low credibility (LC) economy, on the other hand, the required rate of interest on money is higher than in the HC economy, all else being equal, and the demand-for-money schedule starts verticalizing at a lower level of the money stock ($m^{\text{opt}}_{\text{LC}} < m^{\text{opt}}_{\text{HC}}$, see Chap. 13, Appendix 1): unless the interest rate adjusts, new issuances lead wealth holders to convert money into alternative assets including foreign currencies and securities. In the limiting case of an economy characterized by very low credibility, the demand-for-money schedule would tend to be vertical at a very low level of the money stock and money market equilibrium would require a very high interest rate

The government has the option to absorb surplus money by issuing debt. However, this would lead to an increase in the debt stock rather than the money stock, resulting in similar implications for interest rates.

15.5 The Model's Results

Noticing that if saving equals investment ($G = T$ and $NX(\cdot) = 0$), money supply equals demand and the real exchange rate equals the differential between the domestic and foreign real interest, Eq. (15.5) becomes:

$$\frac{W}{P} = \left(\frac{W}{P}\right)_{-1} + I(\mu, i_M + s) = m(Y, i_M|\beta) + \varepsilon(\mathrm{FX}_{-1}), \tag{15.6}$$

then any solutions that solve the IS-MM-BP equation system also solve Eq. (15.6) and make the real wealth equation redundant as a result. Importantly, Eq. (15.6) will become relevant in the context of a disequilibrium situation that will be discussed in Section C.

Thus, replacing Eqs (15.3) and (15.4) into (15.2) and solving for output, the real interest rate and the real exchange rate, with a given general price level, foreign real interest rate, risk factor and inherited stock of wealth, the triplet $\left(Y^*, i_M^*|\beta, \varepsilon^*\right)$ would obtain, conditional on credibility factor β, which would clear simultaneously the three markets, yielding.

$$Y^* = \frac{1}{1-c'_Y}\left\{c'_W \frac{W}{P}(Y^*) + I(\mu, i_M^* + s) + \left[m\left(Y^*, i_M^*|\beta\right) - m_{-1}\right] - \varepsilon^* K\left(i_M^* - i_{\mathrm{RW}}\right)\right\}. \tag{15.7}$$

Based on this equilibrium equation, the effect of MMT policy is now analyzed. A key point to notice—which will underlie the analysis—is that the solution to Eq. (15.7) might not be consistent with MMT's full-employment output policy objective, $Y^* = Y_f$. This follows from observing that full-employment policy $G_f = m_f - m_{-1}$ might imply a current money stock that exceeds its equilibrium (optimal) equivalent (i.e., $m_f > m^*$). In such a case, the real rate of interest required to satisfy Eq. (15.7) might exceed its full-employment equivalent (i.e., $i_M^* > i_M^f$) and hence prevent output from achieving its full-employment level (i.e., $Y^* < Y_f$).

The analysis proceeds by charting the relationships mentioned above for both HC and LC economies. This involves examining them visually and theoretically. The charts illustrate the following dynamics: quadrant I displays the money supply and demand schedules, which establish the equilibrium real interest rate based on a specific money supply. Both schedules are evaluated within the applicable range where the real money supply nears its optimal level and exceeds it due to continued implementation of MMT full-employment policies.

Based on the MMT (ex ante) schedule, in quadrant II, the government decides the additional permanent level of money-financed deficit spending required to bring output to full-employment level, Y_f. The MMT schedule mirrors the simple Keynesian multiplier when stock and price dynamics are not factored into the analysis. In quadrant IV, the $i_M + s$ schedule translates the real interest rate on money into the real cost of investment funding. Finally, in quadrant III, the new level of money-financed spending and the resulting real interest rate on money and real exchange rate cause the IS, MM and BP schedules to shift until they intersect each other (ex post) at a new equilibrium level of output, when stock and price dynamics are incorporated in the analysis. In quadrant III, both the MM and BP schedules are shifted up to reflect the interest rate risk premium, s, that is incorporated in the IS schedule.

The ISLM-based graphical representations used in the analysis do not account for the continuous increase in the money supply relative to output, resulting from permanent additions to the money stock. However, it is important to note that this continuous growth is fundamental to understanding the required rate of return on money balances as an equilibrium mechanism in MMT. This mechanism becomes significant when the circulating money supply approaches and exceeds its optimal level. As illustrated in Chart 15.1 and all subsequent charts, when the money stock perpetually expands in relation to output, leading to it eventually exceeding the optimal level, the economy faces a verticalizing demand-for-money schedule.

15.5.1 Where MMT Policy Can (Exceptionally) Work

This is the case where the economy enjoys high credibility. In terms of the above model, the case is one where the private sector's structural net (desired) saving surplus position impedes the attainment of full-employment output and the government engineers a permanent expansion of public spending financed with new money issuance, $G = \frac{\Delta M}{P}$, to offset the output gap and achieve full employment. As Chart 15.2 shows, benefiting from a low and flat money demand schedule (i.e., $\beta^{HC} \approx 1$) (quadrant I), the higher level of government spending shifts the intersection of the IS-MM-BP schedules to the full-employment output position, with no change in interest rates (quadrant III), and fully in line with the expected policy impact derived from the MMT schedule (quadrant II). The BP schedule has been adjusted because the issuance of new money, whether utilized as a global reserve or exchanged on par with it due to its credibility, facilitates increased imports in line with higher output.

This case is the MMT "prototype." If the money issued by the HC economy remains completely trusted by domestic and international agents, as in a reserve issuing economy, the solution depicted in Chart 15.2 can be sustained over time. While there is a risk of the money stock growing infinitely relative to output, potentially exceeding its optimal level, leading to a scenario where the demand for money starts to rise, triggering discussed effects for less credible economies—this situation is not inevitable for an HC economy. Given the full trust in its currency, reducing the

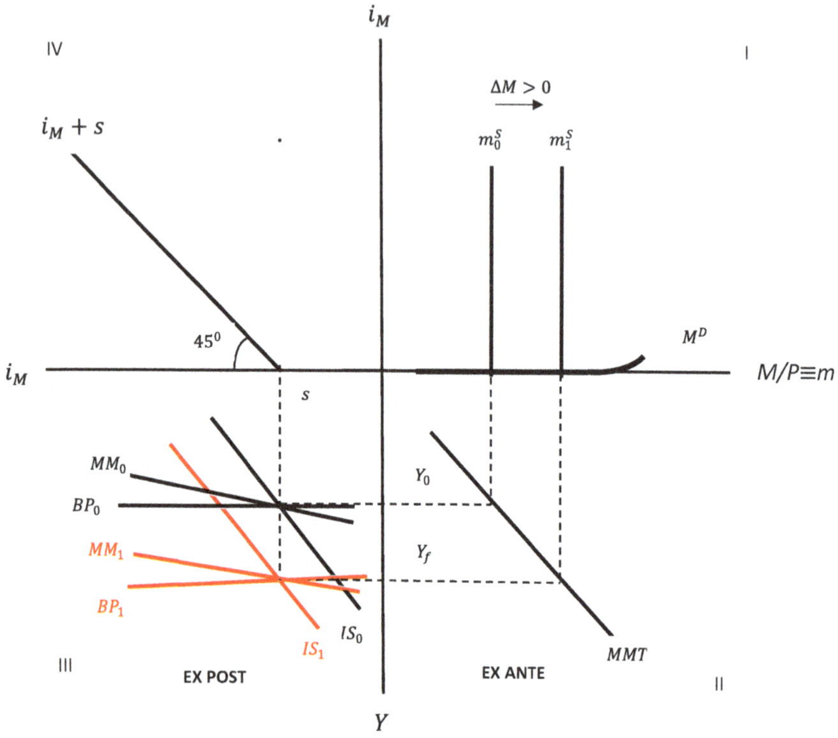

Chart 15.2 MMT policy in an HC economy

budget deficit in such an economy would stem from the wealth effect on consumption, spurred by a series of money supply injections through the budget.[11] Increased real money, when utilized for consumption, expands the IS curve, boosting output, decreasing private sector saving surpluses, and lessening the required fiscal deficits to maintain aggregate demand. This process leads to the economy stabilizing at full-employment output with stock-flow equilibrium, eliminating sector surpluses or deficits. In essence, the wealth effect serves to safeguard the economy from potential excessive money supply associated with MMT policies—the wealth effect rescues MMT from itself…!

In terms of Eq. (15.7), to the extent that the wealth effect works and that increases in money supply do not require interest rate adjustments, policy-driven shocks to the supply of *M* are reflected in aggregate output rises until full employment is reached, with no impact on inflation (by design):

[11] Palley (2013) pointed this out, and specifically mentioned the Pigou effect. Also, in a model that would include income taxes as a way of taxation (instead of, or together with, lump sum taxes), the budget deficit would not only be reduced by intentional cuts in public spending (matching the decrease of the private sector surplus) but also, or only, by higher government revenue. The same private sector saving surplus would be lowered not only by the wealth effect, but also by smaller household disposable incomes.

$$\frac{dY}{dM} = 1 - w'_Y = c'_Y > 0. \tag{15.8}$$

Therefore, the outcome of reaching a new equilibrium depends on how well the wealth effect works. It is probable that in HC economies, and especially in economies that issue currencies that are used as international reserves, the effect would work well as the currency is (almost) always in demand, both internally and externally. In a perfect framework of how households decide to consume over time, the wealth effect would increase gradually and might take some time until it drives the economy to full employment, but this would invariably happen at some point (if there are no negative shocks).

MMT advocates mainly base their view on the U.S. (Palley, 2020), which has such economic, political, and military power, as well as a key role in the global economy, that people within and outside the country are eager to buy (especially during crises) as more dollars get printed to boost aggregate demand. MMT advocates also take Japan's seemingly unlimited capacity to absorb the huge amounts of yen that were printed under Abenomics as proof of the viability of MMT policy recommendations. In so doing, they incorrectly generalize to other economies what turns out to be a very exceptional country case: one where even a dramatic shock to the economy may cause the currency to appreciate—not to depreciate, as it would happen almost everywhere else.

In contrast, in economies that have less credibility (or where credibility vacillates), if market expect money supply steadily to grow faster than output, because of the constant issuances of money to cover lasting budget deficits, wealth holders either reduce their money holdings, as their demand-for-money schedule becomes very steep, or ask for a high enough interest rate to make money attractive to hold.

15.5.2 Where MMT Policy Can't Work

Different would be the case when the same MMT policy were executed in an LC economy (i.e., with a low value of β). Here, two options would be available to the government: the latter could either pursue a zero-interest rate policy or pay on money balances the interest rate that the market requires for holding them.

Zero Interest Rate

As above, the government permanently increases spending (from M_0 to M_1, in quadrant I) to expand aggregate output to full-employment level Y_f, based on the (ex-ante) MMT schedule (quadrant II), at a zero-interest rate (Chart 15.3). This would be perfectly in line with MMT's prescription to pursue a zero-interest rate policy. Here, however, as the economy faces a steeper demand-for-money function, the expansionary effect dissipates into higher demand for *FX* (and alternative assets, if these were included in the model), as the larger stock of money supplied exceeds

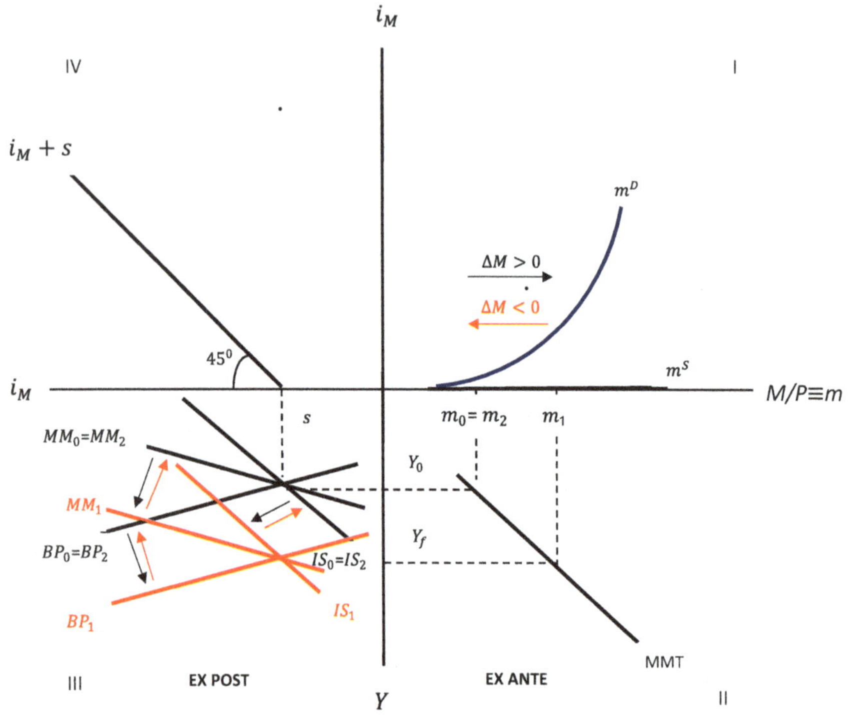

Chart 15.3 MMT policy in an LC economy: zero-interest rate money

its demand at the unchanged interest rate. The dissipation neutralizes the increase in spending.

As the increase in aggregate demand shifts the IS schedule from IS_0 to IS_1, and simultaneously the MM schedule from MM_0 to MM_1, the lack of an interest rate adjustment mechanism that re-equilibrates the money market, causes both the IS and LM schedules to shift back to their initial position, thus offsetting the policy change. Notice, at an invariant interest rate on money, the nominal exchange might depreciate unboundedly due to wealth holders keeping diversifying the increasing stock of M into FX, thereby temporarily shifting the BP schedule outward to BP_1 (from Eq. (15.4)). However, the exchange rate pass-through effect would swiftly translate currency depreciation into higher inflation (in line with empirical research[12]), thus restoring the original value of the real exchange rate and bringing the BP schedule back to its initial position $BP_2 = BP_0$. The higher the expectation of currency depreciation driven by the expected indefinite growth of M, the swifter and more complete the pass-through effect of the nominal exchange rate on inflation: the real exchange rate would not change, but its numerator and denominator would both

[12] For a review of the empirical literature on policy credibility, the exchange rate, and inflation, see Chap. 13, Sect. 2. On the relevance of the exchange-rate pass-through effect especially for developing economies, see Vernengo and Pérez Caldentey (2019).

increase unboundedly. This would neutralize any expansionary effect of currency depreciation on output.

In fact, the story might not end there: a high nominal exchange rate depreciation followed by a large increase in the general price level would further depress output through the contraction in real money supply and real wealth holdings (with further shifts of the MM and IS schedules, respectively, toward the Y axis, which are not reported in Chart 15.3). Notice that an LC economy would stand to gain nothing by adopting a floating exchange rate regime: excess money would either dissipate into larger FX holdings, currency depreciation and inflation, with negative real effects.

In terms of Eq. (15.7), and considering Eq. (15.6) in light of the policy-driven money market disequilibrium, persistent increases in M at interest rate $i_M = 0$ cause $m > m^*$,[13] thereby increasing FX-holdings and driving M-balances back to equilibrium, that is, $m = m^*$, with no changes in real output:

$$\mathrm{d}Y = \frac{(I' - \varepsilon K')i'_M|\beta}{(1 - c'_Y)(1 - c'_W)}(d\mathrm{M} - \varepsilon \mathrm{dFX}) = 0. \tag{15.9}$$

Market-Determined Interest Rate

Another option is that the government does the same thing as before, but instead of following the usual MMT's target of zero interest rate (regardless of the rising demand-for-money schedule), it pays the needed interest rate, i_M, to keep the money market balanced. Chart 15.4 shows the result of this policy choice. As before, the intended effect along the MM curve is to achieve full-employment output, but the lasting increase in aggregate demand due to the larger money-financed fiscal deficits reduces output in the end, because the higher interest rate paid by the government on M makes both the MM and BP curves move inward (toward the axes) along the IS curve, until they meet again at a lower level of equilibrium output (quadrant III), leading to an increase in the real exchange rate.

Specifically, the MM schedule must move back because, as output goes down, the money demand goes down and the money interest rate must go up to make sure that the money demand is equal to the new (larger) supply. The BP schedule also has to move back because, as output goes down, the import demand goes down and the resulting better external surplus boosts the real exchange rate; at the new equilibrium levels of output and the exchange rate on the BP schedule, any rise in output (and, therefore, in imports) would need a rise in the interest rate enough to draw more capital from abroad.

Observe that if the output multiplier were (realistically) assumed to change in the opposite direction of the interest rate, the higher interest rate that the government must pay on M would not only move the MM and BP schedules along the IS schedule, as above, but would also shift the IS schedule inward, thus increasing the contractionary effect on output. This would happen if the households' marginal propensity to consume from current income were to decrease with the real interest

[13] Notice that it is always the case that $m^* = m^{\mathrm{opt}}$, while the reverse is not necessarily true.

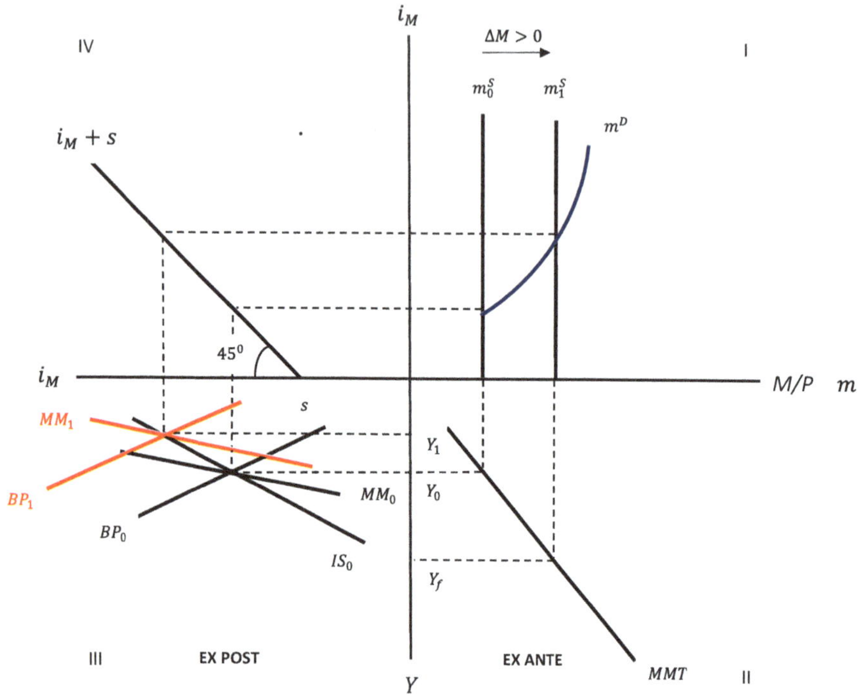

Chart 15.4 MMT policy in an LC economy: positive-interest rate money

rate (Hviid & Kuchler, 2017). Finally, observe that, as the money stock exceeds its optimal level, the increase in the equilibrium interest rate and its contractionary effect can occur at output levels that are lower than full employment: the more the money that accumulates over time, the higher the equilibrium interest rate that wealth holders demand to hold it, and the lower the equilibrium output level achieved compared to its full-employment equivalent.

This case leads to an important finding that MMT theorists overlook: if the reason for policy action is the presence of private sector net (desired) saving excesses (i.e., the cause of an economy's tendency to have Keynesian unemployment or underemployment), this does not mean that savers are happy to hold all the money supply that derives from persistent monetized fiscal deficits. Money will need to pay a positive and rising rate of return to satisfy wealth holders. If this is not done, wealth holders change their portfolios, making money lose its (internal and external) value even when employment is not full. This would be especially the case in those economies where wealth holdings are concentrated, wealth is managed by professional investors, and domestic financial markets are internationally integrated (as discussed in Chaps. 13 and 14). Conversely, if the required interest rate is paid to wealth holders, there may not be a way to ensure it is compatible with full-employment output (Chart 15.4).

In terms of Eq. (15.7), persistent policy-driven increases in M require interest rate adjustments, which eventually cause aggregate demand, and hence output, to decline:

$$\frac{\mathrm{d}Y}{\mathrm{d}M} = \frac{(I' - \varepsilon K')i'_M(m - m^*|\beta) - 1}{(1 - c'_Y)(1 - c'_W)} < 0 \quad \text{for} \quad m > \mu, \tag{15.10}$$

that is, considering the derivative signs of Eq. (15.10) and the properties of the interest rate on money function, $i_M = i_M(\cdot|\beta)$ (see Chap. 13, Appendix 1), there is always a critical level of money, μ, such that for any $m > \mu \geq m^{\mathrm{opt}}$, Eq. (15.10) is negative since $(I' - \varepsilon K')i'_M(m - \mu|\beta) - 1 < 0$. Notice that, as the stock of money is due to grow indefinitely under MMT policy, the above result will inevitably hold at some point. Also the effect of policy credibility on $i_M = i_M(\cdot|\beta)$ is such that, all else equal, $\mu_{LC} < \mu_{HC}$, that is, the critical level of money will be lower for economies with weaker credibility, thus constraining their policy space more than would be the case for HC economies.

15.6 Conclusion

As this chapter has explained, two major internal problems invalidate MMT. The first is that, because of the way money is created in the economy, according to the theory, the money that the government spends in the economy through the fiscal deficits keeps accumulating somewhere in the economy (unless it is taxed away, or public debt is issued) and someone must hold it. This means that either wealth holders receive on their money holdings an interest rate high enough to make them willing to keep holding them, or they will try to get rid of them exchanging money with other assets, since at some point the money stock will inevitably exceed its optimal level (all else being equal). In fact, the more the economy is internationally financially integrated, and the more unequal is its wealth distribution, the more likely is that wealth holders will diversify their holdings out of money and into other (domestic and foreign) assets, causing money to lose (internal and external) value at any level of output. If a price mechanism is not used to ensure balance in the money market, taxation and/or debt issuances may have to be used even before full employment is achieved. In both cases, therefore, the goal of full employment is compromised.

The second problem is that the constant creation of "excess" money becomes a serious issue when an economy suffers from low or declining credibility. In today's open and internationally highly financially integrated (globalized) economies, the money and debt instruments issued by governments trade in financial markets and their prices at which they trade is determined based on the level of credibility that markets assign to the issuing governments. Whether the market assessments of credibility levels are correct or incorrect is not the issue; what matters is that money and debt instruments are "valued" in, and by, the markets based on those assessments. This valuation process determines the policy space available for national policymakers to make an active use of the macroeconomic tools and affects their effectiveness: some countries are more policy constrained than others, depending on their credibility, and only few enjoy a very large policy space.

The fact that a country has monetary sovereignty and therefore cannot be forced to default on its financial obligations (indeed, one of the most essential MMT tenets) does not automatically imply that the money issued maintains its value. On the contrary, any prospects of this sovereignty being misused or abused by the government leads the markets to expect the value of money to decline. Well informed wealth holders with easy access to markets want their money to (at least) preserve its (internal and external) real value: to them, default events are not only when the government cannot pay its debt back, but also when it pays its debt with devaluing money. If wealth holders expect such future occurrences and are not adequately compensated ex ante for potential losses, they can opt out of the money quickly, at any time and at no (or negligible) cost, and shift their portfolios into alternative assets, causing money to depreciate further. As regards the money issued by a poorly credible government of a globalized economy, a stock of such money that were to grow indefinitely relative to output would be expected to lose external value (that is, to devalue) as well as internal value (through inflation) due to the exchange rate pass-through effect.

This is an inherent feature of MMT policy, whereby the money stock is bound to grow indefinitely with the monetary financing of the future fiscal deficits intended to offset the private-sector's structural net saving surplus position. Only the wealth effect, earlier discussed, can break these dynamics; yet its effectiveness relies on the policy credibility of the money-issuing economy: if the credibility is low, the opting out of money from wealth holders neutralizes the wealth effect on aggregate demand and output.

The government might try to bring balance in the money market by paying an adequate interest rate on money holdings. However, the equilibrium interest rate required to restore balance would be increasing (as the money stock would grow indefinitely) and it would soon become unsustainable and inconsistent with full-employment output.

Once again: policy sustainability depends on the credibility attributed by the markets to the national economies. A country that issues a currency that is used as international reserve and is always in high demand (especially in times of crisis) is largely unconstrained and can pursue MMT policy until the wealth effect allows private sector net (desired) saving surpluses to be eliminated; as a result, the need for monetizing additional fiscal deficits would be removed. At the other extreme, a country whose currency nobody wants to hold would not even be able to make it more attractive by paying extraordinarily high interest rates on it, which would be inconsistent with full-employment output anyway. As the only remedy, the country would have to reform its own policy regime and try to acquire credibility in the eyes of the markets by acting in a financially prudent way. This would most likely come at the cost of less than full employment.

As this chapter has shown, Modern Money Theory (or MMT) full-employment policy—understood as the permanent monetary financing of fiscal deficits aimed to offset the negative impact on output deriving from private sector structural net (desired) saving surpluses—would not be a solution for an economy's persistent tendency to Keynesian unemployment or underemployment (except, perhaps, in very few country circumstances). Unless the economy were perceived to be highly credible, the systematic implementation of MMT policy would expose it to significant risk of instability.

The next chapter, which will conclude the Part III of this book on "money and macroeconomic policies," discusses a groundbreaking monetary instrument that I had a role in inventing. This instrument was designed as a policy tool to aid heavily indebted countries lacking monetary sovereignty in overcoming recessions or economic stagnation without exacerbating their fiscal situation.

References

Aspromourgos, T. (2018). Keynes, public debt, and the complex of interest rates. *Journal of the History of Economic Thought, 40*(4), 493–512.

Backus, D., & Driffill, E. J. (1985a). Inflation and reputation. *American Economic Review, 75*, 530–538.

Backus, D., & Driffill, E. J. (1985b). Expectation and policy credibility following a change in regime. *Review of Economic Studies, 52*, 211–221.

Bossone, B. (2021). Why MMT can't work. *International Journal of Economic Policy Studies, 15*(1), 157–181.

Bossone, B. (2023). The *devils*: From real life to movie fiction, and economic theory and practice. *World Economics, 24*(1).

Cochrane, J. H. (2015). *A new structure for U.S. Federal debt, No. 15108*. Economics Working Papers, Hoover Institution, Stanford University.

Davidson, P. (2019). What is modern about MMT? A concise note. RWER (2019), 72–74.

Forstater, M., & Mosler, W. (2005). The natural rate of interest is zero. *Journal of Economic Issues, XXXIX*(2).

Hviid, S. J., & Kuchler, A. (2017). *Consumption and savings in a low interest-rate environment*. Denmark National Bank Working Paper No. 116.

Jayadev, A., & Mason, J. W. (2018). *Mainstream macroeconomics and modern monetary theory: What really divides them?* Institute for New Economic Thinking.

Kelton, S. (2020), *The deficit myth: Modern monetary theory and the birth of the people's economy*. Public Affairs.

Kreps, D., & Wilson, R. (1982). Reputation and imperfect information. *Journal of Economic Theory, 27*, 253–279.

Krugman, P. (2019, February 25). Running on MMT (Wonkish). *The New York Times*.

Mitchell, B. (2012, September 26). *Investment and interest rates*. Bill Mitchell—Modern Monetary Theory, August 10.

Mitchell, B. (2018a, September 26). *MMT and the external sector—Redux*. Bill Mitchell—Modern Monetary Theory.

Mitchell, B. (2018b, September 11). *The divide between mainstream macro and MMT is irreconcilable—Part 2*. Bill Mitchell—Modern Monetary Theory.

Mitchell, B. (2019). *Macroeconomics*. Macmillan Publishers.

Mosler, W. B. (2018, March 27). Soft currency economics. Mimeo. https://web.archive.org/web/20060904234833/http://epicoalition.org:80/docs/soft0004.htm

Palley, T. I. (2013). *Money, fiscal policy, and interest rates: A critique of modern monetary theory.* Mimeo.

Palley, T. I. (2020). What's wrong with modern money theory (MMT): Macro and political economic restraints on deficit financed fiscal policy. *Review of Keynesian Economics, 8*(4), 472–493.

PERI. (2012). *Modern monetary theory: A debate.* Political Economy Research Institute, Working Paper Series No. 279, University of Massachusetts Amherst.

Sawyer, M. (2019). Modern monetary theory: is there any added value? *Real-World Economics Review, 89*, 167–178.

Summers, L. H. (2019, March 4). The left's embrace of modern monetary theory is a recipe for disaster. *The Washington Post.*

Tymoigne, E., & Wray, L. R. (2013). *Modern money theory 101: A reply to critics.* Working Paper No. 778, Levy Economics Institute of Bard College.

Vernengo, M., & Pérez Caldentey, E. (2019). *Modern money theory (MMT) in the tropics: Functional finance in developing countries.* Working Paper, Political Economy Research Institute, University of Massachusetts Amherst.

Wray, L. R. (1998). *Understanding modern money: The key to full employment and price stability.* Edward Elgar.

Wray, L. R. (2015). *Modern money theory—A primer on macroeconomics for sovereign monetary systems* (2nd ed.). Palgrave Macmillan.

Wray, L. R. (2019, October 14). MMT: Report from the front (Part 2). *New Economic Perspectives.*

Chapter 16
Fiscal Money

Abstract This chapter discusses the concept of "Fiscal Money," a policy tool put forth after the 2010 European sovereign debt crisis, aimed at invigorating domestic demand in heavily indebted Eurozone nations without escalating public debt or breaching Eurozone regulations. Conceived by financier Marco Cattaneo and further developed by a collaborative group of researchers, Fiscal Money seeks to facilitate economic recovery in countries ensnared in stagnation and deflation, constrained by traditional fiscal strategies. The proposal, originally framed as Tax Credit Certificates (TCCs), highlights a fresh approach that combines fiscal and monetary policy principles. The chapter explores the theoretical underpinnings of Fiscal Money, presents simulations illustrating its practical application in Italy, and assesses its potential effectiveness in combating economic malaise. By establishing a non-debt fiscal instrument, Fiscal Money seeks to provide a viable alternative for Eurozone countries to stimulate their economies while adhering to stringent fiscal rules, paving the path toward sustainable economic growth.

16.1 Preamble

In 2012, amidst the European Sovereign Debt Crisis, Italian financier Marco Cattaneo posed the challenge of revitalizing an economy burdened by a large public debt and lacking monetary autonomy—a case epitomized by Italy. He outlined a solution in an op-ed for Italy's primary financial newspaper, "Il Sole 24 Ore." Cattaneo proposed the introduction of Tax Credit Certificates (TCCs), a special type of fiscal instrument that could effectively fund a long-term initiative to stimulate both public and private sector expenditure.[1]

After meeting online and engaging in discussions, Marco's proposal impressed me greatly. I believed it deserved further analysis and then to be promoted publicly. As a result, a team consisting of him, me, and other researchers formed to delve deeper into the TCCs. We eventually formulated the idea of Fiscal Money and became known as the Group of Fiscal Money. Through various means such as policy papers,

[1] See Appendix 1 for details on the origin of the idea and his further development.

B. Bossone, *Trailblazing Visions of Money in Economic Theory*, Contributions to Economics, https://doi.org/10.1007/978-3-031-82544-6_16

commentaries on newspapers, participation in seminars and conferences, posts on specialized blogs, and contacts with political and financial institutions, we invested significant time and effort in advocating for the concept and its associated policy program. We reached out to diverse audiences including academia, political circles, business communities, representative of government institutions, and civic societies, both at home and abroad. I especially contributed to establishing Fiscal Money on solid theoretical foundations, ensuring that its use be protected against potential government abuse, and assuring that proposed policy program was aligned with the rules and regulations of the Eurozone.

There are two aspects of great interest regarding Fiscal Money. One is the instrument's innovative economics, which, as its name implies, springs from the clever combination of fiscal and monetary elements to create a powerful tool for macroeconomic policy. This will be the subject of this chapter.

The other equally interesting aspect is how our proposal was publicly received in Italy. While it was appreciated by several progressive economists, grassroots communities, the industrial world, and opposition parties (the Fiscal Money program inspired two draft laws officially submitted to Parliament by the Movement Five Stars and Fratelli d'Italia, respectively), it was aprioristically rejected by the Establishment (the governing parties, the euro-linked institutions, economists and commentators closed to the government), which dismissed our proposal without even giving it a fair consideration. They accused us of attempting to undermine the role of the euro and bypass Eurozone regulations on fiscal discipline, without truly understanding our proposal. They were not interested in debating it, they just wanted to silence it as something that challenged the euro framework. They went to the extent of blocking our responses from being published in the same media outlets where the criticisms had been aired.

All this will not be further discussed in this chapter,[2] which focuses only on the economics of Fiscal Money. To do so, I will revisit the work that Marco Cattaneo and I prepared for the academic international symposium organized by the FernUniversität in Hagen, Germany, and held in Hagen on November 24–25, 2016, where we were invited to present our Fiscal Money proposal.[3]

16.2 Introduction

In 2016, the European sovereign debt crisis had been ongoing for eight years, and the economic recovery in the Eurozone remained weak and inconsistent. The policies implemented to address the crisis, which were guided by the rules governing the region, failed to stimulate growth in peripheral countries and did not prevent their slide into dangerously low inflation or deflation, as well as a liquidity trap. These

[2] An excellent narration is in the book written by Stefano Sylos Labini (2022), one of the Group members who has done his best to defend the proposal publicly.

[3] See Bossone and Cattaneo (2016).

rules, based on a macroeconomic perspective that emphasizes the supply side of the economy, limited the role of discretionary policies in managing the business cycle, thereby greatly restricting policymakers' ability to respond to severe economic challenges.

As such rules could not be changed and there was no national political will to violate them, and if exiting the single currency was deliberately discarded as an option, what could the authorities of a Eurozone country do to resume domestic growth in circumstances where the national economy was caught in a deep depression or stagnation and deflation?

This chapter recounts how the "Group of Fiscal Money" addressed this issue by suggesting the adoption and implementation of a new policy tool by the government, known as "Fiscal Money."[4] This tool aimed to stimulate overall demand by providing households and businesses with additional spending power. It is important to notice from the very outset that Fiscal Money had never been intended by the Group to replace the euro but rather to serve as a supplementary, non-debt fiscal policy instrument. As the Group argued all along in its uncountable public pronouncements and published materials, the implementation of Fiscal Money would adhere to all then existing European regulations and not cause new public debt.

The chapter is organized as follows: Sect. 16.2 examines the limitations posed on demand management policy by the regulations and structure of the Eurozone, and the economic principles that support them. Section 16.3 outlines the origins and developments of the Eurozone crisis, as well as the actions taken to address it. Section 16.4 presents the official definition of Fiscal Money proposed by Marco Cattaneo and myself during the symposium, subsequently adopted by the Group. It explains the key characteristics of Fiscal Money and its compliance with the euro rules. Moreover, it demonstrates the practical application of Fiscal Money by outlining and simulating the effects of a multi-year program in Italy during the crisis. This section also identifies precautionary measures necessary to safeguard the budget against potential drawbacks. Section 16.5 concludes the article. Appendix 1 provides information on the origination of the Fiscal Money concept, the Group of Fiscal Money and some bibliographical references to the Group's contributions from 2014 to 2021.

[4] On the origin of the Fiscal Money program, see Appendix 1.

16.3 Constraints on Macroeconomic Policies in the European Union[5]

The Eurozone's economic governance was fundamentally built on the idea of not recognizing a role for the implementation of macroeconomic policies. The foundation of the Eurozone's economic governance was primarily centered around the principle of excluding the implementation of macroeconomic policies.

The institutions that oversee the economic governance of the European Monetary Union were established through the Maastricht Treaty, which was agreed upon by EU member states in 1992. The Treaty identified five criteria to be fulfilled by countries wishing to adopt the euro,[6] and built on two pillars: the Stability and Growth Pact and the Statute of the European Central Bank (ECB).

The first pillar, the Stability and Growth Pact—introduced by the Amsterdam Treaty in 1997, reinforced by the Fiscal Compact in 2012, and further revised in 2023—became a key component of the European economic governance and was intended to provide the fiscal framework that would induce Eurozone member states to be responsible for their own fiscal policies and act responsibly on them. The Pact includes two elements: a preventive arm that encourages peer pressure among member states, and a system of penalties for countries that do not adhere to the requirement of a balanced budget throughout the economic cycle. As part of this framework, Eurozone member states can only rely on automatic stabilizers to address economic fluctuations.

As the other pillar of economic governance, the Maastricht Treaty mandates the ECB to ensure price stability as its primary objective, as stated in the current article 127 TFEU. The same provision in the Treaty adds that while prioritizing price stability, the ECB should also support the overall economic policies within the

---

[5] The contents of this section and the next, as in the original work with Marco Cattaneo, draw and expand on Saraceno (2015). I am still grateful to Francesco Saraceno for pointing his valid contribution to our attention.

[6] The five criteria, aimed at guaranteeing nominal convergence before the adoption of the single currency, were: (1) Inflation close to the average between the lowest inflation rates in the zone; (2) long-term interest rates close to the average between the lowest interest rates in the zone; (3) two years at least in the exchange rate mechanism, without realignments; (4) public deficit lower than 3% of GDP; (5) public debt lower than 60% of GDP, or approaching that level at a sufficiently fast pace. By the decision date of June 1998, 11 countries fulfilled the criteria, with Greece joining shortly afterwards. As of January 2015, the Eurozone has 19 members.

Community.[7] It is worth noticing that the ECB is given considerable independence by the Treaty in the definition of price stability and its conduct toward it.[8]

As well argued by Fitoussi and Saraceno (2013), the macroeconomic policy framework of the Eurozone is based on neoclassical Walrasian theory. This theory suggests that markets with rational agents and flexible prices and wages can achieve optimal equilibria, where resources are fully utilized and allocated efficiently. The focus of economic policy is on increasing the economy's capacity to produce, with little emphasis on demand management. Any negative effects on demand from supply side policies are believed to be outweighed by export-led growth from increased competitiveness.

According to Walrasian theory, money is only demanded for transactions and has no impact on the real sector of the economy in the long run. Monetary policy can have short-term effects due to price rigidities or surprise effects on expectations, but its overall impact is limited. The best approach for central banks is to maintain a strict inflation target to anchor expectations and minimize deviations in output from its optimal path. By stabilizing inflation, the unemployment rate can be kept at the natural rate, which is the best rate achievable through policy.[9]

The belief that fully rational individuals and a self-stabilizing economic process (in line with Walrasian theory) make active fiscal policy ineffective has implications for the fiscal side. In this view, inefficient government spending can displace productive private investment, and deficits financed by debt do not stimulate economic growth. Instead, adjusting fiscal imbalances can contribute to economic growth by reducing country risk and increasing market confidence (known as the expansionary fiscal-contraction hypothesis). Therefore, the priority for fiscal policy should mainly focus on preventing policy pro-cyclicality and ensuring debt sustainability. This means striving for balanced or surplus budgets in the medium term (across the economic cycle) and reducing government debt levels.

In essence, according to the underlying principles of the euro architecture, the aim is to ensure that monetary and fiscal rules effectively reduce the possibility of government interference causing distortions, alleviate uncertainty caused by policies, and create a stable atmosphere conducive to investment and economic growth.[10] In such

---

[7] In the United States, instead, the Full Employment and Balanced Growth Act of 1978 (the Humphrey-Hawkins Act) amended the Federal Reserve Act and established that monetary policy would serve the dual objective of price stability and full employment. The different institutional arrangements characterizing the ECB and the Fed reflect the different intellectual environment in which they emerged. The Humphrey Hawkins Act dates back to when the Keynesian view of macroeconomic policy dominated economics. Consistent with this view, monetary policy should include full employment as one of its fundamental objectives.

[8] The ECB's Governing Council defines as a "year-on-year increase in the Harmonised Index of Consumer Prices (HICP) for the euro area of below, but close to 2%."

[9] Olivier Blanchard and Jordi Gali call this proposition the "divine coincidence." Additional distortions typically lead to deviations of the natural rate from the constrained efficient rate, but the divine coincidence remains a useful theoretical benchmark (Blanchard 2016).

[10] The construction of the European Monetary Union has been heavily influenced, if not determined, by Germany, as discussed by Bofinger (2016). The macroeconomic policy paradigm in Germany and the Eurozone is based on three key elements: a focus on balanced fiscal budgets, an emphasis on

an environment, policymakers are not expected to make choices other than removing the obstacles to the unrestricted unfolding of market forces (e.g., monopolies, asymmetric information, rigidities) through "structural reforms," thereby enabling the economy to achieve the "bliss" state characterized by full resource employment and Pareto efficient resource allocation.

In this kind of setting, policymakers are anticipated to exclusively focus on eliminating barriers that hinder the natural functioning of the market, such as monopolies, unequal access to information, and inflexibility. This can be achieved through implementing "structural reforms," which facilitate the economy reaching a state of optimal resource utilization and efficient allocation of resources, commonly referred to as the "bliss" state.[11]

From a political economy perspective, technocracies play a vital role due to their possession of technical knowledge that allows them to make appropriate decisions at the right time. Additionally, their actions are not hindered by vested interests or political objectives, which can distort market incentives. Furthermore, technocrats can act quickly and efficiently compared to politicians who are bound by the lengthy and complex processes of democracy. However, the 2007 crisis presented a significant challenge to this view of economic policy and posed difficult decisions for policymakers in the Eurozone. The European institutions established based on this perspective were proven to be ill-suited for the task.

---

price stability as the main goal of monetary policy, and the belief that flexible prices are crucial for addressing unemployment issues. Germany's approach to the Eurozone crisis and its insistence on austerity at all costs is shaped by its skepticism towards the effectiveness of demand management. The German perspective also includes an asymmetric tolerance for inflation, with rates above the ECB's target seen as dangerous, while the current Eurozone inflation rate of 1% is not a concern. The strategy of "wage moderation" adopted by Germany from 2000 to 2007 is a reflection of the belief that flexible prices can help reduce unemployment. This explains the German government's focus on structural reforms as the primary solution to the problems within the Eurozone.

[11] Blanchard (2014) acknowledges that the prevalent macroeconomic policy perspective, which is deeply embedded in the European treaties, rules, and economic institutions, has also influenced mainstream macroeconomics doctrine, thereby reflecting its shortcomings and unrealistic assumptions. "The techniques were best suited to a worldview in which economic fluctuations occurred but were regular, and essentially self-correcting. The problem is that we came to believe that this was indeed the way the world worked... We in the field did think of the economy as roughly linear, constantly subject to different shocks, constantly fluctuating, but naturally returning to its steady state over time. Instead of talking about fluctuations, we increasingly used the term 'business cycle'. Even when we later developed techniques to deal with nonlinearities, this generally benign view of fluctuations remained dominant. That small shocks could sometimes have large effects and, as a result, that things could turn really bad, was not completely ignored by economists. But such an outcome was thought to be a thing of the past that would not happen again, or at least not in advanced economies thanks to their sound economic policies."

16.4 The Eurozone Crisis and the Policy Response

16.4.1 Policy Action

The policy response to the 2007–2008 crisis, when the interbank markets were on the verge of collapse, was effective. Central banks worked together and implemented both traditional and innovative measures to infuse liquidity into the markets and improve credit conditions.[12]

The Federal Reserve implemented aggressive rate cuts and injected liquidity, while the ECB focused on providing liquidity initially and only decided to reduce rates in October 2008, after previously increasing them in July 2008, shortly before the collapse of Lehman Brothers. Both approaches were effective in supporting interbank markets and preventing short-term interest rates from increasing. However, they had varying impacts on long-term rates and consequently influenced the overall macroeconomic environment.[13]

Despite initial success in preventing a financial collapse, monetary policy was unable to restore confidence. Banks held onto the liquidity injected into the system and invested it in secure public bonds, resulting in economies falling into a liquidity trap. As a result, fiscal policy took center stage in the winter of 2009, with many advanced and emerging economies implementing stimulus programs. Although these programs did not fully resolve the crisis, they did prevent further economic decline. Throughout 2009, the ECB and other central banks maintained an accommodating stance but played a more passive role.

However, in Europe, the sovereign debt crisis in the peripheral countries of the Eurozone brought monetary policy back into focus. The crisis was seen as a result of irresponsible government spending, despite the fact that countries like Ireland and Spain had low levels of public debt before the crisis. Austerity measures and structural reforms were implemented in both the peripheral and core countries, leading to a double-dip recession and a weak recovery. This crisis exposed the flaws in the Eurozone governance, such as the lack of flexible exchange rates and a single fiscal budget. Joining the Eurozone also made countries vulnerable to speculative attacks on their public debt. The decision to impose a haircut on Greek debt in 2010 increased the risk of sovereign defaults and raised borrowing costs for other countries.

In response, Eurozone policymakers focused on reducing public deficits through austerity measures. The Fiscal Compact further emphasized the need for budget balancing and reducing public debt. However, this simultaneous restrictive action worsened the downturn and created instability in the Eurozone, which raised concerns about the future of the single currency.

---

[12] Central banks strengthened their open market operations by broadening the types of assets accepted as collateral, even those with uncertain market value. In addition, they increased their involvement by providing longer-term loans to the banking sector.

[13] European rates remained substantially higher than their US equivalent.

16.4.2 The Response from the ECB

Due to the governments' inability to cooperate on a regional recovery effort, the ECB had to step in to prevent a disaster. Since 2010, the ECB took five major actions, all of which were necessitated by extraordinary circumstances. These included the launch of the Long-Term Refinancing Operations (LTRO) program in late 2011, Mario Draghi's famous "whatever it takes" speech in London on 26 July 2012, followed by the implementation of the Outright Monetary Transactions (OMT) program in September of that year. Additionally, the ECB introduced European Quantitative Easing, implemented negative interest rates on banks' excess reserves, and launched the Corporate Sector Purchase Programme (CSPP) on 10 March 2016.

Long-Term Refinancing Operations

The LTRO program, introduced in two stages in late 2011 and February 2012, aimed to address the ongoing weakness of the Eurozone interbank market. The ECB launched a substantial three-year lending initiative, worth one trillion euros, with an interest rate of 1%. Additionally, the range of collateral that borrowing banks could provide was expanded. While the program achieved some success, particularly among peripheral banks in Ireland, Italy, Spain, and Greece, it did not fully resolve the credit crisis or stimulate economic growth. In fact, a significant portion of the LTRO funds were utilized by banks to purchase sovereign debt from struggling countries, exacerbating the interconnected issues of banks and sovereign debt. This situation created a challenging cycle where banks were exposed to the risk of default due to their substantial holdings of sovereign debt, ultimately straining public finances as governments worked to support these increasingly vulnerable banks, thus raising the risk of default even further.

Outright Monetary Transactions

In 2012, after ECB chairman Mario Draghi's "whatever it takes" speech,[14] the ECB introduced the OMT initiative, where they pledged to purchase unlimited quantities of troubled countries' sovereign bonds upon request, effectively taking on the role of a lender of last resort. To avail this protection, countries had to commit to fiscal austerity measures and structural reforms, monitored by the European Commission, the International Monetary Fund, and the ECB (known as the "Troika"). The availability of ECB protection via the OMT program acted as a deterrent against speculative attacks on peripheral countries. This program represented a significant milestone in the European crisis.

[14] During the speech, delivered in London, Draghi (2012) famously stated that, *"Within our mandate, the ECB is ready to do whatever it takes to preserve the euro. And believe me, it will be enough."* The statement calmed to the markets overnight. It was seen as a commitment from the ECB to intervene in the sovereign bond market and potentially exceed its mandate by becoming a lender of last resort for troubled countries. However, ECB President Draghi clarified that the ECB was not stepping outside its mandate, as a collapse of the euro and the resulting financial turbulence would undermine the price stability that the ECB aims to achieve. The Outright Monetary OMT program was approved by the ECB Governing Council in September 2012 with strong support.

The LTRO and OMT succeeded in restoring calm in financial markets, and since their introduction the political and economic turbulences that frequently stroke the Eurozone never triggered the financial turmoil experienced before then. However, the two programs failed to restart growth in the Eurozone. This goal they were not able to achieve in the absence of supporting fiscal policy, and indeed when fiscal policy was pro-cyclical.

The implementation of LTRO and OMT effectively stabilized financial markets and prevented the recurrence of previous financial crises during periods of political and economic instability in the Eurozone. However, these programs were unable to stimulate economic growth in the region, mainly due to the lack of accompanying fiscal policies and even worsened circumstances when fiscal policy was counterproductive.

European Quantitative Easing

In June 2014, the ECB Governing Council decided to change its approach and acknowledged that the Eurozone inflation rate was dangerously low. This allowed for the implementation of new measures to inject liquidity into the economy. The European Quantitative Easing program began in September 2014 and initially involved the purchase of covered bonds and asset-backed securities. However, the program has had little impact on growth due to the persistent weak demand for credit. To address this issue, the ECB made a significant announcement in January 2015, stating that it would start purchasing sovereign bonds outside of the OMT program.

Negative Interest Rates

The ECB implemented a below zero policy interest rate on its deposit facility in June 2014 and made another reduction in September 2014.[15] These decisions primarily aimed to further loosen the already accommodative monetary policy to combat the increasing risk of deflation. The downward pressure on inflation expectations in the latter part of last year and early 2015 led to the adoption of negative deposit rates. The intention behind this was to incentivize banks to invest in alternative assets, thereby driving up their prices and reducing borrowing costs. This would subsequently be reflected in the economy through an overall relaxation of credit conditions. It is worth noting that negative policy rates, both in the Eurozone and non-Eurozone countries like Denmark and Switzerland, have been accompanied by negative market rates on

[15] Commercial banks typically keep deposits at the central bank to settle payments and meet reserve requirements. The central bank pays interest on these reserves, referred to as the deposit rate, for any reserves held above the minimum requirement. In normal circumstances, banks try to minimize excess reserves since the central bank's deposit rates are lower than other money market rates. However, since the global financial crisis, banks have been more cautious and have increased their reserves at central banks due to increased risk aversion and low returns on lending opportunities. Unconventional monetary policies, and the expansion of central bank balance sheets have also contributed to the rise in excess reserves held by banks. One more important reason for banks to hold more reserves was the decision by some central banks to raise the remuneration of reserves so as to offset their opportunity cost.

government bonds, particularly at shorter maturities.[16] The effects of negative rates are qualitatively similar to those of extremely low, yet positive rates.[17] In light of the policy decision, there has been an observable uptick in bank lending within the Eurozone, indicating that negative interest rates have played a supportive role. The results of a recent survey conducted by the ECB further indicate that this policy has had a favorable effect on mortgage lending, particularly for households seeking loans to purchase a house.[18] Overall, the program had a relatively modest impact on the growth of the area.[19]

Corporate Sector Purchase Programme

Following its announcement on 10 March 2016, the European Central Bank (ECB) introduced a new initiative called the Corporate Sector Purchase Programme (CSPP), as part of its efforts to enhance monetary policy measures. Under this program, the ECB will purchase euro-denominated bonds issued by non-bank corporations in the euro area, with investment-grade ratings. The aim of the CSPP, along with existing and new measures, is to provide further policy accommodation and strengthen the impact of the Eurosystem's asset purchases on the financing conditions of the real economy. By directly injecting newly created money into the economy, the CSPP aims to avoid the risk of the funds being absorbed by an unresponsive banking sector. This program is expected to have a greater impact than previous measures taken by

---

[16] For example, the 2-year bond yields on highly rated European countries such as Austria, Denmark, Germany, the Netherlands, and Switzerland have been negative since the first half of 2015. Besides the role of negative policy rates, however, several other potential factors may explain the emergence of negative yields, particularly those beyond the short-end of the yield curve. See "Negative Interest rates in Europe: A glance at their Causes and implications", in World Bank (2015), Box 1.1, pp. 13–19.

[17] Negative nominal rates can have positive effects on the economy in several ways. Firstly, they can contribute to keeping real interest rates below the neutral level, which can encourage consumption and investment. Secondly, lower or negative nominal rates can increase cash flow for businesses and households with limited access to funds, allowing them to increase their expenditure. Thirdly, these low rates can also stimulate lending by financial institutions. Fourthly, when domestic interest rates decrease, it can lead to a devaluation of the currency, as seen with the euro falling against the US dollar. This depreciation can boost exports and improve the balance of trade. Finally, in countries like Switzerland and Denmark, negative rates discourage capital inflows, which helps prevent appreciation pressure on their currencies driven by capital flows.

[18] See ECB's 2015 Euro Area Bank Lending Survey. The survey results indicate that the negative deposit facility rate has decreased lending rates for the purpose of a house purchase and increased lending volume. However, non-interest rate charges have also increased.

[19] Apart from the intended positive consequences outlined by policymakers, negative nominal interest rates have had adverse effects on financial stability and the functioning of capital markets. These effects include the erosion of bank profitability and increased pressures on non-bank financial institutions, such as pension and life insurance companies, to meet their long-term liabilities that were offered at fixed nominal rates. Additionally, negative interest rates have led to increased risk-taking as investors are driven to seek positive yields. A comprehensive analysis of these undesirable effects can be found in the cited publication "Negative Interest rates in Europe: A glance at their Causes and implications".

the ECB. As it was only implemented in June 2016, it is still too early to assess its effectiveness.[20]

Remarks Overall, based on analysis of financial markets' response to the ECB's interventions during the crisis, the ECB's response did not seem to have instilled confidence in the economy (Nedeljkovic & Mody, 2019). The temporary calm achieved through liquidity injection increased the banks' risk-taking behavior. Additionally, the lack of a clear strategy in the stimulative measures led to market uncertainty and a lack of faith in their sustainability. As a result, these measures did not have a significant positive impact on the overall situation.

More broadly, there remains a crucial question as to whether relying solely on monetary policy was enough to revive and sustain higher output growth and overcome lowflation or deflationary pressures in the stagnant economies of the Eurozone. The evidence suggested that this was not sufficient. In extreme crisis situations, particularly when there is a liquidity trap and demand is severely depressed, active use of fiscal policy and potentially coordination between fiscal and monetary actions seem to be necessary responses. However, the European rules and structure would have made it nearly impossible to implement this type of response. Additionally, economies with high levels of public debt, denominated in a currency they do not control, and lacking market confidence may not have the fiscal capacity to implement adequate stimulus measures, regardless of what the existing rules require. In light of these constraints and challenges, policymakers in Eurozone countries should have considered using alternative policy instruments, if any were available to them.

16.5 Fiscal Money as a New Demand-Management Policy Tool

Considering the constraints and challenges discussed earlier, a country in the Eurozone that is stuck in a liquidity trap indefinitely appears to have limited options to escape, except for leaving the single currency and returning to a national currency. However, we were highly skeptical that the European economic institutions' rules and structure, particularly those governing macroeconomic policy, could be reformed in a timely and sufficient manner to revive growth in crisis countries. I, in particular, in disagreement with my co-author, was against Italy leaving the euro, if not under special policy safeguards that would very hardly materialize (Bossone, 2017). Thus, the solution we proposed started from assuming a country wishing to remain in the Eurozone and adhering to its rules, while maximizing its fiscal sovereignty within the confines of the Fiscal Compact. Nevertheless, our proposed solution was adaptable enough that it could also facilitate the implementation of a new national currency, should the country choose to exit the Eurozone.

[20] For a discussion, see Bossone and Sylos Labini (2016), and Tyler (2016).

We proposed that countries facing stagnation and lowflation, with neither monetary sovereignty nor fiscal space available (as it would typically be the case of a largely indebted member of a monetary union) introduce and actively use "Fiscal Money," which we defined as:

> Any claims, private or public, which the state accepts from holders to discharge their fiscal obligations either in the form of rebates on their full value (tax rebates) or as effective value transfers (payments) to the state. Fiscal money claims are not legal tender and may not be convertible by the state in legal tender. However, they are negotiable, transferable to third parties, and exchangeable in the market.

Accordingly, a national state may issue Fiscal Money in two ways: as a promise to provide tax rebates to its holders in future, or as a payment method for settling tax obligations or other financial liabilities to the state, which the state can then use for its own payments (if the recipient agrees to accept it). Importantly, the acceptance of Fiscal Money as a payment method is completely voluntary for individuals or businesses operating within the country, and the state cannot force its usage. Furthermore, holders of Fiscal Money are not entitled to convert it into cash or other assets, but they have the freedom to sell it to others in exchange for local or foreign currencies or any other assets, goods, or services at a price determined by the market. In addressing the challenges and limitations mentioned before, we proposed that countries adopt a specific type of Fiscal Money, as explained next.

16.5.1 The Objectives of Fiscal Money

The idea of Fiscal Money was based on the state's power to recognize a specific instrument as valuable for meeting financial obligations. This concept can be traced back to "Chartalism," a theory devised by the German economist Georg Friedrich Knapp,[21] who already in 1905, in his *"State Theory of Money,"* discussed the authority of the government to produce paper currency and assign value to it through its acceptance as a means of paying taxes.[22] In recent times, scholars like Randall Wray, Matthew Forstater, and Warren Mosler have delved deeper into the concept of Modern Money Theory. Pilkington and Mosler (2012) and Pilkington (2013) examine the feasibility of allowing Eurozone governments to use their own government bonds to settle tax obligations if the issuer is unable to make interest and/or principal payments. This proposal aims to decrease the financial burden on specific Eurozone countries when seeking funding.

Our Fiscal Money proposal for the Eurozone was broader. We suggested addressing the critical economic issues facing the region by introducing a distinctive

---

[21] Note that the term "Chartalism" derives from the Latin "charta", that is, "paper", in relation to the nature of paper money as legal tender and in contrast to "Metallism" the economic principle that money derives its value from the purchasing power of the commodity upon which it is based.

[22] Knapp's work was originally published in German as *"Staatliche Theorie des Geldes"*, München u. Leipzig, Duncker & Humblot, 1905 and translated into English in 1924.

type of Fiscal Money instrument called the "Tax Rebate Certificate" or TRC.[23] Originally denominated Tax Credit Certificate, the new denomination was introduced specifically to avoid the misunderstanding that the word "credit" may inadvertently cause by conceptually associating the nature of the instrument to a debt obligation falling upon the issuing entity. In fact, as discussed in detail below, one of the key features of the TRC is that it *does not* raise or imply any financial obligation for the issuing state.

Our proposal can be summarized in three points. Firstly, we suggested utilizing the TRC as a tool for managing demand, specifically to provide the necessary support for Eurozone countries to escape the then ongoing state of depression, liquidity trap, stagnation, lowflation, and high unemployment. Secondly, we aimed to realign competitiveness within the Eurozone to prevent the creation of current account imbalances, which had been a major factor in the Eurocrisis. Lastly, implementing demand reflation through the introduction of the TRC would enable the Eurozone countries to achieve the goals of the Fiscal Compact without increasing sovereign public debt. This approach allowed for a gradual reduction in government indebtedness relative to national GDP by allowing the latter to grow, instead of being further depressed by austerity measures.

16.5.2 How Would the TRC Work?

Our proposal suggested issuing and distributing TRCs digitally to various recipients free of charge. The aim was to stimulate domestic demand and enhance the competitiveness of local businesses. Here's how the allocations were supposed to work:

- Employees would receive a portion of TRCs based on their income levels. This served the purpose of promoting social equity and encouraging consumption by providing higher after-tax incomes.
- Enterprises would also receive a portion of TRCs to reduce their labor costs. Allocations would be determined in relation to their labor expenses, effectively cutting costs and improving competitiveness.
- TRCs would be used to fund social expenses such as minimum vital income programs, unemployment benefits, and improving public education and healthcare systems.
- Some TRCs would be allocated to finance public investments and provide relief for natural disasters.

---

[23] The idea of the TRC was originated by Marco Cattaneo and presented in Cattaneo and Zibordi (2014). The idea was further elaborated by Biagio Bossone, Marco Cattaneo, Enrico Grazzini, and Stefano Sylos Labini in a public manifesto. The proposal was then the subject of the e-book on fiscal money, see Bossone et al., (2015a). The e-book collects a number of in-depth studies of the various (economic, legal, accounting, and institutional) aspects of the proposal. For a concise description of the proposed TRC, see Bossone et al., (2015b).

TRCs would trade in the financial market similar to government bonds. Their discount rate would be similar to that of a two-year zero-coupon government bond. TRCs would be sold by households and enterprises in need of immediate liquidity and purchased by those looking to save on taxes. Financial intermediaries would buy TRCs at a discount from sellers, either using them for future tax rebates or selling them at a lower discount to make a profit.

In an alternative option, the TRC could circulate in a dedicated digital national payments platform, where all the economy's agents would (voluntarily) hold accounts through which they can make, receive and settle payments directly in TRC.[24] This option would avoid agents having to go through costly and time-consuming conversions of TRCs into and from euros before or after making payments and transform the TRC into a form of immediately accessible liquidity to be used for any kind of purchases. In this case, payment of an interest rate by the state on the TRC balances would eliminate any discount between the market value of the TRC and the euro and would avoid double-pricing issues of goods and services denominated in either of the two instruments.

By reducing labor costs and increasing competitiveness, TRCs would stimulate exports and import substitution. This would lead to more output and employment, offsetting the impact of increased demand on the external trade balance. In a depressed economy with a large fiscal multiplier, TRC issuance would stimulate spending, resulting in output and employment growth. The two-year deferral provision for TRC redemptions allows the multiplier effect to take place and generate enough tax revenue to offset the fiscal rebates, preventing the deficit-to-GDP ratio from rising.

TRC issuance grants immediate spending power to the private sector, while the government faces deferred revenue shortfalls that would be compensated through new revenues generated by output growth. The higher GDP, fueled by increased demand and the fiscal multiplier effect, would boost tax revenues prior to TRC redemptions. Even under conservative estimates, these increased tax revenues would exceed the fiscal revenue shortfalls caused by the tax rebates.

Importantly, TRCs are not debt liabilities for the government and do not carry credit or exchange rate risks. They can be exchanged for equivalent reductions in fiscal obligations and pose no risk to financial stability.

To ensure fiscal stability, special safeguard measures would be implemented in the event of fiscal underperformance.

Overall, the TRC proposal involved a transfer of resources over time from the public to the private sector through future tax rebates that can be liquidated in the market at a present discounted value. These transfers could be spent to stimulate demand, increase employment and output, and generate the necessary fiscal revenues to cover the tax rebates in future.

---

[24] See *Un'Infrastruttura Digitale per l'Uso dei Certificati di Compensazione Fiscale (CCF) come Strumento di Pagamento: Opzioni Tecniche*, Il Gruppo della Moneta Fiscale, La Bottega Partigiana, available at http://bottegapartigiana.org/wp-content/uploads/2020/05/GMF_CCF_Infrastruttura-di-pagamento_25-maggio-2020.pdf.

16.5.3 TRCs Are Not Debt[25]

According to European Union law, the TRCs are not debt instruments. Based on EU Regulation 549/2013 of 21 May 2013 (in particular, par. 5.05 and par. 5.06), they are non-payable tax credits and, as such, they are not subject to reimbursements. Also, according to European System of Accounts 2010, issuing non-payable tax credits does neither originate a financial asset nor a financial liability since there is no money obligation binding a debtor to a creditor.[26] Therefore, when TRCs are issued, they only represent a contingent liability for the issuing government, and should not be recorded in national accounts. They are recorded as reducing tax revenue only when they are effectively used to pay less tax in the relevant accounting period.[27] In fact, the tax revenue reduction is only a contingent event. What matters, in the end, is the overall budgetary impact of TRC redemptions net of the higher tax revenues due to the expansionary effect of TRC issuances on GDP; if the second effect were to exceed the first, the overall (net) ex-post budgetary impact would be positive.

More broadly, fiscal rebates may not be considered liabilities (debt) under current international accounting standards, whereby "*a liability is a present obligation of the entity to transfer an economic resource as a result of past events.*"[28] While they reduce the revenue the government or issuing entity will receive, they do not create an obligation for the government to make payments or transfer resources to other parties. Therefore, Fiscal Money as defined in Section 16.4 would not originate any debt obligations for the issuing state and could not be accounted for as a liability of the issuing state.

16.5.4 Tax Rebate Certificates and the Fiscal Multiplier

The success and sustainability of our TRC proposal depended on the fiscal multiplier mechanism of the Keynesian tradition, which would be activated by changes in domestic aggregate demand resulting from TRC allocations. Based on empirical evidence that was produced at the time of our original article, the multiplier tended to be above 1 when the economy was in a depression or stagnation, such as a liquidity trap. As shown later, our projections indicated that with multiplier values above 0.8, implementing TRCs would not lead to additional budget deficits. This factor alone

---

[25] I grateful to Massimo Costa for having provided us with a thorough analysis of the accounting nature and legal status of the TRC, of which this section only gives a brief account.

[26] See Eurostat Guidance Note on Deferred Tax Assets (DTAs) and Recording of Tax Credits related to DTAs in ESA (2010), 29 August 2014.

[27] Thus, a 2-year TRC issued in 2017 would not be recorded in the national account until it would be used for tax reduction, which would not happen prior to 2019. Notice, also, that any time the TRC changes hand (digitally), it immediately recovers its full 2-year maturity.

[28] See IAS 37 *Provisions, Contingent Liabilities and Contingent Assets*. Section 4.26 of the Conceptual Framework for Financial reporting, (IASB 2018).

ensured the effectiveness and sustainability of the proposal, especially in economies facing depression, stagnation, and low inflation.

However, while a value of 0.8 could be considered relatively low compared to then recent evidence, we wanted to consider how robust our proposal was against factors that could weaken the multiplier effect through leakages or crowding out effects. We have identified three such factors: (1) the increase in imports due to growing demand, (2) the rise in interest rates resulting from higher demand, and (3) the increase in risk premia on government bond prices due to market expectations regarding the budgetary impact of the TRC program. I will discuss each of these factors individually.

In relation to the increase in imports, this would be compensated by the growth in exports and import substitution resulting from improved competitiveness due to reduced labor costs. The impact of this cost reduction, we argued, was similar to that of a currency devaluation, making domestic industries more competitive compared to foreign competitors.

The second factor, the increase in interest rates caused by growing demand, would be moderated or even nullified by the significant output gap, persistently negative price growth, and the anticipated continuation of an accommodative monetary policy stance in the Eurozone for the foreseeable future, reinforced by the extension of unconventional measures until a robust economic recovery takes place.

Lastly, market uncertainty surrounding the initiation of a TRC program, particularly its potential impact on future budget deficits and debt, could result in higher risk premia on government bond prices. Evidence then suggested that fiscal multipliers tended to be weaker when the fiscal position of governments was weak. Specifically, although multipliers were typically larger during recessions, they became smaller in the presence of high government debt, relative to what they would be with lower debt. This implied that TRC programs in countries with a large debt burden might be less effective than expected (an argument that resonates with my Portfolio Inflation Theory discussed in Chap. 13).

We concluded, however, that this type of uncertainty should not affect our proposed TRC program, as this included safeguard measures that would trigger corrective action in the event of fiscal underperformance, discouraging any anticipation that the fiscal revenue shortfalls resulting from TRC redemptions would exceed the expected increase in fiscal revenues due to a larger GDP. By addressing the market uncertainty ex-ante, the safeguard provision would prevent a potential rise in interest rates due to higher risk premia. Additionally, the design of the fiscal safeguard provisions would limit the negative impact of contingent fiscal adjustments on consumption decisions.

Three notations are important. First, The TRC program was designed to promote a sustained demand shock in the economy, lasting long enough to influence the agents' expectations and set in motion a durable, non-inflationary growth environment, which would influence investment decisions by enterprises and traverse the economy permanently on a higher real output trend. Yearly injections of TRC would in turn kick in and generate new stimuli as the stimulus of the previous injections naturally wear out, thus supporting the materialization of a higher multiplier on an ongoing basis, until output is stabilized at full employment consistent with low inflation. Second, the effectiveness of TRCs as producing additional purchasing power and their use for/in transactions would reduce their use as fiscal discounts, thereby diminishing their impact on the budget: in the limit, if (hypothetically) all TRCs issued by the state over time were only used by all agents receiving them to finance new transactions, they would end up serving purely as money and none would be presented to the state for tax compensations, thus removing entirely their impact on the budget. Finally, while usable as payment instruments, the TRCs would be denominated in euro and their value would be the same as that of the euro; also, they are non-defaultable fiscal instruments. Together, these features imply that the TRCs could not suffer from credibility issues of the issuing state, they would not be subject to any additional exchange rate risk than the one face by the euro and, therefore, could not raise any inflationary risk from exchange rate pass through effects other than those raised by the euro itself. In other words, the TRCs would fully reflect the credibility of the euro, and its value would not be affected by idiosyncratic country effects. On the other hand, the modest amount of yearly TRC injections relative to the total stock of euros outstanding would not per se compromise the stability of the euro exchange rate. However, should this happen (perhaps, as a consequence of more than one country injecting TRCs at the same time), the depreciation of the euro, if anything, would stimulate the competitiveness of the Eurozone country exports, while leaving the value of euro-denominated public debts unaltered by definition.

16.5.5 Projections

The fiscal multiplier was an estimation of the real GDP generated through the implementation of expansionary fiscal policies, such as higher government expenditure or lower taxes. We assumed a conservative fiscal multiplier value of 1.25 based on estimates derived from economies with severely depressed demand.[29] As detailed below, the program would provide for a significant share of total TRC issuances to be allocated to enterprises with a view to reducing their gross labor costs. This corresponded to a 9% reduction in total Italian companies' employee costs (currently about € 450 bn p.a.) and significantly enhanced competitiveness of domestic firms. This would allow for higher exports, plus substitution effects of certain import with internal production, to compensate the higher imports (including of raw materials) that the strong economic recovery led by the TRC program would generate. As already noted, the intervening on the gross labor cost i) would prevent Italy's external trade balance from deteriorating, and ii) would avoid demand leakages through import that weaken the effect of the fiscal multiplier on GDP growth.

[29] We conservatively took a 1.3 low-middle point value within the range of existing estimates spanning the 0.9 – 2.0 (and higher) interval and reduced it to 1.25 to take into account the discount that would apply to TRCs traded before maturity.

Table 16.1 TRC program for Italy: issuances and uses

Year TRC	2017	2018	2019	2020	2021	2022 (and beyond)
Issuances	30	60	90	120	120	120
Uses	0	0	30	60	90	120

Table 16.2. TRC program for Italy: economic and fiscal impact (changes in billion euros)

Year impact	2017	2018	2019	2020	2021	2022
Real GDP changes	38	75	113	150	150	150
Higher cumulated inflation (%)	1.0	2.0	3.0	4.0	5.0	6.0
Price effect on GDP	7	34	51	68	85	102
Nominal GDP changes	55	109	164	218	235	252
Gross total tax rate (%)	47.5	47.5	47.5	47.5	47.5	47.5
Gross government revenue change	26	52	78	104	112	120
Uses of TRC			−30	−60	−90	−120
Net government revenue changes	26	52	48	44	22	0

Note that the projected impact above did not take into account the additional effects that would derive from the expansion of private credit—including to fund new corporate investment—which would likely occur especially from the second and third year of the program as Italian corporate investments had been depressed for many years

Setting a two-year maturity for TRCs and planning for a gradual attainment of the € 120 bn TRC stock target, TRC redemptions would keep under TRC issuances up to the sixth year of the program (Table 16.1):

In addition to the € 150 bn additional real GDP, as estimated above, it was reasonable to predict that higher inflation would be generated as the economy recovered and the output gap was progressively reduced. Higher inflation of 1% p.a. would imply more than € 100 bn in additional nominal GDP (due to price effects) in six years ($1.700 \times 6\% = 102$). Total nominal GDP would then be higher by more than € 250 bn (in 2022) due to the TRC program. As gross government revenues as a percentage of GDP were almost 50% in Italy, € 250 bn in higher nominal GDP implied € 120 bn in higher gross revenues in 2022, which offset the revenue shortfalls due to TRC redemptions. In addition, before 2022 the TRC program would generate gross government revenues in excess of the rebates, thus allowing for a reduction of the gross public debt / GDP ratio (Table 16.2):

16.5.6 Safeguards

Our proposal suggested incorporating a series of safeguard measures into the TRC program to prevent any negative impact on the budget, such as increased deficits and additional public debt. In the case of Italy, we suggest allocating the annual € 120

Table 16.3 TRC program for Italy: impact issuances and uses

Year impact	2017	2018	2019	2020	2021	2022 (and beyond)
TRC issuances	**30**	**60**	**90**	**120**	**120**	**120**
Wage increases	10	20	30	40	40	40
Tax wedge reduction	10	20	30	40	40	40
Social expenditures	5	10	15	20	20	20
Public investments	5	10	15	20	20	20
TRC uses			**30**	**60**	**90**	**120**
Max potential trigger for safeguards			**30**	**60**	**90**	**120**
Increase in VAT rates			14	28	42	56
Increase in property taxes			8	16	24	32
Expenditure cuts			8	16	24	32

billion target TRC issuances as follows:

Wage increases: €40 bn
Tax wedge reductions: €40 bn
Social expenditures: €20 bn
Public investments: €20 bn

As previously mentioned, the projections were based on reasonably conservative assumptions, indicating that the increased GDP would generate government revenues that are equal to or greater than tax rebates each year of the program. However, we developed a plan of actions to be taken in case the expected positive effects on the economy did not fully materialize, resulting in lower fiscal performance than anticipated. The safeguards could be structured in the following manner[30]:

Increase in VAT rates: up to €56bn
Increase in property taxes: up to €32bn
Expenditure cuts: up to €32bn

and the impact projections are reported in Table 16.3.

In addition to the safeguard measures just discussed, a range of additional measures could be considered to manage temporary, negative deviations from fiscal consolidation targets. For example, the government could announce a commitment to pay a fraction of public expenditures with TRCs. Also, taxpayers could be entitled to receive TRCs as compensation for additional euro tax payments: this would

[30] The way these measures were designed would also reduce possible Ricardian effects on consumption, since a large part of the contingent adjustment would take the form of spending cuts and VAT increases. The latter, if expected, would accelerate current consumption (D'Acunto et al., 2015).

be equivalent to replacing tax raises with compulsory TRC-for-euro swaps. Furthermore, holders of TRCs could be induced to postpone TRC redemptions for tax rebates by offering them an increase in the face value of their TRC holdings in exchange for their decision to postpone redemptions. Further still, long-term TRCs could be issued to refinance euro-denominated debt, thus speeding up the consolidation of the total stock of public debt outstanding. Note that these measures would be "non-procyclical safety clauses," and would not imply the recessionary impact created by the "debt brakes" that were at the time envisaged by the Eurozone rules (which is the reason why they were difficult or even impossible to enforce in practice).

16.5.7 Remarks

In the debates on the proposed Fiscal Money program illustrated above, it was opined by various participants that the program resembles MMT policy. This is not so, for different reasons. First, the TRCs issued under the program by Italy (or, for that matter, by any other eurozone countries) would be denominated in euro and, therefore, they would reflect the credibility of the euro issuing institutions and the whole Eurozone, as perceived by the markets, whereas MMT policy would rest on the issuance of domestic currencies, each currency reflecting the credibility of its own issuing and policy institutions (see Chap. 15). If a country with a large external public debt were to push on its money supply as policy response to recession or stagnation, this would weaken the currency (with inflationary consequences), perhaps with some beneficial effects on the country's net export position, but more significantly worsening its external debt situation. Second, the proposed Fiscal Money program was not intended for using the TRC as an instrument to permanently monetize the budget deficits (at least, until full employment is achieved, and inflation sets in thereon). It was, rather, a program of future planned (and controlled) issuances of an instrument—the TRC—that would supplement the supply of euros that were not being spent by the private sector, with a view to stimulating aggregate demand and thus allowing the economic recovery that would not be possible otherwise (given the constraints on policy).

Finally, I want to address a significant misconception that emerged in the debate, often stemming from ignorance and, in some cases, deliberate misinformation. Some commentators—including pundits, public opinion makers, and even some notable academics—have stated that if the TRCs are considered money, then they must be classified as debt. This assertion is incorrect for both legal and economic reasons.

Legally, even if the TRCs were deemed a form of state-issued fiat money, they would not fall under the Maastricht definition of debt. Consequently, they might not be included in the public debt statistics relevant for compliance under the Stability and Growth Pact. Therefore, they would not be classified as debt.

Finally, as noted (and worth reemphasizing), the more and longer TRCs are used as money, the less likely they will be viewed as fiscal claims by their holders. Ultimately, if they are solely used as money, they will never be returned to the state as fiscal claims, resulting in no revenue losses for the issuing state and, consequently, no deficit or debt formation.

16.6 Conclusions

Fiscal Money, specifically in the form suggested in the TRC program illustrated in this chapter, appears to be a suitable solution for highly indebted countries that are part of a monetary union and have fallen into a recession, stagnation or liquidity trap. This is the situation that characterized several countries of the Eurozone since 2009—notably Italy among them—in the aftermath of the Global Financial Crisis, due to the inherent malfunctioning of the union's economic policy framework.

By introducing our proposed Fiscal Money the program, those countries could have accomplished three crucial objectives: ending the economic depression, restoring competitive balance within the region, and gradually reducing government indebtedness that contributes to instability and the risk of disruptions in global financial markets. Importantly, with the proposed program, these goals could have been achieved without necessitating any type of fiscal or financial transfers within the Eurozone, as the necessary political consensus for such measures was (and still is) nonexistent.

This chapter has illustrated the concept of Fiscal Money and its possible utilization as an innovative policy tool for economic revamping, in situations where conventional fiscal and monetary instruments are not available, or their use is constrained by institutional or structural limitations.

We have now reached the conclusion of this book. The next chapter will conclude with some final remarks.

Appendix 1: To Know More About Fiscal Money

The term "Fiscal Money" (from the Italian, "Moneta Fiscale") was coined in *Per una Moneta Fiscale Gratuita: Uscire dall'Austerità Senza Spaccare l'Euro*, a manifesto-public appeal launched by Biagio Bossone, Marco Cattaneo, Lucian Gallino, Enrico Grazzini, and Stefano Sylos Labini in November 2014, and later featured in the e-book by the same title, edited by B. Bossone, M. Cattaneo, E. Grazzini, and S. Sylos Labini (with a preface by L. Gallino) and published in the Italian political review MicroMega, on June 15, 2015.

The Group of Fiscal Money was founded in 2014 by Bossone, Cattaneo, Grazzini and Sylos Labini. Grazzini left it shortly after its foundation, and Massimo Costa joined it. Bossone left the group in 2021.

Fiscal Money was originally proposed by Marco Cattaneo in the form of "tax credit certificates" in the article "Tax Credit Certificates for the Tax Wedge," published in Il Sole 24 Ore on October 31, 2012, as an intervention tool to support the Italian economy, and later discussed by Cattaneo himself in the book written with G. Zibordi, "The Solution for the Euro," Hoepli, March 2014. Cattaneo's proposal was then developed in the manifesto-public appeal and the e-book referred to above. Noteworthy among the numerous contributions is "Fiscal Money: The State of Affairs" by the Fiscal Money Group, published in MicroMega on June 17, 2017. Regarding the individual contributions of GMF members: Stefano Sylos Labini has written articles on the topic in the press (Sole 24 Ore, Left, Sinistra in Rete, L'Idea Socialista) and given interviews (RadioPopolare, Money.it, PandoraTv). Massimo Costa has mainly studied the legal-accounting aspects of Tax Credit Certificates.

Following the collaboration between the Group of Fiscal Money and Pino Cabras, Member of Parliament of Italy's political party Movement Five Stars (M5S), the term "Tax Credit Certificate" was replaced with "Fiscal Compensation Certificate," which is not only a more precise denomination but also eliminates the confusion that the original word "credit" would originate on the non-debt nature of the instrument. The Fiscal Compensation Certificate discussed in this chapter is a specific subset of the general definition of Fiscal Money introduced by Bossone and Cattaneo (2016).

The blog "Basta con l'Eurocrisi," created and edited by Marco Cattaneo, is entirely dedicated to the topic of Fiscal Money. A proposal for Fiscal Money was launched by Gennaro Zezza in 2017 on the M5S website, becoming the second most voted proposal by the website subscribers. Various forms of Fiscal Money were proposed in other countries, see for example: "Sortir de l'austérité sans sortir de l'euro… grâce à la monnaie fiscale complémentaire," by G. Giraud, B. Lemoine, D. Plihon, M. Fare, J. Blanc, J.-M. Servet, V. Gayon, T. Coutrot, W. Kalinowski, and B. Théret, published in Libération on March 8, 2017; "Monnaie fiscale complémentaire: sortir des impasses européiste et souverainiste," by T. Coutrot, published in Mediapart on June 27, 2018; and the proposal launched in 2015 for Greece by former Minister of Finance Yanis Varoufakis, illustrated in "The Promise of Fiscal Money" on Project Syndicate on August 29, 2017, and later commented on by GMF in "Making Fiscal Money Work" on Project Syndicate on September 19, 2017. For a comparison of alternative forms of Fiscal Money, see the contribution (in two parts) by B. Bossone and M. Cattaneo, "A Parallel Currency for Greece," on VoxEu, May 25–26. Finally, the issuance of Fiscal Money falls under the category of "unconventional fiscal policies" (which also include fiscal devaluations and pre-announced indirect taxation), juxtaposed with the "unconventional monetary policies" adopted by some major central banks since the 2008 crisis, see Bossone, B., "Unconventional" Fiscal Policies, EconoMonitor, February 16, 2019.

Below is a selection of commentaries on Fiscal Money published on various sources by the group or some of its members between 2014 and 2020.

Writings on Fiscal Money

2020	Thinking Out of the Box: "Unconventional" Fiscal Policies for Economic Recovery After Covid-19, EconoMonitor, 30 June https://www.thestreet.com/economonitor/financial-markets/fiscal-policies

(continued)

(continued)

The Euro after COVID-19 and the "Three Germanies", The Group on Fiscal Money, EconoMonitor, 22 May 2020 https://www.thestreet.com/economonitor/europe/covid19-debt-fiscalmoney-ecb
E se di Germania ce ne fossero tre? Meglio fare da soli, Economia & Politica, 13 Maggio 2020 https://www.economiaepolitica.it/l-analisi/e-se-di-germania-ce-ne-fossero-tre-meglio-fare-da-soli-coronavirus-bond-spread-corte-costituzionale-tedesca/
Siamo a un bivio: altro debito o Moneta Fiscale?, MicroMega, 14 aprile http://temi.repubblica.it/micromega-online/siamo-a-un-bivio-altro-debito-o-moneta-fiscale/
Perché i certificati di compensazione fiscale non sono (e non possono essere) "debito", Economia & Politica, 7 Aprile 2020 https://www.economiaepolitica.it/?s=costa+bossone
Coronavirus e intervento economico dello Stato: siamo in guerra, MicroMega, 27 marzo http://temi.repubblica.it/micromega-online/coronavirus-e-intervento-economico-dello-stato-siamo-in-guerra/
Moneta Fiscale per la Tempesta Perfetta, Scenari Economici, 10 marzo https://scenarieconomici.it/moneta-fiscale-per-la-tempesta-perfetta/
Le Caldaie e la Moneta Fiscale, MicroMega, 4 febbraio http://temi.repubblica.it/micromega-online/le-caldaie-e-la-moneta-fiscale/
L'Italia e l'Euro: solo "Super Mario" può trovare la quadra, MicroMega, 8 gennaio http://temi.repubblica.it/micromega-online/l-italia-e-l-euro-solo-super-mario-puo-trovare-la-quadra/
2019Perché alla Germania serve un 'Nuovo Draghi' per la BCE, MegaChip, 24 aprile https://megachip.globalist.it/kill-pil/2019/04/24/perche-alla-germania-serve-un-nuovo-draghi-per-la-bce-2040498.html
Moneta Fiscale: la via giusta per l'economia italiana, MegaChip, 7 aprile https://megachip.globalist.it/kill-pil/2019/04/07/moneta-fiscale-la-via-giusta-per-l-economia-italiana-2039806.html
CESifo and Fiscal Money: Omissions and Blunders, EconoMonitor, 18 March https://moneymaven.io/economonitor/europe/cesifo-and-fiscal-money-omissions-and-blunders-MrsmrT-_x0SrN1YovPBaPA/
"Unconventional" Fiscal Policies, EconoMonitor, 16 February https://moneymaven.io/economonitor/financial-markets/unconventional-fiscal-policies-_SpvZXjWSEOMJqE4czre3g/
2018Moneta Fiscale per l'Italia, L'Idealogia socialista, 10 novembre https://www.ideologiasocialista.it/index.php/home/canali-tematici/economia/item/99-moneta-fiscale-italia-bossone-cattaneo-costa-syloslabini
Aumentare il deficit non è l'unica strada, MegaChip, 28 settembre
Una valuta parallela per l'Italia è possibile, Sinistrainrete, 21 agosto https://www.sinistrainrete.info/europa/13050-biagio-bossone-marco-cattaneo-massimo-costa-e-stefano-sylos-labini-una-valuta-parallela-per-l-italia-e-possibile.html
The Diagnosis of Italy's Disease: Where we think Charles Wyplosz is Wrong, Economonitor, 19 July https://moneymaven.io/economonitor/europe/the-diagnosis-of-italy-s-disease-where-we-think-charles-wyplosz-is-wrong-5TogNXN34UOYJFF5sxK3Ww/

(continued)

(continued)

Il debito pubblico si può ridurre facendo crescere l'economia. La proposta del gruppo della Moneta Fiscale, Business Insider, 8 luglio https://it.businessinsider.com/debito-pubblico-troppo-alto-la-proposta-del-gruppo-della-moneta-fiscale/
A parallel currency for Italy is possible, Politico.Eu, 7 July https://www.politico.eu/article/parallel-currency-italy-possible-eurozone/
Fiscal money as a solution to Italian eurowoes, Group of Fiscal Money, Telos, 23 May https://www.telos-eu.com/en/european-economy/fiscal-money-as-a-solution-to-italian-eurowoes.html
Moneta Fiscale: Aspetti Finanziari e Contabili, Economia & Politica, 18 aprile 2018 https://www.economiaepolitica.it/banche-e-finanza/moneta-banca-finanza/moneta-fiscale-aspetti-finanziari-e-contabili/
2017Moneta Fiscale: la guerra dell'establishment agli spaventapasseri, MicroMega, 27 dicembre http://temi.repubblica.it/micromega-online/moneta-fiscale-la-guerra-dell'establishment-agli-spaventapasseri/
Moneta Fiscale, le bugie di Bankitalia, MicroMega, 14 dicembre http://temi.repubblica.it/micromega-online/moneta-fiscale-le-bugie-di-bankitalia/
Il futuro dell'Italia: come uscire dalla crisi?, Economia & Politica, 5 dicembre http://www.economiaepolitica.it/politiche-economiche/europa-e-mondo/il-futuro-dellitalia-come-uscire-dalla-crisi/
Spesa in deficit, debito pubblico e mercati finanziari, Economia & Politica, 13 agosto http://www.economiaepolitica.it/il-pensiero-economico/spesa-in-deficit-debito-pubblico-e-mercati-finanziari/
La moneta fiscale per rilanciare economia e sistema bancario, Fixing, 20 Giugno http://www.sanmarinofixing.com/smfixing/fixing/archivio-fixing/23872-la-moneta-fiscale-per-rilanciare-economia-e-sistema-bancario.html
Moneta Fiscale: il punto della situazione, MicroMega, 17 giugno http://temi.repubblica.it/micromega-online/moneta-fiscale-il-punto-della-situazione/
Una moneta fiscale in aiuto all'euro, Il Sole 24 Ore, 26 maggio http://www.ilsole24ore.com/art/commenti-e-idee/2017-05-26/una-moneta-fiscale-aiuto-all-euro-202751_PRV.shtml?uuid=AE4dteTB
La via possibile della moneta fiscale, Il Sole 24 Ore, 9 maggio http://www.ilsole24ore.com/art/commenti-e-idee/2017-05-09/la-via-possibile-moneta-fiscale-202415_PRV.shtml?uuid=AE0vg1IB
Uscire dalla crisi con la Moneta Fiscale, Economia & Politica, 20 April http://www.economiaepolitica.it/politiche-economiche/europa-e-mondo/uscire-dalla-crisi-con-la-moneta-fiscale/
Italy's Predicament is Europe's Predicament, EconoMonitor, March 8 http://www.economonitor.com/blog/author/bbossone/
2016Crescere senza debito: idee per una moneta fiscale, Limes, 7 April http://www.limesonline.com/cartaceo/crescere-senza-debito-idee-per-una-moneta-fiscale?prv=true
'Helicopter tax credits' to accelerate economic recovery in Italy (and other Eurozone countries), (with M. Cattaneo), VoxEu, 4 January http://www.voxeu.org/article/fiscal-stimulus-helicopter-tax-credits

(continued)

(continued)

2015L'eurozona e la stagnazione secolare, EuNews, 28 November http://www.eunews.it/2015/11/28/leurozona-e-la-stagnazione-secolare/45941
Rilanciare l'economia italiana con la Moneta Fiscale: l'analisi di Mediobanca, MicroMega, 25 November http://temi.repubblica.it/micromega-online/rilanciare-l'economia-italiana-con-la-moneta-fiscale-l'analisi-di-mediobanc
Dentro l'euro ma anche oltre l'euro. Il Piano B dei Certificati di Credito Fiscale, Sinistra in Rete, 3 October http://www.sinistrainrete.info/europa/5807-b-bossone-m-cattaneo-e-grazzini-e-s-sylos-labini-dentro-l-euro-ma-anche-oltre-l-euro.html
Fiscal Debit Cards and Tax Credit Certificates: The Best Way to Boost Economic Recovery in Italy (and Other Euro Crisis Countries), EconoMonitor, 8 September http://www.economonitor.com/blog/2015/09/fiscal-debit-cards-and-tax-credit-certificates-the-best-way-to-boost-economic-recovery-in-italy-and-other-euro-crisis-countries/
I Certificati di Credito Fiscale e John Maynard Keynes, Keynesblog, 20 July, 2015 http://keynesblog.com/2015/07/20/i-certificati-di-credito-fiscale-e-john-maynard-keynes/
From Grexit to Exitaly? Let's Stop This Madness, EconoMonitor, 7 July http://www.economonitor.com/blog/2015/07/from-grexit-to-exitaly-lets-stop-this-madness/
A Parallel Currency for Greece: Part II, VoxEu, 26 May http://www.voxeu.org/article/parallel-currency-greece-part-ii
A Parallel Currency for Greece: Part I, VoxEu, 25 May http://www.voxeu.org/article/parallel-currency-greece-part-i
Greece Still Has a Fighting Chance, EconoMonitor, 18 May http://www.economonitor.com/blog/2015/05/greece-still-has-a-fighting-chance/
Greek Parallel Currency: How to Do it Properly, EconoMonitor, 21 April http://www.economonitor.com/blog/2015/04/greek-parallel-currency-how-to-do-it-properly/
Tax Credit Certificates to End the Greek Euro-Stalemate, EconoMonitor, 23 March http://www.economonitor.com/blog/2015/03/tax-credit-certificates-to-end-the-greek-euro-stalemate/
Saving the Eurozone from Stagnation: Can Draghi Do it Alone?, 16 March http://www.economonitor.com/blog/2015/03/saving-the-eurozone-from-stagnation-can-draghi-do-it-alone/
2014 Free fiscal money: exiting austerity without breaking up the euro, Associazione Paolo Sylos Labini, 26 November http://www.syloslabini.info/online/wp-content/uploads/2014/11/Appello-Inglese-rivisto_9-03-2015.pdf
Per una nuova moneta fiscale: uscire dall'austerità senza spaccare l'euro, Manifesto/Appello, Associazione Paolo Sylos Labini, 26 November http://www.syloslabini.info/online/risolviamo-la-crisi-dellitalia-adesso/
Ricetta per l'Eurozona: Più Pil Senza Nuovo Debito, LaVoce.info, 30 September http://www.lavoce.info/ricetta-per-eurozona-piu-pil-senza-nuovo-debito/#comment-57960
Rilanciare la domanda senza creare nuovo debito, Sbilanciamoci, 24 September http://www.sbilanciamoci.info/Sezioni/italie/Rilanciare-la-domanda-senza-creare-nuovo-debito-26305

(continued)

(continued)

Presidente Renzi, Rilanciare la Domanda Senza Creare Nuovo Debito Si Può, OnEuro, 24 September http://www.eunews.it/2014/09/24/presidente-renzi-rilanciare-la-domanda-senza-creare-nuovo-debito-si-puo/22020
Which Options for Mr. Renzi to Revive Italy and Save the Euro?, EconoMonitor, July 3rd http://www.economonitor.com/blog/2014/07/which-options-for-mr-renzi-to-revive-italy-and-save-the-euro/#sthash.VIXB5wj8.dpuf

References

Blanchard, O. (2014). *Where danger lurks*. VoxEu, 3 October.

Blanchard, O. J. (2016). *The US Phillips curve: Back to the 60s?* Policy Brief, Number PB16–1, Peter Institute for International Economics.

Bofinger, P. (2016, June 7). German macroeconomics: The long shadow of Walter Eucken. *VoxEu*.

Bossone, B. (2017). *The costs and benefits of «ExItaly»*, Il Sole 24 Ore, 30 Maggio.

Bossone, B., & Cattaneo, M. (2016). New ways of crisis settlement: Fiscal Money as a tool to fight economic stagnation. Presented at the Conference *A single model of Governance or tailored responses? Historical, economic and legal aspects of European Governance in the Crisis*, FernUniversität in Hagen, on November 24–25, and published in the conference proceedings.

Bossone, B., & Sylos Labini, S. (2016, April 4). Strengthening 'Mario's Plan'. *EconoMonitor*.

Bossone, B., Cattaneo, M., Grazzini, E., & Sylos Labini, S. (Eds.) (2015a). Per una moneta fiscale gratuita. Come uscire dall'austerità senza spaccare l'euro. *MicroMega*.

Bossone, B., Cattaneo, Grazzini, E., Sylos Labini, S. (2015b, September 8). Fiscal debit cards and tax credit certificates: The best way to boost economic recovery in Italy (and other Euro crisis countries). *EconoMonitor*.

Cattaneo, M., & Zibordi, G. (2014). *Soluzione per l'euro*. Hoepli, Marzo.

D'Acunto, F., Hoang, D., & Weber, M. (2015). Inflation expectations and consumption expenditure. *Mimeo*.

Draghi, M. (2012, July 26). *Speech at the global investment conference in London*. ECB.

ESA. (2010). *European system of accounts*. Eurostat, European Commission.

Fitoussi, J. P., & Saraceno, F. (2013). European economic governance: The Berlin-Washington consensus. *Cambridge Journal of Economics, 37*(3), 479–496.

IASB. (2018). *Conceptual framework for financial reporting*. International Accounting Standards Board, IFRS Foundation.

Nedeljkovic, M., & Mody, A. (2019, January 14). The ECB's performance during the crisis: Lessons learned. *Vox/CEPR*.

Pilkington, P. (2013). *The continued relevance of tax-backed bonds in a post-OMT Eurozone*. Policy Note 2013/10, Levy Institute.

Pilkington, P., & Mosler, W. (2012). *Tax-backed bonds—A national solution to the European debt crisis*. Policy Note 2012/4, Levy Institute.

Saraceno, F. (2015). Challenges for the ECB in times of deflation. Employment Working Paper No. 183, ILO Employment Policy Department. International labor Organization.

Sylos Labini, S. (2022), *La battaglia della Moneta Fiscale. L'idea, i rapporti politici, gli attacchi, le prime applicazioni, le prospettive*, Firenze: Il Ponte Editore.

World Bank. (2015). *Global economic prospects: The global economy in transition*. The World Bank Group.

Conclusion

This book has revisited several central aspects of monetary theory and policy and has proposed new perspectives on money. It has sought to mark new trails through and across existing theories of money to overcome some of their shortcomings on such fundamental issues as the nature of money and money creation by commercial banks, as well as to recognize the power that money confers on banks, and to gauge the economic consequences of banks exercising such power.

In writing the book, I also thought that trailblazing was necessary to imagine new solutions for establishing less fragile and more stable financial systems than the existing ones. Trailblazing, I thought, was also necessary to show analytically that the Lucas' Critique can be superseded and that (following Keynes) secular stagnation can originate from high liquidity preference and to identify which policy approaches can or cannot work, under the circumstances.

Trailblazing, I finally thought, was essential to appreciate correctly how money and government budgets interact in today's open and internationally highly financially integrated ("globalized") economies and how their interaction differently shapes (and limits or expands, depending on country circumstances) the space available for policy making.

The book has thus offered a detailed exploration of the foundational principles that underlie the nature of money, the role of banks as money creators, and the intricate relationship between national economies and the global financial system within the international allocation of money process. It has also forged new understandings that can guide to the development of innovative policy frameworks and institutional solutions for achieving more robust and stable financial systems, looking forward.

B. Bossone, *Trailblazing Visions of Money in Economic Theory*, Contributions to Economics, https://doi.org/10.1007/978-3-031-82544-6

1 A New Understanding of Money: Beyond Traditional Theories

At the heart of Part I of the book was a fundamental rethinking of what money is and what it represents within a contemporary capitalist economy. In this context, the book has presented the Accounting View of Money (AVM), which I have developed with accounting expert Massimo Costa, as a groundbreaking perspective that challenges the conventional view of money as predominantly a form of debt. In Chap. 2, the AVM has been presented not just as a theoretical framework but as a practical tool for understanding how money functions within both public and private sectors. The AVM argues that current accounting standards and regulatory frameworks fail to capture today's true nature of money and by reframing money as equity—particularly in the case of state-issued money and a significant share of commercial bank money—the AVM offers a more nuanced and accurate portrayal of money's role in the economy.

This redefinition has profound implications. It suggests that money is not merely a neutral medium of exchange but a dynamic component of financial equity of the issuing entity, which can influence economic outcomes in significant ways. Moreover, by delving into the dual nature of money as both debt and equity, the AVM encourages a reassessment of how we account for money within the economy. This reassessment is not just theoretical but has practical implications for the design of financial regulations and economic policies.

Chapter 3 has delved into the intricate dynamics of how money and other financial assets generate utility for their holders within an environment marked by time, uncertainty, and fluctuating market sentiments and has illustrated the analytical framework I have developed in earlier works to explore these dynamics, highlighting three central features. First, the framework uses a choice-theoretic model that quantifies the utility that economic agents derive from holding assets with different levels of liquidity. This model provides insights into how preferences for liquid versus less liquid assets can influence individual decision-making and overall economic behavior. Second, the framework features a variable transaction cost structure for asset liquidation, which is determined endogenously within the model. This cost structure reflects the time required for transaction execution, the (in)efficiencies of the financial infrastructure where transactions are executed, and how these conditions change with changes in market sentiment. By accounting for these variations, the chapter has offered a realistic portrayal of the costs associated with converting assets into cash, particularly in times of economic stress or optimism.

Finally, the framework incorporates a model of expectations formation, capturing how agents form and adjust their expectations in the face of uncertainty and changing market conditions. This aspect is crucial for understanding how collective market behavior can lead to phenomena such as speculative bubbles and the subsequent busts that often follow. Together, these elements shed light on the broader implications for resource allocation and asset price dynamics.

The model proves useful to understand how capital allocations and asset prices change under various sources of economic uncertainty and shifting market sentiment. Even more than that, the model provides a unifying tool that allows money to be compared and comparable to anything else (goods, services, and other assets), anytime, anywhere. Interestingly, the model also allows to integrate Keynes' liquidity preference theory—of which I have always been a strenuous supporter—within a rational-choice, micro-founded framework, which can explain the occurrences in an economy of Keynesian macroeconomic disequilibria (or underemployment equilibria) triggered by confidence crises and pessimistic expectations. Finally, the model points to market-specific prudential policy tools to mitigate the risks associated with speculative bubbles and boom-bust cycles. Most notably, however, the model has turned out to be extremely helpful for studying how to address secular stagnation problems (Chap. 12) and for analyzing resource allocations and macroeconomic policy effectiveness in internationally highly financially integrated national economies whose currencies trade in global markets dominated by a relatively small class of large investors (Chap. 12).

2 The Economic Power of Banks: Unveiling Hidden Dynamics

A significant portion of the book was dedicated to exploring the immense power that banks wield within modern economies, due to their special role as creators of money, even in a world were nonbank financial institutions have become highly relevant. Traditionally, banks have been understood primarily as intermediaries that facilitate the flow of money between savers and borrowers. However, this view is increasingly seen as insufficient in capturing the true influence that banks have on economic outcomes. Chapters 4-7 of the book have provided a detailed examination of how banks create money and the economic consequences of this process.

In Chap. 4, banks have no longer been represented as passive intermediaries but as active creators of money, a role that gives them a unique power over the economy vis-à-vis all other types of market actors. When banks issue loans, they do more than just allocate existing resources—they create new money, effectively expanding the money supply and influencing economic activity. Using a modified version of the Circuit Theory of Money, the chapter has shown how money is injected by the banks at circuit-start and circulates in a sequence economy, represented as a circuit, and how it reflows back to the issuing banks (or fails to do so) at circuit-end, depending on the portfolio choices of funds allocation by investors and nonbank financial intermediaries. This process of money creation and destruction remains central in contemporary capitalist economies where the financial dimension has far exceeded the mere sphere of production, and it directly impacts everything from relative price dynamics to income distribution and financial stability.

One of the key concepts analyzed in both chapters is seigniorage—the rent that banks obtain from creating money at a cost lower than its face value. While seigniorage has traditionally been associated with state money, the chapters have highlighted how commercial banks also extract seigniorage through their money creation activities. This extraction of seigniorage is not just a technical detail; it has significant implications for the distribution of wealth and power within the economy.

By shedding light on the dynamics of bank seigniorage, the ability of banks to create money and extract seigniorage has been examined, which gives banks an outsized influence over the economy, an influence that is often underappreciated or misunderstood in existing economic models.

Chapter 5 has expanded on the role of commercial banks in the creation of money and has focused on two key aspects: the process of money creation and the extraction of seigniorage by banks. The chapter has acknowledged the limited amount of research on bank seigniorage despite the growing literature on banks as money creators. It has examined how banks create money and the limitations they face in this process due to their payment activities and the rules and technologies of the payment system in which they operate. The chapter has also explored how banks generate seigniorage from the economy and how this differs from profits obtained through financial intermediation alone. Finally, the chapter concludes by discussing the nature of bank seigniorage.

Chapter 6 has then investigated the broader economic implications of bank seigniorage, particularly in terms of its impact on resource allocation and income distribution. By examining how banks' money creation activities can lead to distortions in the economy, the need for policies has been highlighted that can mitigate these negative effects. For instance, the potential has been discussed for using taxation or other regulatory tools to redistribute the gains from seigniorage more equitably across society, ensuring that the benefits of money creation are shared more broadly.

Finally, Chap. 7 has presented my recent work with quantum physicist Fabio Bagarello, further inquiring into the nature of bank money. Drawing on the AVM discussed in Chap. 2, the money issued by the banks in the form of demand deposits exhibits a complex and hybrid nature, embodying characteristics of both debt and equity. The proportion of these debt-like and equity-like characteristics within a deposit can shift based on various factors, such as the specific operational practices of the issuing banks, the regulatory environment, and broader economic conditions. Building on this foundational understanding, the chapter has illustrated the innovative connection between the hybrid nature of bank money and the dual nature of objects in quantum physics, where entities can simultaneously exhibit characteristics of both particles and waves. This analogy is not merely theoretical but serves as a basis for applying quantum analysis methods to the study of bank money. This approach allows for the extraction of valuable economic information that might be obscured by traditional financial analysis methods, offering deeper insights into how money functions in dynamic and uncertain environments. The quantum perspective on bank money not only enriches the theoretical discourse but also has practical implications for how we understand and manage financial stability, risk, and innovation in banking.

3 Innovations in Monetary Stability: Toward More Stable Financial Systems

One of the central themes of the book was the pursuit of monetary stability in an increasingly complex and financially interconnected global economy. Traditional monetary systems, based on fractional reserve banking and the close link between money creation and lending, have proven vulnerable to economic shocks, as evidenced many times through economic history worldwide, and once again by the global financial crisis of 2007–2008. These vulnerabilities are not inherent to all monetary systems but are the result of specific design choices that can be rethought and restructured.

Part II of the book has considered various forms of "sound" money, introduced the concept of "superstable" money as a key innovation in achieving more robust financial systems, and articulated it across different models. In this context, I could not neglect my earlier contribution to the debate on "narrow banking," which had once again re-emerged after the global financial crisis of 2008, with proposals by some scholars to restrict deposit-issuing banks from lending to the private sector and limiting nonbank intermediaries from funding investments with demand deposits. Proponents argued that such reforms would enhance financial stability and efficiency by reducing the risks associated with traditional banking practices, particularly those related to the creation of money through lending, and Chap. 8 has reported my critical arguments against these conclusions.

Chapters 9 and 10 have illustrated two distinct approaches to creating a more stable monetary environment. The first approach—which I developed in cooperation with economist Abdou Sarr, based on Abdou's original proposal—involves severing the traditional link between money creation and bank lending. By establishing specialized institutions that issue money on a non-lending basis, it is possible to create a monetary system that generates purchasing power without increasing private-sector debt or contributing to financial instability. This approach has several key advantages. First, it reduces the economy's reliance on debt, which is a major source of financial risk. Second, by creating money independently of lending activities, it makes possible to maintain a stable flow of money into the economy, even during times of crisis when traditional lending may contract. And, finally, it has the potential to democratize access to purchasing power, as it would allow individuals and businesses to access money without needing to take on debt.

The second approach, discussed in Chap. 10, involves the introduction of a central bank digital currency (CBDC) in a way that preserves the role of banks as lenders while eliminating the risk of depositors (or other bank funding sources) running on them, due to perceived risks, which is inherent in all fractional reserve regimes. The proposed "CBDC next-level model"—which I developed in cooperation with entrepreneur Michael Heines, based on his original proposal—allows the central bank to create money by lending to banks, with deposits being moved from the balance sheets of banks to the central bank. This system would provide unparalleled financial stability by ensuring that no individual bank failure could threaten the broader financial system or depositor confidence. At the same time, it would preserve the essential function of banks in providing credit to the economy.

This innovative approach to CBDCs reflects the book's broader commitment to finding practical solutions to the challenges facing modern monetary systems. By proposing a model that enhances financial stability without disrupting the credit functions of banks, the chapter has provided a roadmap for policymakers seeking to modernize their monetary systems in a way that is both effective and sustainable.

Furthermore, the discussion of CBDCs has highlighted the potential for central banks to play a more effective role in maintaining financial stability. By taking deposits off the balance sheets of commercial banks, while not disrupting their traditional lending business, the central bank can reduce the risk of bank runs and ensure that the monetary system remains stable even in times of economic stress. This approach also has the potential to enhance the central bank's ability to implement monetary policy, as it would give the central bank more direct control over the money supply.

The innovations in monetary stability discussed in the book are not just theoretical and could be used by countries to build more robust financial systems. By decoupling money creation from lending and introducing new forms of digital currency, the book has suggested that it is possible to create monetary systems that are both more stable and equitable, reducing the risk of financial crises and ensuring that the benefits of money creation are shared more broadly across society.

4 Macroeconomic Policy in a Globalized World: Navigating New Realities

The focus of the book was then shifted to the broader macroeconomic implications of money and fiscal policy in globalized economies. The interconnectedness of global financial markets has fundamentally altered the landscape in which national economies operate, imposing new constraints on the effectiveness of traditional macroeconomic policies. Part III of the book was thus dedicated to exploring these challenges and offering new theoretical frameworks that better capture the realities of a globalized world.

Chapter 11 has addressed the Lucas' Critique and shown how it can be superseded by bringing it to the next level. Accordingly, the effectiveness of any policy regime depends on the reference model that people consider to be the correct representation of the economy: if the existing reference model changes, and is replaced by a new one, the way people's expectations and behaviors are shaped also change, and the impact of new policy rules differs from what it would be under the old model. Building on Keynes's idea of "conventional beliefs" and Hahn's "conjectural equilibria," the chapter has argued that the impact of monetary policy depends on whether agents adopt a Keynesian, monetarist, or other model as their guiding convention. These conventions guide agents' responses, making policy outcomes align with their beliefs rather than an objective "true" model of the economy. The chapter has ultimately underscored the need for policymakers to understand and consider the impact of prevailing economic conventions on the effectiveness of macroeconomic policy actions, especially in today's globalized economies.

Chapter 12 has revisited the concept of "secular stagnation," a condition characterized by prolonged periods of low economic growth and high unemployment. Drawing on Keynesian principles, the chapter has argued that secular stagnation can be understood as a consequence of high liquidity preference driven by pessimistic expectations and persistent uncertainty. The chapter has developed a micro-founded theoretical model that explains how asset stock dynamics, influenced by liquidity considerations, can lead to stagnation.

This model challenges the traditional focus on the relationship between saving and investment as the primary drivers of economic growth. Instead, it emphasizes the role of liquidity preference and market sentiment in shaping economic outcomes. The model brings new insights into the causes of secular stagnation and evaluates various possible policy actions—ordered by their level of effectiveness—to reduce liquidity preference, stimulate aggregated demand, and drive the economy out of stagnation, but it also serves to highlight the limits of such actions if they are intended to provide steady solutions to keep the economy at full employment in situations where output potential has been permanently lowered by stagnant demand. Starting from this awareness, the chapter has drawn lessons from Keynes' view of how to stabilize a capitalist economy at its full-employment potential.

Building on this analysis, Chap. 13 has explored the effectiveness of monetary and fiscal policies in globalized economies, using the Portfolio Theory of Inflation (PTI) that I have developed in recent years. The chapter has examined how global capital flows interact with domestic monetary and fiscal policies, shaping the space available for national policymakers to maneuver. The PTI framework offers a new way of understanding the dynamics of exchange rates, inflation, and output in open economies, highlighting the limitations that globalization imposes on traditional policy tools.

The implications of this analysis are significant. In globalized contexts, the choices of global investors—driven by considerations of risk, return, and liquidity—can have a profound impact on the national economies. This means that the effectiveness of domestic macroeconomic policies is constrained by external factors beyond the control of national governments. Notably, the policy space available to countries is endogenous to global investor choices and strongly depend on the policy credibility of the individual countries, as it is perceived by the investors: stimulative macro-policies are more effective (in terms of resource employment gains) in countries considered to be credible, whereas they are less effective in less credible countries where their effects dissipate into currency devaluation and higher inflation.

Chapter 14 has further explored these themes by introducing the Neutrality Theorem for globalized economies. Drawing on the capital structure irrelevance principle of Modigliani and Miller, the chapter has argued that in a globalized economy, the cost of capital for governments is independent of the form of deficit financing, whether it be through debt or money. The theorem suggests that traditional distinctions between different forms of government financing are less relevant in a globalized context, where capital allocation decisions are driven by global investors who are indifferent to the specific forms of debt or money issued by national governments.

This new Neutrality Theorem challenges the conventional wisdom that governments can achieve specific economic outcomes by choosing one form of financing over another. Instead, the global nature of financial markets imposes constraints on the ability of governments to manipulate economic variables through fiscal or monetary policy. This has important implications for how we think about the role of the state in managing the economy in a globalized world.

The chapter has also highlighted the importance of understanding the global financial environment in which national economies operate. In a world where capital flows freely across borders, national policymakers must be aware of the limitations imposed by global financial markets. Traditional macroeconomic policies, which were developed in a context of financially less open national economies, are often ill-suited to the challenges of globalized economies, notably if they are not perceived as credible. Instead, new approaches are needed that consider the realities of global capital flows and the interconnectedness of financial markets.

5 A Critical Examination of MMT: Limits and Possiblities

The book offers a critical examination of Modern Money Theory (MMT) and its limitations in the context of globalized economies. MMT has gained popularity in recent years as a framework for understanding the relationship between government spending, money creation, and economic growth. Proponents of MMT argue that governments can achieve full employment and economic stability by financing fiscal deficits through money creation, without the need for borrowing or raising taxes.

Chapter 15 has presented a detailed critique of MMT-based macroeconomic policy, arguing that its effectiveness is limited in globalized economies where the value of money is determined by international financial markets. The chapter has shown that unless specific conditions are met—such as high policy credibility or the issuance of an international reserve currency—MMT policy is likely to lead to unsustainable growth in the money supply or the need for domestic interest rates that are inconsistent with the policy objectives. While appealing in theory, the MMT framework would not be a viable basis for sustainable macroeconomic policy in most globalized economies.

The critique of MMT presented in the book is grounded in a detailed analysis of the global financial system and the constraints it imposes on national economies. The MMT's focus on domestic policy is too narrow, failing to consider the impact of global capital flows and the interconnectedness of financial markets. In globalized economies, the actions of global investors and financial institutions can have a significant impact on the effectiveness of domestic macroeconomic policy, limiting the ability of governments to achieve full employment while controlling inflation.

The chapter has also noted the importance of understanding the political and institutional context in which macroeconomic policy is implemented. MMT's emphasis on the ability of governments to finance deficits through money creation assumes a high degree of policy credibility and institutional stability—conditions that may not exist in many countries. In countries with lower levels of policy credibility or weaker institutions, the risks associated with MMT policy—such as currency devaluation, higher inflation, and loss of investor confidence—are significantly higher.

Finally, the chapter has discussed the potential for MMT policy to be effective in certain specific contexts, such as in countries that issue an international reserve currency or have very high levels of policy credibility. In these cases, MMT may be able to provide a useful framework for achieving full employment and economic stability; however, these cases are the exception rather than the rule, and policymakers should be wary of applying MMT principles in contexts where the risks outweigh the potential benefits.

6 Fiscal Money: A Novel Policy Tool

The final chapter, Chap. 16, has illustrated the concept of Fiscal Money as a macroeconomic policy tool for countries facing economic recession or stagnation but whose policy space is constrained by high levels of public debt and limited monetary sovereignty or by institutional restrictions—as was the case for several Eurozone countries that were hit by the debt crisis of 2010.

Specifically in the Eurozone context, the economic governance framework under which those countries operate (established through the Maastricht Treaty and the Stability and Growth Pact) was focused on fiscal discipline and price stability, leaving little room for active fiscal intervention. In some cases, the fiscal space available to country authorities was effectively limited by considerable imbalances accumulated by these countries over the years. The crisis exposed the framework's limitations in addressing deep economic recessions since, unlike countries that control their own currency, Eurozone members could not independently adjust their monetary policy to respond to economic shocks. This constraint made it difficult for them to implement effective countercyclical policies, causing them to fall into prolonged periods of economic stagnation.

The idea of Fiscal Money was then introduced as a creative alternative approach to macroeconomic policy. By issuing the Tax Rebate Certificates (TRCs)—originally conceived by financier Marco Cattaneo and further refined by a team of economists of which I was part—governments could inject new liquidity into the economy to boost consumption and investment, without increasing public debt or violating the fiscal constraints imposed by the Eurozone's economic governance framework.

The introduction of Fiscal Money would have marked a significant departure from conventional monetary and fiscal policy approaches, offering a novel tool that could help overcome the structural limitations of the Eurozone's economic framework.

The concept of Fiscal Money raises broader implications for the future of macroeconomic policy in the Eurozone (as well as in any countries facing similar policy constraints). The introduction of Fiscal Money could pave the way for a more flexible and responsive economic governance framework, one that allows for greater fiscal autonomy while maintaining the stability of the common currency.

7 Trailblazing Visions of Money

My aim for writing this book was to challenge current views of money, question some long-held assumptions on which those views are grounded, and propose new frameworks that are better suited to comprehend critical monetary and financial issues of the globalized economies of our times and to design effective policy solutions for better economic performance and financial stability.

With this book, I wanted to provide fresh viewpoints on the concept of money by redefining its nature, analyzing the special role of banks as money creators, presenting groundbreaking ideas for achieving financial stability, and delving into the intricacies of macroeconomic policy when money is traded as an asset in globalized markets. I have then compiled and integrated in it many of my own studies, published over my life as a professional economist, and I have revised and expanded them to submit a comprehensive treatment of the role of money in the current global landscape.

The book calls on scholars, policymakers, and practitioners to engage with its ideas and to debate its insights and proposals. It invites readers to think critically about the role of money in contemporary capitalist economies, to question existing theories, and to embrace new approaches. The book is a reminder of the power of innovative thinking for the correct understanding of economic issues and a signal that the solutions to the challenges confronting the existing economic realities lie in reimagining the way we understand the world around us. Hopefully, the book also suggests useful orientations for navigating the many, inevitable complexities within the field of money.

The manufacturer's authorised representative in the EU is Springer Nature Customer Service Centre GmbH, Europaplatz 3, 69115 Heidelberg, Germany. If you have any concerns regarding our products, please contact ProductSafety@springernature.com

Printed and bound by CPI Group (UK) Ltd, Croydon, CR0 4YY
01/10/2026
02225913-0018